THE LATIN DOSSIER OF ANASTASIUS THE PERSIAN
Hagiographic Translations and Transformations
Carmela Vircillo Franklin

This book examines the cult of an eastern saint in the medieval Latin West, bridging traditional linguistic and geographical boundaries in the study of early medieval Europe. The movement of the cult of Anastasius the Persian monk (d. 22 January 628, in Kirkuk, modern Iraq) from Persia, Jerusalem, and Constantinople to Rome and Italy in the mid seventh century, and from there to Anglo-Saxon England and northern Europe, is documented by an extensive literary dossier, as well as by the veneration of the martyr's relics and other evidence of liturgical commemoration. The book surveys the cult's historical beginnings in the East, and its early development in Rome within the context of the city's Greek-speaking population and the religious controversies of the seventh and eighth centuries. The entire Latin literary tradition of the cult of Anastasius goes back to two Greek texts (one composed in Jerusalem, the other in Rome itself) that were translated into Latin in Rome, the most important center of cultural exchange between Greek and Latin in the period. The Latin dossier's relationship to the Greek texts affords us the almost unparalleled opportunity to observe early medieval translators at work and to understand more fully their tools, methodologies, and motivations at a time when the knowledge of Greek and its literary culture was in sharp decline in the Latin West.

The second part examines the diffusion and metamorphoses of the Latin dossier of Anastasius as a case study of the fluidity of hagiographic works, "living texts" that were constantly adapted to suit different settings and the changing functions of the books into which they were copied. Among the most significant of these revisions is one that may be identified with a lost work of Bede.

Critical editions of ten texts are included: the three original translations from the Greek and seven revisions, produced in various regions and across different periods, from the Greek communities of seventh-century Rome to the Cistercian abbeys of Flanders in the twelfth century and later. These editions exemplify the critical methodologies that are most appropriate to unstable texts and to texts transmitted exclusively within larger collections.

This study of the *fortuna* of the dossier of Anastasius in the Middle Ages shows the value of exploring both the cultural and codicological contexts in which hagiographic texts were composed and transmitted.

STUDIES AND TEXTS 147

The Latin Dossier
of Anastasius the Persian

Hagiographic Translations
and Transformations

by

CARMELA VIRCILLO FRANKLIN

PONTIFICAL INSTITUTE OF MEDIAEVAL STUDIES

ACKNOWLEDGMENT

This book has been published with the aid of a grant
from the Stanwood-Cockey-Lodge Foundation
of Columbia University.

National Library of Canada Cataloguing in Publication

Franklin, Carmela Vircillo
  The Latin dossier of Anastasius the Persian : hagiographic
translations and transformations / by Carmela Vircillo Franklin.

(Studies and texts, ISSN 0082-5328 ; 147)
Includes bibliographical references and index.
ISBN 0-88844-147-9

  1. Anastasius, the Persian, Saint, d. 628—Cult—Europe—History.
2. Christian Saints—Cult—Italy—Rome. 3. Christian hagiography—
History. 4. Christian literature, Byzantine—Translations into Latin—
History and criticism. 5. Transmission of texts. 6. Bede, the
Venerable, Saint, 673-735—Contributions in hagiography. I. Pontifical
Institute of Mediaeval Studies. II. Title. III. Series: Studies and texts
(Pontifical Institute of Mediaeval Studies) ; 147.

BX4700.A43F72 2004   270.2′092   C2003-906725-4

BX
4700
.A43
F72
2004

© 2004
Pontifical Institute of Mediaeval Studies
59 Queen's Park Crescent East
Toronto, Ontario, Canada M5S 2C4

Printed in Canada

Contents

THE TEXTS

Preface

The subject of this book is the cult of an eastern saint in the medieval Latin West. My work follows an ecumenical approach[1] to the study of early medieval European culture, one that disregards traditional linguistic and geographical boundaries. The movement of the cult of Anastasius the Persian monk (d. 22 January 628, in Kirkuk, modern Iraq) from Persia, Jerusalem, and Constantinople to Rome and Italy in the middle of the seventh century, and from there to Anglo-Saxon England, and then to northern Europe in the following centuries is documented by an extensive literary dossier, as well as by the veneration of the martyr's relics, by church dedications and other evidence of liturgical commemoration. In Chapter I, I survey the historical beginnings of the cult of the Persian in the East, and its development in Rome and Italy particularly within the context of the religious controversies of the seventh and eighth centuries. I also provide a translation of the two texts that laid the foundation of the movement in the West, the original *Acta* of Anastasius and the so-called Roman Miracle of 713. My English version of these two works is based on both the Latin and Greek source texts.

The prominent literary expression of the cult of Anastasius in the West constitutes by far the largest part of my study. Chapters II-IV examine three texts translated from the Greek: an early Latin translation of the Greek *Acta* executed in Rome before 668, when Theodore of Tarsus may have taken it to England; a second version of the *Acta*, also carried out in Rome in the ninth or tenth century, which can be seen as part of the revival of Greek learning in Rome of which the papal diplomat Anastasius Bibliothecarius is the best-known exponent; and the Roman Miracle, the account of an exorcism composed in Greek in Rome in 713 and translated

---

1. I borrow Bernice Kaczynski's terminology, used to describe the recent shift in medieval historiography in her "Review Article: The Seventh-Century School of Canterbury: England and the Continent in Perspective."

into Latin not much later. The translation of Greek texts into Latin during the early Middle Ages is a subject that remains in need of substantial scholarly exploration, despite the appearance of several important studies in recent decades. Editions and detailed investigations of individual texts are needed from which to draw broad conclusions on the methods of translation, the tools and strategies employed by translators, as well as their motivations at a time when the knowledge of Greek and its literary culture was in sharp decline in the Latin West. I hope that my analysis of these three texts translated directly from the Greek will contribute to this work. Taken together, they exemplify the history of translation as it was practiced in early medieval Rome, the most important outpost for the cultural exchange between Greek and Latin in the period.

The diffusion and metamorphoses[2] of the two translations of the *Passio S. Anastasii* are examined in chapters V-VII. This examination serves as a case study of the fluidity of hagiographic works, "living texts" that were constantly adapted to suit various needs, or to be included in a variety of books by scribes and editors throughout the Middle Ages. Among the most significant of these revisions is one that, as I discuss at length, is Bede's lost correction of the translation brought to England by Archbishop Theodore, and another revision that Bede may have utilized in preparing his own work.

I provide critical editions of ten texts in the third part of my book, the three original translations from the Greek and seven Latin reworkings discussed in chapters V-VII that show no significant connection with the Greek originals. These texts were produced in various regions and across different periods, from the Greek communities of seventh-century Rome to the Cistercian abbeys of Flanders in the twelfth century and later. Each one is preceded by an introduction that summarizes the conclusions derived from the study and collation of the manuscript witnesses. The "Descriptive List" of the final section is meant to provide a comprehensive and

---

2. The use of this word is inspired by another work that has served as a model to my own, that of Pelagia the Penitent by Pierre Petitmengin et al.

systematic survey of all the manuscripts discussed in this study, including lost manuscripts.

Just as my work was going to press, Xavier Lequeux published, without my knowledge, a short article inspired by the unpublished first draft of my work, which had been made available to him.[3] In this piece, published in 2003, Lequeux takes issue with the translation methodology of the first Latin translation of the *Acta* of Anastasius as I had postulated in an article published in 1995.[4] Lequeux has known that my edition of the first Latin translation was being readied for publication in the present book. Had he waited, he could have considered the updated and greatly expanded treatment of the methodologies of medieval translators, and not focused artificially on material published more than eight years ago that is superseded by the fuller treatment included in chapters I-IV and VI of this book.

This study began many years ago when Paul J. Meyvaert invited me to assist in the identification of the "librum uitae et passionis sancti Anastasii male de greco translatum et peius a quodam inperito emendatum" listed among Bede's works at the end of the Ecclesiastical History (V.25). I dedicate this book, which grew out of that original collaboration, to Paul, with gratitude for all that he has taught me over the years, and with deep affection.

I have incurred many debts to individuals and institutions during my extended manuscript hunt. Both Saint John's University in Collegeville, Minnesota, where I began this project, and Columbia University in the City of New York, where I completed it, supported my research. I also owe thanks to the National Humanities Center and to the National Endowment for the Humanities for support during my sabbatical leave in 1990-1991 when some of the

---

3. Xavier Lequeux, "La plus ancienne traduction latine (*BHL* 410b) des actes grecs du martyr Anastase le perse. L'oeuvre d'un interprète grec?," *Analecta Bollandiana* 121 (2003), 37-44. See n. 3 (p. 37), where Lequeux states that he had occasion to examine "une edition provisoire réalisée par Carmela Vircillo Franklin." M. Lequeux had access not only to the unpublished edition of *BHL* 410b, but also to an early draft of my entire study, which included the discussion of this Latin translation, not just its text.

4. Franklin, "Theodore and *the Passio S. Anastasii.*"

research for this work was begun. I am extremely grateful to all the many libraries that have allowed me access to their collections. While it is impossible to list them all here, I wish to single out in particular the Biblioteca apostolica vaticana, the Biblioteca nazionale in Turin, and the Hill Monastic Manuscript Library at Saint John's University.

I wish to acknowledge also the extraordinary help I received from the following colleagues: Fr. Leonard Boyle, OP (†); Mirella Ferrari and R.C. Barker-Benfield, who kindly replied to my written queries; Alan Cameron; François Dolbeau; Bernard Flusin; Michael Lapidge; Giovanni Verrando (†). I am particularly grateful to Carol Lanham and Claudia Rapp who read large parts of this work and provided valuable suggestions, and to the anonymous readers for the press who read it all in a most constructive way. I am happy to acknowledge the contribution of Robert Franke, who prepared all stemmas and diagrams. I thank Fred Unwalla for coordinating this project for the press, and Clare Orchard for her help in revising the manuscript. My greatest debt is to my editor Jean Hoff. She has been a learned reader of Greek, Latin and English, a generous advisor, and a great teacher. The love of my husband R. William Franklin and my daughters Corinna and Beatrice has sustained me throughout the vicissitudes of this project.

For

PAUL J. MEYVAERT

Abbreviations

ASS	*Acta Sanctorum.* Ed. Jean Bolland et al. Antwerp and Brussels, 1643ff; 3rd ed., 1863-1869.
BAV	Biblioteca apostolica vaticana
BHG	*Bibliotheca hagiographica graeca.* 3rd ed. Ed. F. Halkin. Subsidia Hagiographica 8a. Brussels, 1957 (repr. 1985).
BHL	*Bibliotheca hagiograhica latina antiquae et mediae aetatis.* Ed. Socii Bollandiani. Subsidia Hagiographica 6. Brussels, 1898-1899 (repr. 1992).
BHL. Supplementum	*Bibliotheca hagiograhica latina antiquae et mediae aetatis. Novum Supplementum.* Ed. Henryk Fros. Subsidia Hagiographica 70. Brussels, 1986.
BN	Bibliothèque nationale de France.
CCSL	Corpus Christianorum. Series Latina.
CGL	*Corpus Glossariorum Latinorum* II: *Glossae latinograecae et graecolatinae.* Ed. Georgius Goetz. Leipzig, 1888 (repr. Amsterdam, 1965).
Du Cange	*Glossarium ad scriptores mediae & infimae latinitatis.* Ed. Charles Du Fresne Du Cange. (repr. Paris, 1938).
CLCLT	*Cetedoc Library of Christian Latin Texts.*
Flusin	Flusin, Bernard. *Saint Anastase le Perse et l'histoire de la Palestine au début du VIIe siècle* I *Les Textes*; II *Commentaire. Les moines de Jérusalem et l'invasion perse.* Paris, 1992.
MGH	*Monumenta Germaniae Historica.*
PL	*Patrologia Latina.* Ed. J.-P. Migne.
TLL	*Thesaurus linguae latinae editus auctoritate et consilio academiarum quinque* ... Leipzig, 1900- .

I

FROM PERSIA TO ROME:
A MARTYR AND HIS RELICS

The Roman sanctoral[1] was from its very beginning enlarged by the cult of eastern[2] saints, particularly those martyrs whose popularity became widespread in the Mediterranean world during late antiquity. SS. Cosmas and Damian, for example, the physician brothers whose cult originated at Cyrrhus in Syria, had basilicas built in their honor in Constantinople, Jerusalem, Edessa, Cappadocia, and Egypt, and even in Sardinia in the fifth and sixth centuries. In the early sixth century Pope Felix IV dedicated an ancient edifice in the Roman Forum placing it under the name of Cosmas and Damian. Its apsis mosaic is still preserved today; its allusive inscription—"Martyribus medicis populo spes certa salutis fecit"—testifies to the healing miracles with which the veneration of the two saints was associated.[3] Similarly, the cult of the Libyan St. Mennas spread throughout the West beginning in the fourth century, and a church was dedicated to him on the left bank of the

---

1. By "sanctoral" I mean the collection of saints commemorated in various ways—both within the liturgy and outside it—by a religious community. The Latin word "sanctorale" which is its source frequently has a narrower, more specialized meaning, for it encompasses only those saints included in a calendar for liturgical celebration and can be defined as "the annual cycle of feast-days": see Harper, *The Forms and Orders of Western Liturgy from the Tenth to the Eighteenth Century*, pp. 51-53.

2. I use this term as well as "oriental" to refer in general to the Hellenized regions around the Mediterranean.

3. Jounel, *Le culte des saints dans les basiliques du Latran et du Vatican au douzième siècle*, p. 293. The source is the *Liber pontificalis* (Duchesne I, 279). But even before the pontificate of Felix, we learn from the *Liber pontificalis* that Symmachus (498-514) had dedicated an oratory to the *anargyres* on the Esquiline (Duchesne I, 262).

Tiber where Gregory I preached his thirty-fifth homily on the Gospels.[4] Cults for other eastern saints developed in Rome at this early date for very specific reasons. The veneration of the soldier Theodore, martyred in Amasia in Pontus, is most likely connected with the presence of imperial troops stationed in Rome. The small, round church that bears his name, and whose mosaic dates from the sixth or seventh century, is close to that of St. George *in Velabro*, another soldier saint and, like Theodore, a patron of the imperial troops.[5]

But it was during the period when the city was under direct Byzantine control from the second half of the sixth century, and particularly in the seventh century, that the influx of eastern saints was more rapid, and the cult of those already venerated was strengthened.[6] The reasons for the establishment of these cults in Rome during the Byzantine period are complex. They include the role of Greek-speaking communities in Rome, especially monastic ones, but also the influence of clerical and secular groups; the support of the Roman clerical establishment and its complex relationship to Byzantine cultural influences; the character of the cult, and the presence and efficacy of relics and miracles associated with them; and finally the creation of Latin texts, which were essential for the liturgical celebration of the saint. All of these elements are present in the early history of the cult of Anastasius the Persian monk, making it perhaps the most richly documented eastern cult first established in Rome during the Byzantine period. Its literary and historical dossier permits us to follow in detail the early development of an oriental cult in the city, its spread in the early Middle Ages, and the diffusion and transformation of hagiographic texts across linguistic, chronological, and geographical borders.

---

4. Jounel, *Le culte*, p. 309; *Homeliae in Evangelia* ii, 35 (PL 76, 1259). No trace of this church remains today.

5. Jounel, *Le culte*, pp. 307-308. The head of St. George was also brought to Rome, perhaps in 682 but rediscovered at the Lateran only in the 740s. Both churches are located in the area north of the Palatine, which grew up into a sort of Byzantine quarter in the course of the sixth and early seventh century (Krautheimer, *Rome. Profile of a City, 312-1308*, pp. 76, 90).

6. Sansterre, *Les moines grecs et orientaux à Rome aux époques byzantine et carolingienne* I, 146-156.

According to the Greek *Acta,*[7] chronicling the saint's life and works, Magundat, the future Anastasius, had been a soldier in the army of the Persian king Chosroes II (590-628), who invaded Palestine at the beginning of the seventh century. Although the son of a *magus* and himself trained in "the magical arts" of Zoroastrianism, the Persian soldier became curious about the religion of the cross when he witnessed its arrival at Ctesiphon, where the cross was brought as a trophy to the Persian ruler after the fall of Jerusalem in 614. After the siege of Chalcedon in the same year, Magundat deserted the Persian army, and began a long journey that led him finally to Jerusalem, where he was baptized in 620 by Modestus, the vicar of the exiled patriarch of Jerusalem, and assumed the fitting Christian name Anastasius. He then joined a monastery outside the holy city called "of abbot Anastasius," where he remained for seven years. Enflamed with a desire to emulate the example of the martyrs whose remarkable deeds he saw represented on the walls of the church—a detail that, as we shall see, would be of great significance in later generations' perception of the saint—Anastasius left his community, and embarked on wanderings that culminated in his capture by the Persians in Caesarea of Palestine. Unwilling to renounce his Christian religion, he was sent to Persia, where he was tried and executed by strangulation at Bethsaloe (Kirkuk in modern Iraq) on 22 January 628. His head was then severed so that the seal that had been placed around his neck could be brought unbroken to the Persian king, whose imminent defeat and death Anastasius had prophesized. Anastasius's body was buried in the monastery of St. Sergius, near the place of execution. Within ten days, the victorious armies of the Byzantine emperor Heraclius arrived at Bethsaloe.

---

7. *BHG* 84, edited in Bernard Flusin, *Saint Anastase le Perse et l'histoire de la Palestine au début du VIIe siècle* I, 39-91 (hereafter Flusin). Both *Acta* and *Passio,* frequently joined in *Acta uel/seu passio,* were widely used to refer to the account of the life, passion, and death of a martyr. I use *Acta* for the Greek text, and *Passio* for its early Latin translation (*BHL* 410b, discussed in the next chapter; its text is found below, pp. 259-298; and a Latin translation is appended to this chapter), and for other, later Latin redactions.

The Persian convert soon became a symbol of the triumph of Christianity and its emperor over the power of paganism and Persia, and his relics became a precious and empowering possession.[8] The Greek *Acta* of the Persian soldier turned Christian monk were commissioned by the patriarch of Jerusalem, Modestus, who had baptized Anastasius. They were written during his brief patriarchate between March and December 630 by a member of the monastery of "abbot Anastasius" in Jerusalem. They may even have been conceived while Anastasius was still alive, for they were based on the eyewitness account of another monk who had been sent to accompany Anastasius on his journey to Persia for trial and execution, and had returned to Jerusalem with the armies of the victorious Heraclius.[9]

Soon, however, the desire to recover the martyr's body and head from Bethsaloe and house them at the Jerusalem monastery led the same monk who had been the eyewitness informant for the author of the *Acta* to embark on a second trip to Persia. The account of how the relics were transferred—they were in fact stolen—to Palestine is provided by the Greek *Translatio*. This work was written soon after the triumphant arrival of the relics in Jerusalem on 2 November 631, probably by the same monk who wrote the *Acta*.[10]

Bernard Flusin has shown the exceptional interest that these works hold for the history of the Persian occupation of Palestine; their documentary value is unique. Just as importantly, these texts depict the reaction of the Palestinian monastic community to the powerful cataclysms that had seemed to overwhelm them—the invasion of Palestine, the capture of Jerusalem, and the abduction of the holy cross. These larger events form a counterpoint to the narrative of Anastasius's personal story in the *Acta* and *Translatio*.

---

8. This is one of the themes of Flusin's discussion, particularly at II, 329-352.

9. See Chapter II, pp. 71-73 for a discussion of Modestus's involvement and dating; and Flusin II, 185-190, who refutes earlier proposals that assigned authorship to known figures.

10. The Greek *Translatio* (*BHG* 88) is published in Flusin I, 93-107. The work would certainly have been completed before 1 September 632. See Flusin I, 8.

Thus, the capture of the cross by the Persians becomes the means of the Persian soldier's conversion, the Persian magician becomes a model Christian monk and glorious martyr, and the restoration of the cross to Jerusalem is paralleled by the return of the martyr's relics to his monastery near the holy city. The story of Anastasius thus becomes an analogue of the history of Palestine during the Persian conquest.

The development of the cult of Anastasius is closely tied to the relics of his body. A collection of miracles records the wondrous events surrounding the relics as they travel from Persia to Jerusalem.[11] They mark the principal sites where the knowledge of Anastasius was spreading: Ctesiphon in Persia, Palmyra in Syria, and in Palestine Caesarea, Diospolis, and finally Jerusalem, where, at the monastery of "abbot Anastasius," the principal parts of the relics, including the head, were deposited.[12]

But the Arab invasions, and specifically the capitulation of Jerusalem in 638, swept away both the monastery and the tomb of the martyr. Nothing remains of these sites, and nothing is known of the geographical organization of the cult of Anastasius in Jerusalem. Our only evidence for the cult in Jerusalem are the *Acta* and the *Translatio*, which were written there. In Palestine, the cult of Anastasius began with the victory over the Persians but quickly disappeared with the arrival of Islam.

11. See *BHG* 89g-90; the collection of miracles is edited in Flusin I, 109-153 (see also II, 329-337, 381). It is made up of separate parts. The principal part, *Miracles* 1-14, which describe events taking place along the route traveled by the relics, was put together at Constantinople around 650 by an editor or reviser who might have integrated a collection from the monastery "of abbot Anastasius" with other smaller collections; *Miracles* 15-18, which concern the adventures of a monk who travels from Jerusalem to Constantinople and back with a piece of the relic, were added by a continuator or perhaps by the same editor, and do not fit into the narrative quite as well (Flusin II, 337).

12. An oratory was built at Ctesiphon around fragments of the relic left there by the monk who had stolen the major part of it (Flusin II, 344-348). At Caesarea, where Anastasius had been venerated while still alive, a large part of the relic was kept at the church of St. Anastasius of the Tetrapylos. The details of the narrative that follows rely principally on Flusin II, 348-352.

The cult had by then taken hold in Constantinople, brought there already perhaps by the victorious armies of Heraclius.[13] Certainly, between 631 and 638 the *Acta* were known in the imperial capital, for they served as the basis for an *Encomium* of the Persian saint composed by George of Pisidia, the famous court poet and deacon of Hagia Sophia.[14] The importance of the cult of Anastasius is signaled by the details surrounding the composition of this work. The *Encomium* was commissioned by Patriarch Sergius of Constantinople, and recited by George of Pisidia before a gathering that included the patriarch as well as Anastasius's former teacher Pyrrhus, himself a future patriarch of Constantinople.[15] The importance of the cult of Anastasius in Constantinople is supported as well by the collection of ancient miracles. Several of the miracles were written in the capital, and the entire compilation was put together there.[16] The last three tell how a monk of Jerusalem went to Constantinople with the body and an icon of the saint, after passing through Syria, Cilicia, and Cappadocia. While the narrative is a pretext for the telling of miracles, the account may reflect the actual itinerary of the relic and icon.[17]

But then for one hundred and fifty years nothing is heard of the cult's development in the East. By the time the silence is broken, at the Council of Nicea II in 787, it is beyond doubt that the cult of Anastasius is now centered in Rome. The Fathers of the council, in their condemnation of iconoclasm, made three references to

---

13. Pertusi, "L'encomio di S. Anastasio martire persiano," p. 23 n. 5.

14. The *Encomium* (*BHG* 86) has most recently been edited in Flusin I, 191-259.

15. Pertusi, "L'encomio di S. Anastasio," pp. 5-63. Pertusi argues convincingly that the work should be attributed to George of Pisidia rather than Sophronius of Jerusalem; Pyrrhus, here identified as Anastasius's nameless teacher in the *Acta*, was to succeed Sergius on the patriarchal throne of Constantinople. For further discussion see Flusin II, 381-389 and Chapter II below.

16. See n. 11 above.

17. In 1200 a visitor to the church of St. Luke to the west of Constantinople reports the presence of the relic of "St. Anastasius, who is without head, because his head has been stolen" (Anthony of Novgorod in Khitrowo, *Itinéraires russes in Orient*, p. 103; Sansterre, *Les moines grecs* I, 15 and n. 58).

the cult of Anastasius, all to strengthen the veneration of icons.[18] The first reference is provided by Gregorius, deacon of the Church of the Holy Apostles, who cites the passage in the *Acta* (9.1-10) that describes how Magundat's conversion was inspired by the images of the saints' lives painted on the walls of the churches in Hierapolis.[19] Second, there is the reading of a *Miracle*, taken from the collection compiled in Constantinople, telling how the icon of St. Anastasius, placed on the outside of the oratory built near the Tetrapylos in Caesarea, healed the incredulous woman Arete.[20] Thirdly, the representatives of the pope, Peter, archpriest of St. Peter, and Peter, hegoumenos of St. Sabas on the Aventine, report to the gathering that the miraculous icon is now found in Rome's monastery of St. Anastasius together with the head of the martyr. The location of the icon in Rome is confirmed by John, bishop of Taormina in Sicily, who declares that a possessed woman from his island traveled to Rome, where she was cured by the miraculous icon.[21]

18. Mansi, *Sacrorum conciliorum nova et amplissima collectio* XIII, 21-23. In accordance with the procedure of the council, the citations are quoted verbatim, and not paraphrased. For a discussion of Nicea II and its links with St. Anastasius, see Flusin II, 389-392.

19. I cite the editions of the Greek texts in the first volume of Flusin by chapter and line number.

20. *Miracles* 7 (Flusin I, 131-133).

21. There is no evidence to support the contention that the icon from Caesarea is the same as the one described at the council as being in Rome. However, as Flusin points out, from a moral perspective, it is the same. More perplexing is the absence of any mention of an icon in Rome in any source other than the conciliar acts of Nicea II. The exorcism of 713 described in the Roman Miracle makes no mention of an icon (see below n. 45 and pp. 14-15) and if the bishop of Taormina speaking at Nicea was referring to the Roman Miracle (as Bertelli, "'Caput Sancti Anastasii,'" pp. 13-14 maintains), his account is inaccurate. The speculation (Bertelli, ibid.) that the icon in Rome may have been burned when a fire ravaged the basilica and the monastery where it was kept during the pontificate of Hadrian I (772-795) has no support, nor does it explain the failure of earlier sources, most importantly the Roman Miracle and the *Liber pontificalis*, to refer to the object that is so in evidence at Nicea. See further below, pp. 18-20.

That Rome has become the center of the cult of the martyr by the time of Nicea II is thus indicated by, first, the witness of the two speakers from Rome, including a high official of the Roman church; secondly, by the report of the Sicilian bishop, John of Taormina, of an exorcism taking place in Rome. While the citations of the *Acta* and *Miracles* recall the settings of the life and martyrdom of St. Anastasius, the living expressions of the cult of the Persian—relic, icon, miracles—are found in the western capital.

The quotations taken directly from the Greek *Acta* and the *Miracles* of Anastasius in the conciliar acts have been seen as an indication that these works were available at the council in 787, for the passages are carefully cited, including the title as well as the *incipits* of the works quoted. It has been supposed that the hagiographic dossier would have been available at the library of the ecumenical patriarchate or at some Constantinopolitan sanctuary or monastery, and thence brought to Nicea. If this is true, the dossier may possibly have been used in the liturgy, since Anastasius was part of the calendar of the church of Constantinople from the time of the patriarchate of Sergius.[22] But it seems much more likely that the citations from the *Acta* and *Miracles* of Anastasius read at Nicea were extracted from originals kept in Rome, emphasizing further how Anastasius's cult had become identified with the city, and even with the anti-iconoclastic ideology of its church.

It has been convincingly argued that the texts used at Nicea II constituted an iconodule florilegium brought from Rome, assembled from an extensive compilation of Greek documents and theological works, put together perhaps from the contents of the papal library at the Lateran palace.[23] This source has been described as a *florilegium florilegiorum* copied in 774/5, one of the "dogmatic weapons stored in the patristic arsenal of the Roman church," containing authoritative material on "every major disputed issue of the

---

22. Flusin II, 389-390.

23. Alexakis, *Codex Parisinus Graecus 1115 and Its Archetype*, esp. pp. 255-260. Parisinus gr. 1115 is shown by Alexakis to be a descendant of the iconodule florilegium, refuting earlier views, which had seen it as embodying an earlier collection.

Christian faith."[24] As a consequence, it is possible to assume that the iconodule florilegium utilized at Nicea contained also the passages from the *Acta* of St. Anastasius and the miracle account as quoted at the council.[25] These extracts therefore would have been copied in Rome along with the other authoritative texts cited at the council against iconoclasm. It would have been in Rome, and not in Constantinople or its surrounding monasteries, that the dossier of Anastasius had been mined as an authoritative source against the heresy. There is speculation that Anastasius regained his popularity in Constantinople as a result as his reemergence as a champion of the cult of images of Nicea II. The empress Irene and her son the emperor Constantine, who called the council against iconoclasm, built a sanctury in his honor there.[26] But the martyr's status as a champion of orthodoxy had been constructed in Rome, and lay at the very origin of the cult of the Persian in the western capital.

Indeed, the origin of the cult in Rome dates back to the early years of the cult itself. Within little over a decade after the translation of the relics of Anastasius from Persia to Jerusalem in 631, what was believed to be the relic of the head of the martyr is found at the Cilician community *ad Aquas Salvias* in Rome. One of the most important Greek monasteries of the city, it was located southeast of St. Paul Outside the Walls, along a road that joined the *via Ostiensis* to the *via Ardeatina* or, according to others, the *Laurentina*, at a place where the decapitation of the apostle Paul was reputed to have taken place. The rise of the cult

---

24. Alexakis, *Codex Parisinus Graecus 1115*, p. 255.

25. We can make this assumption since Parisinus contains the passage from the *Acta* as well as part of the miracle account; see Flusin I, 36 and 114 for a brief discussion of the hagiographic dossier of St. Anastasius at Nicea, and Alexakis as in n. 23.

26. See Flusin II, 392-393 for the last stages of the cult of Anastasius in Constantinople. Flusin suggests that the area chosen for the new building—the quarter where oriental monks resided—also shows the emperors' desire to honor the eastern saint and his devotees. As Flusin points out, it may not be a coincidence that the church of St. Luke, where in 1200 the relic of St. Anastasius was venerated (see above, n. 17), also enjoyed the empress's liberality.

of Anastasius in Rome must be connected to the arrival of the relic of the head of the saint in the eternal city. Its presence there is first mentioned explicitly in the seventh-century regional catalogue known as *De locis sanctis martyrum quae sunt foris Romae*.[27] This precursor of the modern guidebook includes in the pilgrim's itinerary on the via Ostiense not far from the basilica of St. Paul "the monastery of the Aquae Salviae, where is found the head of St. Anastasius, and the place where Paul was beheaded" ("Inde haud procul in meridiem monasterium est Aquae salviae, ubi caput sancti Anastasi est, et locus ubi decollatus est Paulus").[28]

The date and circumstances surrounding the origin of the monastery remain uncertain. A tradition that attributed the foundation to the Byzantine general Narses in the second half of the sixth century has been completely discredited.[29] It has been suggested, also unconvincingly, that the founding of the monastery by Cilicians at a place where tradition placed the beheading of Paul, the apostle venerated at Tarsus in Cilicia, should be connected with the capture of Tarsus by the Persian general Shahrbaraz around 611.[30] The earliest evidence for the monastery at the Aquae Sal-

27. It was composed between 650 and 682-683 (Geertman, *More veterum: il 'Liber Pontificalis' e gli edifici ecclesiastici di Roma nella tarda antichità e nell'alto medioevo*, pp. 198-202). The *De locis sanctis* is edited in Valentini and Zucchetti, *Codice topografico della città di Roma* II, 109.

28. For its history, see Sansterre, *Les moines grecs* I, 13-17, with earlier bibliography, and especially Ferrari, *Early Roman monasteries. Notes for the history of the monasteries and convents at Rome from the V through the X century*. Broccoli, *L'abbazia delle Tre Fontane. Fasi paleocristiane e altomedievali del complesso 'ad Aquas Salvias' in Roma* provides a survey of the early archeological evidence. I have covered some of this material in my "Theodore and the *Passio S. Anastasii*."

29. The tradition goes back to the *Chronicon* of Benedict of Soracte written at about the end of the tenth century. Most recently, Broccoli, *L'abbazia delle Tre Fontane*, pp. 21, 28, 32, tried to show that a monastery of the Cilicians already existed there in the sixth century. Sansterre's contrary arguments (*Les moines grecs* II, 229) are completely convincing.

30. Flusin II, 372. However, the chronology does work out, for it seems certain that there was no monastery there as late as 604 since it is not mentioned in a letter of Gregory I instructing Felix, a church administrator, to give to the basilica of St. Paul Ouside the Walls the *massa quae Aqua Salvias*

viae is contained in the minutes of the second session of the Lateran Synod in October 649, called to combat the heresy of monotheletism, the belief that Christ has one will.[31] The minutes of the synod present this monastery as a well-established community of Cilician monks who voice their opposition to the heresy of monotheletism favored by the imperial court at Constantinople. The Lateran Synod of 649 provides telling evidence that the struggle for orthodoxy was led by the Greek-speaking monasteries of Rome,[32] established by monks from Syria, Palestine, and neighboring regions, whose invasion first by the Persians and then by the Arabs, caused a massive exodus westward, particularly to southern Italy and Rome. The early development of the cult of Anastasius within the monastic communities engaged in the orthodox resistance against the heresy of monotheletism, which will be further explored in the following chapter, helps to explain the early link forged between the veneration of his relics and the defense of orthodoxy.

How and by whom the relic of Anastasius the Persian monk was brought to Rome and deposited at the Cilician monastery *ad Aquas Salvias* remains unclear. But it seems most likely, given what we know of the monastic settlements of Palestine and their activities in Rome in the middle of the seventh century, that it was monks from the Jerusalem area, who in flight from Arab advances—Jerusalem itself fell in 638—took with them their precious cargo. The relic of the head of St. Anastasius may have been at the Cilicians' monastery by 645, when the martyr's fame as a thaumaturge was already commemorated in Rome's liturgy. A gospel pericope, Mark 5.21-34 on the healing of the hemorrhaging woman, had been included into the Roman evangeliary on St. Anastasius's feast day, 22 January.[33] The cult of St. Anastasius provides a clear

---

nuncupatur to provide for its illumination (*Gregorii I Papae Registrum Epistolarum* II, 433-434; discussed by both Ferrari, *Early Roman monasteries*, p. 36 and Sansterre, *Les moines grecs* I, 14). It is also possible that an oratory dedicated to St. Paul existed at this location: see Ferrari, p. 46.

31. Mansi, *Concilia* X, 904A [=903A]. For full discussion, see Sansterre, *Les moines grecs* I, 9-10.

32. These have been studied most recently by Sansterre, *Les moines grecs*; see also his "Le monachisme Byzantin à Rome."

33. Sansterre, *Les moines grecs* I, 15.

example of the influence exerted by the exiled monastic communities of Rome on the city's sanctoral.[34]

Why only the head of the saint, and not the rest of the body, was transferred to Rome remains unknown. Since the Arabs' conquest of Palestine and Jerusalem was accomplished in stages, a hasty flight by the Jerusalem monks who would have grabbed only what they could easily carry is not convincing.[35] On the other hand, the decapitation of Anastasius by his executioners facilitated the exaltation of the relic of the head over the rest of the saint's body, a common practice in the Middle Ages.[36] At the monastery in Jerusalem, the relic of the head may have been preserved separately from the rest of the body, which already had undergone fragmentation during its trip from Persia, as we learn both from the *Translatio* and the collection of ancient miracles.[37] The removal of the head to Rome may be seen

34. The role played by Greek monks in the promotion of the cult of oriental saints in Rome has been difficult to gauge, and scholars have disagreed in their estimation. For a discussion of the ways in which the Anastasius dossier provides us with a window onto the milieu of the Greek population of early eighth-century Rome, see Sansterre, *Les moines grecs* I, 147-162 and II, 176-177 n. 23 and below, Chapter II.

35. Flusin II, 356-359. Of course there are other historical examples: the monks of Saint-Pair near Granville, fleeing the Normans in the early tenth century, took the bodies of their founders from their tombs but in their haste left many important bones behind; and Hariulf's *Chronicle of St. Riquier* III, 11 (in Lot, *Hariulf. Chronique de l'Abbaye de Saint-Riquier*, p. 120) notes that the head of St. Riquier was separated from the body for ease of transportation, should invasions force the monks to flee. Both examples are discussed in Herrmann-Mascard, *Les reliques des saints. Formation coutumière d'un droit*, p. 63.

36. This was certainly true in the West. For a very recent discussion of the "hierarchy" of relics, see Boehm, "Body-Part Reliquaries: The State of Research," p. 15. For the fragmentation of relics see, in general, Herrmann-Mascard, *Les reliques des saints*, p. 62.

37. See, for example, *Translatio* 6, which tells how the people of Caesarea wished to prevent the body of Anastasius from leaving the city, forcing the abbot himself to come from Jerusalem to retrieve it. He was able to do so only after leaving a large part of the relic for the faithful of Caesarea. See n. 12 above.

as continuing the fragmentation and dispersion of the relics of the martyr Anastasius.[38]

The importance of the cult of the Persian to the community *ad Aquas Salvias* was such that the monastery of the Cilicians, called by different names at first,[39] by the end of the eighth century came to be known generally as "S. Anastasius ad Aquas Salvias."[40] The presence of the relic helped make the monastery a regular stop on the tour of the eternal city by pilgrims. The *De locis sanctis*, as mentioned above, singles out as its most important attraction the head of Anastasius. The Malmesbury catalogue, compiled by William of Malmesbury (†ca. 1143), but based on a source from the second half of the seventh century or the beginning of the eighth, also mentions the relic of the head, but not the monastery.[41] The

38. There is some evidence suggesting both an intermediate stop at Constantinople and further peregrinations, during which the objects connected with the veneration of Anastasius may have come into the possession of Cilician monks. See further Franklin, "Theodore," pp. 180-181. For a possible stop in North Africa, see below, pp. 75-76 and n. 73.

39. In the minutes of the Lateran Synod of 649 it is called "de cilicia qui ponitur ad Aquas Salvias"; Bede's entry in the *Chronica maiora* ("monasterio beati Pauli apostoli, quod dicitur ad Aquas Salvias" [ed. Mommsen, p. 310; ed. Jones, p. 524])—discussed further in Chapter VI—is tied clearly to the martyrdom of St. Paul, which tradition placed here, and where there might have been some dedication to the apostle from Tarsus (Ferrari, *Early Roman monasteries*, p. 46); the title of the Roman Miracle refers to it as *monasterio quod appellatur Aqua Salvia*.

40. See the section on Hadrian I below, p. 19 and n. 59. The name of the monastery should not be confused with the name of the church within the monastery, which is identified as "mansionem sanctae Dei genitricis semperque virginis Mariae ubi sanctus ac beatus Paulus apostolus decollatus est in loco qui appellatur Aqua Salvia, ubi requiescunt venerabiles reliquiae beati martyris Anastasii" in the Roman Miracle (p. 350, ll. 46-50) and as "oratorio sancte Marie qui ponitur in monasterio aque Salviae" in the *Liber pontificalis* (Duchesne II, 24). Here, the monastery is differentiated from the church, most clearly in the list of gifts of 807 (see below, p. 19). The Roman Miracle also makes it clear that there is another church, dedicated to St. John the Baptist, outside the monastic enclosure ("quia in ipso monasterio mulier non ingreditur, iuxta monasterium est basilica beati Iohannis Baptistae et precursoris" [ll. 50-52]).

41. Also edited in Valentini and Zuchetti, *Codice topografico* II, 150.

martyr's popularity on the pilgrimage route is also demonstrated by a lamp inscribed with the name Anastasius found in a Roman archaeological deposit from the late seventh century.[42] One of the great relic hoards assembled in the early Middle Ages at Sens during the seventh and eighth centuries includes a relic of St. Anastasius, who has been identified with the Persian martyr; it seems most likely that the relic came from Rome.[43] When Sigeric, archbishop of Canterbury, traveled to Rome to collect the pallium in 990, he visited twenty-three major pilgrimage sites in the city. Nine of these sites were situated outside the walls, one of which was the monastery of St. Anastasius.[44]

The miraculous powers of the relic, and the prestige of the monastery that possessed it, are manifest in the story told in the Roman Miracle. The work was written in Greek in 713-714, no doubt at the monastery of St. Anastasius itself, but soon translated into Latin.[45] It recounts in uncommon detail the exorcism of a young woman from 1 October to 1 November 713 through the relic of the head of Anastasius at the church of St. John the Baptist, an oratory connected with the monastery, because the church dedicated to the Virgin where the relic was kept was within the monastic enclosure and inaccessible to women. The relics are brought into increasingly close contact with the possessed girl: at first, they are placed on the altar in their container;[46] a tooth of the saint is taken out of the reliquary and hung around the girl's neck, but the devil makes it disappear; finally, the entire skull of the saint is taken out of its container and placed on a plate directly

---

42. Panella and Saguí, "Consumo e produzione a Roma tra tardoantico e altomedioevo: le merci, i contesti," pp. 798-799. This artifact suggests the large-scale production of similar objects for the consumption of pilgrims.

43. McCormick, *Origins of the European Economy. Communications and Commerce AD 300-900*, pp. 295 n. 34, 307 n. 69.

44. Birch, *Pilgrimage to Rome in the Middle Ages. Continuity and Change*, p. 98.

45. The Greek text is found in Flusin I, 155-187. The Latin translation is discussed in Chapter IV and edited on pp. 339-361. An English translation can be found in an appendix to this chapter.

46. There is no specific mention of a reliquary until later in the text (10.17), but it clear that the relics had been held in some container all along.

on top of the head of the stricken girl. For nearly a month the devil torments the girl, and taunts those assembled in the church through her words and actions, until he finally succumbs to the greater might of the saint.[47]

The report given by Bishop John of Taormina at the Council of Nicea II in 787 echoes, to a certain extent, the events narrated in the Roman Miracle about three quarters of a century earlier. In both cases, the saint effects the liberation of a possessed woman: through his relic in the Miracle, but through his icon in the Nicea report. Sicily features in both accounts: Taormina is in Sicily, and its bishop describes a woman "from Sicily" who travels to Rome to be cured. The Roman Miracle describes how the magic incantation wrapped in fig leaves, by which the devil enters the girl, was procured in Sicily by a spurned suitor. But here, the girl's father is said to be a Syrian bishop who had arrived in Rome only a few years before, and therefore the girl is not a Sicilian.

These differences preclude the identification of the story narrated by Bishop John of Taormina at Nicea with the Roman Miracle. But the veneration of St. Anastasius in early medieval Sicily, and particularly within its Greek-speaking communities, must have been significant, for it finds serendipitous support in a tenth-century Greek inscription carved on a marble architrave in Syracuse, reading ...*νων μάρτυρος 'Αναστασίου*. It has been taken as evidence that a church or oratory dedicated to the saint existed in Syracuse in the tenth century; no further trace remains. If the fragment is reconstructed to contain a reference to the relics of the martyr Anastasius in the genitive plural (*λειψά]νων μάρτυρος 'Αναστασίου*), this would certainly suggest the presence of some relics in Syracuse. On the other hand, a reconstruction as *τοῦ ἐν ἁγίοις πατρὸς ἡμ]ῶν μάρτυρος 'Αναστασίου*, is just as plausible, and would simply indicate the existence of a building dedicated to the cult of the martyr.[48]

---

47. Most extraordinarily, the devil, through the girl, says that he will put down in writing the torments he will suffer if he should enter her body again (... *διότι ἐγγράφως ποιῶ τῷ ἁγίῳ 'Αναστασίῳ* [11.32; cf. l. 270]).

48. Guillou, *Recueil des inscriptions grecques médiévales d'Italie*, plate 198 and p. 233 (no. 213).

An unambiguous witness to the veneration of the relic of the head of Anastasius, however, is to be found at the northern end of the Italian peninsula: an epigraphic monument erected by the Lombard King Liutprand but surviving today only on parchment. After his conquest of Ravenna from the Byzantine exarch Eutychius in 732, or perhaps after his next trip to Rome in 739,[49] Liutprand built a church and monastery dedicated to St. Anastasius in his royal estates at Corteolona, not far from the Lombard capital of Pavia.[50] The contents of three of the hexameter inscriptions that decorated the church have been preserved.[51] One of them describes the beauty of the building at Corteolona, its mosaics, columns and precious marbles.[52] Another describes how Liutprand abandoned his original intention to build baths with precious marbles and columns when the king kissed the relic of St. Anastasius:[53]

49. Bertolini, *Roma e i Longobardi*, pp. 38-42, proposes the earlier date for the building of the church, and argues against the date of 739 that had been proposed by Giorgi, "Il Regesto del monastero di S. Anastasio ad Aquas Salvias," p. 53. Bertolini contends that the triumphal tone of the inscriptions better befits the moment after the capture of Ravenna, and discounts the fact that the biographer of Gregory II in the *Liber pontificalis* makes no mention of Liutprand's visit to the relic of Anastasius, describing instead the king's devotion to the tomb of Peter, prince of the apostles (Duchesne I, 403, 407-408). Liutprand is known to have made only two trips to Rome.

50. Paulus Diaconus, *Historia Langobardorum* VI, 58 (ed. Waitz, pp. 185-186).

51. The inscriptions, preserved in BAV, Palatinus latinus 833, fols. 48v-49r, of the ninth century, are published in de Rossi, *Inscriptiones christianae urbis Romae septimo saeculo antiquiores* II, 168-169, numm. 21-23; and also in Duemmler, *Tituli saeculi VIII*, 106, numm. X-XII. The three inscriptions relating to this building are prefaced with the title: *In Ecclesia Beati Anastasii quam construxit Leutbrandus Rex in Italia.* They are discussed in Bertolini, *Roma e i Longobardi*, pp. 38-42. On the manuscript, see now Franklin, "The Epigraphic Syllogae of BAV, Palatinus latinus 833." There have been no studies of Liutprand's monumental inscriptions; they are not included in De Rubeis, "Le iscrizioni dei re longobardi," which treats only funerary inscriptions still preserved on stone.

52. Paul the Deacon in his history also emphasizes the splendor of the church: "miro opere in honore sancti Anastasii martyris Christi."

53. We are not told whether Liutprand in fact kissed the relic itself or the reliquary that contained it. Kissing was a common practice in the veneration of relics: see Herrmann-Mascard, *Les reliques des saints*, pp. 213-214.

Quando Leo cecidit misero doctore suasus
Scismatis in foueam recto de culmine caesar
Tunc ego regales statui his mihi condere thermas
Marmoribus pulchris Leudbrant rex atque columnis
Sed Romam properans postquam deuotus ad ipsam
Perueni atque sacro capiti mea basia fixi
Sancti Anastasii seruus tuus ecce repente
Paterna de sede meo hanc in pectore Christe
Praeclaram fundare domum sub culmine monstras
Talibus unde meas tendens ad sidera palmas
Vocibus oro Dei fili pro plebe fideli
Qui regis angelicos coetos qui cuncta gubernas
Fac precor ut crescat mecum catholicus ordo
Et templo concede isti ut Salomoni locutus.[54]

The hexameter inscription contrasts the orthodox faith of Liutprand (*seruus tuus*)[55] with the heresy of the Byzantine ruler Leo (III Isauricus), the supporter of iconoclasm, who is "misero doctore suasus" and thus falls "scismatis in foueam." It portrays Liutprand as a pilgrim (*devotus*), going to Rome, where he reverently kisses the head of St. Anastasius, whereupon Christ himself "paterna de sede" intervenes and inspires him to build a church dedicated to his martyr.[56]

One is left to wonder why Liutprand chose to honor St. Anastasius and place his kiss on this particular relic among so many in

54. I transcribe from the manuscript (BAV, Pal. lat. 833, fols. 48v-49r). The ending of the word *praeclar[am]*, in line 9, has been rubbed off; I read *coetos* in line 12, and not *coetus*. Duemmler (p. 106) tentatively emends *his*, in line 3 to *hic*, but I do not think that this change ("Then I decided to build royal baths for me *here* with beautiful marbles") is necessary. The manuscript's reading ("Then I decided to build for me royal baths with *these* beautiful marbles") emphasizes the king's use of the ancient marbles (*spolia*?) for a better purpose. This interpretation finds some support in the first inscription's description of the church, glimmering with precious metals, marbles and columns.

55. Bertolini (p. 40) takes *seruus tuus* to refer to St. Anastasius, but the grammar certainly indicates that it refers to Liutprand, paralleling the other modifier also referring to the king, *devotus*.

56. The first inscription also highlights Liutprand's agency in the building of the church (fol. 48v): "Euge auctor sacri princeps Leutbrando (Leutbrande?) laboris / Te tua felicem clamabunt acta per aeuum / qui proprie gentis cupiens ornare triumphos / his titulis patriam signasti denique totum (totam?)."

Rome, and why he then decided to build a church commemorating that experience. No historian has discussed what may have led Liutprand to venerate the relic and erect the church in Anastasius's name in his suburban residence. Paulus Diaconus's list of the churches built by the Lombard king, where the church of St. Anastasius is included, is not very extensive; Liutprand is not remembered particularly as a church-builder.

It may have been the thaumaturgic powers of the saint, for which the Roman Miracle and the acts of Nicea II provide evidence both before and after the visit of the king, that exerted a great attraction. However, there are no references in the inscriptions to the power and miracles of Anastasius. Indeed, the emphasis in the inscription is on the orthodoxy of the Lombard king and the heresy of the Byzantine emperor. Liutprand's veneration of the relic of Anastasius during his journey to Rome was meant to portray the Lombard king as "re d'inconcussa ortodossia cattolica."[57] The association of the cult of Anastasius with orthodoxy may have played a role in the king's choice that has not been directly recognized. Since Anastasius's status as a witness against iconoclasm is evident at Nicea II, such a reputation may have already been established by the time of Liutprand's visit to Rome. This status may have been built on the monastery's traditional alliance with the church of Rome going back to the Lateran Synod of 649. St. Anastasius may have assumed "something of the nature of a symbol of resistance to imperial tampering with doctrine" partly through the memory of two seventh-century Anastasii (a papal legate and a disciple of Maximus the Confessor) who had been prominent in Roman resistance to monotheletism.[58] In the Roman Miracle, which took place just two decades before Liutprand's visit, the devil (7.15-17; ll. 147-150) boasts of his allegiance to the heretic emperor Philippicus (Philippikos Bardanes) who had attempted to revive monotheletism, and displays anger that St. Peter has instead ensured the success of the orthodox, and aptly named, Anastasius II.

During the eighth and ninth centuries the prestige of the relic and the monastery where it was housed attracted many papal gifts,

---

57. Bertolini, *Roma e i Longobardi*, esp. p. 34.
58. Llewellyn, *Rome in the Dark Ages*, p. 164.

as the *Liber pontificalis* attests. When the church of the monastery "beati Anastasii Christi martyris," together with the *vestiario* (the building where the church's vestments and other precious objects were probably kept) and the *ygumenarchio*, that is the abbot's house, burned down in 789-790 because of the "carelessness of the monks," Pope Hadrian I himself hastened to the site and found the "arca eiusdem martyris lympsani eruta in media corte iacente." He restored the church "cum vestiario et ygumenarchio" as well as the other buildings and placed the arca "in meliori statu."[59] After this event, the *Liber pontificalis* records several more papal gifts to the monastery of St. Anastasius. During the pontificate of Leo III (†816) the monastery and its church are included among the recipients of papal largesse on three occasions. The first time was in 800-801 when the pontiff bestowed on the monastery "a gold-studded cloth depicting that martyr's passion, and a silver light with an eight-sided canister weighing 25 lbs."[60] Secondly, and particularly noteworthy, is the list of the donations made by Leo III in 807 to the monasteries and churches of Rome according to hierarchical principles.[61] Of the Greek monasteries, St. Anastasius (ranking second in importance after St. Sabas) was given "coronam ex argento, pens. lib. VIII, unc. IIII semis."[62] On a third occasion, a silver *canistrum* of two pounds was presented to the "oratorio sanctae

---

59. Duchesne I, 512-513 (transl. Davis, in *The Lives of the Eighth-Century Popes*, pp. 169-170). This passage is the first attestation of the monastery's specific name as "beati Anastasii"; it is also the last specific reference to the relic in the *Liber pontificalis*.

60. Duchesne II, 11: "Immo et in monasterio sancti Anastasii fecit vestem cum chrisoclabo eiusdem martyris passione depicta; et farum de argento cum canistro octogonii, pens. lib. XXV" (transl. Davis, in *The Lives*, p. 197, which also points out that a *corona* is a circular lamp fitting and a *canistrum* is a dish placed under a lamp to catch drips [p. 237]).

61. Geertman (*More veterum*, pp. 82-129, esp. p. 94) has shown that the real importance of each monastery or church in 807 is determined by the size of the gift, indicated by the weight of the silver *coronae* or *canistra* given to it. See also Sansterre, *Les moines grecs* I, 32-37.

62. Duchesne II, 22. St. Sabas's gift *corona* weighs 8 lbs. 10 oz. Sansterre, *Les moines grecs* I, 90-92, presents a very balanced picture of the ecclesiastical and economic status of the Greek monasteries in the late eighth and early ninth century.

Mariae qui ponitur in monasterio aque Salviae."[63] Papal gifts continue to be recorded until the pontificate of Nicholas I in 856-867.[64] In the ninth century, the monastery constituted a small fortified enclosure outside the walls of the city. The relations, both spiritual and economic, most probably forged between the monastery and the surrounding rural population, would have made the monastic complex a virtual parish center.[65]

The decline of organized monastic life that occurred in Rome toward the end of the ninth century did not spare the Greek communities.[66] Many Greek monasteries disappeared or became Latin, as fewer Greek monks moved to Rome after the final defeat of iconoclasm in 843. St. Anastasius persisted longer and perhaps better than others. Greek monks were still living in the monastery not long after the 1010s or 1020s when the biography of St. Nilus

63. Duchesne II, 24. As Geertman points out (*More veterum*, p. 124), it is anomalous to include this church, situated in a monastery outside the walls, at this point in the list, among the less important Latin monasteries within the walls. He attributes this "al residuo di una situazione che risale a prima della metà del secolo VII, quando cioè il monastero non era stato ancora assegnato a monaci greci. L'oratorium sanctae Mariae potrebbe esser rimasto un edificio pubblico servito dal monastero greco ma non riservato ad esso. La menzione di ambedue gli edifici, fatto unico nella lista dei doni dell'807, per giunta in due diverse categorie e ciascuno con un dono proprio, non è spiegabile altrimenti." Geertman's opinion is refuted by the Roman Miracle, which explicitly locates this church within the monastic enclosure. Another reason must be found to explain the anomaly.

64. There are gifts listed under Gregory IV (Duchesne II, 79); Leo IV (Duchesne II, 109); Benedictus III (Duchesne II, 145); and finally Nicholas I (Duchesne II, 158).

65. The church of St. John the Baptist, where the exorcism described in the Roman Miracle takes place, may have functioned as a parish church. See also Sansterre, "Le monachisme byzantin," p. 745 with references in particular to Broccoli, *L'abbazia delle Tre Fontane*, pp. 32-34.

66. Sansterre, *Les moines grecs* I, 206-212. Sansterre (p. 212) suggests that the decline in the number of recruits can also be attributed to fewer travelers visiting the papal areas after the Muslims established settlements in southern Italy. An overview of the later history of Roman Greek monastic communities is provided in Sansterre, "Le monachisme byzantin," pp. 701-746, esp. 709ff.

(†1004) was being written.[67] St. Nilus, searching for a new monastic locale, visited the monastery but refused to take it over, choosing instead the more isolated area where Grottaferrata would be built. St. Bartholomew the Younger, to whom the Life of St. Nilus is attributed, composed a hymn cycle for the feast of St. Anastasius, which emphasizes the power of the relic of the head of the saint.[68] If Peter Damian's sermon for the feast of St. Anastasius was delivered at the Aquae Salviae ca. 1044,[69] it would be the last recorded event to have taken place at the monastery in the first phase of its history. For by 1081 the monastery of St. Anastasius appears to have been abandoned because the site is mentioned among the properties Gregory VII confirmed to St. Paul's Outside the Walls.[70] Around 1140, St. Anastasius was given to the Cistercians, under whose rule it has continued to the present, except for a brief interruption in the nineteenth century.[71]

The relic of the head of Anastasius retained its significance for the Cistercian community, who exploited its miraculous power to strengthen the abbey's claims to twelve fortified towns in Tuscia,

67. Sansterre, "Le monachisme byzantin," p. 717 n. 40; Life of St. Nilus 90 (PG 120, 149-150).

68. The Life of St. Nilus does not mention the relic of the head of Anastasius in its description of the visit by St. Nilus. St. Bartholomew's hymns do not give certain evidence that he had actually seen the relic. For the hymns see Giovanelli, *Gli inni sacri di S. Bartolomeo Juniore*, pp. 134-138, 383-387.

69. See pp. 158-160 below.

70. But there have been some questions raised about this donation, summarized in Sansterre, "Le monachisme byzantin," p. 717 n. 40.

71. On the monastery's artistic activities in the thirteenth and fourteenth century, see Bertelli, "'Caput'," and "L'enciclopedia delle Tre Fontane." The Cistercian monastery was suppressed in 1812, then restored to the Franciscans in 1826, and returned to the Cistercians of the Trappist observance in 1868. Belardi, et al., *Abbazia delle Tre Fontane: il complesso, la storia, il restauro* is a showcase for the recent restoration of the buildings, although the history of the monastery on which it relies completely, [Barbiero], *S. Paolo e le Tre Fontane. XXII secoli di storia messi in luce da un monaco cisterciense (trappista)*, is frequently inaccurate. The name "Tre Fontane" derives from the legend that when Paul's head was cut off, it bounced three times, and at each bounce a spring emerged, whose water tasted unusually milky to Jean Mabillon, who visited in the seventeenth century.

disputed by the neighboring St. Paul's Outside the Walls. According to a diploma forged in the twelfth century, the twelve towns were granted to the abbey of St. Anastasius in 807 by Charlemagne himself after one of them, Ansedonia, fell to his army when the relic of the head of Anastasius was carried in procession around the long-besieged city.[72] The fresco cycle adorning the abbey's so-called "Arco di Carlomagno," depicting the fall of Ansedonia before the relic of Anastasius, was also executed in the twelfth century, at the time of the dispute between the Cistercians and St. Paul's.[73] A century later, this same event was memorialized on the silver reliquary commissioned by Abbot Martin I in 1283 to contain the relic of the head of Anastasius.[74]

The continuing devotion to the relic of the Persian is evident again on 14 June 1408, the day of Corpus Domini, when its recovery from the church of S. Maria in Trastevere was celebrated by a large contingent of ecclesiastical and secular officials and much of the population that lived in the neighborhood of Rome's ancient basilica across the Tiber. At the sound of the bells, those gathered processed into the sacristy of S. Maria where they broke open a box, and there they found the head of Anastasius enclosed in a gilded tabernacle, and another glass and silver reliquary containing the "cellabro [the brain] supradicti capitis." These events are recorded in the diary of an eyewitness, a Vatican official who

---

72. Kehr, *Italia Pontificia* I, 173, 175 (numm. 1 and 11).

73. Bertelli, "'Caput'," p. 21 n. 11. The frescoes are reproduced in [Barbiero], *S. Paolo e le Tre Fontane*, Tavola XIX.

74. It carried the inscription "Domnus Abbas Martinus fecit fieri hoc opus sub anno 1283," according to Onofrio Panvinio (1529-1568) in his devotional guidebook (*Le sette chiese romane*, p. 109). Martinus was abbot from 1283 to 1306 (Bertelli, "'Caput'," p. 22 n. 21). The description of the reliquary provided by Carlo Bartolomeo Piazza (1632-1713) in his devotional guidebook for pilgrims (*Hieroxenia overo, Sagra pellegrinazione alle sette chiese di Roma*, pp. 154-155) mentions its decoration: "... dodeci Castelli nel Territorio di Siena, elegantemente espressi in un Reliquiario d'argento da noi con godimento già osservato, nel venerare ivi rinchiusa la Testa del Santo Martire (hora non senza ingiuria della venerabile antichità disfatto)." Bertelli concludes that the reliquary was destroyed sometime after 1674 ("'Caput'," p. 15 and n. 20).

vaguely attributes the earlier removal of Anastasius's relics to S. Maria's sacristy to disputes over tax payments.[75] When the relics were returned to the church of S. Anastasius, an icon of the saint's head in Cistercian garb was manufactured, perhaps in order to complete the relic with a "memoria" of the long-lost miraculous icon, thus recreating the twin objects that once animated the deliberations of Nicea II.[76] No better strategy could be found to remind the contemporary viewer of their old power to defeat demons and to heal the sick.[77] The relic of the head of Anastasius,

75. "... et ibi in dicta sacristia franserunt unam cassam, et in dicta cassa invenerunt pulcerrimum tabernachulum deauratum cum smaltis, in quo tabernachulo stabat caput sancti Anastaxii martiris, et unum alium tabernachulum parvum de cristaldo ... Quare erant in dicta sacristia supradicte reliquie, quia dominus cardinalis de Sancto Angelo posuerat, quando inposuit datam omnibus ecclesiis Urbis, etcetera. Item supradicte reliquie fuerunt restitute coram omni populo domino abbati Sancti Anastaxii, et factum sibi mandatum per supradictos dominos, quod deberet eas bene custodire" (*Il Diario Romano di Antonio di Pietro dello Schiavo dal 19 ottobre 1404 al 25 settembre 1417*, pp. 32; 22). Pietro dello Schiavo describes the "datam" as a tax imposed by the titular cardinal of S. Maria in January 1408. This passage should not be read, *pace* Bertelli, as a traditional relic "inventio," in which an unknown relic is miraculously discovered, but rather as the recovery and return to the rightful owners of a well-known relic.

76. We cannot be certain that the reliquary described during these events of 1408 is the same as the one seen by Panvinio more than a century later, and by Piazza, more than another century after that at the Tre Fontane (above, n. 74). Since the reliquary they describe appears to have been manufactured in 1283, however, it is difficult to believe that another reliquary was substituted. The invention account of 1408 describes it as a "tabernachulum deauratum cum smaltis." Panvinio and Piazza both agree the reliquary was silver; they do not specify that the reliquary was in the shape of a tabernacle. However, the writer of the 1408 account may be using the word "tabernachulum" more generally in the meaning of precious box.

77. Bertelli, "'Caput'," pp. 15-17. The icon contains the inscription "Imago S. Anastasii Monachi et Martyris Cuius Aspectu Fugari Daemones Morbosque Curari Acta Secundi Concilii Niceni Testantur"; there is a picture of it in [Barbiero], *S. Paolo e le Tre Fontane*, Tavola XVIII. Jean Mabillon viewed the icon on 25 January 1686 and included its depiction in his "Iter Italicum" (*Museum Italicum* I, 142 and apposite illustration). Although his discussion includes a reference both to Nicea and to the Roman Miracle, it does not include the inscription. Indeed, Mabillon does not mention the relic at all, perhaps because by then the reliquary of 1283 had already been destroyed.

enclosed in a reliquary in the shape of a small sarcophagus, is still exhibited today, along with the Cistercian icon, on the feast day of the martyr in the main church of the abbey, which is known as SS. Vincenzo ed Anastasio alle Tre Fontane.[78]

According to another tradition, however, the relic of the head of Anastasius the Persian monk is found today at the Domschatz at Aachen, in a stunning Byzantine silver reliquary dating to the tenth century.[79] The reliquary, in the shape of a domed church, with an external apse and doors on three sides, was originally an artophorion, a container for the reserved host, manufactured for Eustathius Maleinus when he was strategos, or military commander, of Antioch in 969-970. It is not known when the artophorion was transformed into a skull reliquary,[80] or when or how it ar-

78. The name of St. Vincent was added in the thirteenth century when his relics were transferred from Spain. See Ferrari, *Early Roman monasteries*, pp. 46-48, for the present architectural complex. The sarcophagus-reliquary was manufactured in 1868, when the Cistercians returned to Tre Fontane; it also contains other bones, supposed to be of Anastasius's body (Bertelli, "'Caput',", p. 23 n. 24). A picture of it appears in [Barbiero], *S. Paolo e le Tre Fontane*, Tavola XVIII. There is no further mention of the "cerebrum" found in 1408.

79. Much recent scholarship on the reliquary makes this claim, but without further discussion: see, for example, Grimme, *Der Dom zu Aachen: Architektur und Ausstattung*, p. 115. The reliquary was exhibited most recently (1997) at the Metropolitan Museum of Art in New York, and illustrated in the exhibit catalog, with a brief description and bibliography (Evans and Wixom, *The Glory of Byzantium. Art and Culture of the Middle Byzantine Era. A.D. 843-1261*, pp. 460-461). The Greek inscription around the surface of this object, its artistic characteristics and its earlier history are discussed most thoroughly in Saunders, "The Aachen Reliquary of Eustathius Maleinus (969-970)," pp. 211-219, which includes two photographs of this magnificent piece. Saunders, however, does not cite any of the works that discuss this object as a reliquary.

80. Braun, *Die Reliquiare des Christlichen Kultes und ihre Entwicklung*, the standard work on Christian reliquaries, includes the Anastasius reliquary (p. 496 and no. 577) in its survey of reliquaries according to shape, and remarks on its earlier function as an artophorion (a discovery not acknowledged by subsequent scholars), but does not comment on the significance of this transformation. There are of course examples of simpler reliquaries transformed into more elaborate ones (such as the Aachen reliquary containing the relic

rived in the old imperial capital's Marienkirche,[81] whose important relics are still the focus of a septennial pilgrimage that began
in the middle of the thirteenth century.[82]

The Byzantine container and its contents were officially investigated on 3 March 1874 under the direction of Dr. Franz Bock, a
canon of the cathedral of Aachen. The reliquary was opened, the
relic was found wrapped in cloth; an "authentic," a parchment
piece authenticating the relic, was discovered in the folds of the
cloth with an inscription that read "Caput beati Anastasii mrs" and
dated by those present to the eleventh century.[83] The skull contained in the Aachen reliquary was then identified with the "caput
Anastasii monachi et martyris" that, together with the relics of St.
Speus the Confessor and the arm of St. Simeon the Just,[84] were
moved by Emperor Henry IV in April 1072 from Aachen to Harzburg, the fortified town he built as a bulwark against the Saxons,
according to the Annals of Lampert of Hersfeld (ca. 1025-1081/
85).[85] Lampert's Annals had also proposed a reason for the return

---

of St. Simeon) and of reliquaries whose contents change (such as the arm reliquary of St. Lawrence in the Guelph treasure, which was originally made for
the relics of St. Bartholomew: see Hahn, "The Voices of the Saints," p. 22).
However, the transformation of the Anastasius reliquary remains highly unusual.

81. The artophorion may have arrived at Aachen on any number of occasions (for example, after Antioch was taken by the Crusaders in 1098; as part
of the dowry of the Byzantine princess Theophanu, who married Otto II in
Rome in 972; as part of the gift exchanges for the affiancement of Otto III
and a Byzantine princess between 1000 and 1002; among the gifts sent to
Henry IV by Emperor Alexius upon his accession to the throne in 1081). It
seems more likely that its transformation into a reliquary took place in the
West, where the Greek inscription pertaining to its former function would
not have been understood.

82. On the relics and the development of the pilgrimage see Rice, "Music
and Ritual in the Collegiate Church of Saint Mary in Aachen 1300-1600."

83. Kessel, *Geschichtliche Mitteilungen über die Heiligthümer der Stiftkirche
zu Aachen ...*, pp. 110-114.

84. On these relics, see Grimme, *Der Aachener Domschatz*, pp. 46-47, 56-
57, 82-84.

85. This identification may have been suggested by Holder-Egger's edition
of Lampert's Annals published in 1866, where appended to Lampert's passage, "Rex Aquasgrani profectus, sanctum Speum confessorem et brachium

of the relics from Harzburg to Aachen just two years later. In March of 1074 Harzburg was attacked and completely leveled to the ground by the "vulgus Saxoniae." The relics of the saints preserved in the church, disrupted and scattered as the altars were dismantled by the rebels, were rescued by an unidentified neighboring abbot.[86] The destruction of Harzburg and the salvaging of the relics from the ruins have been taken as the opportunity for the return to Aachen of the relics preserved there today.

The head of the Persian is supposed to have first arrived in Aachen during Charlemagne's reign, for references to relics of an Anastasius, although without further specification, are found in Carolingian sources.[87] No medieval source, however, has survived

---

iusti Simeonis, cuius mentio est in euangelio, et caput Anastasii monachi et martiris aliorumque sanctorum reliquias ibi accepit atque in Hartesburc transtulit," is the note "Persae, ut videtur," but without any further comment (Lampertus, *Annales*, in *Lamperti Monachi Hersfeldensis Opera*, ed. Holder-Egger, pp. 135-136).

86. For the insurrection and destruction of Harzburg see Lampert's *Annales* s.a. 1074 (pp. 183-184). The discontent of the rebellious "vulgus" stemmed principally from the fact that the king had used the relics to consolidate his position to the detriment of the region's inhabitants: "Non detulisse regem cultui divino, sed sub pretextu religionis crudelitatis suae patrocinium quesisse" (p. 184). The striking emphasis on the hoarding of the relics highlights and perhaps even justifies the outrage committed in this account. But no details are given by Lampert or any other source after the "Reliquae sanctorum, quae effractis altaribus erutae fuerant, et effossa defunctorum corpora abbas ex vicino suum monasterium cum honore transvexit" (ibid.). The abbot is tentatively identified by Holder-Egger as Herrandus, the abbot of Ilsenburg at this time.

87. The list "sanctorum martyrum" from ca. 1200 in Bonn, Universitäts-bibliothek, S. 1559, fol. 6v includes "Anastasii," whose relics were contained in the Carolingian reliquary attached to the altar of Mary (the so-called Marienschrein), although there is no indication of the exact nature of the relic. This is the earliest inventory of the church's relics. I thank Eric Rice for providing me with the precise reading of this manuscript (see Rice, "Music and Ritual," Appendix 1.A for the Aquensian liturgical books). Angilbert of St. Riquier also lists a relic of Anastasius among those contained at Centula. Schramm and Mütherich, *Denkmale der deutschen Könige und Kaiser*, p. 25 and Kessel, *Geschichtliche Mitteilungen*, p. 113 have taken this reference to reflect the relics enshrined at Aachen.

from which a plausible account of the translation of the skull of the Persian to Aachen from Rome could be constructed. The historical circumstances under which the skull was placed in its beautiful container, and the unusual way in which the object came to be used as a reliquary, remain also completely unknown. Aachen's oldest liturgical sources, dating from the late twelfth century, do not show that the feast of Anastasius the Persian was celebrated in the old imperial capital.[88] And a "pilgerblatt" of 1615 with the images of the principal reliquaries displayed in the septennial ostension at Aachen portrays the artophorion-reliquary with great verisimilitude, but the inscription reads "Caput S. Anastasiae."[89]

The long journey of the head of Anastasius, begun in Persia, with intermediate stages in Jerusalem and Constantinople, and ending finally in Rome according to one version, or concluding in northern Europe according to another, is not unique. The most venerated relics now resting in Aachen, for example, those originating from the life of Christ and his mother and known as Aachen's Great Relics, are reputed to have made similar journeys.[90] The

88. A lectionary ordo from ca. 1200 for the use of Aachen prescribes that "In festo sancti Anastasii leguntur in magno passionali VI lectiones" (Bonn, Universitätsbibliothek, S. 1559, fol. 3r, col. A). But this is not Anastasius the Persian; rather he must be Anastasius of Salonae (in Dalmatia), martyred under Diocletian and commemorated on 26 August in the Hieronymian Martyrology. Although the lectionary ordo does not specify dates, the date of 26 August can be derived from the placement of this feast, after that of the apostle Bartholomew (24 and 25 August) and preceding that of the third-century martyr Hermes (28 August). See *Bibliotheca sanctorum* I, 1058-1059 with additional bibliography. The date of 26 August is further confirmed by later Aachen liturgical sources, the calendars in Aachen, Domarchiv HS G 18, a missal from the second half of the fifteenth century (fol. 4v); and in HS G 39, a Psalter from 1517 (fol. 4v). I thank Eric Rice for providing me with these details.

89. Grimme, *Der Aachener Domschatz*, p. XI, reproduces the pilgrimage poster. The artophorion-reliquary is numbered twenty-five, and can be seen in the lower third of the poster. The history of Aachen's large collection of relics remains for the most part unexplored.

90. The relics of the dress of the Virgin, of both the swaddling cloth and loin cloth of Jesus, and the cloth associated with the decapitated head of John the Baptist are preserved in a magnificent thirteenth-century reliquary (the

relic of Anastasius can be considered extraordinary, however, in its early connection to events and to literary documents, whose historical authenticity can be subjected to scrutiny by means of more conventional scholarly criteria. What remains certain is the arrival in Rome before the middle of the seventh century of what was believed to be the skull of the Persian monk, and that this event was immediately responsible not only for the rise of the cult of Anastasius in the West documented in the previous discussion, but also of a fertile literary tradition in Latin, whose spread from Rome to various parts of Europe, including Anglo-Saxon England, will be examined in the following chapters.

No direct testimony tells us that a copy of the Greek *Acta* of the Persian monk also found its way to Rome with the relic of the head. But the *Acta* must have accompanied the skull, as we can deduce, first, from the fact that the Greek *Acta* were in Rome in the latter part of the eighth century, when the compiler of the iconodule florilegium, as we saw, copied extracts from them. Two surviving manuscripts of the Greek text copied in southern Italy in the eleventh and twelfth century provide additional support.[91] These indicators, however, are only circumstantial. Much more substantial is the evidence provided by the first Latin translation (*BHL* 410b) of the Greek *Acta*, which is the focus of the next chapter. It will show how the Latin literary dossier of Anastasius also begins with the arrival in Rome of a precious object, a copy of the Greek *Acta* of Anastasius that had belonged to, or been closely connected with, Patriarch Modestus of Jerusalem, who had known and baptized the former Persian soldier. It was Modestus's own annotated copy that served as the source from which derived the first Latin translation of the story of Anastasius.

Marienschrein). These relics are also reputed to have been obtained by Charlemagne: Grimme, *Der Aachener Domschatz*, passim.

91. See next chapter. The oldest manuscripts of the Greek *Acta* go back to the tenth century.

APPENDIX

ENGLISH TRANSLATIONS
OF THE *PASSIO S. ANASTASII*
AND THE *MIRACULUM ROMANUM*

The following translations render into English the two texts on which the entire Latin literary dossier of Anastasius depends. The first is the *Acta S. Anastasii*, composed in Jerusalem by a monastic confrere of the martyr in 630. The original Greek composition, as I will argue fully in the next chapter, was translated into Latin toward the middle of the seventh century in Rome by a Greek speaker with a limited command of Latin (=*BHL* 410b, edited below, pp. 259-298). The second text is the Roman Miracle, an account of the exorcism performed by the relic of the head of Anastasius, composed in Rome in 713-714 originally in Greek but later translated into Latin, which is the subject of Chapter IV (=*BHL* 412, edited below, pp. 339-361).

My translations of the *Acta* and the *Miraculum* of Anastasius follow the Latin versions primarily, but they also take into consideration the Greek originals. I have thus provided a parallel triangulation to Flusin's French translations, which were based on the Greek texts, but also took the Latin versions into account. My translations ideally should be read alongside the Latin texts, with reference to the Greek. Reference should also be made to the notes to the original texts, both Flusin's historical notes to the Greek text, and my notes to the Latin edition. I have tried to provide as literal a translation as possible, and to give a reasonable approximation of the stylistic features of the Latin texts, which are fully discussed in Chapters II and IV: hence, for example, the inclusion in the translation of the repetitive vocabulary and syntactical constructions of the Latin, and the overuse of conjunctions and personal pronouns. At the same time, I hope that the English translations can stand on their own, and be useful to readers who do not need to refer to the original Latin and Greek versions. I have used square brackets to indicate phrases not contained in the Latin, but supplied from the Greek texts.

THE LIFE AND PASSION OF THE BLESSED MONK ANASTASIUS

1. The only begotten Son and Word of God, through whom all things were made, who is coeternal and consubstantial with the Father and the holy and life-giving Spirit, took pity on humankind under the tyranny of death and corruption, and "bowed the heavens, and came down" (2 Sm 22.10) according to what has been written. By his birth from a virgin "taking the form of a servant" (Phil 2.7), and living with

humankind (cf. Bar 3.37), he arranged all things for our salvation. By his own death he destroyed the one who had "the power of death" (Heb 2.14), by his three-day burial he purified decay, and by his descent into hell he destroyed the long-lived reign of Hell, and thus by his glorious resurrection he "raised us up with him and made us sit with him in the heavenly places" (Eph 2.6), as the apostle says.

2. Hence, the blessed apostles, those who had been "eyewitnesses and ministers of the Word" (Lc 1.2), and who had witnessed his sufferings (cf. 1 Pt 5.1), clothed with the power from above, traversed the entire earth with their divine preaching. They reconciled to piety every city and region and nation and people and tribe and language, and eradicated from the root the long-standing ancestral error of impiety, and planted on earth the angelic way of life. From that time, all things were "full of the knowledge of the Lord, as the waters cover the sea" (Is 11.9), as it is written. From that time, the earthly was mingled with the heavenly, and life eternal was established on earth. From that time, all of the human race has rejoiced in the great and ineffable gifts of God.

3. But the one who was from the beginning the ensnarer and seducer of humankind and the deceitful enemy of the pious could not bear such great gift of good things enjoyed by men through the grace of Christ; and seeing himself thrown out from the heavens like a bad slave, he devised a plot worthy of his malice. But he was not so much able to harm those who were nourished by piety, as rather to benefit them greatly. Thrusting himself by many and various ways into those who then held the scepters of the Romans, he caused manifold persecutions against the church, and he subverted and confused the entire world as much as he was able. But his mission turned against him, and he caused little or no harm to God's followers, while he himself was confused. Indeed in no different a fashion than once when the deceiver had been banished by the holy apostles, he was cast out by the steadfastness of the victorious martyrs. And again the church of Christ recovered its proper ornament of piety, and the fruits of God's grace flourished and increased each day, stretching their glory over a long succession of years.

4. But we men—as if sated with the good things that God had given us, or as if sickened by the complete forgetfulness of the great and ineffable gifts of Christ, and inscribing against ourselves a long and varied list of sins, reddening the earth with human blood, inflaming God's anger against us by fornications, adulteries, and other innumerable evils and crimes—we called upon ourselves the whole hand, so to speak, of God's discipline. Hence he delivered us into the hands of lawless enemies, and "to an unjust king, the most wicked in all the world" (Dn 3.32 [addi-

tions to Dn 3 between capp. 23 and 24]) who delivered entire cities and regions to fire, while others he razed to the ground, and took into captivity the choicest and most desirable among people and goods, and destroyed the rest in his insatiable rage. But benevolent, loving God did not disdain us unto the end, as events themselves show, but he gave us sweet hope to hold on to, for even now he is glorified in his true servants and martyrs.

5. Fittingly at this point in our account we are struck with the same astonishment as the great apostle before the inscrutable judgments of God, and we say: "O the depth of the riches and wisdom and knowledge of God! How unfathomable are his judgments and how inscrutable his ways!" (Rom 11.33). Behold, for their punishment he delivered his own children and heirs according to grace unto the Persians, and from Persia he elected martyrs who confessed their love and faith for him unto death. And, what is most astonishing, not only men, but also women were there who manifested their capacity to bear every suffering and who in the end for the sake of the faith of Christ were crucified and put on the martyr's crown. One of these is our crowned victor Anastasius, whose life from the beginning until his martyrdom I have been commanded to write. And putting at the head of my account our Lord and God Jesus Christ, whom he confessed, I will thus begin.

6. He was from the region of Persia called Razech, from the village of Rasnouni. His name was Magundat. He was the son of a magician named Bau, a teacher of magic learning, who instructed him also from childhood in the magic arts. When he became a young man, it happened that he was enlisted with many others and came to be in the royal city of the Persians under King Chosroes. After the holy city of God (i.e. Jerusalem) had been destroyed, and the venerable and holy places had been set on fire in the anger that, as was said above, was caused by our sins, the precious wood of the life-giving and most sacred cross of Christ was seized and carried into Persia. And—astonishing event!—the cross of the Lord, while it was being led captive according to the belief of the godless people, was instead capturing there those who were worthy of its salvation.

7. For indeed, when the venerable and precious cross of the Savior was in Persia, as has been said, and was shooting forth its rays of love and power everywhere, it brought fear and wonder among the unbelievers, joy and gladness into the believers' hearts. As the fame of the cross was resounding throughout the region, the aforesaid recruit Magundat, that is Anastasius, asked what it was. And hearing those who said that the God of the Christians had come there, as the good earth, having received

the appropriate rain, is made fit to bear fruit, thus immediately even he, having received through his hearing the most precious name of God, placed it as a treasure in the depth of his heart. Then, wondering within himself, "How the great God who dwells in the heavens, the one whom the Christians worship, as I have heard, has come here," he inquired with great curiosity from some, and he learned that, "This is the cross itself on which Christ the son of God, whom the Christians worship, was crucified." Full of wonder and astonishment over this, the predestined servant of God Anastasius did not from that moment restrain his exploration of Christianity. And the more he received the truth through his hearing, the more magic's enticements departed from his heart. Indeed, just as darkness yields to the light, and shadows to the sun, and smoke to the fire, thus error is exterminated by the doctrine of truth.

8. The blessed Anastasius had a brother in the flesh who was a soldier, and he went with him to Chalcedonia with the army that was led by Sain, the general of the Persians. But Philippicus, of blessed memory, diverted him (i.e. Sain), and entered into Persia. Sain, learning this, turned back after him. And thus it happened that the servant of God Anastasius came to the regions of the East with the army of the Persians. There, he abandoned the army, and, leaving his own brother, he came to Hieropolis, and turned to a certain Persian, a Christian, a silversmith, and lived at his house. He became his apprentice and worked with him.

9. As his desire to be baptized was overflowing, he relentlessly requested from the above-mentioned man to be graced with holy baptism. But he, mistrustful on account of his fear of the Persians lest he be endangered, put him off. Nevertheless, he (i.e. Anastasius) went with him to the churches and prayed, and he saw the pictures of the holy martyrs and inquired from him what these were. And hearing from him the miracles of the saints, and the atrocious torments that had been inflicted on them by tyrants, and their superhuman endurance, he marveled and was spellbound. He remained a little while at the house of this abovementioned Christian man, and his soul was seized by the worthy desire to go to Jerusalem, and there to receive holy baptism.

10. In accordance with God's will, he accomplished this, and came to the holy city. There he settled at the house of a good Christian silversmith, and disclosed to him his desire to embrace Christ and to receive the gift of holy baptism. He was thus presented to Helias, the saintly priest of the Holy Anastasis. Helias received him as a son sent by God, and referred his case to Modestus, the most holy priest then vicar of the apostolic see, who had him baptized with another companion of like character, of the same region and religion. He also suffered the same blessed death for Christ in Edessa and was crowned with the martyr's crown.

11. After Anastasius had spent eight days in his (i.e. Helias's) house for the baptismal observance, the most holy priest Helias asked the blessed Anastasius what more he desired. And Anastasius begged him saying: "Make me a monk." After this period, Helias took him right away to the monastery of abbot Anastasius of blessed memory, which lies four miles from the holy city. And after he and others with great persistence had begged Justinus, the prior of the monastery, a man illustrious in all things, and full of the gifts of God, they entrusted to him the servant of God Anastasius. Justinus received him and joined him to his congregation, in the eighth indiction, in the tenth year of the rule of the most pious and Christian emperor Heraclius. The abbot assigned also to him as teacher one of his brotherly disciples, a man full of discernment, who taught him Greek letters and the Psalter. And he tonsured him and clothed him with the holy monastic habit, and trained him as his true son.

12. The blessed Anastasius discharged many duties in the monastery, both in the kitchen and also in the garden, excelling in their performance through the grace of the Lord. He was indeed very diligent both in his service to the brothers and in the work of his hands, and above all in the observance of the divine liturgy. And he applied his mind diligently while he listened without cease to the reading of the holy Scriptures and of the Lives of the holy Fathers. If he did not understand something, he asked his teacher, a man capable in all things, or one of the senior brethren. And learning from them what he was seeking, he marveled, glorifying God. Reading on his own in his cell the combats and struggles of the victorious martyrs, he shed many tears, and fed the desire in the secret chamber of his heart to be made worthy himself to be equal to the saints in their combat for the praise and glory of Christ. We learned this ourselves, as he admired and was amazed at the steadfastness of the saints, and he wanted to read nothing else, except these things that fed the flame of his desire. He spent seven years in these occupations within the monastery.

13. But the evil spirit, seeing such love of Christ in him, and so great, desiring to enfeeble it and to drive the servant of God Anastasius into desperation, suggested to him evil thoughts and memories of the magic words he had learned from his father, as I said above, and thus troubled him vehemently. But he, knowing the wiliness of the deceiver, prayed to God to be snatched from the snares of the devil. He revealed to his abbot the secrets of his heart with many tears, and asked him to pray God to free him from the snares of the enemy. And the abbot, admon-

ishing him and comforting him according to the understanding given to him by God, and offering prayers for him in church, delivered him from this battle.

14. After a few days, the servant of God Anastasius saw a vision during the night. He saw himself standing on a high mountain. And he saw a man coming toward him and handing him a golden jeweled goblet full of wine and saying to him: "Take this and drink it." And he took it and drank it. Immediately, almost as if filled by the Spirit, and as if he had obtained what he was desiring, he rose up and went to church for the nocturnal office, at dawn of the Lord's day. Summoning the abbot of the monastery into the diakonikon, he fell down before him, begging him in tears to pray for him, for he was going to die soon. And he began to utter words of farewell, saying: "I am aware, father, of all the troubles you took for my wretched sake. I know that I have troubled you much, and that through you God has led me from the darkness into the light. Pray God for me." The abbot said to him: "What is the matter? How do you know that you are soon going to die?" Anastasius told him his vision, and assured him that he was going to die either by an ordinary death or in some other way. He feared however to speak openly, lest he be reprimanded.

15. Then, his heart consoled by the many and varied exhortations of his abbot, he completed the office with his brethren. After mass and the reception of the sacrament of the divine mystery, he took his meal with the brethren, he slept a little, and then, rising and unable to bear the fire of his heart, he secretly left the monastery, taking nothing with him except the clothes he was wearing. He went to Diospolis, and from there to Mt. Garizim to pray, and to the other revered places. Led by the grace of God, he came to Caesarea of Palestine, and remained for two days in the sanctuary of the glorious Mary mother of God.

16. Then he proceeded to St. Euphemia to pray, in accordance with the dispensation of divine Providence, which governs all things wisely, justly and mercifully. As he passed a particular house, he saw certain Persians performing their magical rites. And led by divine zeal, he went up to them and said: "Why do you err, and lead others astray by your sorceries?" They were stupefied by his great vehemence, and they asked him who he was, and where he came from that he spoke such things to them. And he said to them: "Even I was such as you, and I know your spells." And as he began to argue against them, they did not know what to say, but asked him not to divulge their business, and dismissed him.

17. After he had departed from them, some knights sitting in front of the derbas, which is the praetorium of the sellarius, saw him and said

among themselves in their language: "This is a spy." When the blessed Anastasius heard them saying these things, looking at them he said: "What nonsense are you saying? I am not a spy, but a servant of Jesus Christ. And I am better than you, for even I was a knight as you are." But they rose and took hold of him. The sellarius came out and asked him where he was from, and having considered carefully all that pertained to him, imprisoned him for three days. During this time, Anastasius did not agree to take any nourishment from them, fearing their trickery.

18. When the marzabanas returned—for he was not in Caesarea when the servant of God Anastasius had been arrested—the above-mentioned sellarius reported to him what he knew about Anastasius, and brought him to his praetorium. While the marzabanas was busy with other affairs, there chanced to be there a certain Christian who had known the blessed Anastasius in the sanctuary of Mary the blessed mother of God. And speaking with him and learning what had happened, he blessed him for his good beginning and encouraged him with holy words to fear neither torments nor death for the sake of Christ but to answer courageously to the marzabanas, reminding him: "But the one who endures to the end will be saved" (Mt 10.22).

19. The servant of God Anastasius was brought in and he stood in front of the marzabanas, but did not pay homage to him according to the rite that they observed. The marzabanas stared at him, and said: "Where are you from, and who are you?" He said in answer: "I am a true Christian. If you want to learn where I am from, I am a Persian by birth, from the region of Razech, from the village of Rasnouni. I was indeed a knight and a magician, and I abandoned the darkness and came to the light." The marzabanas said to him: "Abandon this error, and return to your first religion, and we will offer you horses and money and you shall have great favor." But he said in answer: "May God keep me from denying my Christ." The marzabanas said to him: "Does it please you to wear this habit with which you are clad?" And he said truly: "This habit is my glory." The marzabanas said to him: "You have a demon." The blessed Anastasius answered saying: "When I was in error, I had a demon. Now I have my Christ who persecutes the demons." The marzabanas said to him: "Don't you fear the emperor, lest he order that you be crucified when he learns these things about you?" But he answered: "Why should I fear? He is a corruptible man, such as you are."

20. Then the marzabanas, angry, commanded him to be led in chains to the camp and to carry stones without rest. While the servant of God carried the stones, he bore many and insufferable tribulations. Some

people from his region saw him and considering their own shame in what was being done to him, said: "Why did you do this to us? Nobody from our region ever became a Christian. And here you have caused ridicule to fall upon us." And with all sorts of fallacious arguments they tried to recall him back to them. But he insulted them and repulsed them. They became angry, and every day they would come and pull his beard and beat him without mercy and tear at his clothes. In addition, four of them would lift up large stones and would place them on him while he was chained with another person and had a chain also around his neck and another around his foot. And they inflicted even fiercer cruelties upon him. But truly the brave athlete bore all things joyously for the sake of Christ.

21. Again the marzabanas commanded him to come before him and said to him: "If truly as you said you were the son of a magus, and have knowledge of the magical arts, tell me something from them so that I may know." But he answered: "May God not allow anything of this sort to come out of my mouth." The marzabanas said to him: "What then? You persevere in these things? Return to your first religion, for I will write to the emperor about you." Anastasius said to him in reply: "You wrote, and have received an answer. Do what you want." And the marzabanas said: "I did not write, but I will; and whatever he commands, I shall do." Anastasius said: "Go and write as many bad things about me as you wish. For indeed I am a Christian." The marzabanas said: "Let him be taken down and beaten until he agrees to do what is being commanded to him." As they began to tie him, the servant of God Anastasius said: "Let me be. I do not need fetters." And sitting down he composed himself in the same position into which they were going to tie him. And they began to beat him with sticks. The saint said to them: "Take off my habit so that it may not be dishonored, and beat upon my flesh. These things that you are doing are jests. Even if you cut me into pieces, I shall not deny my Christ."

22. Again the marzabanas said: "Obey me, for I am going to write to the emperor about you." But he answered: "Go write to your emperor whatever you want." And the marzabanas: "What then—he said—don't you fear the emperor?" The blessed Anastasius answered: "Why should I fear your emperor? Is he not a man like you? And will he not die as you will die? Is he not corruptible just as you are? Whom should I then fear more, him, who is subject to corruption as you are, mud like you, or Christ, who made the sky and the earth, the sea and all things that are in them?" The arrogant man, shocked by the confidence of the martyr, ordered that he be taken to the camp.

23. After a few days, he commanded that he be brought before him and said to him: "Pick up magic's tools, and sacrifice so that you may not die a bad death and be deprived of this life." The servant of God answered and said to him: "To which gods are you commanding me to sacrifice? To the sun and the moon, and to fire and the horse, to mountains and hills and all the rest? May God never permit me to worship the objects you worship. For Christ made all these things for the service of us men. You indeed err, when you serve beasts and demons. You have been created, yet you ignore the God who created you. If you knew Christ, even you could turn toward the light, and be snatched from the demons who lead you astray." God, who does not lie, who promised to give those who suffer for his sake such speech and wisdom that no opponent will be able to contradict (cf. Lc 21.15), was pleased by what came out of the mouth of an unlearned man and a foreigner, both for his glory and for the strengthening of the faithful. With these God-inspired words, the martyr of Christ stupefied his adversaries, the champion of faith was crowned by a triple confession, and adorned with the fetters he wore for the sake of Christ was led back into the camp.

24. When the most holy abbot of the monastery in which the martyr had resided learned of the great steadfastness of his confession in Christ, and of his astonishing and eager perseverance, he rejoiced greatly with the entire community. And he prayed God night and day with all the brethren that Anastasius might complete the course of his confession. He sent two brethren to Caesarea to the blessed Anastasius with a letter in support and encouragement of his zeal.

25. While the martyr of Christ Anastasius was in prison, he did not cease to glorify God night and day with psalms and hymns. He had, as it has been said, a companion chained with him, a young servant who had been imprisoned for a certain reason. Since he (i.e. Anastasius) did not want to distress him when he rose at night to celebrate the office of divine praise, he would stand while bending his neck to the chained companion who was lying down, and would place his foot next to his foot, so as not to disturb him through the extension of the chain. One night, as he was singing the psalms, one of the prisoners, a Hebrew in religion, a personage of high status, and a man of honorable habits, as we learned, heard him. As he observed the blessed martyr laboring during the day in the transport of stones, and at night in prayer to God, he was full of admiration, wondering who this man might be.

26. Lying on the pavement in the darkness of the night, he stared for a long time at him, standing and singing the hymns at daylight. And he saw all of a sudden several men, clothed in white, entering through the door of the prison and surrounding the blessed martyr, and a copious light was shining around them. He was astonished by this vision and he said to himself: "Holy God, these are angels." Having reached this conclusion, he saw the same men enwrapped with pallia decorated with crosses, and said to himself: "These are bishops." Astonished by these things, as he looked at the martyr of Christ Anastasius, he noticed that he also was encircled by the same light as they were. And he saw him also clothed in white as the others, and behold! a young man, standing in full glory before him, and carrying a thurible, was censing him. Seeing all these things, the man began to shake forcefully with his hand his neighbor who was asleep, a Christian, the governor of Scythopolis, so that he might show him what he was seeing. But he was unable to do this, but rather remained with his mouth agape, his mind fully conscious of what he was seeing, but his body immobile. Finally however, with great effort he threw his entire body over the man who was lying down asleep. And this man was terrified and inquired from him what was happening. The Jew said to him: "Do you see, there?" and turning to look, they saw nothing. But he told him all that he had seen, and together in one spirit they glorified the Lord.

27. Now, because, as was shown above, the marzabanas had learned from the first and second interrogation the steadfastness of the servant of God Anastasius, he wrote about him to the emperor Chosroes. And so it happened that within a few days he received the emperor's command. And he sent his chamberlain to the prison for him, and said to him: "The emperor has commanded that you only say the words 'I am not a Christian' and immediately I will release you, and you can go wherever you wish, and if you want to be a monk, you can, or if you want to be a knight as before and be with us, you can; do as you wish." The martyr of Christ answered: "Let it not be that I should deny Christ." The marzabanas made him many promises and appeals through his chamberlain, but did not prevail in convincing him.

28. At the end, he declared to him through the same official: "I know that you feel shame because of your compatriots, and do not want to recant in their presence. But since such is the command of the emperor, that you speak in front of me and two other sellarii, just say the word and I will release you." But he sent back a message replying: "May I never deny my God in front of you or anyone else." Then the marzabanas said to him in person: "The emperor commands that you go to Persia in chains." And the blessed martyr of Christ said in answer: "If you should release me, I will go alone to the emperor on my own." As he saw that the martyr stood steadfast against every attack, that he did

not yield to threats, nor was persuaded by blandishments, he commanded that a seal be placed on his neck and that thus he be led to the
public prison, where he was obliged to wait for five days to undertake
the journey with two other followers of Christ whom the marzabanas
was sending with him and who like him were also bearing a seal.

29. In the meanwhile, the Feast of the Exaltation of the precious and
venerable cross of the Lord had arrived. The blessed martyr himself,
and the two brothers from his monastery, the two above-mentioned
followers of Christ, and some of the city's faithful kept the vigil in
prison, spending the entire night in the singing of psalms and hymns
and in other spiritual celebrations, so that all the prisoners forgot their
miseries and together they glorified God. At dawn, the merchant, who
was a Christian, went to the marzabanas and asked him that the chains
be removed so that Anastasius could attend church. And this was done,
and a great joy came upon all the faithful, and a great consolation for
the tribulations that afflicted them, because the martyr of Christ was
present in the church. For indeed the people of the city had fallen into
great desperation, and it was as if their souls had lapsed into torpor
because of their indescribable and severe tribulations.

30. Indeed, when they saw the blessed martyr's great faith in Christ and
his steadfastness, they blossomed, as it were, and they became alive
again in the faith, and forgot their own tribulations because of the
overpowering consolation they received through the martyr. And para-
doxically, those very ones, who in their misfortunes had recanted and
who over time had fallen into faithlessness, became the anointers of the
blessed martyr, kissing his chains and saying: "If we are ready to die for
you for the sake of Christ, how much more you ought to bear with
absolute zeal all this for the sake of Christ the common Lord of all."
And in a word both men and women showed great and indescribable
veneration and goodwill toward the saint. When the church assembly
was released, the merchant, after many appeals and much pressure, took
Anastasius with the two brothers of the same monastery to his own
house, and after banqueting with them, he led him, rejoicing and exult-
ing in the Lord, back to prison. There also there was great joy, while
all glorified the Lord.

31. After the period of five days came to an end, Anastasius left the city
of Caesarea together with the two other followers of Christ, who had
been denounced on account of a certain reason. He was escorted with
many tears by the citizens, Christians, Persians, and foreigners, and all
praised God for his (i.e. Anastasius's) good intentions. One of the two
brothers of his monastery went with him, following the command of

the abbot, to comfort and minister to him, and even more so that he might accurately report by the grace of the Lord both to the most holy abbot and also to the community under him all that would happen to him (i.e. Anastasius), from beginning to end. The faithful in each city and in each region were filled with much joy and happiness upon the arrival of the martyr. They all received the martyr of Christ and sent him off with every honor and glory. The martyr himself wrote these things to the superior of his monastery from Hierapolis, asking for prayers so that the Lord might hold him blameless for such honor and glory. He also wrote to him from the river Tigris, similarly requesting him to entreat our loving God to bring to an end his course to the glory of his name.

32. When he arrived in Persia, the martyr of Christ Anastasius was thrown into prison in the village called Bethsaloe, which is about six stadii from Diskarthas, where the emperor was residing. The brother who was with him remained in the same village, in the house of Kortak, the son of Yesdin, the first commerciarius of the Persians, who was a Christian. After the saint had spent several days with the prisoners who were there, his case was presented to the emperor Chosrohes. He sent one of his officials with the command to examine him.

33. This man, coming to the prison with the chiliarch who was in charge of the prison, asked him who he was and where from, and for what reason, leaving their religion, had become a Christian. The martyr of Christ answered through an interpreter—he disdained in fact to speak to them in Persian even though they pressured him greatly—and said to them: "You are wrong in worshiping demons instead of God. Even I once when I was in this error, I worshiped them. Now however I worship [and adore] the omnipotent God who made the heaven and earth and all things that are in them. And I know certainly that the objects of your cult are the deceits and deadly errors of demons." The judge said to him: "Wretch, the one whom you Christians worship, did not the Jews crucify him? How then did you go astray, leaving your religion, and becoming a Christian?" And the holy martyr answered: "You say correctly that he willingly was crucified by the Jews. For he is the one who made the heavens and earth, the sea and all things that are in them, and deigned to come down to earth and become human and be crucified so that he might free humankind from the error of Satan, who is worshiped by you. But you, who worship fire and other things that I blush even to name, you have vain hopes, worshiping what is created rather than the creator." The judge said to him: "What use are these speeches to you? Look, the divine emperor has great honors ready

for you, and golden girdles and horses, so that you may be among his first men. Only return to your first religion." The martyr of Christ answered him and said: "I shall not deny my God; rather I adore and worship him. But the gifts of your emperor, I consider them manure."

34. The above-mentioned judge left and reported back all these things to the emperor. The emperor, filled with anger, dispatched him in the morning, having ordered that Anastasius be punished. [On the next day], the judge thus came and angrily ordered that he be taken out of prison. And he began to terrorize him with terrible threats, expecting and convinced that he would persuade him in this way. The holy martyr, however, answered him saying: "Do not exert and weary yourself, O lord judge. For, as Christ gives me strength, you shall not convince me to abandon my faith. Do whatever you want to." He then commanded him to be bound in the Persian manner and be beaten with sticks without mercy, and he said to him: "Since you did not choose to be persuaded by the emperor's honors and gifts, know that from now on you will have to expect such treatment. For thus I shall wear you down every day with beatings." The holy martyr answered and said to him: "Neither am I swayed by the gifts of the emperor nor do I fear your threats. Whatever you want to do, do."

35. Then he ordered him to be untied and made to lie supine, and a plank to be placed on his tibias, and two very strong men to stand on the two ends of the plank. We all know how unbearable is such a torture. But the holy martyr of Christ gave thanks to God, enduring the pain bravely. The judge, seeing that he was accomplishing nothing more—rather, by divine grace he was hardened by such great pains just as iron is by frigid water—commanded that he be thrown into prison, while again he might report to the emperor about him.

36. Since the sellarius who was in charge of the prison was a Christian, the brother of the monastery who had come with the saint would go confidently without fear day after day to him (i.e. Anastasius), consoling him and urging him toward the good. Many of the Christians of that area, among whom were the children of Iesdin, visited him, falling down at his feet and kissing his chains and asking him to pray for them and to give them a blessed object (eulogia) for their protection. But as the martyr rejected such entreaties, they placed wax on his chains and took this impression as a eulogia.

37. Again, after a few days, the same judge returned to the prison and said to him: "What do you say? Will you do what the emperor commands or will you persist in these positions?" The holy martyr shaking his head as if he abhorred him, said: "I said to you once, twice and

more that it is impossible for me to deny Christ. Do quickly therefore whatever you wish." Then, that impudent and barbaric man commanded that he be bound as before and be beaten with sticks for a long time without mercy, and leaving him in the prison, he retired. After waiting for a few days, returning again to him, using the same arguments, he called on the holy martyr of Christ to apostatize, sometimes with blandishments and promises of money and honors, sometimes however with fearful threats and bitter torments. But as he saw that his mind was unchangeable and that his faith in Christ was steadfast, he commanded that he be tied as twice before, and be beaten similarly with sticks. And when he was again untied, he commanded that he be hung by one hand, and that a large stone be tied to his foot. And leaving him thus, he went away. After the martyr of Christ had bravely endured this torture for about two hours, he sent someone with orders that he be taken down. And he went away and informed the emperor of the martyr's immutability of mind and confidence.

38. After about fifteen days the emperor sent the same judge and others with him to kill the holy martyr and many Christian prisoners. When they arrived, they ordered that the holy martyr himself and about seventy men be led outside the village of Bethsaloe, where the prison was located, to the river. And thus they ordered that all be strangled with ropes in front of the holy martyr. Among these were the two above-mentioned followers of Christ who had come with the martyr from Caesarea. And as they killed each one they said to the saint: "Why do you wish to perish by a bad death like one of these? Rather, obey the emperor and live, accept the honors he offers and reside in the palace as one of us; do not abandon this sweet life." But the victorious martyr of Christ Anastasius looking up to the heavens gave thanks to God that his desire had been fulfilled. And answering he said to them: "I expected to be torn limb from limb by you for the love of Christ. But if this is the death that you threaten for me, I give thanks to my God that through a little suffering you make me a participant in the glory of his martyrs." And thus with much joy and eagerness he died by the same death. After they strangled him, they cut off his precious head, and took the seal, and brought it to the emperor.

39. The sellarius in charge of the prison who was a Christian, as was said, wanted the body of the martyr to be placed aside so that it could be identified. But the executioners who were Jews did not allow him. When the sons of Iesdin learned of the death of the saint—for their servants had assisted the holy martyr by holding up his hands (cf. Ex 17. 12) as he was going to his death—they secretly gave much money to the

executioners and convinced them to place his body apart. And on the following night, the brother from the martyr's monastery, taking with him the servants of the sons of Iesdin and some monks of those parts, came to pick up the body of the saint. And he found dogs eating the bodies of the dead, but the body of the martyr, which was lying apart next to them, was intact. "Precious in the sight of the Lord is the death of his faithful ones" (Ps 116.15), and "he keeps all their bones; not one of them will be broken" (Ps 34.20). He thus took the body of the martyr and wrapped it in precious cloths, which the sons of Iesdin had given, and he brought it to the monastery of the holy martyr Sergius, which is about a mile from the above-mentioned village and deposited it there.

40. The victorious martyr of Christ Anastasius completed his contest of the confession in Christ on the twenty-second day of January of the first indiction, in the seventeenth year of the reign of the most pious Heraclius and the fifteenth of his son, God-protected Constantine.

41. On the morrow after the death of the martyr, two of those who were guarding the prison were conversing with each other. And one of them said to the other: "Do you know that dogs came yesterday and sat next to the body of that monk? And they did not touch it, but rather it was as if they were guarding it. And I remained watching for about two hours, and the dogs neither went away nor did they touch the body." The other said to him: "Yesterday when I was on my way home from the prison, I saw something like a star shining on the pavement. As I was going to see what it was, as I got closer, the star disappeared, but I saw the body of the monk lying there on that spot on the pavement."

42. Such things did the guards full of astonishment tell each other in their own language. Some of the prisoners in the jail who were Christians, and who knew Persian, heard them. Two of these, after they were feed with many others, came to the holy city after the death of Chosroes. To these two while in prison the holy martyr Anastasius had predicted his own death, their liberation and the fall of the king, saying: "Know, brothers, that by the grace of God I shall die tomorrow. After a few days you will be released, and the impious and evil king will be killed. But when with God's speed you will come to the holy city, go to the monastery that is called 'of Abbot Anastasius' and report these things to my abbot and my brothers." The men, having heard these things from the saint and having seen the fulfillment of the events with their own eyes, glorified God, who glorifies those who glorify him. And they fulfilled the command of the holy martyr, and narrated these things to us with their own mouth.

43. The brother from the monastery who has frequently been mentioned, having performed the funeral rites for the body of the martyr, buried it properly in the above-mentioned monastery of St. Sergius. He remained there considering how he might return without danger to the one who had sent him. And after about ten days, on the first day of February, our most pious and Christian emperor Heraclius arrived with the army in his following. On seeing them, the brother rejoiced with great joy, and spoke to them in the language of the Romans. And they asked him what he was doing there. And after he recounted to them all things in order, they glorified God and said to him: "Stand up, come with us and keep yourself safe." And he was in great honor among them the entire time they were in Persia, and with them he left through the land of the Armenians.

44. After a year he reached the monastery, and he recounted to the superior everything with great precision. And he brought back to him also the colobium (i.e. tunic) of the martyr, the one in which he had died, and narrated also this to him: "There was a certain young monk in the monastery in which the body of the martyr was buried, who was vexed atrociously by an impure spirit. The superior of that place, after much begging me, took the colobium of the martyr and put it on the patient and immediately he was healed by the grace of the Lord, to the glory of God, who is glorified in his saints."

THE ROMAN MIRACLE

1. In the first year of the reign of our lord the most pious, peace-loving great emperor Anastasius and the first year after the consulship of his serenity, at the time of the most holy and blessed and apostolic supreme bishop Constantine, pope of the city of Rome, [2.] there was a certain bishop by the name of Theopentus, a Syrian, from the city named Constantia. This man had come to this city of Rome a few years earlier. He had a small daughter, and it seemed fitting to him to consign her to a monastery to learn sacred letters. She was instructed in the psalms and hymns, and in the canticles and readings. As the girl was fair of face and beautiful, many wanted to ask her in marriage from her above-mentioned father, not only because of the comeliness and beauty of the girl, but even more because of the wealth of her father. For the venerable bishop was indeed very rich. The venerable bishop, father of the girl, considering these things, recognizing that a handmaiden of the Lord is a good thing, consecrated her in the monastery of St. Cassian among the handmaidens of Christ. And the bishop began to distribute his fortune to the poor and to pious establishments.

3. When the girl had completed eighteen months in the monastery, the malevolent and ancient foe, the enemy of the human race, entered into the girl, and began to rouse her and consume her. Many came to the above-mentioned bishop, the father of the girl, and said to him: "We will make phylacteries and cast out this devil from this girl." And he [hearing these things] began to lament greatly, and, compelled by interior pains, he repulsed all of them and their doings, but rather chose, as the psalm says "to be a doorkeeper in the house of the Lord" (Ps 84.11), and to send up continuous prayers of supplication to his revered martyr Anastasius ...[1] The Christian soul (?) seeks the Lord of majesty, †nor does it abandon God's advice in sadness despising the secret places (?)†;[2] it does not go to the school's teacher to present the arguments of the affair, how .... But the Christian soul does not do this.[3] The Christian soul, rather, freed from whatever tribulations or temptations, having faith within, finds a fitting resting place inside the conscience of its heart and within the cave of its breast. It turns its conscience into a page, its groaning into a pen, and its tears into ink. It holds fast to its interior and most intimate counsel and says: "Hear my prayer, O God (Ps 54.2); give ear to my cry (Ps 39.13); do not be silent from me" (cf. Ps 28.1).

4. And thus also that venerable bishop, whose daughter was vexed by the devil, held fast to his inner counsel and said to himself: "I shall rise and go to our Lord Jesus Christ and to his holy martyr Anastasius; for he has the power to cure my daughter from the vexation of the demon." Thus the venerable man rose up, full of faith in Christ and in the holy martyr Anastasius, and took his daughter who had the impure spirit, and came to the monastery of the holy mother of God, the eternally virgin Mary, where the saintly and blessed apostle Paul was decapitated, in the place which is called "Aqua Salvia," where the venerable relics of the blessed martyr Anastasius are resting. And since a woman cannot enter in the monastery itself, there is next to the monastery the church of the blessed precursor John the Baptist. The bishop went in and gave himself to prayer there, keeping with him a priest and a deacon. And he asked the abbot of the monastery that the relics of the holy martyr Anastasius be brought into the basilica of St.

---

1. The Latin text has a lacuna, and the Greek text has an even longer one.

2. The meaning of the corrupt Latin, and in particular of *iudicem* and *eremum*, is not clear; the Greek has a lacuna.

3. The Latin text that follows varies from the Greek, and most likely preserves more of the original version.

John. [And when this had been done] the entire congregation knelt [in prayer] for the sake of the girl, and beseeched our lord Jesus Christ and the blessed martyr Anastasius. And when these things were done on the Kalends of October of the current twelfth indiction, then the relics of the venerable martyr, that is his head, were brought out and placed on the altar. And the afore-mentioned bishop began to ask the abbot of the monastery to take a particle from the holy and venerable relics and hang it on the neck of his daughter. One of the venerable teeth of the holy martyr was given to him, and they hung it on her neck.

5. But the hateful antagonist by some trick made it fall, and in such a way that it would not be noticed. And what more? While the holy and venerable head itself was being brought to the holy altar, as has already been said, the demon began to perturb the girl, not giving her rest day or night. And the demon itself began to speak blasphemies against the martyrs of Christ and the servants of God through the mouth of the girl, saying: "Why did you take me to Anastasius, this dog-eater? He was mine, but gave his body to be tortured for the Nazarene. He cannot throw me out, because I am an emperor and I have a crown, I have phalanxes, patricians, and there is no one who can throw me out from this body." And one from the congregation said to him: "Our Lord Jesus Christ and St. Anastasius will cast you out." The demon replied: "The Nazarene will not cast me out, because the heavens are his, but the air and the earth are mine." The brothers questioned him saying: "Tell us, most wicked one, how did you dare to enter into a consecrated vessel, where the body and blood of our Lord Jesus Christ have entered?" The demon answered: "Someone conjured me to enter into this body, and thus I did enter." [Having heard these things from him], they took out the head of the blessed martyr Anastasius on a silver platter and placed it over the head of the girl. And as they were sprinkling incense into the thurible, the demon said: "Don't do this because it smells foul to me." But when someone from the assembly brought muck, he smelled it and said: "This is my perfume, for I desire this." And again he cried out and said: "This dog-eater cannot cast me out, for he was mine. I swore an oath over my crown. And I entered by force, and force shall not make me leave this body, because I cannot break the oath which was administered to me on my crown."

6. We questioned him saying: "Who is the one who gave you the conjuration?" The demon answered: "I shall not reveal my friend." And as we were adjuring him in the name of our Lord Jesus Christ and by the eternal judgment that he withdraw from that body, or to tell us how he had entered, the demon began to say: "That young man, who had

asked for her in marriage, traveled to Sicily to a certain [sorcerer], to the place that is called Marathodis, and he made the conjuration in my name, and tied [me] in fig leaves, and took it with him. When the girl[4] went to the baths, he threw it on the road before her; and when she stepped on the bundle, at that moment I entered into her, and on that day I did not toy with her nor did I convulse her. That was on the second day of the month of August, of the eleventh indiction; and in that month I did not vex her, nor did I excite her, nor did I convulse her. On the second day of the month of September, however, I entered into her and began to toy with her and excite her and arouse her." And one of the brothers said to him: "Most wicked one, cursed one, foul one, how can you say you are an emperor and have a crown, when you allow yourself to be tied in fig leaves?" The demon answered: "Do not injure me because I am emperor, and I must rule still. Thus I accepted the conjuration. I swore on my crown, because I have patricians and phalanxes that are in my entourage, and I cannot break my oaths. But if you want me out of this body, go and undo the spells and the charms; and I shall get out of this body." And the afore-mentioned venerable bishop together with the assembly said: "We shall not cast aside our Lord Jesus Christ nor his holy martyr Anastasius, and seek the spells of demons and men." But the demon said: "What are you hoping for? Anastasius is not here; he went to the East, for he has a friend there, who built him a church. He has placed his relics there, and he renders service night and day. And through my plots, I arranged it so that while he wanted to cross a river he fell and broke his legs, and he invoked the name of Anastasius, who went there to heal him. And I tell you, that he shall not come during this entire month of October. And if he should come, I have no doubt that he cannot cast me out of this body."

7. Why say more? He came constantly day and night, making the girl laugh,[5] having fun and laughing, as a man who goes to his friend's for a party; and he entered the girl and said blasphemies and insults against the [divine] majesty and the martyrs and the bishops and priests and deacons and monks. Frequently he said merrily: "Vah, vah, what did I do today? Today I committed three homicides, and I rejoice in my exploits." And on another occasion he said: "Today I made a soldier sleep with a handmaid of God; and I rejoice." After a few days he said again: "I have just come from Spain, and there I committed many homicides

4. The Latin reads *istud corpus*, contrary to the Greek ("young girl").
5. My translation follows the Greek here, rather than the inaccurate Latin translation.

and spilled much blood.[6] And I rejoice even more in my exploits." And one of the brothers said to him: "Accursed one, most evil spirit, enemy of humankind, why do you persecute man who was made in the image of God? The torment of hell is being prepared for you, the inextinguishable flame. Give honor to God and Jesus Christ his son, who will come to judge the world through fire." And the demon answered: "Never shall I bend my head and my crown before the Nazarene. But I shall act according to my decrees because I do not fear anyone." We said to him: "Behold the apostles of our Lord Jesus Christ, Peter and Paul; they will throw you out of this body." The demon responded: "O this evil old man Peter, what has he done? I had caused Philip to rule, because he was my friend; but this old man came on Pentecost and he ordained another one.[7] He did these things against me; but he cannot throw me out of this body." And one of the brothers gave a slap[8] to the girl saying: "You will not curse the majesty of God and his martyrs." The devil said: "Go on striking! What does this body matter to me?" And he did not cease to utter blasphemies against the martyrs and similar things against the servants of God, and other things that would be long to narrate one by one.

8. The girl completed twenty-five days in the basilica of St. John, during which time the demon frequently came into her and stimulated her. On that very night, around the second hour, the most evil spirit came into the girl and began to exclaim through her, saying: "Behold, I say to you, that Mary and Paul and Andrew have offered the tears of this bad old bishop and of these monks to the Nazarene. And the Nazarene issued a command and gave the power to Anastasius, who will come and cast me out from this body on the Kalends of November." And the venerable bishop together with the abbot and the entire congregation did not desist night and day from kneeling, from beating his head on the ground, from stretching his hands, from raising his eyes to the heavens, from striking his bosom, from exclaiming and saying: "O most beloved Lord, you are the living wisdom, you are the fountain of life, you are the sun of justice, you truest light, have pity on me, and pour out the antidote of your generosity,[9] you who free the penitents from sin. Forgive [my] sins, you who give rest to those who have lapsed.

---

6. This is a reference to the Arab invasion of Spain beginning in 711 (Flusin II, 377).

7. See above, p. 18.

8. *palmam* (or *alapam*?) clearly must mean a slap, *pace* Flusin I, 176 n. 56.

9. *largitatis antidotum* is a loose rendering of the Greek.

Raise my daughter from the dead, and snatch her from the harshest torments. Because it was for such reasons that you came down from heaven, to have pity on men. O only-begotten Lord, raise up that which you made, for the sake of the body that you took on earth. Fulfill that which the prophet said: 'He heals the brokenhearted, and binds up their wounds' (Ps 146.3). O only-begotten Lord, you promised us through the gospel, saying: 'Ask, and it will be given you; search, and you will find; knock, and the door will be opened for you' (Mt 7.7). O only-begotten Lord, I am asking, I am searching, I am knocking so that your mercy may heal my daughter and so that I may not perish with her. O blessed Lord, I know that you raised Lazarus from the dead after three days, that you freed your disciple Peter's mother-in-law from fever, and that you healed the centurion's son, already dead; you have shown yourself as a heavenly healer; you raised the daughter of the leader of the synagogue from the dead, and you freed the daughter of the Canaanite woman from the devil; you healed the woman who was hemorrhaging; and as a good master you showed your divinity to the crowds. O Lord, look upon my tears; give me help so that I may have my daughter back, healed from the devil's oppression. For we believe that you are the Lord of angels and man, who live and reign in the centuries of centuries. Amen."

9. And as we said above, there was a candle in front of the venerable relics, burning continuously night and day, and by some trick that most evil, cursed, envious demon was seen to extinguish it. It was at about the third hour. The venerable bishop, seeing this, was very upset and sent a boy to the monastery to bring a light. And behold [while the boy was gone], the candle was lit all of a sudden by itself with great brightness. This happened on the third day before the Kalends of November, [and all gave glory to God for the miracles that the martyr Anastasius performed]. On the day before the Kalends, the venerable bishop asked the abbot of the monastery [Theodosius] that the entire congregation celebrate vespers and matins in the basilica of St. John. And this was done. And in the morning, on the day of the Kalends (i.e. November 1, 713), the brothers left and returned to the monastery; a priest, a deacon and three monks remained with the bishop. And all of a sudden, the most evil, unclean spirit entered into the girl and began to stimulate her. The monks, holding her hands, led her before the holy altar where the holy relics were. And the demon [at the end of one hour] began to speak vain words through [the mouth of] the girl herself. Then he be-

gan to say: "Anastasius brought me to stimulate and afflict me,[10] but now I no longer do harm to Anastasius, nor the bishop, nor the priests, nor the deacons, nor the monks." Immediately, the above-mentioned bishop sent word, and the entire congregation came. And while all were on their knees and saying together "Kyrie eleison," the demon began to exclaim through the girl, and say: "Anastasius, why did you lead me here to be a spectacle before men, to stimulate and torment me?" And the girl began to bend [her head] to the right and the left, as one who is most harshly whipped [by a magistrate] and to shout with a loud voice: "Woe, woe is me! What do I suffer because of this accursed body! I came in derision before all men! I entered it by force [and by force I shall leave it]; I go out, I shall not stay in this accursed body!" And when we said to him: "Go out, accursed one," the demon answered: "I cannot go out, because Anastasius has me tied up. Alas, woe is me! How I suffer!"

10. And after a while, she was lifted from the ground. The demon, who used to make the girl merry, now instead made her sad, and while before he made her laugh and be gay, now however he made her wail and shed tears. She began [again, as before, to bend to the right and then to the left,] and while she was suspended in air, the demon shouted: "Woe to me, Anastasius." Again she was with her head upside down. And the demon exclaimed: "Why do you hang me with my head upside down, Anastasius? I am going out from this body." And we said to him: "Go out, withdraw from this creature, the image of God and bride of Christ." And the demon replied: "Anastasius has tied me down, for he wants to torment me again in the evening because I caused his tooth to get lost." We said to him: "And what happened to that tooth?" The demon said: "When Anastasius came, he picked it up and put it back in its place." And we said to him: "When did St. Anastasius come?" The demon said: "When the candle lit up by itself, at that moment Anastasius arrived and put the tooth back in its place." The bishop said: "You lie, cursed one." The demon said: "Look in the chest where the relics are kept and you will see." And when the chest was opened, the tooth was found among the other relics. And we were reminded that "the Lord is faithful in all his words" (Ps 144.13) as he spoke through the prophet: The Lord "keeps all their bones; not one of

---

10. *ad stimulandum et cruciandum*: The Latin does not make it clear whether the devil is the agent or the recipient of the two actions; the two gerunds have no correspondence in the Greek.

them will be broken" (Ps 34.20). And the Lord said in the gospel: "But not a hair of your head will perish" (Lc 21.18), and many other things.

11. While the liturgy was being performed, the demon did not speak any word through the girl, but she was silent before the altar. When the monks went back for their refection, the bishop and a priest and a deacon and three monks remained. When the eleventh hour came, again the demon began to shout as before and say: "Why do you torture me, Anastasius? I know that you are a saint." And he shouted with a great howl, saying: "Woe, woe is me! St. Anastasius, I know that you are a saint; I did not sin against you; agitate the man who caused me to enter into this body." And again as before, the girl began to twist right and left, as one who is being lashed most harshly in the praetorium. The demon exclaimed: "I am going out from this body with every vice."[11] And he was quiet for a little bit, and again he cried out with a howl: "I am going out. For I swear by the one whom you venerate and worship; I do not perjure." And again he was quiet, and again he cried out with a howl saying: "By that which you are carrying, I am not swearing falsely, I go out; and I shall never return into this body. Woe is me, woe is me! I came into derision among men." And again he exclaimed: "St. Anastasius, I am going out; and I shall never commit injury against your priests, nor against your deacons, nor against your soldiers, that is your monks, for they are your soldiers. And behold I say and confess unto you that I am nothing. I am a wind, an evil and impure spirit, and I am nothing. [But I am powerless against the saints of God.] Wherever a true Christian is found, I flee from him, and I am not able to commit any evil against him."

As we were all crying, the demon said to us: "Do not cry, for when St. Anastasius sees your tears, he will burn me and torment me more harshly. As I have sworn, I am going out and never shall return into this body." And one of the brothers said to him: "Do not do any harm, while you are going out." The demon answered: "St. Anastasius has commanded me that I leave this body causing no injury." After these words, he was quiet for almost one hour. The girl bent her head before the altar and the venerable relics, and was quiet, but we began to say: "Cursed one, go out." The demon answered: "Allow me, for I am [writing down] for St. Anastasius what torments I shall suffer if I should return into this body." And when it was the third hour of the night,

---

11. *vitio*, which appears to translate ἐλαττωμάτων; Flusin took this word in its meaning of "loss, defeat" ("J'en sors completement vaincu") while the Latin translator understood differently.

the girl bent her knees before the icon of our Lord Jesus Christ for almost half an hour; and she got up with her mind and body cured, and stood before the holy altar, and received the body and blood of our Lord Jesus Christ and she was healed from that hour.

[12.[12] Thus we must set forth in fitting manner the miraculous deeds and the praise of the blessed martyr Anastasius, who after the pomp of this world achieved the crown of heaven. Tyrannical fury raged madly against him, but the divine presence shone in his heart. The evil man, Marzabanas the executioner, cut down the limbs of St. Anastasius, but inexhaustible medicine provided refreshment in his heart. The enemy Marzabanas grew weaker in torturing him; and the blessed Anastasius by patient suffering was victorious. It was not a combat fought with human strength, nor was the battle joined for the life of the body; ....[13] rather, the fight was for the heavenly kingdom. He could neither succumb, nor did he fear to arrange his neck for the rope. O good shepherd, whom we praise with our modest voice! He followed the footsteps of the eternal shepherd, our Lord Jesus Christ. He traded death for life, to receive the crown of glory. O great wonder! The body is killed so that the fruit of the martyrs can flower into life. O precious death, from which arises the victory of confession! The innocent is made guilty, while God is not obeyed. The just one is killed, and Christ is crucified in his followers. He chose present death for the sake of the salvation of eternal life. The blessed Anastasius stood firm, armed with the banner of the cross, and protected by the breastplate of faith. The just fought, not so much with the sweat of labor, but with the effusion of blood. The body was victorious among the torments, and the unvanquished soul spilled blood for the sake of our Lord the Savior. O dearest brothers, my heart trembles and my insides are loosened whenever I remember these miracles, which our Lord Jesus Christ accomplished through his martyr the blessed Anastasius. The Lord is wondrous, who accomplishes wondrous things in his saints. Behold, how much they obtained, those who did not deny the Lord Jesus Christ. See, O brothers, how much the faith of the martyrs obtained. May the only-begotten Lord snatch even us from the enemy's oppression through the prayers of his blessed martyr Anastasius so that we may give thanks through our Lord himself Jesus Christ to God the father and the holy Spirit, now and forever and in the centuries of centuries. Amen.]

12. This last chapter is found only in the Latin. See below, pp. 141-144.
13. See n. 69 to the Latin text.

II

THE FIRST LATIN TRANSLATION
OF THE *ACTA S. ANASTASII*: *BHL* 410b

1. INTRODUCTION

The Greek *Acta* of the Persian martyr (*BHG* 84),[1] twice translated into Latin, is the ultimate source of all the Latin passions of St. Anastasius. The first Latin translation of the Greek *Acta* of Anastasius survives in only one manuscript witness, F III 16 (fols. 14-23) of the Biblioteca nazionale of Turin, a passionary[2] copied at the monastery of Bobbio in northern Italy in the late ninth or early tenth century. The work was assigned the number 410b in the 1911 Supplement to the *Bibliotheca Hagiographica Latina* (*BHL*), the Bollandist compilation of Latin manuscripts of saints' Lives.[3]

The Bobbio passionary, containing the early translation of the *Passio S. Anastasii*, is an orderly hagiographical compilation covering the entire calendar year. Its core of twenty-three texts is drawn from the hagiographic traditions of Rome, which included not only the city's own martyrs but also many figures whose cult was imported from abroad. At least twelve of the texts copied into the Bobbio passionary are translations from the Greek; seven of these are found only in this codex. This extraordinary convergence of translated texts in the Bobbio codex has led to the hypothesis that it reflects the translation of an entire Greek hagiographical collection into Latin and perhaps was the work of just one

---

1. See Chapter I, pp. 3-5.

2. A passionary is a collection of passions of martyrs; a legendary contains both passions of martyrs and lives of saints. For further discussion of these, see below, pp. 152-154. A detailed discussion of the unique manuscript witness is found on pp. 259-267.

3. For Albert Poncelet's rationale for assigning this number, see below, p. 259.

translator.[4] Certainly, the passionary copied at Bobbio is the most important witness of the integration of eastern and western hagiographic strands within the multicultural context of early medieval Rome, and its *Passio S. Anastasii* sheds light on the process by which such integration was effected.

2. THE NATURE OF THE FIRST TRANSLATION[5]

The most significant characteristic of the first translation of the *Acta S. Anastasii* is its faithfulness to the Greek text. *BHL* 410b follows the Greek so closely that it contributes to the establishment of the Greek text by providing crucial information in the case of many variant readings.[6] The translator rendered the Greek text word for word, line after line, faithfully following even the word order of its model, and transposing idioms and grammatical constructions, peculiar to Greek, into Latin. Syntactical and lexical choices are determined in this text by the wish, or need, of the translator to remain faithful to the Greek. The Latin text in effect becomes a servile duplication of the Greek. This strict literalism results in the translation of every word, including particles, mechanically and consistently, without regard to the context. For example, δέ, the most common particle, is generally translated as *autem*, occasionally as *vero* and rarely as *at*. Μέν, on the other hand, is generally translated as *quidem*.[7] Greek compound words are rendered by Latin compound words. Greek grammatical constructions are frequently duplicated into Latin.

4. See below, pp. 263-264 and n. 20.

5. Some of the material that follows has already been presented in Franklin and Meyvaert, "Has Bede's Version of the *Passio S. Anastasii* Come Down to Us in *BHL* 408?"

6. These cases are marked in Flusin's *apparatus criticus* with "Lat" (e.g. 3.9). The Latin translation is closest, textually, to two manuscripts of the *Acta*, both of which originate from southern Italy (Flusin I, 30-36): M (=Milan, Biblioteca ambrosiana, F 144 sup. [gr. 377], from the twelfth century) and U (=BAV, Vat. grec. 866, from the eleventh century). These are believed to be the only manuscripts of the Greek *Acta* originating in Italy.

7. Furthermore, καί is regularly translated as *et*, while *atque* appears to correspond more frequently to τε καί.

Coupled with the translator's fidelity to the Greek text is a serious neglect of Latin grammar, syntax, and idiom, most likely the result of the translator's limited knowledge of Latin. As a result, many translated passages remain unintelligible without reference to the original Greek.

A close adherence to the original text is typical of Latin translations from the Greek carried out during the early medieval period, particularly before the Carolingian age. Generally described as following their models *ad verbum*, such word-for-word translations provide a context in which Pope Gregory I's well-known railings against excessive literalism may be better understood.[8] Although numerous *ad verbum* translations have survived, many more have been replaced by more elegant revisions.[9] Of all these translations, it is *BHL* 410b that lays claim to the most confused use of Latin. Just how poor the Latin is can be gauged by comparison with another *ad verbum* translation. The *Passio Febroniae*, for example, which has recently been edited by Paolo Chiesa, provides numerous parallels to the textual history of the *Passio S. Anastasii*. Translated twice, the earlier translation is found in the Bobbio codex. Its fidelity to the Greek model, especially striking in the word order, draws its editor's particular notice. Its translator exhibits only a "modesta competenza" in Latin, and the resulting translation is often unclear and at times incomprehensible.[10] Nonetheless, despite these similarities, the first translation of the

8. "Gravem hic interpretum difficultatem patimur. Dum enim non sunt, qui sensum de sensu exprimant, sed transferre verborum semper proprietatem solunt, omnem dictorum sensum confundunt. Unde agitur, ut ea quae translata fuerint, nisi cum gravi labore intellegere nullo modo valeamus." (*Gregorii I ... Registrum* I, 258). Gregory I also complained about the absence of good translators from Latin into Greek in Constantinople in 597 (see Dekkers, "Les traductions grecques des écrits patristiques latins"). Other examples of complaints concerning the inadequacy of literal translations into both Latin and Greek are given in Sansterre, *Les moines grecs* I, 68.

9. Many works now considered to be direct translations from the Greek are in fact adaptations of lost, more faithful versions (Petitmengin, *Pélagie la Pénitente. Métamorphoses d'une légende* I, 165).

10. Chiesa, *Le versioni latine della 'Passio Sanctae Febroniae.' Storia, metodo, modelli di due traduzioni agiografiche altomedievali*, pp. 67-68, 119-150.

Passio Febroniae, as we know it,[11] does not, unlike the *Passio S. Anastasii*, "translate" the Greek article, and in general has a better command of Latin grammar and syntax.[12]

The Translation of the Greek Article

The greatest impediment to intelligibility resulting from the *Passio S. Anastasii*'s servility to the Greek model is exemplified by the treatment of the Greek article. When the Greek article occurs directly in front of a noun, the translator does not attempt to translate it. Nor is it translated in most cases where the noun is modified simply by an adjective in the attributive position, that is, where the word order consists of *article + adjective + noun*. There are many examples of these simple renditions, such as ʼΟ μονο-γενὴς Υἱὸς καὶ Λόγος τοῦ Θεοῦ (1.1), the opening words, which are rendered as "Vnigenitus filius et uerbum Dei" (l. 3), and "magnarum (*sic*) et ineffabilium Christi donorum" (ll. 46-47) for τῶν μεγάλων καὶ ἀφάτων τοῦ Χριστοῦ δωρεῶν (4.2). These and other examples suggest that the translator was aware of the divergence of Greek and Latin in relation to the definite article. But whenever the Greek text deviates from this simple pattern, that is, when the article is not closely attached to a noun, the translator attempts to translate the Greek article with what appears to be in Latin a relative pronoun. It is almost as if, when the article is close to the noun, it is subsumed into the noun. But when the article is suspended by itself, away from the noun, the translator needed to retain a marker to correspond to the isolated article.

---

11. Chiesa emphasizes the instability of this text, which underwent "un graduale processo di miglioramento stilistico" (p. 67).

12. There are a few other *ad verbum* translations available in critical editions that could be compared to *BHL* 410b. One is the Life of St. Hermule (*BHL* 3858b), a simple text published in Dolbeau, "Le rôle des interprètes dans les traductions hagiographiques d'Italie du sud," pp. 145-162. Despite its literalism and resulting awkward phrasing (e.g. "Diaconus sum horum qui videntur deorum" [p. 158]), one does not find in this text the grammatical and syntactical "howlers" of *BHL* 410b. Another is the dossier of St. Abbibos (=*BHL* 8b and *BHL* 7477b), which survives only in the eleventh-century legendary of St. Peter's Basilica (Chiesa, "Il dossier agiografico latino dei santi Gurias, Samonas e Abibos"). For further discussion, see also Franklin, "Hagiographic Translations in the Early Middle Ages (7th–10th centuries)."

The practice of translating the Greek article with the Latin relative pronoun is not restricted to the *Passio S. Anastasii*.[13] It is found in the early translations of the Bible,[14] and continues into the eighth century, when it occurs, for example, in the *Aratus Latinus*, a translation of a Greek astronomical collection executed in Gaul.[15] In the *Passio S. Anastasii*, this translation procedure results in Latin that is unclear because there is no finite verb completing the relative clause. Since all forms of the Greek article are rendered into Latin, most frequently by either *qui* (for the masculine article) or *quae* (for the feminine and neuter articles) regardless of case or number, while the Latin relative pronoun that translates the Greek relative pronoun is, on the contrary, generally declined, we must not conclude that the translator was confusing the article with the relative pronoun. Rather, he was in effect creating a Latin equivalent to the Greek article, perhaps in an attempt to be consistent with his general practice of translating word for word.

The following examples establish the broad patterns of "translation" of the Greek article that are easily identifiable:[16]

---

13. Priscian, *Institutiones grammaticae* II, 16 (ed. Keil II, 54), attempting to apply Greek grammatical categories to Latin, considers the article to be related to the pronoun. He subsumes the article under *pronomina*, as is shown by his discussion of the Latin pronoun *qui* and its equivalent Greek pronoun ὅστις (which he divides into its two components, *article + pronoun*): "[S]imiliter 'qui', 'ὅστις', articulus subiunctivus intellegitur una cum pronomine." Priscian, however, recognized that Latin does not have "full" articles ("quamvis integros in nostra non invenimus articulos lingua"). It may have been a similar understanding of the article that guided the approach of the translator of *BHL* 410b, and of other translators.

14. Rönsch, *Itala und Vulgata. Das Sprachidiom der urchristichen Itala und der Katholischen Vulgata*, p. 443, where this usage is listed among the Greek-influenced functions of the relative pronoun.

15. Le Bourdellès, *L'Aratus Latinus. Étude sur la culture et la langue latine dans le Nord de la France au viiie siècle*, pp. 198-199. The *Aratus Latinus*, while quite close to the Greek and in some of its usages comparable to the *Passio S. Anastasii*, is more comprehensible than the *Passio*.

16. The references are to Flusin's text by chapter and line, and page; and, by line number, to my edition of *BHL* 410b, pp. 272-298 below.

a. *Article + adjective separated from the noun*

'Ο μονογενὴς Υἱὸς ... ὁ συναΐδιος καὶ ὁμοούσιος (1.1-2)
Vnigenitus filius ... qui coaequalis atque consubstantialis (ll. 3-4)

τὰ πολυχρόνια τοῦ Ἅιδου καταστρέψας βασίλεια (1.8)
quae multa temporum inferi subuertens regalia (ll. 12-13)

τῶν πάλαι αὐτὸν ὑπερορισάντων ἁγίων ἀποστόλων (3.11)
qui olim eum praeterminantium sanctorum apostolorum (ll. 39-40)

The examples above deviate from the simple pattern *article + adjective + noun*, and *qui/quae* are used to mark the presence of the article.[17]

b. *Article + modifying genitive + noun*

ὁ τῆς ἀνθρωπίνης ζωῆς ἀπ' ἀρχῆς ἐπίβουλος (3.1)
qui humanae uitae a principio insidiator (l. 27)

ταῖς τῶν καλλινίκων μαρτύρων ὑπομοναῖς (3.11-12)
quae uictoriosorum martyrum tolerantiis (ll. 40-41)

In these two examples, *qui* and *quae* appear to introduce incomplete relative clauses that lack verbs. In some cases, however, the addition of a finite verb (generally a form of *sum*) improves the Latin by creating a relative clause, as in the following examples:

τούς τῆς εὐσεβείας τροφίμους (3.5)
quae pietatis *sunt* alumnos (l. 32)

τὰ τῆς ἐγχειρήσεως (3.9)
quae inmissionis *sunt* (ll. 37-38)

πάλιν τὸν οἰκεῖον τῆς εὐσεβείας κόσμον (3.12)
rursum proprium quae pietatis *est* ornatum (ll. 41-42)

In some instances, the addition does indeed clarify the Latin (as in the first example), while in others the addition fails to improve the unclear

---

17. There is only one other occurrence of this pattern where the adjective is separated from the noun (2.9), and it is translated quite well: *uniuersa hominum natura* (ll. 25-26). The first example I give above, following the more formal pattern *article + noun + article + adjective*, is unique. A similar word order is found with a participle, however, in place of the adjective in 36.1=l. 483). There are a few cases where a demonstrative pronoun is found before the addition of *qui/quae* (e.g. τὴν μὲν πατροπαράδοτον καὶ πολυχρόνιον τῆς ἀσεβείας πλάνην [2.5]=illam quidem quae paternae traditionem et multis temporibus impietatis errorem [ll. 20-21]). Was this a later attempt to construct a relative clause?

translation. It is not apparent whether such additions were made by a later editor or were also the work of the original translator.[18]

c. *Article + participle*

In the majority of cases, the Latin substitutes a finite verb for the Greek participle, thus in effect creating a relative clause, as in these examples:[19]

Τοῖς γὰρ τότε κρατοῦσιν ... ἐγκατασπείρας (3.6-8)
Eos enim qui tunc *tenebant* ... inseminans (ll. 32-34)

τὰς ἐπαχθείσας αὐτοῖς παρὰ τῶν τυράννων (9.6-7)
quae inlata *sunt* eis a tyrannis (l. 124)

κατὰ τὴν δεδομένην αὐτῷ παρὰ Θεοῦ σύνεσιν (13.8-9)
secundum quae *data est* ei a Deo intellegentia (ll. 179-180)

τὸν ποιήσαντα (22.7)
qui *fecit* (l. 297)

In some cases a more literal translation is followed, and the Greek participle is translated with a Latin participle:

ταῦτα τὰ τὴν φλόγα τρέφοντα (12.13-14)
haec quae flammam alentem (ll. 169-170)

εἰς τὸ κάστρον ἀπήγετο τοῖς διὰ Χριστὸν δεσμοῖς ἐνκοσμούμενος (23.15-16)
ad castrum ducebatur quibus[20] pro Christo uinculis adornatus (ll. 314-315)

οἱ ἀπειρηκότες τοῖς δεινοῖς (30.4)
hii qui desperati atrocibus (ll. 399-400)

d. *Article + prepositional phrase + noun*

In the majority of cases, the translator renders the article followed by a prepositional phrase with *qui/quae*, as in the following examples:[21]

---

18. In some cases, where the genitive is closely related to an adjective and is preceded by an article, a correct translation is provided as in: τῆς μὲν αὐτοῦ πονηρίας ἀξίαν (3.4-5) = eius quidem malignitatis dignam (ll. 31-32). The word order (i.e. not the expected *quidem eius*) suggests revision.

19. Chiesa, *Le versioni latine*, pp. 139-140, notes that in the *Passio Febroniae* the Greek participle preceded by the article is translated generally by a relative clause.

20. One of the few instances of a "declined" Latin form of the article.

21. This usage should be compared to the different (and correct) practice followed by the translator of the *Passio Febroniae* (Chiesa, *Le versioni latine*, p. 140). This translator recognizes the substantive nature of this construction, as in αἱ ἐν τῷ μοναστηρίῳ = qui fuerunt in monasterio.

τὴν ἐξ ὕψους δύναμιν (2.1)
quae de sublimis uirtutem (l. 15)

τῆς διὰ Χριστοῦ χάριτος (3.2-3)
quae per Christi gratia (l. 29)

τοῖς κατὰ πόλιν καὶ τόπον πιστοῖς (31.9)
his qui per ciuitate et locum fidelibus (l. 422)

In some cases, however, this combination is translated correctly:

τῇ εἰς ῞Αιδου καθόδῳ (1.8)
in inferni descensione (ll. 11-12)

In others, a finite verb (generally a form of the verb *sum*) is added to the relative pronoun:

τὴν εἰς αὐτὸν ἀγάπην (5.6)
quae in eum *est* caritatem (l. 67)

τῆς εἰς αὐτὸν ὁμολογίας (24.5)
quae in eum *erat* confessione (l. 321)

τὸ στερέωμα τῆς εἰς Χριστὸν πίστεως (37.11)
soliditatem quae in Christum *habebat* fidei (ll. 504-505)

But, as this last example shows, adding a verb to make a relative clause can cause further problems. Here, the reader must take *quae* to refer to *soliditatem*, while clearly it was meant to go with *fidei*. It is possible that some of the correct translations may be the result of later, editorial revisions, although improvements to the translations were made inconsistently.[22]

Verbal Usage
Verbal usage in the Latin translation also follows the Greek. Greek compound verbs, for example, are translated by Latin compound verbs, as is the case of *ὑπέβαλλεν* (13.2) = submisit (l. 173), or *εἰσήχθη* (6.9) = introducta sunt (ll. 84-85). Such faithfulness betrays a poor grasp of, or indifference to, Latin norms, particularly in the

---

22. Certainly the phrase *μηδὲ θάνατον τὸν ὑπὲρ Χριστοῦ* (18.7-8) = neque mortem quam pro Christo debuerat perpeti (ll. 235-236) should be considered the result of later correction. Likewise, the phrase *τοὺς ἑαυτοῦ κατὰ χάριν υἱοὺς καὶ κληρονόμους* (5.5) = eos qui eius secundum gratiam filios atque heredes exiterunt (ll. 65-66) could be an example of a later correction, since *extiterunt* is not found as the added verb elsewhere in these phrases. However, *extitit* is found in this same chapter (and twice more elsewhere) to translate *ὑπάρχω*.

use of voice. Often the Latin passive is used as though it were a 'middle,' as in *suscepta pluuiam* (l. 95) to translate δεξαμένη (7.7).[23] Some intransitive Latin verbs are used transitively, such as *adquiesco*, which appears correctly in its intransitive meaning,[24] but also as a transitive verb, as in *adquieuerunt eos* (l. 537) translating word for word ἔπεισαν αὐτοὺς (39.6), or *adquiescere eum* (ll. 465-466) translating the compound μεταπείθειν αὐτὸν (34.4-5). The use of the conjunction *quia* in indirect discourse, as in *Scio quia confunderis propter congentiles tuos* (ll. 369-370), is not surprising. Also found here occasionally is the construction *ut* with the subjunctive instead of a verbal noun, as in *amor ut inluminaretur* (l. 118) to translate ὁ πόθος τοῦ φωτισθῆναι (9.1).[25]

The Translation of Participles

Of all the verbal constructions, it is the translation of Greek participles that causes the greatest confusion in the Latin text. Aorist active participles, the most numerous of all participles in the Greek text, are generally translated with present active participles, perhaps because of the impossibility of translating an aorist active participle in Greek with a perfect participle in Latin. The following examples come from cap. 1:

ἰδίῳ θανάτῳ καταργήσας (1.6)
propriae mortis destruens (ll. 9-10)
καταστρέψας βασίλεια (1.9)
subuertens regalia (ll. 12-13)

Five similar aorist participles, found at the beginning of cap. 4 (4.1, 3, 3, 4, 6; ll. 45-51), further illustrate this practice:

λαβόντες = accipientes
νοσήσαντες = languentes
χειρογραφήσαντες = scribentes

---

23. But in the following sentence δεξάμενος (7.8) is translated better as *suscipiens* (l. 97). Another example of a middle Greek form translated as a passive is *suspectus* (l. 120) translating the middle ὑφορώμενος (9.3).

24. E.g. "Adquiesce mihi" (l. 290) or "Nec donis imperatoris tui adquiesco" (l. 473).

25. Another example is *desiderium ... ut ... adueniret* (ll. 127-128) to translate ἐπιθυμίαν ... παραγενέσθαι (9.9).

φοινίξαντες = rubrantes
ἐκκαύσαντες = exardescentes[26]

There are also examples of middle aorist participles translated by a present active participle in Latin: ὑποδεξάμενος (10.6) = suscipiens (l. 134-135); δεξάμενος (10.9) = suscipiens (l. 138); Θεασάμενοι (30.1) = Cernentes (l. 396). As a result of this practice, the Latin text obliterates any distinction between the present participles[27] and the aorist participles of the Greek text. Tenses are thus blended together, following a practice found in other translated texts.[28]

Greek passive participles are generally translated by the Latin perfect participles, as in the following examples:

πυρικαύστων γενομένων (6.7) = igni combustis (ll. 82-83)
προωρισμένος (7.13) = praedestinatus (l. 102)
φερόμενος (16.3) = ductus (l. 212)
πληρωθέντος (31.1) = expleto (l. 412)
συκοφαντηθέντων (31.2) = accusatis (l. 414)
προπεμφθείς (31.3) = praemissus (l. 414)
ἀναγκασθείς (33.4) = coactus (l. 442)[29]

In countless other cases, however, the use of the Latin participles creates confusion in the text. The most puzzling usage is that of the Latin future active participle. In a few cases, a Latin future

---

26. In one case, the perfect participle of a Latin deponent verb is used: οἰκτείρας (1.2) = miseratus (l. 5).

27. These are generally translated also by Latin present participles. For example, λεγόντων (7.6) = dicentium (l. 94); Ἔχων (8.1) = habens (l. 108); ἐνθυμούμενος (7.9) = cogitans (l. 97); παρερχόμενος (16.2) = pertransiens (l. 211).

28. See for example, Chiesa, Le versioni latine, pp. 135-136 where the Greek aorist participle is regularly translated by a present participle. Chiesa points out that the translator of the Passio Febroniae has thus sacrificed the "sfumatura di anteriorità" to maintain a formal correspondence between Greek and Latin. As further examples of this phenomenon, he gives audiens and audientes used fifteen times to translate ἀκούσας, ἀκούσαντες and similar forms; videns is used four times to translate ἰδών, ἰδόντες; dicens for εἰποῦσα; accipiens for παραλαβών. Some of these same translations, such the last example, also occur in the Passio S. Anastasii.

29. There are also examples of aorist passive participles correctly translated by a present participle. For example: ἐκπλαγείς (7.13) = obstupescens (l. 102); συνεστιαθεὶς αὐτοῖς (30.11) = conuescens cum eis (l. 408).

active participle is used to translate an aorist middle participle, as in the following examples:

ποιησάμενος (1.8) = facturus (l. 11)

ἐπιδειξαμένους ... ἐπιδειξαμένας (5.7-8) = ostensuris ... ostensuras (ll. 68-69)

ἀναδησαμένας (5.9) = obligaturas (l. 71)

This problem may arise from confusing the endings of the aorist participle (-σαμενος, -α, -ον) with those of the future participle (-σομενος, -η, -ον). But more generally it may stem from the translator's lack of understanding of the Latin future participle, whose forms are employed to translate a variety of Greek verbal forms:

ἀπολλύμενον (1.3) (passive present participle)[30] = periturum (l. 5)

βλάψας (3.10) (an aorist, which is generally translated with a present participle) = nociturus (l. 38)

γενομένοις (5.1) = factoris (facturis) (l. 61)

ἐκπλαγῆναι (5.2) = stupefacturi (l. 62)

τὸν παρ' αὐτοῦ ὁμολογηθέντα Θεὸν (5.11) = eum quem ab eo confessurus est Deum (ll. 73-74)

ἐπιλαθομένους (29.5) (a second middle aorist) = oblituros (l. 387)

The translation of the participial expression in the genitive absolute also causes confusion in the Latin text. There are examples of the Greek genitive absolute being translated into a Latin genitive absolute:

τῆς δὲ ἁγίας ... πόλεως ἁλούσης καὶ τῶν σεβασμίων, καὶ προσκυνουμένων τόπων πυρικαύστων γενομένων (6.6-7) = Sanctae autem ciuitati excidioni factae et uenerandorum atque adorandorum locorum igni combustis (ll. 81-83)[31]

Φήμης ... διαθεούσης (7.4) = Famae ... personantes (l. 92)[32]

But there are also examples of Latin ablative absolute constructions translating the Greek genitive absolute:

---

30. It is possible that the translator did not know how to translate a present passive participle, which has no direct equivalent in Latin. However, immediately following *periturum*, the word *subiectum* is used to translate τυραννούμενον, although this may be a revision: see textual note 4.

31. Is it possible that *combustis* is a later correction of *combustorum*?

32. *Personantes* could be a misspelling of *personantis*.

Τοῦ δὲ ἐν ἁγίοις Φιλιππικοῦ ἀντιπερισπάσαντος αὐτὸν καὶ εἰσελθόντος
(8.3) = Phylippico circumuallanti eum, et introgresso eo in Persida
(l. 111)
Ἐλθόντος δὲ τοῦ μαρζαβανᾶ (18.1) = Veniente uero marzabana (l.
229)[33]

There are also occasions when the genitive absolute is translated by a nominative absolute:

Τοῦ δὲ μάρτυρος ἀπαναινομένου (36.6-7)
beatus martyr abiciens (ll. 489-490)[34]

Such inconsistency in translating a common Greek construction (the genitive absolute) for which a common Latin construction was available (the ablative absolute) is perhaps an indication of the translator's uncertain Latin.[35]

Confusion of Latin Case Endings
Further evidence for the translator's poor grasp of Latin is found in the use of incorrect syntax and case endings. The genitive, dative, and ablative are frequently used interchangeably and erroneously. As a result, it is often difficult to pinpoint the cause of the incorrect usage. For example, in the sentence "Sanctae autem ciuitati excidioni factae et uenerandorum atque adorandorum locorum igni combustis" (ll. 81-83), translating τῆς δὲ ἁγίας τοῦ Θεοῦ πόλεως ἁλούσης καὶ τῶν σεβασμίων καὶ προσκυνουμένων τόπων πυρικαύστων γενομένων [6.6-7]), was *ciuitati* used instead of *ciuitatis*, as if it were a second declension genitive? Or did the translator think that the genitive of the third declension was the same as the dative by analogy to the first declension feminine adjective *sanctae*? Equally unclear is what the translator intended by the phrase *excidioni factae*. Was this an attempt to parallel the Greek genitive absolute with a Latin ablative absolute in which *excidioni* fell victim to a similar case confusion as above? Or was this actually an attempted Latin ablative absolute in which both noun and adjective are given the wrong endings? The same wavering between Greek

33. Other examples are found in 18.3 = l. 232; 11.9 = ll. 149-150; 34.6 = l. 467; 32.5 = ll. 434-435.
34. Other examples in 16.7 = l. 214; 36.1 and note = l. 483.
35. See also Chiesa, *Le versioni latine*, pp. 137-138.

and Latin usage is found in the final phrase of this sentence, where after *uenerandorum atque adorandorum locorum* (to parallel the Greek genitive absolute) there is an inexplicable switch to the ablative *combustis*.[36]

In other places, however, it is possible to trace the source of the wrong case. For example, the genitive singular and the nominative/accusative endings of the third declension are regularly interchanged; this suggests that the translator's knowledge of Latin was acquired orally.[37] Most frequently, Latin usage imitates Greek usage. The genitive *missas factas* (l. 201) probably derives from the *s*-ending of the corresponding Greek phrase συνάξεως γενομένης (15.2). In the case of *propriae mortis* (l. 9) translating the Greek dative ἰδίῳ θανάτῳ (1.6), presumably the translator intended to use the Latin dative to correspond to the Greek, and extended to the third declension word the same ending of the dative and genitive on the model of the first. In numerous instances, prepositions are followed by the wrong Latin case, by analogy to the Greek: *cum* is frequently followed by the genitive,[38] as is *de*.[39] In some cases, the translator neglected to decline nouns altogether, leaving them in the nominative.[40] In many others, the wrong case is used where the translator is uncertain of the correct gender, as in *mares* (l. 24), or *captiuus ... crux* (ll. 85-86).[41] Some words are attached to the

36. But see n. 31 above. For examples of similar confusion of declensions and cases in the *Passio Febroniae*, see Chiesa, *Le versioni latine*, pp. 146-147.

37. E.g. in the phrase *secte existentes* (ll. 137-138), *existentes* is used instead of *existentis*. Frequently such "mistakes" reflect actual pronunciation. By the same token, *per auditu* (l. 104) might reflect the dropping of final *m* in spoken Latin, and *ciuitati* may reflect the dropping of final *s*. For parallel examples and further discussion, see Stevenson, *The 'Laterculus Malalianus' and the School of Archbishop Theodore.*

38. E.g. *cum duorum ... uirorum* (l. 413).

39. As in the phrase *de quoquine quam etiam de horti* (l. 156). There are also mixed cases, such as *inter me et aliis duobus sellariis* (l. 371). For further parallels, see Stevenson, *'Laterculus'*, p. 81.

40. E.g. *Sellarius ... christiano existenti* (l. 483).

41. However, the gender of *crux* appears to be known, or to have been corrected, in *honoranda atque uiuifica crux* (ll. 88-89).

wrong declension, for example *gestis* (l. 75), which is probably used as a genitive singular to translate τῆς διηγήσεως (5.12).[42]

Lexical Choices

In addition to poor grammar and syntax, the first Latin translation also betrays confusion and ignorance in the choice of words. There are many examples of words chosen inappropriately. Sometimes these are quite common words, such as *amor* (l. 118), which is used to translate πόθος (9.1).[43] In the phrase *quorum a suo patre edocuerat* (l. 174), which translates ὧνπερ παρὰ τοῦ ἰδίου πατρὸς μεμάθηκεν (13.3-4), the word *doceo* is confused with *disco*. In the same passage, ἠξίου εὔχεσθαι (13.7) is translated as *dignabat orare* (l. 178), which probably stems from conflating the two meanings of ἀξιόω (to deem worthy; to request).[44]

The translator's fidelity to the Greek text is revealed in this context, for example, by the tendency to translate Greek simple words with Latin simple words, and Greek compound words with Latin compound words. Hence, Βλέπων (13.1) is translated as *uidens* (l. 171), ἐμβλέψας (17.4) as *intuens* (l. 222), and ὑπερορισάν-των (3.11) as *praeterminantium* (ll. 39-40), which is neither authentic or appropriate. This tendency to duplicate the Greek lexical model is also evident in the translation of compound words, where two Latin words are used even when a single word could be used satisfactorily:

---

42. Unlike other similar, contemporary texts, a prepositional construction is used infrequently to replace simple case construction. The only construction used in this way is *de* + ablative, which occasionally replaces the Greek genitive. The fact that this construction is generally found before proper nouns suggests an uncertain grasp of Latin, e.g. de Persida (l. 76) = τῆς Περσίδος (6.1); de Iesdim filii (ll. 486-487) = οἱ τοῦ Ἰεσδὶν υἱοί (36.4). For comparisons with other texts, see Chiesa, *Le versioni latine*, pp. 146-147.

43. In other cases, the wrong choice of words is not so easily explained. For example, ἔκπληξιν (5.2) is translated as *excessum* (l. 62; a confusion with ἔκπλεος?), while ἐκπλαγῆναι (5.2) is translated as *stupefacturi* (l. 62), a usage found in the pseudo-Cyril glossary, which reads: "Εκπληξις hic stupor stupefactus obstupefactus" (*CGL*, 292).

44. Cf. "Αξιω desidero oro postulo posco mereor dignor" of the pseudo-Cyril (*CGL*, 232). A similar confusion results from translating ἀξιωθῆναι (9.2) as *dignaretur* (l. 119).

μεγαλοδωρεὰν (3.3) = magnale donum (l. 29; where *magnale* corresponds phonetically but not in meaning to the Greek word)[45]

θεοσεβεῖς (3.10) = Dei cultores (l. 38)

πολυτρόπως (4.3) = multis modis (l. 42)

χειρογραφήσαντες (4.3) = manu scribentes (l. 43)

κακοπραγίαις (4.5) = malis actionibus (l. 50)

ἀθέων (6.10) = Deo odibilium (l. 86)

ὑπεράνθρωπον (9.7) = super hominem (ll. 124-125)

εὐδοκίᾳ (10.1) = bonae uoluntatis (l. 129; most probably a biblical influence)

ἐργοχείρῳ (12.3) = opere manus (l. 158)[46]

The translator's lexical choice was also shaped by contemporary usage. This is illustrated most clearly by the use of the word *superistam* (l. 161) to translate the Greek ἐπιστάτην (11.11), a Latin transliteration thought to be an exclusively Roman term.[47]

The Use of a Glossary
The mechanical use of a bilingual glossary may explain the translator's choice of a particular Latin word. For example, the word *submisit* (in the phrase *submisit ei cogitationes malignas* [l.173]) which is used to translate ὑπέβαλλεν (13.2) is found in the pseudo-Cyril glossary, the most extensive Greek-Latin glossary to have survived from late antiquity, which reads "Ὑποβάλλω subicio suggero submitto subdo."[48] If one compares the vocabulary of *BHL* 410b with the two extant Greek-Latin general dictionaries (the fragment *Folium Wallraffianum* and the pseudo-Cyril), connections can be made.[49] That the translator used either of these bilingual

---

45. *magnale*, and more frequently the plural *magnalia*, is found as a noun in biblical usage, meaning "miracles" (Maltby, *A Lexicon of Ancient Latin Etymologies*, p. 359; Blaise, *Lexicon Latinitatis Medii Aevi*, p. 552).

46. The translator of the *Passio Febroniae* uses similar methods to translate compound words. See Chiesa, *Le versioni latine*, p. 125.

47. See Du Cange, s.v., esp. the phrase "Quidam Gregorius nomine, quem Romani Superistam vocant." I owe this suggestion to Chiesa, "Traduzioni e traduttori a Roma nell'alto medioevo," p. 462 (cf. my "Theodore," p. 198).

48. *CGL*, 465.

49. For an overview, see the excellent discussion by Dionisotti, "Greek Grammars and Dictionaries in Carolingian Europe," esp. pp. 6-15. The *Folium Wallraffianum* is edited in Kramer, *Glossaria bilinguia in papyris et membranis reperta*, pp. 51-59.

aids cannot be proved, especially since the *Folium Wallraffianum* is a single leaf from a papyrus codex written in Constantinople in the sixth century and consists of only eighty entries arranged alphabetically, from [πα]ραχειμαζει *hibernat hiemat* to παροιμία. Only three words used in *BHG* 84 are found in the *Folium*. Two of these are translated in *BHL* 410b by the same word as used in the *Folium*. One of these two words, furthermore, occurs three times in the Greek *Acta* and is translated in *BHL* 410b by two different words, both of which are found in the *Folium* entry.[50]

More evidence is available to evaluate the relationship between *BHL* 410b and the pseudo-Cyril glossary, a dictionary with a multiplicity of sources, and by far the most complex and sophisticated such tool compiled in the Middle Ages. While its original purpose was to help Greek speakers understand Latin, the final version may have been compiled in Byzantine Italy for western users. Its compiler was not a Latin speaker, as reflected in numerous mistakes in the Latin grammar and idiom, characteristics that are found also in the *Passio S. Anastasii*.[51] An analysis of random passages in *BHL* 410b reveals that in over sixty percent of the cases the glossary and the text agree in the translation of Greek words.[52]

---

50. These words are: (1) παρρησία (16.5, 22.8, 37.17) respectively translated as *constantiam* (l. 214) and *fiduciam* (ll. 229, 510); cf. *Folium*, p. 53: "παρρησια κατα χαριν fiducia constantiam," and pseudo-Cyril (*CGL*, 399): "Παρρησια licentia fiducia confidentia"; (2) παρέχομέν σοι (19.7-8) translated as *prebemus tibi* (ll. 246-247); cf. *Folium*, p. 52: "παρερχει praestat praevet" and pseudo-Cyril (*CGL*, 398): "Παρεχω adhib[eo pre]beo tribuo" (with my reconstruction of a five-letter lacuna).

The third word is translated in a slightly different way in *BHL* 410b: παρερχόμενος (16.2) is translated as *pertransiens* (l. 211). Cf. *Folium*, p. 52: "παρερχεται transit," but also pseudo-Cyril (*CGL*, 398): "Παρερχομαι pretereo transeo transgredio."

51. Dionisotti, "Greek Grammars," p. 11, points out, for example, that the compiler reproduced the mistakes of his source in the gender of many Latin nouns, and that he created forms such as *sprevo, pepero* and *censuo* from his source's *sprevi, peperi* and *censuit*.

52. I have checked several passages, eliminating the most common words (*ecclesia, sanctus, deus*), proper nouns and articles, as well as words corresponding to a lacuna in the pseudo-Cyril. The results for cap. 6, for example, are as follows: 45 of the 65 words found in cap. 6 have corresponding defini-

This high degree of agreement suggests that while the translator of *BHL* 410b did not use the pseudo-Cyril glossary, at least as we now have it,[53] he may have used something quite similar to it, perhaps a source used by the compiler of the pseudo-Cyril, or another glossary that shared a common source. Indeed, in some cases, where the translation of a Greek word in *BHL* 410b is not found in the pseudo-Cyril, it is found in the pseudo-Philoxenus glossary, the most comprehensive extant Latin-Greek glossary, which most probably shared at least one common source with the pseudo-Cyril.[54] For example, the word μαθημάτων (6.3) is translated as *disciplinae* in *BHL* 410b (ll. 78-79), but as "documentum studium" in the pseudo-Cyril (*CGL*, 33), whereas the pseudo-Philoxenus (*CGL*, 51) reads "disciplina αγωγη επιστημη μαθεσις." Carlotta Dionisotti has suggested that the similarities between the two glossaries are best attributed to a common, shared source rather than to a proto-glossary from which both derive; and perhaps this glossary, or one closely related to it, was available to the translator of *BHL* 410b.[55]

---

tions in the glossary, 11 are not found, 9 are translated differently in the glossary. The rate of agreement is 69 per cent. Similar results are found for cap. 13: of the 45 comparable words in this chapter, 28, or more than 62 percent, correspond to the meaning given in the pseudo-Cyril. Actual agreement would be even higher if words not found in pseudo-Cyril had been eliminated from the sample instead of counted among the non-agreements. In many cases of non-agreement, furthermore, close relatives can be found in the glossary. For example, although τὰ μαγικά is not found in the pseudo-Cyril, μάγος is.

53. For one thing, the pseudo-Cyril glossary may not yet have been available. Dionisotti ("Greek Grammars") has not suggested a date for its compilation; the earliest surviving manuscript, London, British Library, Harley 5792, was written in Italy ca. 800.

54. Dionisotti, "Greek Grammars," pp. 6-11. It is also found in *CGL*, 1-212.

55. Dionisotti, "Greek Grammars," p. 36 n. 23. On some occasions, *BHL* 410b uses translations that find echoes in each glossary. Thus ὑπομονή (9.7, 12.13, 24.3, 30.2) is translated as *tollerantiam* (l. 125) as in the pseudo-Cyril glossary, and as *perseverantiam* (ll. 168, 318-319, 397) as in the pseudo-Philoxenus glossary. But it should also be noted that not every word that occurs in *BHG* 84/*BHL* 410b is found in either the pseudo-Cyril or the pseudo-Philoxenus. My notes to the text of *BHL* 410b include the reading of the pseudo-Cyril where relevant. This is not to suggest the source of the

The results of my detailed and technical analysis of the lexical, grammatical and syntactical characteristics of this first translation of the *Passio S. Anastasii* support the theory that the author's style of translation came from a rigid adherence to a translation methodology that was meant to duplicate in Latin the Greek original.[56] Although such *ad verbum* translations were not untypical of Christian antiquity and the early Middle Ages, it is its extreme conformity to the patterns of the source text that makes *BHL* 410b unique. A closer examination of its historical context will perhaps help to explain the unusual features of this text.

3. THE HISTORICAL AND CULTURAL CONTEXT OF THE TRANSLATION

The first translation of the Greek *Acta*, preserved in the Bobbio codex, reveals that the monks who brought the relic of the head of Anastasius (and possibly a miraculous icon) to the monastery *ad Aquas Salvias* in Rome brought also a particularly noteworthy copy of the Greek *Acta*. This was either the copy of the *Acta* that had belonged to the patriarch of Jerusalem, Modestus, and was annotated in his own hand, or at least a copy closely related to it. This connection between Modestus and the copy of the *Acta* brought to Rome strengthens the suggestion that close ties existed between the church of Rome and that of Jerusalem during the monothelete controversy, and helps to situate the birth of the cult of Anastasius in the West within the political and religious interests of the Palestinian monastic community in Rome.

The text of *BHL* 410b copied into the passionary from Bobbio incorporates two significant phrases that clearly must have been glosses written in the margin of the Greek codex used by the translator, for they do not appear in any other Greek or Latin

---

translator's lexical choice, but rather to help explain the translator's method. There is evidence of the use of a bilingual glossary for the translation of the dossier of St. Abbibos, executed in a similar historical context as *BHL* 410b; Chiesa, "Il dossier agiografico," pp. 229-232.

56. The debate surrounding translation methodologies is discussed in the next chapter.

manuscripts. The first of these phrases occurs in the preface and preserves a unique piece of information about the historical circumstances under which the Greek *Acta* of the Persian soldier turned Christian monk were written. The anonymous author of the *Acta*—a monk of Anastasius's monastery outside Jerusalem[57]—concludes his long prologue with a prayerful invocation to Christ, for whom the Persian gave up his life. The relevant passage and the corresponding section in *BHL* 410b read as follows:

Τούτων εἰς ὑπάρχει καὶ ὁ ἡμέτερος στεφανίτης ᾿Αναστάσιος, οὗ τὸν βίον τὸν ἀπ᾿ ἀρχῆς μέχρι τοῦ μαρτυρίου γράψαι κελευσθείς, αὐτὸν προστήσω τοῦ λόγου τὸν παρ᾿ αὐτοῦ ὁμολογηθέντα Θεὸν καὶ Κύριον ἡμῶν ᾿Ιησοῦν Χριστὸν καὶ οὕτως ἄρξομαι τῆς διηγήσεως (5.9-12)

Horum unus extitit et noster coronator Anastasius, huius uitam quam ab initio usque ad martyrii scribere iussus sum *ego Modestus indignus archiepiscopus Hierusolimae sanctae Dei ciuitatis,* ipsum praeponens sermoni eum quem ab eo confessurus est, Deum et Dominum nostrum Ihesum Christum, et sic incipiam gestis eius. (ll. 71-77)

One of these is our crowned victor Anastasius, whose life from the beginning until his martyrdom I have been commanded to write, *I Modestus unworthy archbishop of Jerusalem, the holy city of God*[. And] putting at the head of my account our Lord and God Jesus Christ, whom he confessed, I will thus begin.

The italicized phrase is not preserved at all in the Greek tradition, nor in any manuscript of any of the other Latin versions, whether based on this first translation or not. It therefore seems likely that this addition must have originated as a marginal comment, which was translated into Latin also as a marginal comment, but then at a later stage transcribed into the main text. The note's humble description of Modestus as *indignus archiepiscopus* differs from the way he is referred to elsewhere as "Modesto sanctissimo presbytero qui tunc uicarius apostolicae sedis" (l. 136).[58] The expression "Hierusolimae sanctae Dei ciuitatis" is also historically accurate.

---

57. Flusin II, 185-190.

58. The Greek source of the Latin *indignus* was most likely ταπεινός. This adjective is always used in Byzantine literary ascriptions when the author is signing his own work or referring to himself in letters. See Cameron, *The Greek Anthology from Meleager to Planudes,* p. 304 and nn. 13 and 14.

Elsewhere in the *Acta* the city is referred to in a similar fashion. Thus, for example, the phrase "sanctae autem ciuitati excidioni factae" (ll. 81-82) renders the Greek τῆς δὲ ἁγίας τοῦ Θεοῦ πόλεως ἁλούσης (6.6). Even more significantly, the phrase Ἱεροσολυμῶν ἁγίας τοῦ Θεοῦ ἐκκλησίας, a version of which must have been the source of the Latin marginal phrase, is attested as the seat of the apostolikos thronos of the patriarch of Jerusalem.[59]

The entire ascription "ego Modestus indignus archiepiscopus Hierusolimae sanctae Dei ciuitatis," therefore, carries authenticating weight, and must go back to Modestus himself,[60] who is thus revealed as the person who commanded the author to write an account of the life and martyrdom of the Persian monk.[61] Modestus's close involvement in the composition of the *Acta* of Anastasius should cause no surprise, since, according to the *Acta*, it was he who had baptized the Persian convert. Modestus's strong interest in the monastic communities of Palestine is also well established. The Bobbio codex thus preserves the evidence that Modestus had written on his own copy of the *Acta* at the very point where the author says he has been ordered to write it (γράψαι κελευσθείς; "iussus sum scribere"). This may mean either that it was Modestus's own annotated copy of the *Acta* that was brought to Rome and translated into Latin, or that his marginal note was transcribed into the margin of the copy that was eventually translated.

That patriarch Modestus was involved in the composition of the *Acta* means that *BHG* 84 can be dated to the brief period of his patriarchate, between March 630 and his death on 17 December 630.[62] Flusin has convincingly shown that two editions of the Greek *Acta* were prepared, one during the patriarchate of Modestus, the other composed after Modestus's death between 2 November 631 and 1 September 632 and including an account of the

---

59. *Acta Conciliorum Oecumenicorum*, p. 18.33.

60. It could not have been added, therefore, by a Latin scribe.

61. For further discussion of Modestus's role in the composition of the *Acta* and in the organization of the cult of Anastasius, see Flusin I, 172-180 and esp. 191-193.

62. This was first pointed out in Franklin and Meyvaert, "Bede's Version," p. 115, and is further discussed in Flusin II, 191-193.

Translatio of the relics of Anastasius from Persia to his monastery near Jerusalem.[63] The Latin translation of the *Acta*, as well as its two most closely related Greek manuscripts, M and U, descend from the first redaction. Since the second redaction of the *Acta*, joined now to the *Translatio*, was executed so soon after the first, it is more probable that it was Modestus's very own copy that was brought to Rome and translated, not a copy made from it. Modestus's comment must have been translated as a marginal note into the original copy of the Latin translation. Only this would explain why *BHL* 408 and 410, revisions based on the first translation, both exclude this comment.[64] That such a remark would be omitted independently from both the Greek and Latin transmissions does not seem likely. It is also worth noting that M and U, the two manuscript witnesses to the first redaction of the *Acta* closest to the Latin text, are from southern Italy. Hence, one might conclude that in the East the new edition replaced the old, whereas in Italy the new redaction with the account of the translation of the relics was not available at this time.[65]

The second marginal note is the phrase "et ille quidem compatiebatur ei," which is also found only in the Bobbio codex incorporated in the following passage (ll. 177-179):

> Abbati uero quae cordis eius erant denudans cum multarum lacrimarum *et ille quidem compatiebatur ei* dignabat orare pro eo ad Deum ut liberaret eum ab insidiis aduersarii.

> τῷ ἀββᾷ δὲ τὰ τῆς ἑαυτοῦ καρδίας ἀπογυμνώσας μετὰ πολλῶν δακρύων ἠξίου εὔχεσθαι ὑπὲρ αὐτοῦ πρὸς τὸν Θεὸν ἐλευθερῶσαι αὐτοῦ τῆς μεθοδίας τοῦ ἀντικειμένου (13.6-8)

> He revealed to his abbot the secrets of his heart with many tears *and he indeed pitied him* and asked him to pray God to free him from the snares of the enemy.

There is no corresponding phrase in any of the surviving Greek manuscripts or later Latin texts. In fact, it is hard to imagine how

---

63. Flusin I, 33-36; II, 329-330.

64. See the chart on p. 271.

65. In the later eighth century, however, a copy of the second redaction of the *Acta*, which included the collection of "ancient miracles," was available at the Lateran library. See above, Chapter I, pp. 8-9.

this phrase could be made to fit into the syntax of the Greek passage; nor does it fit syntactically into the Latin text that preserves it. But as is also the case with the first marginal note discussed above, this phrase makes sense in its historical context. If we take it to mean: "and he pitied him" or "he had compassion for him," the note refers to the monastery in which Anastasius spent those seven years before striking out in search of martyrdom and reflects the feelings of the abbot Justinus to whom Anastasius had gone for counsel and prayer when the devil tempted him with memories of his training as a magician. The note is an addition made by someone who knew the details of that interview in the back of the church, perhaps a monk of the monastery of Abbot Anastasius, or even Abbot Justinus himself. Or perhaps it is another annotation made by Modestus, who must have closely followed the events of Anastasius's life. It may also have been written into the margin by the scribe, or even the author himself, as a correction or amplification to the text and not purely as a peripheral remark. In any case, it could not have been an integral part of the text or its survival only in the Bobbio manuscript could not be explained.[66]

These marginal notes show beyond any doubt that the copy of the *Acta* brought from Jerusalem to Rome was very special, most likely the copy that had belonged to Modestus himself, perhaps the dedication copy by the author and the larger monastic community to the man who had commissioned it. It may have held special meaning for the Jerusalem community, which safeguarded it from destruction by bringing it to Rome together with the precious relic of the head of Anastasius during the flight from Jerusalem. This copy of the *Acta* could even be considered another relic because of its physical association with the patriarch Modestus.

The priceless relic of the head of Anastasius and the authoritative copy of the *Acta* were brought to Rome in the wake of the invasions of Palestine and the monothelete crisis. The removal to Rome

---

66. The grammatical characteristics of this note are in keeping with the Latin of this translation, providing further authentication. The use of the compound *compatiebatur* followed by the dative suggests that the Greek used the middle form of συμπαθέω, which is normally followed by the dative. The Latin translation, as usual, duplicated the Greek.

rather than to Constantinople is an indication of the close political alliance between the Palestinian monastic community and the western capital. They were both opposed to the heresy of monotheletism upheld in Constantinople by Patriarch Sergius and his successor Pyrrhus, and supported by the imperial authority of Heraclius and then Constans II.[67] The opposition to monotheletism was led by Sophronius (†638),[68] patriarch of Jerusalem and Modestus's successor, who must have known the story of the Persian convert, and perhaps even been acquainted with him. After Sophronius's death, the Palestinian church was split asunder when a monothelete hierarchy was imposed by Constantinople. These divisions, coupled with the Arabs' attacks, meant that Rome became the center of the orthodox resistance to the imperially supported heresy. It was in these circles of the orthodox, exiled Palestinian community that the cult of Anastasius in the West was first developed, and became closely connected with the fight against monotheletism.

The clearest condemnation of monotheletism came from Rome in the Lateran Synod of 649 under Pope Martin I, but much of the ground work had already been done by Pope "Theodorus, natione Grecus, ex patre Theodoro episcopo de civitate Hierusolima."[69] The Palestinian influence on the city is most clearly exemplified by Maximus the Confessor, the intellectual force behind the Lateran Synod of 649 who later became a martyr for dyotheletism.[70] A Palestinian monk himself, he had been a pupil and close associate of Patriarch Sophronius of Jerusalem, when the cult of Anastasius was being established there. Before his arrival in Rome in late 645 or early 646, Maximus and his followers had sojourned in

67. Flusin II, 359-365; Sansterre, *Les moines grecs* I, 115-119.

68. Flusin II, 359-360 discusses the reasons for this date, even though in I, 191 the dates for his patriarchate are given as 638-641.

69. He is so described in the *Liber pontificalis* (Duchesne I, 331). For a discussion of the role of Palestinian monks in papal politics, see Sansterre, *Les moines grecs* I, 115ff.

70. Maximus's crucial role at the Synod is reflected in the florilegium of twenty-seven quotations concerning monotheletism that he had sent the preceding year to Stephen of Dora in Jerusalem, and that figure among the texts quoted in the conciliar acts of the Synod (Bischoff and Lapidge, *Biblical Commentaries from the Canterbury School of Theodore and Hadrian*, pp. 66-67).

Africa at the monastery of Hippo Diarrhytus (now Bizerte) not far from Carthage on the North African coast.[71] There they joined Syrian monks from Nisibis who were living in the same monastery. Also present was Pyrrhus, the monothelete former patriarch of Constantinople (638-641) deposed from his throne because of dynastic disputes at the imperial court. This is most likely the same Pyrrhus who as a monk had been assigned by Abbot Justinus to be the teacher of the recently converted Persian soldier when he had joined the monastery outside Jerusalem in 620. Pyrrhus had also been present in Constantinople when George of Pisidia recited his *Encomium* in honor of Anastasius. In Carthage, Pyrrhus debated with Maximus the question of the wills of Christ, and declared himself convinced by Maximus's arguments.[72]

Thus, when Maximus went to Rome ca. 645, he was part of a large retinue that included many Syrian and Palestinian monks from Hippo Diarrhytus, as well as the former patriarch of Constantinople and teacher of Anastasius the Persian, the aged Pyrrhus.[73] They took up residence at the monastery of St. Sabas, and joined the already well-established Syrian and Palestinian monastic community of Rome, which included Pope Theodore and many other monks in flight from the invading Arabs. All of them were engaged in the opposition to monotheletism favored in Constantinople. Among them were those who had witnessed Anastasius's life and martyrdom, for they had known him and his confreres. Many of them had participated in the creation of the cult of the Persian monk in the East, both in Jerusalem and Constantinople, and would promote its development in Rome.

The appropriation of the cult of Anastasius by the Palestinian dyothelete monastic community in Rome is also supported by the

71. According to one source, Maximus went to Africa to escape the Persian invasions in 628; according to another source, he went during the Arab attacks. But his sojourn in Africa is not disputed (Sansterre, *Les moines grecs* I, 25-26; Bischoff and Lapidge, *Biblical Commentaries*, pp. 72-73).

72. On Pyrrhus, see Flusin II, 384-389; Bischoff and Lapidge, *Biblical Commentaries*, pp. 73-74; Sansterre, *Les moines grecs* II, 253 s.v.

73. It is possible that just as many Syrian and Palestinian monks passed through North Africa on the way to Rome, so too did the *Acta* and the relic of the head of Anastasius.

intriguing textual history of the *Encomium* of Anastasius (*BHG* 86), a text written by George of Pisidia between 631 and 638 in Constantinople.[74] One of the manuscripts of the *Encomium* (Berolinensis gr. 54) attributes the authorship of the text not to George of Pisidia, but to Sophronius of Jerusalem. Furthermore, the body of the text in this Berlin manuscript includes two other significant changes: the substitution of the name of Modestus of Jerusalem for that of Sergius of Constantinople as one of the people to be praised by the writer; and the replacement of Pyrrhus as the monastic teacher of Anastasius in Jerusalem by Theodore, who remains unidentified. Since Sergius of Constantinople was the great proponent of monotheletism, George of Pisidia his protégé, and Pyrrhus his monothelete successor on the patriarchal throne, it is clear that the Berolinensis represents an attempt to purge the text of its heretical monothelete connections. It has even been argued that this *damnatio memoriae* is an effort to turn the *Encomium* not only into an orthodox text, but also into a Palestinian one.[75] The person responsible for the changes was "un fin connaisseur de la crise monothélite, et bien au courant des choses palestiniennes."[76]

The Berlin codex, furthermore, is one of the only two surviving witnesses of the original Greek text of the Roman Miracle of Anastasius the Persian, a text composed undoubtedly in Rome (discussed in Chapter IV). The Berolinensis suggests the possibility that the purged copy of the *Encomium* was in Rome, where it was joined to the Greek Roman Miracle, and ties the transmission of the "dyothelete" text of the *Encomium* to Rome, and in particular to the monastery of St. Anastasius at the Aquae Salviae. I sup-

---

74. This *Encomium* is edited in Flusin I, 191-259 and discussed in II, 384-389. See also above, Chapter I, p. 6. There is no evidence that this text was ever translated into Latin.

75. Flusin I, 191-194, II, 384-389. It was Pertusi ("L'encomio di S. Anastasio") who first explained the significance of the changes in the Berlin manuscript, and convincingly proved that George of Pisidia was the author, not Sophronius. He also suggested, however, that the *damnatio memoriae* was carried out under the influence of the VI Ecumenical Council (680-681), which explicitly condemned the adherents of monotheletism, including Sergius and Pyrrhus.

76. Flusin II, 388.

port the suggestion, therefore, that the changes preserved in this branch of the transmission of the Greek *Encomium* could best be explained as originating within the Palestinian anti-monothelete milieu of Rome during the period of the Lateran Synod, when the cult of Anastasius was being established in the city.[77] It is also important to note in this context that the Roman Miracle, written in Rome in 713, most likely by a monk of the Aquae Salviae, shows that the monastery was still identified with the anti-mono- thelete cause.[78] The cult of Anastasius in Rome was promulgated by a community deeply engaged in the orthodox dyothelete strug- gle, and the memory of that struggle was still vivid when the Roman Miracle was written, more than half a century later. More broadly, the "anti-heretical" version of the *Encomium* and the Roman Miracle, two Greek texts produced in Rome, provide fur- ther evidence for the role of the exiled Palestinian community in the creation of papal policy.[79]

The translation into Latin of the Greek *Acta* of the Persian monk must have originated in this same Greek-speaking, Palestin- ian monastic milieu of seventh-century Rome, where the greatest theological preoccupation centered on the fight against monothe- letism. We know that George, hegoumenos of the Aquae Salviae, where the relic of Anastasius was kept and where the translation of the *Acta* into Latin was executed, was present at the Lateran Synod of 649, as was Maximus the Confessor, and other monks and abbots from the refugee community. All of these men would have known the story of the Persian who had become one of their own; some might even have known him personally.[80] Another

---

77. Flusin I, 193-194. There is nothing that ties the Berlin manuscript paleographically to the Roman region or anywhere else (Flusin II, 388).

78. The defeat of Philippicus, the emperor who attempted to revive the heresy, is attributed to the intervention of the apostle Peter in this text (7.15-17 = ll. 147-150)

79. This subject is discussed in Sansterre, *Les moines grecs* I, 115-146 (= chap. V: "Les moines 'grecs' et la politique de l'Église romaine").

80. It is not clear whether the hegoumenos John, specifically mentioned in the acts of the Synod, is to be identified as the head of the monastery of St. Sabas outside Jerusalem—in which case he certainly would be a Palestinian —, or of the new foundation in Rome *(Cellae Novae)*. See Flusin II, 370-372.

monk most likely present at the Lateran Synod was Theodore of Tarsus, who was later sent to England as archbishop of Canterbury by Pope Vitalian in 669.[81] The clearest connection between Archbishop Theodore and the Persian monk is revealed by the presence in seventh-century England of the Latin version of the *Passio S. Anastasii.* I have argued elsewhere that it was Theodore who brought to England a copy of the first translation of the Greek *Acta* of Anastasius, and perhaps even a copy of the Greek *Acta* themselves.[82] The evidence is based on the knowledge that Bede had access to a copy of this first translation, which must therefore have reached England long before his death in 735. We also know that its circulation is tied to other hagiographical texts available at Canterbury in the late seventh century, further connecting *BHL* 410b to the archbishop. We must remember, furthermore, that the life and career of Theodore of Tarsus intersected at several points with the life and cult of Anastasius, both in the East and in Rome. It has been sugested that Theodore may have been in Constantinople when Heraclius's army returned from Persia, bringing with it knowledge of the Persian martyr.[83] It is also very likely that Theodore lived at the monastery of the Cilicians at the Aquae Salviae during his Roman sojourn. Furthermore, given what we know now of the archbishop's Latinity,[84] the possibility that he himself was the translator of the *Acta* of the Persian Monk cannot be discounted. While we cannot be sure of the exact role that Theodore did play in turning the Passion of St. Anastasius into Latin, we can be fairly certain that it originated in the same circles in which he lived in Rome, and that it was he who brought the knowledge of the Persian to Canterbury and England. This connection allows us to date the translation very closely, to some point between 645, the approximate time when the relic and

81. For the identification of "Theodorus monachus," one of the signatories of the Lateran Synod's acts as Theodore of Tarsus, see Bischoff and Lapidge, *Biblical Commentaries*, pp. 77-81.

82. Franklin, "Theodore," and below, Chapter VI.

83. Bischoff and Lapidge, *Biblical Commentaries*, p. 64.

84. See Stevenson, '*Laterculus*,' passim.

the *Acta* reached Rome, and 668, when Theodore embarked for England as archbishop of Canterbury.

The mechanical, literal nature of the first translation of the Greek *Acta* of Anastasius the Persian provides some indications about the conditions under which it was executed. The "barbarity" of the language suggests that this text was not intended to be read in Latin independently of the Greek. It does not seem likely, in other words, that the original translation with its complete disregard for the rules of Latin grammar and diction was meant as a substitute for the Greek text for Latin readers. Rather, such servile rendering of the Greek suggests another purpose. For example, it could have been a first draft, to be reworked later by someone better skilled in Latin. There are numerous examples of such two-step translations in the West, the most famous being Gregory of Tours's version of the Legend of the Seven Sleepers of Ephesus (ca. 580) based on John the Syrian's literal translation into Latin.[85] We also have several examples of two-step translations from Naples and Rome during the ninth and tenth centuries.[86] And the second translation of the *Acta* of the Persian monk (discussed in the next chapter) was undertaken as a two-step translation. It is possible that the first translation was made to assist Latin speakers with their understanding of the Greek text, and may not have been meant to stand on its own. It could also have been a translation exercise executed by someone learning Latin.[87] I have suggested elsewhere that there are some indications that the translator may have initially written his text as an interlinear gloss.[88] These include not only the word-for-word approach to the translation, but also the incorporation into the text of the marginal glosses discussed above, as well as the possibility that the translator left

---

85. *De gloria martyrum*, cap. 95: "passio eorum quam Siro quodam interpretante in Latino transtulimus" (ed. Krusch, p. 109).

86. Some of these have been discussed by Dolbeau, "Le rôle des interprètes," pp. 145-162.

87. We do not know exactly how a Greek monk living in Rome would have learned Latin. Latin would have been more familiar to monks from Palestinian pilgrimage centers (Sansterre, *Les moines grecs* I, 67), and perhaps the translator of the Greek *Acta* was from such an area.

88. Franklin, "Theodore," pp. 196-201.

a few visible blanks over the Greek text.[89] While this last suggestion remains only a speculation, the literalist approach of the translator to the text in front of him is beyond dispute. It is an approach that would have been very familiar to the Palestinian monks who brought the cult of the Persian to Rome.

The purpose and method used by the first translator of the *Passio S. Anastasii* recall in many ways those of the literal translators of antiquity, who produced slavish renderings of legal and business documents, as well as the translators of biblical and patristic literature, whose versions were meant for bilingual readers for whom the original text had overwhelming prestige. Sebastian Brock's study of translations of Hebrew into Greek (biblical) and of Greek into Syriac (both biblical and non-biblical) has isolated a number of features common to literalist translations, all of which are found in *BHL* 410b.[90] These include: the preservation of the word order of the source language[91] and the formal correspondence of grammatical constructions; regular lexical correspondence, including the translation of every particle; the use of etymological calques and of transcriptions, particularly of technical words.

The principal difference between the translations examined by Brock and the *Passio S. Anastasii* is the translator's native language: in the texts studied by Brock, it is the receptor language that was

89. I have hypothesized that these blank spaces led a later scribe to transliterate the Greek letters into Latin words. Further to my study of Theodore, I would include one other Latin expression that may be transliterated from the Greek: προπεμφθεὶς μετὰ πολλῶν δακρύων ὑπὸ τῶν πολιτῶν (31.3) = praemissus cum multarum lacrimarum ut pute ciuium (l. 114) where *ut pute* may be a simple transliteration of ὑπὸ τῶν πολιτῶν. For a recent discussion of an interlinear translation from ninth-century St. Gall, see Kaczynski, "A Ninth-Century Latin Translation of Mark the Hermit's *Peri Nomou Pneumatikou* (Dresden, Sächsische Landesbibliothek, Mscr. A 145b)."

90. The following discussion of translation technique owes much to Brock, "Aspects of Translation Technique in Antiquity." The origins of the medieval western ideal of the word-for-word translation, according to Brock, are found in biblical translation practice, which replaced the classical view of the superiority of the literary, *ad sensum* translation. This is discussed further below, Chapter III.

91. This is a requirement of the format in the case of bilingual texts, such as the bilingual school-texts of Vergil.

the translator's mother tongue, while the native tongue of the translator of the Passion of Anastasius was clearly not Latin. This difference can be seen as arising from the historical circumstances in which the translations were made: in seventh-century Rome, it was the Greek-speaking foreign community that had a primary interest in the translated text, not the native speakers of Latin. Had a Latin speaker undertaken this translation, the result would certainly have been a more polished Latin composition. While there continue to be disagreements on the exact linguistic and ethnic composition of seventh-century Rome, and particularly of its clergy, it is generally accepted that the city contained a very large hellenophone population during the seventh and early eighth century. There were many Greek speakers among the clerical hierarchy; many popes were of eastern background.[92] Yet, the question of bilingualism among the Greek clerical population remains extremely difficult to settle.[93] Maximus the Confessor remained ignorant of Latin, despite his many years of sojourn in Rome. His contemporary Pope Martin I used an interpreter during his trial in Constantinople in 653 even though he had worked as apocrisarius in the eastern capital. However, the Latin translation of the *Passio S. Anastasii* cannot be used as evidence to confirm ignorance of Latin among the clergy of Rome in the second half of the seventh century for two principal reasons. Firstly, its purpose, as discussed, was not to create an independent Latin text. Secondly, its methodology was ancient and well-established in the translator's cultural circles, despite its shortcomings for both medieval and modern readers.

One can well imagine that monks of similar training and background to the representatives of the Syriac school of translation studied by Brock, and, most significantly, with a comparable ap-

92. In addition to the "Greekness" of the Lateran Synod, already discussed above, there is the famous story of the Roman synod of 704, convened by Pope John VI to judge the case of Wilfrid, who had been deposed from York's bishopric. Even though the language of the meeting was Latin, Wilfrid's disciple Eddius remarks that the visiting Anglo-Saxons could not understand the jokes passed around by the local clerics "inter se graecizantes" (Eddius, *Vita Wilfridi* 53 [ed. Levison, p. 247]).

93. Sansterre, *Les moines grecs* passim, but esp. I, 20-21, 68-69, remains the best discussion of this topic. See also below, pp. 139-140.

proach to translation were also to be found in the Syrian and Palestinian community of seventh-century Rome, where the first translation of Anastasius's *Acta* took place.[94] One should not be surprised if the translator of the *Acta* of Anastasius approached his task using a technique that was common in his native land. The approach to translation that Brock assigns to the Syriac school in the early seventh century helps us to understand the literalist impulse behind *BHL* 410b, and the cultural background of the translator. We might wonder, finally, if some of the "mistakes" in Latin usage might in fact be the result of a less than perfect understanding of the Greek by the translator, for whom Greek may have been not the mother tongue.

A word-for-word translation can make sense only in a bilingual context, as Brock has shown. The Syriac school of translators of patristic and biblical literature was the product of a bilingual culture where the source language had overriding prestige. But once Greek disappeared from the Middle East, these works ceased being copied, for in places they verge on being unintelligible without some knowledge of Greek. A similar fate awaited the first translation of the *Acta* of Anastasius: once it moved, chronologically and spatially, out of the historical context in which it was produced, the eastern monastic milieu of early medieval Rome, it was revised, resulting in the texts catalogued as *BHL* 408 and 410, and it was replaced altogether by a new translation (*BHL* 411a).[95]

94. For the translation of Greek into Syriac, Brock, "Aspects of Translation," pp. 80-81, surveyed the works of three early seventh-century translators, all of whom probably trained in the same monastery: Paul, bishop of Tella, who translated Origen's *Septuagint* into Syriac; Thomas of Harkel and his revision of the New Testament (known as the Harklean New Testament); and Paul, bishop of Edessa, who revised an earlier translation of the works of Gregory of Nazianzus. Brock (p. 80) remarks that a similar development of schools of literal translations from Greek into Latin and Armenian, as well as into Syriac, took place in the late sixth and early seventh centuries, and calls for a study of these schools and their methods of translation.

95. For an explanation of its survival in the Bobbio codex, see below p. 267.

III

THE SECOND LATIN TRANSLATION
OF THE *ACTA S. ANASTASII*: *BHL* 411a

1. INTRODUCTION

The second translation of the *Acta* of St. Anastasius is introduced
by an original Latin prologue, which describes the circumstances
in which this new Latin rendition of the *Passio S. Anastasii* was
prepared.[1] Its author calls himself Gregorius clericus, and states
that he was asked by Abbot Athanasius to produce a new redaction of the martyrdom of the Persian monk because of dissatisfac-
tion with the version that "quidam grammaticae artis expertissimus
de graeco in latinum confuse transtulerat" (ll. 3-7; "someone completely ignorant of the art of grammar had translated confusedly
from Greek into Latin"[2]). Gregorius also discusses his translation
method. It seems that he engaged the assistance of the archpriest
Nicolaus, "achivos quidem luculente, latinos vero ex parte apices
eruditum" (ll. 18-19; "excellently learned in Greek letters, but partially learned in Latin"), who prepared a verbatim translation on
which Gregorius's new redaction could then be based. Recalling
the long-running debate over the nature of translation dating back
to antiquity, Gregorius justifies his preference for the *ad sensum*,
rather than the *ad verbum* technique. His revision of Nicolaus's

---

1. All references are by line number to my edition, below, pp. 299-338.
The prologue was published on its own by Angelo Mai from manuscripts in
the Vatican Library in *Spicilegium Romanum* IV (1840), 283-285.

2. *Pace* Walter Berschin, who, misunderstanding the stem of *expertissimus*
to be *expertus* rather than *expers*, interprets this phrase as "This predecessor
who was an 'expert in grammar' ... ," and concludes that the translator may
have been the Venerable Bede (*Greek Letters and the Latin Middle Ages. From
Jerome to Nicholas of Cusa*, pp. 171, 326 n. 53; *Biographie* II, 159).

literal translation is thus presented as an attempt to produce a literary piece, as well as an alternative to the inadequate earlier version, and even as an improvement on the original Greek model.[3]

Gregorius's version of the *Passio S. Anastasii* has been identified with the text published by the monks of Monte Cassino in 1877,[4] and then catalogued as *BHL* 411 by the Bollandists.[5] *BHL* 411 has since been considered to be one of the products of the so-called "translation school" that flourished in Naples during the ninth and tenth centuries.[6] My systematic survey of the manuscripts transmitting this redaction, however, has made it clear that the published *BHL* 411 is not in fact Gregorius's work but a revision of it. The original text—of which *BHL* 411 is but an abbreviation—has remained unstudied and unpublished until now. I have numbered this newly identified text *BHL* 411a for ease of reference, with the understanding that the sequence of numbers is not meant to represent the true relationship between 411a and 411. Furthermore, I believe that Gregorius's redaction of the Passion of the Persian monk was not executed in Naples, but rather in Rome during the late Carolingian period, when a learned coterie incorporated the study of Greek texts into their cultural agenda. The

3. See below pp. 104-115 for further discussion of the prologue.

4. The edition, published in *Bibliotheca casinensis* III. Florilegium, pp. 102-109, was prepared "ex diversis Codicibus"; most likely the codices used were Cod. 144, Cod. 145 and Cod. 146. Cod. 145 is specifically mentioned in the discussion of this text (III, 265), but the other two are incorrectly identified there as Cod. 141 and Cod. 149. This text is also preserved in another Cassinese codex, no. 123.

5. Cesare (Cardinal) Baronio in his edition of the Roman Martyrology of 1586, conflated Gregorius's redaction with the version published by Bolland in the *ASS* (Ian. II, 426-431; 3rd ed. III, 39-45; =*BHL* 408, treated in Chapter V). The identity of Gregorius's work, as distinct from the *ASS* text, was not established until the publication of its prologue by Angelo Mai in 1840, and, in 1877, of what was then believed to be the complete version of its text. Cesare Baronio and the Oratorians are renowned for the collection, preservation and study of hagiographic sources. For an introduction to the history of the Oratorians' Vallicelliana library, see Vichi and Mottironi, *Catalogo dei manoscritti della Biblioteca Vallicelliana*. I discuss Baronio's interest in Anastasius in Chapter VII, Appendix 2.

6. See below, pp. 99ff. and n. 28.

relationship of *BHL* 411a to 411 and to the two earlier accounts of the Passion of Anastasius—namely the Greek *Acta* and the early translation, *BHL* 410b—will be the initial focus of this chapter.[7] This will establish the priority of *BHL* 411a to 411, and clarify its relationship to the Greek text and the early translation, providing the groundwork for an accurate appraisal of the nature of this redaction and of its historical context.

2. THE RELATIONSHIP OF *BHL* 411a TO *BHL* 411, THE GREEK TEXT, AND *BHL* 410b

Before one can examine the problematic issues surrounding the date and place of composition of this new version of the *Passio S. Anastasii*, it is first of all necessary to investigate Gregorius's claim that this is a new translation from the Greek, intended to replace a faulty, earlier version. Although general complaints about the inadequacies of earlier, *ad verbum* translations are not unusual in the prologues of hagiographic and other translations, it is only in the Anastasius dossier that such a claim can both be made and tested because of the survival of both translations.[8] Hence, the importance of establishing the relationship of *BHL* 411a to the first translation to discover whether it was in fact the poor translation referred to in Gregorius's prologue. For if it was, then the aims and methods employed by Gregorius, and other translators and re-

---

7. In addition to *BHL* 411, *BHL* 411a gave rise to another, much shorter abbreviation surviving in only two witnesses, catalogued by the Bollandists as *BHL* 411d. I have found two further abbreviations in manuscripts going back to the thirteenth century, which I call "Abbreviated Version A" and "Abbreviated Version B." Finally, both *BHL* 411a and *BHL* 411 were used to extract readings for the Office. These passages, which I call "411a Extracts" and "411 Extracts," are found in compilations generally called "hagiographic lectionaries." All these later renderings, and their role in the diffusion of the *Passio S. Anastasii*, will be discussed in Chapter VII.

8. Of the prologues analyzed by Dolbeau in "Le rôle des interprètes" only this prologue to the *Passio S. Anastasii* states its intention to replace a "mediocre earlier translation" (p. 149). But clearly there must have been many other literal translations of Greek hagiographic texts that were similarly dismissed, as discussed by Dolbeau (pp. 152-153).

visers of hagiographic texts, can be better understood. Through textual analyses, I shall argue that Gregorius's version is not merely a translation of the Greek text, but a new independent work, which is meant to replace, for a purely Latin audience, both the original Greek and the early translation (*BHL* 410b).

My comparative textual analysis will show clearly that this second translation is in fact based directly on the Greek. This examination will also support, although with less certainty, the view that the early translation was used in the preparation of *BHL* 411a either by Nicolaus or, more likely, by Gregorius, and that therefore *BHL* 410b must be considered the inadequate translation alluded to in Gregorius's prologue. I will also use the following text comparisons to prove that 411a and not 411 is the original text, and that 411 has, up until now, been erroneously attributed to Gregorius.

BHL 411a (ll. 101-103)[9]

His igitur cuneatim Calcedoniam abeuntibus, Phylippicus deicola hos e contra circumvallans introgressus est Persidem.

BHL 411 (cap. 3)

Quo cum exercitu Calcedonam abeunte, Philippicus deicola cum magna manu suorum ingressus est Persidem.

BHL 410b (ll. 110-111)

... et uenit usque Carchaedona. At uero sanctae recordationis Phylippico circumuallanti eum, et introgresso eo in Persida.

Flusin 8.2-4

... καὶ ἦλθεν ἕως Καλχηδόνος. Τοῦ δὲ ἐν ἁγίοις Φιλιππικοῦ ἀντιπερισπάσαντος αὐτὸν καὶ εἰσελθόντος ἐν Περσίδι.

Observations

1. The priority of *BHL* 411a is suggested by its preservation of the phrase *hos e contra circumvallans*, which is not found in *BHL* 411. This expression must be taken as an attempt to render the Greek ἀντιπερισπάσαντος αὐτὸν.

2. Two unusual expressions are common to both translations, *BHL* 411a and *BHL* 410b. The first one, *e contra circumvallans* (411a)/*circumuallanti* (410b), must reflect a misunderstanding of the Greek (περισπάω = divert, draw away).[10] The second is *introgressus* (411a)/*in-*

---

9. Line numbers refer to my edition of *BHL* 411a and *BHL* 410b on pp. 299-338 and 259-298, below. English translations can be found in the Appendix to Chapter I by referring to the chapter numbers for Flusin's Greek text.

10. There is no entry for περισπάω in the pseudo-Cyril.

trogresso (410b), a poetic word whose more prosaic equivalent is in fact found in 411's *ingressus*.[11] Both the shared misunderstanding of the Greek in the first example and the use of the same rather unusual word to translate the common εἰσελθόντος in the second example imply a connection between the two translations.

BHL 411a (ll. 379-383)

Abbas itaque eiusdem monasterii quo ipse deguerat, eius quidem confessionis in Christo stabilitatem, et copiosam sine pavore alacritatem, magnam quoque cum perseverantia promptitatem—fama silicet multivola devehente—omperiens, cum universo suo collegio est nimium laetatus.

BHL 410b (ll. 316-319)

Cognoscens ... abbas ... tantam stabilitatem confessionis eius quae in Christum est et quae sine stupore et copiosam alacritatem atque perseuerantiam eius gauisus est gaudio magno cum uniuersa congregatione sua.

BHL 411 (cap. 19)

Abbas itaque eius monasterii in quo ipse manserat, eius confessionis in Christo stabilitatem et perseverantiam

comperiens cum universo suo collegio nimium est laetatus.

Flusin 24.1-4

Μαθὼν δὲ ... ἀββᾶς ... τήν τε ἔνστασιν τῆς ὁμολογίας αὐτοῦ τῆς εἰς Χριστὸν καὶ τὸ ἀκατάπληκτον καὶ τὴν πολλὴν προθυμίαν καὶ ὑπομονὴν αὐτοῦ ἐχάρη χαρὰν μεγάλην μετὰ πάσης τῆς συνοδίας αὐτοῦ.

Observations

1. This passage again clearly illustrates *BHL* 411a's greater fidelity to the Greek model. The four objects of *comperiens* in 411a (*stabilitatem, alacritatem, perseverantia, promptitatem*; *sine pavore* translates τὸ ἀκατάπληκτον) parallel the Greek, while *BHL* 411 keeps only the first and last object of *comperiens*. But 411a also adds a phrase not present in the Greek (*fama scilicet multivola devehente*), which 411 eliminates. The adjective *multivola* is used here not in its more usual meaning of "wishing much," but rather in its very rare sense of "fast-moving, flying."[12] This addition is typical of those introduced by Gregorius

---

11. But it is worth noting that the pseudo-Cyril glossary reads "Εισερχομαι in eo introeo introgredior ingredior" (*CGL*, 286).

12. *multivolus* is found in *Thesaurus linguae latinae* s.v. only in its common meaning of "wishing much." The word is often found in this sense in Christian writings, for example, in the Vulgate, Cassian, etc., although in Catullus 68.128 it means "lustful," the only meaning attested in the *Oxford*

in his version and justified in the prologue: "decorandae constructionis causa nonnulla adiecimus" ("we added some phrases for the sake of decorating the style").

2. The passage also strongly suggests that the editor of *BHL* 411a made use of the earlier translation, *BHL* 410b. There are six words used in this section of 410b that are also found in 411a: τήν τε ἔνστασιν τῆς ὁμολογίας = stabilitatem confessionis 410b confessionis ... stabilitatem 411a; τὴν πολλὴν προθυμίαν = copiosam alacritatem 410b copiosam ... alacritatem 411a; ὑπομονὴν = perseuerantiam 410b perseverantia 411a; πάσης = uniuersa 410b universo 411a.

These are the entries relating to these words as found in the two major bilingual glossaries that have survived:[13]

Ενστασις instantia (pseudo-Cyril)[14]
Ομολογια confessio professio (pseudo-Cyril)[15]
Πολλα multa, Πολλοι multi, Πολυς multus (pseudo-Cyril)[16]
Προθυμια alacritas (pseudo-Cyril)[17]
Υπομονη patientia tolerantia (pseudo-Cyril)
perseverantia επιμονη υπομονη (pseudo-Philoxenus)[18]
Πασα omnis universa, Πας omnis universus (pseudo-Cyril)
omnis πας πασα (pseudo-Philoxenus)
uniuersi συμπαντες (pseudo-Philoxenus)[19]

Although it is possible that both the translator of *BHL* 410b and Nicolaus, the literal translator of *BHL* 411a, used the same Greek to Latin glossary (or a very similar one), the lexical similarities between these examples are so striking that it must be assumed that there is a direct relation between the two translations. Of the six words listed

---

Latin Dictionary. It is clear, however, that medieval writers used it to mean "fast-moving" as in "singulus quisque eorum ob multivolum variantis animi motum" (Bede, *In primam partem Samuhelis* I, i [CCSL 119,12, l. 40]) or "Grandia multivolum revocant coepta poetam" (Henry of Auxerre, *Vita S. Germani* [PL 124, 1181]).

13. For these glossaries, see above, pp. 67-70.

14. *CGL*, 300. There is no entry for *stabilitas* in the pseudo-Philoxenus.

15. *CGL*, 383. There is no entry for *confessio* in the pseudo-Philoxenus.

16. *CGL*, 412. There is no entry for *copiosa* in the pseudo-Philoxenus which, however, has "Copia παρρησια" (*CGL*, 116).

17. *CGL*, 417. While there is no entry for *alacritas* in pseudo-Philoxenus, "Alacres προθυμοι" is found there (*CGL*, 14).

18. *CGL*, 467; *CGL*, 148.

19. *CGL*, 399; *CGL*, 138, 211.

above, only two (ὁμολογία/*confessio; προθυμία/alacritas*) correspond to the principal equivalent in the pseudo-Cyril glossary and one (πά-σης/*uniuersa, uniuersus*) to the second equivalent.[20] It is the use of the common πολλή that is especially striking. While the use of *uniuersa* to translate the equally common πάσης could have come from a glossary, the translation of a very common Greek word, πολλή, with a much less common Latin word, *copiosa*, not found in the surviving glossary evidence, supports the existence of a relationship between 411a and 410b.

3. There is further evidence that *BHL* 411a did in fact make use of the Greek text directly. The Greek τὸ ἀκατάπληκτον, meaning "undaunted," is translated as *sine pavore* by 411a but *sine stupore* by the early translation.[21] Both Latin terms render the Greek correctly, although clearly the term chosen by the translator or editor of 411a is more appropriate than that chosen by 410b, which strongly suggests that the translator of 411a used the Greek directly.

BHL 411a (ll. 394-414)	*BHL* 411 (capp. 20-21)
Quadam vero nocte dum sanctus Anastasius solicanus Deo psalleret, unus quidem convinctorum, hebraeae scilicet religionis, stemmate praeclarus, moribus quoque probus, eum intentis auribus pervigil auscultabat. Videns quippe illum diurno tempore devectionem lapidum miserabiliter perpessum, nocturno quoque conticuo assiduis orationibus deditum quantus vel qualis esset nimis extupescebat. **26.** Interea dum delitens in nocturna furvitate pavimento accumberet, subito quosdam splendidissime indutos, et vibrantissimo lumine praefulgidos, ingredientes	Quadam vero nocte dum sanctus Anastasius Deo psalleret, unus convinctorum, hebraeae scilicet religionis, stemmate praeclarus, moribus quoque probus, eum intentis auribus pervigil auscultabat. Videns quippe illum diurno tempore devectione lapidum miserabiliter fatigatum nocturno quoque assiduis orationibus deditum nimis obstupescebat. Nocte autem quadam dum beatus Anastasius solo procumberet, subito quosdam viros praefulgidos ergastuli ostium ingredientes eumque circumdantes prospexit.

20. There is also the secondary correspondence of *perseuerantia*/Υπομονη in the pseudo-Philoxenus.

21. There is no entry for this Greek word in the Greek-Latin glossary pseudo-Cyril. The Latin-Greek pseudo-Philoxenus reads "Stupor θαμβος καταπληξις εκπληξις" (*CGL*, 189); "Pavor δεος πτοησις" (*CGL*, 143).

quidem ergastuli ostium et simul circumdantes beatum Anastasium prospexit. Huiusmodi igitur intuitu stupefactus, apud semetipsum dixit: "Sanctus Deus, isti angeli sunt." Et dum talia convolveret, eosdem crucigeris homoforis circumamictos respexit. Et iterum apud se dixit: "Isti episcopi sunt." Intuitusque martyrem Christi Anastasium, eisdem collucentem similiter aspexit ...

... Quem cum excitare nullomodo valeret, quemamodum exsanguis sine flatu manebat, pervigili animo intuens quae videbat.

Huiusmodi igitur intuitu stupefactus, apud semetipsum dixit: "Sanctus Deus, isti angeli sunt." Hoc autem dum aspiceret vidit eosdem ipsos palliis circumdatos habentes cruces in manibus et ait in semetipso: "Isti episcopi sunt." Cum quibus etiam martyrem Christi Anastasium similiter collucentem aspexit.

... Quem cum excitare nullomodo valeret, quemamodum exsanguis sine flatu manebat, pervigili animo intuens quae videbat ...

BHL 410b (ll. 331-353)

In una igitur nocte psallente eo, auscultabatur ei quidam de uinctis, Hebraeus quidem religione et de nobilioribus, clemens autem moribus, sicut didicimus. Et uidens beatum martyrem die quidem in lapidum asportatione miserantem, nocte uero deprecatione Dei sustinente, stupebat mente existimans quis nam esset hic.

26. Tamdiu ergo intuens in eum, iacens super pauimento in tenebras noctis, stante sancto et psallente matutinos hymnos, uidit subito aliquos ueste dealbatos ingredientes per ostium carceris et circumdantem beatum martyrem, quibus et lux copiosa refulsit. Amens vero factus uir super contemplationem dixit intra se: "Sanctus Deus, isti angeli sunt." Hoc autem existimans, uidit hos ipsos pallia circumdatos habentes

Flusin 25.7–26.14

Ἐν μιᾷ οὖν νυκτὶ ψάλλοντος αὐτοῦ, ἐπηκροᾶτο αὐτοῦ τις τῶν δεσμίων, Ἑβραῖος μὲν τὴν θρησκείαν καὶ τῶν ἐμφανῶν, ἐπιεικὴς δὲ τοῖς τρόποις, ὥς ἐμάθομεν, καὶ εἰδὼς τὸν μακάριον τὴν μὲν ἡμέραν ἐν τῇ τῶν λίθων παρακομιδῇ ταλαιπωρούμενον, νυκτὸς δὲ τῇ προσευχῇ τοῦ Θεοῦ προσκαρτεροῦντα, ἐξίστατο τῇ διανοίᾳ λογιζόμενος τίς ἂν εἴη οὗτος.

Ἐπὶ πολὺ οὖν ἀτενίζων εἰς αὐτόν, κείμενος ἐπὶ τοῦ ἐδάφους ἐν τῷ σκότει τῆς νυκτός, ἑστῶτος τοῦ ἁγίου καὶ ψάλλοντος τοὺς ὀρθρινοὺς ὕμνους, θεωρεῖ αἰφνίδιον τινὰς λευχειμονοῦντας εἰσελθόντας διὰ τῆς θύρας τῆς φυλακῆς καὶ κυκλώσαντας τὸν μακάριον, οἷς καὶ φῶς ἱκανὸν συνεξέλαμψεν. Ἐξέστη δὲ ὁ ἀνὴρ ἐπὶ τῷ θεάματι καὶ εἶπεν ἐν ἑαυτῷ· «Ἅγιος ὁ Θεός, οὗτοι ἄγγελοί εἰσιν.» Τοῦτο δὲ λογισάμε-

cruces, et dicit in semet ipso: "Isti episcopi sunt." Admirans autem de his, intuens in martyrem Christi Anastasium uidit et ecce hii qui circa eum erant lux circumfulsit. Videbat enim eum splendide indutum sicut et caeteros ...

et non poterat, sed manebat amens, sobria quidem cogitatione adtendens quae uidebantur, corpori quidem manens immobilis.

νος, ὁρᾷ τοὺς αὐτοὺς ὠμοφόρια περικειμένους ἔχοντα σταυρούς, καὶ λέγει ἐν ἑαυτῷ· «Οὗτοι ἐπίσκοποί εἰσιν.» Θαυμάζων δὲ περὶ αὐτῶν, ἀτενίσας εἰς τὸν μάρτυρα τοῦ Χριστοῦ Ἀναστάσιον, εἶδεν καὶ ἰδοὺ καὶ αὐτὸς τοῖς περὶ αὐτὸν συνεξέλαμψεν. Ἑώρα γὰρ αὐτὸν λαμπροφοροῦντα καθὼς καὶ τοὺς λοιπούς, ... καὶ οὐκ ἠδύνατο, ἀλλ' ἔμενεν ἀχανής, νήφοντι μὲν λογισμῷ προσέχων τοῖς ὁραθεῖσιν, σώματι δὲ μένων ἀκίνητος.

Observations

1. One notes again in this passage how much closer *BHL* 411a is to the Greek than *BHL* 411 is: *delitens* (411a) closely corresponds to the Greek ἀτενίζων, which is omitted by 411; *in nocturna furvitate* (411a) renders ἐν τῷ σκότει τῆς νυκτός, which 411 simplifies to *nocte quadam*; *crucigeris homoforis circumamictos* (411a) provides a calque on the Greek vocabulary which is eliminated by 411.

2. This last expression, *crucigeris homoforis circumamictos*, is a more accurate rendition of the Greek original than *BHL* 410b, and illustrates again the use made of the Greek by *BHL* 411a. In the Greek the word ὠμοφόριον refers generically to a cloak; hence, the addition of ἔχοντα σταυρούς ("having crosses") is necessary to indicate that these are bishops' cloaks. The Latin word *pallium*, on the other hand, refers specifically to a bishop's cloak. Anyone reading *BHL* 410b would understand *habentes cruces* to refer to the bishops, not to the cloaks, because the verbal form *habentes* is masculine plural instead of neuter plural *habentia* agreeing with *pallia*. Both later revisions of the early translation, *BHL* 408 and 410, executed without recourse to the Greek,[22] added *in manibus* (l. 377 and ll. 247-248 respectively), thus revealing their misinterpretation of the original translation.[23] The translator or

---

22. This is discussed further in Chapter V.

23. The expression used in *BHL* 411 in this case should also be noted: *palliis circumdatos habentes cruces in manibus*. This is very close to the expression used in *BHL* 410b, which may suggest that the editor of 411 consulted the original translation, or even one of the later versions, perhaps *BHL* 408, whose text here is quite similar to *BHL* 411. This last possibility can only

editor of 411a, on the other hand, discerned the real meaning because the Greek original was available to him.

3. The last sentence in the passage again illustrates that *BHL* 411a made use of the Greek. For, as has been discussed in the previous chapter, the early translation fails to reproduce the original Greek with accuracy. The word *manens*, in particular, is an inappropriate translation. But 411a, on the contrary, shows its understanding of the Greek by the appropriate use of the expression *exsanguis sine flatu manebat*.

The analysis of the passages above allows us to draw the following conclusions. It proves beyond a doubt that *BHL* 411a is the source text and *BHL* 411 derives from it. The textual analysis also shows conclusively that the second translation of the *Passio S. Anastasii* did in fact use the Greek prototype, and that Nicolaus prepared a fresh translation of the Greek, as Gregorius states in his prologue. However, it seems highly probable that the earlier translation also contributed to Gregorius's composition. The difficulty in determining how much use 411a makes of the primitive translation stems from the slavishly word-for-word approach of the earlier version. It is hard therefore to distinguish between the reliance of 411a on the Greek original and reliance on what is in effect its Latin carbon-copy in sentence structure, grammatical constructions, and, most importantly, in word choice. The similarities between 411a and 410b are most notable in their lexical choice: the same Latin term is often used in both translations to render the original Greek. However, this cannot be taken as proof that 411a simply copied the early translation, for in many cases one would expect the same word to be used, not only because of the exigencies of translation, but also because it could have come from the same or a similar glossary. Only if 410b and 411a agree against the Greek could their mutual dependence be proven beyond any reasonable doubt. This never occurs, since clearly the Greek was used in the later translation, and hence a badly translated passage in the

---

remain a hypothesis since there is no other evidence to support it. The only other explanation, that 411 and 411a are both reworkings of the second, literal translation (i.e. Nicolaus's work), must be excluded because of the overwhelming evidence that 411 is a reworking of 411a.

earlier version was corrected.[24] In fact, the precision of the second translation in rendering the Greek is striking.

It remains very likely that *BHL* 411a is indebted to *BHL* 410b. Both translations frequently use the same unconventional words to translate the straightforward Greek original. The question is whether this can be taken as an indication that 411a relied on the early version. On the one hand, it could be argued that the conscious choice of an unusual word was beyond the capacities or interests of the first translator. When such a word occurs, it must be because he found it in a glossary (if indeed he used one) or because of some other external reason. On the other hand, one could argue that the translator or redactor of *BHL* 411a was aware of the connotations of an unusual word; his choice was very deliberate. Agreement in the use of unusual lexical choices would therefore tend to support the dependence of the later translation on the earlier one. Furthermore, the cases in which 411a and 410b agree in their word selection, whether ordinary or extraordinary, are so numerous that a certain degree of consultation must be assumed unless proven otherwise.

To sum up, the collective evidence gathered from a comparison of *BHL* 411a and *BHL* 410b strongly suggests that the later translation must have made some use of the earlier translation, and that 410b is in fact the inadequate translation Gregorius wished to replace. It would seem more likely that Nicolaus prepared a verbatim translation of the Greek with little or no reference to the earlier version, but that Gregorius in his work as editor of the final version made use of both Nicolaus's and the earlier translation to prepare a more rhetorical, embellished text that resulted in *BHL* 411a.

This reconstruction of the translation process of this text calls into question Gregorius's knowledge of Greek. This may have been very minimal, or even non-existent, since he required the help of Nicolaus, whose knowledge of Latin is admitted in the prologue to be only *ex parte* (l. 19). Gregorius says nothing about

---

24. There is one case where both 410b and 411a misinterpret the Greek by mistranslating ὑπερείδοντες as if it were ὑπερίδοντες. But this may very well have to do with the reading of the Greek text (see *BHL* 411a, l. 610 and n. 20).

his own knowledge of Greek.[25] His justification of an *ad sensum* approach to translation, as I discuss further below (pp. 115ff.), can be seen as a defense of his role as editor or revisor of the text, not as a characterization of the actual translation technique used in rendering the Greek employed by Nicolaus. Nor does the text that has survived reveal whether Gregorius consulted the Greek. There is only one instance that suggests that Gregorius may have corrected what he, with reason, believed to be a mistranslation of the Greek.[26] Still, even if Gregorius was responsible for this emendation of Nicolaus's text, one cannot conclude that he did not know Greek, but only that he did not consult the Greek copy at this point. Furthermore, such a correction could just as easily have been introduced by a scribe early on in the transmission of the text, and therefore it is not conclusive evidence from which to determine Gregorius's use of the Greek text.

Gregorius's contribution as editor or redactor of the finished work, however, remains significant. Almost certainly, he prepared his final version by consulting and comparing at least two texts: the earlier translation and the new translation by Nicolaus. Furthermore, he introduced significant features that resulted in a text with pretensions to literary artistry and historical awareness, a text that altered the original source in significant ways. As we shall see, this second translation of the *Passio S. Anastasii* raises questions about the extent of the bilingualism of individual

25. Real expertise in Greek by Latin speakers at the time of this second translation, during the ninth or tenth centuries, was extremely rare even in Rome as is shown by the extraordinary fame of Anastasius Bibliothecarius, the ninth-century translator and member of the Roman curia; see below, pp. 106; 109-113. The Greek learning of Johannes Hymmonides, Anastasius's contemporary, for example, is disputed; at best, he knew a little, but not enough to translate Greek documents (Sansterre, *Les moines grecs* I, 70-71).

26. This is the rendering of ἵππῳ with *aquis* in 411a (l. 365 and n. 16). Nicolaus, most likely, translated ἵππῳ with *equo* or maybe *equis*. It is easy to understand that when Anastasius chides his persecutors for worshiping the sun, the moon, fire, and the horse, as the Greek text states, the last element in the series could be seen as out of place by anyone who was ignorant of the Persian custom of horse worship. This would explain the instinctive correction in the Latin tradition of *equo* or *equis* into *aquis*.

medieval translators. It also adds to our understanding of the elaborate steps by which Greek hagiographic texts were turned into Latin and adapted to their new audience. However, before addressing these linguistic issues, it is important to look at the historical context in which it was written.

3. PLACE AND DATE OF COMPOSITION

The redaction of the *Passio S. Anastasii* by Gregorius clericus has long been attributed to the Neapolitan milieu of the ninth and tenth centuries.[27] At this time, according to some scholars, Neapolitan culture was characterized by a conscious bilingualism and exemplified by what has been called a "translation school" with its own topoi, vocabulary, and literary aspirations.[28] Recently, however, the distinctive identity of this "translation school" and the extent of the bilingualism of these Latin-speaking hagiographic redactors, who like Gregorius depended on Greek speakers as first-step translators, have been called into question.[29]

27. Although previous scholars in fact referred to *BHL* 411 and not *BHL* 411a, most of their arguments are based on the prologue, which is the same in both texts.

28. For the Neapolitan school of translation, see most recently Brunhölzl, *Histoire de la litterature latine du Moyen Age* II, 291-300; Chiesa, "Le traduzioni dal greco: l'evoluzione della scuola napoletana nel X secolo," pp. 67-86; idem, "*Ad verbum* o *ad sensum?* Modelli e coscienza metodologica della traduzione tra tarda antichità e alto medioevo," pp. 1-51 at pp. 43ff. and esp. n. 166; Berschin, *Greek Letters*, pp. 169-171. Dolbeau, "Le rôle des interprètes," pp. 145-162, and esp. n. 2, summarizes the main issues and previous bibliography. Chiesa believes in the existence of this school ("carattere di scuola è dimostrato sia da una sensibile omogeneità stilistica, sia dall'utilizzo di tecniche e di termini di chiara origine scolastica, sia dalla presenza a monte di un progetto unitario di ampio respiro: quello di dotare la chiesa napoletana di un *corpus* completo di testi agiografici di buona qualità, che sostituissero le cattive traduzioni precedenti e colmassero eventuali lacune nel calendario" ("Le traduzioni dal greco" p. 68).

29. Dolbeau, "Le rôle des interprètes," pp. 151-152, has questioned the idea that bilingualism was widespread in Naples, and has drawn attention to the necessary distinction between "translator" and "reviser." I share Dolbeau's more cautious approach.

My research confirms the rough dating that is implied by associating Gregorius's *Passio S. Anastasii* with the Neapolitan translation school of the ninth and tenth centuries. The earliest manuscripts of *BHL* 411a are from the eleventh century, but the oldest witnesses of the Roman Miracle, with which it is often found, are dated to the late tenth century. One of these is a codex copied at Fleury. If my theory that *BHL* 411a and the Roman Miracle traveled together to France is correct,[30] then the late tenth century can stand as the *terminus ante quem*. There is no precise *terminus post quem*, but prefaces to hagiographical reworkings do not appear in large numbers until the ninth century, and Gregorius's prologue has many similarities to the prefaces of translations composed in Rome, Naples and other parts of central and southern Italy from the late ninth century into the eleventh century. The framework within which this text was composed can then be taken to be the period from the ninth to the late tenth century.

I believe, however, that this second translation of the *Passio S. Anastasii* was not written in Naples, as other scholars have suggested, but rather in Rome.[31] Gregorius's work has traditionally been assigned to Naples for the following reasons:

1. The identification of the dedicatee Athanasius with one of the bishops of Naples: either Athanasius I (†872) or Athanasius II (875-898).[32]
2. The identification of Nicolaus, the first-step translator, with the Nicolaus who had fulfilled a similar role for Ursus in the translation of the *Vita S. Basilii*, whose dedication to *Gregorius loci salvator* of Naples, places it in early tenth-century Naples.[33]

---

30. See below, pp. 147-150.

31. Ermini, *Storia della letteratura latina medievale dalle origini alla fine del secolo VII*, p. 622, also believes this text originated in Rome, but offers no discussion.

32. The prologue published in 1840 by Angelo Mai reads *Anastasio*, which must be a misreading or a typescript error. Paolo Chiesa ("Le traduzioni dal greco," p. 68 n. 3) lists "Atanasio dedicatario della Passio Anastasii Persae [*BHL* 411]" as one of the figures who are to be held responsible for the "progretto di costituire un corpus agiografico di buon livello ..." in Naples.

33. Rabbow, "Zur Geschichte des urkundlichen Sinns," p. 77. Rabbow was followed, for example, by Siegmund, *Die Überlieferung*, p. 228 and n. 1. For the *Vita S. Basili* (*BHL* 1024) see *Bibliotheca casinensis* III. Florilegium, pp. 205-219.

3. The language and style of the text, and in particular the use of translation topoi in the prologue have been likened to the stylistic features of Neapolitan texts from the ninth and tenth centuries.

However, none of the claims for Naples as the place of origin for this translation stand up to scrutiny. In the following discussion, I will show how internal indicators have been wrongly used to place this text in ninth- or tenth-century Naples. I will then present the evidence for Rome as the place of origin of this text, supported, in the next section, by my analysis of the language and translation technique. I will show that the Neapolitan school of translation—if we can in fact still use such a term—shared many characteristics with a broad range of translators from central and southern Italy, including the most famous Roman translator, Anastasius Bibliothecarius. The topoi and stylistic traits used by Gregorius are typical of the genre of hagiographic retranslation and revision, which was prevalent in central and southern Italy in the ninth and tenth century, and is not restricted to Naples.

The principal reason for placing this text in a Neapolitan context is Siegmund's identification of the dedicatee *Athanasio gratia Dei venerabilissimo Christi famulo* as one of the two Neapolitan bishops of that name in the late ninth century.[34] However, this reading is a corruption found in *BHL* 411 and in the one manuscript of *BHL* 411a on which the *BHL* 411 redaction depends and which today is found in the National Library of Naples. All the other manuscripts of *BHL* 411a that contain the prologue read *Athanasio abbati*, who clearly cannot be identified as either of the Athanasii who sat on the episcopal throne of Naples. The identity of this abbot Athanasius remains obscure.[35]

---

34. *Die Überlieferung*, p. 228. This reading is found in Cod. VIII B 3 (s. XII) in the Biblioteca nazionale of Naples and Cod. Cas. 123 (s. XI[2]) at Monte Cassino. Siegmund did not realize, however, that the text he was examining in the Cassinese codex was in reality a different redaction (*BHL* 411) than the one found in the Naples manuscript (*BHL* 411a) (p. 118 and n. 1). The Naples codex is the only witness of 411a with this reading.

35. It would be tempting to assume that the abbot Athanasius is of the monastery *ad Aquas Salvias*. But there is no independent evidence for it. See Bertelli, "'Caput Sancti Anastasii'," p. 20 n. 2.

The second reason given for the Neapolitan origin of this translation is the identification of Nicolaus, the first-step translator, with the Nicolaus who filled a similar role in Ursus's translation of the *Vita S. Basilii,* a text apparently produced in Naples. But, apart from the fortuitous coincidence of the same (not uncommon) name, there is no other reason for making this association.[36]

Hence, one must conclude that the traditional attribution to Naples is founded on the incorrect identification of both Athanasius and Nicolaus, and therefore there is no evidence that places the composition of this work in Naples.

Since that is the case, it is the manuscript evidence and the history and circulation of the collections in which the text has been transmitted, as well as any information provided by the cult of the saint, that one must resort to for determining its place of origin. This methodology has been devised by Siegmund as a way of palliating the absence of internal information in most translations from the Greek,[37] and indeed it can be applied more broadly to locate the origin of hagiographic texts.

All of the surviving manuscript witnesses of *BHL* 411a, with two exceptions, are legendaries composed for churches in Rome or in the immediate vicinity.[38] Furthermore, it is important to note that

---

36. Nicolaus is described in the *Vita S. Basilii (BHL* 1024) as "Nicolaum praesulem peritissimum graecorum atque philosophum" while Gregorius characterizes this Nicolaus as "praelustris archipresbyter," thus providing no evidence one way or another. Nor can any information be elicited from the style of the *Vita S. Basilii,* for that text is a collection of passages from several authors, and the original Latin prologue is the sole responsibility of Ursus, the second redactor. An example of the danger of relying on common names for identification is the claim, completely disproven, that the Nicolaus of the *Vita S. Basilii* was none other than Pope Nicholas I (Sansterre, *Les moines grecs* I, 70).

37. *Die Überlieferung*, pp. 195-213. Siegmund's methodology is also discussed by Sansterre, *Les moines grecs* I, 150 and E. Follieri, "I rapporti fra Bisanzio e l'Occidente nel campo dell'agiografia," p. 359.

38. BAV, S. Pietro A 2 is part of the legendary of St. Peter's Basilica; S. Salvatore 996 in Rome's Archivio di Stato was written in Romanesca and used at the Ospedale di S. Salvatore near the Lateran; BAV, Vat. lat. 1195 was part of the legendary of the church of SS. Giovanni e Paolo; the manuscript now in Cape Town was the legendary of S. Cecilia in Trastevere; the

the earliest witnesses of 411a also contained the Roman Miracle, a text whose Roman origin and early circulation are beyond dispute.[39]

It is important to bear in mind that the translation was carried out in a context where a copy of the earlier translation, now preserved only in the Bobbio passionary, was available to Gregorius. We can be fairly sure that the early translation was done in Rome and therefore it must have circulated there; it seems likely too that the *Acta* in the Greek original were also circulating in Rome, at the monastery *ad Aquas Salvias*, the Lateran library, and perhaps elsewhere. In contrast, there is no evidence to support the hypothesis that these texts were also available in Naples at this time. Although two of the manuscripts of the Greek *Acta* are of southern Italian origin, one from the eleventh and the other from the twelfth century,[40] a more specific locale has not been suggested.

There is no evidence of *BHL* 411a's liturgical use in Naples either. Rather, as I indicate in Chapter VII below, it was *BHL* 411 that appears to have been adapted for liturgical use in the Naples area.[41] In the light of these observations, it seems likely that Gregorius's text originated in Rome.

---

close relationship to the Roman area of the three Subiaco legendaries is expressed most clearly by the oldest, written in Romanesca between 1065-1120; BAV, Chigianus P VIII 15 originated in northern Latium or Roman Tuscia; BAV, Vat. lat. 13012 originates from Assisi; and the Vallicelliana Tomus X perhaps also in Rome. See below, pp. 145-146 and "Descriptive List."

39. The two non-Roman manuscript witnesses of *BHL* 411a (Naples, Biblioteca nazionale, Cod. VIII B 3 and Bern, Bürgerbibliothek Cod. 24) indirectly support a Roman origin for this text through their links with the Roman Miracle. See next chapter.

40. Flusin I, 19-20.

41. Chiesa himself has emphasized that the translations executed in Naples at this time had liturgical purposes and expressed puzzlement at the fact that two translations attributed to the Neapolitan school (the *Vita Mariae Aegyptiacae* [*BHL* 5415] and the *Poenitentia Theophili* [*BHL* 8121-8122]) "non ebbero un'utilizzazione liturgica nell'area napoletana, come dimostra il fatto che la tradizione manoscritta, assai ampia, è quasi solo transalpina, caso unico fra tutte le traduzione elaborate a Napoli in questo periodo" ("Le traduzioni dal greco," p. 71 n. 10).

4. THE NATURE OF THE SECOND TRANSLATION

A. *Style and Cursus*

By comparing the passages quoted above with the earlier translation (*BHL* 410b), it is possible to identify certain stylistic and linguistic characteristics in the work of Gregorius. Whereas 410b is no more than an awkward effort to create a calque on the Greek, the later text constantly endeavors to provide literary refinement and rhetorical elegance. Throughout the text, attempts are made to improve on the simple Greek with a more embellished turn of phrase.[42] Repeatedly, Gregorius's text shows a preference for rare and arcane nouns, especially those with Greek roots, compound verbs and adjectives, symbolic and metaphorical language. Although the earlier version follows the Greek word-for-word, it is less accurate than the later translation, which has greater overall clarity.

Examples of these characteristics can all be found in the last passage quoted above on pp. 90-92. At the very opening, where *BHL* 410b faithfully follows the original by using the ablative absolute, *BHL* 411a uses a different construction—*dum* with the subjunctive—and introduces two very expressive words: *psalleret* and, more remarkably, the rare *solicanus*, which is attested in Martianus Capella.[43] It is not surprising to find a word with such a lineage used by Gregorius, for Martianus's *De nuptiis Mercurii et Philologiae* was a source of much arcane vocabulary, particularly of Greek origin, at this time.[44] Rare and unusual words are found throughout this passage. Examples are *nocturno conticuo* (compare the pedestrian *nocte* of 410b), a word attested only in a few Latin

---

42. This tendency to improve on the simple original by the use of more colorful language is found also, for example, in the "Neapolitan" translation of the *Passio Febroniae* (discussed in Chiesa, *Le versioni latine*, pp. 276-293).

43. According to Du Cange s.v., which quotes "Musae nunc solicanae, nunc concinentes." Lewis and Short, *Latin Dictionary* gives *solicanus* as a hapax in Martianus Capella. The word is not found in the *Oxford Latin Dictionary*, nor in *CLCLT*.

44. The *De nuptiis* was mined extensively for Greek words, for example, by the Carolingian scholar Johannes Scotus (Jeauneau, "Jean Scot Erigène et le grec," pp. 13 and 17).

authors,[45] and the dramatic *delitens in nocturna furvitate*. A predilection for rare and more exotic expressions is also exemplified by such words as *ergastuli*, and particularly by the phrase *crucigeris homoforis circumamictos*, which contains examples of rare words (*crucigeris*),[46] compound words (*circumamictos*), and also Greek terms (*homoforis*).[47] The expression *splendidissime indutos, et vibrantissimo lumine praefulgidos*, combining two separate Greek phrases that clearly belong together, is another example of the redactor's preference for compound words over simple, straightforward ones, even those in very common use.[48] In the next sentence, the same tendencies are found in the embellished phrase, *intentis auribus pervigil auscultabat*.[49]

Another indication that Gregorius was attempting to create a more literary work is his use of cursus, or rhythmic clause endings, throughout his text. The application of the statistical method developed by Tore Janson[50] indicates without doubt that Gregorius strove to follow the cursus, and that he favored certain rhythmical patterns at the end of his clauses.[51]

---

45. *Conticium* is attested according to the *Thesaurus linguae latinae* only once (Censorinus 24,2 "conticium cum galli conticuerunt"); it appears as an alternate form of *conticinium* in Lewis and Short, *Latin Dictionary*. But even this fuller version is found only in Isidore, who provides its definition ("Conticinium est quando omnes silent" [*Etym.* 5.31.4]), and his followers.

46. *Cruciger* is not attested in any dictionaries or data bases. Other examples of uncommon words in *BHL* 411a include *multivolus* discussed above, p. 88, *cuneatim* (l. 102), *atqui* (l. 193), *malesuadus* (l. 287), *ultroneus* (l. 439), *obsequela* (l. 479), etc.

47. In many cases, Gregorius may be coining new words, for they are not attested elsewhere; their meaning, however, is clear. Examples are *intervoco* (ll. 34-35); *percitatus* (l. 125) meaning "fast" (*percito* in Latin dictionaries is given as meaning "to excite strongly"); *inexasperabilis* (l. 153), related to the attested *exaspero*; *promptitas* (ll. 381, 465); *superhaereo* and *immarcescibilis* (l. 599).

48. For example, Gregorius rarely uses the forms of the simple *sum*, preferring to use *adsum* throughout the text.

49. This can be compared to *auscultabatur* of *BHL* 410b, a made-up verbal form introduced to parallel the Greek middle verb.

50. *Prose Rhythm in Medieval Latin from the 9th to the 13th Century*.

51. In the Table, the x2 or critical value for four pairs of clause endings in my statistical analysis of this text (i.e. p 5p, pp 4p, p 4pp, and all others grouped together) is 25.79; the minimal critical value for four pairs should be

TABLE: THE USE OF CURSUS IN *BHL* 411a				
CLAUSE ENDINGS	EXPECTED FREQUENCY	OBSERVED FREQUENCY	%	x2 VALUE
p 5p	14.8	25	11.2	7.02
pp 4p (velox)	33.5	52	23.3	10.07
p 4pp (tardus)	13.3	33	8.7	1.66
p 3p (planus)	28.3	30	13.45	
all others				7.04
TOTAL				25.79
The critical value for four pairs is 7.81.				

The cursus velox, including the variant of a paroxitone word followed by a five-syllable paroxitone (p 5p), is favored, with the cursus tardus and cursus planus in second and third place respectively.[52] The *Passio S. Anastasii* follows a cursus that according to Janson's statistical survey is first linked to eleventh-century authors, and it is therefore surprising to find it in this text whose manuscript circulation goes back to the late tenth century.[53] The other striking characteristic of Gregorius's cursus is the third-place finish of the planus, which was the dominant form in the more traditional cursus of the ninth century. Janson's statistics show that use of the tardus had declined to third place in the papal chan-

---

7.81. Hence, the critical value of the four pairs from this text indicates that their occurrence was not by chance but by design. See further, Janson, *Prose Rhythm*, p. 21.

52. The cursus velox is defined, following Janson's scheme, as a proparoxytone word followed by a four-syllable paroxytone, such as *indefatigabilis medicina*; the *tardus* as a paroxytone followed by a four-syllable proparoxytone, such as *confessione victoria*; the *planus* as a paroxytone followed by a three-syllable paroxytone, such as *fulgebat aspectus*. For a full explanation of this method, see Janson's work, particularly his Chapter 3 and Appendix 2.

53. According to Janson, *Prose Rhythm*, pp. 43-45, 47-49, the preference for the velox developed in northern Italy and France in the early years of the eleventh century; it is found, for example, in Guido of Arezzo (fl. 1030s) and Peter Damian (†1072). Later, it dominated the papal chancery, especially during the pontificate of Alexander II in the 1060s.

cery by the time of Urban II (†1099) as the velox gained in popularity, but they do not show the planus in third place as it is in the *Passio S. Anastasii.*

Indeed, Gregorius's preference for the cursus velox and the distant third place occupied by planus at a much earlier time than that suggested by Janson's survey call into question Janson's outline of the historical development of cursus usage.[54] Certainly, the dominance of the velox in the *Passio* by Gregorius suggests that a different evolution may have occurred. Perhaps, a fuller survey of prose writers from the late ninth to the eleventh century would find more examples of the planus in third place and a preference for the velox earlier than it appears in Janson's survey, particularly if hagiographic works are included, for they, along with letters, made the most consistent use of cursus.

B. *The Latin Prologue*[55]
Gregorius's stylistic elaborations are complemented by the substitution in *BHL* 411a of an original Latin prologue for the one provided by the author of the Greek *Acta.* The prologue introduces

---

54. The problem may lie with the limited material from the tenth century included in Janson's survey: only Liutprand of Cremona and Atto of Vercelli, both of whom follow the traditional cursus. Janson excludes any evidence from the Roman chancery after the pontificate of Hadrian II (867-872), whose letters, written by Anastasius Bibliothecarius, followed the traditional cursus. Still it is noteworthy that, while in Atto (ca. 885-961) the tardus retains its traditional position in second place, in Liutprand (born ca. 920) the velox is now in second place (*Prose Rhythm*, pp. 38-39, 46, 109). Janson's assumption that the new cursus developed in northern Italy in the eleventh century may be undermined by a fuller consideration of the tenth-century material.

55. For hagiographic prefaces, see Strunk, *Kunst und Glaube in der lateinischen Heiligenlegende* and Simon, "Untersuchungen zur Topik der Widmungsbriefe," although neither work includes prefaces to translations and revisions. For prefaces to legendaries (mostly of the *legenda nova* type), see Dolbeau, "Les prologues de légendiers latins." For prose prefaces in antiquity and the patristic period, see Janson, *Latin Prose Prefaces. Studies in Literary Conventions*; and Curtius, *European Literature and the Latin Middle Ages*, pp. 82-89. Of particular relevance to the following discussion is Chiesa, "*Ad verbum o ad sensum?*," which provides an excellent guide to the ancient, patristic, and early medieval discussions of translation theory.

a Latin text that displaces not only the earlier translation, but also in effect the original source, a displacement Gregorius justifies by appealing to the ancient debate on the theory of translation with particular reference to the works of Jerome.

Gregorius's prologue to the new translation has been discussed in the past as part of the literary environment of the Neapolitan translation school of the latter part of the ninth century and the first half of the tenth.[56] The characteristics of this school include a self-conscious discussion of translation that appears to have been inspired by the debates in late antiquity led by Rufinus, Evagrius, and most strikingly by Jerome in his letter to Pammachius, subtitled "De optimo genere interpretandi," where he famously declared the superiority of a translation *ad sensum*:

> Ego non solum fateor, sed libera voce profiteor me in interpretatione Graecorum absque Scripturis Sanctis, ubi et verborum ordo mysterium est, non verbum e verbo, sed sensum exprimere de sensu.[57]

These sentiments are consistently echoed in the prefaces of Neapolitan translators. Scholars who have analyzed these texts have also emphasized their striking similarity in the use of topoi and rhetorical arguments, and in vocabulary and stylistic affectations. In fact, in some cases the presence in a text of these features has been used to determine authorship and localization.[58]

But these topoi and stylistic concerns, as well as the intertextual allusions to Jerome's views on translation methodology, are not restricted to the translation school of Naples. They are found in

---

56. The best-known members of this school are Bishop Athanasius II (ca. 875-898), Guarimpotus, Paul the Deacon, John the Deacon, Ursus the Priest, and Peter the Subdeacon. For bibliography, see above, n. 28.

57. *Ep.* 57, 5, 2 (ed. Bartelink, p. 13). Neither the medieval translators discussed here, however, nor many modern discussions of patristic theories of translation consider the historical and doctrinal context in which Jerome wrote this and similar statements, nor has Jerome's varied translation practice been fully examined. For an example of the complexity of Jerome's position see Kamesar, *Jerome, Greek Scholarship, and the Hebrew Bible. A study of the Quaestiones hebraicae in Genesim*. For the meaning of the phrase *verborum ordo* see Chiesa, "*Ad verbum o ad sensum?*," p. 16 and n. 50.

58. E.g. Dolbeau, "La vie latine de saint Euthyme: une traduction inédite de Jean Diacre napolitain," esp. pp. 318-319.

most original Latin prefaces that are a defining characteristic of works translated or retranslated from the Greek at this time, including those produced in Rome during the ninth century by one of the best-known of all medieval translators, Anastasius Bibliothecarius. My analysis of Gregorius's prologue to the *Passio S. Anastasii* will emphasize the ubiquity of these literary conventions in translated works, and provide support for my contention that this text was not produced in Naples. The next section will then examine in detail some examples of Gregorius's translation practice and relate it to the theories advanced in the prologue.

The principal purpose of Gregorius's prologue is to justify a new version of the *Passio S. Anastasii* that eschews the servility of an *ad verbum* translation, denigrated by the common opinion of the *doctores*.[59] While conceding the value of Nicolaus's literal rendering as a means of ensuring faithfulness to the original source ("Quo magis quippe rivus suo fonti sit propior, eo magis gustantibus solet esse saporior" [ll. 22-23; "The closer the stream is to its source, the tastier it is to those who taste it"]), Gregorius defends his contrasting method of translation. His own text, he says, will be composed "urbanius regulari digestu" (l. 7; "more elegantly, with orderly arrangement"). His work will even be an improvement on the Greek text, for he will eliminate what is unnecessary and add what has been left out, "decorandae constructionis causa" (l. 26; "for the sake of decorating the style"). Yet, despite these changes, Gregorius claims faithfulness to the meaning or truth of the Greek text by declaring that all these interventions have been achieved "salvo manente sensu" (l. 25; "while safeguarding the meaning"). Gregorius compares and contrasts the inferior merits of a translation *ad verbum*, represented by both the early translation and Nicolaus's

---

59. "Communis namque doctorum sententia affirmat, verbum de verbo exprimere, pessimum genus interpretandi esse; ridiculose etenim currens et lectorem praepedit, et auditores fastidit" (ll. 28-31; "Indeed, the common opinion of learned men states that to transpose word for word is the worst kind of translation; for it sounds ridiculous, and trips up the reader and irritates the listener"). Gregory's image of a stream to describe translation is developed further in the passage following.

first-stage rendering, with a translation that boasts stylistic skill and·sanctions additions and deletions in the original model.[60]

Almost every sentence of this prologue echoes Jerome. At the very beginning, when Gregorius pays homage to the classic humility topos by expressing his sense of inadequacy for the task to which he has been called, the image he uses of his critics as dogs, complete with teeth and barks ("oblatrantium suffrementes denticulos" [l. 10]), though an ancient one, is indebted most immediately to the language of Jerome as found in the letter to Pammachius[61] and especially to the opening words of the preface to the Pentateuch, where Jerome is discussing the dangers of accepting Desiderius's plea to translate the Pentateuch from the Hebrew ("Periculosum opus certe, obtrectatorum latratibus patens ...").[62] Similarly, Gregorius's hesitation in accepting Athanasius's request for a new translation of the *Passio S. Anastasii* is patterned after Jerome's letter to Desiderius. And just as Jerome's preference for an *ad sensum* translation is rooted in its pleasing appeal to a broader readership, so also Gregorius claims that "... verbum de verbo exprimere, pessimum genus interpretandi esse; ridiculose etenim currens et lectorem praepedit, et auditores fastidit" (ll. 29-31).[63] Gregorius's use of the adverb *ridiculose* here may also echo Jerome's use of *absurde* and *ridiculum* in his preface to his translation of Eusebius, which is quoted in the same letter to Pammachius ("... si ad verbum interpretor, absurde resonat ... Quodsi cui ... videbit ordinem ridiculum").[64]

---

60. For a fuller discussion of specific additions, see below, pp. 118-120.

61. "Nam quidem pseudomonachus ... deditque adversariis latrandi contra me occasionem, ut inter imperitos contionentur me falsarium, me verbum non expressisse de verbo ..." *Ep.* 57, 2, 1 (ed. Bartelink, pp. 11-12). The image of the critic as a barking dog was widely identified with Jerome: Johannes Scotus refers directly to Jerome when he uses the image of the teeth in one of his poems: "Quod si quorundam mordetur dente feroci, / Hoc leue: namque meo contigit Hieronimo" (*Carmina* 20.15-16 [ed. Herren, p. 108]; Jeauneau, "Jean Scot Erigène et le grec," p. 15).

62. *Biblia sacra*, ed. Weber, I, 3.

63. See above, n. 59, for translation.

64. *Ep.* 57, 5, 7-8 (ed. Bartelink, p. 14).

In justifying his additions and deletions, Gregorius may have been recalling statements of Jerome, who declared that he added material as well as removed what was not worthy of remembrance both in his translation of Eusebius's *Chronicle* and in the *Onomastikon*.[65] More immediately, Gregorius's phrase—"multa quidem superflua, salvo manente sensu, penitus subtraximus; et e contra decorandae constructionis causa nonnulla adiecimus" (ll. 25-27; "We eliminated completely many superfluous things, while safeguarding the meaning; but, on the other hand, we added some things for the sake of decorating the style")—echoes Jerome's reference, again in the letter to Pammachius, to Cicero's practice in his translations of Plato, Xenophon, Aeschines and Demosthenes: "Quanta in illis praetermiserit, quanta addiderit, quanta mutaverit, ut proprietates alterius linguae suis proprietatibus explicaret, non est huius temporis dicere."[66]

Gregorius's appropriation of the rhetorical phraseology used by Jerome in his various discussions of translation theory is one of the most common features found in the prologues routinely added in this period to translations and retranslations from southern and central Italy to justify an *ad sensum* translation.[67] There are parallels in Neapolitan works, such as Guarimpotus's prologue to his translation of the *Life of St. Eustratius (BHL 2778)*:

Fideli quippe sensu, etsi non fideli sermone, haec me transtulisse confiteor, plurimis additis, plurimis ademptis, mutatis et transmutatis

---

65. Cf. Jerome's words in the *Chronicle*'s preface "... quae nova inseruimus, de aliis probatissimis viris libata cognoscant. Sciendum etenim est me et interpretis et scriptoris ex parte officio usum ... et quae mihi intermissa videbantur, adjeci" (PL 27, 225-226). Both passages are discussed by Chiesa, "*Ad verbum* o *ad sensum?*," pp. 14-15.

66. *Ep.* 57, 5, 2 (ed. Bartelink, p. 13). In his preface to the *Chronicle*, Jerome also discussed how Cicero's translation of Xenophon's *Oeconomicus* was marred by too faithful a rendition (PL 27, 223-224).

67. All of Gregorius's obvious echoes of Jerome can be accounted for by the letter to Pammachius and the Pentateuch preface. However, the "intertextuality" of these translation topoi is so dense that we cannot exclude other works as direct sources.

dictionibus aliisque pro aliis positis uti omnes maiores auctores nostros fecisse dinoscimus.[68]

This familiar disclaimer is also found, for example, in Bishop Athanasius II's Passion of Arethas and companions (*BHL* 671):

> Et quia peregrinum idioma latino minime congruit stylo, non verborum folia sed magis sensus ubertatem carpere studentes, superflua resecamus et interdum, serie commutata, ad dilucidandas sententias nonnulla ingerimus nostra.[69]

A similar statement is made in the prologue to the translation of the *Miraculum Michaelis* composed at the Amalfitans' cloister on Mt. Athos toward the end of the tenth century:

> Quod nos magis necessitate fecimus quam voluntate, quia si illud per totum sicut in Graeco habetur eloquio, ita Latinis sermonibus exponere voluissem tam insipidum inconveniensque sonaret, ut non modo aedificationem nullam legentibus, sed fastidium generaret.[70]

This translation approach is also consistently advocated in similar language in the works of Anastasius Bibliothecarius, best known for his political and literary activities as a member of the Roman curia. His considerable efforts as a translator from the Greek span the period between 860 and 880.[71] He could have been, therefore, a contemporary of Gregorius. In the dedicatory letter to Pope Nicholas I, which serves as prologue to his translation of the Life of Patriarch John (the Almsgiver) of Alexandria, Anastasius declares:

> Cum autem beatum hunc in Latinum verterem eloquium, nec Graecorum idiomata nec eorum ordinem verborum sequi potui vel debui. Non enim verbum e verbo, sed sensum e sensu excerpsi.[72]

Similar sentiments are expressed in the letter of Pope Nicholas I to Emperor Michael III, also believed to have been penned by

---

68. Devos, "L'oeuvre de Guarimpotus, hagiographe napolitain," p. 155.

69. Quoted by Devos, "L'oeuvre de Guarimpotus," p. 156. See *ASS*. Oct. X, 761-762.

70. Quoted and discussed by Chiesa, "*Ad verbum o ad sensum?*," p. 49.

71. For Anastasius Bibliothecarius as translator, see the overviews in Brunhölzl, *Histoire*, pp. 282-287 and Berschin, *Greek Letters*, pp. 162-169, with further bibliography.

72. *MGH. Ep.* VII, 395-398.

Anastasius Bibliothecarius,[73] and in the preface to the translation of the acts of the VII Ecumenical Council, in which Anastasius criticizes the existing translation for its excessive literalness:

> interpres pene per singula relicto utriusque linguae idiomate, adeo fuerit verbum e verbo secutus, ut quid in eadem editione intelligatur, aut vix, aut numquam possit adverti, in fastidiumque versa legentium pene ab omnibus hac pro causa contemnatur.[74]

They are found again, with slight apologies for the divergence from a word-for-word translation, in the dedicatory letter to Charles the Bald that Anastasius affixed to his translation of the *Passio Dionysii*,[75] the prologue to the translation of the acts of the VIII Ecumenical Council,[76] and the preface to his translation of Greek documents known as the *Collectanea*.[77]

---

73. Here Pope Nicholas charges that the emperor's translators of Latin documents are so literal as to destroy the text "... qui quando necesse non est non sensum e sensu, sed violenter verbum edere conantur e verbo" (*MGH. Ep.* VI, 459 [discussed by Chiesa, "*Ad verbum* o *ad sensum?*," p. 38]).

74. *MGH. Ep.* VII, 415-418.

75. "... arrepto interpretandi certamine, Latino eloquio tradidi, quantum potui, auxiliante Deo, et si non ex toto verbum e verbo, sensum tamen penitus hauriens" (*MGH. Ep.* VII, 439-441).

76. "... interpretans igitur hanc sanctam synodum, verbum e verbo, quantum idioma Latinum permisit, excerpsi; nonnunquam vero, manente sensu, constructionem Graecam in Latinam necessario commutavi" (*MGH. Ep.* VII, 403-415 at p. 411).

77. "... itaque mihi, interveniente oboedientia, sata ab aliis rustica falce collegisse et ad aream Latinitatis fideli humero transvexisse sufficiat, nihil videlicet addenti vel minuenti. Tuum autem erit, adiunctis sententiis, veluti quodam ventilabro iudicii opus historiae dilatare, et verba nostra, quae in ea inserenda decreveris, quasi quaedam frumenta purgare. Verum nos sic et haec et alia interpretandi propositum sumpsimus, ut nec ab ipsa verborum usquequaque circumstantia discessisse noscamur, nec pro posse a sensu veritate decidisse videamur" (*MGH. Ep.* VII, 422-426). Anastasius's words recall Evagrius of Antioch in the preface to his translation of the *Vita Antonii*, quoted also in Jerome's letter to Pammachius: "Ex alia in aliam linguam ad verbum expressa traslatio sensus operit et velut laeto gramine sata strangulat. Dum enim casibus et figuris servit oratio, quod brevi poterat indicare sermone, longo ambitu circumacta vix explicat" (*Ep.* 57, 6, 1-2 [ed. Bartelink, p. 14]). The agricultural imagery emphasized by their common use of *sata* is particularly striking.

In all of these works, Anastasius Bibliothecarius contrasts impli-
citly. or explicitly his own *ad sensum* approach to the literalism of
earlier translations. In particular, he differentiates his approach
from that of contemporary translators at the Carolingian court.
Anastasius's backhanded praise of John the Scot's translation of
the *Corpus Dionysiacum*, for example, also criticizes the overly
faithful approach by the Carolingian translator.[78] Anastasius Bibliothecarius, Gregorius, and other contemporary Italian translators
thus exhibit an awareness of different translation methodologies;
they portray their method as more accurate and satisfying than the
literal approach of earlier translators still favored by Carolingian
scholars, and claim the authority of the greatest Christian translator as justification for their efforts.[79]

One such translation methodology is the technique of two-step
translation, which we know Gregorius employed in preparing his
version of the *Passio S. Anastasii* from the direct translation
prepared for him by the archpriest Nicolaus. This technique involves as its first step a literal, in some cases interlinear, translation
made by a speaker of the original language, and the second step
involves a revision made by a native speaker of the receptor language. It is known to have been practised by the translators of late
antiquity; Jerome, for example, says in his prologue to the book
of Tobit that he employed an expert in *chaldaeo sermone* to render

---

78. "... quia tanto studio verbum de verbo elicere procuravit, quod genus
interpretationis (licet et ipse plerumue sequar) quantum illustres interpretes
vitent, tua profecto sollers experientia non ignorat" (*MGH. Ep.* VII, 430-434).
See Chiesa, "*Ad verbum o ad sensum?*," p. 38. Chiesa emphasizes the "letteral-
ismo" of Hilduin and Johannes Scotus, and the conservative nature of their
translation, an approach that leaned toward faithful adherence to the Greek
model. For example, Johannes Scotus follows Greek word order and frequently creates Latin calques on the Greek, such as *equordinatu* for ὁμοταγής
(Chiesa, "Traduzioni e traduttori," pp. 189-191; "*Ad verbum o ad sensum?*,"
pp. 35-37). This literalism may result from a belief that Latin vocabulary was
unable to reflect the philosophical precision of the Greek, a belief held by
late medieval translators of Greek philosophical and scientific texts.

79. Some of Anastasius's statements, however, appear to propose a more
literal translation as the more truthful (Chiesa, "*Ad verbum o ad sensum?*,"
pp. 40-41).

it into Hebrew first.[80] Gregory of Tours employed a "Syrian" to provide him with a verbatim translation of the Legend of the Seven Sleepers of Ephesus, which he then revised.[81] Numerous Latin hagiographic translations from the early Middle Ages as well undoubtedly go back to lost verbatim, or even interlinear, translations of Greek originals. Their dependence on a more literal version has been obscured by the disappearance of the earlier Latin text. The procedure of deliberate two-step translation becomes most apparent, however, in Italy in the period from the ninth to the eleventh century, when Italian translators contrasted their translation approach to the literal technique still followed at the other major center of translation activity, the Carolingian court.[82]

The two-step method has been identified particularly with the translation school in Naples[83] though there are numerous examples of two-step translations in other southern Italian locales, such as Benevento.[84] There are Roman examples also. The Latin version of the Life of Pope Martin I, by Anastasius Bibliothecarius

---

80. *Biblia sacra*, ed. Weber, I, 676. It is a method of translating which became popular in the later Middle Ages, when the large-scale translation of scientific and philosophical works was undertaken.

81. *De gloria martyrum*, 95, quoted above, p. 80 n. 85.

82. Even among Carolingian scholars, however, the use of Greek speakers by Latin translators is attested. Hilduin's translation of the *Areopagitica*, for example, may have been done with the help of a number of Greek-speaking collaborators (Lapidge, "Lost *Passio Metrica S. Dionysii* by Hilduin of Saint-Denis," pp. 59-65; Chiesa, "*Ad verbum* o *ad sensum?*," pp. 35-36). In general, the approach to Greek among the Carolingian translators appears to have been more bookish and academic. Johannes Scotus, for example, relied heavily on a bilingual glossary, several of which were in circulation in his circles. Also available to him were "graeca collecta," lists of Greek words culled from Latin authors, such as Priscian, Jerome, Lactanctius, Servius, with an accompanying Latin translation (Jeauneau, "Jean Scot Erigène et le grec," pp. 31-34).

83. Dolbeau ("Le rôle des interprètes") discusses seven examples of these two-step translations composed between 875 and 1000, four of which are from Naples. He makes a distinction between translators and "remanieurs," or revisers/editors, who polish the literal translation.

84. The Life of Gregory Nazienzus (*BHG* 723) was translated by Adhemarus of Benevento in 903 with the help of a Greek interpreter. It remains unedited (*BHL* 3667), but is discussed by Dolbeau in "Jean de Gaète," pp. 84ff.

himself, was based on a translation at least partly executed by somebody else.[85] Anastasius's translation of the acts of the VII Ecumenical Council (Nicea II) was made to replace a word-for-word translation, which may, nonetheless, have been used in preparing his own more polished rendition.[86] In effect Anastasius would have been following the two-step approach in this case. Another work of cooperative translation by Anastasius Bibliothecarius is the Seventy Miracles of SS. Cyrus and John (*BHL* 2080). Twelve of these, he says, had been translated earlier ("Bonifatius consiliarius ... duodecim cum praefatione capitula olim interpretatus est"), and it is reasonable to assume that Anastasius made use of the earlier version.[87] Although the two-step method dates back at least to Jerome, Italian translators like Athanasius Bibliothecarius and Gregorius make no attempt to claim patristic authority for it. Rather, this method is presented as an integral part of the *ad sensum* approach, the first necessary step on which the looser translation can then be based. In many cases the final redactor knew little, if any, Greek. His work should more rightly be classified as one of revision of a translated text, or even, as the composition of a completely new work.

A work whose prologue has striking similarities to Gregorius's *Passio* of Anastasius is the *Vita S. Johannis Chrysostomi* (*BHL* 4376), whose manuscript tradition suggests that it originated most likely in central Italy before 1010.[88] Like Gregorius's prologue, this preface also indicates the name of the person who made the request ("... quondam Iuliano, nunc Lupo nomine"), the first-stage translator ("... Christophori scilicet reverendi sacerdotis") and the reviser ("Leo qui et Iohannes cognomine ... a propria infantia ...

---

85. "Verum huius operis media in aliis implicitus ipse non transtuli, sed ab alio petitu meo interpretata postmodum in quibusdam correxi" (*MGH. Ep.* VII, 422).

86. *MGH. Ep.* VII, 416. See above, p. 110.

87. *MGH. Ep.* VII, 427. On Bonifatius, see Berschin, "Bonifatius Consiliarius. Ein römischer Übersetzer in der byzantinischen Epoche des Papsttums."

88. Published in Poncelet, *Catalogus codicum hagiographicorum latinorum antiquioroum saeculo XVI qui asservantur in Bibliotheca nationali parisiensi*, pp. 17-45. See also Dolbeau, "Le rôle des interprètes," pp. 149-150, which corrects earlier assertions about provenance.

lumine visibili carens ex toto"). The organization of the preface of *BHL* 4376 is strikingly similar to that of *BHL* 411a. Leo also begins by using the topos of humility. His characterization of the first translator as "humana tamen oblivione quadam praepeditus" recalls Gregorius's expression "lectorem praepedit" (l. 31). Similarly, *BHL* 4376's "Plurima tamen, quae ab interprete ad plenum, ut se habebat, dicta sunt, propter fastidium legentium seu audientium praetermisi" echo Gregorius's own "et auditores fastidit" (l. 31).[89] These lexical and thematic similarities are discussed here not to argue that there is a direct connection between the translation of the *Vita S. Joannis Chrysostomi* and 411a, but rather to show that hagiographic translation and revision, as well as the topoi and language employed to describe that process, became extraordinarily common.

Even this brief survey of the translations of one well-known interpreter from Rome, Anastasius Bibliothecarius, and an even briefer comparison with the obscure Leo's *Vita S. Joannis Chrysostomi* show that the literary conventions and vocabulary found in Gregorius's prologue were quite widespread in central Italy, and cannot be used without other evidence to localize a text within one particular city.[90]

89. This in turn also recalls Anastasius Bibliothecarius's words "in fastidiumque versa legentium" in the preface to the acts of the VII Ecumenical Council quoted above, p. 110.

90. The use of topoi and vocabulary to localize a literary work is never sufficient by itself, and may have been overused in the case of Naples during this period. For example, Dolbeau singles out a certain group of words recurring "si régulièrement sous la plume des hagiographes napolitains qu'ils peuvent être considérés comme des caractéristiques d'école" ("La vie latine de saint Euthyme," pp. 318-319). While such words may in fact be commonly found in Neapolitan works, they also appear in other places. Of the words singled out by Dolbeau, two are found in 411a: *stomachari* ("Stomachatus igitur Marzabanas" [l. 280]; "Stomachatus igitur imperator" [l. 526]); and *repedare* ("Quo audito dux Saim retrogrado tramite iterum repedavit" [ll. 103-104]), but this word is found also in numerous medieval Latin texts, as, for example, in Bede's *Historia ecclesiastica* IV, 24 (ed. Colgrave and Mynors, p. 416) "... ad suam domum repedabat ..." and V, 19 (p. 516) "...ad priora repedantes ...". Another word singled out in Dolbeau's study is *uerbosari*, which is not found in *BHL* 411a but is found in *BHL* 410b, the first translation ("'Quid uerbosatis?'" [ll. 222-223]).

Despite their ubiquity, however, the meaning of these translation topoi has never been fully investigated. This can be done only through the careful examination of the actual practice of hagiographic translators, i.e. by comparing their work to their original Greek source and to previous *ad verbum* efforts. In many cases, not all the layers of translation are available, either because they have not survived or because adequate editions of one or the other works do not exist. This analysis can however be made of the *Passio S. Anastasii* of Gregorius clericus, a task that is rendered possible by the fortunate survival of the early translation which Gregorius wished to replace (*BHL* 410b), by Gregorius's theoretical description of his undertaking in his Latin prologue, and by the identification of *BHL* 411a (and not *BHL* 411) as Gregorius's original work.

C. *Hagiographic Revision*

The use of a mannered vocabulary, stylistic elaborations, and prose cursus, as discussed above, reflect Gregorius's assertion that his work is a literary piece composed "urbanius regulari digestu" (l. 7), superior to the early translation and the Greek model. But Gregorius claims more for his opus, for he states that while he maintained the sense or meaning of the source, he also made additions and deletions to the Greek text ("multa quidem superflua, salvo manente sensu, penitus subtraximus; et e contra decorandae constructionis causa nonnulla adiecimus" [ll. 25-27]). This statement is used by Gregorius to contrast an *ad verbum* translation with his own version. It must therefore be taken as Gregorius's definition of a translation *ad sensum*, an expression he never actually uses, but is recalled by his phrase "salvo manente sensu." By examining the cuts and additions made by Gregorius, we should be able to understand and evaluate his claim that his translation retains the meaning of the original Greek.

Certainly, the "factual" story of Anastasius as told by Gregorius remains a faithful account of the life and martyrdom of the Persian. No new episodes are added; no passages are eliminated. There is only one place where the Latin obviously changes a significant detail, and this may be the result of misunderstanding.[91] But just as the substitution of a new Latin prologue for the original preface to·the Greek *Acta* eliminates the specific historical context in which the Greek text was written—seventh-century Palestine in the wake of the Persian victory, occupation and ultimate defeat— and replaces it with Gregorius's own milieu, there are other altera- tions intended to detach the Latin text from the context in which the Greek *Acta* were composed, and to appropriate it for a new audience. Thus, for example, the phrase ὡς ἐμάθομεν (25.9; "as we learned") cannot apply to the author of the Latin text; it is there- fore eliminated from the Latin version as a means of creating an independent Latin text. Similarly, elaborations addressed to a Latin audience are on occasion added to the Latin version, as, for ex- ample, the explanation of the meaning of Magundat's new Chris- tian name as the "resurrected one," and the specification that Ana- stasius was given the Greek not the Latin tonsure (ll. 151, 156). These are meant to create a more erudite text, and parallel Grego- rius's ornate vocabulary and style. They also keep readers aware of their separation from the original text, and of the presence of the author of this version.

Less obvious, but perhaps more germane to Gregorius's defini- tion of a translation *ad sensum,* are the unobtrusive transforma- tions that alter the text in more fundamental ways. These changes can be highlighted only by a detailed comparison of the two ver- sions. The scene described in cap. 36 provides a good example of such subtle changes.

At the chapter's opening, Anastasius is found in prison in the village of Bethsaloe in Persia where the Persian officials attempt to turn him away from Christianity by torture and verbal persuasion. As the officer in charge of the prison (the sellarius) is a Christian, Anastasius's monastic confrere, who has been sent by the abbot to accompany the future martyr to Persia, is emboldened to visit the prison, "alternis eum diebus solacii et obsequii gratia visitabat" (l. 553; "he visited him every other day for the sake of solace and

---

91. The change of what must have been *equo* or *equis* into *aquis* (l. 365), perhaps by Gregorius, is due to ignorance of the Persians' religion. See n. 26 above and my note to the text.

sake of solace and honor."). This renders the Greek, εἰσήρχετο μίαν ὑπὲρ μίαν πρὸς αὐτόν, παραμυθούμενος καὶ προτρεπόμενος αὐτὸν εἰς τὸ ἀγαθόν (36.2-3). The Latin phrase, "alternis diebus" appears to mistranslate the Greek μίαν ὑπὲρ μίαν; the Greek clearly says that the confrere visited Anastasius every day, while the Latin "alternis diebus" would normally be taken to mean "every other day." Most likely, this is the simple result of a mistranslation by Nicolaus or a misunderstanding by Gregorius. But the Latin rendition of εἰς τὸ ἀγαθόν is more significant, for it is a deliberate manipulation of the original material and changes the portrayal of the martyr. While the Greek author emphasized that the monastic confrere visits the emprisoned Anastasius every day to encourage him to remain steadfast, to follow τὸ ἀγαθόν ("the good"), and not to betray his Christian faith, the Latin text says nothing about such encouragement, and instead identifies the motivation of the visits as "solacium"—clearly solace to the prisoner—and "obsequium." This latter word could refer to the confrere's obedience to the abbot who had sent him to follow Anastasius to Persia as a supporter and a witness. But it would be read most immediately in the Latin context as signifying the monastic confrere's own obedience and submission to Anastasius, who is already recognized as a heroic holy figure, as a martyr. This is clearly an alteration of the Greek version. While it might have been dictated by the desire to elevate the style and vocabulary of the simple and vague Greek expression (τὸ ἀγαθόν), the result goes beyond stylistic improvement.

The scene that follows further emphasizes the position of veneration that Anastasius has already achieved. Numerous Christians come to visit him in prison, falling at his feet, embracing his chains, and asking that he pray for them and give them a blessed object, a εὐλογία, for their protection. When the martyr refuses, the visitors place wax on his chains to make an impression thereof, and take that as their εὐλογία, a relic in fact of the still-living martyr. The interpretation of the Latin text here is quite consistent with the Greek. The Latin equivalent of εὐλογία, *benedictio,* a word that could mean an object sanctified by contact with a living martyr or his tomb, a kind of talisman,[92] is used here in the phrase "benedictionis monimentum" (ll. 556-557), which renders the meaning of the custom much more precisely, and certainly more grandly than the early translation *BHL* 410b's "benedictionem aliquam" (ll. 488-489). But the Latin passage in Gregorius's version adds a phrase—"huius modi preces quasi indigno" (l. 557; "[rejecting] such prayers as if he were unworthy")—that is not found in the Greek. This addition fills out the story by explaining Anastasius's refusal to give his visitors a εὐλογία, a refusal left without comment or explanation in the Greek: by the adjective *indignus* the Latin redactor supplies the motivation for Anastasius's refusal, which is thus attributed to his humility. Also, the addition of "benefidi" (l. 559) to characterize the Christian visitors who make an impression of the wax further highlights the veneration of Anastasius as a holy person.

While the tale of Anastasius's conversion or martyrdom is not changed by the deletion or addition of "factual" details, nonetheless this episode illustrates how Gregorius's composition differs from the Greek not only in tone and style but also in content.[93] The presentation of the events is filled out to provide a smoother narrative and to portray Anastasius as a heroic martyr. This is also clearly the purpose of the frequent authorial interventions, the insertions that provide Gregorius's own rhetorical reflections on the events he is narrating, and that are far removed in style from the straightforward Greek text. Many of these rhetorical elaborations are imprecations against the persecutors of the saint (e.g. ll. 334-338) or expressions of wonder at the martyr's stamina and fortitude (e.g. ll. 115-119, 196-198). Some of these simply expand or build on a phrase already present in the Greek. This is true, for example, of the short addition in cap. 1 where Gregorius takes the

---

92. McCulloh, "The Cult of Relics in the Letters and Dialogues of Gregory the Great: a Lexicographical Study," pp. 169-173. See also my note to the text.

93. Although the redactor of the second translation of the *Passio Febroniae* was not interested in changing the dynamic or organization of the story, according to Chiesa, *Le versioni latine*, pp. 263-276, he placed the central figures of the narrative into greater relief by eliminating minor events and details.

Greek phrase (Καὶ—ὦ παραδόξων ... σωτηρίαν [6.9-11]) and elaborates it stylistically by the obvious use of alliteration and irony ("O victoriosissimae crucis gloriosam captivitatem! Quae ideo capta est ut captores caperet, et eos capiendo a captivitate liberaret. O praedam de praedonibus tropaea elevantem, et praedones in praedam salubriter vertentem" [ll. 49-52; "O glorious captivity of the most victorious cross! It was captured indeed so that it might capture its captors, and by capturing them it might liberate them from captivity. O stolen prey, raising a trophy up from the robbers, and salubriously turning robbers into prey"]).[94]

Some of these additions stand out because of their length and learned allusions. The very long intercalation in cap. 21 begins as a commentary on Anastasius's refusal to be bound as he is lashed by his Persian torturers. It plays on the contrast between external fetters, which the martyr refuses, and internal bonds of faith, by which Christ strengthens Anastasius's resolve ("Volebant enim impii invitum extrinsecus ligando concutere, quem iam Christus ultroneum intrinsecus vinciendo coeperat stabilire" [ll. 318-320; "Indeed the impious ones wanted to shake him from his inner resolve by constraining externally him, whom Christ had begun to make steadfast externally by binding him within"]). The martyr's shedding of his monastic habit to keep it from dishonor while he is lashed offers the opportunity for a long discussion of the martyr's humility, represented externally by his shedding of his clothes, and internally by his reliance on Christ. Gregorius then turns directly to the chief persecutor himself whose title "marzabanas" has here been turned into a proper name. Exploiting the logical argument that two contrary things cannot be found in the same essence—a form of argumentation ultimately borrowed from Augustine's works, in particular *Contra Iulianum opus imperfectum*—Gregorius "defeats" the accusations of vice that Marzabanas makes against the martyr, who is shown to be full of virtue. Similarly, the long insertion in cap. 7 begins with a direct address to the "future martyr of God." Anastasius's wonder at the mystery of the Incarnation ("quomodo illocalis Deus et invisibilis ..." [ll.

---

94. See ll. 54-55 for another example.

65-66; "how God, not fixed in any place, invisible"]), represented by the captured cross held by the Persians, leads Gregorius to a discussion of the Trinity, borrowed in large part from Gregory the Great's *Moralia in Iob*, but with echoes of Augustine's *De trinitate*.[95] These additions are noticeably long, and further display Gregorius's learned and rhetorical pretensions. More importantly, they illustrate how distant Gregorius's version is from the source.

Like many medieval translators, Gregorius justifies his revision by echoing the arguments and vocabulary of patristic translators.[96] In many cases, it seems clear that these theoretical statements were lifted out of their historical context, and mechanically repeated. In the case of Gregorius, however, they were used to justify a different practice than that apparently envisioned by the Fathers.[97] Central to the theory of Rufinus and Jerome is the contrast between a translation *ad verbum*, which is described as a literal, word-for-word rendition of the original, much like *BHL* 410b, and one *ad sensum*, less literal in its adherence to the model, but in many ways more accurate according to its proponents. As I have shown, however, this does not correspond to Gregorius's version.

Jerome and his contemporary translators had recast in these terms the ancient discussion on translation found, in particular, in the works of Cicero, who had focused on the contrast between *interpretari* and *aemulari*. The former was the humble task of the

---

95. See my note to the text for full bibliographic reference. There are similar rhetorical-stylistic additions in the *Passio Febroniae*, centered around the martyrdom of the saint, such as "quid hac sancta virgine robustior?" See further, Chiesa, *Le versioni latine*, pp. 270-271.

96. See above, pp. 105ff.

97. I am here indebted to Chiesa's excellent discussion of ancient, patristic and medieval theory in "*Ad verbum* o *ad sensum?*," especially pp. 4-7. Copeland, *Rhetoric, Hermeneutics, and Translation in the Middle Ages: Academic Traditions and Vernacular Texts*, pp. 9-36, discusses Roman and patristic theories of translation within the broader disciplines of grammar and rhetoric, but assumes there was one view held by all the Fathers, including Jerome and Augustine, when in fact there were clearly disagreements, arising principally from their different views on biblical translation. Neither scholar considers the relationship of theory to practice. For a very summary view of Jerome's translation practice, see Kelly, *The True Interpreter: A History of Translation Theory and Practice in the West*, pp. 180-181.

technical interpreter who mechanically translated from Greek into Latin; his purpose was to bring the reader to the original text. An example of this is provided by *BHL* 410b. The latter term (*aemulari*), on the other hand, described an undertaking fit for the orator, who would strive to rewrite the Greek prototype in elegant Latin, and even to surpass the original by rhetorical flourishes or by elaborating and expanding on its argument. This task fell properly under the sphere of *inventio*, by which the rhetorician devised the argumentation with which he would persuade his audience. In antiquity then, the choice was represented to be between translating—which by definition was a verbatim rendition of the model—and a rhetorical reworking or adaptation of the original Greek text, whose ultimate purpose was to create a new Latin work that stood alongside the Greek original.

By the time of Evagrius, Jerome, and Rufinus, however, the educated Latin public had much less familiarity with Greek. Furthermore, the importance and prestige of the source text, in most cases the sacred Scriptures, had increased. The purpose of Christian translators, it was claimed, was to convey as accurately as possible the truth of the original, not to alter it rhetorically. It is within this context that the debate about translation in the fourth century is reduced to a simplified contrast between a literal translation (*ad verbum*), which had been the norm for most Christian translations, and translation *ad sensum*, a new construct to indicate a new translation approach, which appears to correspond to a looser, but still faithful rendition of the original.[98] The earliest use of this term in its meaning "according to the sense" to contrast a literal *ad verbum* translation is found in Evagrius's *Vita Antonii*.[99] It is fully elaborated in the fourth century in reaction to the excessive literalism of early Christian versions from the Greek.[100] Jerome's most famous dictum on the superiority of a translation *ad sensum*

98. Such an approach is complex. It is clear, for example, that Jerome's *ad sensum* embraced a very wide spectrum of translation practices, including the addition and deletion of text. See further the preface to Eusebius's *Chronicle* as in n. 65 above.

99. PL 73, 125-126.

100. See particularly Chiesa, "*Ad verbum* o *ad sensum?*," pp. 11-13.

is expressed in his normative letter to Pammachius, his most extended discussion of translation, and one most frequently cited by translators from all ages. Here Jerome most clearly had declared the value of the *ad sensum* translation for non-biblical texts.[101] While rhetorical artifice to convey the meaning of the original text is not scorned, the work of the translator is no longer seen by Jerome as one that belongs to *inventio*; the role of translator is clearly distinguished from that of author.[102] For Jerome, the validity of an *ad sensum* translation is its ability to reflect the meaning of the original accurately. Gregory I's imprecations against *ad verbum* translations that obscure the meaning of the original rather than illuminate it is but a continuation of the same debate;[103] it is addressed to the widespread practice exemplified by the early translation of the *Passio S. Anastasii, BHL* 410b.

But Gregorius clericus applies Jerome's terminology and arguments to new circumstances. For he is not a translator, since, unlike Jerome and Evagrius, he worked little if at all with the source language. To a very limited degree, the modest results of his approach are closer to the ideals of Cicero, who emphasized that for the rhetorician the goal of translation is to replace and displace the Greek original.[104] Gregorius's lexical tags for these compositions are telling. For the activity of the earlier, anonymous translator of *BHL* 410b as well as for the literal rendition of Nicolaus, he employs the verb *transferre* ("quidam ... de graeco in latinum

---

101. Quoted above, p. 105. Even for biblical translation, Jerome favored the "interpretatio ad sensum" and he blamed excessive literalism for misrepresenting the meaning of the sacred text.

102. Chiesa, *"Ad verbum o ad sensum?,"* pp. 24-25, points out the terminological evolution which results from this different view of translation: *transferre* is the most frequently used word, followed by *interpretari* and *vertere. Sequi, aemulari, imitari*—the ancient terms—have disappeared completely.

103. Discussed above, p. 55 and n. 8.

104. It cannot be argued, however, that Gregorius is following the classical translation approach of Cicero, which contrasted rhetorical *aemulatio* with the literal translations of professional or technical translators, since Gregorius shows no sign that he was familiar with such ancient discussions of translation, except as transmitted in Jerome's works.

confuse *transtulerat*; quatenus ... observata serie *transferret*" [ll. 6-7; 20-21]). This is the term traditionally associated with the technical translators, who produced the verbatim versions of scientific and technical works of antiquity.[105] Gregorius, however, uses the term *componere*, the primary meaning of which is "to write, to compose," for his activity ("ut urbanius regulari digestu *componerem*" [ll. 7-8]). There is no evidence that Gregorius was aware of the evolution of translation terminology from ancient to patristic times, but his lexical choice in this context is a further reflection of his self-conscious authorship.[106]

The second translation of the *Passio S. Anastasii* is part of the transmission of the Greek heritage to the Latin world, and is emblematic of the importance of hagiography in this exchange. Gregorius's version of the *Passio S. Anastasii*, however, is also part of the history of hagiographic *retractatio*, the constant rewriting of hagiographic texts to make them more suitable to the taste of contemporary audiences.[107] In the case of Gregorius's reworking, the primary goal was to provide a polished Latin text which by necessity cannot be a literal, faithful rendition of the original language as the early translation or Nicolaus's version are. This second translation is the product of a different milieu than that which produced *BHL* 410b, or even the Roman Miracle to be considered in the next chapter: this is a translation where the purpose is not to bring the reader to the text, but the text to the reader or the listener, as Gregorius says in his prologue (l. 30). It is not the translator's purpose to make the original available to the reader, but rather to create a new text, one that can stand on its own. Gregorius's description of the audience of his text to include both readers and *listeners* indicates that new versions of hagiographic works were to be read effectively out loud, as, for example, during the performance of the liturgy.

---

105. Chiesa, "*Ad verbum o ad sensum?*," p. 24.

106. Johannes Scotus, on the other hand, refers to himself as "interpres, non expositor." See Chiesa, "*Ad verbum o ad sensum?*," p. 37.

107. For an excellent introduction to the rewriting of saints' Lives, see most recently Lapidge, "Editing Hagiography."

This second version furthermore was composed in a context in which knowledge of and access to the source language, Greek, had greatly diminished over the three centuries since the first translation. By the time the second translation was composed, Rome was much less Greek than it ever had been. Beginning with the late ninth century many of the Greek monastic communities of the city disappear or become Latin because of a lack of new recruits.[108] The monastery of St. Anastasius *ad Aquas Salvas*, perhaps the one that remained Greek the longest, became a Cistercian house in 1140, as it remains today. Yet even so it is important to note that Gregorius clericus uses Latinized Greek words or words with Greek roots as a mark of learning, following a common practice.[109] For knowledge of Greek was a highly sought after and fashionable commodity in the Middle Ages, and Byzantium and its civilization a fount of inspiration in all western artistic and cultural revivals from this time forward.

Gregorius clericus's display of Greek learning and his work on the seventh-century *Passio* of the Persian martyr can best be broadly situated within the revival of interest in Greek and the Greek patristic heritage that was spurred on by a small circle of Roman literati in the second half of the ninth century.[110] Our view of this circle has been shaped in particular by the varied activity of Anastasius Bibliothecarius, whose translations of Greek hagiographic texts have been connected to the ideological commitment to strengthening the papacy against Frankish influence by emphasizing its role in the recovery of the shared Greek and Latin heritage. The saints who thus attracted Anastasius's attention were both Roman martyrs whose Passions existed only in Greek, and eastern saints who resisted political authority for the sake of the true faith.[111] The Persian martyr does not fit neatly in either category, but certainly could be considered a "Roman" martyr,

108. See above, pp. 20-21 and n. 67.
109. This habit was very common in Hiberno-Latin, for example, and the use of *graecolatina* by Anastasius Bibliothecarius has also long been noticed (Berschin, *Greek Letters*, passim).
110. Berschin, *Greek Letters*, pp. 162-169.
111. Leonardi, "L'agiografia romana nel secolo IX," pp. 471-490.

whose Passion still existed in an authoritative form only in Greek, since the early translation was clearly inadequate. Anastasius Bibliothecarius himself knew of the Persian martyr, whose name he shared, no doubt from the complex *ad Aquas Salvias*. But he also knew of the Greek *Acta* and of the Greek collection of ancient miracles, for in about 873 he translated for Pope John VIII the acts of the VII Ecumenical Council (Nicea II),[112] where the discussions of the Fathers had centered on the miraculous powers of Anastasius in Rome, where his relic had become one of the attractions on the pilgrims' tour of the city and its environs. Indeed, the complete Greek *Acta* and collection of ancient miracles—a source of the iconodule florilegium deployed at Nicea II—may still have been available at the Lateran Palace, which was the center of the circles in which Anastasius Bibliothecarius's literary and diplomatic activities took place. There is absolutely no evidence to suggest whether or not Gregorius's translation of the *Passio* was carried out in these same circles dominated by the papal librarian. While the title of the dedicatee, the abbot Athanasius, might at first bring to mind a monastic context, Gregorius's self-appellation as *clericus*, on the other hand, points to a non-monastic background.[113]

In any event, the attribution of this second version of the *Passio S. Anastasii* to Rome is fairly conclusive, and this text can now be added to the body of evidence of Greek learning in Rome in the central Middle Ages. Equally important, Gregorius's version of the *Passio S. Anastasii* teaches that the translation of hagiographic texts was not a mechanical, linguistic transmutation, but that it could involve a deeper and more considered metamorphosis of the original. It foreshadows the complex process of revision and adaptation that characterizes the transmission of hagiographic texts, a subject treated in Chapters V-VII.

---

112. See above, pp. 6-9 and 110.

113. Anastasius Bibliothecarius himself had been given the office of abbot of S. Maria in Trastevere. Arnaldi, "Anastasio Bibliotecario," p. 28.

IV

THE ROMAN MIRACLE[1]: *BHL* 412

1. INTRODUCTION

The Roman Miracle tells the story of an exorcism. It recounts how a young woman was healed of demonic possession by the relic of the head of St. Anastasius during October and November 713 at the church of St. John the Baptist, which was attached to the monastery *ad Aquas Salvias*.[2] The text survives in both Greek and Latin.[3] The title of the Greek text, Θαύματα τοῦ ἁγίου Ἀναστασίου ἐν μερικῇ διηγήσει γενάμενα ἐν Ῥώμῃ τῇ πόλει ["The miracles of St. Anastasius in the particular narrative as took place in the city of Rome"],[4] perhaps results from an attempt to distinguish the miracle (or miracles) performed in Rome from those performed by the relic in the eastern parts of the empire, before its removal to the West, and collected under the title "ancient miracles."[5] Although it seems likely, judging from the available evidence, that the account of the miracles in the East was never

---

1. I use the short title "Roman Miracle" to translate the Bollandists' *Miraculum Romae ad Aquas Salvias* (*BHL* 412), published in Poncelet, "Catalogus codicum hagiographicorum latinorum Bibliothecae ambrosianae," pp. 233-241. My edition is found below, pp. 339-361; I refer to it by line number. The English translation is on pp. 44-52.

2. This was most likely an oratory serving the parochial, and hence public, functions of the monastery, since the church where the relic was kept was within the monastic enclosure and inaccessible to women. See Chapter I, pp. 9-10, 19-20.

3. The Greek text was published first in Usener, *Acta m. Anastasii Persae*, pp. 14-20, and now by Bernard Flusin (I, 157-187 with a facing French translation). As in the case of the *Acta*, I refer to Flusin's edition by chapter and line.

4. The reading of the Greek title is problematic; see Flusin I, 164 n. 1 and my note to the text.

5. *BHG* 89g-90, discussed in Chapter I, p. 5.

translated into Latin, it would be surprising indeed if the earlier miraculous activities of the relics were not known at the Aquae Salviae, where the Roman exorcism took place, and where this account was written down. It is known that by 770 the papal library in Rome contained the Greek collection of ancient miracles, which was cited in the iconodule florilegium compiled for Nicea II.[6] Furthermore, the text of the Roman Miracle itself contains some verbal echoes of the earlier collection.[7] The Latin title, on the other hand, "Incipit Miraculum Anastasii incliti martyris quod factum est temporibus papae Constantini urbis Romae ... in monasterio quod appellatur Aqua Salvia," places the miracle at the monastery at the Aquae Salviae, and makes no reference to the earlier miracles that took place in the East. I believe that the original version of this miracle text was written in Greek, and then translated into Latin. I also believe that the Latin translation was eventually revised and added to Gregorius clericus's second translation of the Greek *Acta, BHL* 411a, to create a "Roman" dossier for the Persian monk, whose cult was being integrated into the ancient martyrial traditions of the city.

The Miracle was composed between 1 November 713 and 31 August 714.[8] Its author, although anonymous, appears throughout the narrative as a witness to the extraordinary events, which he describes in great details in the preface; he refers to Rome as "*this* ancient city,"[9] addresses his audience in the prologue as "dearest brethren," and adds that he is writing at the command of "our holy Fathers."[10] It thus seems reasonable to suppose that he was a monk of the monastery *ad Aquas Salvias* when it was still Greek. This account of the exorcism must have been motivated partly by the desire both to make known the miraculous powers of the saint

---

6. See Chapter I, pp. 8-9.

7. See below, n. 21.

8. The Greek preface, missing in the Latin tradition, specifies that the writer is writing in the year of the world 6222, in the twelfth indiction (1.15-16) i.e. the period between 1 September 713 and 31 August 714. The text itself states that the final events of the exorcism take place on 1 November 713 (9.14), thus narrowing the chronological parameters even further.

9. ταύτης τῆς πρεσβυτέρας Ῥώμης (1.19-20).

10. 1.12, 1.10-11.

and to enhance the prestige of the monastic community that possessed the relic, which, from the outset, had been instrumental
in the development of the cult of the Persian monk. However,
it is possible that the impetus to write down a record of these
events may have come from the bishop Theopentus, the father
of the stricken girl and a principal character in the narrative.[11] It
is the bishop's decision to go to the church, where the relic of St.
Anastasius is kept, to seek help for his daughter, ostentatiously
rejecting the recourse to sorcery and phylacteries suggested by his
advisors.[12] His piety is alluded to on several occasions; his wealth
and prestige accord him and his daughter unusual and direct access
to the relic.[13] It is possible too that the monastery of St. Anastasius was a beneficiary of his munificence.

The *Bibliotheca Hagiographica Latina* lists two versions of the Roman Miracle of Anastasius.[14] A collation of all the known manuscripts of the Roman Miracle shows that in reality there is only a

---

11. It has also been proposed that the author may have been a member
of Bishop Theopentus's entourage. See Flusin I, 157.

12. For the widespread practice of magic, including the use of phylacteries in Rome in the early eighth century, see Llewellyn, *Rome in the Dark
Ages*, p. 130. Sorcerers are frequently found in the Byzantine hagiographic
sources surveyed in Auzépy, "L'évolution de l'attitude face au miracle à Byzance (VII-IXe siècle)," pp. 36-37, which, however, makes no mention of the
Roman Miracle.

13. Since women cannot enter the monastery, the relic is brought out to
the church of St. John the Baptist; a tooth of the saint is hung around the
girl's neck, and the relic of the head is even taken out of the reliquary and
placed on a silver platter on top of the girl's head. On the other hand, Theopentus's wealth is one of his daughter's attractions to suitors and hence an
indirect cause of her predicament. See also Flusin II, 378.

14. P. 68; *Supplementum* p. 53. *BHL* 412 is the number given to the version published by Poncelet as in n. 1 above. The second version, numbered
BHL 413, is identified by the Bollandists with the text from which Cesare
Baronio published excerpts in the *Annales Ecclesiastici*. It differs in specifying
the name—Theopentus—of the *episcopus natione Syrus* in the opening chapter
of *BHL* 412, and in missing a final passage that is contained in the published
text. See below, pp. 339-340. The text classified as *BHL* 413b and found in
BAV, Vat. lat. 1193 (=V in my study), is in reality *BHL* 412, with numerous
revisions and corrections. There is an expurgated Italian translation of the
Roman Miracle in [Barbiero], *S. Paolo e le Tre Fontane*, pp. 82-84.

single version of this text, and that the differences among the manuscripts are merely textual variants. I have retained the first number, *BHL* 412, when referring to the text of the Roman Miracle.

2. THE RELATIONSHIP BETWEEN THE GREEK AND LATIN TEXTS

Even a superficial comparison of the Latin and Greek texts shows that the two versions are very close to each other, and that one must be a translation of the other. That the Greek composition came first is proved beyond doubt by a comparison of the language and sentence structure of the two versions. Such an examination, furthermore, indicates that the writer of the Latin version was not a master of Latin, and that his native tongue was Greek.

Although relatively simple, the Greek version has a richer, more varied vocabulary than the Latin. Frequently, the same Latin word is used to translate two or more Greek words, sometimes unidiomatically, suggesting that the translator did not have a good enough mastery of Latin to render the nuances of the Greek text and that his Latin vocabulary was not as extensive as the Greek text required. An example is provided by the Latin verb *eicio*, which translates every occurrence—eleven altogether—of both ἐκβάλλω and ἐξωθῶ, without any distinction, at times obfuscating in Latin the meaning of the original Greek.

ἐξεούμεθα τοῦτο τὸ δαιμόνιον ἐκ ταύτης τῆς νεάνιδος (3.6-7)
Eiciemus istud daemonium de hac puella (l. 27)

Οὐ δυνήσεταί με ἔνθεν ἐξεώσασθαι (5.9)
Non me potest eicere (ll. 72-73)

οὐδείς ἐστιν ὅστις δυνήσεταί με ἐκβαλεῖν (5.11)
non est qui possit me eicere (l. 74)

Ἐξεοῦταί σε ὁ Κύριος (5.12)
"Eiciet te dominus ..." (l. 75)

Οὐ μή με ἐκβάλῃ ἐκεῖνος ὁ Ναζαρηνὸς (5.13-14)
"Non me eiciet Nazarenus ..." (ll. 76-77)

ἐκβαλόντες τὴν τιμίαν κάραν (5.19)
Eicientes autem caput beati martyris (l. 82)

Οὐ δυνήσεταί με ἐκβάλαι οὗτος ὁ κυνοφάγος (5.21)
Non me potest eicere cynophagus iste (l. 87)

ἵνα ἐξεώσηταί με ἐξ αὐτῆς (6.27)
quia non me potest *eicere* de isto corpore (ll. 126-127)

αὐτοί σε ἐκβάλλουσιν ἐκ ταύτης τῆς κόρης (7.14)
ipsi te eiciunt de isto corpore (ll. 146-147)

οὐ δυνήσεταί με ἐξεώσασθαι (7.17)
de isto corpore eicere me non potest (ll. 150-151)

καὶ αὐτὸς ἐκβάλλει με ἐκ τοῦ σώματος τούτου (8.7-8)
ipse veniet et eiciet me de isto corpore (l. 163)

The problems that can arise from this rote insertion of *eicio* are illustrated most clearly in the fifth example above, where *eicientes autem caput beati martyris* is a misinterpretation of the Greek text.[15] It is noteworthy that the pseudo-Cyril glossary lists *eicio* first under ἐκβάλλω.[16]

An even more striking example of the generic use of a common Latin word to translate a number of Greek words, conflating a range of meanings into one term, is the verb *adduco,* which is used to translate five different Greek verbs. The Greek verb ἄγω occurs seven times in the Greek version of the Miracle, and in all corresponding Latin passages it is translated with a form of the verb *adduco.*[17] In addition, *adduco* is used to translate four other Greek verbs, each of which occurs only once in the Greek text, namely, φέρω, παράγω, προάγω, αἴρω.[18] A third example, which again

---

15. Two of the manuscripts of the Roman Miracle attempt to correct this puzzling reading: N reads *adducentes* and V *extraentes*, both rendering the Greek meaning more accurately. See p. 340 and "Descriptive List."

16. *CGL*, 288. But cf. "Ἐξωθω repello expello extrudo" (*CGL*, 304).

17. I.e. ἠγάγετε (5.7) = *adduxistis* (l. 71); ἤγαγεν (6.6) = *adduxit* (l. 99); ὥστε ἀγαγεῖν (9.6) = *adduceret lumen* (ll. 192-193); ἤγαγέν με (9.22) = *adduxit me* (l. 205); ἤγαγες (9.29) = *adduxisti* (ll. 210-211). There are two other occurrences of ἄγω; one is found in a passage omitted in the Latin (2.8); the other is actually a reconstruction by Flusin based on the Latin phrase *duxerunt eam* (9.18). While this is plausible, *duco* is never found to translate ἄγω; in fact, *duxerunt eam* is the only occurrence of *duco* in the Latin text. Given the translator's strict adherence to the use of *adduco* for ἄγω, one would expect a different Greek word for *duxerunt*. *Adduco* occurs one other time in the Latin text: *adduxit lutum* (l. 85); the Greek text has a lacuna here, however.

18. ἐνεχθῶσιν (4.16) = *adducerentur* (ll. 54-55); παρήχθησαν (4.20) = *adductae sunt* (ll. 58-59); προαχθῆναι (5.2) = *adductum fuisset* (l. 66); ἦρεν αὐτὸν ὅθεν

shows the more varied vocabulary of the Greek, is the use of *ambulare* translating three Greek verbs, ἄπειμι, ἀπέρχομαι, and πορεύω.[19] These examples could easily be multiplied.

Numerous occurrences of unidiomatic Latin expressions also suggest that the Greek text came first. *Quia*, for example, is used to translate ὅτι, and introduces direct discourse.[20] Many words suggest the translator's uncritical reliance on a glossary: *eicientes* to translate ἐκβαλόντες in the passage above, or *periret* (l. 66) for ἐκπέσῃ (5.2). There are also a few cases of Greek words simply transliterated into Latin, such as *cynophagus* (ll. 71, 87) for κυνοφάγος (5.8 and 5.21).[21] Several instances of weak translations may be attributable to the writer's poor grasp of Latin.[22]

Another indication of the anteriority of the Greek text is provided by the biblical quotations, which reveal that the translator was not consistently familiar with the wording of the Latin Bible. There are eight scriptural phrases used in the Latin version of the Roman Miracle. These are all found in the Greek text, except for

---

ἔκειτο (10.12) = *adduxit eum et levavit* (l. 230). This last is another striking example of an inaccurate Latin translation of the Greek.

19. ἐπορεύθη ... ἐν Σικελίᾳ (6.4-5) = *ipse ambulavit in Sicilia* (ll. 97-98); Ἐν δὲ τῷ ἀπιέναι (6.7) = *dum ambularet* (l. 100); ἀπέλθατε καὶ λύσατε (6.16) = *ambulate ac solvite* (l. 114); εἰς Ἀνατολὴν ἀπῆλθεν (6.21) = *in orientem enim ambulavit* (ll. 119-120); Κἀκεῖσε ἐπορεύθη (6.24) = *et ibi ambulavit* (l. 124); καὶ οὗτος ὁ γέρων ἐπορεύθη (7.16) = *et iste ambulavit* (l. 149). Another occurrence of ἄπειμι is translated with *eo*: Ἀναστὰς ἄπειμι (4.1) = *Surgam et eam* (l. 41). But this is very much the exception, and could easily be attributed to the commonness of this word. (Two other occurrences of ἄπειμι are in passages omitted in the Latin.)

20. ὅτι· «Ἡμεῖς ποιοῦμεν ... (3.6) = *quia "Faciemus* ... (ll. 26-27); ὅτι· «Ἐκεῖνος ὁ νεανίας ... (6.3-4) = *quia "Ille adulescens ..."* (ll. 96-97).

21. This word appears also in the Greek collection of miracles performed during the translation of the relics from Persia to Palestine (See Flusin I, 149 [16.18]). This suggests that the author of the Roman Miracle may have been familiar with the ancient miracles collection.

22. Perhaps the most striking example is ἐγγράφως ποιῶ (11.32) by which the devil, in a dramatic scene, makes his formal promise to St. Anastasius to leave the body of the girl forever, by, in effect, signing a contract. This phrase is blandly rendered in Latin as *satisfacio* (l. 270), which could be an example of poor translation. It is, however, possible that *satis* is a correction of an attempt at translating ἐγγράφως ποιῶ literally as "scriptum/scripte facio."

one whose wording suggests, however, that it was there originally and that the pertinent Greek passage now has a lacuna. The translator, therefore, was in all cases attempting to render into Latin the biblical citations he found in the Greek text.[23]

The three phrases from the New Testament show most clearly that the translator did not know the Vulgate well:

1. "Quaerite et invenietis, petite et accipietis, pulsate et aperietur vobis" (ll. 176-177)

   «Αἰτεῖτε καὶ δοθήσεται ὑμῖν, ζητεῖτε καὶ εὑρήσετε, κρούετε καὶ ἀνοιγήσεται ὑμῖν» (8.22)

   Vulgate: "Petite et dabitur vobis, quaerite et invenietis, pulsate et aperietur vobis."

While the Greek text is a direct quotation of Mt 7.7, the Latin translation departs from the Vulgate by the insertion of the middle phrase. In some manuscripts of the Roman Miracle, the middle phrase is omitted,[24] no doubt in conformity with biblical wording.

2. (ll. 181-182): The Greek text (8.28) refers to the story told in Mc 5.22, where the operative word is ἀρχισυναγώγου (rendered as *archisynagogus* in the Vulgate). The Latin text uses *principis*, which is the word used in the story as told in Mt 9.18 (ἄρχων). This again suggests a lack of familiarity with the wording of the Latin Bible, and, though less likely, with the existence of the different versions of the story in Mark and Matthew.

3. Et Dominus in evangelio ait: "Non periet capillus capitis vestri," et alia multa (ll. 238-239)

   Cf. Lc 21.18: καὶ θρὶξ ἐκ τῆς κεφαλῆς ὑμῶν οὐ μὴ ἀπόληται.

   Vulgate: et capillus de capite vestro non peribit.

This phrase is missing in the Greek version of the *Miraculum*. But the wording of the Latin text suggests that its source is the Greek biblical verse, which must have been quoted in the Greek text. The use of the genitive *capitis vestri*, corresponding to the Greek ἐκ τῆς κεφαλῆς ὑμῶν, is particularly telling. The Latin phrasing indicates that the translator was not familiar with the Vulgate text; several Latin manuscripts of the Roman Miracle changed the text into *de capite vestro*.

---

23. Two of these citations are too short to be significant (Prv 13.14 and Ps 33.19, both in cap. 7).

24. The phrase is not found in manuscripts NVMG.

In stark contrast to the citations from the Gospels, however, the Latin text demonstrates that the translator was quite familiar with the Latin Psalter, and in particular with the Roman version that antedates the so-called LXX or Gallican version and was in common use in Rome up to the modern period.[25] These are:

1. Adimple quod dixit propheta: 'Qui sanat contritos corde et alligat contritiones eorum' (ll. 173-175)

   ἐκπλήρωσον ὅπερ ὁ σὸς προφήτης ἐκήρυξεν λέγων· «'Ο ἰώμενος τοὺς συντετριμμένους τῇ καρδίᾳ καὶ δεσμεύων τὰ συντρίμματα αὐτῶν» (8.19-20)

   Ps 146.3 qui sanat contritos corde et alligat contritiones eorum.[26]

2. Et rememorati sumus, quia fidelis dominus in verbis suis (l. 236)

   καὶ ἐγνωμεν σαφῶς <ὡς πιστὸς Κύριος ἐν τοῖς λόγοις αὐτοῦ> (10.18-19)

   Ps 144.13 fidelis Dominus in verbis suis[27]

3. "Dominus custodit omnia ossa eorum: unum ex eis non contereretur" (ll. 237-238)

   «Κύριος φυλάσσει πάντα τὰ ὀστᾶ τῶν ἁγίων αὐτοῦ, ἓν ἐξ αὐτῶν συντριβῆναι μὴ συγχωρῶν» (10.20)

   Ps 33.21 Dominus custodit omnia ossa eorum: unum ex eis non conteretur.[28]

In all three examples, the fidelity to the Latin Bible is evident; the second and third examples, in particular, suggest that the translator was familiar with the Roman version of the Psalter. In the first and third examples, the biblical text cited in the Latin translation departs from the Greek text of the Roman Miracle. One must conclude, therefore, that the translator knew the Latin Psalms, most likely in the Roman version (as we would expect), but not the Gos-

---

25. Weber, Le Psautier romain et les autres anciens psautiers latins, pp. viii-ix and ad psalmos.

26. The Roman and the LXX (Septuagint) version are the same; the iuxta Hebraeos reads: "qui sanat contritos corde et alligat plagas eorum."

27. The LXX version reads: "fidelis Dominus in omnibus verbis suis."

28. "Dominus custodit omnia ossa eorum: unum ex his non conteretur" (LXX); iuxta Hebraeos: "Dominus custodit omnia ossa eius: unum ex eis non confringetur."

pels.[29] This is not surprising: the Psalter, more than any other part of the Bible, is associated with monastic observance, recited regularly during the Divine Office. Even a hellenophone monk living in Rome must have been exposed to the Latin psalms. Another possibility is that the translator had access to a bilingual copy of the Psalter. Unlike other biblical books, bilingual psalters were available throughout the entire medieval period.[30] Certainly, the fact that the three citations from the Gospels are authentic in the Greek text, but not in the Latin, confirms that the Greek version of the *Miraculum* came first.

The Roman Miracle of Anastasius is one of the very few texts known to have been produced by the Greek-speaking community of eighth-century Rome. The only other significant extant original Greek texts composed in the city during the seventh and eighth centuries are the preface to the translation of Pope Gregory's *Dialogues* (741-752), and the Life of Martin I (730-754), the martyr against monothelism.[31] Along with the Roman Miracle of Anastasius, these other near-contemporary works reveal the broader theological and political interests of the Greek community of the city, which, as in the previous century when the *Acta S. Anastasii* was first translated into Latin, still centered on the defense of orthodoxy.[32] But the Roman Miracle alone among these texts is concerned with contemporary events taking place within the community itself. It is a unique witness, and tells us much about the Greek-speaking population of early medieval Rome.

29. Of course it is possible that the faithfulness to the biblical wording in the Psalm citations is the result of correction, but one would then have to ask why the manuscripts do not reveal variation, as they do in the case of the Gospel citations.

30. Berschin, *Greek Letters*, pp. 38-41.

31. A short litany of the saints composed between 687 and 701 also survives (Santerre, *Les moines grecs* I, 138-140, 155-156, 194-196, with further bibliography). Sansterre convincingly supports the claim that the Life of Martin was indeed written in Rome.

32. See Chapter II.

3. DATE AND PLACE OF COMPOSITION

Unlike the Greek original, the Latin translation tells us little about its historical context or when it was composed.[33] This places it in a rather broad timespan: between the date of composition of the Greek text, that is the period November 713–August 714, and the late tenth century, when the earliest surviving manuscript witnesses were copied.

The manuscript evidence suggests that the original translation was done in Rome, where the Greek text originated, and that the major revisions (discussed below, pp. 141ff.) were also made there. The manuscript diffusion of the text appears to begin in the city;[34] some of its oldest witnesses are Roman legendaries; Rome and the surrounding regions to the east and north were the almost exclusive areas in which the text was transmitted. Since the translator's native language was Greek, one can easily suppose that he was a member of the monastic community at the Aquae Salviae, where the Greek text was most likely written and where a copy would be readily available. The fact that the entire Latin transmission of the text as it has reached us omits the name of the abbot of the monastery—Theodosius, the name supplied by the Greek model[35]—might argue against locating the translation at the monastery. However, this omission may reflect an error in transmission rather than an intentional deletion, and the fact that the translator was familiar with the Roman Psalter supports the likelihood that he was based in a monastery in Rome.

4. THE NATURE OF THE TRANSLATED TEXT

The method of translation found in the Roman Miracle differs from both the first and second translations of the *Acta*. The text,

33. Flusin II, 380 n. 164, states that Siegmund, *Die Überlieferung*, pp. 227-228, believes that the Greek and Latin versions are near contemporary. In fact, Siegmund does not refer to the text of the Roman Miracle at all. No one has proposed any date for the translation of the Miracle text.

34. See the introduction to my edition, pp. 339-346 and also below, pp. 144-147.

35. τὸν προεστῶτα τῆς μονῆς Θεοδόσιον ὀνόματι (9.10-11).

as we know it, is neither the literal, word-for-word rendition of the early translation of the *Acta* (*BHL* 410b) nor an attempt to create a Latin literary piece like Gregorius clericus's second translation (*BHL* 411a). A close comparison of the following chapter will allow us to analyze further the translation technique found in this text, and examine the broader relationship between the Greek and Latin versions.[36]

(7.1-19) καὶ τί πολλὰ λέγω; Ἤρξατο ὁ πονηρὸς δαίμων συνεχῶς ἡμέρας τε καὶ νυκτὸς ἱλαρύνειν τὴν κόρην χαίρων τε καὶ γελῶν, καθάπερ τις παραγίνεται πρὸς τὸν φίλον αὐτοῦ· καὶ εἰσελθὼν ἐν αὐτῇ ἀπεφθέγγετο δι' αὐτῆς ὕβρεις τινὰς καὶ λόγους βλασφήμους < ... > καὶ εἰς τοὺς ἐκεῖσε παρατυχόντας μοναχούς. Καὶ πολλάκις βοῶν ἔλεγεν· «Οὐὰ οὐά, τί ἠργασάμην σήμερον; Τρεῖς φόνους ἐποίησα.» Καὶ γελῶν ἔφασκεν· «Ἐπιχαίρομαι ἐν τοῖς ἔργοις μου.» Ἔλεγεν δὲ καὶ τοῦτο, ὅτι· < ... > «Ἄρτι ἐλήλυθα ἀπὸ Σπανίας καὶ πολλοὺς φόνους ἐποίησα, καὶ διὰ τοῦτο καυχώμενος λαλῶ.» Καὶ τις τῶν ἀδελφῶν ἔφη αὐτῷ· «Ἐπικατάρατε, ἵνα τί σὺ ἐκδιώκεις τοὺς δούλους τοῦ Θεοῦ; Ἐχθρὸς καὶ πολέμιος τυγχάνων τοῦ ανθρωπίνου γένους, ἐτοιμάζεταί σοι ἡ τῆς γεέννης κόλασις.» Καὶ ὁ δαίμων ἀποκριθεὶς εἰπεν· «Ἄπιθι εἰς τὸ σκότος, ἀββᾶ· οὐδέποτε ὑποκλινῶ τὴν κεφαλήν μου καὶ τὸ διάδημά μου ἔμπροσθεν τοῦ Ναζαρηνοῦ, αλλὰ κατὰ τοὺς θεσμούς μου, οὕτως ποιῶ, ὅτι τινὰ οὐ δειλιῶ.» Καὶ ἡμῶν λεγόντων αὐτῷ· «Ἰδοὺ οἱ ἀπόστολοι τοῦ Κυρίου ἡμῶν Ἰησοῦ Χριστοῦ Πέτρος καὶ Παῦλος, αὐτοί σε ἐκβάλλουσιν ἐκ ταύτης τῆς κόρης», ὁ δὲ δαίμων εἰπεν· «Οὗτος ὁ κακόγηρος, τί ἠργάσατο; Ἐγὼ ἐποίησα ἵνα χρισθῇ ὁ Φιλιππικὸς εἰς βασιλέα, καθότι φίλος μου ἦν, καὶ οὗτος ὁ γέρων ἐπορεύθη ἐν τῇ ἡμέρᾳ τῆς Πεντηκοστῆς καὶ ἔχρισεν ἕτερον. Διὸ οὗ δυνήσεταί με ἐξεώσασθαι.» Οὐκ ἐπαύσατο δὲ βλασφημίας προσφέρων ῥήματα κατὰ τῶν ἁγίων τοῦ Χριστοῦ μαρτύρων καὶ κατὰ τῶν δούλων τοῦ Χριστοῦ τὰ ὅμοια καὶ χείρονα τούτων.

(ll. 128-155) Et quid plurima? veniebat frequenter die noctuque hilaris, gaudens et ridens per puellam, quemadmodum qui veniet in convivium ad amicum suum, et ingrediebatur in puellam et blasphemias et iniurias faciebat in maiestatem et in martyres et in episcopos et in presbyteros et in diaconos et in monachos. Et multotiens dicebat gaudens: "Vah, vah, quid hodie operatus sum? Hodie tria homicidia feci, et ecce gratulor in operibus meis." Et altera occasione dicebat: "Feci hodie ut miles dormiret cum ancilla Dei; et ecce gratulor." Post modicos autem dies iterum dixit: "Modo veni de Hispania et feci ibi homicidia multa et ef-

---

36. See above, pp. 47-48 for the English translation.

fusiones sanguinum. Et ecce multo magis gratulor in operibus meis."
Et quidam de fratribus dixit ei: "Maledicte, nequissime spiritus, hostis
humani generis, quid persequeris hominem qui factus est ad imaginem
Dei? Praeparatur tibi gehennae tormentus, flamma inextinguibilis. Da
honorem Deo et Iesu Christo filio eius, qui venturus est iudicare saeculum per ignem." Et daemon respondit: "Numquam inclinabo caput
meum et coronam meam ante Nazarenum. Sed secundum canones meos
sic facio quia aliquem non timeo." Dicentibus nobis: "Ecce apostoli
Domini nostri Iesu Christi Petrus et Paulus, ipsi te eiciunt de isto corpore." Daemon respondit: "O iste senex malus Petrus, quid est operatus? Ego feceram ut regnaret Philippicus, quia amicus meus erat; et iste
ambulavit in die Pentecosten et ordinavit alium. Haec operatus est in
me; sed de isto corpore eicere me non potest." Et unus de fratribus
dedit palmam puellae dicens: "Non facias iniuriam in maiestatem et in
martyres." Daemon dixit: "Caedite, quid mihi pertinet de corpore
isto?" Et non cessabat in blasphemia contra martyres et servos Dei,
similia, et alia multa quae per singula enarrare longum est.

In the first two sentences, the Latin carefully follows the Greek,
including some of the word order,[37] but with a few noteworthy
departures. The omission of ὁ πονηρὸς δαίμων is most likely a reflection of the Greek text available to the translator, although it
could be the result of an accident in the transmission of the Latin
account. The elimination of λέγω, on the other hand, may be due
to willful choice, for *Et quid plurima?* does not require a verb.
Respect for Latin idiom is also shown by the use of *die noctuque*
rather than the genitive used in the Greek. While *hilaris* does not
have the force of ἱλαρύνειν, the phrase *veniebat ... hilaris, gaudens
et ridens per puellam* is a good description of the demonic activities. The phrase *in convivium* is not found in the Greek text as we
now have it; the Latin manuscripts suggest that it may have been
there originally, or was added at the very beginning stages of the
Latin transmission. It sounds authentic, and emphasizes the ob-
scene intentions and behavior of the demon, who boasts that he
has caused *ut miles dormiret cum ancilla Dei.* This phrase has been
eliminated in the Greek manuscript tradition, suggesting the possibility of censorship.[38]

37. Note, for example, "veniebat frequenter die noctuque hilaris."
38. These particulars are also omitted from the Italian translation made
by a Cistercian monk, cited in n. 14, above.

On the other hand, the above passage calls attention to the lacunae and other corruptions that mar the integrity of each version, and particularly the Greek text.[39] The Latin text in this chapter, as in the entire work, is generally more full, preserving details not found in the Greek.[40] In addition to the ones mentioned above, there are two other important phrases found only in the Latin: *et iniuriam faciebat ... in diaconos*, and *Feci hodie ... iterum dixit*. The Latin text in turn omits the last part of Καὶ πολλάκις βοῶν ἔλεγεν merging in its place γελῶν ἔφασκεν (*Et multotiens dicebat gaudens*). Given the problems of the Greek transmission, however, it is possible that the Latin is the more accurate witness of the original text. The words uttered by one of the monks (*Maledicte ... saeculum per ignem*) reflect the original, but are not its exact replica. Again, the Latin contains a fuller text than the Greek, but as the

39. The problem is not restricted to this chapter. A comparison of the entire text of the two versions consistently shows that the Greek text available to the Latin translator was fuller than the one that has been preserved in only two manuscripts (Berlin, Deutsche Staatbibliothek, gr. 54, s. X, =A in Flusin's edition; and Vat. grec. 1641, s. X-XI from southern Italy, =W in Flusin's edition). Had it survived, this manuscript would have been extremely useful in reconstructing the Greek archetype. Such a reconstruction, as Bernard Flusin has already indicated, is impossible, however, since there is no way of telling whether all the departures of the Latin from the surviving Greek text in fact reflect the model used by the translator, or are examples of corruption and emendation in the early stages of the Latin tradition. Flusin I, 161 provides this stemma to summarize his conclusions:

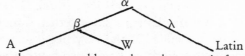

40. Among the most notable are those that contain factual information, such as that in the opening Latin chapter (ll. 9-10=2.1), which transmits the name of the Syrian bishop Theopentus; the detailed report of the early possession and the devil's dislike for incense and desire for filth (ll. 82-86 =5.18ff); and the date on which the devil entered the girl and the beginning of the manifestation of the possession one month later (ll. 102-106=6.7). The Latin passages that can be used to complete the Greek are easily discernible in Flusin's text, where they are printed in bold letters in the *apparatus criticus*. On the relationship of the Latin and Greek texts, see also Flusin I, 158-161. Discrepancies between the two versions are noted in my edition.

additions are generalities (*Da honorem* ...), it is difficult to say whether or not they are pious expansions of the original. The Latin, somewhat significantly, names the apostle Peter as the old man responsible for the defeat of the emperor Philippicus.[41] Only the Latin preserves the incident of the monk who slaps the demon, and the devil's sneering reply. The Latin omission of the demon's words, Ἄπιθι εἰς τὸ σκότος, probably arose from a faulty Greek model. A final departure from the Greek is found in the concluding sentence of the chapter where *contra martyres et servos Dei* translates κατὰ τῶν ἁγίων τοῦ Χριστοῦ μαρτύρων καὶ κατὰ τῶν δούλων τοῦ Χριστοῦ, and *similia, et alia multa quae per singula enarrare longum est* translates τὰ ὅμοια καὶ χείρονα τούτων. These alterations appear to be intentional, rather than accidental.[42]

This chapter confirms that the Latin translation, as a whole, is quite faithful to the Greek text, and that it differs in style from the earlier translations. There are no major rearrangements of the text, no significant additions[43] or deletions.[44] Departures from the Greek model are generally variations in word order or lexical changes. The vocabulary used in the Latin version is frequently less accurate and more bland than in the Greek. The verbs *ambulavit ... ordinavit*, for example, do not convey precisely the meaning of ἐπορεύθη ... ἔχρισεν; *canones* seems a poor equivalent of θεσμούς.

---

41. Emperor Philippicus ruled from 11 December 711 to 3 June 713, and is best known for his attempt to revive monothelism. The Latin text alone preserves (or adds?) the name Petrus ("O iste senex malus Petrus ..." (ll. 147-148); cf. κακόγηρος (7.15). The passage has been seen as a reflection of the strong reaction in Rome against Philippicus. See Llewellyn, *Rome in the Dark Ages*, pp. 164-165.

42. I believe, however, that the Latin equivalent for προσφέρων (7.18) has been accidentally omitted.

43. Except for the addition of *Petrus*, although I am not convinced that it did not appear in the original Greek text.

44. The Greek version shows that there are lacunae also in the Latin text, but these are not as numerous or long as the lacunae in the Greek. The Latin text, for example, does not contain the date (of the year of the world) and the indiction, both preserved in the Greek (1.14-16). These omissions are marked in the notes to my edition. See also Flusin I, 160-161. In effect, only by taking the Greek and Latin documents together can we fully reconstruct the original account of the exorcism.

The Latin Miracle text, as discussed above, employs a very repetitive lexicon,[45] and exhibits many examples of unidiomatic Latin usage, as well as some examples of poor grammar. But there are no systematic constructions that violate the rules of Latin grammar or syntax, as, for example, the attempt to convey the article in Latin, as found in the early translation of the *Acta*. There are indications, however, that improvements may have been made to the Latin text either during its transmission, or perhaps when a final chapter was added to the Latin version, which will be discussed further below.

The translator certainly possessed a working knowledge of Latin; in fact, the translation of the Roman Miracle is one of the very few texts that can be used as evidence for the knowledge of Latin among Greek monks in Rome during the early Middle Ages. It is generally thought that the large majority of Greek ecclesiastics did not need to learn Latin, and that an extensive knowledge of the language of the Romans would have been necessary only for those in high positions. Even Maximus the Confessor, for example, is believed to have learned little Latin while he lived in Rome in the middle of the seventh century.[46] The translation of Gregory the Great's *Dialogues* into Greek by Pope Zacharias (741-752) was made for the benefit of Greek monks living in Rome who had no Latin.[47] The competence of the Latin translation of the Roman Miracle suggests that there were at least some Greek monks living in Rome who managed to learn Latin well enough to be familiar with the Latin Psalter, and to translate a simple text such as this into intelligible Latin.

45. *Dicit* and *respondit* are virtually the only verbs of telling used in the text.
46. Sansterre, *Les moines grecs* I, 20-21, 62-63, 72-75. See above, pp. 82-83.
47. The famous manuscript of the Greek *Dialogues*, Vat. grec. 1666, copied around the year 800 in a Roman Greek monastery, includes some short Latin expressions in the margins (e.g. *ora pro me*) written in Greek characters (Sansterre, *Les moines grecs* I, 72-75).

5. THE DOSSIER OF A "ROMAN" MARTYR

Special consideration needs to be given to two major differences between the Greek and Latin versions of the Roman Miracle. These are not incidental differences arising from discrepancies in the Greek copy used by the translator, or from the transmission of the Latin text, but should instead be viewed as deliberate changes. They reveal how the text of the Roman Miracle was manipulated and joined to the Roman text of the *Passio—BHL* 411a, the second translation redacted by Gregorius clericus—so as to create a literary dossier to support the cult of the Persian soldier who had become enshrined as a Roman martyr.

The first of these divergences is the omission in the Latin text of the Greek author's preface, a passage that places the work in its historical context, the Greek community of early eighth-century Rome, and the monastic complex *ad Aquas Salvias*, and gives the writer an opportunity to present himself to his listeners and readers. The Greek preface is concerned mostly with the writer's justification of his work, which follows a long-standing tradition and employs well-worn topoi. Most prominent among these is the author's claim that modesty and a sense of unworthiness had prevented him from writing, and that these scruples were overcome at last both by his obedience to the commands of his superiors and by the power and glory of the subject.

It is possible to suppose that the original translator may have chosen to eliminate the Greek preface because it was historically irrelevant to the circumstances in which the translation was being prepared.[48] But the faithful, verbatim adherence of the translation to the Greek model does not support the conclusion that the preface was omitted out of a desire for historical accuracy.[49] There is another possibility, namely, that the Greek preface was indeed originally translated along with the rest of the text, but later removed for a specific reason. This deletion could have taken place

48. The language of the Greek preface is particularly obscure, and the text problematic (see Flusin's edition), and this may also explain its omission from the Latin translation.

49. This point is reinforced by the continued presence of the original Greek writer in the Latin: see e.g. the phrase "dicentibus nobis" (l. 145).

at the same time that a final chapter was added to the translation, a passage that is peculiar to the Latin and has no correspondence in the original Greek model.[50] This is the second major difference between the Greek and Latin versions.

The concluding passage appended to the Latin version of the Roman Miracle is a rhetorical peroration, but its function in the Latin text is similar to that performed by the Greek preface. Both, for example, address the audience directly; both emphasize the spiritual value of the narration of the Miracle. The words of the Greek preface are even echoed in the Latin conclusion.[51] It is clear that this added, final chapter would make the insertion of a translation of the Greek preface redundant.

The style and language of this last chapter differ greatly from the main part of the Miracle text. The author of the additional chapter clearly valued literary artifice as reflected in the use of antithesis and rhyme, as in *torquendo deficiebat ... patiendo vincebat* (ll. 281-282).[52] Most striking, however, in this chapter is the evident use of cursus. There are twenty-two clause endings in this final chapter according to my punctuation.[53] Of these, six end in the traditional cursus planus, five in the cursus velox, and one in the tardus.[54] In addition, there are four clauses that have the heterotomous end-

50. Usener, p. VII, without giving any explanation simply says that the last chapter was added by the translator.

51. Cf. the following Latin phrases with the opening sentences of the Greek preface: "Et ideo debemus mirabilia et laudem beati martyris Anastasii suaviter enarrare ..." (ll. 276-277); and "Fratres carissimi, contremescit cor meum et renes mei resolvuntur quotienscumque ..." (ll. 295-296).

52. The following phrases are similarly constructed: "secabat ... membra, reficiebat ... medicina"; "reus ... Deus"; "iustus ... Christus"; "armatus ... munitus"; "meruerunt ... negaverunt" (ll. 280-300).

53. In my count, I have included even the two clauses that end with proper names, i.e. "... Iesu Christi" (ll. 286-287), and "... Anastasium" (l. 298). Neither of these two clauses ends in a favored cadence.

54. Cursus planus is here defined as a clause ending consisting of a paroxytone word followed by a three-syllable paroxytone, such as *fulgebat aspectus*; velox as a proparoxytone word followed by a four-syllable paroxytone, such as *indefatigabilis medicina*; tardus as a paroxytone followed by a four-syllable proparoxytone, such as *confessione victoria*.

ings for the cursus planus,[55] thus bringing the total number of the planus endings to ten. Hence, almost seventy-five percent of the clauses follow the cursus. Even if a full statistical analysis is not possible, because of the small scale of the sample,[56] such a high percentage of cursus endings indicates that the writer of this chapter intentionally sought them out.[57] The use of cursus in the final chapter is in marked contrast to the rest of the text of the Roman Miracle, where no cursus is evident. Indeed, it is difficult to imagine that cursus could have been followed in the text since it so closely emulates the word order of the Greek model.

It seems probable that the editor responsible for this new conclusion was also behind the removal of the Greek preface since the new chapter serves the same purpose, and is more appropriate to the Latin text. It is also possible that this editor revised to a certain extent the literal translation available to him, although the "revision" still contains many examples of poor and unidiomatic Latin.

Most significantly, the editor responsible for this new conclusion to the Latin text makes an important link between the Miracle account and the *Passio* of Anastasius. He does this by recalling the martyrdom of the saint and the iniquity of his persecutors, in particular the marzabanas, the Persian official who interrogates Anastasius, and whose title is transformed here into a proper name, Marzabanas, just as it is in *BHL* 411a. Throughout the Greek text of the Miracle there is no direct reference to Anastasius's life or martyrdom; there are no echoes of the *Passio* whatsoever. The narration is centered exclusively on the physical relic, preserved in the Roman monastery of St. Anastasius. This does not mean that the writer of the Greek account did not know who Anastasius was; on

---

55. These are three clauses ending in a proparoxytone followed by a two-syllable word (*martyrum fructum; attenditur Deus; crucifigitur Christus*); and one clause ending with a one-syllable word followed by a four-syllable paroxytone (*mors pretiosa*). See Janson, *Prose Rhythm*, pp. 13-14 and 37-40.

56. Janson, *Prose Rhythm*, p. 24, suggests a sample of about a hundred clause endings as being sufficient for the statistical method he proposes.

57. In his preference for the planus and velox and the heterotomous variant of planus, a proparoxytone followed by a two-syllable word, our anonymous editor is very similar to Anastasius Bibliothecarius (see Janson, *Prose Rhythm*, pp. 36-40).

the contrary, the saint and his story would be well known to Rome's Greek population, particularly at the monastery where the relic of the head was kept, whose community participated directly in the event and was responsible for commissioning a written record of the Miracle. It seems more likely that the Greek author does not refer to the life and martyrdom of the Persian monk because they are not relevant to the story with which his text is solely concerned: the exorcism taking place in the complex of S. Anastasius *ad Aquas Salvias* in the early eighth century.

The concluding chapter of the Latin Miracle, on the other hand, is linked to the *Passio* itself through its reference to Anastasius's tortures and martyrdom, to the "vir iniquus, Marzabanas carnifex," blamed and condemned for the martyr's sufferings. This suggests that the two works were intended to be placed together, as a kind of hagiographic dossier, a *libellus*, combining *Passio et miraculum* into a unified work. No record exists in Latin of the translation of the relic to Rome; no account of the ancient miracles performed in the East by St. Anastasius seems to have been available in Latin.[58] Yet, the incorporation of miracles within a hagiographic *vita* or at its end was standard practice.[59] The joining of these texts, therefore, might respond to two concerns: it follows an established hagiographic tradition that the Life of a martyr, or saint, be enriched or completed with an account of the miracles performed through his intercessionary power; and it connects Anastasius the martyr and his story to the miraculous relic of the head kept in Rome.

The manuscript diffusion of the two texts, as discussed below, confirms these conclusions. It indicates that the two works in the form that has survived to us began their circulation together in

58. See Chapter I, pp. 3-4, 8-9, for my discussion of the Greek texts of the *Translatio* and ancient miracles, which may have been available at the Lateran.

59. The best-known example of such practice is the *libellus* containing the Life and Miracles of St. Martin of Tours, called a "Martinellus." It is found in numerous legendaries, including, for example, St. Peter's Legendary (BAV, Archivio di S. Pietro A 5, fols. 96-123).

Rome, and that only later did the Miracle and the second translation of the *Passio* have independent dissemination.[60]

The Roman Miracle survives today in fifteen ancient manuscripts
and six *codices rescripti*, all of which show that the text circulated
almost exclusively in Italy. While the Greek version of the Miracle
survives in only two manuscripts, the richer circulation of the
Latin translation is explained in large part by its early association
with the text of the Passion.[61] The Roman Miracle and Gregorius
clericus's version of the *Passio S. Anastasii* are known to have
been found together in five witnesses. The oldest is the legendary-
homeliary from the Ospedale di S. Salvatore at the Lateran from
the first half of the eleventh century.[62] Three other ancient manuscripts, the imposing legendaries of St. Peter's Basilica, the
Basilica of S. Cecilia, and the Church of SS. Giovanni e Paolo al
Celio, which were written during the eleventh century in Romanesca, the peculiarly Roman type of Caroline minuscule, included
the text of the Roman Miracle immediately following that of the
Passio.[63] The layout of the texts in these manuscripts presents
Passion and Miracle as a single unit.[64] These four witnesses are

---

60. Part of this later circulation is the joining of the Miracle to other
versions of the *Passio*, and expecially *BHL* 408. See also Chapter III, pp. 99ff,
the texts' critical editions, and "Descriptive List" for further details.

61. The *only* witnesses to the Roman Miracle alone without the *Passio* are
YUSD in my edition, at the bottom of a branch at whose top the Miracle
text is joined to *BHL* 408 in manuscripts A and F. It is most likely that
YUSD also go back to an exemplar that contained both texts, and that for
some reason, of economy perhaps, only one of them was copied.

62. This book still awaits a thorough study.

63. The legendaries of St. Peter's (=P, in my edition) and of SS. Giovanni
e Paolo de Urbe (=T) still contain it today; the pages of the legendary from
S. Cecilia (=Q) that once contained the Miracle account have fallen out, as
is indicated both by the codex itself and by its 1601 copy.

64. In the St. Peter's Legendary (BAV, Archivio di S. Pietro A 2, fols.
136r, 136v, 143v), for example, the opening words of the *Passio*'s preface
("Athanasio") and of the Miracle ("Imperante") begin with a large decorated
initial, while the opening word of the *Passio* itself ("Beatus") is marked by a
much larger (about twice as large) and much more elaborate initial. The
opening line of the *Passio* is written in capitals occupying two lines; the
opening lines of the *Passio*'s preface and the Miracle are written in one-line

the most conservative Roman hagiographic collections known to us. Their contents preserve texts closely associated with the oldest and most traditional sanctoral of Rome's churches; and they reflect little, if any, influence from outside the city.[65] The four volumes of the legendary of St. Peter's Basilica, in particular, were prepared as a large hagiographic compendium that would encompass all of the texts relating to the *gesta* of the Roman martyrs. Its inclusion of the *Passio S. Anastasii* in Gregorius clericus's "Roman" version and of the Roman Miracle is entirely in keeping with its character as a collection relating to Rome's traditional martyrs. Another ancient witness of both the *BHL* 411a and the Miracle account, which has been localized in the city though not in a specific church, is the legendary written in the thirteenth century in Northern Latium or Roman Tuscia, perhaps for the Monastery of S. Michele de Subripa, or for a Roman establishment with possessions in this area such as S. Pancrazio.[66]

---

capitals. The last (i.e. added) chapter of the Miracle is not marked in any way. Similar layout distinctions occur in the legendary of SS. Giovanni e Paolo al Celio (BAV, Vat. lat. 1195, fols. 98r, 98v, 106r). The legendary of S. Pancrazio/S. Michele (see n. 66) gives even less prominence to the beginning of the Miracle (BAV, Chigianus P VIII 15, fols. 119v, 127r).

65. See Franklin, "Roman Hagiography and Roman Legendaries," pp. 866-868.

66. BAV, Chigianus P VIII 15(=G). Four other witnesses of *BHL* 411a, produced in or around Rome, do not contain the Roman Miracle but are likely to have derived from an exemplar that once included it. One (Vallicelliana Tomus X, =I in my edition) is a small legendary from the turn of the twelfth century. Its contents indicate clearly that it was prepared for a Roman church, but its precise locale has not been determined. Although it does not contain the Miracle, this cannot be used as evidence against the early association of 411a and the Roman Miracle: most of the texts included in this small legendary have been shortened, including the *Passio S. Anastasii*, whose preface and several other passages have been eliminated for the sake of brevity.

The other ancient witnesses of the Roman version of the *Passio* are three hagiographic collections from Subiaco, which have direct links to Rome. The oldest was written in Romanesca between 1065 and 1120. However, because of their textual relation to the Beneventan exemplar of the *Passio*, their ultimate source would have had to include the Miracle, assuming that the arguments presented below regarding the Beneventan manuscript are valid. For the relations of the scriptorium of S. Scolastica of Subiaco to Rome, and of

From Rome, its early center of diffusion, the Miracle text traveled to other parts of central and north-central Italy, and specifically the areas encompassed by southeast Tuscany, Umbria and an area further east to the south around Spoleto, where it was joined in some legendaries to other versions of the *Passio S. Anastasii.*[67] This area produced large numbers of legendaries in the eleventh and twelfth centuries, into which the Roman Miracle alone or with a version of the Passion (*BHL* 408) that achieved wide circulation is this area was introduced. I would like to suggest that the compilers of these collections, when putting them together from various sources, added the text of the Roman Miracle, imported from Rome, to the version of the Passion that was already known in their area. There are indications that this combination of texts was then reverse exported to Rome. The Roman Miracle with the *Passio S. Anastasii* in the *BHL* 408 redaction that circulated in the Tusco-Umbrian region is found in the eleventh/twelfth century legendary attributed to S. Lorenzo in Damaso (=L, in my editon),[68] in a legendary which was modified for use at S. Maria in Trastevere (=V, in my edition), and a twelfth/thirteenth century legendary prepared perhaps for S. Maria Maggiore. These collections are less homogeneous than the Roman legendaries that couple the Miracle with Gregorius's version of the *Passio S. Anastasii.*[69]

Both the Roman Miracle and the *BHL* 411a recension of the Passion share a similar pattern of diffusion from Rome into the Beneventan script area and into France. Each text survives in a single

---

Romanesca to Beneventan script production, see Supino Martini, *Roma e l'area grafica romanesca*, pp. 147-166. Two other manuscripts were copied from Roman models during the early seventeenth century. These two additional witnesses are *codices rescripti* (Vallicelliana H 25, copied from S. Pietro A 2 by Antonio Bosio; and Vat. lat. 6075, copied from the legendaries of S. Cecilia and SS. Giovanni e Paolo).

67. These are manuscripts AFYUSD in my edition.

68. Supino Martini, *Roma e l'area grafica romanesca*, pp. 121-122. The large number of saints from Spoleto and the Umbrian region included in this collection is striking. Perhaps the localization in S. Lorenzo should be reconsidered, although clearly the legendary was copied within the larger Romanesca script area.

69. Franklin, "Roman Hagiography," pp. 868-875.

Beneventan witness: what I call N in my edition of the Roman Miracle, written perhaps in Troia, dates from the eleventh century; E in my edition of *BHL* 411a, now in Naples, was written during the eleventh or twelfth century in the Beneventan area, probably at the scriptorium of Troia, in the Capitanata region of Apulia.[70] Similarly, both texts have only one non-Italian witness: O in my edition of the Miracle, most likely written at Fleury, parallels B in my edition of the *Passio*, which was written in the latter half of the eleventh century in the region of Toul in Alsace, most likely in the abbey of St. Epure, as suggested by the presence of a number of texts associated with the monastery. While Fleury is a long way from Toul, it had close connections with the abbey of St. Epure. This monastery was the first house reformed by Fleury according to Cluniac customs in the tenth century.[71]

The similarities in the patterns of manuscript diffusion of these two works is all the more striking if one considers that in both cases the manuscripts transmitting these single texts are grouped into one branch of the stemma (pp. 305 and 344). In other words, the legendaries from Toul (B) and from Troia (E), which represent the branches of the witnesses of the *BHL* 411a redaction of the Passion excluding *BHL* 412,[72] have a parallel stemmatic relationship to the codices from Fleury (O) and Troia (N), which are ancient witnesses of *BHL* 412 excluding the *Passio BHL* 411a. One may conclude from this evidence that the Roman Miracle and *BHL* 411a traveled together to the Beneventan area and to France, perhaps to Fleury, possibly in the form of a booklet, or even as part of a larger hagiographic compilation. Once in these regions, their common transmission was interrupted as each text was copied separately, in a different collection.[73]

---

70. The abbreviated version, *BHL* 411, comes from this branch.

71. *Dictionnaire d'histoire et de géographie ecclésiastiques* XVII, 448.

72. I do not include I in these comments; it is a shortened text, and its position in the stemma is not assured.

73. The other possibility, namely, that the *Passio* and the *Miraculum Romanum* were transmitted separately seems unlikely, for then we would have to assume that each of the two texts was brought independently into each region, somehow resulting in a parallel diffusion.

While it is not surprising to find the Passion and Miracle of St. Anastasius in a passionary put together for the clergy of Troia,[74] it is somewhat intriguing to find the dossier of Anastasius in France by the late tenth century, the date of the Fleury codex containing the Roman Miracle. How the Passion and the Roman Miracle got to this region remains unclear. It seems likely that these texts came directly from Italy, since there is no evidence that they traveled anywhere else. The library of Fleury had always been supplied with Italian books, and it is known that northern Italian scribes, as well as scribes trained in Beneventan, were found working at Fleury around the year 1000, when the Miracle text was copied.[75] It is possible that one of these Italian scribes could have brought a codex containing the dossier of the Persian to Fleury. Another possibility is that the dossier was brought back home to this part of France by a pilgrim or visitor who spent time in Rome. The identity of the vast majority of these travelers remains unknown; some, however, have left traces behind, such as Flodoard of Reims (†966), Thierry of Metz (†984) who accompanied Otto II to Italy, and Thierry of Fleury and Amorbach, a monk of St. Benoît-sur-Loire who traveled to Rome and Monte Cassino at the very beginning of the eleventh century.[76]

While the descendant of the *Passio* of Anastasius that traveled to France, perhaps with the Miracle account, is preserved in a "proper" legendary written in Toul, the Miracle is found in a disparate collection of hagiographic texts.[77] A similar, though less pronounced differentiation is found with the Beneventan exemplars. While the

74. The textual exchanges between Rome and the Beneventan script area are discussed in Supino Martini, *Roma e l'area grafica romanesca*, pp. 147-166.

75. Lowe, *Paleographical Papers* II, 479; Bischoff, *Latin Palaeography. Antiquity and the Middle Ages*, p. 111; Mostert, *The Library of Fleury: A provisional list of manuscripts*, manuscripts numbered BF 386, 1014, 719, 1267, 460, 461, 462.

76. Thierry's visit to Italy occurred after the current dating of the two non-Italian codices, but not by much. See Poncelet, "La vie et les oeuvres de Thierry de Fleury," pp. 5-27.

77. The Fleury codex includes the Life of St. Athanasius of Alexandria (*BHL* 730), a pseudo-Augustine sermon on the birth of Christ, another sermon on the Exaltation of the Holy Cross, and several ones on the Holy Innocents, and the apocryphal "Liber de ortu B. Mariae."

codex transmitting the *Passio*, E, is a proper, two-volume legendary, the one transmitting the *Miraculum*, N, constitutes an ill-arranged collection, into which were gathered a variety of texts, perhaps excluded from other, better integrated compilations. The reason for the different treatment of the Passion and Miracle in these areas is probably explained by the way the texts were used. In these regions, where the cult of Anastasius the Persian did not have the local associations found in the Roman Miracle, the account of the martyrdom would have sufficed to commemorate St. Anastasius the Persian, whose feast was marked in the calendars under 22 January. The *Passio* would therefore have been included in the legendaries used for liturgical or similar public purposes, while the Miracle would have been preserved in less formal compilations, if at all.

The similarities found in the transmission of the Roman Miracle and the second translation of the *Acta* suggest that *BHL* 411a was part of the historical backdrop to the diffusion of the revised *BHL* 412, and that Gregorius clericus, the author of *BHL* 411a, may also be responsible for the revision of the original Roman Miracle. The language of the last chapter—its use of cursus, its exclamatory emphasis, and attempts at rhetorical artifice and stylistic polish—recalls the style of *BHL* 411a. But, as discussed above, these characteristics do not provide conclusive evidence of authorship. It is possible that *BHL* 412 as we now have it, having been translated by someone who was not a Latin speaker, was brought to the attention of the cleric Gregorius, and that he added the final chapter, having eliminated the preface, and attached the Miracle to the *Passio*. But it is equally possible that the *libellus* of Anastasius the Martyr may have been made in a different context, at a time when much work went into the great Roman legendaries, the oldest of which go back to the tenth century. The principal purpose of these compendia was not simply to provide texts for liturgical reading, but rather to codify the tradition of Roman hagiography.[78]

---

78. Franklin, "Roman Hagiography," pp. 870-872.

The removal of the original preface and the addition of a new final chapter are the elements that transform the original Greek Miracle into a Latin text. The link to Gregorius's version of the *Passio*, even if not forged at the very beginning of the transmission of the Miracle text, was certainly created early in the diffusion of these texts in the Roman region. Together, they make up a hagiographic dossier that has been "Romanized," to reflect the transmutation of the Persian monk into one of the martyrial figures whose cult dominated the sanctoral of the city. The addition of the Roman Miracle to the text of the *Passio* was strategic, for the local context of the exorcism would connect the cult of the Persian more closely to the city of Rome, and to the complex at the Aquae Salviae, whose relic, as we have seen, made it an important cult center for both Romans and pilgrims.

V

THE DIFFUSION OF THE *PASSIO*

Each Latin translation of the *Passio S. Anastasii* gave rise to an entire genealogy of texts—revisions and abbreviations created to be inserted in passionaries, legendaries, and similar books to suit the needs of the church or religious community for which each of these hagiographical collections was assembled. The following chapters survey all of these later recensions.[1] The manuscripts that transmit them are included in the "Descriptive List"; critical editions of the most significant texts are also found on pp. 259-507, below.

My study of the diffusion of the Latin dossier of Anastasius the Persian is not meant to be exhaustive, however. I do not present editions of all the texts I have identified. In some cases, it could even be argued that what I define as a highly corrected textual witness of a particular recension represents in fact an entirely new version. My purpose has been to survey the continuous development of these texts as a way of illustrating characteristic stages in the metamorphosis of hagiographic works. The dossier of Anastasius serves as a case study of the transformations to which saints' *vitae* and martyrs' *passiones* were subjected, particularly under the increasing influence of liturgical requirements.

Before the creation of these comprehensive and ordered collections, *vitae* and *passiones* were copied individually in a *libellus*, such as the one I hypothesize may have contained the second translation of the *Passio S. Anastasii* and the Roman Miracle, or as part of a small group of hagiographic texts. The earliest comprehensive hagiographical collection developed in the eighth century. This new book form known as a *passionarium* is a collection of com-

---

1. I use the *BHL* catalogue number where it exists. For reasons I explain at the end of this study, pp. 247-248, I exclude from my survey the witness of breviaries and *Legendae novae*.

plete *passiones* arranged according to martyrs' feast dates over the course of the liturgical year.[2] The other collection type, the *legendarium*, developed shortly afterwards; it contains not only martyrs' *passiones* but also saints' lives.

Passionaries and legendaries served a variety of functions early on in their development. They provided materials for private study and consultation, for communal reading during meals in religious communities, as well as in liturgical settings.[3] But the liturgical use of their contents became a dominant influence on their later development. By about the year 800, the custom of reading the martyrs' passions and saints' lives at the night Office began to spread throughout the church,[4] and, increasingly thereafter, hagiographic collections were put together to provide the readings for matins, or night Office, for the feast of the saint who was being commemorated on a particular day. The night Office was divided into three services, called nocturns, each of which normally required three or four readings in addition to antiphons, psalms and other prayers. The passionary or legendary was the book from which these nine or twelve readings were taken. Many early hagiographic collections have marks in the margin of the texts, added to alert the lector where he should start and where he should end the public reading. Some manuscripts show multiple sets of markings.[5] It was not necessarily most appropriate, for example, to commence the readings at the very beginning of a *passio* or *vita*, since only a certain amount of text could be read during the allot-

2. I follow the terminology outlined in Philippart, *Légendiers*, pp. 23-26.

3. Useful summaries are provided by Lapidge, "Editing Hagiography," pp. 240-241, and Philippart, *Légendiers*, pp. 116-17.

4. The general consensus is that, as indicated by *Ordo Romanus XII*, Hadrian I instituted the reading of the martyrs' passions in St. Peter's, thus repealing the earlier prohibition against such readings except at the martyr's titular church on his or her feast day. This custom then spread to the rest of Europe. A summary of discussions of this issue is also found in Lapidge, "Editing Hagiography," p. 243, and in Philippart, *Légendiers*, pp. 112-118. The extent of the liturgical use of early passionaries remains in dispute.

5. This is true, for example, of the legendaries from St. Peter. Another, even earlier practice was for the presider to indicate by a sign of his hand when to stop the reading (Poncelet, "Le Légendier de Pierre Calo," p. 13).

ted time.[6] Reading aloud obviously imposed certain demands on written texts—demands for clarity, simplicity and brevity, as well as conformity to the literary conventions of hagiography. One can see that the requirements of liturgical reading were responsible, to a large extent, for the manipulation of hagiographic texts and profoundly affected their transmission.

The earliest point that we can return to in the diffusion of the *Passio S. Anastasii*, beyond its origin within the Greek community of mid-seventh century Rome, is Anglo-Saxon England. We can conclude from the information that the Venerable Bede provides in the *Chronica maiora* and in his Martyrology that he was in possession of a copy of what has come down to us as *BHL* 410b, the first translation into Latin. Furthermore, it seems quite plausible that this early translation was brought to England by Theodore of Tarsus, who had been a member of a Greek monastic community in Rome—most likely the monastery *ad Aquas Salvias*—before his appointment to the see of Canterbury in 669. There was extensive knowledge of the story of the Persian in Anglo-Saxon England. Anastasius, for example, is found in the Old English Martyrology and several of the earliest surviving calendars from Anglo-Saxon England.[7] Most of this information derived ultimately from the *Passio*, but some, as I will argue in Chapter VI, came from a copy of the Hieronymian Martyrology that also had links with Archbishop Theodore. Since no manuscripts of the text of the *Passio* in any form survive from medieval England, we do not know whether the early translation was brought from Rome to England in a small booklet on its own, or whether it was part of a larger compendium containing a small group of texts, or even a full-fledged hagiographical collection.

6. Lapidge, "Editing Hagiography," pp. 247-248, shows how the Life of St. Swithun written by Lantfred had to be modified to make it suitable for liturgical reading.

7. He is included in calendars, from the late ninth to the eleventh century, numbered 1, 2, 3, 4, 6 and 7 in Wormald, *English Calendars before A.D. 1100*. Clearly, it was through Bede's works that the information contained in the *Passio* was spread.

While Bede provides the earliest *literary* witness to the transmission of the *Passio S. Anastasii*, the oldest *manuscript* witnesses are complete *passionaria* covering the entire liturgical year, which were prepared in the ninth century in eastern Francia. They are part of a cluster of ancient passionaries, closely related by reason of contents, all created before the year 1000, and most, if not all, in Bavaria or German Switzerland.[8] Two of the manuscripts, dated to the beginning and the first half of the ninth century respectively, are especially old, given the fact that the earliest surviving passionary has been dated to the middle of the eighth century.[9] It was in the Frankish north, and not in Italy, the ultimate source of the earliest *passiones*, that the *passionarium* most likely was developed, as the fragmentary evidence suggests.[10]

These earliest collections are not localized by their contents, but are instead universal, and contain the passions of martyrs venerated throughout the entire church.[11] The *Passio S. Anastasii* is included as part of a core group of texts representing the martyrial traditions of the city of Rome. Although radically different from the *gesta* of the Roman martyrs, the fictitious romances created to give literary support to the well-established cult of traditional Roman and eastern martyrs,[12] the *Passio S. Anastasii* reflects the Persian

8. For further discussion of these manuscripts, see "The Early Diffusion of *BHL* 408," pp. 377-381.

9. The oldest is the Codex Velseri (Monacensis latinus 3514), and there are a few others also from the eighth century. There are many from the ninth century. See Philippart, *Légendiers*, pp. 27ff.

10. Philippart, *Légendiers*, pp. 33-49. The notion that there was an official Roman passionary from which these northern exemplars originated has long been rejected.

11. They consist mostly of the passions of the martyrs of the early church both from the East and the West, but some of them also include the lives of the great ascetic figures at the beginning of the monastic movement, bishops and other venerated leaders of the early Christian period. The earliest legendaries are also "universal."

12. The term *gesta* was famously used by Albert Dufourcq in his *Études sur les Gesta martyrum romains* (4 vols.; Paris, 1900-1907). Dufourcq wanted to signify, first of all, his belief that the deeds of the early Roman martyrs had been compiled in an official collection. In addition, for Dufourcq, as well as for others who rejected the concept of an official Roman collection, these

martyr's developing cult in the city, and the importance of his relic. The *Passio S. Anastasii* and the other *passiones* were copied into these collections as whole texts; they have not been shortened by the elimination of prefaces, for example, or altered in any serious ways. In essence, these texts are transmitted in these early collections as "fixed" texts. Even in these early passionals, however, the *Passio S. Anastasii* shows evidence of corrections and improvements to its language. It begins to exhibit signs of the "fluidity" that characterizes the transmission of hagiographic texts.[13]

In the case of the *Passio S. Anastasii*, however, factors other than the requirements of the liturgy contributed to its fluidity. The opacity of the original translation caused by its "bad grammar" and lexical obscurity invited continuous improvement. Also, its length, the abundance of precise historical details, its complex characterization, and multiple story-lines were not suitable for public reading within a liturgical setting. Hence, we find in the transformations of the *Passio S. Anastasii* a growing historical schematization and a more focused typological characterization. The historical and geographical context of the original account, the details of its political and ecclesiastical settings are steadily eroded until the only biographical information about Anastasius to be retained are the facts needed to establish the typology of an ancient martyr. The rhetorical, stylistic, and narrative changes made in Gregorius's version (*BHL* 411a) or the complex relationship between martyr and monk found in *BHL* 408 are lost as the text is simplified and shortened. The historical figure of Anastasius becomes the classic martyr, who through his conversion, martyrdom, and death proves the superiority of Christianity to paganism and the secular world. The result of these transformations will come to represent a distillation of the stylistic and narrative conventions of hagiography.[14]

---

gesta constituted an epic cycle, a collection of related texts, homogeneous in style and in hagiographic and literary topoi. A *passio*, on the other hand, is seen as an isolated text, not one episode within a textual cycle. See Franklin, "Roman Hagiography," pp. 857-859.

13. Lapidge, "Editing Hagiography," p. 257.

14. See, for example, Grégoire, *Manuale di agiologia. Introduzione alla letteratura agiografica*, pp. 250-255.

The earliest revisions based on the first translation (*BHL* 410b) are, to a large extent, attempts to perfect the text. The clearest example of this development is *BHL* 408. It is motivated exclusively by a desire to improve and clarify the inadequate translation. There is no shortening, no elimination of historical detail, although there are subtle modifications in content. Another revision (*BHL* 410) of the same early translation has been shortened. This trend toward compression continues, and many details are eliminated as the *Passio* is copied into larger hagiographic compendia, some of which comprise hundreds of texts.

With the passage of time, legendaries become very specialized through the inclusion of many local saints and local versions of earlier texts. It is even possible to identify various redactions of the *Passio S. Anastasii* that were restricted to specific geographic areas. The redaction of the *Passio* that was transmitted in the exemplars of the Cistercian legendary put together in Flanders and northern France in the twelfth century and later, for example, is different from the redaction contained in the legendaries produced at several Austrian Cistercian houses around the same time.[15] The version of *BHL* 408 that I identify as the r-redaction illustrates most strikingly both the increasingly local characteristics of hagiographic collections and the growing fluidity of hagiographic texts.[16] Distinct variations of this recension were copied into several legendaries in the Roman and north-central Italian regions beginning in the eleventh century and continuing with greater frequency into the twelfth century. This was a time when this area, which had trailed behind northern Europe in the production of legendaries, witnessed a sudden efflorescence of hagiographical collections.[17] The books from this area that transmit the *Passio S. Anastasii* in the r-recension are large and beautifully decorated. They are display books, prepared for use during the celebration of the liturgy, not for private reading and study. The revisions of *BHL* 408(r) origina-

15. See below, pp. 364, 382-383, and my introduction to the text of *BHL* 410, pp. 417-426.

16. See pp. 232-234 and my introduction to the text of *BHL* 408(p), pp. 362-377.

17. Philippart, *Légendiers*, p. 45.

ting in this area most clearly reflect the desire to provide a text more suitable for public liturgical reading.

A similar, but even more pronounced transformation can be seen in the family of texts resulting from the second translation of the Greek *Acta* (*BHL* 411a).[18] Originating in the milieu of late Carolingian Rome, where familiarity with Greek was the mark of intellectual sophistication, this later translation is an attempt to produce a more ambitious text, with a rarified vocabulary and an observance of *cursus*. The versions descending from this second, highly literary translation shortened and simplified Gregorius's sometimes turgid text for liturgical use. They circulated only in Italy, and each version was circumscribed geographically. *BHL* 411, for example, is a shortened, less rhetorical redaction than *BHL* 411a that has survived mostly in traditional legendaries written in the Beneventan script area of Italy from the eleventh and twelfth centuries. It is the version of the *Passio S. Anastasii* that was included in some of the most handsome liturgical books produced at the Abbey of Monte Cassino during the "Golden Age" of its scriptorium, under abbots Desiderius and Oderisius I. Another reworking of the second translation, which I have labeled the Beneventan Redaction, is found in two books only, one from the cathedral of Benevento (edited below, pp. 493-499). The texts I refer to as Abbreviated Version A and Abbreviated Version B are preserved exclusively in specialized liturgical lectionaries used in two Roman churches, not in traditional hagiographical collections (edited below, pp. 500-507). These revisions show how the detailed account of Anastasius's life and sufferings was being transformed into an increasingly generic account of martyrdom and death.

The metamorphosis that the *Passio S. Anastasii* underwent can perhaps best be understood by comparing the different uses to which the text was put by two men at the beginning and toward the end of the diffusion process: the Venerable Bede and Peter Damian. For the Anglo-Saxon monk, the *Passio* was a historical document. It served as a source for the history of the Holy Land in the seventh century in the composition of his Chronicle. It

18. See below, pp. 234-244.

provided him, as a philologically-minded student of the Scriptures, with another example of the complexities that translated texts present to their readers. Even in the Martyrology, where he naturally concentrated on the sufferings and martyrdom of the Persian, Bede took pains to include many factual details that place these events in a well-defined historical context. Three centuries later Peter Damian preached a sermon on the feast of Anastasius sometime between 1044 and 1067, most likely at Rome and perhaps even at the monastery *ad Aquas Salvias* itself.[19] For Peter Damian, the story of Anastasius had lost its historicity; it had become a simplified paradigm of conversion from idolatry and of steadfastness of faith, the basis of the sermon's multi-layered tropological message.

Peter begins his sermon by invoking the text's authority ("ut eius testatur historia") for the statement that Anastasius "magi extitit filius, et paternis insuper fuerat sacrilegiis institutum."[20] This note about Anastasius's parentage and early training, and the mistaken report that the martyr was killed by drowning[21] are the only historical details about Anastasius that are mentioned in the entire sermon, unless we include here the etymology of Anastasius's name as "resurrectionis filius,"[22] which was most likely also in-

19. "Sermo III. In festivitate beati Anastasii martyris" (ed. Lucchesi, pp. 9-14); Lucchesi, "Il sermonario di s. Pier Damiani come monumento storico, agiografico e liturgico," pp. 33-34. I reach this conclusion by establishing that Peter Damian's version of the *Passio S. Anastasii* was BHL 411a. This text circulated primarily in Rome, whereas in the north-central region of Italy, including Peter Damian's own city of Ravenna, we find versions of BHL 408(r). But one should note that Peter Damian makes no reference to the relic of the head of the martyr in this sermon. It is surprising that he would not refer to the local relic if he was indeed preaching in Rome, and at the Aquae Salviae in particular.

20. "Sermo III," 1 (ed. Lucchesi, p. 9).

21. "... tandemque, post immania poenarum suppliciorum tormenta, in flumine necatus occubuit" ("Sermo III," 8 [ed. Lucchesi, p. 13]). Many, including Bede, misstated the manner of Anastasius's death. See pp. 191, 211, 219.

22. "Sicut enim Seth, qui uidelicet primi fuerat hominis filius, hebraice 'resurrectio' dicitur, ita et Anastasius de graeca in nostram linguam 'resurrectionis filius' interpretatur. Conuenienter itaque filius resurrectionis dicitur, quia mortuus est in eo magus atque sacrilegus, pro quo surrexit uerae fidei christianus ..." ("Sermo III," 5 [ed. Lucchesi, p. 11]). Cf. "... de mortuo Ma-

spired by the *Passio*. These particulars are singled out simply as starting points for Damian's elaborate pastoral and exegetical constructions. There is nothing in the sermon about Anastasius's Persian nationality, for example, or his encounter with the Holy Cross while a soldier in the army of Chosroes, or his wanderings in the Holy Land, or his life as a monk. All the details that so intrigued Bede are ignored by the preacher. Yet, it is clear that Peter Damian knew the text. He refers to it at the beginning in a way that suggests that his audience was familiar with it, perhaps having heard it, or at least extracts from it, read during the service. Furthermore, Peter Damian's words in the few passages referring to Anastasius echo the text specifically enough to allow us to detect which version of the "historia" was available to him. We can be fairly confident that he is referring to *BHL* 411a, the second translation, and not to a version derived from the first translation.[23] Despite such verbal echoes, however, the figure of Anastasius is barely visible in Peter Damian's discussion.

---

gundag, suscitavit Anastasium. Denique beatus Anastasius suam resurrectionem praetendit in nomine, quam e magicis erectus volutabris meruit Christi munere. Anastasius namque in latino resurrectionem sonat." (*BHL* 411a [ll. 155-158]). This etymology is not in the original Greek text; it is added in the *BHL* 411a translation, further evidence to support my belief that Peter Damian was referring to the 411a version of the Passion.

23. In addition to the passage discussed in the previous footnote, Peter Damian's phrase "Beatus enim Anastasius ut eius testatur historia magi *extitit* filius, et paternis insuper fuerat sacrilegiis *institutum*" should be compared to "Beatus itaque Anastasius ... *extitit* oriundus ... Filius vero cuiusdam magi ... qui et eum ... magicam disciplinam *instituit*" of *BHL* 411a (ll. 39-43). *BHL* 408(p) (ll. 79-82) reads here "Hic quidem *erat de* ... Filius vero erat magi cuiusdam ... qui etiam doctor *extiterat* ... *Erudivit*que eum ... magicam artem." It is also clear that it is not one of the revisions of 411a that Peter Damian knew. None of them echoes the passage above, except for *BHL* 411, but 411 does not preserve the etymology of Anastasius's name. Additional evidence that 411a and not 411 was Peter's source is provided by the following passages: "Tandem ad iudicem tractus, modo *blandiciis* attemptatur, modo *minarum* asperitatibus deterretur" ("Sermo III," 5 [ed. Lucchesi, p. 11]), cf. "*blanditoriis* pecuniae et dignitatum promissionibus, tum terribilibus *minis*" (411a [ll. 569-570]) and "tum pecuniae et dignitatum promissionibus, tum terribilibus *minis*" (411 [cap. 32, in *Bibliotheca casinensis* III, Florilegium, p. 108]).

It is to be expected that the treatment of the text by these two monks would be, to a great extent, dictated by the conventions of their different compositions, as well as by their personal interests. Peter Damian was fundamentally a reforming theologian and political activist, while one of Bede's most important commitments was to historical writing. Yet, the differences in their approach to the text of the *Passio S. Anastasii* are so vast that they transcend the norms of literary genre. They mirror the transformations of the text itself that are revealed during the course of this study.

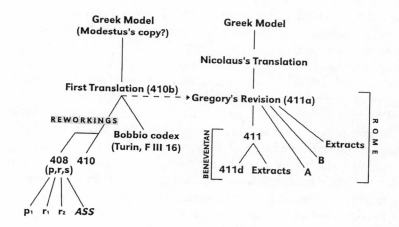

Revisions of the First Translation:
BHL 408 and *BHL* 410

1. Introduction

The early Latin translation (*BHL* 410b) of the *Passio* of Anastasius the Persian monk resulted in two direct revisions known as *BHL* 408 and *BHL* 410. It is my belief that their textual and manuscript history, combined with the historical evidence provided by Anglo-Saxon sources, suggests that the original *BHL* 408 is the work of Bede, and that he also used *BHL* 410 in his revision of the early translation. I also believe that this evidence shows that Archbishop Theodore played a larger role in English hagiographic traditions than previously acknowledged. In this introductory section, I look at the complex textual and manuscript data, an analysis of which precedes the critical edition of each revision.[1] The rest of Chapter V considers the nature of each text, and their relationship to each other and their common source. Chapter VI considers the Anglo-Saxon material relating to the hagiographic dossier of Anastasius the Persian, and in particular the works of Bede and the English redactions of the so-called Hieronymian Martyrology.

BHL 408 is the version of the *Passio S. Anastasii* that, until the correct identification of *BHL* 410b, was believed to be the translation of the Greek source *BHG* 84. Published in the *ASS* from two manuscripts,[2] it survives today in about fifty witnesses, and is the version of the Passion that achieved the greatest diffusion. There is a great deal of contamination and fluidity, as well as corrections, in the transmission of this version, resulting from the attempts of scribes or editors to improve the often complex and impenetrable text. Some of these later revisions are so different

---

1. Below, pp. 362-386 and 417-427.
2. Ian. II, 426-431; 3rd ed. III, 39-45. All references are to the third edition. See further, Chapter VII, Appendix 1: The *ASS* Text.

from those represented in the earliest manuscripts that they should be regarded as new redactions.[3] *BHL* 408 does not in fact designate a single text, but a group of texts, all ultimately linked through their common derivation from a single revision of the first translation.[4] I call this original revision *BHL* 408(p)—or simply p, to indicate my edition of this text—after its oldest complete manuscript witness, BAV, Palatinus latinus 846, written in the first half of the ninth century, probably at Lorsch. I make this identification by following two lines of inquiry (see the introduction to p's critical edition). Firstly, I look at the earliest surviving redactions, *BHL* 408(p), *BHL* 408(r) and *BHL* 408(s). I compare them with each other and with the early translation (*BHL* 410b) to determine which most likely represents the original revision. Secondly, I look at the manuscript context, the collections in which these early redactions are preserved, to determine which is most likely the oldest collection. This can be done because the oldest surviving witnesses of *BHL* 408 are part of a cluster of passionaries, closely related through their overlapping contents, compiled before the year 1000 in Bavaria and German Switzerland. Each passionary is unique, and reflects not only the time and place where it was put together, but also its position within this cluster of hagiographic collections. These parallel, but independent, investigations suggest that *BHL* 408(p) is more likely the original redaction. The close reading of the text as a literary and cultural artifact, which is presented primarily in this chapter, and the conclusions extracted from the Anglo-Saxon sources, which are considered in Chapter VI,[5] confirm this view.

The text that was catalogued by the Bollandists as *BHL* 410, but has never been published, is another revision of the first transla-

---

3. The clearest example of this is what I call the Roman Revision (=r_2), because it survives in two Roman legendaries; another is the redaction that survives in Paris, BN lat. 9741 (=p_1). See pp. 231-234 and the editions on pp. 449-492.

4. It is thus appropriate to consider the version now numbered *BHL* 410 as a different text since it is derived from a different revision of *BHL* 410b.

5. I have attempted to consider each set of data independently to avoid circular reasoning.

tion of the *Passio S. Anastasii*.[6] *BHL* 410 has a parallel relationship to *BHL* 408, but it represents a very different editorial approach that serves to highlight the skill and meticulousness of the editor of the original *BHL* 408, the p-redaction.

BHL 410 had a much more restricted geographical circulation than *BHL* 408, and generated no surviving revisions. Although there is no internal evidence for date or place of composition, the surviving manuscripts originate from the area centered on northwestern Switzerland and southwestern Germany and Austria. The *terminus ante quem* is the date of its earliest manuscript (Vienna, lat. 357 = V in my edition), from the late ninth century. An even earlier date is possible, if this work can be identified with the poor correction of the early translation discussed by Bede.[7] If this hypothesis is correct, the presence of this version of the *Passio* in England by the late eighth century and its association with *BHL* 410b, which almost certainly came to England from Rome, could point to Roman provenance. It is also possible that this revision of the early translation was executed in England, and then brought to the Continent, following a well-worn path.[8] No clues, however, have been uncovered in support of these, or other, hypotheses.

Despite its limited manuscript diffusion, the *BHL* 410 version of the *Passio S. Anastasii* is significant for two principal reasons. Firstly, it deserves special consideration because of the possibility that it circulated in Anglo-Saxon England. Secondly, it was included in several of the large hagiographic compendia that are characteristic of the twelfth and thirteenth centuries. *BHL* 410 is a component of the six-volume legendary written at the Premonstratensian abbey of Windberg in Bavaria during the second half of the twelfth

---

6. *BHL* I, 68. It is important to note that the *BHL* numbering obscures the fact that *BHL* 410b is the original text.

7. *Historia Ecclesiastica* V, 24 (ed. Colgrave and Mynors, pp. 568-570).

8. There is a large bibliography on the cultural exchanges between England and continental Europe; see especially Levison, *England and the Continent in the Eighth Century*; Ortenberg, *The English Church and the Continent in the Tenth and Eleventh Centuries: cultural, spiritual, and artistic exchanges*; Parkes, *The Scriptorium of Wearmouth-Jarrow*.

century.[9] It was also incorporated in the so-called *Magnum legendarium austriacum* (=*MLA*),[10] an even larger, multi-volume collection of hagiographical legends, surviving in six exemplars from Benedictine and Cistercian monasteries in southern Bavaria and Austria between the end of the twelfth century and end of the thirteenth.[11] The other manuscripts preserving this version are legendaries compiled for monastic houses during this same period and in these same regions. The stemma of the manuscripts of *BHL* 410 (p. 423) contributes to the broader task of mapping the links between these large hagiographic anthologies.

Unlike *BHL* 408(p) and the second translation of the Greek *Acta*, *BHL* 411a, *BHL* 410 did not create a genealogy of texts. The reasons are simple. *BHL* 410 was not widely adapted for liturgical reading, as in the case of *BHL* 411a and most of the versions grouped under *BHL* 408. The collections that included *BHL* 410 are too large and inclusive to be intended exclusively or even primarily for liturgical use. The goals of the *MLA*, which contains about five hundred entries, are expressed in the compiler's prologue, interposed within an elaborate system of borrowed prologues and other literary discussions of the value of hagiography.[12] His task, the anonymous compiler claims, is inspired by the love of his brethren, and the desire to emulate those whose deeds are being narrated:

> Vestrae igitur catervae me amor provocat, vester affectus trahit. Pro certo enim habeo, fratres, animari conatus nostros eorum meritis, quorum vitam narrantes veneramur. Ita ergo castis moribus aemulandum honoremus, ut quod in propriis virtutibus deest, in patrum gloria praesse videatur.[13]

---

9. Now preserved in Munich, Bayerische Staatsbibliothek, latt. 22240-22245 (=I, in my edition) (Poncelet, "De legendario Windbergensi," pp. 97-122).

10. But Poncelet in his monumental study of the *MLA* ("De *Magno legendario austriaco*"), which appeared in the same volume of the *Analecta Bollandiana* as "De legendario Windbergensi," did not notice that the *Passio* of Anastasius in the *MLA* was the same as the one found in the Windberg Legendary. The *BHL* failed to refer to the *MLA* version of the *Passio S. Anastasii*.

11. Poncelet's seminal article cited above remains the fundamental study on the *MLA*. For further bibliography, see p. 421 and n. 12.

12. Dolbeau, "Les prologues," pp. 353-354.

13. Quoted in Poncelet, "De *Magno legendario austriaco*," p. 38.

The large compilations that transmit *BHL* 410 are clearly intended to produce hagiographic summas; most likely, they replace earlier, smaller collections.[14] Their editors integrated ancient and newer collections into one, exercising little discrimination in their selection of texts. This may also help to explain why there is a hiatus of more than two centuries between the two oldest manuscripts of this revision. Unlike the ninth-century compilers of passionaries and legendaries whose aim was to put together hagiographic collections to provide readings for the liturgy, the purpose of the twelfth- and thirteenth-century compilers was to gather all the available hagiographical resources into one single, well-ordered, encyclopedic series to serve as models to be emulated by monastic confreres. During the collection of these older texts, *BHL* 410 may have been rediscovered and included into new and larger compendia.[15]

2. THE NATURE OF THE *BHL* 408(p) REDACTION

The original redaction of *BHL* 408, p, is a revision based directly on the first translation of the Greek *Acta*. *BHL* 408(p)'s dependence on the earlier translation is striking even from a cursory reading of the two texts side by side. Because the early translation is such a close rendition of the Greek, it is difficult to establish whether the redactor of *BHL* 408(p) had access to the Greek source. Although there are no cases where the editor of 408(p) corrects the early translator's misunderstanding of a Greek passage, there are some instances where 408(p)'s more accurate lexical usage might more easily be explained by its editor's recourse to the original Greek word, rather than by his resourceful and subtle skill as an editor. The relationship of 408(p) to the Greek and Latin models of the *Passio S. Anastasii* can be most efficiently illustrated by close textual comparison.[16]

14. Philippart, *Légendiers*, pp. 107-108.

15. The *MLA*'s text of *BHL* 410, for example, is slightly more polished, and grammatically more correct, than the original version.

16. Some of this material already appears in Franklin and Meyvaert, "Has Bede's Version of the *Passio S. Anastasii* Come Down to Us in *BHL* 408?," pp. 386-391. I use the siglum t to refer to my edition of *BHL* 410b, and p̄ to refer to my edition of *BHL* 408(p). An English translation is found on p. 38.

Flusin (26.4-17)

'Εξέστη δὲ ὁ ἀνὴρ ἐπὶ
τῷ θεάματι καὶ εἶπεν
ἐν ἑαυτῷ· «῎Αγιος ὁ
Θεός, οὗτοι ἄγγελοί εἰ-
σιν.» Τοῦτο δὲ λογισά-
μενος, ὁρᾷ τοὺς αὐτοὺς
ὠμοφόρια περικειμέ-
νους ἔχοντα σταυρούς,
καὶ λέγει ἐν ἑαυτῷ·
«Οὗτοι ἐπίσκοποί εἰ-
σιν.» Θαυμάζων δὲ περὶ
αὐτῶν, ἀτενίσας εἰς
τὸν μάρτυρα τοῦ Χρισ-
τοῦ 'Αναστάσιον, εἶδεν
καὶ ἰδοὺ καὶ αὐτὸς τοῖς
περὶ αὐτὸν συνεξέλαμ-
ψεν. 'Εώρα γὰρ αὐτὸν
λαμπροφοροῦντα κα-
θὼς καὶ τοὺς λοιπούς,
καὶ ἰδοὺ νεανίας τις ἐν
πολλῇ δόξῃ ἔστη ἔμ-
προσθεν αὐτοῦ, ἔχων
θυμιατήριον καὶ θυμῶν.
'Εωρακὼς δὲ ταῦτα
πάντα ὁ ἀνὴρ ἐβιάζετο
τῇ χειρὶ νύξαι τὸν πλη-
σίον αὐτοῦ κοιμώμενον,
ὃς ἦν χριστιανός, ἄρ-
χων Σκυθοπόλεως,
πρὸς τὸ δεῖξαι αὐτῷ
τὰ ὁραθέντα· καὶ οὐκ
ἠδύνατο, αλλ' ἔμενεν
ἀχανής, νήφοντι μὲν
λογισμῷ προσέχων τοῖς
ὁραθεῖσιν, σώματι
δὲ μένων ἀκίνητος.
῎Ομως ἐπὶ πολὺ βια-
σάμενος, ὅλον ἑαυτὸν
ἤνεγκεν ἐπὶ τὸν κείμε-
νον. Θροηθεὶς δὲ ὁ εἰρη-
μένος ἀνήρ, ἐπύθετο

t (ll. 341-357)

Amens uero factus uir
supercontemplationem
dixit intra se: "Sanctus
Deus, isti angeli sunt."
Hoc autem existimans,
uidit hos ipsos pallia
circumdatos habentes
cruces, et dicit in semet
ipso: "Isti episcopi
sunt." Admirans autem
de his, intuens in mar-
tyrem Christi Anasta-
sium, uidit et ecce hii
qui circa eum erant lux
circumfulsit. Videbat
enim eum splendide in-
dutum sicut et caeteros,
et ecce iuuenis quidem
in multa gloria stetit
ante eum, habens turi-
bulum et incensum mit-
tentem. Aspiciens au-
tem haec omnia uir
uim faciebat manu pul-
sare proximum suum
dormientem, qui erat
Christianus, ut iudex
Scythopoleos, qualiter
ostenderet ei quae uisa
sunt, et non poterat,
sed manebat amens, so-
bria quidem cogitatione
adtendens quae uide-
bantur, corpori quidem
manens immobilis. Ta-
men super multum
uim faciens, totum se
ipsum ducens super ia-
centem. Territus uero
praefatus uir, comperit
ab eo quid hoc esset.

p (ll. 375-391)

Amens vero factus prae-
fatus vir super visione,
dixit intra se: "Sanctus
Deus, isti angeli sunt."
Hoc autem aspiciens,
vidit hos ipsos pallia
circumdatos habentes
cruces, in manibus, et
ait in semetipso: "Isti
episcopi sunt." Admi-
rans autem de his, in-
tuens in martyrem
Christi Anastasium, et
qui cum illo erant,
immensum lumen, et
candidis vestibus eum
indutum cum eis qui ei
apparuerant. Et ecce iu-
venis quidam in magna
gloria stetit ante eum,
habens thuribulum au-
reum et incensum mit-
tens. Aspiciens autem
vir qui contemplabatur,
pulsabat manu proxi-
mum suum dormien-
tem, qui erat Chris-
tianus, iudex Cytopo-
lim, qualiter ei osten-
deret quae videbat, et
non poterat quia gravi-
ter dormiebat. Ille
autem attendebat quae
videbat, corpore qui-
dem manens immobi-
lis, tamen iactans se
super proximum suum
cum quo iacebat. Et
expergefactus, quan-
doque comperit ab eo
quid hoc esset. Dicit ei

παρ' αὐτοῦ τὸ τί ἂν εἴη. Λέγει αὐτῷ ὁ 'Εβραῖος· «Θεωρεῖς ὧδε;» Καὶ ἀτενίσαντες, οὐκέτι εἶδον οὐδέν. Διηγήσατο δὲ αὐτῷ πάντα τὰ ὁραθέντα καὶ ἐδόξασαν ὁμοθυμαδὸν τὸν Θεόν.

Dicit ei Hebraeus: "Cernes hic?" Et intuentes non uiderunt nihil. Enarrauit autem ei omnia quae uisa sunt et glorificauerunt unianimiter Deum.

Hebraeus: "Consideras aliquid?" Et intuentes iam nihil uiderunt. Insinuavit autem ei omnia quae viderat, et glorificaverunt simul Dominum Ihesum Christum.

The close dependence of p on t is evident in every line of this passage. In relation to the Greek text, the following should be noted:

1. The expression ἐν ἑαυτῷ occurs twice, and is translated *intra se* the first time and *in semet ipso* the second time by t. These same variations are repeated in p.

2. t's *existimans* is a poor translation for λογισάμενος. The redactor of p, in his attempt to create a meaningful text, changes it to *aspiciens*, which is a perfectly reasonable solution, but deviates even further from the meaning of the Greek text.

3. t's *sed manebat amens* does not render the meaning of the Greek text accurately, which is that the Jew is not able to awaken the Christian sleeping next to him because he is so astonished by what he sees that he cannot even open his mouth, but remains ἀχανής, mute with astonishment. The redactor of p—not using the Greek original—cannot understand the meaning behind *sed manebat amens* and makes a creditable attempt at interpreting what it means by writing *quia graviter dormiebat* ("because he [i.e. the Christian] was soundly asleep"), which is, however, not true to the Greek.[17]

On the other hand, the following passages make it impossible to say categorically that the redactor of p did not have access to the Greek.

1. αὐτὸν καὶ ἰδίαν αἰσχύνην νομίζοντες τὰ εἰς αὐτὸν γινόμενα (20.4)
   t: proprium existimantes pudorem quae in eo fiebant (ll. 260-261)
   p: videntes quae in eum fiebant, erubescebant (ll. 287-288)

2. «Οἶδα ὅτι αἰσχύνη τοὺς ὁμοφύλους σου ... (28.1-2)
   t: "Scio quia confunderis propter congentiles tuos ... (ll. 369-370)
   p: "Scio quia erubescis propter concives tuos ... (l. 404)

---

17. A similar passage is discussed in Franklin and Meyvaert, "Bede's Version," pp. 390-391.

3. λέγειν αἰσχύνομαι (33.15)
    t: dicere erubesco (l. 454)
    p: dici nefas est (l. 493)

In all three passages, we find the use of the same Greek stem αἰσχύν- (meaning shame or to be ashamed; these are the only occurrences of this word-group in the Greek text). In the first two cases, t does not translate the Greek word properly, and uses two different Latin words for it. p's use of the verb *erubesco*, with its biblical connotations, is quite accurate, however, and is used twice to render the same Greek word. It could be argued that the redactor of p was somehow able to identify the Greek word within the larger Greek text, knew its meaning, and used the Latin equivalent in both cases. It is also possible that the author of p was able to surmise the real meaning behind the poor translation. One can argue that he is not correcting a mistake here, but simply improving the text of a weak translation.

In the last passage, however, p's redactor willfully changes *erubesco* (the correct Latin translation for the Greek word) to *nefas est*. If the redactor of p was aware that the same Greek word was being used, he must have had some reason for this uncharacteristic divergence from the model. This revision reflects the redactor's attempt to find a more precise vocabulary, especially in "technical" areas, as discussed below. He is emphasizing the point that the new convert considers it a sacrilege even to name the Persians' false gods, a sentiment that the word *erubesco* cannot convey. This same impulse may be behind the change, in the second passage, of *congentiles* to *concives*. *Concives* is in fact a more accurate rendition of ὁμοφύλους than *congentiles*, which suggests that Anastasius and the Persians follow the same religion, when in reality it is only their ethnic or national origin that they have in common. Interestingly, the word *concivis* is not widely found in patristic authors, occuring only in the works of Bede and Gregory the Great.[18]

The evidence therefore is only slight and inconclusive that in rare instances the redactor of p may have made use of the Greek text to achieve greater lexical precision. On the other hand, the above passages, to which many more examples could be added,[19] demonstrate that the redactor of p did not, or could not, refer to the Greek text, during his process of revision. Nowhere, for example,

---

18. A search in *CLCLT* (first volume) found only seventeen occurrences, the largest number in Bede (five), followed by Gregory the Great (four).
19. See my notes to the edition of p.

does p correct t's misinterpretations of the Greek.[20] We must conclude that this redactor relied systematically on the early translation, in preparing his own version of the Passion of the Persian saint. This cannot have been an easy task given the fact that among the numerous examples of verbatim and inaccurate translations from Greek unearthed by scholars, there are few, if any, that can compare with *BHL* 410b in their deficient handling of the Latin language.

Nonetheless, a comparison of p and t makes it clear that the redactor of p showed a remarkable degree of skill in revising the poor text available to him, carefully avoiding major alterations.[21] Many of the changes introduced by p's redactor result in lexical improvement. Obvious Greek calques are eliminated and standard Latin words, or words that would be better understood in the context in which the editor is writing, are substituted. Hence, for example, *primarius* replaces *sellarius*, and *officialis* or a paraphrase such as *in officio fui* replace *caballarius* in cap. 17; rather than *comerciarius* we find *dispositor rebus publicis* in cap. 29; *ad religionem christianam* is used rather than *de Christianismo* in cap. 7; *magnale donum* becomes *magnum donum* (cap. 3); *incarnari ex Spiritu Sancto* is written in place of *humanari* (cap. 33). Closely related to the elimination of Greek calques is the constant effort to use a more precise vocabulary. Among the countless examples of this effort, one could single out the following: *litteris consolatoriis* for *litteris adhleticis* (cap. 24); *quadrupediis* for *iumentis* (cap. 23); *prosternatur in terra* for *ponatur* (cap. 21); *sociavit* for *connumeravit* (cap. 11); *malleator* for *argentariae artis* (cap. 8); *diligenter* for *curiosius, perquirebat* for *comperiebat,* and *diffamabatur* for *personantes* (cap. 7).

Another area of change involves grammatical and syntactical improvements. The relative pronoun, used as an equivalent to the Greek article, is eliminated; closer attention is given to the proper use of case (e.g. *incensum mittens* for *mittentem* in cap. 26); the correct voice is restored to verbs (e.g. *auscultabat* for *auscultabatur*

---

20. Access to the Greek preface, in particular, would have clarified the very confused early translation.

21. This subject has also been discussed in Franklin and Meyvaert, "Bede's Version," pp. 392-393.

in cap. 25); adjectives are made to agree with nouns, and simple verbs are substituted for awkward circumlocutions (e.g. *timeam* for *habeo metuere* in cap. 19). Such changes are found in every line of the text.

More significant perhaps are those alterations that are not strictly needed in order to clarify the problematic text, but are added to present the editor's standpoint. An example is provided by the description of Anastasius's desire to seek martyrdom (cap. 14). In the Greek *Acta*, this is vividly portrayed with much emphasis on his desire to suffer and die for the sake of his new religion. Anastasius's hesitation in confessing openly to his abbot his conviction that he will die a martyr's death is attributed by the narrator to fear of reprimand. This is repeated in the early translation ("Metuebat enim palam dicere, ut non increparet ei" [l. 199]). Some small but significant changes are introduced in p, which reflect the redactor's awareness of the inherent conflict between monastic stability and the desire for martyrdom, and his attempt to justify Anastasius's departure from his monastic community. Contrary to the original translation, the p redactor states that Anastasius does not lie to his abbot, but tells him plainly that he knows that he will die soon, "sive propria morte, sive per martyrium, quomodo cupiebat," adding, however, "Timebat tamen palam dicere de martyrio ut non increparent eum fratres." (ll. 212-214). In this version, Anastasius secretly confides in the abbot because he fears reprimand from his brethren.

The redactor of p makes a similar intervention in the scene in which the devil attempts to subvert Anastasius's monastic observance (cap. 13). *BHL* 410b, faithful to the Greek text, reveals that the devil's intent is to remind Anastasius of the magic he learned as a child "ut qualiter eam [caritatem] euitaret et in desperationem adduceret famulum Dei Anastasium" (ll. 172-173). In *BHL* 408(p), likewise, the devil wants Anastasius to recall the magic arts, but the redactor renders the devil's motivation as "et volens eum a bono proposito revocare, et de praedicto monasterio suadere exire" (ll. 183-184), adding the notion that Anastasius's decision to leave the monastery results from the devil's temptation. In the early translation, Anastasius chooses to flee from the monastery convinced by the vision of cap. 14: "prandens cum fratribus, soporatusque modicum et surgens, non ferens cordis eius incendium, exiit clam de monasterio, nihil accipiens omnino, nisi ea quae uestieba-tur" (ll. 202-205). This sequence of events, however, becomes in p "... sumpsit cibum cum eis. Soporatusque est modicum, et evigi-lans, non ferens cordis sui incendium, *volens adimplere desiderium suum quod erat placitum Domino*, egressus est clam de monasterio, nihil secum tollens nisi eam vestem qua indutus erat" (ll. 217-221). The addition of the phrase that describes God's approval of Ana-stasius's action is significant because the p redactor usually remains faithful to his text. He must have felt, therefore, that Anastasius's abandonment of his monastic community needed further justification.

Another small change—t's "prandens cum fratribus" into "sump-sit cibum cum eis"—shows attention to proper monastic conduct and terminology.[22] This awareness of monastic procedure is appa-rent in other minor changes. For example, Anastasius's life in the cloister (cap. 12) is described in the early translation as, "Erat enim sedulus ualde in ministerio fratrum et in opere manus et *prae om-nibus in regulam diuinae Missarum aderat*" (ll. 157-159). This be-comes, in p, "Erat enim sedulus valde in ministerio fratrum et in opere manus et *prae omnibus in regulam monachicam intentus et in Missarum solemniis frequentans*" (ll. 166-168).[23] In the early trans-lation, the praepositus prays for Anastasius "faciens orationem pro eo *coram aecclesiae*" (ll. 180-181); in p, the abbot is described as "faciens orationem pro eo *coram omnibus fratribus in ecclesia*" (ll. 193-194). Greater precision in the use of monastic terminology can also be discerned in the change from t's *nocturna psalmodia* (ll. 188-189) to p's *matutinales hymnos* (l. 201). Also found in p is a more precise use of liturgical terms. Compare, for example, the original "Et missas factas, percipiens diuini mysterii sacramentum"

22. The story refers to the simpler evening meal, and not the principal meal of the monastic day (*prandium*), which would be normally consumed at noon or mid-day. See, for example, Benedict's Rule for monks (passim, and esp. chapter 39).

23. Cf. *BHL* 410 "et in opere manuum et in regula prae omnibus." (ll. 92-93). The use of *regula* in t for κανόνι misled the revisers of *BHL* 408(p) and 410 as to the real meaning of this phrase, which describes Anastasius's faithfulness "in the observance of the divine liturgy."

(ll. 201-202) to p's revision, "Missarum vero sollemnia celebrans cum fratribus et percipiens divina mysteria ..." (ll. 216-217); or the use of *sacrario* in p (l. 203) for t's *ministeriali loco* (l. 190). Some revisions may stem from the editor's understanding of theological concepts. Thus, for example, the change in l. 454 of t's *erubesco* (the correct translation of αἰσχύνομαι) into p's *dici nefas* (l. 493) mentioned above may indicate a reluctance to name idolatrous objects. In the same passage, the phrase *divinitas imperatoris* (l. 456) used by one of the interrogating judges to refer to the Persian king is changed into *pietas imperatoris* in p (l. 495). The editor of *BHL* 410, on the other hand, retains both phrases of t.

On other occasions, the redactor of p intervenes to present events more plausibly. When Anastasius reaches Caesarea and chances upon some Persian magicians, he reproaches them. They are forced into silence by his arguments against magic, and, after asking him not to divulge their activities, send him away (cap. 16). The Persian magicians' request for secrecy is puzzling.[24] The editor of p makes the story more plausible by changing t's "dimiserunt eum" (l. 218) into "dimisit eos" (l. 237). This small alteration improves the logic of the narrative by strengthening the authoritative stance of Anastasius: he initiates the altercation with the magicians, he reproaches them, he is asked not to betray them, and he is the one to make the dismissal. After Anastasius's arrest, several interrogations, and various tortures, a Persian official, a Christian, is shown asking the marzabanas for permission to free the monk of his chains and take him to church for the Feast of the Exaltation of the Cross (cap. 29). All t has to say about this is: "Et hoc facto" (l. 390), which must seem extraordinary to any reader of the *Acta*, as it must have seemed to the redactor of p. He tries to explain why the marzabanas might have granted permission by adding the official's reassuring words, "Quia ego iterum reduco in custodiam" (ll. 425-426).

---

24. Flusin (I, 58 n. 56) remarks that the "attitude of the magicians is surprising," and explains it within the context of the city's population, the majority of which was Christian and Jewish.

Later in this same episode, the redactor of *BHL* 408(p) introduces an even more significant change. In the original account, the Christians are shown encouraging the would-be martyr to remain steadfast. Just as they feel they are placing themselves in danger by encouraging him, and becoming his "anointers," so too must he feel ready to die for the sake of Christ in the coming struggle. The difficulty of this passage for the careful redactor of p was not simply the problematic word "unctores" (rendering the technical Greek term ἀλείπται), which may already have been corrupted through misunderstanding, but also the idea that the faithful would be encouraging the heroic martyr, and not the other way around. The response of *BHL* 410 to this difficulty is to omit the entire passage. In p the order is inverted, and it is the faithful who state that now that they see him ready to die for Christ, they too are strengthened and willing even to risk death. In p, the "unctores" overcome their fear and become "victores," ready for martyrdom. This can be termed a double revision: an emendation of the text and a modification to its meaning to match the development of the story, and perhaps also the viewpoint of the redactor.

A similar concern for verisimilitude is found near the end of the text. After the execution of the martyr, the first miraculous events are witnessed and recounted by Persian guards (capp. 41-42). They are overheard by captive Christians who know Persian and who are later freed. Both the Greek *Acta* and the early Latin translation imply that it is through these captives that knowledge of the first miraculous events reach the author of the *Acta*. *BHL* 408(p)'s redactor makes clear the importance of these details by adding "ipsi nobis retulerunt quid inter se custodes confabularentur" (ll. 606-607). He clarifies the role of the eyewitnesses, which is only implicit in t, perhaps to emphasize the reality or credibility of these first miraculous manifestations.[25] The omission of the word *latine* in p may also reflect a concern for verisimilitude. This word mistranslates the Greek ῥωμαϊστί, "the language of the Romans" spoken by Anastasius's confrere to the victorious imperial troops

---

25. Another indication of the importance the *BHL* 408(p) redaction attaches to the Passion of Anastasius as an eyewitness account is found in cap. 31. See p. 409 n. 63.

(noted in the commentary on t, l. 585). Both *BHL* 410 (l. 440) and the second translation *BHL* 411a (l. 668) keep *latine*. Its omission in p may indicate the redactor's concern about the historical accuracy of the use of Latin in this context.

The redactor of *BHL* 408(p) takes a more sensitive and scholarly approach to the imperfect original. An example of his use of emendation and conjecture to make sense of the text available to him is found in the passage recounting Anastasius's baptism (cap. 11).[26] After observing Anastasius for eight days, the priest Elias is satisfied that the new convert genuinely wishes to become a monk and takes him to the monastery. The text of the early translation reads: "Post ergo abbas continuo adsumens eum, perduxit in mansionem sanctae recordationis abbatis Anastasii" (ll. 143-144). Clearly, *abbas* is a corruption. The corresponding Greek word is ἀπόλυσιν, rendered in the glossaries as "absolutio missio,"[27] but one witness has instead ἀπόλουσιν, which might have been translated as some form of *ablutio*.[28] Though it remains unclear what the original translation read, the erroneous *abbas* must have been the reading available to p's redactor. Hence, he emended *abbas* to *albas*, taking into account that those about to be baptized wore white garments for one week, removing them on the Sunday after Easter, which thus was called "Dominica in albis depositis."

There are other examples of this redactor's scholarly approach. For example, when the marzabanas asks Anastasius to perform the traditional Persian sacrifices and avoid execution, the saint answers in t: "Quibus diis iubes me sacrificare? soli et lunae et igni et equo et montibus et collibus caeterisque omnibus? Sed ne det mihi Deus adorare cultoribus uestris aliquando ..." (ll. 302-304). This appears in p as: "Quibus diis iubes me sacrificare? Soli, et lunae, et igni, et mari, monti et colli ceterisque omnibus elementis, et metallis? Ne praestet mihi Dominus ut adorem sculptilia vestra aliquando ..." (ll. 331-334). There are two major changes in this passage. The first

26. This passage is also discussed in Franklin and Meyvaert, "Bede's Version," p. 393.

27. *CGL*, 239.

28. 11.4 (Flusin I, 53 and note). There is no entry in the pseudo-Cyril for ἀπόλουσις but the one for ἀπολούω is *abluo* (*CGL*, 238)

is the transformation of *equo* to *mari*. The redactor of p was puzzled by the reference to a horse in this context, being unaware of the historical accuracy of this word in relation to the Persian gods and their representations in the natural world.[29] He must have surmised that this word was a corruption, perhaps of *aquae* or *(a)equori*; hence, his change to *mari*, which fits in very well with the other elements in the list. The editor of *BHL* 410, on the other hand, eliminates it completely (ll. 215-217).[30] More interesting is the change of *cultoribus*, a word misused here,[31] to the learned and allusive *sculptilia*, which echoes the biblical phrase, *confundantur omnes qui adorant sculptilia* (Ps 96.7).

These changes result in a text that works hard at presenting a factually accurate account. Only rarely does a word-for-word comparison with t reveal that p has omitted a word or short phrase. Most of these brief omissions could simply reflect the manuscript available to the reviser. Unlike the editor of *BHL* 410, this editor is unwilling to delete large passages of the text. The problem that confronted him in deciding what should be done with those portions of his model where the meaning is completely obscure must have seemed insoluble. For the only solution—to cut them out—seems to be contrary to this redactor's practice. Since the redactor of p was clearly reluctant to delete any material at all, obscure, even nonsensical passages remain in his text. This is particularly true of the preface, which contains theoretical material, and is especially apparent in capp. 3-5, where the Greek author attempts to establish a theological interpretation of the struggle between the Persians and the Christian empire, and of the early triumphs of the heathen.

Another category of problematic passages in p may result from incomplete corrections, where the redactor has changed the original reading but has not removed it altogether. An example is found in cap. 7 where Anastasius considers how he can become a

---

29. ἵππῳ: See Flusin I, 66 n. 88 on this passage. This example also supports the theory that the redactor of p had no access to the Greek text.

30. See also above, p. 95 and n. 26, and p. 116 and n. 87.

31. There is no entry in the glossary for σέβασμα, but it is easy to see how the confusion arose.

Christian. t reads: "Deinde cogitans in semetipsum quomodo qualiter Deum magnum qui habitat in caelo, quem ut audiebat et Christiani colunt inueniret hic" (ll. 97-99).[32] This is rendered in p as: "cogitans qualiter Deum magnum, qui habitat in caelo, quem Christiani colunt, ad culturam eius pertingeret" (ll. 103-104). One can imagine that the redactor of p intended to keep *Deum ... inueniret* as his main clause, but changed his mind and decided to use another expression instead of, or in addition to it. Perhaps he meant to write *Deum inueniret et ad culturam eius pertingeret*; or, he meant to substitute *ad culturam eius pertingeret* for t's *Deum ... inueniret*, but in the process of revision forgot to change the first part of the phrase to correspond to the end. A similar example may be found in cap. 38, when Anastasius and the others are being suffocated. t's "funibus suffocari uniuersos iusserunt" (l. 516) becomes in p "illos sanctissimos viros ... funes mitti in gutture eorum, et sic suffocari universos iusserunt" (ll. 557-558). The phrase "funes mitti in gutture eorum," which breaks up the grammatical flow of the sentence, is possibly an example of an incomplete correction.

From the evidence presented above we can build up a picture of the author of redaction p. Clearly, he was keen to preserve the meaning of the text as best he could. Although unwilling to cut out even the most garbled passages, he did emend and clarify the story by short additions and explanations. Not surprisingly for a composition that must date well before its oldest manuscripts of the ninth century, the author took great care in his choice of monastic and liturgical vocabulary. All these considerations, when added to the other evidence to be discussed in the next chapter, lead me to believe that the redactor of p was in fact the Venerable Bede at the Northumbrian monastery of Wearmouth and Jarrow.

32. For t's *inueniret*, see p. 277 n. 38.

3. THE NATURE OF *BHL* 410

The main purpose in the revision of *BHL* 410b that results in *BHL* 410 was to shorten the text.[33] The redactor of 410 was not as concerned as the redactor of BHL 408(p) with the accuracy of his revision, as the following examples indicate:[34]

t (ll. 341-357)

Amens vero factus uir super contemplationem dixit intra se: "Sanctus Deus, isti angeli sunt." Hoc autem existimans, uidit hos ipsos pallia circumdatos habentes cruces, et dicit in semet ipso: "Isti episcopi sunt." Admirans autem de his, intuens in martyrem Christi Anastasium, uidit et ecce hii qui circa eum erant lux circumfulsit. Videbat enim eum splendide indutum sicut et caeteros, et ecce iuuenis quidem in multa gloria stetit ante eum, habens turibulum et incensum mittentem. Aspiciens autem haec omnia uir uim faciebat manu pulsare proximum suum dormientem, qui erat Christianus, ut iudex Scythopoleos, qualiter ostenderet ei quae uisa sunt, et non poterat, sed manebat amens, sobria quidem cogitatione adtendens quae uidebantur, corpori quidem manens immobilis. Tamen super multum uim faciens, totum se ipsum ducens super

410 (ll. 245-256)

Amens vero factus super contemplatione hac, dixit intra se: "Isti angeli sunt." Hoc autem existimans, vidit eos palliis circumdatos, habentes cruces in manibus et dicit in semetipso: "Isti episcopi sunt." Intuens autem martyrem Christi Anastasium,

vidit

eum splendide indutum sicut et caeteros et iuvenem quendam in multa gloria stantem ante eum et habentem turibulum et incensum mittentem. Aspiciens autem haec omnia cepit manu pulsare proximum suum

ut ostenderet ei quae videbat, et non poterat quia manebat amens.

---

33. This is true of many other texts found in the principal collections containing *BHL* 410. See Poncelet, "De *Magno legendario austriaco*," passim. On the topos of *brevitas* in the *MLA*, see Dolbeau, "Les prologues," p. 354. While I assume that 410 has come down to us in its original redaction, it is possible that changes were made before it was included in its earliest witness.

34. A more extensive comparison is made in Franklin and Meyvaert, "Bede's Version," pp. 386-393.

iacentem. Territus uero praefatus uir, comperit ab eo quid hoc esset. Dicit ei Hebraeus: "Cernes hic?" Et intuentes non uiderunt nihil. Enarrauit autem ei omnia quae uisa sunt et glorificauerunt unianimiter Deum.

Territus uero factus, interrogabat ab eo quid hoc esset. Dicit ei Hebraeus: "Cernis hoc." Et intuentes iam nihil viderunt. Enarravit ergo ei ille omnia quae viderat et glorificaverunt unanimiter Deum.

This passage reveals the very different style of the redactor of *BHL* 410, whose deletions included both long sections, as for example, the phrase *sobria ... super iacentem*, as well as short ones, such as *Sanctus Deus*. The deletions appear to serve two purposes: firstly, to remove problematic passages; and, secondly, to shorten the text. This would explain, for example, the omission of brief phrases that serve as simple links in the story, such as *Admirans autem de his*, or of factual details, such as the specific description of the other prisoner as *Christianus, iudex Scythopolis*.

Another characteristic of the text revealed by this passage is that the editor of *BHL* 410 made very few significant changes in vocabulary, or in grammatical or stylistic constructions. The only word substitution is *interrogabat* for *comperit*, and the addition of *in manibus*.[35] The word order remains mostly unchanged, and the only grammatical improvements are simple ones. For example, *ecce iuuenis ...* is changed to an accusative in order to fit within the structure of 410. The result is that *BHL* 410 remains much closer to the original translation *BHL* 410b than *BHL* 408(p),[36] and is frequently as unclear and confusing as its model. An example of how such an approach can lead to a misrepresentation of the story is shown in the passage recounting the efforts of local Christians to recover the body of the martyr through the intervention of the sons of Yesdin, a Christian who was a chief official in the Persian administration.[37]

35. For the addition of *in manibus* see below, pp. 180-183.

36. This verbal similarity explains why the Bollandists catalogued the text found in the Bobbio manuscript, which is in reality the early translation, under the *BHL* 410 category as *BHL* 410b.

37. Yesdin and his son Kortak have already appeared in cap. 32. See Flusin I, 76 n. 122 for details of Yesdin's life and career. This passage is discussed further in Franklin and Meyvaert, "Bede's Version," pp. 390-391; see also below, p. 183.

t (ll. 533-537)

Cognoscentes uero filii de Iesdim finitionem sancti martyris—et enim pueri eorum simul aderant sancto martyri eunti ut finiretur super despicientes manus eius—dederunt clam quaestionariis argenteos multos et adquieuerunt eos separatim ponere corpus eius.

410 (ll. 398-401)

Cognoscentes vero fideles de Gesdim finem sancti martyris et pueri eorum

dederunt clam quaestionariis argenteos multos et permiserunt eos separatim poni corpus eius.

Fideles may reflect a textual corruption rather than carelessness on the part of the redactor of *BHL* 410. But the sloppy elimination of the following passage without revising the remaining text misrepresents the story as told in *BHL* 410b.[38] Only by such close textual analysis and comparison does it become clear that, by deleting the more obscure material, the redactor of *BHL* 410 altered the meaning of the model text.

4. The Relationship Between *BHL* 408(p) and *BHL* 410

As discussed above, it is clear that *BHL* 408(p) and *BHL* 410 are revisions of *BHL* 410b, the early translation of the Greek *Acta*. Yet, a comparison of the two revisions reveals similarities that cannot be satisfactorily explained by their sharing of a common source. Such links are not fortuitous, nor can they be accounted for by the textual history of the early translation. For example, in the passages cited above, the phrase *in manibus* has been added to both redactions but is not found in t or in the Greek. Clearly, then, the addition of *in manibus* cannot be considered a variant of another witness of the original translation. Such similarities instead suggest the possibility of a direct connection between the two revisions. I list below the instances where 408(p) and 410 agree with each other against 410b in a significant way. Most of these examples show lexical similarities; a few, however, illustrate how 408(p) and 410 reflect a meaning that differs from t:[39]

38. The Greek text is confused here: see my editions of *BHL* 411a (ll. 607-610 and n. 20) and of p (ll. 577-580). Both these redactions, however, remained largely true to the Greek text.

39. I have not included examples of minor alteration, e.g. the change of t's *uisa sunt* (l. 351) into *videbat* in both p (l. 385) and 410 (l. 253). Such

1. (cap. 6)
   ob admirandorum rerum t
   O admiranda res p 410
2. (cap. 8)
   secessit ab exercitu t
   recessit ab exercitu p
   recedens ab exercitu 410
3. (cap. 11)
   At uero rogabat eum t
   Ipse vero rogavit eum p
   At vero ipse rogabat eum 410
4. (cap. 13)
   submisit ei cogitations malignas t
   immisit ei cogitationes iniquas p
   immisit ei cogitationes malignas 410
5. (cap. 13)
   ab eum effugauit pugnae t τοῦ τοιούτου ἀπήλλαξεν πολέμου
   effugavit ab eo pugnam diabolicam p
   effugavit ab eo insidias diaboli 410
6. (cap. 14)
   sed ora pro me propter deum t
   sed rogo, pater, ut pro me Dominum ores p
   sed nunc peto ora pro me ad Dominum 410
7. (cap. 14)
   narrauit ei uisionem et conualescebat t
   narravit ei somnium quod viderat et confirmans asserebat p
   narravit ei visionem confirmans 410
8. (cap. 20)
   uidentes eum et proprium existimantes pudorem quae in eo fiebant accedebant ei dicentes t
   videntes quae in eum fiebant, erubescebant et increpabant eum
   dicentes p
   videntes quae in eum fiebant accesserunt ad eum dicentes 410
9. (cap. 21)
   Ne det mihi Deus egredi ultra ex ore meo quicquam huiusmodi t
   Ne permittat Deus ultra ut egrediatur quicquam ex ore meo de
   tali re p
   Non det mihi Deus ut egrediatur quicquam huiusmodi ex ore
   meo 410

---

minor changes could have been made independently, and do not provide significant links between the two texts.

10. (cap. 26)
   iacens super pauimentum in tenebras noctis t
   iacens super pavimentum in noctis silentio p *410 omits the phrase*
       but cf. later in the same chapter cum esset in silentio noctis 410
11. (cap. 26)
   hos ipsos pallia circumdatos habentes cruces t
   hos ipsos pallia circumdatos habentes cruces in manibus p
   eos pallis circumdatos habentes cruces in manibus 410
12. (cap. 28)
   minis praebentem neque blandimentis suasum t
   minas paventem neque blandimentis suadi p
   minis territum neque blandimentis suasum 410
13. (cap. 29)
   ut oblituros uniuersos uinctos cladibus eorum t
   ita ut obliviscerentur habere sibi vincula p
   ut obliviscerentur universorum vinculorum 410
14. (cap. 35)
   quia nihil plus exigit t
   quia nihil proficeret p
   quia nihil ei proficit 410
15. (cap. 37)
   blanditiis atque promissionibus t
   blandimentis atque promissionibus p
   blandimentis et promissionibus 410
16. (cap. 39)
   adquieuerunt eos separatim ponere corpus eius t
   permiserunt separatim reponi corpus eius sanctum p
   permiserunt eos separatim ponere corpus eius 410
17. (cap. 43)
   reuocare ad transmissorem suum t
   remearet ad abbatem, et mansionem suam p
   remearet ad transmissorem suum 410

Some of these cases (especially examples 7, 13, 17) may not be significant, since t's inaccurate rendition of the Greek may reflect a corruption of the original translation as it survives. It is possible, therefore, that the agreement between p and 410 goes back to an uncorrupted, original translation, which may have rendered the Greek with greater accuracy. Example 8 may also be deemed irrelevant because a similar expression (*quae in eo fiebant*) is found in t, although in a different sequence. Yet, there are enough significant echoes in the examples above to suggest a closer link between

BHL 408(p) and 410, other than their common derivation from *BHL* 410b. The addition *in manibus* (example 11) is especially striking. In the Greek, the crosses are on the ὠμοφόρια, which are identified as bishops' cloaks by the crosses that decorate them. The Latin revisions place the crosses in the hands of the bishops. It is easy to see how this misunderstanding of the Greek arose from the use of *habentes* in t, rather than the correct *habentia* modifying *pallia*, and from the technical meaning of *pallia*. The question remains, however, as to why both revisions agree in the correction—*ferentes cruces*, for example, could have been used.[40] The addition of *diabolicam* (p)/*diaboli* (410) in example 5 for t's precise translation of πολέμου is similarly striking. Also noteworthy is the parallel revision of t's *praebentem*—a poor attempt at translating the Greek (εἴκοντα=unyielding)—into *territum/ paventem* (example 12), and the alteration of *adquieuerunt* into *permiserunt* (example 16), both of which alter the meaning of the Greek. Finally, the appearance of *in silentio noctis* (example 10) in both p and 410 (in contrast to *in tenebras noctis* of t) is revealing, even though it occurs at different points in the sentence. The word *tenebrae* occurs four times in t, translating the four occurrences of σκότος in *BHG* 84 (Flusin 7.17, 14.11, 19.6, 26.1=ll. 106, 194, 245, 337-338). The first three of these are retained by both 410 and p; the last one is replaced by *silentio noctis* in both revisions. The use of this expression in this context is particularly appropriate. In the three previous examples, *tenebrae* is used metaphorically, meaning "ignorance"; here, instead, it means "night." This is the most striking link between the two texts, and suggests that the redactor of one text may have copied the other.[41]

That *BHL* 410 may have used *BHL* 408(p) is unlikely. The comparison on pages 178-180 above repeatedly shows that 410 reflects *BHL* 410b verbatim, even duplicating problematic words and passages that are better interpreted in 408(p). If an editor had access to 408(p), it is inconceivable that he would imitate it only in a

---

40. See above, pp. 92-93.

41. It may be significant that Bede shows a particular awareness of the word σκότος, on which he commented twice in his *Retractatio* (II, 20 and XIII, 11 [ed. Laistner, pp. 100, 130]).

very few cases, and for the most part follow 410b instead. It is more likely that the editor of 408(p) had access to 410 in some form,[42] and that he used it carefully and prudently to add to his understanding of the poor translation. In this case, the person responsible for 408(p) would have created a text that was fundamentally his own, based on 410b, but consulted 410 for help in deciphering the unclear translation.

Such a procedure is apparent in the examples above. In example 5, the change of t's *ab eum effugauit pugnae* into *effugavit ab eo insidias diaboli* (410) is typical of this editor's method. In responding to the ungrammatical text, the editor of 410 simply adapted a phrase that he had already used twice in the preceding sentences (*insidiis diaboli* and *insidiis adversarii*). The editor of 408(p), on the other hand, has a much more respectful attitude to his text. He is able to see through the early translation's grammatical mistakes and corrects them, without making deletions. The addition of the adjective *diabolicam*, missing from t but suggested by 410's *diaboli*, can be explained since the battle that is being described does indeed pit Anastasius against the devil, as the preceding narrative had made clear. Such an approach is typical of the redactor of 408(p). Similarly, example 12 suggests that 410 could have been accessible to 408(p), and not vice versa. The change of t's *minis praebentem* into 410's *minis territum* is readily conceivable (note, in particular, the retention by 410 of *minis* in the ablative), even though the original meaning is stretched and therefore altered. The change of p's *minas paventem* into 410's *minis territum* would be harder to explain. It is quite feasible that the editor of 408(p), faced with the unclear *minis praebentem* of t, might have been influenced by 410's *minis territum*, and written *minas paventem*. This is further supported by the use of the present participle in p, which may reflect an attempt to duplicate the temporal meaning of the present participle of t, and may also reflect his suspicion that *praebentem* could have been a scribal corruption or misunderstanding of *paventem*.

This solution may be another example of how the redactor of 408(p) remained faithful to the original translation, while still

42. There is no way to ascertain in what form *BHL* 410 may have been accessible to the redactor of p.

resorting to the revision of *BHL* 410. Such practice matches exactly Bede's description of his approach in preparing his redaction of the *Passio S. Anastasii*.[43] Similarly, the redactor who emerges from this analysis of *BHL* 408(p) is a subtle and learned editor, an adept narrator, concerned with evidence and verisimilitude, and perhaps also a committed monk—characteristics that also fit what we know of the Venerable Bede. These initial conclusions will be further explored in the next chapter.

43. See n. 7 above, and below, pp. 194-196.

VI

THE *PASSIO S. ANASTASII* IN ANGLO-SAXON ENGLAND[1]

1. BEDE AND THE *PASSIO S. ANASTASII*

In the short autobiography inserted at the end of the *Ecclesiastical History of the English People* (=*HE*), Bede provides a list of his works among which he includes a Passion of St. Anastasius: "librum vitae et passionis sancti Anastasii male de greco translatum et peius a quodam inperito emendatum, prout potui, ad sensum correxi."[2] Bede also displays a detailed knowledge of the life of the Persian monk in the so-called *Chronica maiora* (=Chronicle), the universal chronicle attached to his second computistical work composed in 725, the *De temporum ratione*; he also drew from the Chronicle the notice of Anastasius's feast day on 22 January in his Martyrology.[3]

It had always been assumed that Bede's version of the *Passio S. Anastasii* had not survived because no manuscript text of it named Bede as its author nor was its existence documented in any medie-

---

1. First discussed in Franklin and Meyvaert, "Has Bede's Version of the *Passio S. Anastasii* Come Down to Us in *BHL* 408?" Much of the material presented in that article is incorporated in this chapter.

2. *HE* V, 24 (ed. Colgrave and Mynors, pp. 568-570); the relevant passages are cited below, p. 194. There has never been any doubt that Bede meant Anastasius the Persian monk, despite Bertram Colgrave's note in the edition of 1969. See Franklin and Meyvaert, "Bede's Version," pp. 373-374 and notes.

3. "Ad Aquas Salvias sancti Anastasii monachi et martyris de Persida: qui post plurima tormenta carceris, verberum et vinculorum quae in Caesarea Palestinae perpessus fuerat a Persis, postremum in Perside multa poena affectus, atque ad ultimum decollatus est a rege eorum Chosroe." See Quentin, *Les martyrologes historiques du moyen âge. Étude sur la formation du Martyrologe Romain*, p. 106; Dubois and Renaud, *Édition pratique des martyrologes de Bède, de l'Anonyme lyonnais et de Florus*, p. 20.

val library.[4] Furthermore, no text had surfaced that might reasonably be identified as Bede's source. But the discovery of the early
translation, *BHL* 410b, in the Bobbio passionary supplied a crucial
piece of evidence. It seemed most likely that this, at least, could be
said to be one of the texts discussed by Bede, namely, the "librum
male de greco translatum." It became clear, furthermore, that both
BHL 408, as known through Bolland's edition in the *Acta Sanctorum*,[5] and *BHL* 410 were based directly on the early translation.
In Chapter V it was suggested that, while *BHL* 410 could not be
Bede's text (because its editorial style is so different from what
we know of his textual approach), *BHL* 408, and specifically the
original p-recension, could, on the other hand, be accepted as the
work of Bede. Let us consider this possibility further by comparing the *BHL* 410b, 408(p), and 410 versions of the *Passio S. Anastasii* with Bede's discussion of Anastasius in the Chronicle.

Anastasius and Bede's Chronicle
Even though Bede's Chronicle by necessity summarizes and, occasionally, rearranges the material presented in the *Passio*, a detailed
comparison of the passage relating Anastasius's life and martyrdom
with the early translation *BHL* 410b (or, more accurately, with t,
which is my edition of 410b), leaves little doubt that the major
source for the Chronicle's entry is the Latin tradition originating
in the early translation. This comparison also highlights the lexical
links between *BHL* 408(p) (=p, in my edition) and Bede's writing.
This is Bede's discussion of Anastasius in the Chronicle:[6]

> 537: ... Persae ... destruentes ecclesias sancta quaeque profanantes inter
> ornamenta locorum vel sanctorum vel communium, quae abstulere,
> etiam vexillum dominicae crucis abducunt ...

4. Laistner, *A Hand-List of Bede Manuscripts*, p. 87.

5. *ASS* Ian. III, 39-45; for further discussion see Chapter VII, Appendix 1.

6. The *Chronica maiora* has been edited independently of the *De temporum ratione* in Mommsen, *Chronica minora* III, 231-327; and reedited with
insignificant corrections by Charles W. Jones (in CCSL). A translation is
found in Bede, *The Ecclesiastical History* (ed. McClure), pp. 307-340. The passage concerning Anastasius is found on pp. 310-311 (*MGH*), p. 524 (CCSL),
and pp. 331-332 (ed. McClure).

539: Anastasius persa monachus nobile pro Christo martyrium patitur. qui natus in Persidae magicas a patre puer artes discebat, sed ubi a captivis Christianis Christi nomen acceperat, in eum mox animo toto conversus relicta Perside Calcidoniam Hierapolimque Christum quaerens ac deinde Hierosolymam petit, ubi accepta baptismatis gratia quarto ab eadem urbe miliario monasterium abbatis Anastasii intravit. ibi septem annis regulariter vivens, dum Cesaream Palestinae orationis gratia venisset, captus a Persis et multa diu verbera inter carceres et vincula Marzabona iudice perpessus tandem mittitur Persidem ad regem eorum Chosronem, a quo tertio per intervalla temporis verberatus ad extremum una suspensus manu per tres horas diei, sic decollatus cum aliis LXX martyrium complevit. mox tonica eius indutus quidam daemoniacus curatus est. inter ea superveniens cum exercitu Heraclius princeps superatis Persis Christianos, qui erant captivati, reduxit gaudentes. reliquiae beati martyris Anastasii primo monasterium suum, deinde Romam advectae venerantur in monasterio beati Pauli apostoli, quod dicitur ad aquas Salvias.

Obervations

537: ... *Persae ... abducunt*: Although the information about the abduction of the Holy Cross from Jerusalem in the entry for the year 537 is not part of the notice concerning Anastasius, its source could have been the Passion of Anastasius, which contains a long discussion of the removal of the cross to the Persian capital (cap. 6).[7]

539: ... *a captivis ... conversus*: Bede says that Anastasius learns about Christianity from captives, while in the *BHL* 410b tradition it is the captive cross that converts the Persian soldier ("captiuus ille ... crux ... captiuabat ... eos" [ll. 85-86]), who then learns about the religion of the cross *per auditum* from *dicentium* (t [l. 94]), and from *fidelibus* (p [l. 96]). However, Bede could have concluded that the Christians responsible for the instruction of Anastasius in Persia, like the cross itself, are there as captives. There are verbal similarities between the Chronicle (*magicas a patre puer artes discebat; ...Christi nomen*) and the Latin Passions:

> t : erudiuitque eum a pueritia magicam artem. ... suscipiens per auditu praetiosissimum nomen Dei (ll. 79, 96-97)
>
> p : Erudivitque eum pater suus a pueritia magicam artem. ... suscipiens per auditum ... Ihesu Christi mirabile nomen (ll. 81-82, 100-101)

---

7. As noted by Mommsen in his edition of the Chronicle, p. 310 n. 1.

410 : eruditvitque eum a pueritia magica arte. ... suscepit per auditum nomen Dei (ll. 29-30, 44-45).

It may be significant that only the Chronicle and p read *Christi nomen*, while t and 410 keep *nomen Dei*.

relicta Perside ... intravit: Bede omits the fact that Anastasius was a soldier and that he left Persia with the army. Since this fact does not play a major role in the story told in the *Passio*[8] nor was Anastasius commonly identified as a soldier saint,[9] the omission of this detail in the Chronicle is not surprising. What is most striking about these lines is Bede's particular attention to the geographic itinerary, listing accurately the major stops on Anastasius's travels (Chalcedon, Hierapolis, and finally Jerusalem), and the precise location of the monastery in which Anastasius eventually lives as a monk. Bede's interest in geography, and especially in holy places, has been well documented,[10] and is here clearly evident in the details he chooses to retain at the expense of others. The wording of the Chronicle ("quarto ab eadem urbe miliario monasterium abbatis Anastasii intravit") recalls specifically the Latin *Passiones*:

t : in mansionem sanctae recordationis abbatis Anastasii, quae a quarto miliario sanctae ciuitatis adiacenti (ll. 143-145)

p : ad monasterium sanctae recordationis Anastasii Abbatis quod quarto miliario distat a sancta civitate (ll. 152-153)

410 : ad mansionem abbatis Anastasii quae a quarto miliario sanctae civitati adiacet (ll. 81-82)

It is significant that the Chronicle and p use the term *monasterium* while 410 keeps t's *mansionem*.

ibi ... venisset: Bede summarizes Anastasius's monastic life with the word *regulariter*, matching the emphasis in the *Passio* on Anastasius's observance of monastic discipline.[11] The statement that Anastasius went to Caesarea *orationis gratia* represents a slight modification of

---

8. Although contrary to the historical reality: see Flusin II, 226-227, 235-241.

9. Instead he was known as a thaumaturge.

10. This interest is clearly evident in his composition of the *De locis sanctis* (ed. Fraipont, CCSL 175, 251-280), based largely on the report of the Gallic bishop Arculf, who had visited the Holy Land, Egypt, and Constantinople. See Levison, *England and the Continent in the Eighth Century*, pp. 42-43.

11. *septem annis* also corresponds to the *Passio*: per septem annos (t [l. 170]); *per annos septem* (p [l. 180]).

the story as told in the *Passio* (cap. 16). There, Anastasius leaves his monastery out of a desire to seek maryrdom; once in Caesarea, he goes to the church of St. Euphemia *orationis gratia*. Perhaps no significance should be attached to the way the Chronicle passes over Anastasius's unauthorized departure from his monastery; on the other hand, it could be an attempt to explain his breach of monastic discipline, not unlike the attempt in p to justify Anastasius's actions by having him reveal his intentions to his abbot.[12]

captus ... complevit: Bede summarizes the events leading to the capture of Anastasius and his interrogations under the marzabanas. The Chronicle's wording—"et multa diu verbera inter carceres et vincula Marzabona iudice perpessus"—provides a striking verbal reminiscence of p, particularly in comparison to 410:

> t : ... iussit eum inferratum duci in castro ... multas atque insufferentes tribulationes sustineret famulus Dei (ll. 257-259)
>
> p : ... iussit eum in vinculis ferreis duci in castrum ... multas atque innumeras tribulationes perpessus est famulus Christi Anastasius (ll. 284-287)
>
> 410 : ... iussit eum ferro alligari, et duci in castrum ... insufferentes tribulationes sustineret famulus Dei (ll. 175-178)[13]

It is significant that the Chronicle and p use the words *vincula/vinculis* and *perpessus*, while t and 410 do not. *Perpessus* obviously held some importance for Bede since it is found in his works several times.[14] The change of *inferratum* into *in vinculis ferreis* into *vincula* also suggests that Bede's Chronicle derives from p, which in turn derives from t.

Chosroes is consistently called a king in the Chronicle; t uses both *rex* and *imperator* while p, with two exceptions, uses *imperator*.[15] The general use of *imperator* in p may be an attempt to unify the nomenclature, while the use of *rex* in the Chronicle might reflect a more

---

12. See above, pp. 171-173.

13. It is striking that p changes *famulus Dei* to *famulus Christi* since Bede refers to himself as *famulus Christi* (*HE* Preface [p. 2]; V.24 [p. 566]). But one must also remember that Bede used the word *famulus* numerous times in the *HE*, frequently associated with *Christi*, but also with *Dei*. See Jones, *A Concordance to the Historia Ecclesiastica of Bede*, p. 202.

14. He used it once in the *HE* (Jones, *Concordance*, p. 392) and three other times as attested in *CLCLT*.

15. (l. 56) "regi iniusto" (which may not refer specifically to Chosroes, but to an unjust king in general); and (l. 613) "malignus rex interficietur." *BHL* 410 is less consistent, following *BHL* 410b's usage.

mature historical work written late in Bede's life (in 725),[16] which makes a careful distinction between a real emperor (like Heraclius) and a mere king (like Chosroes).

When Anastasius finally reaches Persia, he is beaten three times and is subjected to two particular tortures according to the Chronicle.[17] However, Bede omits a third episode of torture, described at the beginning of cap. 35, when two men stand on a plank placed on Anastasius's tibias. Bede also omits a detail relating to one of the tortures, namely the attachment of a stone to one foot as Anastasius is suspended by one hand. Furthermore, while the *Passio* says that this torture lasted "quasi horarum duarum spatio," according to the Chronicle it lasts three hours. These are minor inconsistencies, however, and probably resulted from a need to condense an overlong text.

Far more significant is the discrepancy concerning the manner of Anastasius's execution. Bede tells the readers of the Chronicle that Anastasius was decapitated along with seventy others, while the *Passio* describes how the seventy companions and then Anastasius himself were strangled. Only then was his head cut off so that the sealed collar—the *bulla*—which had been fastened around his neck at Caesarea, could be taken unbroken to the king, following the Persian custom. This mistake is found also in Bede's Martyrology.[18] A possible explanation is that Bede, writing from memory or perhaps looking over his source hurriedly, is conflating the strangulation and the decapitation. His knowledge of the presence of the relic of the head in Rome may also have influenced this conflation.[19] Furthermore, he would have been unaware of the significance of the decapitation, as proof, rather than cause, of death.[20] There is no question, however, that this remains a major and troubling inconsistency between Bede's Chronicle and Martyrology, and the *Passio*.[21]

---

16. Laistner, *Hand-List of Bede Manuscripts*, pp. 144-145.

17. The Chronicle's *tandem* may reflect the delays before Anastasius's final departure for Persia, including the letter sent to the king, the attempts at compromise, etc. The three beatings correspond to three separate episodes in the *Passio* (capp. 34 and 37).

18. It is also found in the Old English Martyrology, providing further evidence that Bede, rather than the *Passio* directly, was the source of the Martyrology. See below, pp. 224-225.

19. See further below, pp. 211ff.

20. Flusin I, 184 n. 149.

21. Bede is ultimately responsible for introducing this error into later summaries of the martyr's death, including breviaries. It should be noted,

mox tonica ... curatus est: Bede's account of the first miracle follows the order of events chronologically, unlike the sequence in the *Passio*, where the healing is told retrospectively by Anastasius's confrere when he returns to their community in Jerusalem (cap. 44). Bede's sequence appears much clearer and simpler. The key words in his account (*tonica, daemoniacus*) do not appear in the *Passio*. The word *daemoniacus* may have been chosen as a simple alternative to the circumlocution of the Passion stories (t: quidam frater iuuenis ... uexatus atrociter ab spiritu immundo [ll. 593-594]; p: iuvenis ... qui nequiter vexabatur a spiritu immundo [ll. 637-638]). Less easily explained is why Bede would use *tonica* in the Chronicle rather than *colobium*, the literal equivalent of the Greek word and used in all Latin redactions, including p. The answer may have to do with the intended audience for this work. While *colobium* would be well-known in monastic circles,[22] Bede might have wished for a more common, less specialized, word for his Chronicle. Or, he might have decided, when he composed the Chronicle, to avoid a word so clearly calqued on the Greek.

superveniens ... gaudentes: This sentence corresponds to the last portion of the *Passio* (capp. 43-44), in which the emperor Heraclius and his army play an important role in escorting Anastasius's companion, and witness to the martyrdom, back to Jerusalem. There is, however, an inconsistency between the Chronicle and the *Passio*. While the former states that Heraclius, following his victory in Persia, returns with "Christiani, qui erant captivi," the *Passio* indicates that it is only the companion whom Heraclius's soldiers invite to accompany them home. The remark in the Chronicle, however, can be explained by comparing the preceding chapter in the *Passio*. This chapter concludes the account of the miraculous events taking place around the body of the martyr, as witnessed by Persian soldiers, by stating that "Christiani captivi qui erant in carcere" would subsequently be freed and would return to Jerusalem, where they would make these events known (p; "absoluti vero a vinculis et venientes in sanctam civitatem hoc diffama-

---

however, that the same mistake has been made by others. Even Sansterre, who is a model of precision, says (*Les moines grecs* I, 15): "Le saint moine Persan avait été torturé par ses compatriotes et finalement decapité le 22 janvier 628." And Peter Damian states that Anastasius drowned (above, p. 159).

22. *Colobium* would be familiar to monks from monastic writings. *CLCLT* indicates that *colobium* is found almost exclusively in the writings of John Cassian. It also appears in Isidore's *Etymologies* (19, xxii, 24) and in Jerome's *Liber quaestionum hebraicarum in Genesim* (37,3).

bant ubique" [ll. 605, 607-608]). There is in addition the striking use of the adjective *gaudentes* to describe the freed Christian prisoners. This recalls the verb *gavisus est*, used in all three Latin redactions, to describe the companion's reaction when he sees Heraclius's soldiers.

reliquiae ... ad aquas Salvias: This information, that the saint's relics were first translated to his monastery in Jerusalem and are now in Rome, is not found in the *Passio* and suggests that Bede had another source. The identity of this source will be discussed below in the section on "The Hieronymian Martyrology."

A comparison of Bede's Chronicle with the *Passio* shows a great deal of agreement, and demonstrates that Bede drew from the Latin tradition that began with the early translation, *BHL* 410b (=t in my edition). There are clear verbal echoes between the Chronicle and t, and, even more striking, between the Chronicle and *BHL* 408(p).

Bede's Description of the "librum vitae et passionis sancti Anastasii"
There remains little doubt that *BHL* 410b must be the *male translatum* work Bede is referring to when he states that his "librum vitae et passionis sancti Anastasii" was based on a work that had been "male de greco translatum" and "peius a quodam inperito emendatum." It remains unclear what Bede means by *et peius emendatum*. Certainly, he may have wished to indicate that his source had been corrected in some unsatisfactory way, but he gives us no further details about the nature of the emendations and how the correction has been made. Nor is it absolutely clear whether Bede meant "a quodam inperito" to refer to the individual who both translated and corrected the work, or to the person responsible only for the emendations, not for the translation. The Colgrave-Mynors edition follows the former option. I, on the contrary, think that the word order indicates that "a quodam inperito" refers to *emendatum* only, since it seems unlikely that a poor translator would emend the text. Since *BHL* 410 is a badly corrected version of *BHL* 410b, and since it was likely used by the redactor of *BHL* 408(p), the conclusion that 410 was Bede's *peius emendatum* would follow if indeed Bede was the author of 408(p).[23]

---

23. For further discussion of p's use of *BHL* 410, see above, pp. 180-185.

While the identification of *BHL* 410b as Bede's inadequate source seems quite certain, the identification of *BHL* 408(p) as Bede's revision is much more complex. In addition to the factual discrepancies, there are the textual and linguistic deficiencies, which argue against Bede's authorship.[24] Clearly, 408(p) was not purged completely of 410b's obscure and uncouth phrases, and appears in stark contrast both to Bede's style, which has been praised "for its straightforwardness and simplicity," and to his Latin "worthy of the simple, pious, learned scholar who wrote it."[25] Since there is no overwhelming external evidence to support Bede's authorship, the case for p as Bede's corrected text must be based for the most part on the internal evidence of 408(p) itself.

Any comparison of the *Passio S. Anastasii* with Bede's well-known and popular works, however, must first take into account Bede's own description of the *Passio* within the autobiographical passage at the end of the *Ecclesiastical History*.[26] Bede omitted any verb—such as *scripsi*—in listing his works, with three exceptions. Firstly, in the entry "In Apostolum quaecumque in opusculis Augustini exposita inveni cuncta per ordinem transcribere curavi"; secondly, in the Martyrology, a detailed description of which was necessary to account for the major innovations introduced by Bede into the traditional genre; and thirdly, in the item detailing his hagiographical pieces:

> Item de historiis sanctorum: librum uitae et passionis sancti Felicis confessoris de metrico Paulini opere in prosam transtuli; librum uitae et passionis sancti Anastasii male de greco translatum et peius a quodam inperito emendatum, prout potui, ad sensum correxi; uitam sancti patris monachi simul et antistitis Cudbercti et prius heroico metro et postmodum plano sermone descripsi.

> Also about the histories of the saints: I transposed into prose from the metrical work of Paulinus a book of the Life and Passion of St. Felix the Confessor; I corrected according to the sense as best I could the

---

24. Jean Bolland describes his text of *BHL* 408 as "certe impolitus sermo est" (*ASS* Ian. III, 35).

25. Colgrave and Mynors, pp. xxxvi, xxxviii. This praise presumably applies specifically to the *HE* rather than to Bede's Latinity in general.

26. *HE* V, 24 (pp. 568-570).

book of the Life and Passion of St. Anastasius badly translated from the Greek and worse emended by some unskilled person; I also wrote down the Life of the holy father Cuthbert, monk and bishop, first in heroic meter and later in plain prose.[27]

Bede grouped these works under one heading because all three belong to the same category, the genre of the *historiae sanctorum*.[28] Despite belonging to the same category, Bede notes the different nature of each work. To describe his prose adaptation of Paulinus of Nola's poem on the life of St. Felix, Bede used the expression "... de metrico Paulini opere in prosam transtuli." This last word indicates precisely the transformation of a work from poetry into prose.[29] For his composition of the verse and prose Lives of St. Cuthbert, Bede employs the verb *descripsi*, which means "write, compose," and which recalls the author's careful discussion of his methodology in the preface to this work.[30] But for the *Passio S. Anastasii* Bede makes use of the much more modest *correxi*. By using such a word, Bede was assigning to himself a more limited role than the one he assumed in his composition of the other two hagiographic pieces. Bede's description is almost apologetic—"I corrected according to the sense as best I could the book of the Life and Passion of St. Anastasius badly translated from the Greek

27. My translation, which departs from the translation of Colgrave and Mynors facing the Latin text.

28. Although Bede treated saints and their Lives in numerous works, only these three belonged to the distinct genre he calls the *historiae sanctorum*, that is works that concentrate exclusively on one saint's Life. The three works are listed chronologically according to the time in which their subjects lived, which may have been Bede's organizational principle here.

29. Bede uses the verb *transferre* in only one other passage in *HE* to describe Caedmon's transformation of material into song—and therefore verse. See Jones, *Concordance*, pp. 539-540. Bede added his own preface to the Life of Felix. The edition of J.A. Giles has a colophon in Bede's name (*Venerabilis Bedae Opera* IV, 200), but it is not clear to me whether this is authentic.

30. I.e. for publication, not in the sense of note taking, I believe. It is noteworthy that Bede here also (as in the preface of his prose *Vita Sancti Cuthberti* [ed. Colgrave, pp. 141-144]) fails to mention the Anonymous's *Life of Cuthbert*, on which his own work is believed to have been based. The three works are not, or at least not explicitly, joined here then by their common chararacteristic of being based on earlier works.

and worse emended by some unskilled person." *Pro ut potui* implies that the resulting text was deficient, and that Bede was well aware of its shortcomings. He may have used *ad sensum* to indicate that the result would be an approximation based on his own interpretation of the text, not a literal *ad verbum* rendering of the original, which was not possible since his source was not the original Greek and was furthermore faulty.[31] By using the word *correxi*, Bede may also mean revision and adaptation, which were appropriate for non-literal translation. He is therefore displaying his knowledge of the technical terminology of translation theory, learned from patristic sources, such as Gregory and Jerome, and from his own direct experience of translation.[32]

Bede does not reveal how he knew that the *Passio* of the Persian saint had been badly translated from the Greek. It is possible that he may have surmised that this text was a translation from its title or colophon, although its language and content could have supplied sufficient evidence for Bede to label it *male translatum*. Another possibility is that the Greek text may have been brought to England from Italy by Archbishop Theodore, and then found its way to Bede, along with the bad translation and poor correction. The format in which the earliest version of the *Passio S. Anastasii* traveled from Rome to England with Theodore, and the form in which it was available to Bede remain unknown. Our knowledge of the early dissemination of hagiographic texts is very sketchy because of the paucity of evidence.[33] The transmission of

---

31. The Colgrave-Mynors edition translates *ad sensum* as "to clarify the meaning." I see no support for such an interpretation. Rather, *ad sensum* must mean that Bede distinguishes between a literal adaptation and an *ad sensum* adaptation, based on the *general* sense he can establish under the circumstances. This word, and even this very expression, is used in this way in *HE*, as for example in V.17 (pp. 512-513; "Haec de opusculis excerpta praefati scriptoris ad sensum quidem uerborum illius, sed breuioribus strictisque conprehensa sermonibus ..."), or in IV.24 (pp. 416-417, the story of Caedmon; "Hic est sensus, non autem ordo ipse uerborum ..."). It is clear then that Bede is contrasting a literal with a more approximate meaning. Bede's understanding of a literal, or word-for-word, translation was probably shaped by biblical glossing.

32. See below, pp. 197-198, 223.

33. Philippart, *Légendiers*, pp. 28-29.

some of the texts in the manuscript that contains the first translation suggests that a group of them may have traveled to Canterbury together.[34] Further research into the availability and transmission of the hagiographic texts known in Anglo-Saxon England is needed to resolve these issues.[35]

My comparison in the preceding chapter of *BHL* 408(p) with the Greek has revealed that the redactor of p did not make systematic, active use of the Greek text to correct the language or meaning of the early translation.[36] As discussed above, p at most suggests only occasional awareness of the meaning of a Greek word. The method followed by the editor of p corresponds to the method that Bede followed in his own work: "pro ut potui ad sensum correxi" concedes the inadequacy of his version of the *Passio S. Anastasii* because it was not based on the Greek.

The question of Bede's knowledge of the Greek language has frequently been addressed, but only recently has the complexity of the material that must be taken into consideration been illustrated.[37] Bede's passionate philological preoccupation with the text of the Bible made him especially sensitive to the problems of translation. His interest in the *Passio S. Anastasii*, the only hagiographic piece that Bede cited extensively in his Chronicle, may have stemmed partly from its nature as a translated text. Bede knew well enough that a translation is but a pale reflection of the original.[38] By the time he composed the *Retractatio* on the Acts of the

---

34. See my preliminary conclusions in "Theodore and the *Passio S. Anastasii*," pp. 184-185. For general comments, see Lapidge, "Editing Hagiography" and "The Saintly Life in Anglo-Saxon England."

35. Evidence for the early circulation of hagiographic collections in England is provided in BN 10861, a collection of eighteen hagiographic texts of third- and fourth-century martyrs which may have been copied in southern England in the ninth century. See Brown, "Paris, Bibliothèque Nationale, lat. 10861 and the Scriptorium of Christ Church, Canterbury," pp. 119-157.

36. See above, pp. 166-170.

37. On Bede's knowledge and use of Greek, see Dionisotti, "On Bede, Grammars, and Greek," pp. 111-140.

38. Meyvaert, "Bede the Scholar," p. 49, points out that Bede was keenly aware that the only way to determine the validity of a translated text was to master the original language, a teaching that went back to Augustine.

Apostles, when he was in his fifties most likely, Bede had taught himself enough Greek to be able to apply a rigorous, critical-philological approach to the biblical text, comparing different Latin readings with the Greek. But such knowledge of Greek was acquired in his maturity: the result of his careful study of bilingual biblical texts, and his knowledge of patristic authors and Latin grammatical works. He did not have any kind of Greek grammar from which to learn, nor any bilingual glossary or dictionary to which he could refer. We cannot be sure whether the Greek text of the Passion was available to Bede, but his meticulous choice of words in the *Historia Ecclesiastica* indicates without a doubt that he was not able to refer to it at that time. His inability to use the Greek source, whether or not he had access to it, is another reason why Bede was apologetic about the text, and why he used the phrase "pro ut potui ad sensum correxi." Clearly, Bede believed that the Passion of Anastasius, being a revision of a translation, belonged in a different category from all his other writings.

Bede and the Latin Style of BHL 408(p)

Out of Bede's prolific corpus, it is the *Historia Ecclesiastica* that survives in the most authentic form. It is found in copies almost contemporary with the author's own lifetime, the products of the scriptorium of Wearmouth-Jarrow itself. Yet, even in the *Historia Ecclesiastica* there are occasional instances of what might be termed "mistakes." One editor has found thirty-two examples "where some defect of sense or syntax suggests that correction is required."[39] Twenty-six of these instances are found in passages Bede is transcribing from an earlier source. It is disconcerting that Bede, "an excellent Latinist," incorporated so many documents into his text of the *HE* without making corrections.[40] It is possible that Bede's reluctance to make changes stemmed from the respect he had for his source and its historical accuracy.[41] For example, in the epi-

39. Mynors, *HE*, pp. xxxix-xl.

40. This puzzled Meyvaert: "Nevertheless one is left with the enigma of a man who had a shrewd sense of textual problems failing to bring it to bear on material replete with such problems" ("Bede the Scholar," p. 51).

41. This is most likely in the cases where Bede is quoting Pope Gregory's *Libellus responsionum*. See Meyvaert, "Bede the Scholar," pp. 50-51.

sode recounting the martyrdom of St. Alban, which is based on the *Acta* of the martyr, there is a geographical description that simply does not make sense.[42] This erroneous reading, as it turns out, is also contained in a ninth-century copy of the *Acta*, and it is assumed that Bede was simply copying his source verbatim. It remains puzzling, however, why Bede did not make the obvious textual emendation to clarify the story. A similar observation could be made in the case of the grammatical error that occurs in the Life of St. Fursey, again arising from Bede's faithfulness to his source.[43]

In addition to errors resulting from a close adherence to the source, the editors of the *HE* have singled out six additional problems. These discrepancies should be considered genuine authorial mistakes, which could have occurred "if the author had changed his mind and not removed all traces of the change."[44] Three of these mistakes show lack of gender agreement between noun and adjective or relative pronoun. In these cases, it is possible that Bede could have first used a word of a different gender, then inserted another one but neglected to change the noun's qualifiers. In another case, one finds the double use of a pronoun, resulting perhaps from the fusion of two phrases.[45] These examples, in other

42. *HE* I.7 (p. 30): "pervenit ad flumen quod muro et harena, ubi feriendus erat, meatu rapidissimo diuidebatur," where "ad fluuium quo murus" is the better reading.

43. *quartus* where *quartum* is required (*HE* III.19 [p. 272]).

44. *HE*, p. xl. Taking into account both the excellent state of the transmission and the nature of the mistakes, it is unlikely that these discrepancies are due to scribal error.

45. *HE* IV.22(20) (p. 402): "promittens se nihil ei mali futurum pro eo ..." which Mynors suggests may be the result of the fusion of *nihil ei mali facturum* and *nihil mali futurum pro eo*. The other two examples of errors identified by Mynors are the omission of *ut* in the heading of II.5 (p. 118), which is probably just a slip; and the omission of a word to serve as object of *habentes* in V.13 (p. 500). In this last case, Mynors suggests that Bede may have been uncertain as to what word to use, a problem compounded by the fact that he needed to find a Latin word to render accurately the vernacular one. It is interesting to note that later scribes added *vomeres*, not in the common meaning of "ploughshares," but in its more arcane meaning of "small point," "stylus."

words, are not unlike the linguistic problems found in the p redaction, which I have called examples of "incomplete correction."[46]

The death scene in Cuthbert's *Life* (chapters 37-39) has been recently singled out as uncharacteristic of Bede's style. The language in this scene is much less polished and sophisticated than in the rest of Bede's work. There is a much greater use of short paratactic sentences and unnecessary personal and possessive pronouns in chapters 37 and 38. It is possible that Bede was anxious to report the account of the death scene in the very words of his informant, Herefrith.[47] However, Bede goes on to improve Herefrith's Latinity when reporting the very last words of the saint (chapter 39), a point in the story where one would expect the text to remain faithful to its source. Fidelity to Herefrith's language can only play a small role in an explanation of Bede's awkward Latinity.[48] Bede's *Capitula lectionum*, only recently identified, provide additional material that broadens the range of Bede's Latin usage. While the literary quality of these chapter summaries—the use of variety in word order and syntax, the balancing of construction, the attention to story development, etc.—betray the hand of a master, here too occasionally is found a more casual Latin style than one would expect from the general estimates of Bede's Latinity.[49]

If we accept that Bede's Latin was much more varied, and even less "correct" than is generally admitted, and that Bede himself characterized his "librum vitae et passionis S. Anastasii" as a modest

46. See pp. 176-177.

47. Berschin, "*Opus Deliberatum ac perfectum*: Why Did the Venerable Bede Write a Second Prose Life of St. Cuthbert?," p. 102. Berschin quotes as examples of phrases that one "cannot imagine that Bede could have written": "Qui cum ad nonam usque horam *intus* cum illo maneret, *sic* egrediens vocavit me: Episcopus, *inquiens*, te iussit *ad se* intrare. Possum autem tibi rem referre novam *permirabilem*, quia ..." where the italicized words represent what Berschin regards as redundancy.

48. Berschin himself pointed out the need for further study of these particular passages. Another issue to be addressed is whether it was Latin or English that Herefrith and Cuthbert used.

49. Meyvaert points out the "misuse" of indirect discourse: "Apparuit Deus ad Isaac sponte impleturum se quod pollicitus est Abrahae" ("Bede's *Capitula lectionum*," p. 370 and n. 2).

achievement, we can proceed to a more balanced estimation of *BHL* 408(p) as a possible work of Bede. Considered within this more limited perspective, the only passages that would strain belief in Bede's authorship are found in the preface of the *Passio S. Anastasii*. As an examination of the text will show, the preface frequently follows the early translation almost verbatim, and, like its model, it is rife with problems.[50] In numerous places, it is incomprehensible. But it would be hard to imagine how an editor who did not have access to the Greek could have improved it. Only the Greek original can reveal the meaning behind the obscure Latin of the preface; there is no story line to guide the Latin editor, as there is in the rest of the text. Hence, the only real option would be to eliminate the preface altogether, a practice that is contrary to the approach taken by this editor. The rest of *BHL* 408(p), however, is much clearer, and could be attributed to Bede, within the parameters delineated above. An example chosen for its linguistic peculiarity from cap. 23 illustrates how the language and style of p match Bede's established practice.

t : Si enim noueratis Christum, habueretis conuerti ad lucem, et erui
   a daemonibus qui errare uos faciunt (ll. 307-308)

p : Si enim cognovissetis Christum qui vos fecit, quandoque converti
   habuissetis ad veram lucem, et erui a daemonum potestate qui vos
   errare faciunt (ll. 337-338)

The phrase *converti habuissetis* seems awkward, and unworthy of a good Latinist. While the past-contrary-to-fact condition in t is cleaned up by the use of the pluperfect subjunctive (*habuissetis*) as Latin grammar requires, one might have expected a less awkward phrase, such as *conversi essetis*. However, the editor of p here must have understood the source text as expressing not only past-contrary-to-fact, but also necessity, and it is this meaning that he rendered with *converti habuissetis* = "you would have had to be converted," "you would have been converted." Such an interpretation might also explain the addition of *quandoque*. In the *HE*, one frequently finds the use of *habeo* in the meaning of "have to" or "must,"

---

50. The prefaces to *BHL* 410b and 408(p) are found on pp. 272-276 and 387-392 respectively.

as, for example in "... supplicia tu soluere habes,"[51] or "... tu in ipsa domo mori habes"[52] and "Sed primum expectare habes."[53] The use of *habeo* and the infinitive to indicate necessity parallels the subjunctive and the infinitive of p's example above. The strained language of p is an attempt both to accommodate the meaning of the translation while at the same time correcting its blatant errors. Such practice could be described, using Bede's words, "pro ut potui ad sensum correxi."

It is in this context that we might reexamine Bede's factual mistakes about the Persian in the Chronicle and Martyrology, in particular his account of the way in which Anastasius died. We should perhaps consider that Bede was capable of error. Bede's first redaction of the metrical *Vita S. Cuthberti* shows him "capable of minor slips in comprehension of the anonymous prose *Life*" on which his own work is based.[54] Even his final metrical version contains inconsistencies when compared to his prose Life.[55] A better known error, acknowledged by his contemporaries, is the mistaken chronology of the reigns of Samuel and Saul in Bede's commentary on Acts 13.21, even though in an earlier work he had given the correct number of regnal years.[56]

---

51. *HE* I.7 (p. 30), the account of the *Passio* of St. Alban.

52. *HE* III.22 (p. 284).

53. *HE* IV.14 (p. 376).

54. Lapidge, "Bede's Metrical *Vita S. Cuthberti*," p. 83. For example, at one point in the early redaction, Cuthbert is said to be prior of Melrose when in fact, as the anonymous *Vita* states, he was already prior of Lindisfarne.

55. For example, in the poem, Bede says that Cuthbert was recalled after his departure from Melrose by Bishop Eata, while in the prose Life he is called *Abbot* Eata. Eata was made bishop in 678, and Bede's inconsistency confuses the date at which this occurred. See Stancliffe, "Cuthbert and the Polarity between Pastor and Solitary," p. 33. Another "mistake" (perhaps made by a student rather than Bede himself) is the inclusion of the book of Daniel and the exclusion of Ezechiel in the list of *Capitula lectionum* for the Old Testament that Bede says he composed, when in fact it appears to be the other way around (Meyvaert, "Bede's *Capitula lectionum* for the Old and New Testaments," p. 361).

56. Laistner, *Expositio in Actus apostolorum et Retractatio*, pp. XV-XVI. Laistner suggests that in his commentary on Acts Bede used earlier, uncorrected notes.

Bede and the Nature of BHL 408(p)

One can also ask whether the nature of p provides evidence of Bede's language, interests, and personality. The characteristics of p that have been singled out in the previous chapter certainly fit Bede's style. For example, p's emphasis on monastic discipline and its more precise monastic vocabulary are reminiscent of Bede. This is evident in the phrase, "Erat enim sedulus valde in ministerio fratrum et in opere manus, et prae omnibus in regulam monachi-cam intentus et in Missarum solemniis frequentans" (ll. 166-168), which is a revision of the translation's "Erat enim sedulus ualde in ministerio fratrum et in opere manus et prae omnibus in re-gulam diuinae missarum aderat" (ll. 157-159). This reworking in-troduces more rigor and precision to the monastic and liturgical description of Anastasius's new life. Furthermore, the term *mona-chicam* is first found in Gregory the Great's *Dialogues* and Letters, and not found again until Bede uses it in his description of Ecbe-rectus's *monachica vita*.[57]

The redactor of p, as discussed in the previous chapter, perceived a conflict between the requirements of monastic vows, in particu-lar that of obedience, and Anastasius's desire for martyrdom, which led him to abandon his monastery in secret without the permission of his abbot, and he modified the text accordingly.[58] The changes introduced by the editor of p to portray Anastasius as a dutiful monk recall, for example, Bede's emphasis on Cuth-bert's obedience to his abbot, or Ceolfrith's diligent monastic behaviour. In his efforts to portray these two men as models of cenobitic monasticism, Bede, it has been argued, even glossed over evidence to the contrary.[59] The author of p was just as willing to

---

57. Gregory uses the word sixteen times. According to *CLCLT*, Bede's only use is in the *Chronica maiora*, chapter 66 (ed. Jones, pp. 532-533). But it is also found in the *Vita Sancti Cuthberti* (ed. Colgrave, p. 208), e.g. *instituta monachica*, which is not included in the *CLCLT*. The point I am making here is that the editor of p probably learned this word from Gregory, and we know that the word was known to Bede.

58. See above, p. 171.

59. While the anonymous source describes Cuthbert's departure from Melrose to Lindisfarne using words such as *fugiens, abscedens, enavigavit*, in Bede's *Vita* it is Abbot Eata himself who transfers Cuthbert to Lindisfarne

edit his text in order to strengthen the description of Anastasius as a good monk.

The textual approach of the editor responsible for p is also reminiscent of Bede's methods.[60] His attempts to maintain the integrity of his source while making sense out of it, his ingenuity in emending a very inadequate text, correspond to Bede's scholarly habits, particularly if one compares p to the other reworking of the early translation, *BHL* 410, and to *BHL* 411a.[61] His use of 410, which would correspond to the text that he characterized as *peius emendatum*, emphasizes his careful methodology, the primary goal of which was to restore the meaning of the original text exploiting every tool at his disposal. The *Passio S. Anastasii* is the only work that Bede describes as a reworking or a correction of an earlier one.[62] His principal concern was to render the meaning as best he could ("pro ut potui ad sensum correxi"). This was also the main concern of the redactor of p, to render the meaning of the original text faithfully, in contrast to *BHL* 411a and *BHL* 410.

As we have seen, lexical echoes also couple Bede's Chronicle and p. It is important to note that in a few cases p and the Chronicle agree against *BHL* 410b and *BHL* 410.[63] Rather than the result of chance, this might mean that the redactor of p and the author of the Chronicle willfully used the same word. This could therefore be taken as evidence for Bede's authorship of p. We can reasonably reject the other possibility, that p was the version he characterized

---

(ed. Colgrave, p. 207). Even in his treatment of Ceolfrith, contrary to the anonymous Life, Bede omits Ceolfrith's departure from Monkwearmouth while he was prior during Benedict Biscop's absence (*Historia abbatum* 7 [ed. Plummer, pp. 390-391]). See Stancliffe, "Cuthbert and the Polarity," pp. 32-33). For Bede's didactic tendencies, see Campbell, "Bede," pp. 176-184.

60. See above, pp. 168-171, 175-176.

61. For Bede's scholarly approach, see in particular Meyvaert, "Bede the Scholar," pp. 4-50.

62. The *Vita S. Felicis* evolved in a different way, and Bede never claims that the *Vita S. Cuthberti* is based on what we call the anonymous *Life*. See above, p. 195 and n. 29.

63. Of particular significance, the Chronicle and p agree in changing t's *mansionem* to *monasterium*; in reading *Christi nomen*; in their common use of *perpessus*. See above, pp. 187-193.

as "worse emended," for it is difficult to believe that Bede or anyone with textual expertise could consider p as a worse text than
the *BHL* 410b translation.[64]

The results of any broader lexical comparison between p and
Bede's works in general can only be used with caution because
there is no other writer who can be used in comparison,[65] and
also because p is to a very large extent conditioned by its source,
a situation limiting the lexical and stylistic choices of its author.
There are, however, particular instances of lexical usage that recall
Bede's habits, and that, taken together with the other considerations adduced so far, help to strengthen the case for attributing
BHL 408(p) to Bede.

The first is the use of the verb *insinuo* as a replacement for *nar-
ro*. The verb *insinuo* occurs twice in p:

p : "Insinuavit autem ei omnia quae viderat" (ll. 389-390)
t : "Enarrauit autem ei omnia quae uisa sunt" (ll. 356-357)[66]
p : "et insinuavit eis minutius" (ll. 627-628)
t : Et ipse insinuauit eis minutatim (l. 586)[67]

Hence, p in one place substitutes the word *insinuavit* for *enarravit*,
and keeps it in another place where it is already being used. The
verb *insinuo* is found 343 times in the works of Bede; it is a word
that Bede clearly used a lot.[68] This verb, as defined in standard

---

64. The third possibility, that the redaction I call *BHL* 408(r) might have
been Bede's "badly translated text" and p the "worse emended," can be rejected both because p is in fact better than r, and also because it would have
to accommodate the anteriority of p over r (cf. below, pp. 365ff.). Given the
survival of *BHL* 410b, furthermore, one can also reject the possibility that p
was the translated text referred to by Bede.

65. In other words, we can only tell whether a specific word is found in
Bede's works, or how frequently.

66. *BHL* 410 reads: "Enarravit ergo ei ille omnia quae viderat" (ll. 255-
256). One of the revisions of *BHL* 408, r_2 (the "Roman Revision"), keeps *insinuavit* (l. 367); another, p_1, changes it to *dixit* (l. 377).

67. *BHL* 410 keeps *insinuavit* (l. 441); p_1 changes it to *narravit* (l. 606);
r_2 to *notificavit* (l. 605).

68. 334 times as surveyed in *CLCLT*, and nine more in the *HE* (Jones,
Concordance, p. 265). But it is also used frequently in Gregory (439 times)
and Augustine (517 times).

dictionaries, generally means "to wind one's way into" and, secondarily, "to make favorably known, to introduce, to recommend." In Bede's theoretical works, and particularly in the biblical expositions, it often means "to signify." In the *HE*, the verb occurs four times in direct quotations from papal letters; in another case, Bede is citing Archbishop Augustine. But in the other four cases, Bede uses it directly, in the unusual meaning of "tell," which is the way it is used in the Passion of Anastasius.[69]

Another lexical link is the unusual word *zona*. In his *Life of Cuthbert*,[70] Bede uses the word *zona* to describe the girdle of the saint, which is used to cure Abbess Aelfred. In p, t's *cingulas* (l. 457), used to describe one of the gifts the king offers Anastasius in exchange for apostasy, is changed into *zonas* (l. 495). This is a word found numerous times in Bede, referring principally to a component of monastic garb.[71] It is possible that the Greek-sounding word was used in p as an attempt to achieve historical accuracy.[72]

The use of the phrase "ad culturam eius pertingere" in p (l. 104) is also reminiscent of Bede, who uses the word *cultura* frequently in the more unusual meaning of "worship," as it is used here.[73] The substitution of t's *argentariae artis* with p's *malleator* (l. 120)

---

69. See *HE* I.7 (p. 30); I.10 (p. 38); II.22 (p. 136); IV.11 (p. 366). See also *In Marci euangelium expositio* III, 9 (ed. Hurd, p. 545 l. 124): "et quasi manifestius fidem aduentus eius illis insinuans, hic uir, inquit, hic est ille quem moyses iste uobis saepius in mundo nasciturum promisit."

70. Chapter 23 (ed Colgrave, pp. 230-232).

71. There are 267 citations in all of *CLCLT*; by far the largest number is found in Jerome (41 times) and Bede (26 times).

72. However, it is also possible that *BHL* 410b's reading originally may have been *zonas*. *BHL* 410 has, unfortunately, cut this passage out. Although *zonas* is used in *BHL* 411a, this could be considered another indication of this text's preference for Greek-sounding words.

73. As, for example, in *In Lucae euangelium expositio* IV, 15 (ed. Hurd, p. 287): "qui in unius dei permansere cultura." *CLCLT* reports twenty-one occurrences of this word in Bede, most of them signifying a religious activity, and occasionally meaning agricultural cultivation.

is also striking, for this word, found only in a few authors, occurs three times in Bede.[74]

The change of t's *disciplinam* (l. 65) into p's *correptionem* ([l. 68] not *correctionem*) is also significant. In the *HE* and Bede's other works, *disciplina* is never used in the sense of "correction," the meaning in the early translation, but rather always as "monastic discipline" or "ecclesiastical discipline" or "learning."[75] This is another example of p's careful attention to monastic terminology, which is also found in the works of Bede.

2. THE MANUSCRIPT EVIDENCE

The *Passio S. Anastasii* is not included in any English hagiographic collection.[76] Nor is it found among Ælfric's homilies and saints' lives composed in Winchester at the end of the tenth century.[77] There is no manuscript of the *Passio S. Anastasii* that names Bede as the author, and there is no surviving evidence that any library in the Middle Ages possessed such a document.[78] This does not

---

74. The word *malleator* is a biblical one (found in Gn 4.22 and Jb 41.15). It is found thirty-one times in *CLCLT*, and only in Jerome—six times, all in his *Book on Hebrew Names*—does it occur more frequently than in Bede.

75. *correctus* comes from *corrigo*=to correct, while *correptus* (post-Augustan) comes from *corripio*=to snatch; to correct (secondary meaning). *Correptio* is found thirty-four times in Bede's works according to *CLCLT*; it does not occur in the *HE*, but II.6 is entitled "Ut correptus ab apostolo Petro Laurentius ... ."

76. The earliest surviving collection (now Paris, BN 10861) was probably written at Canterbury in the early ninth century and contains only eighteen texts; the oldest multivolume legendary to survive is the so-called "Cotton-Corpus legendary," which was copied from a northern French original. For an introduction, see Jackson and Lapidge, "The Contents of the Cotton-Corpus Legendary."

77. See Lapidge, "Ælfric's *Sanctorale*," p. 25.

78. On the contrary, its absence from medieval libraries was often noted, since Bede's catalogue of his own works in the *HE* served as an obvious checklist for well-organized librarians. This occurrred, for example, in the ninth-century catalogue of the library at Murbach, where Bede's own description of the Passion (as taken from the *HE*) is included under the rubric "Sequentes libros adhuc non habemus" (Cf. *AB* 90 [1972], 216); and in the list

mean that Bede could not have been responsible for *BHL* 408(p).
Although Bede listed this revision among his writings, he may not
have formulated a new title or colophon for a work that was merely
a correction of a poor text to begin with. This might explain why
p itself did not survive in a collection of Bede's works,[79] but only
in passionaries and legendaries. Texts included in such hagiographic compendia generally do not carry the author's name. There are
a number of reasons for this. Firstly, most of these texts are in
fact anonymous. Secondly—and perhaps more crucially—in these
books the saint in question is far more important than the author
of the *vita* or *passio*. For example, in the oldest complete witness
of p (BAV, Palatinus latinus 846), Walafrid Strabo is not mentioned as the author of the Life and Miracles of St. Gall.[80] The
absence of Bede's name on any of the manuscripts of p is therefore
not conclusive. Its absence would have been of greater significance
had p survived in some context other than regularly organized
hagiographic collections.

The location of the earliest manuscripts of p and the *BHL* 408
tradition as a whole is generally consistent with Bede's authorship.
The region of western Germany where the earliest manuscripts of
the 408 version were written match the areas where Bede's writings were used from early on, and where the earliest copies of
Bede's works have survived, most of them brought to the Conti-

of books available in various English libraries prepared by Henry of Kirke-
stede (d. after 1378) (Rouse, "Boston Buriensis and the Author of the *Catalogus Scriptorum Ecclesiae*," p. 495. It should be noted that Rouse's study
corrects an earlier assertion by James regarding the presence of Bede's *Passio*
at Bury St. Edmund's Library, *The Abbey of St. Edmund at Bury*, p. 38,
repeated by Laistner, *Hand-List of Bede Manuscripts*, p. 87).

79. Similarly, the remnants of the early verse Life of Cuthbert survive
anonymously in the Besançon collection discussed in Lapidge, "Some Remnants of Bede's Lost *Liber Egigrammatum*."

80. This text is included in the first part of the codex, ascribed to the
tenth-century scriptorium at Lorsch. The Leningrad Bede, containing the *HE*
and attributed to the Wearmouth scriptorium in the 740s, does not name the
author, since the last line of the colophon is believed to be a fake (Parkes,
The Scriptorium of Wearmouth-Jarrow).

nent for the use of Anglo-Saxon missionaries.[81] The *Historia Ecclesiastica* is the only one of Bede's numerous works whose extensive circulation in England between Bede's death and the Norman Conquest is documented by surviving manuscripts. The earliest copies of Bede's other works are mostly found in ninth-century continental manuscripts, written in northern France and Germany, which is where the passionaries containing *BHL* 408 were generated.[82]

There are also connections between the circulation of p and its direct revisions *BHL* 409 and p$_1$ (discussed in the next chapter) and Anglo-Saxon England. The manuscript tradition of *BHL* 409 and p$_1$ has close links with that of the anonymous Life of Cuthbert, a text used as a source in Bede's own Life of the Northumbrian saint: all three legendaries containing *BHL* 409 and p$_1$ also contain the anonymous Life, whose circulation was extremely limited, surviving today in only seven manuscript witnesses, all of them from the Continent. The three legendaries therefore provide evidence for a possible Anglo-Saxon origin of the p-redaction.[83] In addition, a late manuscript of p (Cambrai 816) also contains Bede's prose Life of Cuthbert, the account of the translation of St. Cuthbert in 1104, and the *Brevis Commemoratio* of Bede (*BHL* 1071).[84] This is another manuscript link between p and English texts of particular relevance to Bede.

81. Lapidge, "Some Remnants," p. 78; Parkes, *Scriptorium*, pp. 14-20.
82. Many of Bede's minor works survive only in continental copies (Brown, "An Historical Introduction to the Use of Classical Latin Authors in the British Isles from the Fifth to the Eleventh Century," p. 281).
83. My study of the circulation of the *BHL* 409 and p$_1$ versions of the *Passio* confirms the relationship between these three legendaries proposed by Colgrave in his study of the *Vita S. Cuthberti*, and further links the circulation of the Anastasius texts and the Cuthbert text. Colgrave noted that two of the legendaries (Harley 2800 and Brussels 207-208) share a common ancestor for the Life of Cuthbert, a "parent legendary" composed some time in the twelfth century in the diocese of Trier, while the third, the legendary of St. Maximin of Trier, preserves a different tradition (*Two Lives*, p. 43).
84. Colgrave, *Two Lives*, pp. 33-34. See my edition of p and "Descriptive List."

Bede was the author of a great number of works that circulated widely in England and in areas where Christian culture was being established. The fact that so many of his works survive is proof of their wide circulation.[85] There is evidence that there was a great demand for the works of Bede in western Germany by the middle of the eighth century, as reflected in the letters of Boniface, archbishop of Mainz, both to Archbishop Egbert of York and to Hwaetberth, abbot of Wearmouth, urgently requesting copies of Bede's writings. These demands continued into the next generation, when Boniface's successor, Lull, wrote to Aethelbert, archbishop of York, requesting copies of Bede's hagiographical works.[86]

One can easily understand, however, that while Bede's exegetical and didactic works were needed by the missionaries of northern Europe at this time,[87] the revision of the Passio of an obscure Persian saint was not so much in demand, and its exclusion from Anglo-Saxon compendia containing Bede's works should not be surprising. However, its inclusion in the passionaries compiled in western Germany suggests that the reworking of the Passio S. Anastasii was brought into this area by the same route as the better known works of Bede.[88]

85. See Gorman, "Wigbod and the Lectiones on the Hexateuch Attributed to Bede in Paris Lat. 2342," pp. 343-345. Since Gorman first compiled his useful list, Meyvaert has identified the various Capitula lectionum; see p. 200 and n. 49 above.

86. Parkes, Scriptorium, has illustrated how heavy demands for the works of their house author placed a huge strain on the human and financial resources of the scriptorium of Wearmouth-Jarrow, so much so that a new, more efficient script was adopted as the common bookhand to replace the monastery's traditional Roman uncial.

87. The interest in the HE, whose many continental copies testify to its popularity, is more difficult to explain. Perhaps it served as a model for the conversion and transformation of a pagan nation into a Christian one. See Parkes, Scriptorium, p. 16.

88. There are, however, a few scribal slips in the π branch of BHL 408(p) that may suggest an ultimate exemplar copied in England: these "symptoms of insular transmission" include the reading of perfectum rather than praefatum (l. 124) suggesting the confusion of an open a for ec; the confusion of qui for quod (l. 153); the misunderstanding of enim for autem (l. 166). See Brown, "An Historical Introduction," pp. 237-299; Beeson, "Paris Lat. 7530: a Study in Insular Symptoms."

3. The Hieronymian Martyrology

The information in both Bede's Chronicle and his Martyrology suggests that Bede depended on another source in addition to the *Passio S. Anastasii* for his knowledge of the Persian monk. This conclusion is contrary to that of editors of his works, who believed that the *Passio* was, ultimately, Bede's only source.[89] The following "additional" information taken from the Chronicle and Martyrology is not reported in the *Passio*:

1. The first translation of the relics from Persia to Jerusalem: "reliquiae beati martyris Anastasii primo monasterium suum" (Chronicle);

2. Aquae Salviae as cult location: "Ad Aquas Salvias sancti Anastasii monachi et martyris de Persida" (Martyrology); "[reliquiae] deinde Romam advectae venerantur in monasterio beati Pauli apostoli, quod dicitur ad aquas Salvias" (Chronicle);

3. Anastasius's execution by decapitation: "ad ultimum decollatus est" (Martyrology); "sic decollatus cum aliis LXX" (Chronicle).

(1.) Bede would not have learned about the removal of the relics from Persia to Jerusalem from the Latin *Passio*. The *Passio* ends with the return of Anastasius's confrere to Jerusalem, before the removal of the relics took place. The account of the first removal of the body of the martyr from its original burial place at the monastery of St. Sergius in Persia to the monastery near Jerusalem is given by *BHG* 88 (= *Translatio*).[90] If Bede had known this work,

---

89. Quentin concluded that the source for the entry on the Persian monk in Bede's Martyrology was the Chronicle, and not the *Passio* (*BHL* 408) (*Les martyrologes historiques*, p. 106). Mommsen, in his edition of the Chronicle, had supplied the *Passio* as the source of the Chronicle passage. He reached this conclusion, however, without noting either the "additional information" that the Passion could not have provided to Bede, or the inconsistencies between the Chronicle and *BHL* 408 (*Chronica* 539 [p. 310]; Jones's edition [p. 524] adds nothing).

90. Flusin has argued convincingly that when the relics arrived in Jerusalem, a second edition of the Greek *Acta* was redacted, which circulated with the *Translatio*. The Latin tradition, however, was based on a copy of the first edition of the Greek *Acta,* which did not contain the account of the translation of the relics. Moreover, as far as we know, the *Translatio* was never translated into Latin. See pp. 72-73. Sansterre, *Les moines grecs* II, 71-72

we would expect some reference to the journey of the relics, to the miracles that took place along the route, and perhaps also to specific topographical features, given his interest in the geography of the Holy Land. More crucially, had Bede been familiar with this text, he would have known that the emperor Heraclius had restored the Holy Cross to Jerusalem, an event surely worthy of notice in the Chronicle.[91]

The entry in the Chronicle reporting the first removal of the body from Persia to Jerusalem is of great significance since Bede appears to be the *first Latin writer* to be aware of this fact. Such knowledge is likely to have come from someone who had a particular interest in the story of Anastasius: a member of the monastic community *ad Aquas Salvias*, or someone who might in some way be connected with Anastasius's monastery near Jerusalem, or the places of his martyrdom and death. It is possible then, that Bede's information originated from such a person, directly or indirectly, orally or in writing. Theodore of Tarsus, who most probably brought the copy of the *Passio* of Anastasius, when he came to England as archbishop of Canterbury and who may well have been a member of the community at the Aquae Salviae, could have brought this information as well, perhaps noting it in a colophon on his copy of the text. Alternatively, it could have come from someone in contact with Theodore, such as Benedict Biscop who traveled with the archbishop from Rome to Canterbury in 669.[92] Likewise, one of Theodore's pupils at Canterbury could have taken this information with him to Wearmouth-Jarrow. There is no evidence for these hypotheses, however.

(2.) Similarly, Bede would not have learned about the cult status of Aquae Salviae from the *Passio*. There is no written source, in Greek or Latin, to explain how the head reached Rome, although it seems most likely that it was brought there by monastic exiles.[93]

---

n. 66, states that Bede knew both *Acta* and *Translatio*, but offers no supporting evidence. He was presumably following the Chronicle and Martyrology entry.

91. For Bede's notices on the feasts of the Holy Cross, see below, p. 222.
92. Meyvaert, "Bede and the Church Paintings at Wearmouth-Jarrow," p. 63.
93. For the relic and its travels, see pp. 9ff.

It is certainly possible that Bede received information about the relic from Anglo-Saxon pilgrims who had seen the head at the monastery outside of Rome, a favorite pilgrimage stop.[94] It is also possible that a liturgical calendar or even a list of the major relics preserved in Rome, or a guide to the holy places in the city[95] could have provided Bede with this piece of what I call "additional information."

There is, however, evidence that Bede learned about Anastasius's relics from a more formal liturgical work linked to Archbishop Theodore, perhaps a martyrology, a book that is concerned primarily with the death and the final resting-place of the bodies of the saints. This evidence is provided by the earliest martyrology to include Anastasius, the Epternacensis recension of the *Martyrologium Hieronymianum*. Its entry for January 22 reads: "... et rōm ad aquas salvi sci anastasi episcopi,"[96] which is very similar to the opening of Bede's own Martyrology entry: "Ad Aquas Salvias sancti Anastasii monachi et martyris." The Hieronymian's use of *rōm* is also found in Bede's Chronicle.

The Hieronymian Martyrology, the oldest surviving Latin martyrology, was compiled in northern Italy in the fifth century, probably in the region of Aquileia.[97] It was then worked over in northern Gaul, most likely at Auxerre, at the very end of the sixth century. A copy of this reworking was transmitted to Anglo-Saxon England, where it received further revision. This English recension was then brought to the Continent, for it survives exclusively in one manuscript, the Epternacensis (=E), so called because of its

---

94. The traffic of Anglo-Saxon travelers to Rome has been documented for the early eighth century. Among the best known are Benedict Biscop and Ceolfrith, both of whom traveled to Rome several times, and King Caedwalla (see n. 92 above and the reference to the *Historia abbatum*. See also Moore, *The Saxon Pilgrims to Rome and the Schola Saxonum*). Bertolini, *Roma di fronte a Bisanzio e ai longobardi*, p. 40 n. 43, says that Bede must have learned that Anastasius's relics were in Rome from "un itinerario romano."

95. Such as the *De locis sanctis* (Chapter I, p. 10).

96. Delehaye, *Commentarius Perpetuus in Martyrologium Hieronymianum*, p. 55. The word *episcopi* is clearly a scribal mistake for *martyris* or *monachi*. The Hieronymian Martyrology is plagued with scribal errors.

97. See Dubois, *Les martyrologes du Moyen Âge latin*, pp. 29-36.

association with the household of St. Willibrord (658-739) at Echternach (Luxemburg). Willibrord, a native of Northumbrian and contemporary of Bede, known as the "missionary to the Frisians," was also the founder of the monastery of Echternach. It was there most likely that the Epternacensis redaction of the Hieronymian Martyrology was copied by an Anglo-Saxon scribe named Laurentius in the early part of the eighth century,[98] before the death of Willibrord in 739.[99] The Echternach Martyrology occupies the first part (fols. 2-33) of Paris, Bibliothèque nationale, lat. 10837. The second part (fols. 34-41), with which the Martyrology has been associated from before the middle of the eighth century,[100] is the personal calendar of St. Willibrord, also written by an English hand between 703 and circa 710, and well known for the marginal entry in St. Willibrord's own hand on fol. 39v commemorating the anniversay of his ordination.[101]

The Echternach Martyrology reveals its origin primarily by its inclusion of five Anglo-Saxon commemorations: St. Augustine of Canterbury, St. Paulinus, the bishop of York buried at Canterbury, King Oswald of Northumbria, St. Cuthbert, and Oidiwald

---

98. It seems clear to me that the Martyrology was copied at Echternach because of the scribe's links with Echternach charters. Laurentius, who identifies himself in a colophon ("Tuorum, domine, quorum nomina scripsi sanctorum eorum queso suffragiis miserum leva Laurentium; tuque idem lector ora"), is known to us from four Echternach charters (dated 704, 710, 711, 721/2: see Wampach, *Geschichte der Grundherrschaft Echternach im Frühmittelalter*, nos. 8, 17, 28, 32); he is also commemorated in an acrostic poem in the Maihingen Gospel (Duchesne and de Rossi, *Martyrologium hieronymianum*, p. viii). The controversial issue of whether the Echternach scriptorium followed the scribal traditions of Ireland or Northumbria is irrelevant here (Ó Cróinín, "Is the Augsburg Gospel Codex a Northumbrian Manuscript?" pp. 189-201; and Metzer, "Willibrord's Scriptorium at Echternach and its Relationship to Ireland and Lindisfarne," pp. 203-212).

99. The death and deposition of the saint in 739 are noted in the margin of fol. 28v (Ó Cróinín, "The Augsburg Gospel Codex," p. 192).

100. Duchesne and de Rossi, *Martyrologium*, p. viii.

101. Duchesne and de Rossi, *Martyrologium*, p. viii. The note was written in 728. A facsimile of the calendar is found in Wilson, *The Calendar of St Willibrord from MS Paris. Lat. 10837. A Facsimile with Transcription, Introduction and Notes*.

of Ripon.[102] It also reflects the influence of a liturgical book of Campanian origin by its notices of saints such as Castrensis of Castel Volturno, Juliana of Cuma, Sossius of Miseno, Augustinus and Felicitas of Capua, and Nicander, Cassianus and Felicissimus also of Capua.[103] It has been convincingly argued that the Martyrology made use of a liturgical book brought to England by Hadrian, who had been a monk at a monastery near Naples before traveling with Archbishop Theodore to Canterbury, where he became abbot of the monastery of SS. Peter and Paul.[104]

Just as the Epternacensis recension has English additions, so too could the information it contains concerning St. Anastasius and the Aquae Salviae be considered an English insertion. This has not been noted by scholars investigating the links between the Epternacensis redaction and Anglo-Saxon England because Anastasius is not thought of as an English saint.

The entry on Anastasius in the Hieronymian Martyrology could not have been introduced during its reworking in northern France for obvious chronological reasons.[105] Nor does it seem likely that it came from the Campanian liturgical source. First of all, the commemoration of Anastasius is not found in the calendar of Willibrord. As the same Campanian liturgical book was a source for both the Epternacensis Martyrology and the calendar of Willibrord, this argues against the presence of Anastasius in the Campanian book.[106] Secondly, it seems unlikely that the cult of Anasta-

---

102. Duchesne and de Rossi, *Martyrologium*, pp. viii-ix.

103. Duchesne and de Rossi, *Martyrologium*, p. ix.

104. On Abbot Hadrian, see Bischoff and Lapidge, *Biblical Commentaries*, passim, esp. pp. 82-132 and 160-167. There is some disagreement among scholars as to whether it was Hadrian or Benedict Biscop who brought this Campanian sacramentary to England. However, this controversy does not alter the belief that the liturgical book was of Campanian origin.

105. The edition prepared by Quentin clearly singled out the entry on Anastasius as an addition peculiar to E (Delehaye, *Commentarius*, p. 55).

106. The calendar contains all the Campanian saints found in the Martyrology, with the addition of St. Lupulus of Capua. There is no reason to believe therefore that Anastasius would have been excluded. Another witness of the influence of the Campanian source in Anglo-Saxon England is the Walderdorff Calendar, a fragmentary liturgical calendar which covers only

sius would be commemorated in a Campanian liturgical book that appears to have reached England at the same time as Abbot Hadrian, especially since Anastasius's cult was just beginning to be established in Rome itself, as Hadrian and Theodore embarked for England.[107] It seems likely, therefore, that, as in the case of the text of the *Passio*, this martyrological entry, which confirms the presence of the cult in Rome, came to England via Rome, and that it was in England that it was added to the developing English version of the Hieronymian Martyrology.

It could be argued, on the other hand, that the addition was the result of continental influence, that it came to be added at Echternach, where the manuscript preserving this recension was copied. The fact that the commemoration of St. Anastasius is also found in the oldest representative of the other family of manuscripts of the Hieronymian Martyrology, B, written for the monastery of Saint-Avold near Metz toward the end of the eighth century, could be cited as support for this argument.[108] The entry in B, however, is much later and more basic than the one found in the Epternacensis, reading merely *anastasi martyris*.[109] It does not contain the topographical information preserved in the Epternacensis, and also found in Bede's Martyrology, and thus only provides evidence that the *Passio* and/or the date of Anastasius's feast were known in the region of Metz.[110] It is also clear that the saints who may

---

the months July to October, and therefore has no bearing on the present question. See Siffrin, "Das Walderdorffer Fragment saec. viii und die Berliner Blätter einer Sakramentars aus Regensburg," pp. 201-224; and Bischoff and Lapidge, *Biblical Commentaries*, pp. 164-165.

107. The earliest notice of the commemoration of Anastasius in the Neapolitan region is the so-called Marble Calendar, dating from after the middle of the ninth century; see Delehaye, "Hagiographie Napolitaine," pp. 8-11, 59.

108. Dubois, *Les martyrologes*, p. 31. The same addition is found in C (Paris, Bibliothèque nationale, lat. 12410), a manuscript from the eleventh century, and of the same family as B, hence irrelevant to our discussion (Delehaye, *Commentarius*, pp. xi; 55). The manuscripts of the Hieronymian Martyrology are divided into two families, both of which go back to a "Gallican archetype."

109. Delehaye, *Commentarius*, p. 55.

110. This is not surprising: some of the oldest manuscripts of *BHL* 408 come from this region of Germany.

have been included in the Epternacensis at Echternach are by and large monastic figures from Ireland and continental Irish foundations—for example, St. Bridget of Ireland, or St. Attala of Bobbio or St. Patrick[111]—who reflect Echternach's or Willibrord's cultural background. Anastasius the Persian monk has no special connection with Willibrord or his household, and therefore there is no reason to connect him with these notices.[112]

If the Anastasius entry did not originate in Echternach, we need to look elsewhere for a source. Bede tells us himself that he used a copy of the Hieronymian Martyrology in his *Retractationes in Actus Apostolorum*.[113] Quentin's study of the historical martyrologies has shown that the Anglo-Saxon monk used a version of the Hieronymian Martyrology that is closest to the Echternach recension.[114] In addition, the entry for St. Dula in Bede's Martyrology in particular indicates that the copy of the Hieronymian Martyrology used by Bede was more extensive (or "less abridged" in Quentin's words) than the one surviving in the Epternacensis

---

111. Found respectively in Delehaye, *Martyrologium*, pp. 70, 135 (17 March). St. Willibrord spent twelve years in Ireland before his Frisian mission. I do not mean to imply that these saints would not be venerated in England; their addition could just as easily be the result of English influence. In fact there are no saints found in E who, for chronological reasons, must have been Echternach additions. According to Duchesne, the latest chronological entry may be the commemoration of Oidiwald (Ethelwald) of Ripon, buried at Farne, who died between 699 and 705 (*Martyrologium*, p. viii). As the earliest dated document by Laurentius is the charter of 704, it is conceivable that even the commemoration of Oidiwald was not original to E but was found in its source. Clearly, a more complete study of E is called for.

112. Although it is known that Willibrord wrote in the calendar, we have no such physical evidence to link him to the Martyrology (Wilson, *Calendar*, p. XIV).

113. "Quibus adstipulatur et liber martyrologii qui beati Hieronimi nomine ac praefatione adtitulatur, quamvis idem Hieronimus libri illius non auctor sed interpres, Eusebius autem auctor extitisse narretur" (I, 13; ed. Laistner, p. 96).

114. Quentin, *Les martyrologes historiques*, pp. 109-111. For example, see the mention of St. Juliana of Cuma discussed on p. 109.

codex.[115] Given the agreement between the opening words of Bede's Martyrology notice and the Epternacensis recension, it is tempting to identify Bede's fuller copy of the Hieronymian Martyrology as the source that supplied him with the "additional information" concerning the cult of Anastasius at the Aquae Salviae. At the very least, it suggests that Bede and the Martyrologist used the same source.

The next question to address is whether the information about the relics' first translation from Persia to Jerusalem was also contained in Bede's copy of the Hieronymian Martyrology/common source. This detail would not be out of place in a martyrology, since martyrologies commemorate the death and deposition of saints and are closely preoccupied with relics.[116] The Epternacensis here provides no clue. It should be noted, however, that a characteristic of the Epternacensis singled out by Delehaye is its tendency to delete topographical detail.[117] In other words, the elimination of the detail of the translation from Persia to Jerusalem is consistent with known excisions in the Epternacensis. As we know that Bede's copy of the Hieronymian was more extensive than the version surviving in the Epternacensis, it is possible to maintain that there was one single source for both relic translations. This is certainly a tidy solution. Otherwise, we would have to postulate two extra sources for Bede besides the *Passio S. Anastasii*, one of which would also be the source for the Echternach Martyrology.[118]

---

115. Quentin, *Les martyrologes historiques*, p. 110.

116. Dubois, *Les martyrologes*, pp. 13-14: "les premiers martyrologes anonçaient tout au plus avec le nom du saint, le lieu de son culte et sa qualité ..."

117. "Recordasse iuverit in codice Epternacensi, ceterum praestantissimo, non pauca consulto resecta esse quae pertinent ad indicia topographica, ecclesiarum dedicationes et elogia quae hinc inde in martyrologium inserta sunt" (*Commentarius*, p. XI).

118. If Bede obtained this information about the double translation—first to Jerusalem, then to Rome—from the same source, this could explain Bede's use of the term *reliquiae* in the Chronicle. For while it was the *relics* of Anastasius that were translated to Jerusalem, it was only his *head* whose presence is attested in Rome. Hence, it is conceivable that Bede's source used the term *relics* to refer to this double translation. On the other hand, it is also very possible that *reliquiae* was Bede's own choice of words, either

(3.) As for the discrepancy in Bede's account of Anastasius's execution, it is difficult to attribute this to Bede's copy of the Hieronymian Martyrology or to another source. If we assume that this source was a martyrology or a source similarly interested in the relics, especially the head of the martyr, then it is possible to see how Bede could have mistakenly concluded that the cause of the martyr's death was decapitation. Learning that the relic of the head was kept and venerated at the Aquae Salviae could easily have led to that belief. It is also worth bearing in mind the probable haste in which the 114 full entries for Bede's Martyrology were composed, thereby introducing the possibility of error.[119]

A number of conclusions, some of them tentative, can be drawn from the above discussion of the history of the Hieronymian Martyrology and Bede's treatment of the Persian martyr. It seems certain that the information concerning the commemoration of Anastasius at the Aquae Salviae contained in the Echternach recension of the Hieronymian Martyrology was added in England, at the same time that the English saints were added to the martyrology. Secondly, it seems likely that the detail concerning the cult of the relic of the head at Aquae Salviae in Bede's Martyrology may have come from his copy of the Hieronymian Martyrology, a version of this ancient text identified by Quentin as close to the Epternacensis, but fuller and more detailed. This same copy of the Hieronymian Martyrology may have also provided Bede with information about the relics' first translation from Persia to Jerusalem. Alternatively, the Martyrologist and Bede may have shared a source for their treatment of Anastasius, but Bede would have had an additional source containing the detail about the translation from Persia to Jerusalem, perhaps a colophon or other note on his

---

because he did not know whether the head and the relics had traveled together, or because he wished to subsume both translations under one heading for brevity's sake.

119. Dubois, *Les martyrologes*, p. 14. There could be a similar explanation for Bede's error concerning the regnal years of Samuel and Saul; see above, p. 202 n. 56. In both cases, an earlier work (*De temporibus*, BHL 408[p]) was correct, but a later work (*Expositio in Actus, Chronica maiora*) relied on earlier misinformation (Josephus, Hieronymian Martyrology).

copy of the *Passio*. In any case, it is clear that this little known fact must have ultimately come to Bede from Archbishop Theodore or someone closely associated with him. Scholars who have searched for the influence of Theodore and Hadrian on the cult of the saints in England have concentrated on St. Willibrord's Calendar, the Old English Martyrology, and Bede's *Martyrologium*.[120] The Echternach Martyrology should be added to this list.

The evidence presented in earlier studies supports the conclusion that the Latin translation of the Greek *Acta* of the Persian saint was brought to England by Theodore.[121] The archbishop is also the most likely source for Bede's knowledge of the translations of the saint's relics. Therefore, a copy of the Latin *Passio* would have come to Bede from Canterbury rather than Rome. This is not surprising: the connections between Canterbury and Wearmouth-Jarrow during Bede's lifetime have been well documented.[122] Bede was on good terms with Albinus, abbot of SS. Peter and Paul at Canterbury, as reflected in the exchange of books between the two monastic centers. There is evidence that Bede's works were sent to Canterbury, including the famous letter in which Bede tells Albinus that he is sending him a copy of the *Ecclesiastical History* together with the *De templo Salomonis*.[123] It is clear that Bede was in turn a beneficiary of the Canterbury collection of books and documents. Materials relating to the councils of Hertford and Hatfield held under Archbishop Theodore in the 670's must have come from Canterbury,[124] and Pope Gregory's *Libellus responsionum* as well as Gregory's letter to Archbishop Augustine dealing with the structure of the Anglo-Saxon church may have come from there.[125] The *Libellus*, in particular, may have derived from

120. See in particular, Christopher Hohler, "Theodore and the Liturgy," and the works by Michael Lapidge cited throughout this section.

121. Franklin, "Theodore," and above, pp. 78-80.

122. This topic is treated most recently in Kirby, *Bede's Historia Ecclesiastica Gentis Anglorum: Its Contemporary Setting.*

123. PL 94, 655-657.

124. *HE* IV.5 (pp. 348-352) and 17 (pp. 384-386).

125. The *Libellus* contains the pope's answers to questions from Augustine (*HE* I.27 [pp. 78-102]). See also *HE* I.29 (pp. 104-106).

a penitential collection associated with Archbishop Theodore.[126] Bede was familiar with some of the teaching of the Canterbury school, for he tells us how he learned of Theodore's exegesis of 2 Cor 11.25 from some of Theodore's own pupils.[127] Benedict Biscop also provides a link between Wearmouth-Jarrow and Canterbury. He traveled with Theodore from Rome to England in 669, and then was in Canterbury for two years as abbot of SS. Peter and Paul before he founded Wearmouth and Jarrow.

The question of Bede's interest in this obscure Persian saint still remains unanswered. It could be that Bede recognized that the *Passio* was an historical work, an important source for his own interest in world history, and, more specifically, in universal Christian history. Anastasius's early life was lived against the background of sensational events. The *Passio* begins with the Persian conquest of the Holy Land and ends with the emperor Heraclius's victory over the pagan Persians. It is the only hagiographic piece that is used at length in the Chronicle, and Anastasius's martyrdom is the only incident in the war between the Byzantines and Persia recorded there.[131] The *Passio* was also used as a source for Bede's Martyrology, another work concerned with the worldwide history of Christian saints. It connected Bede to Rome and to the East, places rich in the precious relics of Christian martyrs. Both in the Chronicle and the Martyrology Bede is careful to specify the fate of the relics of Anastasius, part of the treasure held by the city of Rome and venerated by Wearmouth and Jarrow.[132]

126. Meyvaert, "Bede's Text of the *Libellus Responsionum* of Gregory the Great to Augustine of Canterbury," p. 16.

127. Bischoff and Lapidge, *Biblical Commentaries*, pp. 41, 160 and n. 116. It is worthy of note that Albinus had been one of the Canterbury pupils whose Greek learning—under the teaching of Theodore—Bede praised: "... in tantum studiis scripturarum institutus est, ut Grecam quidem linguam non parva vero parte, Latinam vero non minus quam Anglorum, quae sibi naturalis est, noverit" (*HE* V.20 [p. 530]).

131. Goffart, *The Narrators of Barbarian History (A.D. 550-800): Jordanes, Gregory of Tours, Bede, and Paul the Deacon*, p. 248.

132. For the influence of Rome on Wearmouth-Jarrow, see, most recently, Ó Carragáin, *The City of Rome and the World of Bede*. Bede shows his interest in relics and their translation elsewhere in his Martyrology, where he

The link between Anastasius and the Holy Cross is another like-ly reason for Bede's interest in the saint.[133] The cult of the cross was very powerfully expressed in Anglo-Saxon England through artistic, literary, and liturgical monuments. The icon of Christ exalted on the cross brought to Jarrow by Biscop, the jeweled cross of Abbess Bugga's church described by Aldhelm, and the Old English poem *The Dream of the Rood* provide well-known testi-mony to the veneration of the cross in Anglo-Saxon England.[134] The liturgy, and not only on Good Friday, emphasized the adora-tion of the instrument of Christ's death and human salvation. Ceolfrith's last liturgical act was to kiss and venerate the cross before his departure from Wearmouth-Jarrow for Rome, where he would be able to venerate relics of the True Cross at the Vatican and Lateran basilicas, and at S. Croce in Gerusalemme.[135]

Bede's own interest in the cross is evident in his writings. In the Martyrology, for example, he notes both the feasts of the Inven-tion of the Holy Cross on 3 May, and of the Exaltation on 14 Sep-tember.[136] In the Chronicle, Bede quotes the *Liber pontificalis* at length to provide an account of Pope Sergius's discovery of a lost relic of the cross in the sacristy of the Vatican, which would be venerated from that time on at the Lateran on the Feast of the Ex-altation.[137] Also in the Chronicle is Bede's account of the abduc-tion of the cross from Jerusalem by the Persians, most likely based

---

notes—the first writer to do so—the translation of St. Augustine's relics to Pavia by King Liutprand, an event, dated variously between 710 and 733, during Bede's lifetime (Quentin, *Les martyrologes*, p. 109).

133. For much of what follows, see Ó Carragáin, *The City of Rome*, p. 14 and passim.

134. Mayr-Harting, *The Coming of Christianity to Anglo-Saxon England*, pp. 187, 194, 204.

135. Ó Carragáin, *The City of Rome*, p. 14.

136. However, he does not reveal any knowledge of the events com-memorated by these two feasts. The first feast marks the discovery of the relic by the Empress Helena; the other feast marks Constantine's consecra-tion of the *Martyrium* and *Anastasis*, the places of Christ's crucifixion and resurrection in Jerusalem, as well as the Exaltation of the Cross.

137. Duchesne I, 374; *Chronica maiora*: pars 568-569 (ed. Mommsen, p. 316).

on the *Passio* of Anastasius, which singles it out as one of the scourges visited upon God's people during the Persian advances. Bede remained unaware, however, that the emperor Heraclius restored the cross to Jerusalem, for which the *Translatio* of Anastasius's relics from Persia is an important source.[138]

It could also be that the *Passio* was of interest to Bede in his role as textual scholar. The nature of the *Passio* as a translated and revised text no doubt appealed to Bede's general interest in the process of translation, as he investigated the translations of the scriptural text for his exegetical treatises and as part of his community's preparation of a new edition of the Bible.[139]

Through the Martyrology and the Chronicle, which later scholars routinely incorporated into their works, Bede became responsible for spreading the knowledge of the Persian monk in the Latin West throughout the Middle Ages. Many medieval chroniclers of world histories included the paragraph about the Persian's conversion and martyrdom from Bede's Chronicle.[140] The early-ninth-century Old English Martyrology was largely indebted to the Chronicle. Florus of Lyon in the later ninth century combined Bede's Martyrology and Chronicle for his own Martyrology entry on Anastasius,[141] an entry that was repeated almost verbatim in the historical martyrologies of Ado of Vienne (†875) and of Usuard (†ca. 877).[142] Usuard's Martyrology, adapted to local use, was

---

138. *BHG* 88; see Flusin I, 98, II, 293-309; and above, pp. 211-212.

139. Marsden, *The Text of the Old Testament in Anglo-Saxon England*, esp. pp. 107-139; Franklin, "Bilingual Philology in Bede's Exegesis."

140. A good example is Ordericus Vitalis, who simply repeats Bede's discussion verbatim (*Historia Ecclesiastica* I, I [PL 188, 81]).

141. Florus: "Ad Aquas Salvias, natale sancti Anastasii monachi et martyris de Persida: qui post plurima tormenta carceris, verberum et vinculorum quae in Caesarea Palestinae perpessus fuerat a Persis, postremum in Perside multa poena affectus, atque ad ultimum decollatus est a rege eorum Chosroe cum aliis septuaginta. Reliquiae corporis ejus primo Hierosolymis ad monasterium suum, deinde Romam delatae, venerantur in monasterio beati Pauli apostoli, quod dicitur ad Aquas Salvias" (Dubois and Renaud, *Édition pratique*, p. 20).

142. For Ado's Martyrology, see Dubois and Renaud, *Le Martyrologe d'Adon. Ses deux familles. Ses trois recensions*, p. 68; Rabanus Maurus depended

read at the Office of prime in monastic and collegiate chapters, which means that the commemoration of St. Anastasius, as Bede had fashioned it, became the standard for the Middle Ages.

APPENDICES

1. THE OLD ENGLISH MARTYROLOGY (=OEM)

The Old English Martyrologist, probably writing in the early ninth century, composed the following entry for St. Anastasius:

> On the same day is the martyrdom of the holy man St. Anastasius, who was at first a sorcerer in the country of Persia, but afterwards he believed in Christ. Cosroas, king of Persia, ordered him be hung up by one hand and urged him to forswear the belief in God. As he would not consent to this, the king ordered him to be beheaded. The emperor Heraclius seized his body in Persia at the head of an army and brought it to Rome, and it rests in St. Paul's minster at the waters called Aquae Salviae; there his head is carried about in these days as a relic for Christian men.[143]

It is immediately apparent that Bede's Chronicle is the principal source for the Martyrologist: the suspension of Anastasius by his hand is singled out in both the OEM and in the Chronicle; the mistaken belief, found in the Chronicle, that Anastasius was executed by decapitation is repeated in the OEM. In fact, all the details contained in the Martyrology's entry are found in the Chronicle, with two important exceptions. The first is the erroneous statement that Heraclius brought back the body of Anastasius from Persia to Rome. It is my belief that the Martyrologist simply misread the Chronicle passage, which I cite here without punctuation, in an attempt to duplicate what the Martyrologist may have read:

> inter ea superveniens cum exercitu Heraclius princeps superatis Persis Christianos qui erant captivati reduxit gaudentes reliquiae beati martyris Anastasii primo monasterium suum deinde Romam advectae venerantur in monasterio beati Pauli apostoli quod dicitur ad aquas Salvias

---

exclusively on Bede's Martyrology: Dubois, *Le martyrologe d'Usuard. Texte et commentaire*, p. 166.

143. This is Herzfeld's translation of the Old English original (*An Old English Martyrology*, pp. 29-30). Herzfeld (p. xxxvii) gave Bede's Chronicle as the source for this entry. The edition prepared by Kotzor, *Das altenglische Martyrologium* II, 287 adds nothing further.

It seems likely that the Martyrologist took "superatis Persis Christianos qui erant captivati" to belong together, and "reliquiae" to be the object of "reduxit"[144] and thus concluded that Heraclius brought the relics from Persia to Rome.

The other difference between the OEM and Bede's Chronicle is the added fact that the *head* of St. Anastasius "is carried about as a relic for Christian men." This has been interpreted as an indication that the Martyrologist was updating his source—Bede—by adding new material culled from the Roman Miracle, where indeed the relic of the head is carried during the exorcism of the possessed girl.[145] The Miracle's presence in England is explained by claiming an English scribe for the Orléans manuscript (=O, in my edition). As I show in "Descriptive List" (pp. 523-524), the Orléans copy of the Miracle was copied at Fleury, not in England.

There is, furthermore, no evidence whatsoever that the Miracle was known in England. Rather, it is more likely that the OEM's information about the head of Anastasius was provided by a version of the English redaction of the Hieronymian Martyrology, which, as discussed above, might also have been a source for Bede's knowledge of the relics' presence in Rome.[146] Alternatively, the Martyrologist's information may simply have been provided by a pilgrim or visitor to Rome who would have seen the relic of Anastasius in ceremonial use.

By specifying that the *head* was *carried about*, the OEM shows that its compiler consulted sources other than Bede's Chronicle to cull material for this entry. Nonetheless, the central reliance on Bede is confirmed by the erroneous description of Anastasius's death by decapitation.

144. Either through carelessness or because of a defective copy. In Mommsen's critical edition of the Chronicle, there is a variant reading *Christianis* but no other reading for *reliquiae* is reported; only five manuscripts are systematically used for the edition, however, out of a total of 245 listed for the entire *De temporum ratione* (pp. 242-256). Jones's edition is basically a reprint of Mommsen's edition.

145. Cross, "On the library of the Old English martyrologist," pp. 239-240 and n. 65, and "The Use of a *Passio S. Sebastiani* in the Old English Martyrology," p. 50 and n. 39.

146. For the Hieronymian Martyrology as a source of the OEM, see Kotzor, *Das altenglische Martyrologium* I, 178*-179*.

2. ADO OF VIENNE

Ado of Vienne, through a misinterpretation of Bede's Chronicle, is responsible for the mistake in the Latin tradition that it was the emperor Heraclius who brought the relics of Anastasius from Persia to the monastery in Jerusalem, and even to Rome. In his influential universal chronicle, *De sex aetatibus mundi*, Ado used Bede's Chronicle, especially the treatment of Anastasius's life therein, as his principal source to cover the events surrounding the Persian wars during the reign of Heraclius. In the following passage, the sections in italics were copied by Ado straight from Bede's work, with only an occasional lexical change, while those in roman letters come from other sources or are original to Ado:[147]

Persae adversus rem publicam gravissima bella[148] gerentes multas Romanorum provincias et ipsam Hierosolymam capiunt: ac destruentes ecclesias, sancta quoque loca profanantes, etiam vexillum Dominicae crucis auferunt. Heraclius imperator, annis viginti sex. Anastasius Persa monachus, nobile pro Christo martyrium patitur: qui natus in Perside a patre puer magicas artes didicit; sed ubi a captivis Christianis nomen Christi accepit, in eo mox animo conversus, relicta Perside Chalcedoniam Hierapolimque, Christum quaerens, ac deinde Hierosolymam petiit, ubi accepit baptismatis gratiam. Quarto ab eadem milliario monasterium abbatis Anastasii introivit, ubi septem annis regulariter vivens, dum Caesaream Palaestinae orationis gratia venisset, captus a Persis, et multa diu verbera inter carceres et vincula Marcebana judice perpessus tandem in Persidem mittitur ad regem eorum Chosroam : a quo tertio per intervalla temporis verberatus, ad extremum una suspensus manu per tres horas, sic decollatus cum aliis septuaginta martyrium complevit. Mox tunica eius indutus quidam daemoniacus curatus est. Sigebutus Gothorum res in Hispania ... Persae Chalcedoniam usque pervenerunt. Aeunni murum longum irrumpentes, et moenia Constantinopolis accedentes cum Heraclio imperatore mutuo in muro stante colloquuntur, acceptoque ab eo pretio pacis ad tempus recedunt. Aetherius Viennensis .... a Dagoberto constituitur.

147. PL 123, 112-130. Examples of the minor changes introduced by Ado are: *Hierosolymam capiunt* for *Hierosolymam ... auferunt; vexillum ... auferunt* for *vexillum ... abducunt*. Ado's Chronicle—at least as printed in PL—removes a few words, and occasionally changes Bede's word order.

148. Ado's use of *bella gerentes multas* here shows his direct dependence on Bede (cf. the Chronicle s.a. 537 [ed. Mommsen, p. 310]), and not on Isidore's *Chronica*, Bede's source according to Mommsen, which reads: "Proelia quoque Persarum grauissima aduersus rem publicam excitantur" (*Isidori Hispalensis Chronica*, ed. Martin, p. 202).

Heraclius imperator cum exercitu superveniens Persis victor, Christianos qui ibi erant captivi reduxit, ac vexillum Dominicae crucis Hierosolymam triumphans reportavit. *Reliquiae* quoque *beati martyris Anastasii, primo ad monastrium suum, deinde Romam advecate, venerantur in monasterio beati Pauli apostoli, quod dicitur ad Aquas Salvias. Anno Heraclii imperatoris octavo decimo, indictione quinta, Eduinus excellentissimus rex Anglorum* ...

Typical of his method of composition, here Ado intersperses three quotations from Bede with text from other sources.[149] Following the second quotation taken from Bede, Ado adds the phrase *ac vexillum Dominicae crucis Hierosolymam triumphans reportavit,*[150] and then returns to Bede, adding, after *Reliquiae,* the conjunction *quoque* to connect these last two sentences.[151] The addition of *quoque* indicates that Ado misinterpreted Bede's text and believed that Heraclius brought back the relics along with the cross. Hence, in Ado's universal history the fate of the relic of the cross is linked to the body of St. Anastasius, leading to the mistaken tradition that Heraclius brought back the body from Persia. This error is followed, for example, by John the Deacon, the twelfth-century canon of the cathedral of St. John the Lateran, in his *Descriptio Ecclesiae Lateranensis.*[152] Similar misinformation is con-

149. A complete study of Ado's sources is still needed.

150. Bede gives no evidence that he knew that Heraclius had returned the True Cross to Jerusalem. Ado, on the other hand, was very familiar with *BHL* 4178, the *Exaltatio seu Reversio sanctae Crucis,* the account of the abduction of the Holy Cross by Chosroes and its return to Jerusalem by Heraclius, for in his Martyrology under September 14 he quotes at length from this work (as well as, again, from Bede's Chronicle).

151. No variant textual tradition adding *quoque* is indicated in the critical apparatus of Bede's Chronicle; I have checked several manuscripts of the Chronicle not consulted by Mommsen and found no *quoque* or any other textual variant suggesting that the misunderstanding might be due to the textual transmission of the Chronicle.

152. PL 194, 1556: "Est iterum ibi alia capsa deaurata, ubi est de ligno illo sanctae crucis, quam Eraclius devicto Chosroe secum tulit de Perside, una cum corpore sancti Anastasii martyris, et est in altare, quod ibi est Sancti Laurentii de marmore."

veyed in the *Pantheon* of Gotfredus of Viterbo (†1192/1200),[153] and in Martin von Tropau's *Chronicle* from the thirteenth century.[154]

153. "His diebus Anastasius ... Huius corpus Eraclius de Perside absportavit" (ed. G. Waitz, p. 196).

154. "Cuius corpus Eraclius imperator devictis Persis deducens Romam in monasterio sancti Pauli ad aquas Salvias collocavit" (ed. Weiland, p. 423). A further elaboration of this tradition, based no doubt on a misreading of John the Deacon's description of the relics found at the Lateran, maintains that the body of Anastasius was found together with the relic of the Holy Cross at the Church of the Saviour at the Lateran (discussed in *ASS* Ian. III, 38).

VII

THE OTHER REVISIONS

1. THE REVISIONS OF *BHL* 408(p)

I have argued in the previous two chapters that Bede was most likely responsible for the original revision *BHL* 408 of the poorly translated text of the *Passio S. Anastasii* preserved in *BHL* 410b. If so, then we have to assume that this version of the *Passio* was brought by missionaries from Anglo-Saxon England to eastern Francia, the area where many works of Bede were imported and where the earliest surviving passionaries containing *BHL* 408 originate. From there, *BHL* 408 spread to other regions, and was included in a growing number of hagiographic collections. During this process of diffusion, it gave rise to four revisions, each of which circulated in a restricted geographical area, reflecting the increasing localization of hagiographic texts. These are *BHL* 409, as inventoried by the Bollandists, and the revisions I have identified and named p_1, r_1, and r_2 (=Roman Revision), none of which are included in the *BHL* inventory.

BHL 409 and p_1 are descended from the form of *BHL* 408 that I have called BHL 408(p), or the p-recension. This version circulated, as far as the evidence indicates, principally in eastern Francia and Flanders.[1] It is not surprising, therefore, that these two revisions of p are found exclusively in the diocese of Trier, within the geographic parameters of their source text.

BHL 409 is preserved in only two legendaries. One is the three-volume compilation from the Premonstratensian monastery of Arnstein in Limbourg (in the diocese of Trier), copied ca. 1200, now preserved as London, British Library, Harley 2800. The other manuscript, closely related to the Arnstein compilation in terms

---

1. See below, pp. 381ff. for a discussion of all manuscripts.

of contents, is a legendary, also in three volumes and also from Trier, copied at the end of the twelfth or early in the thirteenth century (Brussels, Bibliothèque Royale, 207-208).[2]

The other revision of p, p₁, was incorporated in the legendary prepared at the Benedictine monastery of St. Maximin of Trier ca. 1235. Originally consisting of nine volumes, this collection has rightly been described as "the most comprehensive of all legendaries written on German soil."[3] The *Passio S. Anastasii* is included in the first volume, which encompasses the saints of January (Paris, Bibliothèque nationale, lat. 9741).[4]

As discussed in the previous chapter, there is a striking similarity in the circulation of these revisions of *BHL* 408(p) and that of the anonymous Life of St Cuthbert, a text used as a source in Bede's Life of the Northumbrian saint. All three legendaries containing the two revisions of p also contain the Cuthbert text, which survives today in only seven manuscript witnesses, all from the Continent. This connection with the Life of Cuthbert supports a possible Anglo-Saxon origin of the p-redaction.[5]

BHL 409's only departure from its source *BHL* 408(p) is the omission of the preface, the most obscure part of the text. Instead, it begins as follows:[6]

Temporibus Cosdroe imperatoris qui destruxit (cepit *corr. Harley*) Iherusalem extitit unus noster coronator Anastasius. Huius vitam quam ab initio usque ad finem scribere iusssus sum ipsum proponens testem quem ipse confessus est Deum et Dominum Ihesum Christum, ac sic incipiam enarrationis sermonem Domino protegente. Hic quidem erat ...

---

2. For bibliography on these manuscripts, see "Descriptive List."

3. Colgrave, *Two Lives*, p. 19.

4. It is edited below, pp. 449-468. This manuscript was also used by Jean Bolland in his edition of the *Passio S. Anastasii*. See below, Appendix 2.

5. My study of the text of the *Passio S. Anastasii* circulating in the Trier region (*BHL* 409 and p₁) confirms the relationship between these three manuscripts noted by Colgrave in his study of the *Vita S. Cuthberti* (see n. 83 of the previous chapter).

6. It could be argued that *BHL* 409 does not qualify as a discrete redaction from *BHL* 408; I have kept it separate, however, following the Bollandists' classification.

The *Passio* of St. Anastasius from the monastery of St. Maximin in Trier (p_1) has been shortened in places, in the interest of clarity. In general, only the most obscure passages are eliminated; others are successfully revised.[7] New biblical citations are incorporated, and, on occasion, simple explanations elucidating a passage have been added.[8]

These two adaptations of the p-redaction are related to the textual tradition of *BHL* 408(p) included in several exemplars of the *Liber de natalitiis*.[9] This large Cistercian legendary was compiled during the twelfth and thirteenth centuries in the area of Flanders and eastern Francia.[10] These four legendaries—the Premonstratensian Arnstein Legendary and its close relative now in Brussels (containing *BHL* 409), the St. Maximin Legendary (containing p_1), and the Cistercian *Liber de natalitiis* (containing p)—were based on the same core texts; each one was then tailored to meet local needs and interests. Thus, for example, the legendary from St. Maximin includes the saints Agricius, Poppo, and Maximinus, all of whom had close associations with the abbey. The *Passio S. Anastasii* was one of the core texts. Yet, even this text (and presumably others) was altered and manipulated by the compilers, reflecting the individualistic nature of each collection, and the fluidity of hagiographic textual transmission. Most of these revisions, however, are aimed at clarifying obscure passages to render the text worthy of inclusion in some of the largest hagiographic compendia of the Middle Ages.

7. See, for example, the preface, ll. 18ff, 52-56. One change is particularly significant, and may indicate that the reviser was not aware of the veneration of the relic of the head of St. Anastasius in Rome. According to this version, the head is sent to the Persian ruler (ll. 552-554).

8. For example, "omnia quae sunt hominis absque peccato sustinuit, *videlicet famem, sitim, sompnium ...*" (ll. 8-9).

9. As suggested by the textual evidence provided by the *Passio S. Anastasii* as well as the contents of these compilations. See p. 382.

10. These are the manuscripts under the "α" designation in my discussion of the p text.

2. THE REVISIONS OF THE *BHL* 408(r) REDACTION

The version of *BHL* 408 that I have identified as the r-redaction and discuss in the introduction to the edition of *BHL* 408(p) provides a good example of how hagiographic collections became increasingly localized and how individual hagiographic texts became tied to liturgical use. The r-redaction, and the third version of the *BHL* 408 group, the s-redaction, were copied into several legendaries in north-central Italy and the Roman region in the eleventh century. Production increased in the twelfth century, as indicated by the number of manuscript witnesses. This was a time when this area, which had previously produced fewer legendaries than northern Europe, became engaged in the large-scale production of hagiographic books.[11] Evidence from the surviving legendaries suggests that the diffusion of the r-recension began in north-central Italy, particularly around Ravenna, and then moved into the Roman region.[12] These are traditional legendaries, in general preserving complete texts, containing minor corrections. The most distinctive feature of these later legendaries is the inclusion of passions and lives of figures connected with local cults. The two revisions of r originated in these regions, possibly in response to the need to provide a text more suitable for public reading than the unrevised r-recension.

The first of the revisions, here designated as r_1, originated most likely in Emilia Romagna or Tuscany, in the late eleventh or early twelfth century. This is suggested by the contents of the collections in which this adaptation has survived: two legendaries from Tuscany (Rome, Biblioteca casanatense 718; Florence, Biblioteca medicea laurenziana, Strozzi I), and the legendary compiled at the beginning of the twelfth century for the cathedral church of Rimini.[13] These manuscript witnesses provide only partial evi-

---

11. Philippart, *Légendiers*, p. 45.

12. As discussed in Chapters III and IV, the more traditional Roman legendaries contain instead the second translation of the *Passio S. Anastasii* by Gregorius clericus (*BHL* 411a). See also Franklin, "Roman Hagiography and Roman Legendaries."

13. Biblioteca del Seminario diocesano, Codex s.n., a fragmentary legendary of the cathedral.

dence with which to determine the place of this recension in the textual development of *BHL* 408. But it is clear that they preserve a text that developed out of the r-recension.[14] The contents of these three legendaries overlap with a Ravenna legendary transmitting the original r-recension (BAV, Vat. lat. 6073).[15] This confirms that the area of diffusion of the r-recension centered on Tuscany and the region to the northeast, Emilia Romagna.[16]

The r₁ version of the Passion of St. Anastasius has been shortened so radically that entire passages have been cut out for the sake of brevity. So drastic in fact was the editing that even the death of the martyr is eliminated from the narrative, and the text is brought to a speedy, if somewhat abrupt, conclusion with the announcement that the martyr and seventy others are to be executed.[17] It is impossible to tell whether this was the intended ending, or whether the version as it survives is fragmentary.

14. As is indicated by the informative reading, for example, on fol. 136v of Strozzi I: "docuit eum litteras graecas simul et placentem dei doctrinam." (For the significance of *graecas* in the identification of the r-recension, see p. 365).

15. Of the first thirty-eight texts in Vat. lat. 6073—the period of the liturgical year roughly covered by Casanatense 718—all but four are contained in the Casanatensis codex. Similarly, there is a very close match between the corresponding sections of the Rimini legendary and Casanatense 718, but the Rimini book is a much bigger collection, embracing also the celebration of Christ's feasts and those of his mother, which are not found in the Casanatensis.

16. Since Vat. lat. 6073 cannot be considered a source for these volumes because of its later date (s. XII), their relationship may be explained by a common source. The textual evidence—at least as far as the abbreviated nature of Vat. lat 6073 allows such a comparison—shows several textual discrepancies between that text and the r₁ revision. For example, "erat enim sedulus valde *in monasterio* fratrum" (Vat. lat. 6073, fol. 64v) : "Erat enim sedulus *in ministerio* fratrum" (Casanatense 718, fol. 114r; Strozzi I, fol. 136v); "et linguis" *om.* (Vat. lat. 6073, fol. 63r) : "et linguis" (Strozzi I, fol. 135v) (Casanatense 718 has a lacuna here).

17. The text ends as follows: "... Qui veniens (*sic*) iusserunt eos educi foris predio Bethaloe in quo beatum Anastasium cum aliis circiter septuaginta viris interfecerunt propter nomen (fidem *Strozzi I*) domini nostri Iesu Christi. Qui vivit et regnat cum Deo patre in unitate spiritus sancti per omnia secula seculorum. Amen."

A more satisfying revision of *BHL* 408 in the r-recension is preserved in three twelfth-century legendaries compiled for Roman
churches (edited below, pp. 469-492). This revision, which I have
defined as the "Roman Revision" or r₂, is an attempt to provide a
clearer text, with a more precise and correct vocabulary.[18] The
reviser's pastoral intentions are revealed by a few additions to the
text. Two of these (ll. 28-30, 551-553) emphasize the Christ-like
forbearance of Anastasius during his trials and final execution.
Another is made in the preface's discussion of the triumph of the
Church in the face of persecutions by worldly powers (ll. 42-47;
i.e. the addition of Augustine's exegesis of Abraham's wife Sarah
as the Church). The three legendaries also show the continuing
evolution of this text toward greater simplicity and clarity. While
the legendary of S. Maria in Trastevere (Vat. lat. 1193)—the oldest
of the three—retains the preface (and includes the Roman Miracle),
the other two witnesses (Vat. lat. 1196; Vat. lat. 5696) have
eliminated it. The S. Maria Legendary offers clear evidence of the
liturgical use of this version. Although the text itself shows no sign
of division into readings by the original scribe, notes in the
margins, marking the text into five readings, are clearly visible.[19]

3. REDACTIONS ORIGINATING
FROM THE SECOND TRANSLATION (*BHL* 411a)

BHL 411: *The Beneventan Version*
This redaction of Gregorius clericus's version of the *Passio S. Anastasii*, previously published by the monks of Monte Cassino, is a
shortened version of *BHL* 411a.[20] I have found it in nine witnesses, most of them traditional legendaries dating from the second

18. For example, the text insists that the Persian ruler be addressed as *rex*
rather than as *imperator*.

19. See Vat. lat. 1193, fols. 73v-86v, where the abbreviation for "lectio"
plus the appropriate Roman numeral marks the end of each of the readings,
for both the *Passio* and the Roman Miracle. A copy of the Miracle text from
Vat. lat. 5696 made by Antonio Gallonio (1556-1605) is contained in
Biblioteca vallicelliana H 16.

20. As discussed above, pp. 86-93. The text is published in *Bibliotheca
Cassinensis* III. Florilegium, pp. 102-109. I refer to it by chapter.

half of the eleventh century to the seventeenth century. It derives from the manuscript branch of *BHL* 411a now represented by three Subiaco legendaries and the only surviving witness of that text in Beneventan script: Naples, Biblioteca nazionale VIII B 3 (=E in my edition), written in or around Troia in Apulia in the twelfth century. *BHL* 411, as I show in my introduction to the edition of *BHL* 411a, breaks off from this stemmatic branch below the Subiaco manuscripts and above E.[21] The four earliest legendaries in which *BHL* 411 is found (Codd. Cass. 123, 144, 145, 146), all from the second half of the eleventh century, are products of the scriptorium of Monte Cassino, even though some may have been used at other churches connected with the abbey.[22] At least three of these, and maybe even the fourth, were copied during the "Golden Age" of the scriptorium, during the abbacies of Desiderius and Oderisius I. They are to be considered display books, elaborately copied and decorated, intended for public use in the performance of the communal liturgy. The latest Beneventan witness is a legendary written at the end of the eleventh century or the beginning of the twelfth for the church of Valva and Sulmona in the Abruzzi (Vat. lat. 1197). The text of *BHL* 411 is also found in two twelfth-century legendaries written in common minuscule from Pisa (Rome, Casanatense 726; Vat. lat. 6933). One of these may have been copied for a monastic church.[23]

The evidence provided by the manuscripts containing *BHL* 411—as related to both their origins and their script—justifies the term "Beneventan version." Given the close relationship of *BHL* 411 to E, the only Beneventan manuscript of *BHL* 411a, it is possible that a copy made its way from the Roman region, where 411a originated, to a Beneventan-script region. Whether this was Monte

---

21. See below, p. 305.
22. For descriptions of these manuscripts, see "Descriptive List."
23. The text was also copied into a thirteenth/fourteenth-century legendary from Benevento (Rome, Biblioteca vallicelliana Tomus VI).

Cassino itself is unclear.[24] Although the exact place of origin of this text remains uncertain, we can be sure that *BHL* 411 was produced in an area where Beneventan script was employed, and that it spread from there. The presence of *BHL* 411 in the Sulmona (Abruzzi) legendary written in Beneventan indicates how far this text traveled. It is likely that one Beneventan copy found its way to Tuscany, to the neighborhood of Pisa, where the minuscule codices were copied.[25] The presence of this Beneventan text here may have something to do with the local economic interests of the abbey of Monte Cassino, which had possessions in Pisa from the early twelfth century.[26]

The Nature of BHL 411

The redactor of *BHL* 411 was attempting to create a simpler version of the Passion of the Persian monk by cutting out the stylistic and rhetorical embellishments of *BHL* 411a unnecessary to the narrative. For the most part these sections were the very ones that Gregorius clericus had added to adorn his version of the Life of the Persian.[27] The editor of *BHL* 411 also replaced longer circumlocutions with simpler ones, and on occasion eliminated unnecessary details. This can be illustrated most effectively by comparing the passages presented on pp. 87 and 88 above. In the first, *hos e contra circumvallans* is replaced with *cum magna manu suorum* (cap. 3), which, while well fitted to the story, does not correspond to the Greek model. In the second passage, 411a's elaborate phrase *eius quidem confessionis in Christo stabilitatem, et copiosam sine pavore alacritatem, magnam quoque cum perseverantia*

---

24. No manuscript of *BHL* 411a survives from Monte Cassino. Most of the early witnesses of *BHL* 411 are Cassinese products (Codd. Cas. 123, 144, 145, 146), while Vat. lat. 1197, the latest of the Beneventan codices, was written in the Abruzzi.

25. The earlier one, Casanatense 726, dates to the end of the eleventh century or the beginning of the twelfth. This copy ultimately led to the other minuscule codex, Vat. lat. 6933, from the latter part of the twelfth century.

26. Bloch, *Monte Cassino in the Middle Ages* I, 436-438.

27. The only "Gregorian" elaboration that escaped elimination is found in cap. 6 ("O cuncti creatoris—sonat" [411a, ll. 153-158]). Its survival helps to prove that *BHL* 411a and not *BHL* 411 is the original text.

promptitatem has been whittled down into 411's *eius confessionis in Christo stabilitatem et perseverantiam* (cap. 19).

The editor of *BHL* 411 also simplified the vocabulary of his model, replacing arcane words with simpler ones, or eliminating them altogether. Thus, for example, he consistently replaces *adsum* with a form of the plain *sum*. In the third passage on p. 90, he simply removes the rare *solicanus* (cap. 20), which is not necessary to the meaning of the story, and in fact has been added by Gregorius. He also replaces the precious *in nocturna furvitate* with the straightforward *nocte quadam*. Further down in the same passage, *BHL* 411a's Greek calque *eosdem crucigeris homoforis circumamictis respexit* is turned into the much simpler *eosdem ipsos palliis circumdatos habentes cruces in manibus*. This is a particularly important change because it recalls the revision that *BHL* 408(p) made to the early translation, most notably the addition of *in manibus*.[28] This suggests that the editor of *BHL* 411 may have consulted a copy of *BHL* 408, perhaps because he did not understand the unusual *crucigeris homoforis*. However, there are no other indications that *BHL* 408 was consulted, and it is possible that the addition of the phrase *in manibus* was arrived at independently as a way of improving the Latin text. To sum up, the redactor of 411 needed a shorter, simpler work than *BHL* 411a, and he achieved his goal by eliminating rhetorical passages, simplifying vocabulary and grammatical constructions, and correcting or emending his text.[29]

28. p: "vidit hos ipsos pallia circumdatos, habentes cruces in manibus" (ll. 376-377).

29. An example of editorial correction can be found in cap. 1, where the editor of *BHL* 411 emended the apparently ungrammatical *defertum* of E to *delatum*, not realizing that *defertum* is a corruption of the original reading, *devectum* (411a, l. 49). In a few cases, the changes in *BHL* 411 are due to the particularly poor copy of *BHL* 411a that was available to the redactor, for example, the phrase in the prologue rendered in 411 as "oblatrantes suos frementes denticulos in me exacuerent." Manuscript E, from which the 411 tradition descends, reads "oblatrantium suffrementes denticulos in me exacuerent," suggesting that perhaps the plural verb (*exacuerent*) rather than the singular *exacueret* of 411a (l. 10-11) may have led the redactor to change the *oblatrantium* to the nominative *oblatrantes*.

Apart from these basic, stylistic changes, no important factual details are cut. No revisions are made to Gregorius's prologue; the names of people and places are retained; and none of the secondary characters or scenes is eliminated. The changes introduced by the 411 redactor, therefore, were not nearly as drastic as in some of the other redactions of the Latin dossier of the Persian monk; rather, this version attempts to simplify style and language in a manner better suited to reading out loud in a liturgical or other common setting for which the rhetorical and lexical refinements of Gregorius's text (as well as his authorial intervention) seemed less appropriate.

BHL 411d: *The Benevento Revision*

Yet another redaction of the *Passio S. Anastasii* is the text inventoried by the Bollandists as *BHL* 411d[30] and published below (pp. 493-499). It survives in only two manuscripts. One is a legendary copied at Monte Cassino at the beginning of the twelfth century; the other is a hagiographic lectionary-homeliary written for the cathedral of Benevento in the first half of the twelfth century. A textual comparison proves beyond a doubt that *BHL* 411d is an abbreviation of *BHL* 411 and not of the original source of this family of texts, *BHL* 411a. The following comparisons provide a couple of examples to prove the point:

BHL 411a (ll. 177-179) ... *inconventaneos* ei cogitatus et magicorum quos a profano patre didicerat sermonum memoriam callide suggerebat.
BHL 411 (cap. 8) ... *nefarios* ei cogitatus et magicorum quos a profano patre didicerat sermonum memoriam callide suggerebat.
BHL 411d (ll. 26-27) ... magicarum artium memoria et *nefariis* illecebrosisque cognitationibus angebatur

BHL 411a (ll. 425-428) ... ut solo quidem verbo te esse christianum *abdicis*, et statim te absolvam; et quocumque volueris abire sive monachus volueris adesse, sive eques ut prius et nobiscum manere, tuae prorsus aderit potestatis.
BHL 411 (cap. 22) ... ut solo quidem verbo te esse christianum *abneges*, et statim te absolvam; et quocumque volueris abire permittam; et

---

30. *BHL. Supplementum*, p. 233.

sive monachus volueris esse, sive eques ut prius et nobiscum manere, tuae prorsus erit potestatis.

BHL 411d (ll. 79-81) ... ut si verbo tantummodo christianum te *abneges*, protinus te dimittam, et sive eques ut prius, sive monachus esse volueris, facultatem tibi tribuam liberam.

The use of *nefarious/nefariis* in *BHL* 411 and *BHL* 411d joins these two texts against 411a, which has *inconventaneos* instead. The presence of *abneges* in both 411 and 411d as opposed to *abdicis* of 411a illustrates again the dependence of 411d on 411, not 411a.

This is a revision clearly intended for liturgical use. In the Benevento book, *lectio* markings are part of the original lay-out of the page. The *Passio S. Anastasii* is divided into two *lectiones* supplying two readings for 22 January. The other ten lections to complete the liturgical *cursus lectionum* for 22 January are supplied in the same codex by the *Passio* of St. Vincent, the early Spanish martyr also venerated on this day. The Monte Cassino legendary (Cod. Cas. 141) does not appear to have *lectio* markings. But other texts have been shortened and simplified in much the same way as the *Passio S. Anastasii*, suggesting a similar purpose.[31] We may conclude that the redaction which I call the Beneventan revision was made for the precise purpose of being part of a liturgical book of the sort that now preserves it, in the Beneventan script area, since both the transmission of *BHL* 411d, and the earlier circulation of its "parent" text *BHL* 411, are confined exclusively to this script tradition.

The Nature of BHL 411d

This revision has been drastically cut; entire episodes are removed and the plot simplified by omitting secondary characters and factual details.[32] Chapters are sometimes eliminated in their entirety. Such large omissions include capp. 24-25 (=*BHL* 411a, capp. 29-30),

31. For example, also contained in this codex is *BHL* 2245, a Life of St. Dominic of Sora, also revised twice, and with a very similar redaction history. See Franklin, "The restored *Life and Miracles of St. Dominic of Sora* by Alberic of Monte Cassino," pp. 320-324. A detailed textual study of other lives in this codex might reveal similar reworkings.

32. The only addition made to *BHL* 411d, presumably by the redactor, is the biblical quotation from Ps (*iuxta LXX*) 123.7-8, in cap. 13.

which recount Anastasius's church visit on the Feast of the Exaltation of the Holy Cross and his interaction with the local Christians. Also eliminated are capp. 20-21 (=*BHL* 411a, capp. 24-26), which are principally concerned with the nocturnal visitation of bishops and angels to Anastasius's cell, as witnessed by the imprisoned Jew. All of the events that take place after the death of the saint—the miraculous phenomena marking his exposed body as holy, the return journey of his companion with Heraclius's victorious troops, and the first miracle performed by the colobium— are likewise excluded. So too is the entire prologue.

Secondary story lines are suppressed to simplify the plot. For example, only the events relating directly to Anastasius's interrogation and torture are recounted in cap. 8 (=*BHL* 411, capp. 26-28; *BHL* 411a, capp. 31-33), while the sub-plot relating the visit of Anastasius's two confreres to his jail is omitted. One of these monks is instrumental in the burial of the martyr's body, and, more crucially, in providing the eyewitness account on which the original *Acta* were based. Yet, these details are excluded from *BHL* 411d. Other factual information is also omitted: the names of Magundat's home city, of the monastery where he became a monk and of its abbot, of the patriarch Modestus who baptized him, of the Persian Christian Yesdin and his sons who supported and buried him.[33] As a result of these drastic excisions and simplifications, *BHL* 411d is reduced to less than a third of its model, and the richly detailed historical account that is found even in the reworked redaction *BHL* 411 is transformed into a more general story of martyrdom and death.

The Abbreviated Versions A and B

These abbreviated versions of *BHL* 411a were composed specifically for use as readings for the Divine Office on Anastasius's feast day. This is confirmed by the manuscripts that transmit Abbreviation A and Abbreviation B: specialized books, dating from the thirteenth and fourteenth centuries, more accurately called "Office lectionaries," for they contain all the readings for the liturgical

---

33. The Christian Persians who bury the body are simply described as "quidam christiani."

Office—biblical, patristic or homiletic, and hagiographical.[34] The Office lectionaries that transmit these abbreviations of *BHL* 411a were copied for Roman churches, St. Anastasius *ad Aquas Salvias* (Abbreviation B), S. Croce in Gerusalemme, and another that remains unidentified (Abbreviation A). These texts were radically cut to provide the requisite number of readings for the commemoration of Anastasius, in balance with the readings for St. Vincent.

The two abbreviations achieve a very different measure of success. While Abbreviation A follows *BHL* 411a quite closely on occasion,[35] its preoccupation with condensing the text required the elimination of entire sections (especially the rhetorical ones) and scenes, and the compression of one or two episodes into a few words. Thus, for example, it eliminates completely the nocturnal visit of bishops and angels to Anastasius's prison cell, as witnessed by the Jewish prisoner, but retains the earlier dream-vision, in which Anastasius drinks from a bejeweled cup, which is interpreted as a prefiguration of his martyrdom. Many cuts are made to the text describing Anastasius's efforts to become a monk and his training in monastic learning and discipline.[36]

The redactor of Abbreviated Version A, however, seems to have consulted at least two other works in preparing his version of the Passion. One of these must have been a member of the *BHL* 408 family of texts. After Anastasius's baptism, the abbreviated version tells us that "Octava vero die post albas depositas in monasterio sancti Anastasii ..." (ll. 14-15). The expression *post albas depositas* is found only in the *BHL* 408-family redaction, and was provided

---

34. Again, here I am relying on Philippart's nomenclature (*Légendiers*, pp. 24-25). He notes that in this sort of book, the text was divided into *lectiones* by the original copyists (as in these cases), and emphasizes the distinction between the "Office lectionary" and the "homiliary-lectionary": not only are the contents different, but in the latter the division into *lectiones* is not generally the work of the original scribe's hand. In the Benevento homiliary-lectionary containing *BHL* 411d (Biblioteca capitolare 7; see pp. 508-509), however, the division into readings is made by the original scribe.

35. For example, in the first part of the interrogation by the marzabanas, where even descriptive phrases (e.g. *torvo vultu* [l. 41]) are retained.

36. The word *universa* (l. 17) is generically used to encompass all the various monastic activities which are individually listed in the source text.

to make sense of the nonsensical passage of the first translation.[37] *BHL* 411a reads at this point "cum ... octo dies ut dici solet suae illuminationis moraretur" (ll. 136-138). It seems likely that the redactor, puzzled by this expression, looked at another copy of the Life of Anastasius and found a text more to his liking.[38] As the Roman Revision (r$_2$) also uses this expression, and as both manuscripts preserving the Abbreviated Version A betray a Roman origin, it seems more likely perhaps to assume that the Roman Revision may have been its source.[39]

Clearly, the redactor of this abbreviation of the *Passio S. Anastasii* also consulted Ado of Vienne's Martyrology when composing the beginning and the ending.[40] The words setting the scene for the events that lead to Anastasius's encounter with Christianity—"Cum itaque Phoca romanis imperante perse sub Chosroe rege Ierosolimam invasissent, et inter ornamenta sacra quae abstulerunt etiam lignum vivifice crucis in Persidem abduxissent" (ll. 5-8)—are taken verbatim from Ado's entry on the Exaltation of the Cross on September 14. Likewise, the conclusion of this redaction—"Reliquie corporis eius una cum capite primo ad monasterium suum deinde Romam delate venerantur in monasterio ad Aquas Salvias" (ll. 127-129)—repeats the last part of Ado's entry for St. Anastasius on 22 January, with two significant changes.[41] The redactor added *una cum capite* and removed the name of the monastery *beati Pauli apostoli*, reflecting his knowledge of Rome, and in particular of the monastery of St. Anastasius *ad Aquas Salvias*. He must have been puzzled by the reference to

37. See my edition of p (ll. 151-152 and n. 39).

38. Alternatively, this expression might have been added at some point as a marginal note on a copy of *BHL* 411a and in due course was brought to the attention of the redactor.

39. There are no other expressions in Abbreviated Version A that must derive from Roman Revision or *BHL* 408.

40. This version of the Passion of Anastasius provides an unusual example of how a martyrology could influence a legendary, a topic which, as Dubois has pointed out (*Les martyrologes*, p. 58), needs further investigation. For Ado of Vienne, see Appendix 2 to Chapter VI.

41. Both of these entries ultimately go back to Bede's *Chronica* and his Martyrology, important sources for Ado's composition.

the monastery "of the Apostle Paul," as it was known in Bede's lifetime, when it had long been known as *S. Anastasii.* He also knew that the relic of the head in particular was venerated at the Aquae Salviae, a fact not mentioned by Ado. It is likely that he retained the reference to the relics of the body as a way of acknowledging the tradition that grew when the monastery became Cistercian, that not only the head but also the body of the saint were kept at the Aquae Salviae.[42]

Abbreviation B survives in a single manuscript, an Office lectionary from the fourteenth century that once belonged to the church of St. Anastasius *ad Aquas Salvias.*[43] The dependence of this redaction on *BHL* 411a is made apparent by a textual comparison.[44] The redactor did not provide a summary of the full text. Rather, he began with a summary of the prologue, which formed the first reading, and then, in the remaining seven readings, he brought the story up to the middle of cap. 19 of *BHL* 411a, the first interrogation of Anastasius by Marzabanas. It is puzzling that the rest of the tale is not included, or at least that, if the redactor had only limited space, he did not include the more central parts of the story recounting the saint's actual martyrdom and death.[45] Perhaps, the rest of the story was omitted because it would be read on another occasion during the celebration of the saint's feast in his own monastery.

Such idiosyncracies in the text of Abbreviation B, on the other hand, could suggest that the redactor of this text wrote his revision directly onto this codex, and that this is an incomplete or imperfect result. One example, in *lectio vii,* ll. 93-94, reads: "visitavit loca sancta et sanctorum ibi quiescentium et in monte Garizim corpora." One would have expected the phrase to read: *visitavit*

---

42. See Chapter I, p. 24 and n. 78.

43. Rome, Biblioteca nazionale, Sessorianus 4.

44. For example: l. 100 "Quid garrientes?" retains "Quid garrientes strepitis?" of 411a (l. 239; cf. 411: "Quid inter vos verba confertis?" [cap. 12]).

45. The "Extracts for the Office," which I discuss below, generally include the martyrdom and death scenes, and occasionally burial. The manuscript does not suggest a physical lacuna, but this does not preclude the possibility of a defective source.

loca sancta et sanctorum ibi quiescientium corpora. The phrase *et in monte Garizim* gives the impression of an afterthought. It is possible that the redactor included it here, rather than later in the narrative, in an attempt to save time and space.[46] Despite such occurrences, this redaction is much less abbreviated than Version A. The proper names of the participants in the story, such as Iustinus or Helias, are retained. The redactor often departs from his source text to add his own digressions, suggesting that compactness and brevity were not his principal concerns. As in the case of Abbreviation A, relatively little of the source text is cut from the episode of Anastasius's dream-vision, and even Gregorius clericus's rhetorical, authorial intervention at the end is retained, with modification.[47] A few details are new to this version, including the addition of a metaphor to the discussion of Anastasius's conversion, "tamquam granium seminis" (ll. 26-27). While *BHL* 411a provides one etymology for the name Anastasius, the redactor of this version adds another of his own, "Vel dicitur Anastasius quasi sursum stans" (ll. 55-56), building on the prophetic meaning of the name of Anastasius, and emphasizing the perfection of his monastic practice.[48]

Both of these redactions, in effect, represent a new phase in the metamorphosis of the *Passio S. Anastasii*, one in which the redactor intervenes in an authorial fashion by adding materials or details. This phase foreshadows future developments in the history of hagiographic texts, when the creation of new texts became preferable to the revision of old ones. While this tendency recalls the work of Gregorius clericus, these new editors, unlike Gregorius, do not claim to be faithful to their source text.

---

46. This might also explain the awkward position of the subject in the phrase "de presentia christiani et miraculis crucis dominice letarentur" (ll. 24-25).

47. As is the rhetorical passage after the dream-vision: "O predulce et plenissimum misterii sompnium. Qui enim in excelso montis fastigio se stare vidit, postea contemplative vite tutissimum atque sacratissimum cacumen ascendit" (ll. 78-80). Cf. *BHL* 411a (ll. 192-195).

48. *Incipt prologus beati Gregorii papae* (ll. 1-2). The attribution of this version to Pope Gregory may have been a way of giving the text greater (monastic?) authority.

All the revisions of the *Passio S. Anastasii* listed so far were the work of editors or redactors who in some way altered the text they had before them. Another method of preparing readings for the Office was to extract material from existing texts without revision, and collect them in a hagiographic lectionary.[49] The dossier of Anastasius provides particular examples of this method of compilation as well. *BHL* 411a as contained in St. Peter's Legendary was mined for passages to include in several hagiographic lectionaries for Roman churches. Several used in the basilica itself have survived, the oldest from the end of the twelfth century, but some as late as the fifteenth.[50] We must suppose that the selection

49. Philippart, *Légendiers*, p. 24, uses this term to designate a separate volume containing hagiographical readings for the Office, which he distinguishes from the legendary, whose function is not "strictly liturgical," and whose texts are not divided into lections by the original scribe. Philippart does not remark on the nature of the texts contained in these two kinds of books. My study of the manuscripts transmitting the *Passio S. Anastasii* in its different versions suggests that the texts as well as the lay-out are different in the two book formats, although there are no rigid boundaries between them. Legendaries transmit complete texts, while hagiographic lectionaries transmit selections; legendaries are more inclusive (containing even poems), while hagiographic lectionaries are much more narrowly focused. Hagiographic lectionaries, at least for Rome, seem to me to be smaller on the whole than the very large legendaries that have survived from the great basilicas. Clearly, more work needs to be done here.

50. The oldest hagiographic lectionary to be copied from the basilica's legendary (BAV, Archivio di S. Pietro A 2, A 4, A 5) is BAV, Archivio di S. Pietro A 3; the most recent may be A 8, from the fifteenth century, whose scribe wrote: "Legendae sanctorum quae in sacrocancta basilica principis apostolorum de Urbe in matutinali officio leguntur" (fol. 1). The Basilica of St. John the Lateran has a hagiographic lectionary from the late thirteenth or early fourteenth century whose readings for the feast of St. Anastasius also derive ultimately from St. Peter's Legendary, as revealed by my collation of the texts (Archivio storico del Vicariato 67, fols. 39-40). A similar fifteenth-century book that includes readings for St. Anastasius related (but not identical) to those in the Roman books is found in Naples (Biblioteca nazionale VIII B 9, fol. 131). Extracts from *BHL* 411 must have also been used in hagiographic lectionaries, as is indicated by one early-twelfth-century fragment written, following its source, in Beneventan script (Rome, Biblioteca vallicelliana G 98).

and transcription of the pertinent passages from traditional legendary to hagiographic lectionary was done for ease and convenience, for only the passages read aloud were extracted. While each volume may contain a different number of readings to suit the local Office, those passages narrating the death and burial of the saint were included.[51] It is also possible that the hagiographic lectionaries reflect a general reduction in the length of the readings performed at the Office.[52] In many cases, the original scribe noted the genesis of the book, as did "B. de Novaria," who wrote at the end of the collection he put together, apparently for the church of SS. Apostoli: "Expliciunt legende et passiones sanctorum, quorum proprium potuit inveniri per anni circulum; quas fecerunt scribi domini prior et capitulum basilice apostolorum de Urbe anno dominice incarnationis M°CCC°XXXVIIII° pontificatus domini pape Benedicti anno V° scripte per me presbiterum B. de Novaria."[53]

From the evidence discussed above it is clear that the second translation *BHL* 411a underwent a number of transformations to conform to the range of uses to which the translation itself and its revisions were put. The same range is not found in the textual genealogy of the first translation, except for the versions of *BHL* 408 that circulated in Italy. In France and Germany, the earliest witnesses of the *Passio S. Anastasii* are found exclusively in traditional legendaries. After this initial circulation, we find the Passion of Anastasius included only in very large hagiographic compendia. Revisions made to texts in northern collections are attempts to perfect the unclear or ungrammatical text. In Italy, on the contrary, the celebration of Anastasius was incorporated into the

---

51. Since the hagiographic lectionary played only a specialized liturgical role, it is possible that the legendary (from which it was copied) was used for other purposes, such as reading in the refectory. The relationship between Office and refectory reading needs further investigation. See Philippart, *Légendiers*, pp. 115-116.

52. The Office appears to have been greatly abbreviated at the end of the twelfth century. In his study of a group of twelfth-century manuscripts, Suitbert Baümer has noted that the marks for the *explicits* have been moved to make the readings shorter (*Dictionnaire d'archéologie chrétienne et de liturgie* s.v. Légendes Liturgiques).

53. BAV, Archivio di S. Pietro A 9, fols. 264v-265.

regular cycle of the liturgy—hence its preservation in a variety of books created specifically for liturgical use and therefore demanding significant modifications to the text. The evidence presented throughout this survey shows how the form of the text corresponds largely to the function, and the format, of the book wherein it is contained, and how the style and content of a hagiographic text were responsible for how and where it circulated.

The story of the dossier of the Persian monk does not end here, even as the decline in the number of legendaries made room for new kinds of hagiographic collections.[54] Readings ultimately derived from Anastasius's *Passio* were also included in breviaries, the liturgical books encompassing all the materials necessary for the recitation of the daily Office. In these books, the tendency to abbreviate and simplify liturgical readings is even more apparent. Their exclusive liturgical function and purpose place them in a different category from the various kinds of legendaries so far considered. Their hagiographic components can only be viewed as integral parts of a newly created whole. While recognizing that breviaries have functions similar to some of the books I have considered, I have therefore excluded the Anastasius readings found in them from my discussion.

An account of Anastasius was also included in Jacobo da Voragine's *Legenda Aurea* and the similar, so-called *Legendae novae* or abbreviated legendaries.[55] The texts included in the abbreviated legendaries have in general been radically transformed to create a larger, homogeneous literary work by a named author. Rather than borrowing and rewriting traditional texts, these authors in fact created new ones, uniform in tone and style, and gathered them into one book, usually providing an author's preface. The versions of the *Passio S. Anastasii* that resulted from the efforts to create the *Legendae novae* belong more properly with a study of their authors. Furthermore, the function of the *Legendae novae*

54. For the decline of the legendary after its high point during the twelfth century, see Philippart, *Légendiers*, pp. 45-48.

55. The earliest manifestations of the *Legendae novae* date from ca. 1250. For a brief definition, see Philippart, *Légendiers*, p. 24. Poncelet, "Le Légendier de Pierre Calo," provides a very thorough discussion.

was not the private and public reading of the saint's *vita*, as it was principally for traditional passionaries, legendaries, and breviaries. Rather, it was primarily to serve the needs of preachers. The manner of manuscript transmission for the abbreviated legendaries also differs. The *Legendae novae* were copied as fixed literary works.[56] This is in stark contrast to the manner in which old, and generally anonymous, *passiones* and *legendae* were manipulated for inclusion in a great variety of passionaries or legendaries, resulting in the varied and diverse transmission of the *Passio S. Anastasii*.

APPENDICES

1. THE *ASS* TEXT

In the introduction to his text of the *Passio S. Anastasii*, Jean Bolland writes that he made use of two "pervetusti codices MSS. monasteriorum Gladbacensi in Julia et S. Maximini Treviris, sed in hoc nonnihil variante ac fere fluente et laciniosa phrasi."[57] There is little doubt that the codex from S. Maximin was either the present Paris, BN, lat. 9741 (whose text of the *Passio S. Anastasii* I label p_1), or another codex containing the *Passio* in the same redaction. There are four occasions in which Bolland gives the precise reading of his Trier manuscript, and in all of these cases the readings correspond to the text of BN, lat. 9741.[58] In addition, the text printed in the *ASS* has other similarities with p_1: the addition *cum ligare eum vellent* is found in Bolland's text (cap. 21) and in 9741 (l. 303).[59] But as Bolland does not indicate that this is a

---

56. Philippart, *Légendiers*, p. 46.

57. *ASS* Ian. III, p. 35.

58. These are: p. 41 n. e *sine dubio* as in BN, lat. 9741 (l. 205); p. 43 n. d *similiter bullatis* as in 9741 (l. 402); p. 44 n. i *supra capita ligni* as in 9741 (*super capita ligni* [ll. 496-497]); p. 45 n. d *Accipiens tribunus secum fratrem* is quite close to 9741's *Tribunus ergo ille sequenti nocte accipiens secum fratrem* (l. 561). In this last example, Bolland was interested in the singular *accipiens* as opposed to the plural (*accipientes*) of his other witness.

59. *ASS* Ian. III, cap. 22 (p. 42). I call this an addition because it is not found in the Greek text nor in *BHL* 410b, nor in *BHL* 408(p). A very similar phrase is found in the Roman Revision (*Cumque vellent eum ligare* [l. 295]) suggesting a general attempt to clarify the meaning. There is no evidence to

reading from his Trier manuscript we cannot be sure whether it was also the reading of his Gladbach witness. The identity of this second codex remains uncertain. But it is clear that, as the text printed in the *ASS* belongs to the *BHL* 408(s) tradition, Bolland followed principally this manuscript witness.[60] This text has been revised and corrected in numerous small ways, and results in a much clearer version of *BHL* 408 than the one found in earlier witnesses.[61] There is at least one example of an editorial decision that can only have been made after consulting the Greek text, or *BHL* 410b, or a witness going back to an earlier model of *BHL* 408.[62] As there is no evidence to support the latter possibilities, one must conclude that in this problematic passage Jean Bolland consulted the Greek text, and emended the Latin.

2. Cesare Baronio and the Dossier of St. Anastasius

In a note to the Roman Martyrology of 1586, Cesare Baronio says, "... habemus in nostra bibliotheca eiusdem [*St. Anastasius's*] res gestas a Gregorio quodam clerico a Grecis latine redditas, quibus praemittitur

---

suppose that the Roman Revision had a direct connection with the text found in 9741.

60. There is full agreement between the passages I single out as most clearly differentiating the s and p text (*ASS* cap. 1 [p. 39] *sub mortis atque* ...; cap. 16 [p. 41] *ea quae* ...; cap. 30 [p. 44] *cum ira furoris ad carcerem*). Cf. p. 365.

61. See, for example, the beginning of cap. 9, where the *ASS* text is much corrected.

62. This is the preservation of the phrase *ut didicimus* in cap. 25 (p. 42) of *ASS*, which corresponds to *BHL* 410b's *sicut didicimus* (l. 333). No other manuscript witness in the Latin tradition developing from the first translation that I have examined preserves this phrase. It comes in the middle of a poorly transmitted passage, and it is possible that Bolland consulted the Greek text here, especially since the *ASS* text is quite accurate in its rendition of the original. On the other hand, in cap. 30 (p. 44), Bolland's text (*Veniens ... cum ira furoris*) shows that in this instance he did not consult the Greek, or he would have corrected the text to reflect the meaning of the original. Rather, this reading may reflect a medieval correction of the text in the s tradition (*cum ira foris ad carcerem*; cf. *BHL* 408(p), l. 503).

praefatio, cuius est exordium: Unigenitus filius, etc."[63] These remarks confused Bolland because the life of Anastasius beginning "Unigenitus filius, etc." (i.e. *BHL* 408) provided no indication of authorship by Gregorius. Bolland was not aware of the existence of *BHL* 411a or 411, which refers to Gregorius clericus's authorship in the prplogue. Baronio, however, must have read, albeit superficially, both *BHL* 408 and *BHL* 411a/411 since several copies of all these texts were at the Oratorians' library, the Biblioteca vallicelliana.[64] Given the similarities between these two texts, it is not surprising that he should have thought of them as being one text, for which Gregorius was responsible. Furthermore, Baronio was greatly interested in the original Greek *Acta* of Anastasius, which he discusses at length in the *Annales ecclesiastici*, even speculating on their authorship.[65]

He was also interested in the Roman Miracle of Anastasius, although, judging from his reliance on the Latin version, it seems unlikely that he knew the Greek text. In the same passage in the Martyrology, he added: "Habentur illic insuper post eadem acta elegans historia de arreptitia puella virtute martyris liberata Romae in ecclesia S. Mariae ad Aquas Salvias." And in the *Annales*, he returns to the Roman Miracle of Anastasius "quem ... hactenus conservatum invenimus in bibliotheca Vallicelliana, positum velut appendicem ad vitam eiusdem sancti martyris Anastasii ... ," quoting at length from this work to illustrate an ancient custom, whereby public cures performed by the saints in a church were written down by notaries, so that they might be preserved in the church's archives and read publicly to the faithful.[66]

63. *Martyrologium Romanum*, p. 44. I believe that the 1586 edition is the one Bolland refers to, since it contains Baronio's notes and treatise on the sources. Baronio had been asked by Cardinal Sirletus to undertake the expansion of the 1584 edition in anticipation of negative reactions to the first edition.

64. See the "Descriptive List" for all codices containing a version of the Latin *Passio* and/or the Roman Miracle at the Vallicelliana today.

65. *Annales* XI, 221ff. Baronio suggested either the monk Antiochus of St. Sabas, or Patriarch Sophronius of Jerusalem, both contemporaries of St. Anastasius, as possible authors.

66. *Annales* XII, 240; *BHL* 412, l. 150.

The Vallicelliana library's Tomus V (=L, in my edition of the Roman Miracle) has long been believed to be the one used by Baronio.[67] In fact, it is the only pre-Baronio manuscript at the Vallicelliana today that contains the *Passio* (*BHL* 408) and the *Miraculum* alongside each other, just as Baronio describes. The manuscript is "ancient," and Baronio's introduction to the Roman Miracle implies that his source was similarly old. Although Baronio tends not to quote verbatim, preferring instead to summarize and simplify, there is some textual evidence that confirms Baronio's use of Vallicellianus V. For example, in the middle of the devil's speech in cap. 7, Baronio and Vallicellianus V omit the words "Haec operatus est in me" (l. 150).[68] This is particularly significant because, unlike narrative passages, speeches are faithfully reported by Baronio. Minor textual agreements also support Vallicellianus V as Baronio's source.[69]

But it is the manuscript itself that confirms Cardinal Baronio's use. In the introduction to the miracle story, Baronio states that the text will prove that the Emperor Philippicus ruled one year and six months, and not two years or more as some believed.[70] Two passages in Vallicellianus V are underlined,[71] and these very passages are cited in a note in the *Annales* entitled "quot annis regnavit Philippicus."[72]

---

67. Giorgi, "Il Regesto di S. Anastasio," pp. 51-52 n. 6; Bertelli, "Caput," p. 21 n. 4. Neither of them gives any reasons for this assertion. On this manuscript, see "Descriptive List."

68. *Annales* XI, 242.

69. For example, both the Vallicellianus and Baronio read "ancillas Dei" rather than "ancillas Christi" (*Annales* XII, 240; *BHL* 412, l. 21).

70. "... ut temporis Philippici Imperatoris certa ratio habeatur ad redarguendum illos, qui non duos tantum annos, sed et aliquot etiam menses post duos annos eum vixisse in Imperio tradiderunt" (*Annales* XII, 240).

71. "anno primo et post consolatum eiusdem serenitatis anno primo" and "die kalendarum octobris istius duodecimae indictionis" (fol. 138r). These passages concern the dates of Emperor Anastasius's rule, and are directly relevant to Philippicus's dates.

72. *Annales* XII, 241 note. The text of the Roman Miracle has notations and corrections throughout, perhaps in Baronio's own hand.

CONCLUSION

The veneration of the material relics of Anastasius the Persian monk was, not surprisingly, one of the most important factors in the development of the cult and its hagiography, which has constituted the focal point of my study. The translation of the body of Anastasius from its original burial site in Persia to Jerusalem is amply chronicled in written sources that validate the theft and fragmentation of the martyr's remains by a series of miracles performed along the route. Their arrival and relocation at the monastery "of Abbot Anastasius" outside Jerusalem are similarly documented. On the other hand, the circumstances of the translation of the relic of the head to Rome—an event that transferred the principal locus of the cult of the Persian—are not the subject of any surviving written account, and we can only surmise that the holy relic left Jerusalem as a result of the disruptions caused by war and exile. However, the creation and early elaboration of the Latin dossier of Anastasius, and in particular the textual history of the first Latin version of the *Passio S. Anastasii* and its affinity to the copy annotated by Patriarch Modestus of Jerusalem, allow us to recreate portions of the missing narrative. As was the case for the earlier translation of the relics of the body, so also the removal of the head to Rome was part of the political and religious interests of the Palestinian monastic community, now established in the western capital. It seems almost incredible that Bede in Northumbria should know of the first translation of the relics of Anastasius from Persia to Jerusalem, a fact recorded in no other surviving Latin source. The astonishing survival of this precious piece of information is an appropriate metaphor for the extraordinary journey of the literary dossier of the Persian martyr, and of its value for students of hagiography and cultural history.

The traditional view that after the end of antiquity no one in the Latin West knew Greek except for a few Irish clerics has long been discredited.[1] Still, there is no certain evidence that from the middle of the sixth century until the beginning of the ninth century any literary translation from Greek into Latin was executed anywhere in Europe except in Rome.[2] It is ironic then, that, while much consideration has been given to a better and more complete understanding of the continuing cultural interactions between the Greek East and the Latin West in the early Middle Ages, Rome's position as the most vigorous cross-cultural entrepôt, while generally recognized, has not been fully explored. There is still no large-scale treatment of the translation of Greek hagiographic texts in early medieval Rome, for example, nor is there an up-to-date, comprehensive study of the *corpus translationum* of the most famous of all early medieval translators, Anastasius Bibliothecarius of the Roman church. The most useful preliminary resource to remedy this scholarly oversight is the investigation of a body of texts whose history in both Greek and Latin can be adequately documented. In the case of hagiography—which constitutes by far the single largest group of translations—the history of the text frequently offers the only clues for dating and localization.[3] The hagiographic dossier of Anastasius the Persian offers a particularly rich subject for study, for the abundance of evidence for the cult is accompanied by an even richer literary record. Its history embraces a large array of surviving Greek and Latin texts; its traces can be followed from Persia to Northumbria; its connections to Rome are explicit and specific.

Paolo Chiesa recently singled out three well-known events as emblematic of Rome's mediating role in the relations between the Latin West and the Greek East from the seventh to the ninth century.[4] The Lateran Synod of 649 condemned monotheletism in a series of canons composed in Greek within the Palestinian circle

---

1. See Berschin, *Greek Letters*, pp. 3-17 for a review of the scholarship on Greek in the Middle Ages.

2. Chiesa, "Traduzioni e traduttori a Roma nell'alto medioevo," pp. 457-458. This lack of evidence is not conclusive, however.

3. This is the case for the *Vita* of Theodora, discussed by Chiesa, "Traduzioni," pp. 463-465.

4. Chiesa, "Traduzioni," pp. 455-457.

of Maximus the Confessor during his sojourn in Rome, and then translated into Latin. Our best manuscript witness of the acts of this synod most likely derives from a papyrus roll that was sent from Rome to Bishop Amand of Maastricht (†679/684). It is important in this context to remember that a copy of the Latin acts of the Lateran Synod was brought to England from Rome by John the Archchanter in 679, that a copy of this Roman copy was made at the command of Benedict Biscop, and that Bede used the Lateran acts as a source in both his historical and exegetical works.[5] Chiesa's second emblematic event is the translation of Gregory the Great's *Dialogues* at the command of Pope Zacharias around 750, executed for the benefit of Greek monks living in Rome, "qui latinam ignorant lectionem."[6] Pope Zacharias's Greek version became so popular in the Greek East that Gregory acquired the sobriquet ὁ Διαλογός. Chiesa's third illustrative example of Rome's mediating role between East and West is Anastasius Bibliothecarius's retort to Emperor Charles the Bald in 875 concerning John Scotus Eriugena's recent translation of the *Corpus Dionysiacum*. Anastasius transmitted his critique to the emperor by writing his own corrections and explications in the margin of a copy of Eriugena's translation, and adding his own Latin translation of the commentary on pseudo-Dionysius attributed to Maximus the Confessor and John of Scythopolis. The version of the *Corpus Dionysiacum* read in the West until the later Middle Ages was in the form corrected and glossed by Anastasius Bibliothecarius. Rome was the center for the composition, exchange and dissemination of translated texts—both from Greek and from Latin—in the early Middle Ages.

The early phases of the dossier of Anastasius the Persian intersect, strangely enough, with the three emblematic events discussed by Chiesa. The Latin dossier of Anastasius includes the only significant hagiographic composition (*BHL* 410b) whose connections to the Greek community of the city active at the Lateran Synod of 649, and even to a specific member of that community, Theodore

---

5. For further bibliography, see Ganz, "Roman Manuscripts in Francia and Anglo-Saxon England," pp. 618-619.

6. *Liber pontificalis* (Duschesne, I, 435).

of Tarsus, can be charted in detailed fashion (Chapter II). The composition of the Roman Miracle in Greek, as I discuss in chapters III and IV, took place not long before the translation of Gregory's *Dialogues* into Greek. It was the product of the monastic community for which Zacharias's translation was intended. The Greek Roman Miracle and its association with the purged, anti-monothelete version of the Greek *Encomium* result from a movement to represent Anastasius and his Roman relic as symbols of the community's orthodoxy and attachment to Rome.[7]

Finally, Gregorius's version of the Greek *Acta* of the Persian martyr, *BHL* 411a (Chapter III), is to be viewed alongside the better-known translations of Anastasius Bibliothecarius. I argue that this text was composed in Rome. It may have been executed or shaped into a *libellus* with the revised Roman Miracle within the same Roman cultural circles in which Anastasius Bibliothecarius plied his trade as translator and revisor. Anastasius has been portrayed as an isolated figure within the cultural history of Rome, both because of his extraordinary productivity as a translator, but also because his translations are the only ones from Rome judged to have identifiable cultural and political goals: the construction of Rome's autonomy between Frankish and Byzantine power. Other translations executed in Rome have been seen instead as occasional pieces, responding to the needs of particular cults or individual communities.[8] The Roman dossier of Anastasius the Persian both confirms and undermines these conclusions. The creation of what I call in Chapter III the "Dossier of a Roman Martyr," which joins Gregorius's literary version with a similarly erudite revision of the Roman Miracle, expands our view of the agenda of Roman translators, and suggests that Anastasius Bibliothecarius was not as singular as we have thought. It is possible that there existed a "translation school" of Rome also, to parallel the one associated with Naples, where Gregorius's version has been, wrongly, in my judgment, so far located.

---

7. See Chapter II, pp. 76-77, for a discussion of the purged Berolinensis gr. 54.

8. Chiesa, "Traduzioni," esp. pp. 478-482, with further bibliography. Anastasius Bibliothecarius is also discussed above, pp. 109-124.

In parallel to some of the translations singled out by Chiesa, so too was the literary dossier of Anastasius transmitted from Rome to the West. We can be almost certain that Theodore of Tarsus brought a copy of the first translation to England, and it is possible that he may even have been responsible for its composition. We can also consider it likely that Bede transformed this early translation into the original *BHL* 408, which became the most widely diffused redaction of the *Passio S. Anastasii* circulating in the West. Through Bede's Chronicle and Martyrology, the memory of Anastasius, and of his relic preserved in his Roman monastery, was celebrated all over Latin Christendom.

The Latin dossier's relationship to the Greek texts affords us the almost unparalleled opportunity to observe early medieval translators at work and to understand more fully their tools and methodologies. The fortunate survival of the early *ad verbum* translation and its comparison to Gregorius's *ad sensum* version shows that the methodological jargon that saturates the prefaces of hagiographic texts in fact represents a more complex activity than simple translation, and provides an illustration of the blurred boundaries between translation and hagiographic adaptation.

The dossier of the Persian martyr is further proof of the extraordinary fluidity of hagiographic texts, and of the difficulties inherent in their edition. While the task for the editor of a "fixed" or "stable" text is clearly that of establishing as far as possible the "original" text, the editor of a fluid text faces a number of questions.[9] For example, when does the editor decide that the corrections and modifications imposed upon a text cannot be confined among the variants at the bottom of the page, but have resulted in a new and different text, worthy of its own independent existence? Even more fundamentally, what is the function of an *apparatus criticus* that includes not only what might still be called "errors" but also willful corrections? In considering these issues, I have been restrained in separating or isolating texts that are fluid by nature. I have, on the other hand, been most inclusive in the *apparatus cri-*

---

9. Lapidge, "Editing Hagiography," cited throughout, summarizes some of these issues.

ticus, in the hope that its details will help with the identification of texts in manuscript witnesses unknown to me.

The transmission of the various texts within hagiographic collections has been another necessary consideration in my study. The approach of "materialist philology," which is generally understood to apply to collections of disparate texts, can also be usefully applied to hagiographic books, almost all of which are unique compendia, reflecting the particular needs of the compiler and the community for which the collection was put together. The texts in the dossier of Anastasius the Persian are contained in a variety of hagiographic collections, different *qua* collection. The earliest of these are traditional legendaries, comprising full texts arranged according to a general liturgical calendar. Increasingly, more specialized and localized collections required the revision and adaptation of the traditional texts. The textual manipulations of the Latin dossier of Anastasius are determined by the format and function of the book in which each text is transmitted, and not just by the literary preference of the reviser.

Too often textual analyses of hagiographic collections go no further than the texts themselves.[10] My study of the *fortuna* of the dossier of Anastasius in the Middle Ages has shown, I hope, the value of exploring both the cultural and codicological contexts in which hagiographic texts were composed and transmitted.

---

10. This point is made very forcefully by Philippart, *Légendiers,* p. 59

1

THE FIRST TRANSLATION
BHL 410b

The Manuscript
The first Latin translation of the Greek *Acta* of Anastasius survives
in only one manuscript witness, F III 16 (fols. 14-23) of the Biblioteca nazionale universitaria of Turin, a codex of the late ninth or
early tenth century that came to Turin from the monastery of Bobbio.[1] When Albert Poncelet described the hagiographical manuscripts of Turin's national library in 1909, he must have been
struck by the similarities between this text and the only published
Latin Life of Anastasius, in the *ASS*,[2] to which the Bollandists had
assigned the number 408, for he added "cf. *BHL* 408."[3] But when
the first *Supplementum* to the *BHL* was published in 1911, the
Turin text was grouped instead as *BHL* 410b under the redaction
found in the Windberg Legendary and in the Great Austrian Legendary (*BHL* 410). My comparisons of these three texts (*BHL*
410b, *BHL* 410 and *BHL* 408) with the original Greek *Acta* and
with each other (see Chapters II and V), however, have shown
that the text found in the Bobbio manuscript is the only surviving
witness of an original translation of *BHG* 84, the ancient Greek
Acta of Anastasius, and that *BHL* 408 and 410 are later reworkings

---

1. It survived the great fire that devastated Turin's Biblioteca nazionale
on 25-26 January 1904 because it had been taken to Göttingen's University
Library to be studied by W. Mayer. The most complete physical description
of the manuscript is given in Cipolla, *Codici bobbiesi della Biblioteca nazionale
universitaria di Torino con illustrazioni*, p. 154. Other treatments of this codex are found in Chiesa, *Le versioni latine*, pp. 46-49 with extensive previous
bibliography; Poncelet, "Catalogus codicum hagiographicorum latinorum Bibliothecae nationalis taurinensis," pp. 431-434; Ottino, *I codici bobbiesi nella
Biblioteca nazionale di Torino*, pp. 20-22; Siegmund, *Die Überlieferung*, passim.
   2. *ASS* Ian. II, 422-440; 3rd ed. Ian. III, 35-54.
   3. Poncelet, "Catalogus codicum ... taurinensis," p. 431.

of this first Latin version. I present here a full discussion of this manuscript because of its extraordinary importance in the history of hagiographic collections, and specifically as a witness of early passionaries representing the cults of the city of Rome. I will argue that the codex, notable for its unusually large concentration of translations from the Greek, was copied from an already existing collection whose roots reach back to Rome, and that this copy was made at the monastery of Bobbio, and not in some other area of northern Italy, as has sometimes been claimed.

Turin, Biblioteca nazionale, Codex F III 16 (Ottino, no. 24), is a passionary, the main part[4] of which was written by various hands toward the end of the ninth century.[5] Since Bobbio's saints do not figure in this passionary, the claim has been made that this manuscript was not written at Bobbio.[6] Such a conclusion, however, would demand that monastic scriptoria copied only hagiographic collections made to order, so to speak, to their own liturgical celebrations or hagiographic traditions. It also ignores the fact that early passionaries and legendaries such as the Bobbio collection—regardless of where they were copied—encompassed almost exclusively universal saints, the martyrs and early saints venerated in Rome, whose cult thence spread to the rest of the

---

4. There is a page added at the beginning of the codex (fol. A) containing part of Ado's *Laudatio* of St. Augustine; fols. 206-232 were written in the eleventh century, even though these folia must have been part of the original book, as their size, prickings and rulings indicate. For an eleventh century palimpsest inserted to replace a missing quire, see below.

5. Ferrari, "Manoscritti e cultura," pp. 270-271. Prof. Ferrari in a letter to me of 19 August 1992 repeated this date without excluding the possibility, however, that the codex may have been written slightly later, though certainly no later than the beginning of the tenth century. Ottino dates it simply to the tenth century as does Poncelet; and Cipolla attributes it "al sec. X in. o piuttosto al sec. X indeterminatamente." A ninth-century dating had also been repeated by Bernt ("Die Quellen zu Walahfrids Mammas-Leben," p. 142 n. 1).

6. Chiesa, *Le versioni latine*, p. 47. But Cipolla's remark (*Codici bobbiesi*, p. 154: "Per il suo contenuto è quindi affatto estraneo al monastero di Bobbio") on which later claims are perhaps based does not pass any judgment on where the manuscript was copied, and in fact one would conclude that Cipolla's treatment tacitly assumes that the codex was copied at Bobbio.

church. Only slowly were local and more contemporary saints included in hagiographic collections.[7]

But even disregarding these considerations, the claim that the contents of the Bobbio passionary do not have a Bobbio flavor is not true, for a close examination of the texts contained in this collection, as well as what we can learn of the manuscript's history, do reveal connections with Bobbio's traditions.[8] We know that the manuscript was at Bobbio in the eleventh century when it was supplied with a palimpsest quire (fols. 176-181), replacing one that had most likely fallen out, thus completing the Life of St. Mary the Egyptian.[9] The lower script of these pages was an Irish minuscule

7. See Philippart, *Légendiers*, pp. 30-36, for a discussion of early passionaries. The earliest hagiographic collections to survive date from the middle of the eighth century; none of these is from Italy. Of the manuscripts used systematically by Philippart (pp. 13-16) the oldest Italian one is Vat. lat. 5771 (s. IX-X), contemporary to our Turin codex. Vat. lat. 5771 is generally attributed to Bobbio, yet its sanctoral is certainly not "Bobbiese." For a description, see Philippart, *Légendiers*, passim; Poncelet, *Catalogus codicum hagiographicorum latinorum Bibliothecae vaticanae*, pp. 140-149.

8. As far as I have been able to discern, the belief that this codex originates from the Emilia (Chiesa, *Le versioni latine*, p. 47) is based on a misunderstanding of a footnote in Garrison ("Notes on Certain Italian Mediaeval Manuscripts," p. 23 and n. 37), who points out that the celebration of St. Christopher of Lycia on 7 January (rather than on 25 July or 9 May) is found north of the Appenines only in two calendars of Brescia and in "Emilian books and calendars," among which he includes the Bobbio passionary, without any discussion or support. But one must note that Garrison considers Bobbio to be part of the neighborhood of the Emilian city of Parma (p. 24) and hence the greater Emilian region. Garrison's footnote cannot be interpreted to mean that the art historian questioned the writing of this passionary at Bobbio on paleographic grounds. Esposito, "The Ancient Bobbio Catalogue," pp. 337-344, noted the desirability that "some expert should make a systematic study of the extant Bobbio MSS (about 180), with a view to fixing as closely as possible their dates and palaeographical characteristics." No one has undertaken this task, and there is as yet no systematic investigation of the extant Bobbio manuscripts, with the exception of the numerous learned studies by Prof. Mirella Ferrari.

9. Ferrari, "Spigolature bobbiesi. I. In margine ai *Codices latini antiquiores*," pp. 13-14. This quire had been dated by earlier scholars to the twelfth century. In this article, Prof. Ferrari repeats Garrison's opinion that the co-

(s. VIII-IX); their text an "opus astronomicum."[10] An addition on fol. 59r-v in a twelfth-century hand holds a list of the monastery's possessions.[11] Finally, the manuscript contains the Bobbio version of Paulinus's Life of Ambrose.[12] The codex was included as no. 121 in the famous Bobbio library catalogue of 1461.[13]

A closer look at the passionary's compilation also finds evidence that supports its Bobbio origin. The codex was compiled principally from a Roman collection that included many texts translated from the Greek, to which were added several hagiographic pieces from Bobbio's own tradition. The texts contained in the Bobbio manuscript can clearly be divided into two groups. The first part, comprising fols. 1-95,[14] all written by the same hand, consists of a passionary made up of twenty-three texts arranged *per circulum anni*, beginning with St. Anastasia whose feast is celebrated on 25 December, and ending with the Passion of SS. Crisantus, Maurus, Daria, et al., which is celebrated on 25 October. Thus, the entire liturgical year from Christmas almost to the beginning of Advent is contained in this first part. We have to assume that the saints of Advent are absent here accidentally, either because the codex as

---

dex was written in the Emilia in the tenth century, an opinion that she corrects later (see n. 12 below).

10. Vat. lat. 5755, fols. 7-94 and 132-147 are also palimpsests originating from the same codex containing the "opus astronomicum" as the quire from Turin, F III 16. Ferrari, "Spigolature," pp. 13-14.

11. Cipolla, *Codici bobbiesi*, p. 154; and idem, *Codice diplomatico del monastero di S. Columbano di Bobbio fino all'anno MCCVIII*, pp. 368ff.

12. Ferrari, "Manoscritti e cultura," pp. 270-271. The Life is found in four distinct textual families that circulated in the ninth century: one is northern French, another is localized at St. Gall, a third at Milan, and a fourth one at Bobbio, in F III 16 and in G V 3, also now in the Biblioteca nazionale, Turin.

13. As a note on top of fol. 1r reminds us: "Liber Sancti Columbani de bobio. Istud passionarium est monachorum Congregationis sancte Justine de observantia ordinis sancti benedicti residentium in monasterio sancti Columbani de bobio. Scriptus sub numero 121."

14. Fol. A containing only the last part of Ado's *Laudatio* of St. Augustine is extraneous to the original codex.

we now have it is defective at the beginning,[15] or, more likely, because these texts were never copied into it. Almost all the titles, written by the same hand that wrote the texts, note the feast day of the saint, thus emphasizing the unified nature of this part of the codex.[16]

The sanctoral of the first part of the codex also presents a homogeneous picture. All of the saints included in this section are either early martyrs celebrated in the church of Rome, such as Nereus and Achilleus, Eleutherius, and Anatholia and Victoria; or eastern or Palestinian martyrs whose cult was most likely introduced into the West through Rome.[17] An unusually large number of these texts, at least twelve,[18] are translations from the Greek, and seven

15. The codex is not defective at the end of this first group of texts since it ends on fol. 95 within a quire (comprising fols. 92-99); on the other hand, it seems improbable that the codex is defective at the beginning because of the larger than usual space allotted for the initial, which is decorated with green in addition to the usual red. While it is unusual for a passionary from Italy to begin with Christmas or January 1st rather than with Advent (Philippart, *Légendiers*, p. 79), it should be noted that Vat. lat. 5771, also from Bobbio, begins its sanctoral proper with April (p. 83).

16. There are five exceptions (S. Anastasia, S. Eleutherius, SS. Nereus, Achilleus et Domitilla, SS. Anatholia et Victoria, SS. Crisantus, Maurus et Daria), which are, however, placed in the correct chronological sequence. The omission of a feast date is most likely an oversight of the scribe (if he was responsible for adding the date) or of his model. There are also some minor "errors" in the chronological order: S. Anastasius and S. Triphon should change place with each other (22 January and 4 January), as should Anatholia and Symphorosa, who should be on 9 and 18 July respectively.

17. Berschin, *Greek Letters*, p. 91; Sansterre, *Les moines grecs* I, 147-150; Philippart, *Légendiers*, pp. 32-33.

18. I reach this number from a comparison of the texts as described in Poncelet, "Catalogus codicum ... taurinensis," and Appendix V in *BHL. Supplementum* (pp. 922-923); but for a different opinion see Chiesa, *Le versioni latine*, p. 48. While it is probably true that some additional texts to the ones listed in the Appendix V would be added if a careful study of all the texts in the Bobbio codex were made, some of them were clearly written in Latin to begin with, such as the Passion of Anatholia and Victoria or Symphorosa and her sons.

of these are found in this codex and nowhere else.[19] It is this extraordinary convergence of translated texts that has led to the hypothesis that the Turin codex may provide evidence for the wholesale translation of an entire Greek hagiographical collection into Latin.[20] The only text that at first glance appears not to belong to this Graeco-Roman sanctoral is the *Vita uel Actus* of Eusebius, first bishop of Vercelli (d. 371), best known for his opposition to Arianism and the ensuing conflict with the emperor Constantius.[21] In the tradition originating from Jerome's *De viris illustribus*, Eusebius is not presented as a martyr; rather, after the death of Constantius, he returns from exile to Vercelli where he dies a natural death. But another tradition going back to a *Passio*, a copy of which is included in the codex, tells the story of Eusebius's gruesome torture and martyr's death at the hands of Arians. This, rather than Jerome's more sober account, is the story followed, for example, in the principal medieval martyrologies, including Bede's.[22] The *Vita uel Actus* of Eusebius in the passionary is not an intrusion

19. Siegmund lists *BHL* 5191d S. Mammes from Cappadocia; *BHL* 5259b SS. Marcianus, Nicander et soc. martyred in Alexandria; *BHL* 6716b SS. Petrus, Paulus, Andrea et Dyonysia "apud Lamsacum"; *BHL* 6887b SS. Polieuctus, Candidianus et Philoromus from Alexandria; *BHL* 8596d SS. Victorinus, Victor et soc. from Alexandria; *BHL* 8338b S. Tryphon from Nicia (*Die Überlieferung*, pp. 222, 228, 239, 247, 248, 254, 273). We must now add *BHL* 410b S. Anastasius to Siegmund's list.

20. This hypothesis was first advanced by H. Delehaye, "Les martyrs d'Égypte," p. 126 n. 1, where he calls for the comprehensive study of translations of hagiographic texts from the Greek. Siegmund, *Die Überlieferung*, pp. 204-208, also addresses the question of group translations. My examination of the Turin manuscript texts to date has revealed a variation in style that does not support the theory of a single translator, although only a comparison with the Greek texts will ultimately reveal whether the translation approach is similar or not.

21. The text is on fols. 60-72; it has been identified as *BHL* 2748, 2749 (Chiesa, *Le versioni latine*, p. 47).

22. Quentin, *Les martyrologes historiques*, p. 100, and Cross, "Two Saints in the *Old English Martyrology*," pp. 101, 102-103.

among the ancient and eastern martyrs, nor does it mar the homogeneity of the contents of this first part of the Turin codex.[23]

Beginning with fol. 95v, the contents of the rest of the codex do not maintain the homogeneity of the first part, even if one discounts the last section of the book (fols. 206-232) written in the eleventh century.[24] The hagiographic texts included here are not arranged in any particular order nor are they consistently marked as they are in the first part with the calendar date of the saint's commemoration.[25] They consist of the Passions of a number of early Roman and eastern martyrs[26] and, more importantly, the Lives of several monastic saints, some of whom are connected with continental Irish foundations, of which Bobbio was one.[27] Although these saints are not of Bobbio itself, they are associated with monastic houses whose history and traditions are tied to those of Bobbio. It is in this section that the Bobbio version of the Life of Ambrose is found (fols. 119-131v). The same hand that had copied

23. The *Passio S. Symphorosae* ends, complete, in the middle of fol. 59r. This half page and the next one (fol. 59v) must have been left blank because this is where a twelfth-century hand added the list of Bobbio's possessions. The *Vita uel Actus Eusebii* begins at the top of fol. 60r. It seems to me very possible that with fol. 60 we may have the beginning of what originally was the second volume, which has since been bound together with the first. There is no positive proof of this, except the following *inditia*: 1) Fol. 60 is the beginning of a new quire. 2) Fol. 59v, a hair side, appears to me unusually dark suggesting that it may have been the end sheet before binding (fol. 1r is also darker than usual, offering a similar possibility at the other end). 3) The initial Q of fol. 60r (at the beginning of the Passion of Eusebius) is similar to the initial O of the first page (the beginning of the *Passio S. Anastasiae*) in the use of green in addition to the usual red.

24. But these folia were part of the original book, cf. n. 4 above. From a codicological point of view, the only heterogeneous section of the codex is the palimpsest discussed above and fol. A.

25. Hence, for example, while the title for St. Christopher's Life contains the date, there is no date for Ambrose, Filibertus, Otmar, etc.

26. For example, St. Felicity (*BHL* 2853), St. Mary the Hermit (*BHL* 5417), St. Febronia (*BHL* 2844, a translation from the Greek).

27. For example, St. Valery (Walaricus), pupil of Columbanus, monk at Luxeuil and later abbot of Leucomaus; St. Otmar, abbot of St. Gall; St. Philibert, abbot of Joumières and Noirmoutier.

the first part of the codex continued to copy the texts up to fol. 140v, after which a succession of contemporary hands is found.

It appears, therefore, that the Bobbio passionary presents two different groups of hagiographic texts: one comprised a collection arranged *per circulum anni* (up to fol. 95), perhaps incomplete because it is missing the saints for Advent.[28] The rest of the codex contains an heterogeneous collection of hagiographic texts including a few similar to the ones comprising the first part, as well as others relating to Bobbio's broader monastic traditions. But both the scribal hands—the first of which continued to copy well beyond the end of the first group of texts on fol. 95—as well as the physical composition of the manuscript show the book to be an organic whole.[29] Such a configuration indicates that the first part of the codex, in which the Passion of St. Anastasius is found, was not compiled at Bobbio from separate *libelli* or even disparate hagiographic collections, but rather that it was copied *en bloc* from an already existing collection. This anthology of Roman and oriental passions must have been transcribed first; then the other, more disparate texts were added in the large amount of space still left in the codex, first by the original scribe, and then by others. These additions, on the other hand, could very well have been copied from separate *libelli* or other collections; one of the aims of the additional compilation seems to have been to avoid duplication of the texts already included. Unless the first part was copied from a single source, it would be difficult to understand how and why a Bobbio scribe would form a passionary consisting exclusively of texts treating Roman and oriental martyrs from several sources and arrange them chronologically in the first part of the book, only to begin to add various and disparate texts in the second part.

28. There is some evidence that an original first volume may have ended with fol. 59. See above, n. 23.

29. There is absolutely no evidence that fols. 60-232 ever constituted more than one volume.

The *Passio S. Anastasii* found at Bobbio therefore was contained not in an independent *libellus*, but rather in a small passionary[30] comprising Roman, oriental, and other early martyrs. The principal characteristic differentiating it from the primitive passionaries that were then in circulation in the Latin church is its inclusion of an unusually large number of texts translated from the Greek. This suggests that the ultimate origin of this collection was Rome, and in particular its Greek milieu. No other place in western Christendom had the resources from which such a collection could have been compiled. Whether it came to Bobbio directly from Rome or by way of an intermediate place is a question that cannot be answered at present.

The preservation of this early translation of the *Passio S. Anastasii*, as well as of other rare translated texts, is certainly in large part due to Bobbio's remoteness from more active centers of culture at this time. While more recent versions of the Passion of the Persian saint were being copied in other places, at Bobbio a passionary whose Greek flavor represents the interests and concerns of Rome of several centuries earlier was still providing a model for copyists in the latter part of the ninth century.[31]

About This Edition

My objective in preparing this edition has been to recreate as much as possible the original translation of the Greek *Acta* based on its unique exemplar, Turin, Biblioteca nazionale universitaria, F III 16 (=T).[32] The extreme fidelity of T to the Greek suggests that it has remained fairly close to the original translation. But there is

---

30. When placed within the charts of Philippart, *Légendiers*, pp. 39-40, the size of the sanctoral of the Bobbio passionary is rather small, even disregarding the missing saints for Advent. For it contains only two feasts for September, while the smallest sanctorals in Philippart's charts have three. In its physical size, cm. 30x21.5, however, the codex is standard for its age.

31. The survival of this early translation in an isolated library can be compared to the case of the first translation of the *Vita* of Pelagia the Penitent also in a unique witness, in a manuscript preserved at Udine (Petitmengin, *Pélagie* I, 165).

32. There are a few corrections in the original hand; these are marked T[1]. Others made in a later hand are marked T[2].

enough evidence to conclude that, in addition to the inevitable scribal errors, it has undergone some intentional revisions. Therefore, other witnesses have been taken into account. The Greek *Acta* (=g) are of the greatest importance in establishing the text of the original translation.[33] Also important have been the texts *BHL* 408 (=p) and *BHL* 410, which are revisions of the original translation;[34] their evidence is included in the apparatus criticus when it bears on the text. My edition therefore is based on all this eclectic evidence, which crosses both textual and linguistic lines, as well as on the recognition that the primary textual authority is held by the unique witness, the Bobbio passionary preserved at Turin, and fully described above. It is my hope that this hybrid approach can serve as a model for editions of other medieval texts whose transmission cannot be subjected to the rigid requirements of the classic stemma.

As I discuss more fully in Chapters I and II, the original Latin translation (Latin 1; see following diagram) was based on a copy of the Greek *Acta* that had been brought to Rome and that preserved two notes in the margins. It is very possible that this Greek copy had belonged to Patriarch Modestus of Jerusalem, and been annotated by his very hand. Latin 1 must have also contained the translation of these marginal notes since they were incorporated into the text only as it came down through T, but not through the tradition that produced *BHL* 408 and *BHL* 410.

Both the tradition (=o) from which depend *BHL* 408 and *BHL* 410 and the one that resulted in T go back to a common archetype Latin 2 (containing the notes still in the margin) marked by the following common errors:[35]

(11.3) μετὰ οὖν τὴν ἀπόλυσιν : post ergo abbas T : post depositas uero albas p : *om.* 410

---

33. For the use of the text of the Latin translation in the establishment of the Greek text, see Flusin I, 30-34.

34. Their relationship to each other and to the original translation is discussed in Chapter V.

35. Since *BHL* 408 and *BHL* 410 are revisions, rather than other witnesses of Latin 1, and because 410 is abbreviated, the occasions where they would yield such textual evidence must necessarily be limited.

The original translation of ἀπόλυσιν may have been a form of *absolutio*, corrupted into a word that gave rise to T's *abbas* and p's *albas*.

(18.6) μαθὼν : dicens T : requirens p : *om*. 410
I postulate that Latin 1 read *discens*, already corrupted at the common archetype Latin 2, thus explaining the reading of p.

(23.12) ἐκ στόματος : eorum T 410 : *om*. p
Latin 1 must have read *ex orum*, corrupted to *eorum* already at Latin 2.

The following readings are less clear but they suggest errors that may go back to the common archetype:

(9.7) ὑπεράνθρωπον : super omnem tormentam T : *om*. p 410
I postulate that the original translation read *super hominem*, corrupted, perhaps, into *super omnem* in the common archetype, not understood and therefore eliminated in the 408/410 branch, and emended in the T tradition.

(30.5) ἀλεῖπται : iunctores T : victores p : *om*. 410
Latin 1 must have read *unctores*. The reading of p may indicate a corruption already at the common archetype, or simply a lack of understanding of *unctores* and a consequent correction in BHL 408.

In cases where the text as preserved in the codex deviates from the Greek while p and 410 present a common reading more faithful to the Greek source, I have emended T. In general, these are small words omitted by T. But in cases where p and 410 do not agree, I have been more cautious, even if one of the revisions has preserved the Greek reading. Thus, for example, T reads *quidam* in cap. 5 to translate μέν. While p reads *quidem*, 410 reads *quidam*. This suggests that perhaps the original translator did in fact misspell or confuse *quidem* and *quidam* even though in many instances he spells them correctly. Also, I have not corrected even the most egregious examples of T's orthographical errors (e.g. *aecclesia, factoris*), in the belief that in many cases they may reflect the translator's Latinity. Unless there is independent confirmation from the indirect tradition, however, one cannot be certain that each of these inconsistencies goes back to the translator. These impediments to recovering the original text are compounded because there are no clear boundaries as to what is linguistically or grammatically possible in this work of translation. The original translator, as I argue above, did not intend to create a finished, independent work, at least not in the form in which this text has survived to us.

In my attempts to reconstruct the original translation both by following the best witness, T, but also by using the indirect evidence, I cannot claim that the resulting text is in fact the original translation, but only that it is as close an approximation of it as possible. In some places where T departs from a close adherence to the Greek, we should suspect that the original translation has been corrected.

Punctuation: The only marks of punctuation in T are the medial stop (i.e. a period suspended in the middle of a line), and the interrogation mark (;). The medial stop is followed by either a lower-case letter, or an upper case to indicate a longer pause. In the majority of cases, the punctuation of the manuscript has been followed by using a comma in the case of the former and a period in the latter cases. But on some occasions the punctuation has been altered either for the convenience of the reader, or because the manuscript's punctuation reflects a misunderstanding of the text.

Chapter Division: I have divided *BHL* 410b into chapters to correspond to Flusin's Greek text.

Orthography: The orthography reproduces exactly that of T even in its inconsistencies and "errors." The most erratic usage concerns the diphthong *ae*. Sometimes the cedilla is used, in which case I have used *ae*; in the absence of the cedilla, my spelling has been *e*. In the case of an abbreviated prefix, I have consistently used the diphthong. T capitalizes only after certain medial stops. I have added the capitalization of proper nouns.

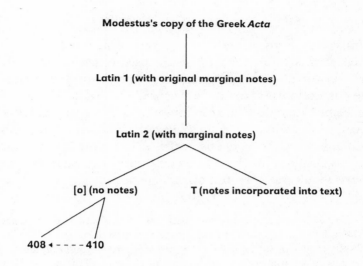

Modestus's copy of the Greek *Acta*

Latin 1 (with original marginal notes)

Latin 2 (with marginal notes)

[o] (no notes)   T (notes incorporated into text)

408 ◄ - - - - 410

CONSPECTUS SIGLORUM CODICUM ET RECENSIONUM

T   Turin, Biblioteca nazionale universitaria F III 16

g   *BHG* 84, Flusin ed. (aut graecum)

p   *BHL* 408(p) *infra editum*

410   *BHL* 410 *infra editum*

INCIPIT VITA ET PASSIO BEATI ANASTASII MONACHI
Quod est Xl K. Februar.

1. Vnigenitus filius et uerbum Dei per quem omnia facta sunt,
qui[1] coaequalis[2] atque consubstantialis patri et sancto atque uiuifi-
5 catori spiritui, miseratus genus hominum periturum[3] et sub mortis
atque corruptionis tyrannide subiectum,[4] inclinauit quidem caelos
et descendit[5] secundum quod scriptum est. Per uirginis natiuitatem
formam serui accipiens,[6] conuersatusque cum hominibus,[7] omnia
dispensauit ad salutem generis nostri, et quidem propriae mortis[8]
10 destruens eum qui habebat mortis imperium,[9] triduanae autem eius
corporis sepulturae corruptionis emundationem facturus, atque in

---

1. *qui coaequalis atque consubstantialis ... inclinauit quidem caelos et descendit*: In the Latin translation as it has come down to us, the verbs *inclinauit*
and *descendit* appear to be dependent on the relative pronoun *qui*; hence, one
at first might assume that the main verb is *dispensauit*. In the Greek text,
however, ἔκλινεν and κατέβη (for which *inclinauit* and *descendit* are the
translated equivalents) are the main verbs of this clause, while ᾠκονόμησεν
(=*dispensauit*) is the main verb of the next clause. It is doubtful therefore that
the translator meant to change the structure of the sentences here by adding
a relative clause. In reality this construction is an unintended result of the
mistranslation of the pattern Greek article + adjective as *qui* + adjective,
which occurs very frequently in this translation. See Chapter II, p. 58 for
additional examples and a discussion of such translations.

2. *coaequalis* is an inaccurate translation for συναΐδιος. Not in the pseudo-
Cyril, but cf. "Αεΐδιος perennis aeternum ..." (*CGL*, 219).

3. For a discussion of the future participles see Chapter II, pp. 62-63.

4. The use of a rare word (*tyrannide*) is uncharacteristic. It may indicate that
the original translation read *sub mortis atque corruptionis tyrannice subiectum* to
correspond literally to ὑπὸ τοῦ θανάτου καὶ τῆς φθορᾶς τυραννούμενον and has
been corrected as it came down to us in T. Prepositional phrases introduced by
ὑπό in the Greek original are translated in various ways in T; some are accurate
(e.g. 33.11 ὑπὸ 'Ιουδαίων=l. 450 *a Iudei*; 44.4-5 ὑπὸ πνεύματος=l. 594 *ab spiritu*);
others are very literal (e.g. 8.2 ὑπὸ τοῦ Σαΐν στρατηγοῦ=l. 109 *sub Sain magistrato*) and support the suggestion that *tyrannide subiectum* may be a revision. The
pseudo-Cyril reads "Υπο sub" (*CGL*, 465).

5. *inclinauit-descendit*: 2 Sm 22.10.

6. *formam-accipiens*: Phil 2.7.

7. *conuersatusque-hominibus*: cf. Bar 3.37.

8. *propriae mortis*: ἰδίῳ θανάτῳ. The use of the Latin genitive to translate
the Greek dative is a frequent mistake. See Chapter II, pp. 64-66.

9. *propriae-imperium*: cf. Heb 2.14.

inferni descensione quae multa temporum inferi subuertens regalia,[10] ita gloriosae eius resurrectioni consurgere fecit et consedere
nos in caelestibus[11] sicut inquit apostolus.

15 **2.** Ex hinc quippe quae de sublimis uirtutem induti hii qui per semet ipsi prospecti et ministri uerbi facti sunt,[12] atque eius passionum testes[13] beati apostoli peruenerunt quidem cunctum orbem di-
uino praedicamento, conuenerunt[14] autem ad pietatem uniuersam
ciuitatem et regionem et nationem et populum et tribum et lin-
20 guam, et illam quidem quae paternae traditionem et multis temporibus impietatis errorem radicitus euulserunt, angelicam uero con-
uersationem super terram deplantauerunt. Ex hinc repleta sunt cuncta
ut noscerent Dominum, secundum quod scriptum est, sicut aqua
multa cooperiet mares.[15] Ex hinc terrestria caelestibus conmixta
25 sunt, et uita aeterna in mundo conuersata est. Ex hinc uniuersa
hominum natura magnis et inenarrabilibus Dei donis laetabatur.

3. Sed qui humanae uitae a principio insidiator et fascinator atque
dolosus et piorum inimicus non habens qualiter induceret in tantam bonorum quae per Christi gratia in hominibus magnale donum,
30 et uidens semet ipsum ut quodam mancipium malignum eiectum
caelestibus inuenit concinnationem eius quidem malignitatis dignam,[16] nihil autem magnum eos qui pietati sunt alumnos laedere
posse, sed magis prodesse quod maximum est. Eos enim qui tunc
tenebant Romanorum sceptra uarietate et multis modis semetipsum
35 inseminans, insurgere quidem fecit uniuersales persecutiones aduersus aecclesiam, et hoc quod super se ipso cunctum orbem subuertit
atque confusit, in meliori autem ei circumstetit ea quae inmissionis

---

10. *quae ... regalia*: τὰ ... βασίλεια. For a discussion of the translation of
the Greek article in similar circumstances see Chapter II, p. 58.

11. *consurgere–caelestibus*: cf. Eph 2.6.

12. *qui–facti sunt*: cf. Lc 1.2.

13. *eius–testes*: cf. 1 Pt 5.1.

14. It is clear that *conuenerunt* and not *conuerterunt* (as one might have
expected) must have been the original translation for μεθήρμοσαν: cf. *convenerunt* of p and "Αρμοξη conuenit" in the pseudo-Cyril (*CGL*, 245).

15. *repleta–mares*: cf. Is 11.9.

16. *concinnationem eius quidem malignitatis dignam*: ἐπίνοιαν τῆς μὲν αὐτοῦ πονηρίας ἀξίαν. An example of a literal but correct translation of the
pattern Greek article + modifying genitive + noun. See Chapter II, p. 58.

sunt, et parua et si[17] nihil nociturus Dei cultores, maxime ipse con-
fundebatur. Nihil enim deterius horum qui olim eum praetermi-
40 nantium[18] sanctorum apostolorum quae uictoriosorum martyrum
tolerantiis eiectus erat dolosus, et rursum proprium quae pietatis
est ornatum Christi recipiebat aecclesia, et quae Dei sunt gratiae
florebat, atque addebatur per singulos dies in annorum numerum
multam[19] gloriam protendentem.

45 **4.** Satietatem autem quasi quae nos facta sunt ex Dei bonorum accipientes homines, et si obliuionem perfectam magnarum et ineffabilium Christi donorum languentes et uariate atque multis modis
delictum manu scribentes, et sanguine quidem hominum terram
rubrantes, fornicationibus uero atque adulteriis seu aliis innumeris
50 malignitatibus atque malis actionibus iram Dei aduersus semet ipsos exardescentes, totam ut dicerem super nos[20] Dei manu discipline traximus. Vnde tradidit quidem nos in manibus inimicorum
nequissimorum, et regi iniquo et malignissimo praeter uniuersam
terram,[21] ciuitates omnes et regiones quasdam quidem igni tradi-
55 tas,[22] quasdam autem a funditus euellenti et captiuanti quidem omne
quod electum et desiderabile in corporibus quoque et in pecuniis,
in perniciem autem fecit uniuersum quod derelictum insatiabili insania. Sed non usque in finem despexit benignus atque humanus[23]

17. *et si:* ἤ καὶ, as also below l. 46.
18. *praeterminantium:* ὑπερορισάντων. The Latin word (which did not
turn up in the *CLCLT* data base search) is a mirror of the Greek compound
verb. Cf. the pseudo-Cyril (*CGL*, 386) "Ορίζω ... finioterminolimito" and
(*CGL*, 463) "Υπερ prae pro super."
19. *multam:* πολὺν. The original translation may have been changed to
multam to modify *gloriam.*
20. *nos:* ἑαυτοὺς. Cf. *super nos* p.
21. *regi–terram:* cf. Dn 3.32.
22. *traditas:* παραδόντι; cf. *traditas* p. This passage is emblematic of the
way in which the aorist participle is translated (see Chapter II, pp. 61-62).
The following two aorist participles are translated with present participles,
according to the more common usage (ἀνασπάσαντι καὶ αἰχμαλωτίσαντι =
euellenti et captiuanti); ἐξολοθρεύσαντι, however, is translated as *in perniciem
autem fecit*, which, though grammatically correct, obscures the real subject.
23. *humanus:* φιλάνθρωπος. Cf. 31.14 (l. 428). Cf. the pseudo-Cyril (*CGL*,
471) "Φιλάνθρωπος humanus clememens" (*sic*); and *Passio Febroniae*, where
Φιλάνθρωπε = "amator hominum" (Chiesa, *Le versioni latine*, p. 125).

Deus, sicut manifestant res ipse, sed suaues habere nos spes dedit,
60 ut usque nunc glorificari inter germanos eius seruos et martyres.

5. Oportunum autem hic sermone factoris[24] eundem magni apostoli excessum stupefacturi[25] super inuestigabilibus Dei iudiciis et
dicere, "O altitudo diuitiarum et[26] sapientiae atque scientiae Dei,
quam inscrutabilia iudicia eius, et inuestigabiles uiae eius."[27] Ecce
65 enim Persibus quidem tradidit in disciplinam eos qui eius secundum gratiam filios atque heredes extiterunt,[28] ex Persida autem
martyres sibi elegit usque ad sanguinem quae in eum est caritatem,
fidem atque confessionem ostensuris, et quod glorificum est,[29] quia
non solum uiros sed et mulieres omnem ostensuras †malexitudi-
70 nem†,[30] et quod ultimum est propter Christi fidem per crucis martyrii coronam obligaturas. Horum unus extitit[31] et noster coronator[32] Anastasius, huius uitam quam ab initio usque ad martyrii scribere iussus sum, ipsum praeponens sermoni eum quem ab eo con-

---

63 et *om.* T; *cf.* πλούτου καὶ et p   73 sum] ego Modestus indignus archiae-
piscopus Hierusolimae sanctae Dei ciuitatis *add.* T

24. *factoris*: γενομένοις. But the correct spelling is found, e.g. in l. 11
(*facturus*). For a discussion of the future participle, see Chapter II, pp. 62-63.
25. I have found no other examples of a passive aorist infinitive translated
with a future participle. Cf., for example, κρατηθῆναι=*teneri* (l. 80). For the
occurrence of the Latin future participle, see Chapter II.
26. The omission of *et* in T's tradition may have resulted from the influence of the biblical passage.
27. Cf. Rom 11.33. T's major variant from the biblical phrase is the use of
inscrutabilia for *incomprehensibilia* of both Vulgate and Old Latin versions. *Inscrutabilia*, however, is found in many writers, including Augustine and Bede.
28. *extiterunt*, which has no equivalent in Greek nor in p or 410, should
most likely be considered a later addition, an attempt to correct the text, as
is also suggested by *eos qui*, corresponding to the Greek article.
29. *quod glorificum est*: τὸ παράδοξον. This Greek expression occurs three
times, and is translated differently each time (6.9=l. 85 *ob admirandorum rerum*; 30.3=l. 399 *quod demum est*).
30. *malexitudinem*: κακοπάθειαν. Clearly, a problematic and puzzling word.
410 eliminates the passage; p revised it into *ostensuras agonem et certamen*.
31. *extitit*: A change in tense from the Greek present tense.
32. *coronator* is found generally in the active meaning.

fessurus est, Deum et Dominum nostrum Ihesum Christum, et sic
75   incipiam gestis eius.

6. Hic regionis quidam[33] erat de Persida Razech uocabulo, de fundo autem Rasnuni, nomen autem ei Magundat. Filius uero erat magi
quoddam Bau nomine, qui etiam doctor extiterat magicae disciplinae, erudiuitque eum a pueritia magicam artem. Factum autem iu-
80   uenem contigit teneri eum in tyronem cum aliis multis et esse in
regia ciuitate Persarum sub Chosdrohe rege. Sanctae autem ciuitati
excidioni factae et uenerandorum atque adorandorum locorum igni
combustis in praedicto irae propter peccata nostra sumpta sunt et
onoranda ligna uiuificatoris et preciose crucis Christi, introducta
85   sunt in Persida. Et—ob admirandorum rerum—captiuus ille[34] quidem
ducebatur Domini crux secundum Deo odibilium suspectionem,
captiuabat autem magis ibidem eos qui digni erant sibi in salutem.

7. Superstans enim ut dictum est ciuitati Persidae honoranda atque
uiuifica crux saluatoris et quae gratiae atque uirtutis eius radia ex-
90   plendens ubique, metum quidem et stuporem infidelibus inpone-
bat, gaudium uero atque laetitiam cordibus fidelium conferebat.
Famae autem ubique regionis personantes de eo, interrogabat praedictus tyro Magundat qui et Anastasius quid hoc esset. Et audiens
dicentium quomodo Deus Christianorum hic ueniret, statim sicut
95   terra bona suscepta pluuiam idoneam ad fructificationem efficitur, ita et ille tunc suscipiens[35] per auditu praetiosissimum nomen
Dei in profundo cordis eius[36] intromittebat. Deinde cogitans in

---

75 eius] Incipit passio beati Anastasii martiris et monachi *add. in marg.* T[2]
76-77 Hic–Rasnuni] erat quidem de Persida Razech uocabulo *corr.* T[2]   77
autem *om.* T δὲ autem p 410   83 praedicta ira *corr. supra lin.* T[2]   84 honoranda *corr. supra lin.* T[1]   uiuificationis *corr. supra lin.* T[2]   92 personantis *corr.* T[1]

33. *quidam*: μὲν; cf. *quidam* 410, *quidem* p.

34. *ille* is added in 410b but omitted in p and 410. *Ille* may have been a
retranslation of the *-os* ending of αἰχμάλωτος.

35. *suscepta ... suscipiens*: δεξαμένη ... δεξάμενος. See p. 61 and n. 23.

36. ὥσπερ θησαυρὸν is omitted in the Latin tradition of the first translation (T, p, 410), but not in 411a, additional evidence that the 411a family of
texts goes back to a new translation.

semetipsum quomodo qualiter Deum magnum qui habitat in caelo, quem ut audiebat[37] et Christiani colunt inueniret hic,[38] curiosius
100 comperiebat a quibusdam, et didicit quomodo ipsa est crux in qua Christus filius Dei crucifixus est, quem Christiani adorant. Admirans autem et obstupescens super hoc praedistinatus Dei famulus Anastasius, non desinebat a tunc de Christianismo. Et quanto plus per auditu quae ueritatis sunt percipiebat, tanto magis ab eius corde
105 magicae seductiones abscedebant. Sicut enim effugiunt a luce quidem tenebrae, a sole autem umbra et ab igne fumus, ita et quae ueritatis sunt dogmata[39] exterminantur.

8. Habens uero fratrem carnalem beatus Anastasius[40] militem, factus est cum eo in exercitu qui sub Sain magistrato Persarum duce-
110 batur, et uenit usque Carchaedona. At uero sanctae recordationis Phylippico circumuallanti eum, et introgresso eo in Persida, audiens Sain reuersus est post tergum eius, et sic contigit famulum Dei Anastasium cum Persarum exercitu uenire usque in partibus Orientis.[41] Exinde secessit ab exercitu, et derelinquens proprium fratrem,
115 uenit in Hierapolim, et deuertit ad quendam Christianum Persam

---

103 a] at T ἀπὸ τότε πολυπραγμονῶν

37. *ut audiebat*: ὡς ἀκούω. The change in person is most likely the result of correction. The phrase is not found in p nor 410.

38. The mistranslation of ἐλθεῖν as *inueniret* changes the meaning of the phrase. This misunderstanding is followed in p and 410.

39. ἡ πλάνη is omitted in 410b. This slip garbles the Latin text even more, suggesting a meaning contrary to the Greek. In the other passages where πλάνη occurs (2.5; 7.18; 19.7, 12; 33.6, 8, 14) it is always translated with a form of *error*. It is possible that the original translation contained *error* here, which was then omitted in its textual transmission, leading perhaps to this phrase in which *dogmata* became the subject and the verb was shifted to the plural. This would be supported by p's reading *et fallacia exterminatur a doctrina veritatis*, although p's editor could have surmised the correct meaning behind his confused model.

40. The Latin frequently adds *Anastasius* where the Greek uses only the descriptive phrase (ὁ μακάριος, ὁ τοῦ θεοῦ δοῦλος).

41. Ἀνατολῆς: Cf. *orientales partes* used in the *Passio Febroniae* to translate τὴν Ἀνατολήν, an example of the use of a Latin periphrase to translate a Greek word (Chiesa, *Le versioni latine*, p. 144).

argentariae artis, et mansit apud eum. Didicit autem et ipse, et operabatur cum eo.

9. Cum uero habundauit ei amor ut inluminaretur, rogabat multum praedictum uirum qualiter dignaretur gratiae baptismatis sanc-
120 ti. At ille suspectus propter metum Persarum ne periclitaretur ob hoc clandestinabatur. Verum tamen cum eo ibat ad aecclesias et orabat, et picturas sanctorum martyrum uidebat et scissitabatur ab eo quidnam haec essent. Et audiens ab eo sanctorum mirabilia et atrociora tormenta quae inlata sunt eis a tyrannis, et quae super
125 hominem[42] eorum tollerantiam, persistebat[43] mirabatur et pauebat. Manens igitur paruum tempus aput praedicto Christo amabili uiro, optimum desiderium perceptus est in animo ut in Hierusolima adueniret et illic sancti mereretur baptismatis perceptionem.

10. Et quin etiam hoc in demum ducens in Dei bonae uoluntatis,
130 deuenit ad sanctam ciuitatem et manens apud quendam Christo amabilem uirum argentarium arte, et manifestans ei omne eius desiderium quomodo uult Christo accedere et digne accipere gratiam sancti baptismatis, oblatus est ei tunc Helias sanctissimus presbyter[44] Sanctae Resurrectionis. Qui hunc sicut a Deo missum susci-
135 piens filium et suggerens quae erga eum erant Modesto sanctissimo

---

122-123 ab eo *om.* T παρ' αὐτοῦ ab eo p 410 *cf.* ab eo T *l. 354 infra*
124-125 super hominem] super omnem tormentam T ὑπεράνθρωπον

42. *tormentam* has no equivalent in Greek. It must have been added in T's tradition to make sense of *super omnem*, a corruption of *super hominem*, translating literally the Greek ὑπεράνθρωπον (see Chapter II, p. 67).

43. *persistebat* has no direct equivalent in Greek, nor in p and 410. It may be a corruption of *perseverantiam*, translating ὑπομονήν (cf. l. 168 and ὑπομείνας : *perseuerauerit* [l. 238]). In this case *tollerantiam* may be a later addition. However, *persistebat* might also derive from a correction or marginal note that made its way into T.

44. Cf. προσήχθν ... 'Ηλίᾳ. Both p (*perductus est ab eo Heliae sanctissimo presbytero*) and 410 (*Oblatus est autem ab eo Helyae sanctissimo presbytero*) maintain the correct Greek meaning (that Anastasius is brought to Elias by the Christian artisan), suggesting that T's tradition has undergone revision, and that *ei tunc* corresponds in some way to παρ' αὐτου. p and 410, however, could easily have inferred the correct interpretation.

presbytero qui tunc uicarius apostolicae sedis erat fecit eum baptizari cum et socio simili moris[45] id id[46] eisdem regionis et secte
existentes, qui etiam et ipse beatam finem pro Christo suscipiens
in Edissam ciuitatem martyrii coronam obligatus est.

140 **11.** Faciente uero in domo eius dies octo pro inluminatione sua[47]
interrogabat beatum Anastasium sanctissimus presbyter Helias quid
nam uult de reliquo. At uero[48] rogabat eum dicens: "Fac me monachum." Post ergo †abbas†[49] continuo adsumens eum, perduxit in
mansionem sanctae recordationis abbatis Anastasii, quae a quarto
145 miliario sanctae ciuitatis adiacenti, et multa rogans cum et aliis praedicti uenerabilis monasterii praepositum, Iustinum fateor, uirum in
omniaqueque illustrem et plenum ex his quae a Deo sunt,[50] tradidit
ei famulum Dei Anastasium. Qui etiam[51] hunc adsumens, eius congregationis connumerauit, in indictione octaua, imperante Heraclio
150 piissimo atque Christo amabili anno decimo imperii eius. Dedit
autem ei et[52] magistrum unum de eius germanis discipulis abbas,
uirum intellectu plenum, qui etiam et docuit eum tam litteras gre-

137 moris] modis T ὁμοιοτρόπου   151 autem *om.* T δὲ autem p 410   153
eum *om.* T αὐτὸν eum p 410

45. While ὁμοιότροπος does not occur again in the Greek text, τρόπος occurs four times (21.11=l. 284; 25.9=l. 333; 34.7=l. 469; 37.6=l. 497) and is
translated as *admodum, moribus, morem,* and *admodum,* respectively. But the
first and last occurrences are both translations of the phrase ὃν τρόπον. Cf.
also "Τροπος secta mos" (pseudo-Cyril, *CGL,* 460).
46. *id id*: ὡσαύτως. A very puzzling translation. It does not occur again.
47. *sua* is added in the Latin tradition.
48. Perhaps the original translation read *at uero ipse.* Cf. ὁ δὲ; *Ipse vero*
p; *at uero ipse* 410.
49. T's textual tradition is clearly corrupt. Perhaps the original translation
for ἀπόλυσιν was *absolutionem.* Cf. "Απολυσις absolutio missio" (pseudo-Cyril,
CGL, 238). *BHL* 410 eliminated this phrase while p's *post depositas vero albas*
may be a learned conjecture. In 30.9, ἀπόλυσιν is translated as *dimissam
aecclesiam.*
50. It seems quite possible that the translation of ἀγαθῶν (*bonorum?*) may
have been omitted in T's tradition. Cf. *praeceptis* p *bonis* 410
51. *etiam* seems to be an addition in the Latin tradition (T, p).
52. T as well as p and 410 add *et.*

cas quam et psalterium. Et attundens eum atque sanctum habitum monachorum induens, ut filium edocabat germanum.

155 **12.** Fecit autem et ministrationes diuersas in monasterio beatus Anastasius tamque de quoquine quam etiam de horti, placens in eis per Domini gratiam. Erat enim sedulus ualde in ministerio fratrum et in opere manus et prae omnibus in regulam diuinae missarum aderat.[53] Et audiens sine intermissione diuinas scripturas recensi-

160 tas[54] et uitas sanctorum patrum ponebat mentem suam diligenter, et siquid forte non intellegebat interrogabat superistam[55] idoneum uirum in omnibus uel qui praeerant fratribus. Et discens ab eis ea quae requirebat, mirabatur glorificans Deum. Legens autem intra semetipsum in cella certamina uel[56] athlos uictoriosorum marty-

165 rum, lacrimabat multum et cupiebat, in abscondito cellarii cordis sui desiderium malens ut et eum dignum efficiat quandoque coequari sanctorum certaminis ad laudem et gloriam Christi. Hoc autem nouimus cum miraret se et stuperet perseuerantiam sanctorum et nihil aliud paene legere uolentem, nisi haec quae flammam alen-

170 tem desiderii illius < *** >[57] per annos septem.

13. Videns uero malignus spiritus huiusmodi eius ac tantam in Christo caritatem, ut qualiter eam euitaret et in desperationem adduceret famulum Dei Anastasium, submisit ei cogitationes malignas et memorias magicorum illorum uerborum quorum a suo patre edocuerat[58]

---

171 eius ac tantam] αὐτοῦ καὶ τοσαύτην (MSS BGKV)

---

53. *aderat*, echoed by p's *frequentans*, has no direct correspondence in Greek.

54. *recensitas:* ἀναγινωσκομένας. The translator must have used *recensere* in its meaning of "to read aloud" (cf. Du Cange s.v.), distinguishing it from Ἀναγινώσκων below which he translated as *Legens autem intra semetipsum.*

55. *supersistam*: this calque on the Greek is a term found exclusively in Rome. See Chapter II, p. 67.

56. *et* for *kai* is omitted in T and p (410 is irrelevant).

57. A phrase corresponding to Διετέλεσεν δὲ ἐν τούτοις ἐν τῇ μονῇ has dropped out of T's tradition. Cf. *Perseuerauit autem in eadem mansione per annos septem* p; *Perseuerauit autem beatus Anastasius in mansione illa annis vii* 410.

58. This is the only instance of a mistranslation of μανθάνω. The Greek verb occurs ten other times, and is translated with a form of *disco* in eight, and *cognosco* in the other two.

175   sicut supradixi, et tribulabat eum[59] uehementer. At ipse cognoscens dolosi astutiam orabat quidem Deo eripi ab insidiis diaboli.
Abbati uero quae cordis eius erant denudans cum multarum lacrimarum, dignabat orare pro eo ad Deum ut liberaret eum ab insidiis aduersarii. Ammonens quoque eum et confortans secundum
180   quae data est ei intellegentia a Deo praepositus monasterii, et faciens orationem pro eo coram aecclesiae, huiuscemodi ab eum[60] effugauit pugnae.

14. Et post dies paucos uisionem uidit in nocte Dei famulus Anastasius huiusmodi. Videbat se ipsum in monte stare excelso, et quen-
185   dam uirum ad eum uenientem et porrigentem ei poculum uini
aureum et lapillatum et dicentem ei: "Accipe et bibe." Quod et
suscipiens bibit. Statim autem ut quasi suspectus factus est et impe-
trans quod cupiebat, surgens uenit ad aecclesiam in nocturna psalmodia, delucescente sancto dominico die. Et adortans abbatem mo-
190   nasterii ingredi in ministeriali loco, ceciditqué[61] ante pedes eius
rogans cum lacrimis ut oraret pro eo qui quasi futurum se mori in
his diebus credebat,[62] et coepit euentura sonare uerba, ita dicens:
"Scio, pater, quantos labores habuisti in me miserabilem, et quia
multum te tribulaui, et quia per te adduxit me Deus de tenebris ad
195   lucem, sed ora pro me propter Deum." Dicit ei abbas: "Quid enim est
in re, et unde scis quia futurus es mori in his diebus?" Ipse uero
narrauit ei uisionem, et conualescebat,[63] quia per omnia futurus

---

177-178 lacrimarum] et ille quidem compatiebatur ei *add.* T *Vide "Chapter
II"*   186 et[1] *om.* T καὶ et p 410   et[2] *om.* T καὶ MS U et p 410

59. ἐν τούτοις is omitted in T; p and 410 provide no information on
whether the omission was in the original translation.
    60. *ab eum* is absent from the Greek tradition. Cf. *ab eo* of p and 410.
    61. The *-que* is added in the Latin; it is possible, however, that the Greek
text available to the translator had τε, which is generally translated with the
enclitic in Latin (cf. [18.6] ἐμακάρισέν τε = *beatificauitque*).
    62. *credebat* has no immediate equivalent in the Greek.
    63. *conualescebat* is a puzzling translation for διοχυρίζετο. Could the trans-
lator have mistaken διοχυρίζετο for διοχύω? On the other hand, p reads *confirmans asserebat*; BHL 410, *confirmans*, and the pseudo-Cyril (*CGL*, 277) "Δι-
οχυριζομαι confirmo autumo." It is not clear therefore whether the original

sit in his diebus mori siue communem mortem, siue et aliter quoquo-
modo. Metuebat enim palam dicere, ut non increparet ei.

200 **15.** Ita[64] uero consolatus est corde[65] multisque modis ammonitionibus abbatis, compleuit canonem cum fratribus. Et missas factas,
percipiens diuini mysterii sacramentum et prandens cum fratribus,
soporatusque modicum et surgens, non ferens cordis eius incendium, exiit clam de monasterio, nihil accipiens omnino, nisi ea
205 quae uestiebatur. Et abiit in Diospolim, et exinde in Garizin montem orans, atque in caetera ibidem ueneranda loca. Deductus per
gratiam Christi,[66] deuenit usque Caesaream Palestinae, et mansit
in domo super laudabili et Dei genitricis Mariae duos dies.

16. Secundum dispensationem uero quae omnia sapienter et iustae
210 et humaniter deducentes[67] diuina prouidentia procedens usque ad
Sanctam Eufemiam orationis causa, uidit pertransiens in quandam
domum Persarum magice operantes. Et zelo deifico ductus, ingressus ad eos dicens: "Quid erratis et errare facitis in maleficiis uestris?" Stupentes autem hii uiri super huiusmodi eius constantiam
215 interrogabant eum quis esset, et unde, quia haec dicit ad eos. Ipse
uero ait eis: "Et ego sicut et uos fui aliquando, et scio incantationes

---

210 deducentes] iubente *add.* T   211 causa] et *add.* T

---

translation used some form of *confirmo*, preserved by p and *BHL* 410, or
whether *confirmans* was a correction introduced by 410 and picked up by p.

64. *ita* (omitted in both p and 410) corresponds to εἶτα. In the *Passio Febroniae* εἶτα is also translated by *ita*, and the editor suggests that this may be
an example of a phonetic influence—that the sound of the Greek word
suggested a similar sounding Latin word (Chiesa, *Le versioni latine*, p. 123).

65. πολλαῖς is absent in the surviving Latin tradition; the awkward literal
rendering *multis multisque modis* may have been subsequently corrected.

66. *Christi* appears to have been added in the original translation. Cf. *per
Domini gratiam* in p.

67. *iubente* has no equivalent in Greek nor in the rest of the Latin tradition. It must be considered an addition to T's own tradition, and probably
was a later attempt at the ablative absolute with *diuina prouidentia* to make
sense of the unclear Latin text.

uestras." Et incipiens arguere eos, obmutescentes illi rogauerunt eum[68] ne diuulgaret quae erga eos erant, et dimiserunt eum.

17. Et cum abisset < *** >[69] ab illis uiderunt eum quosdam de
220 cauallariis sedentes ante derbas quod est praetorium sellarii, et dicunt inter se propria lingua: "Iste dilator est." Audiens autem beatus Anastasius haec eos dicentes, intuens eis[70] dicit: "Quid uerbosatis? Ego dilator non sum, sed seruus sum Ihesu Christi. Et melior uestri sum, nam et ego aliquando sicuti uos caballarius fui."
225 At illi surgentes tenuerunt eum. Et exiens sellarius et discutiens eum unde esset, et omnia diligenter quae erga eum erant examinans, custodiuit eum tres dies. In quibus diebus non adquieuit suscipere quicquam ab eis alimenti causa suspectus dolum eorum.

18. Veniente uero marzabana—non enim erat in Caesaria quando
230 tentus est famulus Dei Anastasius—suggessit ei quae erga eum cognouit[71] praedictus sellarius, et adduxit eum in praetorium suum. Occupato uero marzabana circa alias res, inuentus est quidam Christo amabilis qui agnouit beatum Anastasium in domum Dei genitricis Mariae, et confabulatus est ei et discens ea quae de eo senserat, bea-
235 tificauitque eum de bono initio et confortauit diuinis sermonibus, ut non metueret tormenta neque mortem quam pro Christo debue-

---

222 eis *om.* T *supplevi ex* eos p *cf.* αὐτοῖς   225 et² *supplevi ex* p *cf.* καὶ
234 et² *om.* T καὶ et p 410   dicens T μαθὼν requirens p 410

68. *eum* in the Latin tradition of the original translation is absent in g.

69. T has no equivalent for ὀλίγον. p has *modicum*, and this or a similar word must have been present in the original translation.

70. *intuo* occurs also followed by *in* + accusative (e.g. 19.2=l. 241), but there it translates ἀτενίζω + εἰς + accusative. This is the only occurrence of ἐμβλέπω.

71. The phrase τὰ κατ' αὐτὸν is generally transformed into a relative clause by the addition of a form of the verb *sum* (cf. 16.8=l. 218 *quae erga eos erant*, 17.8=l. 226 *quae erga eum erant*). Here we find instead the addition of the more elaborate *cognouit* and further down (18.6=l. 234) of *senserat*. This suggests that these passages may have been revised. Cf. p's *suggerens de eo primus officiorum*.

rat perpeti,[72] sed fiducialiter responderet marzabanae dicens quomodo "qui perseuerauerit usque in finem hic saluus erit."[73]

19. Introductus est autem Dei famulus Anastasius, et stetit coram
240 marzabana, non adorans eum secundum ritum quod ab eis tenetur.
Et intuens in eum marzabanas[74] dicit: "Unde es, et quis extiteris?"
Ipse uero respondens dixit: "Ego Christianus uerax sum. Si autem
uelis discere[75] unde sim, Persarum quidem sum genere, de regione
Razech, de uilla Rasnuni. Cauallarius uero eram et magus, et reli-
245 qui tenebras et ueni ad lucem." Dicit ei marzabanas: "Dimitte errorem hunc et conuertere ad primam tuam religionem, et prebemus
tibi iumenta et miliaresia et continentiam[76] habeas magnam." Ipse
uero respondens dixit: "Ne det mihi Deus negare Christum meum."
Dicit ei marzabanas: "Ergo placet tibi uestire schemam quam indu-
250 tus es?" Ipse uero ait: "Hic habitus gloria mea est." Dicit ei marzabanas: "Daemonium habes." Respondens beatus Anastasius dicens[77]
"Quando fui in errorem habui daemonem. Nunc autem habeo
Christum meum qui persequitur daemones." Dicit ei marzabanas:
"Non metuis imperatorem, ne quando didicerit quae erga te sunt
255 iubeat te crucifigere?" Ipse uero dixit: "Quare habeo timere? Homo
est corruptibilis sicut et tu."

247 et miliaresia] ut scis militaris T *cf.* καὶ μιλιαρήσια

72. *debuerat perpeti* has no direct equivalent in g, p or 410. It could very
well be an addition to the T tradition to complete the original translation's
quam pro Christi. See previous note for other evidence that this passage has
been revised.

73. *qui–erit*: Mt 10.22.

74. *marzabanas* is added in the Latin tradition; ἐπὶ πολὺ is omitted.

75. καὶ is omitted in the Latin tradition.

76. It is possible that the translator read συγκράτησιν ("retention, holding
together") instead of συγκρότησιν ("welding; approval, favor; support"; cf. the
pseudo-Cyril [*CGL*, 440] "Συγκροτησις sustentatio"). On the other hand, on
the same page, cf. "Συγκροτω contineo sustento." *Habeas* has no equivalent
in the Greek, nor in p or 410. Could it be an incomplete correction (*ut conti-
neantiam habeas magnam*)?

77. *dicens* is not in g; cf. *dixit* p, 410.

20. Tunc indignatus iussit eum inferratum duci in castro et asportari lapides sine cessatione. Cum uero asportaret lapides, multas
atque insufferentes tribulationes sustineret famulus Dei. Quosdam
260 enim de regione eius uidentes eum et proprium existimantes pudorem quae in eo fiebant accedebant ei dicentes: "Quid hoc fecisti
nobis? Nemo aliquando de regione nostra factus est Christianus.
Et ecce fecisti nobis ridiculum." Atque omnibus uerbis fallacibus
aduocabant eum in semetipsos. Ipse uero iniuriabat eos et repelle-
265 bat. Illi autem insania uersi, per singulos dies accedentes auellebant
ei barbam et percutiebant sine parcitate et scindebant uestimenta
eius. Non solum autem hoc, sed et saxos magnos[78] quos quattuor
ex eis baiulantes imponebant ei et haec conuinctum[79] habentem
et unam quidem catenam a collo, alia uero a pede ferentem. Et
270 multa atrociora ostensi sunt in eum. At uero fortissimus adhleta
omnia ferebat propter Christum gaudens.

21. Iterum autem iussit marzabanas adsisti[80] eum et dixit ei: "Si
ueraciter sicut dixisti magi filius fuisti et scis magicam artem, dic
mihi aliqua ex his ut cognoscam." Ipse uero respondens dixit: "Ne
275 det mihi Deus egredi ultra ex ore meo quicquam huiusmodi." Dicit
ei marzabanas: "Quid ergo? permanes in his? conuertere in primam
tuam religionem, nam scribo imperatori de te." Ipse uero ait ad
eum: "Scripsisti et suscepisti rescripta. Fac quod uis." Et marzabanas dixit: "Non scripsi, sed scribo; et quicquid iusserit mihi[81] fa-
280 cio." Ipse uero ait ei: "Vade, scribe quanta uolueris mala de me.
Ego enim Christianus sum." Dicit marzabanas: "Ponatur et caedatur usque dum confiteatur facere quae iubentur ei." Incipiens au-

257-258 asportari] *sed cf.* παρακομίζειν deportare p asportari 410   268 con-
uinctum] cum uinctum T   274 mihi aliqua] μοι τι (MS I)   279 dixit] εἶπεν
(MS I)   280 ei *non est in* g

77. *magnos* is not in g; cf. *lapides magnos* p, *lapides multos* 410. Converse-
ly, there is no equivalent of *hoc*.
79. συνδέτην is found as *conuinctum* below (l. 326).
80. Perhaps this passive (or "deponent"?) infinitive was the result of confusing the active 2nd aorist infinitive, as here, with the passive 1st aorist infinitive. Cf. 19.14 σταυρωθῆναι=l. 255 *crucifigere*.
81. *mihi* is added in the Latin tradition.

tem alligari famulus Dei Anastasius dicit: "Sinite me. Non habeo necesse uincula." Et sedens designauit semetipsum quem admodum
285 incipiebat alligari ab eis, et coeperunt ferire in⁸² eum fustibus. Dixit autem sanctus ad eos: "Expoliate me habitum, ut non iniurietur, et sic caedite super carnes meas. Haec enim quae facitis ludibria sunt. Me enim si membratim abscidatis Christum meum non negabo."

290 **22.** Iterum autem inquid marzabanas: "Adquiesce mihi, nam scribo imperatori de te." At ipse respondens dixit: "Vade scribe imperatori tuo⁸³ quicquid uolueris." Et marzabanas: "Quid igitur," inquid, "non times imperatorem?" Beatus Anastasius respondit: "Quare habeo metuere imperatorem tuum? Non est homo sicut et tu? et
295 sicut tu morieris non moritur? Sicut corrumperis non corrumpitur? Quem igitur magis timeam, illum qui corrumpitur sicut et tu, similem tibi lutum, aut Christum qui fecit caelum et terram mare et omnia quae in eis sunt?"⁸⁴ Stupefactus autem superbus ille super fiduciam martyris, iussit eum duci in castro.

300 **23.** Et post dies paucos iussit eum adsisti et dicit ei: "Accipe magica, sacrifica ut non moriaris male et frauderis lucis huius." Respondit Dei famulus et dicit ei: "Quibus diis iubes me sacrificare? soli et lunae et igni et equo⁸⁵ et montibus et collibus caeterisque omnibus? Sed ne det mihi Deus adorare cultoribus uestris aliquando.
305 Haec enim omnia Christus fecit in seruitium nostri hominum. Vos uero errando seruitis iumentis et daemonibus, homines facti ignorantes qui fecit uos Deum. Si enim noueratis Christum,⁸⁶ habueretis conuerti ad lucem, et erui a daemonibus qui errare uos faciunt."

292 Et marzabanas *non est in* g   294 et² *non est in* g   295 non² *om.* T οὐ
non p 410   301 sacrifica] sacrificia T θῦσον et sacrifica p 410   303 et equo]
? Ergo T καὶ τῷ ἵππῳ et mari p *om.* 410   et⁴] οὐκοῦν καὶ

82. *in*, with the Latin transitive verb, might be taken as meaning "against."
83. *tuo* is not found in g.
84. *mare–sunt* appears only in the Latin tradition.
85. It seems likely that p's *mari* originates from a misreading of *equo* (*aequo?*) for, perhaps, *aequori* or *aqua*.
86. καὶ ὑμεῖς is omitted in T and 410 (p is irrelevant).

Haec qui non mentitur Deus qui promisit[87] his qui pro nomine
310 eius patiuntur dare os et sapientiam cui non poterunt resistere[88]
omnes aduersarii[89] ex orum idiota et alienigena procedere uoluit,[90] in gloriam quidem eius, roborem autem credentium. His
Deo spiratis sermonibus, stupefaciens contrarios Dei martyr, et
trinis coronatus confessionibus pietatis certator statim[91] ad
315 castrum ducebatur quibus pro Christo uinculis adornatus.

24. Cognoscens autem sanctissimus abbas monasterii in quo existebat martyr tantam stabilitatem confessionis eius quae in Christum est et quae sine stupore et copiosam alacritatem atque perseuerantiam eius gauisus est gaudio magno cum uniuersa congregatione
320 sua. Et Deum quidem supplicabat die noctuque cum omni frater-
nitate pro ut finiret eius cursum quae in eum erat confessione.
Duo autem fratres dirigens in Caesarea ad beatum Anastasium cum
litteris adhleticis confortauit eius alacritatem.

25. Cum uero esset in custodia[92] martyr Christi Anastasius, non
325 cessabat psalmis et hymnis glorificans Deum die ac nocte. Habens
uero conuinctum, ut dictum est, iuuenem quendam ex seruorum
pro quadam causa tentum et nolens contristare eum, cum surgebat
quidem nocte ut caelebraret consuetum canonem Dei glorificatio-
nis, super inclinabat uero eius collo uincto iacenti, stans et pedem
330 suum iuxta pedem eius, ut non per catenarum extensione laborem

---

309 promisit] fidelibus suis *add.* T   310 resistere] et contradicere *add.* T
311 ex orum] eorum T 410 *om.* p ἐκ στόματος *cf. quoque* ex ore meo (ἐκ τοῦ
στόματός μού) *l. 275 supra.*   327 eum] sed cum *add.* T *cf.* 410

87. T's *fidelibus suis*, most likely, was a marginal explanatory note that
was integrated into the text.
88. T's addition makes the biblical quote conform to the Vulgate text.
89. *os–aduersarii*: cf. Lc 21.15.
90. The mistranslation of εὐδόκησεν (also translated as *uoluit* in l. 451
[33.13]) obscures the meaning of the sentence.
91. The Greek text of the translator may have read εὐθύς instead of αὖθις. Cf. 37.8 αὖθις =l. 500 *rursum.* Cf. the pseudo-Cyril (*CGL*, 317) "Ευθυς
statim." *Statim* in all other occurences translates εὐθέως.
92. τοῦ κάστρου is omitted in the Latin tradition.

praestaret ei. In una igitur nocte psallente eo, auscultabatur ei quidam de uinctis, Hebraeus quidem religione et de nobilioribus, clemens autem moribus, sicut didicimus. Et uidens beatum martyrem[93] die quidem in lapidum asportatione miserantem, nocte uero

335 deprecatione Dei sustinente, stupebat mente existimans quis nam esset hic.

26. Tamdiu ergo intuens in eum, iacens super pauimento in tenebras noctis, stante sancto et psallente matutinos hymnos, uidit subito aliquos ueste dealbatos ingredientes per ostium carceris et

340 circumdantem beatum martyrem, quibus et lux copiosa refulsit. Amens uero factus uir super contemplationem[94] dixit intra se: "Sanctus Deus, isti angeli sunt." Hoc autem existimans, uidit hos ipsos pallia circumdatos habentes cruces, et dicit in semet ipso: "Isti episcopi sunt." Admirans autem de his, intuens in martyrem

345 Christi Anastasium, uidit et ecce hii[95] qui circa eum erant lux circumfulsit. Videbat enim eum splendide indutum sicut et caeteros, et ecce iuuenis quidem in multa gloria stetit ante eum, habens turibulum et incensum mittentem. Aspiciens autem haec omnia uir uim faciebat manu pulsare proximum suum dormientem, qui erat

350 Christianus, ut[96] iudex Scythopoleos, qualiter ostenderet ei quae uisa sunt, et non poterat, sed manebat amens, sobria quidem cogitatione adtendens quae uidebantur, corpori quidem manens immobilis. Tamen super multum uim faciens, totum se ipsum ducens super iacentem. Territus uero praefatus uir, comperit ab eo quid

355 hoc esset. Dicit ei Hebraeus: "Cernes hic?" Et intuentes non uiderunt nihil. Enarrauit autem ei omnia quae uisa sunt et glorificauerunt unianimiter Deum.

27. Quia uero sicut superius praememoratum est a prima et secunda interrogatione discens marzabanas immobilitatem serui Dei

---

93. T often uses the phrase *sanctus* or *beatus martyr* in places where the Greek has either the adjective ἅγιος/μακάριος or the noun μάρτυς but not both, cf. below ll. 340, 375, 377, 384, 396, 400 and passim.

94. καί is omitted in the Latin tradition, and in Flusin's manuscript B.

95. *hii*: a corruption of the translation of καὶ αὐτός (*et is? et ille?*)?

96. *ut*, not in g, is found only in T. It could be an attempt by the translator to indicate that his translation is only an approximation of the original, and easily have been eliminated from p and 410.

360 Anastasii scripsit imperatori Chosdrohi de eo. Et[97] contigit inter
paucos dies suscipere eum imperatoris iussionem, et transmittens
ad eum de carcere per maiorem eius dicit ei: "En iussit imperator
ut uerbum solum dicas quia 'non sum Christianus,' et statim te
dimitto et ubi uolueris uade, siue monachus uis esse, esto, siue ca-
365 uallarius sicut eras antea et esse nobiscum; ut uis fac." Respondit
autem martyr Christi et dixit: "Ne fiat mihi negare me Christum."
Multas uero promissiones et consolationes proferens ei per maiorem eius non ualuit suadere eum.

28. Postmodum uero mandauit ei per eidem dicens: "Scio quia con-
370 funderis propter congentiles tuos, et ideo non uis coram eis negare.
Sed quia iussio imperatoris est uel inter me et aliis duobus sellariis,
dic uerbum et dimittam te." At ipse remandauit ei dicens: "Absit
mihi neque coram te, neque coram alios negare aliquando Deum
meum." Tunc dicit ei per se ipso: "Ecce iussit imperator ut ferro
375 uinctus uadas in Persidam." Beatus uero martyr Christi respondens
dixit: "Si dimiseris me, ego solus uadam ad imperatorem." At autem uidebat beatum martyrem ad omne experimentum fortiter
stantem, neque minis praebentem, neque blandimentis suasum,
bullatum eum iussit duci in custodia publica. Futurum erat post
380 quinque dies iter facere cum aliorum duo Christo amabilium uirorum quos etiam bullatos cum eo transmisit.

29. Adpropinquante autem inter quibus die festo exaltationis prae-
tiose[98] crucis Domini, fecerunt lucrationem[99] in carcerem, ipse
quoque beatus martyr et duo fratres monasterii eius[100] et praefati

---

362 ad eum de carcere] ad eundem carcere T αὐτὸν ἐκ τοῦ δεσμωτηρίου ad
eum in carcere p ad eum 410   363 uerbum solum] μόνον λόγον (MS A)
373 negare] me *add.* T *non est in* g p 410   381 cum eo *om.* T σὺν αὐτῷ cum
eo p 410

---

97. *Et* is added in the Latin tradition.
98. καὶ πανσέπτου is omitted in the Latin tradition.
99. Did the translator confuse *lucratio* for *lucubratio*, which would have
been a suitable translation for ἀγρυπνίαν? Cf. the pseudo-Cyril (*CGL*, 217)
"Αγρυπνια lucubratio excubitum peruigilium ..." Or is T's reading a corruption of *lucubratio*? p eliminates this phrase, and 410's *sollempnitatem* suggests
that *lucubratio* was not the reading available.
100. *eius* is added in the Latin tradition.

385 duo Christo amabiles uiri et quosdam de ciuitate reuerendissimo-
rum, psalmis et hymnis et caeterae spiritali festiuitati noctem per-
ducentes, ita ut oblituros uniuersos uinctos cladibus eorum communi Deum glorificarent. Diluculo autem ingressus comerciarius
uir Christo amabilis ad marzabanam postulauit ab eo uincula tolli,
390 ut eum adueniret in aecclesia. Et hoc facto, gaudium magnum factum est uniuersis fidelibus et consolatio multa de frequentium
eorum tribulationum, ut pute martyres[101] Christi aduenientes in
aecclesia. Et enim[102] multam uenerunt desidiam hii qui de ciuitate erant uiri, et quasi torpentes eorum anime de immensis atque
395 saeuissimis tribulationibus.

30. Cernentes uero tantam beati martyris fidem in Christum et
perseuerantiam refloruerunt, uerum etiam et reuixerunt fidei, atque
obliti sunt suorum tribulationum propter super eminentem in martyres[103] consolationem. Et quod demum est, hii qui desperati atroci-
400 bus et in modico fidei tempore corruentes, unctores beati martyris
facti sunt, osculantes eius uincula et dicentes: "Si nos parati[104] ha-
buimus mori pro te et[105] propter Christum, quanto magis tu propter communem et omnium dominum Christum debueras hoc cum
multa alacritate sustinere." Et multum ut dici[106] et ineffabilem
405 honorem atque alacritatem in sanctum ostenderunt uiri pariter et
mulieres. Postquam uero dimissam aecclesiam multum rogans et
uim faciens ei commerciarius perduxit eum in propriam domum

396 et *om.* T καὶ et 410   400] unctores] iunctores T ἀλεῖπται victores p
403 et *non est in* g

101. The Latin translation (especially the use of the plural *martyres*)
obscures the meaning of the Greek. Neither p nor 410 retain the Greek idea
that the faithful are rejoicing in the presence of a martyr in the church,
suggesting that the confusion occurred early on in the Latin tradition.
102. εἰς is omitted in T.
103. *super eminentem in martyres*: the translation's confused Latin, particularly the use of the plural, may explain the shortening of the text in p and 410.
104. Was the original translation *parate* (ἑτοίμως)? But cf. *parati fuimus*
410 (p is irrelevant).
105. *et* is added in T.
106. *ut dici*: a corruption of the original translation for ἁπλῶς (which
does not occur again)?

cum duobus fratribus de monasterio eius, et conuescens cum eis restituit eum in carcerem gaudentem et exultantem in Dominum.
410 Similiter autem ibidem factum est gaudium magnum, omnium glorificantium Dominum.

31. Expleto itaque termino quinque dierum, exiit de ciuitate Cesarea cum[107] duorum Christo amabilium uirorum super quadam causa accusatis, praemissus cum multarum lacrimarum ut pute[108]
415 ciuium Christianorum atque Persarum et aliorum gentilium[109] pariter glorificantium Deum super bonum eius propositum. Ibit autem cum eo unus ex duobus fratribus monasterii eius secundum iussionem praepositi ad solatium atque ministerium eius. Plurimum autem ut ea quae execuntur in eum ab initio usque in finem, haec
420 per Domini gratia retulerit tamque sanctissimo abbati atque etiam quae sub eo est congregationi. Multum enim gaudium et laetitiam his qui per ciuitate et locum fidelibus fiebat super aduentum martyris. Et cum omni honore et gloria ut pute Christi martyrem suscipiebant et praemittebant uniuersi. Haec autem ipse martyr
425 scripsit ab Hierapolim praeposito monasterii sui rogans orare pro eo ut incondemnabilem eum Dominus super huiusmodi honor et gloria custodiat. Scripsit uero ei et a Tigridis flumine, similiter poposcens obsecrare humanum Deum ut finiret eius cursum in gloriam nominis sui.

430 **32.** Ingrediens autem in Persida Christi martyr Anastasius missus est in carcere in praedio qui uocatur Bethsalohe, qui est a stadiorum sex de Discarthas, in quo degebat imperator. At uero frater qui cum eo erat mansit in eodem praedio, in domo Cortac fili de Iesdim primi comerciarii Persarum qui erat Christianus. Et faciente
435 sancto martyre dies aliquos cum eorum qui ibidem erant captiuorum, suggestum est quae erga eum erat imperatori Chosdrohi. Et mittens unum de iudices iussit examinari eum.

420 gratia] σαφῶς *om.* MSS GKV

107. καὶ is omitted in the Latin tradition.
108. *ut pute*: This phrase (omitted in p and 410) here corresponds to ὑπὸ τῶν, while in two other occurrences (ll. 423, 392) it translates οἷα. It might go back to a transliteration of ὑπὸ τῶν.
109. πάντων is omitted in T and 410 (p is irrelevant).

33. Qui etiam[110] adueniens in carcerem cum tribuno qui erat super carcerum et[111] interrogabat eum quis esset et unde et quam ob rem relinquens eorum religionem factus est Christianus. Respondit martyr Christi per interpretem—dedignauit enim eis loqui persica lingua, et quidem multa coactus[112]—dixit eis: "Erratis uos daemones pro Deo colentes. Et enim ego aliquando cum essem in errore hos colebam. Nunc autem colo[113] omnipotentem Deum qui fecit caelum et terram et omnia quae in eis sunt. Et scio diligenter quia culturae uestrae perditio et error daemonum sunt." Dicit ei iudex: "Miser, numquid quem colitis uos Christiani crucifixerunt Iudei? Quomodo ergo errasti relinquens religionem tuam et factus es Christianus?" Et sanctus martyr respondit: "Quamquidem crucifixus est sponte a Iudeis, uerum dicis. Ipse autem est qui fecit caelum et terram, mare[114] et omnia quae in eis sunt, et uoluit descendere super terram et humanari et crucifigi ut liberaret genus hominum de errore Sathanae qui a uobis colitur. Vos uero colentes ignem et caetera que dicere erubesco, uanas habetis spes, creaturae colentes praeter qui condidit." Dicit ei iudex: "Quid tibi et sermonibus istis? Ecce diuinitas imperatoris parauit tibi dignitates magnas et cingulas aureas et equos,[115] ut sis inter primatos eius. Tantum conuertere in pristinam religionem tuam." Respondit martyr Christi et dixit: "Ego Deum meum non negabo, sed potius eum adoro ac colo. Dona uero imperatoris tui ut stercora computabo."

34. Haec autem omnia abiens intimauit imperatori praedictus iudex. Furore uero repletus imperator iussit eum iterum in carcerem

---

441 per interpretem] per inter interpretem T   445 et² *om.* T καὶ et p 410
460 vero *supra lin. add.* T¹

110. *etiam* is added in T and p; cf. *quique* 410.
111. *et* is added in T and p.
112. καί is omitted in the Latin tradition.
113. καὶ προσκυνῶ is omitted in the Latin tradition.
114. *mare* is added in the Latin translation.
115. καί is omitted in the Latin tradition.

retrudi[116] ut in crastinum poenis afficeret. Altera namque die[117]
ueniens igitur iudex cum ira iussit trahere eum foris carcerem, et
465 coepit minis terribilibus obstupesci eum, ut putabat, suspicans adquiescere eum. Sanctus uero martyr respondit ei dicens: "Ne labores, domine iudex, neque fatiges. Me enim Christo confortante non
adquiesco sermonibus tuis.[118] Quicquid ergo uis fac." Tunc iussit
eum ligatum secundum morem Persarum fustibus caedi sine par-
470 cim, et dicit ei: "Honoribus et donis imperatoris adquiescere non
adsentis? Cognosce quia a modo haec tibi adhibetur. Sic enim te
per singulos dies plagis consumam." Respondens autem sanctus
martyr dixit ei: "Nec donis imperatoris tui adquiesco neque minas
tuas timeo. Quicquid ergo uis fac."

475 **35.** Tunc iussit eum solutum supinum poni et lignum super tibias
pedum eius inponi et duos uiros fortissimos stare super duarum
partium ligni. Omnes uero nouimus quod insufferens est tormenti
species. Sanctus autem martyr Christi gratias agebat Deo sustinens
dolores fortiter. Videns uero iudex quia nihil plus exigit—sed per
480 huiusmodi magnis doloribus sicut ferrus frigidi aquae limabitur

465 putabat *ex* potabat *corr.* T¹ *aut* T²   466 ei dicens *non est in* g   479-
481 exigit–iussit] exigit per huismodi magnis doloribus <u>sed</u> sicut ferrus frigidi
aquae limabitur <u>ita</u> divina gratia corroboratus <u>immobilis permanebat</u> iussitque
T. *Cf.* Sed magis huiusmodi doloribus sicut ferrum frigidis aquis limabatur
per divinam gratiam et confortabatur, iussit ... p; *cf.* g

116. *iterum–retrudi,* which changes the meaning of the Greek text, is
most likely the result of revision. The version closest to g here, and probably
therefore also to the original translation, is p's *Furore uero repletus imperator
iussit mitti eum in carcerem in crastinum, uolens eum poenis affici,* where only
the addition of *in carcerem* departs from the transmitted Greek text. Cf. *BHL*
410's *Qui statim furore repletus misit eum in carcerem.* ἀποστέλλω is translated
as *transmisit* (28.12=l. 381); *misit* (38.1=l. 511); *transmissorem* (43.4=l. 581).
Retrudo does not occur again.
    117. *Altera namque die* is added in the Latin tradition.
    118. T's text may have been edited. Cf. μὴ πείσῃς ἀποστῆναι τῆς πίσ-
τεως; *non adquiescam tibi neque recedere facies a fide quam coepi* p, *non facies
recedere a fide Christi* 410.

diuina gratia corroboratus—iussit[119] eum mitti in carcere donec iterum intimaret imperatori de eo.

36. Sellarius uero qui erat super carcerem Christiano existenti,[120] frater e monasterii qui etiam et abiit cum sancto martyre ingredie-
485 batur unam infra unam ad eum, consolans et adortans eum in bonum. Multi uero Christianorum qui ibidem erant in quibus et de Iesdim filii introibant ad eum corruentes atque osculantes eius uincula, et rogabant[121] ut dignaretur orare pro eis et daret eis benedictionem aliquam ad custodiam eorum. At uero beatus martyr
490 abiciens haec, ipsi uero ceram supermittentes uinculis eius exprimentesque eam et in benedictionem hoc percipiebant.

37. Iterum ergo post dies paucos ingrediens iterum ipse iudex in carcere dicit ei: "Quid dicis? Facis iussionem imperatoris aut permanes in his?" Sanctus uero martyr mouens caput suum quasi abo-
495 minauit eum, dicens: "Et semel et secundo et sepius dixi tibi quam inpossibile est negare me Christum. Quicquid ergo uis, fac citius." Tunc temerarius ille et barbarus iussit ligari eum quem admodum et pridem, et caedi eum diutius fustibus sine parcim, et derelinquens eum in carcerem secessit. Recuperans autem dies aliquos,
500 rursum ingrediens ad eum, his ipsis sermonibus utens ad negationem sanctum martyrem prouocabat, aliquando quidem blanditiis atque promissionibus pecuniis quoque et dignitatibus, aliquando autem minis terribilibus amarisque tormentis. Cum uero uideret eius immutabilem mentem atque soliditatem quae in Christum
505 habebat fidei, iussit eum ligari sicut semel et bis caedi similiter fustibus. Et iterum solutum eum iussit suspendi eum ex una manu, et

---

488 et rogabant *om.* T καὶ ἀξιοῦντες et rogabant p rogabant 410   491 eam et *non est in* g   492 iterum² *non est in* g *sed cf.* p 410

119. Given the habit of the translator to remain quite close to the Greek text, the insertion of *ita ... immobilis permanebat* must be considered a later revision or a marginal note integrated into the text. This view is supported by p.

120. θαρρῶν is omitted in the Latin tradition deriving from this translation. Note as well that the translator may have considered *Christiano existenti* as the ablative absolute, rather than *sellarius ... existenti*.

121. Despite the agreement of p and 410, the original translator may have rendered the Greek more closely, as *rogantes* perhaps.

saxum magnum alligari in pede eius. Et sic relinquens eum abiit.
Sustinebat autem fortiter martyr Christi huius modi supplicium
quasi horarum duarum spatio, mittens iussit deponi eum. Et abiens
510   suggessit imperatori incompositum mentis atque fiduciam martyris.

38. Et post dies quindecim misit imperator ipsum quoque iudicem
et socios cum eo interficere sanctum martyrem et multos Christianorum captiuorum. Qui etiam uenientes iusserunt eos[122] adduci
foris praedio Betsalohes in quo existebat carcer, ipsumque sanctum
515   martyrem et circiter septuaginta uiros secus amnem, et sic coram
sancto martyre funibus suffocari uniuersos iusserunt, inter quibus
erant et praedicti duos Christo amabiles uiri qui cum eo abierant[23]
a Caesarea sancto martyre. Et per unumquemque qui interficiebant-
tur dicebant sancto: "Quare uis sicut unus horum male perire? Sed
520   magis adquiesce imperatori et uiue et accipe honores ab eo et esto
in palatio sicut unus ex nostris et ne derelinquas dulciam uitam
hanc." At uero uictoriosissimus Christi martyr Anastasius aspiciens
in caelum gratias egit Deo quam impletum est desiderium eius. Et
respondens ait ad eos: "Ego optabam membratim concidi a uobis
525   pro caritate Christi. Si uero iste est obitus quem comminatis mihi,
gratias ago Deo meo quia per modico dolore participem me facitis
gloriae martyrum eius." Et ita cum multo gaudio atque alacritate
defunctus est simili morte. Post quam autem suffocauerunt eum,
absciderunt eius praeciosum caput et accipientes bullam perduxe-
530   runt eam imperatori.

39. Christianus igitur existens sellarius, ut dictum est, qui erat super carcere uoluit corpus martyris seorsum ponere ut cognitum eo
esset. Sed non sinebant ei questionarii cum essent Hebraei. Cognoscentes uero filii de Iesdim finitionem sancti martyris—et enim
535   pueri eorum simul aderant sancto martyri eunti ut finiretur super

---

519 unus *om.* T εἷς unus p 410   523 Et *om.* T καὶ et p 410

122. *eos* is added in the Latin tradition.
123. *cum eo abierant:* συναπελθόντες

despicientes manus eius[124]—dederunt clam quaestionariis argenteos multos et adquieuerunt eos separatim ponere corpus eius. Et sequenti nocte, accipiens secum frater de mansionem martyris pueros de Iesdim filiis et quosdam monachos qui ibidem erant, uenit sus-
540 tulere corpus sancti martyris, et inuenit canes aedentes corpora interfectorum, corpus uero martyris iacentem de parte proximae eorum intactum. Praetiosa enim est[125] in conspectu Domini mors sanctorum eius[126] et custodit Dominus omnia ossa eorum, unum ex eis conterere non permittens.[127] Accipiens igitur corpus
545 martyris et inuoluens linteis praeciosis quos dederunt filii de Iesdim, deducens reposuit ipsud in monasterio sancti martyris Sergii, ferme miliario uno praedicti castelli.

40. Finit uero certamen suum in confessione Domini uictoriosissimus Christi martyr Anastasius in secunda et uicesima die ianuarii
550 mensis primae indictionis, anno XVII imperii Heraclii piissimi et XV Constantini a Deo conseruato filio eius.

41. In crastino igitur post defunctionem sancti martyris, duo quidam qui erant in custodiam confabulabantur ad inuicem. Et quidem unus dicebat ad sotium[128]: "Scis quia uenerunt[129] canes et
555 sederunt iuxta corpus de monacho illo? Et non adtrectabant eum, sed erant custodientes illud? Et mansi ferme duas horas aspiciens, et neque recedebant canes, neque contingebant corpus eius."[130]

555 erant] ὥσπερ *om.* T

124. *super–eius*: cf. Ex 17.12. But it is clear that the translator read ὑπερ-ιδόντες (from ὑπεροράω) rather than ὑπερείδοντες (from ὑπερείδω). Cf. pseudo-Philoxenus (*CGL*, 464): "Υπερορω perspicio despicio sprevo." The later translator (*BHL* 411a) made the same mistake.
125. *est* is added in the Latin tradition.
126. *Praetiosa–eius*: Ps 116.15.
127. *custodit–permittens*: Cf. Ps 34.20.
128. T appears to have misread the Greek ἑτέρῳ as ἑταίρῳ.
129. χθὲς is omitted in the Latin tradition.
130. *eius* is added in the Latin tradition.

At uero socius eius dixit: "Et ego uespere recedens de uincla in
domo mea uidi sicut stellam lucentem super pauimento. Et[31] abiens
560   ut uiderem quid hoc esset, ut autem propinquius factus sum,
quidem stella nusquam comparuit, corpus uero monachi iacentem
uidi super pauimento."

42. Et haec quidem qui custodiebant dicebant ad inuicem admiran-
tes[132] propriae linguae. Quidam uero qui erant in carcere captiuo-
565   rum, uiri Christiani scientes persicam linguam, auscultabantur eos.
Ex quibus duo dimissi cum et aliorum multorum uenerunt in sanctam ciuitatem post interfectionem Cosdrohe. Quibus praedixerat
sanctus martyr Anastasius dum esset cum eis in custodia de eius
finitione et de eorum liberatione et de regis ruinae ita dicens: "Ut
570   sciatis, fratres, quia per Dei gratia ego quidem crastinum finior.
Post paucos autem dies uos quidem relaxabimini, iniquus uero
atque malignissimus rex interficietur. Sed Domino prosperante aduenientes in sanctam ciuitatem, ite ad mansionem quae dicitur abbatis Anastasii et dicite abbati meo et fratribus haec." Viri autem
575   audientes a sancto ista et propriis oculis rerum exitum cernentes,
Deum quidem glorificauerunt qui glorificat glorificantes eum. Mandatum uero sancti martyris impleuerunt, proprio ore haec nobis
enarrati sunt.

43. Saepe memoratus uero frater mansionis, sepeliens corpus mar-
580   tyris et reponens decenter in praefato monasterio sancti Sergii,
mansit ibidem tractans qualiter citra periculo reuocare[33] ad transmissorem suum. Et post dies decem, prima die mensis februarii,

---

560 sum] et *add.* T   563 haec *supra lin. add.* T[1]   572-573 *ex* aduenientis
corr. T[1] *aut* T[2]   575 ista] ita T ταῦτα

131. *Et* is added in the Latin tradition.
132. One of the few occasions where the word order differs from that of
the Greek text.
133. *reuocare*: ἐπανέλθῃ. p and 410 agree in their reading *remearet* here,
a correct translation for ἐπανέλθῃ (Cf. pseudo-Cyril [*CGL*, 305] "Ἐπανερχο-
μαι remeo redeo"). It is possible, therefore, that the original translation read
remearet, corrupted in T's transmission to *reuocare*. ἐπανέρχομαι occurs only
here; *remeo* does not occur nor is *reuoco* found again in T.

adproximauit et piissimus atque Christo amabilis noster imperator
Eraclius cum sequenti eo exercitu. Quos cernens frater, gauisus est
585 gaudio magno, et locutus est latine.[134] Et ipsi interrogauerunt
eum quid ibidem faceret. Et ipse[135] insinuauit eis minutatim. At
illi[136] glorificauerunt Deum et dixerunt ei: "Surge ueni nobiscum
et salua animam tuam." Et erat cum eis in honore quos dies demo-
rati sunt in Persida et cum eis exiuit per Armeniorum regione.

590 **44.** Adpropinquans uero circiter[137] per anni circulum monasterium, intimauit praeposito uniuersa cum omni diligentia, perceptus
est ei et colobium martyris in quo finitus est, enarrans et hoc, quia
"erat quidam frater iuuenis in monasterio in quo depositum fuerat
corpus martyris uexatus atrociter ab spiritu immundo. Rogans
595 me[138] multum praepositus de illic, accipiens induit eum qui paciebatur colobium martyris, et confestim sanus factus est Domini
gratia in gloria Dei qui glorificatur in sanctis eius."

---

591 omni *non est in* g   592 et¹ *om.* T καὶ et p etiam 410   595 me] eum
T με me 410   597 *om. ult. cap.* T. *Cf.* Cui est honor et gloria et potestas
atque maiestas per immortalia saecula saeculorum Amen. p cui est honor gloria in saecula saeculorum. Amen. 410

134. ῥωμαϊστί, that is Greek, the language of the "Romans," as opposed
to Syriac which was most likely the language spoken by the companion of
Anastasius. But cf. pseudo-Cyril (*CGL*, 429) "Ρωμαΐζω latino." p omits
the word completely, but 410 and the second translation (*BHL* 411a) also
used *latine*.

135. *Et ipse* is not in g.

136. *At illi* is added in the Latin tradition.

137. *circiter* is found only in T, and has no correspondence in g. Perhaps
it is a later addition.

138. 410's *me* keeps the meaning of the Greek; p is defective here. A corrector or scribe did not understand that *quia* here introduced direct speech,
translating ὅτι.

2

THE SECOND TRANSLATION
BHL 411a

About This Edition

My edition, based on the existing manuscripts of this version known to me,[1] attempts to restore the original translation of the *Acta* of Anastasius as revised by Gregorius clericus; there is no way of course of getting at the text translated by "Nycolaus praesul" (l. 18). The stemma that resulted from the collation and examination of the manuscripts has been my principal guide in deciding which reading to adopt in cases of disagreement. In a few cases, however, the uncertain evidence of the stemma required a more direct editorial decision, which I based on my observation of the linguistic context.

Most hagiographic texts transmitted in legendaries contain a large number of variants. In addition to errors resulting from manual copying, compilers as well as scribes of hagiographic collections routinely introduced willful improvements, some major and some insignificant, into the texts, especially if these were used to supply readings for the Office. It is difficult therefore to construct accurate stemmata of hagiographic texts using the traditional methodology of common errors. These general observations apply to the text of *BHL* 411a and to all the other texts in this study.

1. There are in addition two other, late manuscripts that have been examined but not used in this edition since they are copies (one a partial copy) of surviving witnesses. One is Vallicelliana H 25, assembled by Antonio Bosio (1575-1629) from a number of Roman manuscripts. The *Passio S. Anastasii* was copied from S. Peter's Basilica's legendary, S. Pietro A 2 (Poncelet, *Catalogus codicum hagiographicorum latinorum bibliothecarum romanarum praeter quam vaticanae*, pp. 443-447). The other is codex IV 4 of Subiaco's Monastero di S. Scolastica, a thirteenth-century Office lectionary. This book contains capp. 1-8 of *BHL* 411a divided into four readings (numbered 9-12). The text was copied from Subiaco II 2, as is shown by the fact that IV 4 repeats all of II 2's errors, including, for example, such peculiar readings as (l. 61) illorum K; (l. 70) magi dum K; (ll. 102-103) contra *om.* K; (l. 155) mutavit K.

The surviving manuscript witnesses of this version of the *Passio S. Anastasii* appear to be divided into two groups, which correspond to the geographical diffusion of the text. One error common to all witnesses, the reading *gestiebat* for *gestabat* (l. 295), suggests that all the witnesses go back to a single common archetype. Another possible common error may be *aquis* for *equis* in cap. 23 (l. 365), which is further discussed in the notes to the text.

B, a legendary prepared after the middle of the eleventh century in Toul, perhaps for the abbey of St. Epure, is the unique witness of one main branch of the manuscript stemma. It represents the only evidence that this version traveled beyond the Alps, most likely joined to a copy of the Roman Miracle, as I discuss in Chapter IV. B contains the text freest from errors. In cap. 23 (l. 363), for example, only B reads *praesentialiter*, most likely the correct reading. In cap. 36 (l. 557), only B preserves what must be the correct reading, *praeces*, while all other witnesses present various corrupted readings or attempts at corrections. B, as the only surviving witness of its tradition, has carried great weight in the establishment of this edition, and it has always been followed when its evidence has been confirmed by the Greek text. But in cases where the testimony of the Greek is irrelevant or missing or doubtful, and in cases where B omits words or phrases, I have given equal weight to the evidence of the other manuscripts.[2]

The other side of the stemma breaks down into two branches. One branch is represented by the two legendaries from the monastery of S. Scolastica in Subiaco (J and K), and by the only witness to the text of *BHL* 411a written in Beneventan script, E. The shortened redaction *BHL* 411, surviving only in Beneventan exemplars copied in the area to the south of Rome, derives from this branch, which thus provides evidence of the movement of texts from the Roman region to the Beneventan area, and the pivotal role exercised by the Benedictine abbey of Subiaco in their transmission.[3] The other, the [c] subarchetype group, comprises the

---

2. B's reading *saevissime* instead of *semotissime* (l. 335) in a long passage added in the Latin version, for example, is clearly wrong.

3. For the Subiaco scriptorium and its relations to Beneventan books, see Supino Martini, *Roma e l'area grafica romanesca*, pp. 167-184.

legendaries copied in Rome and its surrounding region, where the *Passio* circulated together with the *Miraculum Romanum*. The earliest manuscripts of this group were copied in Romanesca, the typical version of Caroline minuscule as practiced in the Roman region.

Many of the Roman group of manuscripts present only partial witness for the text. C, the legendary from Assisi, deliberately omits the prologue, all of the text from the middle of cap. 19 to the end of cap. 39 (ll. 276-603), and from cap. 41 to the end. G has a lacuna from the middle of cap. 38 to the beginning of cap. 44 (ll. 597-676) caused by the excision of an entire folium from the codex. I, a twelfth- or thirteenth-century legendary compiled for a Roman church, presents a shortened text characterized by the elimination of some sections, including most rhetorical passages, the prologue, the entire central section from cap. 24 to the beginning of cap. 34 (ll. 379-526), and the last chapters (capp. 41-44) ending with the burial of the martyr.

Q, the legendary of S. Cecilia in Trastevere now in South Africa, is lacking a central quire, leaving the text of the *Passio Anastasii* incomplete. X (= Vat. lat. 6075) was copied from it in 1601.[4] The titular cardinal of S. Cecilia, Paulus Sfondratus, vouched for the copy's faithfulness to the original, even in preserving confusing passages ("... summa fide atque diligentia descripta esse testamur; immo, licet aliquibus in locis verba aliquando deesse viderimus ideoque sensum satis obscurum esse, tamen veritati studentes nihil immutari, nihil addi permisimus ..." [fol. 208v]). And in fact, a comparison of X with Q's fragment of the *Passio S. Anastasii* confirms the cardinal's statement. The scribe of X copied the text faithfully as he found it in Q, incorporating into his copy all the corrections made directly on Q, and even substituting in his text the few words written in the margin of Q by a still later hand glossing the text.[5] Errors and omissions common to QX also support the relationship of the two codices.[6]

Despite the claim of faithfulness, it is clear that the scribe of X resorted to another codex to fill the substantial lacuna that he found in Q's text of the *Passio S. Anastasii*. That codex is either

4. Vat. lat. 6076, for the second half of the year, was also copied from Q.
5. E.g. (l. 117) vestigia; (l. 142) intervallo; (l. 151) grece.
6. E.g. (l. 94) visitandae] ut si tandem QX.

T, the legendary connected with the church of SS. Giovanni e Paolo, or a codex copied from it.[7] Beginning in the middle of cap. 19 (l. 267: *Ad haec Marzabanas* ...), the text in X repeats all of T's errors, omissions, and all corrections introduced into T's text described below;[8] here I will point out just a few examples from the latter part of cap. 19, where both the lacuna in Q and the correspondences between T and X begin, up through cap. 21:

> (ll. 270-271) Non permittat mihi deus meum Christum negare] Non permittat dominus meus me (*add. supra lin. alt. manus*) Christum negare T Non permittat dominus meus me Christum negare X
>
> (l. 278) timuerim] timuero *ex* timuerim *corr.* T timuero X
>
> (l. 280) igitur] *om.* TX
>
> (l. 284) agebantur] agebatur TX
>
> (l. 285) quidem] *eras. (non legi potest*) T *om.* X
>
> (l. 285) quidem] quidam TX
>
> (ll. 286-287) tantum nobis] nobis tantum TX
>
> (l. 313) hunc habitum] hoc habitu *corr.* T hoc habitu X
>
> (l. 335) semotissime] remotissime TX
>
> (l. 342) pectoris] peccatoris TX

A few readings make the direct dependence of X from T less than absolutely certain:

> (l. 331) fastidiam] fastidiant T (fastidiam X)
>
> (l. 379) quo] quo *ex* quod *corr.* T (quod X)
>
> (l. 491) quae] qui T (quae X)
>
> (l. 605) ut esset] ut esse T (ut esset X)

These cases, however, seem insignificant, and could be explained by supposing that X's scribe realized the error in T and corrected it (*fastidiam, quae, ut esset*), or failed to note T's correction (the expunction point under the 'd' in *quod*). In either case, it is clear

---

7. The possibility that T was corrected from the tradition from which X was copied (i.e. an undamaged Q) can be eliminated since this would not explain the cases where the original T text and X agree in common error after the lacuna in Q, while they do not share common errors in the earlier part of the text.

8. The corrections in T made over the line were executed by a slightly later hand; corrections written over the scraped text are more difficult to attribute. See "Descriptive List," pp. 536. Readings of X in the *apparatus criticus* are provided only to illustrate the relationship between T and X.

that Q was already defective when X was copied from it.[9] In my stemma codicum, I designate as X(a) the first part copied from Q, and by X(b) the part copied from T.

Despite the fragmentary evidence, the Roman group of manuscripts—PHTCQ(X)G—can be traced to a common subarchetype because of the lacuna of cap. 41 ([l. 635] *sed–invigilantes*) shared by PHTX. Since the other two manuscripts of this group lack this section and thus can provide no evidence on this lacuna, their association can be deduced by their connection to subgroups, such as (l. 173) quid] quod PHTCQ; (l. 181) fidissimo] fidelissimo PTGQ.

PHTC form a clearly discernible subgroup characterized by their common "error" in alone preserving the phrase in cap. 9 (l. 116) *invicta certamina triumphos vel victorias martyrum*. This must have been a marginal note, a gloss written by a reader or editor to explain the word *indalmata*, a transliteration, in effect, of the Greek word ἰνδάλματα meaning "images," which at some point was integrated into the text. The close relationship of these manuscripts is also supported by a number of common errors peculiar to them, such as, for example, *fastigii* instead of *fatigii* (l. 204); *athleta sanctas* (PH), *sanctis* (T) for *adletacis* (l. 386); *quibus* (PHT) for *qui ibi* (l. 454), or *et cogitans* (PHT) for *excogitans* (l. 663).[10]

The abbreviated text preserved in I may also belong to this branch, for there is, despite its truncated nature, some evidence to suggest that it forms a subgroup with PHTC.[11] In my stemma, I attach I above the branch with a broken line to indicate that this conclusion is based on sketchy evidence.[12] While this witness has minimal importance in the establishment of the text of *BHL* 411a,

---

9. X of course contains some mistakes of its own (e.g. the omission of *nimium* [l. 383] or *mali suadere* for *malesuadis* [l. 545]).

10. But one must not forget that all too frequently only partial evidence is available. The omission in cap. 41 ([l. 635] *sed–invigilantes*) is shared by PTX at a point in the text where, unfortunately, G's long lacuna occurs, and Q is no longer available. Similarly, in cap. 21 (l. 340), PTG share the common error *etiam* (for *vitia*) at a point where Q is no longer available.

11. (l. 193) Atqui] Utqui PTC atque I; (l. 591) fato] facto JK PHTXI.

12. For example, the passage in which PHTC preserve the marginal gloss on *indalmata* has been excised as was also the most significant passage omitted by PHT, *sed–invigilantes* (l. 635).

I have included it in the apparatus to provide another illustration of the editorial reworkings of hagiographic texts.

Further subdivisions of this group are not clear because of the carelessness of H's scribe, and the truncated evidence provided by C. However, the most likely grouping is for P and H to form a branch,[13] and T and C another branch.[14]

The two legendaries from Subiaco—J (S. Scolastica X 10) written in Romanesca in the late eleventh century, and K (S. Scolastica II 2) copied in the second half of the twelfth century in common minuscule—and E, the twelfth-century legendary from Troia in Apulia written in Beneventan script, form a separate branch altogether. This is suggested first of all by the separation of the last section of the text (capp. 41-44), which is entitled in all three manuscripts "Item miraculum eiusdem." None of these manuscripts contains the Roman Miracle.[15] Furthermore, a number of textual errors clearly group these manuscripts together.[16]

The group KE is further highlighted by a very large number of common errors indicated in the apparatus criticus. Among these, most prominent are numerous omissions,[17] as well as many other errors that reflect their common origin.[18] It is clear, however, that E cannot have been copied directly from K.[19] These manuscripts show the increasing corruption of the text, as it moves

13. This is suggested particularly by (l. 317) hostilibus] hostibus P hostilis H; (l. 345) unieidemque] unieidem PH; (l. 403) ergastuli] ergastulo PH; (ll. 406-407) circumamictos] circum amictis PH.

14. This is suggested by (l. 104) retrogrado] retrogra TC; (l. 198) devotissime om. E TC; (l. 230) adesset] esset T esse C.

15. See Chapter IV, pp. 144-150, for the diffusion of the conjoined *Passio et Miraculum*.

16. E.g. (l. 66) isse] ipse JKE; (ll. 191-192) est hylaratus] exhilaratus JE irradiatus K; (l. 286) regionis] religionis JKEI.

17. E.g. (ll. 211-212) Ad–praedicebat; (ll. 244-246) Sanctus–accepit; (ll. 402-403) indutos–lumine.

18. E.g. (Prologus l. 24) insulse compositum] insule composita K infule composita E; (l. 533) persico more devictum] percommovere devictum K iam invictum E; (l. 670) unanimiter glorificantes] una uoce glorificantes K unaglorificantes E.

19. E repeats almost all of K's mistakes, but in a few cases preserves the correct reading: e.g. (l. 190) edicere] ei diceret K; (ll. 440-441) immote] in monte K.

away from Rome, where it originated, to Subiaco and then even further to the Beneventan script area in the south.[20] It is from this branch before E itself breaks off from it that the abbreviated redaction *BHL* 411, copied mostly in Beneventan script, depends.[21]

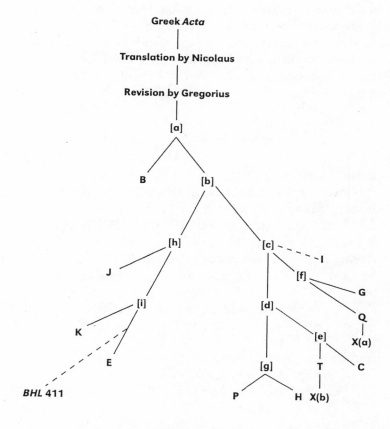

20. There are some scribal slips that suggest that K and E were copied from an archetype written in Romanesca, particularly their mistaking a "d" for a "t" (e.g. [l. 434] duos] tuos KE), which may be the result of the practice in Romanesca of flattening the extender.

21. There are numerous examples where *BHL* 411 and JK agree in preserving the correct reading against E (e.g. [ll. 269-270] cavallos et miliarisia cum magno beneficio] equos et militiam E; cf. caballos et pecuniam cum magno beneficio [*BHL* 411, *Bibliotheca Casinensis* III. Florilegium, p. 105]; [l. 281] sine interstitio] sine intermissione E; cf. sine interstitio (*BHL* 411, p. 105).

In my *apparatus criticus*, I give all variant readings, except those that would be considered only spelling variations. I have standardized the spelling, except for proper nouns. X's variant readings are given from cap. 19 on only to show that X here was copied from T, not from Q, and cannot therefore be used to reconstruct the text of this last witness, which is missing from here on. I indicate also all the visible corrections and additions on T made by a later hand as described above. Unless I specifically note it, the correction has been from the text I consider the correct text.

My chapter divisions match those of Flusin's text, followed in my edition of *BHL* 410b.

CONSPECTUS SIGLORUM

B	Bern, Burgerbibliothek 24
C	Biblioteca apostolica vaticana, Vaticanus latinus 13012
E	Naples, Biblioteca nazionale VIII B 3
G	Biblioteca apostolica vaticana, Chigianus P VIII 15
H	Rome, Archivio di stato, S. Salvatore 996
I	Rome, Biblioteca vallicelliana, Tomus X
J	Subiaco, Biblioteca del monastero di S. Scolastica X 10
K	Subiaco, Biblioteca del monastero di S. Scolastica II 2
P	Biblioteca apostolica vaticana, Archivio di S. Pietro A 2 (alias A)
Q	Cape Town, The South African Public Library, Grey Collection, Ms 48 b 4
T	Biblioteca apostolica vaticana, Vaticanus latinus 1195
X	Biblioteca apostolica vaticana, Vaticanus latinus 6075
411	*BHL* 411, *Bibliotheca casinensis* III. Florilegium, pp. 102-109
g	*BHG* 84, Flusin ed.

INCIPIT PROLOGUS IN PASSIONEM
BEATI ANASTASII MARTYRIS.

Athanasio gratia Dei venerabilissimo abbati Gregorius clerorum in-
fimus perpetuam in Christo salutem.

5   Vestrae benignitatis excellentia nos ammodum rogavit, ut beati
Anastasii martyrium quod quidam grammaticae artis expertissimus
de graeco in latinum confuse transtulerat, urbanius regulari digestu
componerem. Quod onusculum bina excusatione obtrectare volueram, ne scilicet aut a maioribus intemptato nostri ingenioli scintilla
10   succumberet, neve oblatrantium suffrementes[1] denticulos[2] in me
exacueret. Sed illud quidem divini suffragii et huius celebratissimi
martyris atque vestri interventus gratia compescui; hoc vero, prae-
monendo ut quicumque irruerint, aut meum emendent aut suum
componant, similiter suppressi. Denique perpauci sunt parati ad

---

3 abbati] Christi famulo E   clericorum EG   5 rogitavit K rogitant Q
7 transtulerant E   regulari digestu] digestum E   8 Quod–bina] quod onus
columbina E   abiectare K ablectare (abiectare?) E   9 a] ei JKEPTGQ
corr. ad a Q   11 exacuerent JET   divinis suffragiis E   celeberrimi E
12 interveniente E   13 suum] emendent aut suum *add. E*   14 similiter]
denique T

---

1. The lack of parallellism is troubling in this phrase (*ne ... aut ... neve*). Furthermore, it is not clear whether the subject of *exacueret* is *scintilla* or *onusculum*.
The use of the rare *suffremo* ("to growl") should be noted, although one wonders
if Gregory could possibly have written the even rarer *suffrendentes* ("gnashing").
2. The image of the critics' bark and teeth is ancient, and was commonly
used among translators. Most immediately, Gregorius's inspiration for these lines
was Jerome both in his letter to Pammachius ("Nam quidem pseudomonachus
... dedit adversariis latrandi contra me occasionem, ut inter imperitos concionen-
tur ..." *Ep.* 57, 2, 1 [ed. Bartelink, pp. 11-12]) and especially in his preface to the
Pentateuch, where Jerome is discussing the dangers of accepting Desiderius's plea
to translate the Pentateuch from the Hebrew ("Periculosum opus certe, obtrectatorum latratibus patens ..." *Biblia sacra*, ed. Weber, I, 3). Johannes Scotus refers
directly to Jerome when he uses the image of the teeth in one of his poems:
"Quod si quorundam mordetur dente feroci, / Hoc leue: namque meo contigit
Hieronimo" *Carmina* 20.15-16 (ed. Herren, p. 108). (For full discussion, see
pp. 104-115).

15 scribendum, sed parvo pauciores inparati ad iudicandum. Castrensi
etenim vulgus circumseptum munimine, proeliantium eventus visit
securo pectore.

Nycolaum igitur praelustrem archipresbyterum, achivos quidem
luculente, latinos vero ex parte³ apices eruditum, obnixe postula-
20 vimus, quatenus praedictum martyrium de graeco in latinum observata serie⁴ transferret ut et nos deinceps retextu promptiore illud
prosequeremur. Quo magis quippe rivus suo fonti sit propior, eo
magis gustantibus solet esse saporior. Sed quia idem apud Graecos
etiam ipsos in plerisque locis insulse compositum adesse prospexi-
25 mus, multa quidem superflua, salvo manente sensu, penitus subtraximus; et e contra decorandae constructionis causa nonnulla adiecimus. Graecam vero seriem licet minus quam decuit quantumcum-
que mutavimus. Communis namque doctorum sententia affirmat,
verbum de verbo exprimere, pessimum genus interpretandi esse;
30 ridiculose etenim currens et lectorem praepedit, et auditores fastidit. Quanto magis igitur etiam sine eo eloquium honestare non potui, tanto magis cum eodem omnino deturpare obhorrui. Ceterum
tam vos quam quoslibet hoc opusculum inspecturos suppliciter exposco, ut gloriosissimum Dei martyrem Anastasium devote inter-
35 vocent;⁵ quatenus id sibi dicatum devote accipiat, et ad eum per
quem hoc promeruit, et a quo coronatus est pro nobis intercedat,
Dominum nostrum Ihesum Christum, cui cum Patre et Spiritu
sancto semper inest gloria in saecula saeculorum. Amen.

15 inparati] imperiti KE   16 visit] *eras.* + sit J vixit K lusit E sui fit T
18 igitur *om.* E   18-19 achivo siquidem ... latino ... apice KE   21 retex-
tum KET   promptiore illud *om.* KE promptiores T   22 prosequeremur]
sequeremur E prosequerer G   Quo] Quanto G   24 etiam ipsos *om.* PT
insule composita K infule *(?)* composita E   25-26 multa–subtraximus *om.*
KE   26 decorandae] huius *add.* KE   27 Graeca ... serie B Graegam G
30 ridiculo P   31 eo *om.* JT   33 tam] tamen G   34 quolibet P   34-35
invocent PT   35 dictum dignanter KE   36 a *om.* Q   intercedat] ad *add.* T

3. An echo of Jerome's prologue to Job ("hebraeum sermonem ex parte
didicimus" [*Biblia sacra*, ed. Weber, I, 732])?

4. Word order is most likely meant here.

5. Although *intervoco* is not attested in dictionaries nor in *CLCLT*, it is
the *lectio difficilior* and may be another manifestation of Gregorius's pen-
chant for rare and newly coined words.

6.⁶ Beatus itaque Anastasius de quadam regione Persidis quae Razech
40   nuncupatur extitit oriundus, de villa videlicet Rasnuni; proprium
quoque nomen eius Magundag primum fuit. Filius vero cuiusdam
magi nomine Bau, qui et eum a crepundiis magicam disciplinam
instituit, fuisse dinoscitur. Regnante igitur Chosroe in imperiali
Persarum civitate, hunc effectum iam iuvenem tyronicae professio-
45   ni contigit adfuisse. Verum propter Dei iudicium nostris exigentibus commissis maturatum, sancta Dei civitas ab hostibus est capta;
venerabilia quoque sanctorum loca quae ibidem sunt intersita miserabiliter sunt igne concremata. Praetiosissimum etiam vivificae crucis lignum devectum est in Persidem. O victoriosissimae crucis glo-
50   riosam captivitatem!⁷ Quae ideo capta est ut captores caperet, et
eos capiendo a captivitate liberaret. O praedam de praedonibus tropaea elevantem, et praedones in praedam salubriter vertentem. Infinita namque gratia inexaustaeque virtutis potentia ibidem radiabat.

7. Omnibus⁸ etenim infidelibus metum cum stupore cumulabat,
55   gaudium vero et laetitiam fidelium cordibus aggregabat. Denique

39 *Hic incipiunt* C (Passio S. Anastasii) I (Passio S. Anastasii martyris edita
a Gregorio episcopo)   Ralech E Rezech P   40 extitit oriundus *transpos.*
post Rasnuni KE   Rasnoni PC   proprium *om.* G   41 primum *om.* TI
vero *om.* BJI *cf.* δὲ, vero 411   42 et *om.* B per T (*alia manu?*)   43 institutum T*corr.*   fuisse *om.* GQI   dinoscitur *om.* QI   44 civitatem I   44-
45 professionis JKE PHTCI   45 propter *om.* B   46 mature I   47 quae-
sunt *om.* KE   48 cremata EQ   49 devectum] defertum KE   Persidam T
51 a] de KE   praedam *om.* G   51-52 trophaema BE   51-52 tropaea elevan-
tem] evacuantem T   53 inexhaustaeque] et exaustae KE

6. From this point the chapter numbers correspond to Flusin's Greek text,
also followed in my edition of 410b. Gregorius's version of the *Passio* lacks the
Greek preface (=Flusin, 1-5)
7. Gregorius expands on the rhetorical exclamation already present in the
Greek. At the beginning of the next chapter there is also a slight lengthening
of the rhetorical passage (ll. 56-58 *nec est dictu ... ante ligavit*).
8. Here we find an example of Gregorius's building upon the literary de-
vices already present in the Greek: the contrast between *infidelibus/fidelium
cordibus* is already in his model; the use of the verbs *cumulabat ... aggregabat*
is his own.

huius ligni non est rudis victoria, nec est dictu mirabile quod Persas devicerit, cuius videlicet fructus eorundem principem diabolum paulo ante ligavit. Huius itaque fama eandem provinciam passim pervolante, ante dictus tyro Magundag quid huiusmodi rumor per-
60 streperet, sollicite disquirebat. Audito itaque quod christianorum Deus illorsum advenisset, ille continuo non secus ac gratissima tellus exhausta pluvia confovendis seminibus christianae institutioni coaptatur, et divinae excellentiae nomen auditu percipiens, quemammodum thesaurum in secreto sui pectoris latibulo recondebat.
65 Sed cum ipse cunctabundus apud se convolveret quomodo illocalis Deus et invisibilis illuc isse crederetur, indagantius quibusdam interrogatis, salvificae crucis lignum in quo Dei filius Ihesus Christus pependerat, illuc venisse comperit; et exinde huiusmodi causa stupidatus, rimari de christianismo penitus non cessabat; et quo magis
70 auditu veritatem perceptabat, eo magis de eius corde magicum proludium discedebat. Sicut enim lux tenebras, sol umbras, ignis fumum effugat, ita dogma veritatis sinuosum errorem in eius pectore annihilabat. O⁹ future Dei martyr, quod fieri potuisse attonitus ambigis, in te ipso experturus certum esse comprobabis. Qui enim
75 incircumscriptus Persidem visitavit, idem incircumclusus cor tuum illuminabit. Divinae namque excellentiae atque essentiae nihil aliud

---

57 videlicet] scilicet KE   58 ligaverat G   59 tyro *om.* B   quod J qui KE
60 itaque *om.* BJ   61 illorsum] illuc B illorum K *om.* E   ille *ras.* T   hec
T ac T*corr.*   62 seminibus] hominibus E   christiana institutione T   64 in
secreto] secretum in E   66 isse] ipse JKE   indagantium KE indegantius
I   67 quod B   68 pependit E   et *om.* HGQ   70 de-corde *om.* G
magicum] magi dum K dudum E   73 anelabat J   potuisset KE   74 in-
ipso] ante ipse P a te ipso T   75 Persides T   76 illuminavit KEPTCG *cf.*
comprobabis (l. 74) excellentiae atque *om.* KE

9. This passage, to the end of the chapter, is one of Gregorius's additions. The first part of this long theological discussion is clearly inspired by Gregory the Great's *Moralia in Iob*; cf. especially, "Incircumscriptus namque spiritus omnia intra semetipsum habet, quae tamen et implendo circumdat, et circumdando implet et sustinendo transcendit et transcendendo sustinet" (XVI, xxxi, 38 [ed. Adriaen, p. 821]). The discussion of the Trinity goes back to Augustine's *De trinitate* (especially IV, xxi [ed. Mountain, pp. 202-205]).

quam quod simpliciter et naturaliter inest accidere potest; nihil ei qualitatis variat diversitas; nihil auget vel minuit quantitatis varietas. In trium distinctione personarum non scinditur, ubique in se
80 tota nullo loco concluditur. Dum qui sit semper quod est, tempore non movetur, minime fatigatur omnia gubernando, nec etiam ditatur omnia possidendo. Ineffabilis namque deitatis ut diximus essentia, quae non est aliud quam ipsa deitas, nihil sibi accidentialiter asciscit, sed quaecumque ei insita catholici inesse profitentur, haec
85 adesse ingenita substantialiter creduntur. Et licet quidem multa pro variis virtutum vocabulis edicantur, non tamen esse multa, sed unum atque idem ut et ipsa est deitas singulariter comprobantur. Sicut enim omnipotentia vel misericordia vel tale aliquid virtutum in eadem supersubstantiali essentia non esse diversum vel aliud quam
90 ipsa est astruuntur, ita etiam et eadem omnipotentia vel misericordia et cetera virtutum similia, unum atque idem esse fideliter sentiuntur. Aeterna namque atque una deitas, non est hoc atque hoc multipliciter, sed est hoc unum esse simpliciter. Qui igitur nulli loco quantum ad se est absens, visitandae Persidi coepit adesse
95 praesens, Deus scilicet omnipotens qui totum mundum implet circumdando, et circumdat implendo, praesidendo sustinet, sustinendo praesidet. Supra quem nihil, extra quem nihil, infra quem nihil; sub quo omnia et cum quo omnia. Cui illud quod in est gloria est aeterna. Amen.

100 **8.** Sed ut quod instat prosequamur. Erat quidem illi germanus commilito, Saim scilicet persicae militiae principi subiugatus. His igitur cuneatim Calcedoniam abeuntibus, Phylippicus deicola hos e con-

---

77 quam *om.* HI   accidere potest *om.* E   78 qualitates G   quantitatis *corr. ad* unitatis Q   78-79 varietatis I   79-80 in se tota] insecuta I   81 omnia *om.* G   81-82 dicatur B   82 omnia *om.* B   84 ascit K scit E esse BJ   85 creduntur] geruntur E   86 dicantur P edificantur G   88 aliquid] quid KE   89 superstantialem G   esse] est G   90 ipse E   90-92 ita–sentiuntur *om.* C   91-92 sentiunt B   92 atque[1] *om.* PT   atque hoc *om.* B   93 simpliciter] multipliciter B   Qui] ille *add.* KE   94 visitandae] ut si tandem Q   96 residendo Q   97 extra quem nihil *om.* B   100 quidam KET *cf.* ῎Εχων δὲ   102 cuncatim BKEIQ cuncantim (?) P   Calcedonam KEH   deicolam T deicola T$^{corr.}$ 102-103 contra *om.* K   e contra *om.* E

tra circumvallans introgressus est Persidem. Quo audito dux Saim
retrogrado tramite iterum repedavit. Interea quidem Magundag, qui
105 et paulo post Anastasius, cum Persarum acie in orientales plagas
contigit emeasse, et exinde tyrocinio et germano postpositis, ingressus Gerapolim apud quendam christicolam argentificem fabrum
eundemque et persam, ibidem mansitavit. Eidem quoque arti et
etiam operi cum eo desudabat.

110 **9.** Exuberante igitur in eius pectore futurae illuminationis ardore,
praefatum artificem ut se almi baptismatis latice dignaretur ablui
subnixis rogaminibus exposcebat. Quod licet ille Persarum timore
intricatus abnueret, iste tamen impigro comitatu ecclesias cum illo
oraturus adibat. Triumphales quoque martyrum picturas suspiciens
115 quid ipsae praetenderent ipsum interrogabat. O devotissime Dei fa-
mule; eia age, diligenter gloriosorum suspice martyrum indalmata,
quorum orbitam sequendo mox et tua facies esse perspicienda; et
quo eos interim emersisse gloriaris, illo te ipsum paulo post pervenisse gaudebis. Addiscens itaque sanctorum miracula et inestimabi-
120 lia a barbarie tyrannorum ingesta cruciamina, illorum sufferentiam
hominem supergressam stupidus mirabatur. Cum igitur ibidem
pauxillum temporis deguisset, eundi Hierusolimam ut ibi baptizare-
tur, quod postea fine tenus Deo favente perduxit, immenso desiderio medullitus exarsit.

125 **10.** Cum igitur illo usque percitato itinere devenisset, apud quemdam christianum similiter argentarium fabrum illic est hospitatus.

---

103 Persidam B   Aim P   104 retrograde JI retrogradu H retrogra TC
105 plagas *om.* E   106 remeasse KE   germanio B   107 Hierapolim
ETG   108 Eidem] ei KE   quoque] et *add.* PHTC   109 etiam] re iam
B artis (s *add. supra lin.*) *add.* T   cum eo *om.* B   desudavit T   111 dignaretur ablui] haberetur digni G   112 subnixe PHTC   113 illo] eo KE
114 ornaturus aiebat G   114-115 Triumphales–interrogabat *om.* G   115
ipsae] ipsum JI   115-121 O devotissime–mirabatur *om.* I   115 Dei *om.* KE
116 diligenter *om.* T   gloriosorum *om.* B gloriosum TC   indalmata] invicta certamina triumphos vel victorias martyrum *add.* PHTC   117 orbita
PHT vestigia *in marg. add.* Q   est B   118 interum BE   118-119 gloriaris–pervenisse *om.* H   118 paulo post *om.* G   120 ingesta] gesta E   125
pervenisset E

Cui quicquid affectaret animi, quod scilicet christianus desideraret fieri et salutari lavacro vellet regenerari, intrepido affatu fidissime propalavit. Ab ipso quoque est adductus ad Heliam venerabilissimum
130 Sanctae Resurrectionis presbyterum. Qui et eum non aliter quam a Deo sibi destinatum filium suscepit, et quaeque erga eum aderant Modesto sanctissimo presbytero pontificalis sedis custodia tunc temporis sublimato prorsus notificavit. Hic igitur cum altero eiusdem provinciae et religionis viro iussit eum baptizari, qui et ipse
135 pro Christo in Edessa civitate ad martyrii palmam pertingere meruit.

11. Beatus vero Anastasius qui et pridem Magundag cum apud Heliam probabilem presbyterum octo dies ut dici solet suae illuminationis moraretur, et ab eo quid deinceps agere disponeret crebro inquireretur, continuis precibus ut se monachum faceret illum depre-
140 cabatur. Octavo igitur die advoluto, sanctus Helias sacerdos perduxit eum ad Sancti Anastasii monasterium a sancta quidem civitate quattuor ferme stadiorum intercapedine diremptum. Huius quoque monasterii abbatem Iustinum videlicet in omnibus praeclarum, et Dei omnipotentis gratia refertum, ut eum fraterno aggregaret colle-
145 gio admodum rogitavit. Ille igitur presbyteri Heliae rogatibus adquiescens, suae congregationi illum attitulavit, octava videlicet indictione, piissimo regnante Heraclio, anno quidem eiusdem imperii decimo. Unum quoque de suis discipulis divinae scilicet scripturae apicibus elimatum eidem instruendo assignavit. Qui eum tam grae-

127 animo E   scilicet] acceptatus *add.* G   128 salutari] salutando G generari H   affatu] affectu KEP   fidissime] fidissimo *et transpos. ante* affatu G   129 est *om.* P   adductus] perductus KE   131 destinatum sibi *transpos.* E   quaeque] quae (*corr. ex* neque K) KE   eum] *non legi potest* T ei T*corr.*   133 sublimata KE   136 apud] praephatum *add.* KE *cf.* apud praefatum Heliam 411   137 solent E   138 ageret G   141 eum *om.* P   142 neriscapedine T*corr.*   intervallo *add. in marg.* Q   143 videlicet] scilicet KE *cf.* scilicet 411   144 omnipotenti P   145 cogitavit P   146 rogantibus JPHCT rogatibus T*corr.*   146-147 octava–indictione] octava die licet G 147 Heraclio] Cladio G   148 ipsius E   discipuli P   149 Qui] cum *add.* B

150 ca helementa quam etiam psalterium luculente instruxit. Eius[10]
quoque ut graecae est consuetudinis attondens capillitium nec non
et habitum induens monachicum, non secus ac proprium filium
sustentabat. O cuncti creatoris inexasperabilem clementiam! et
quaecumque decreverit agendi potentissimam quae versiformem
155 magum vertit in monachum; et de mortuo Magundag, suscitavit
Anastasium. Denique beatus Anastasius suam resurrectionem praetendit in nomine, quam e magicis erectus volutabris meruit Christi
munere. Anastasius namque in latino resurrectionem sonat.

12. Ille igitur suppetente Dei gratia diversis ministeriis tam culinae
160 videlicet quam horti vel etiam quorumcunque iniunctis, in monasterio assidue fungebatur. Tantae quippe efficacitatis aderat, ut et
obsequio fratrum et laboribus manuum agilis insisteret, et in divini
ministerii regula ceteros anteiret. Sacras vero scripturas legentibus
sic animum inquisite attendebat ut quibuscumque intellectu pertin-
165 gere nequiret, ea suum magistrum vel anteriores fratres statim in-
terrogaret. Quando autem victorialia martyrum agonismata ut spe-
cialius assueverat in propria cella apud se relegebat oborsis affatim

---

150-151 quam–graecae est *om.* T   151 ut graecae] gregis E ut grave HI graecae *om. et* grece *add. in marg.* Q   adtollens JE   152 habitu] abbitu P
monachum *(?)* P *non legi potest* T monachicum T^*corr.*   ac] si *add.* E filium
om. T   153 inasperabilem KET   et *eras.* T   154 quae qui KE quem P
155 magum vertit] mutavit E   vertit] mutavit K   157 e] a T^*corr.* et C
ereptus B   voluntabris T volutabris T^*corr.* volutatabris C   159 culinae]
coquinae JE   161 Tanto P   ut *om.* KE   162-163 divinis ministeriis T
divini mysterii I   163 regulam T regula T^*corr.*   164 *om.* E animo BT^*corr.*
inquisite] *emendavi* in dies B inquies (*corr. ex* quies Q) J(?)PIGQ inquiens
KET inquirens H *cf.* ἐτίθει τὸν νοῦν ... ἀκριβῶς   cuiuscumque intellectum
T   165 ea] eas E eam *sed* m *eras.* T   167 cella] *om.* Q cellula KE *cf.* cellula
411   apud *om.* E   redigebat E   oborsis] aborsis J aborsis E

---

10. Another addition in the Latin version. Both the reference to the
Greek tonsure and the etymology of the Greek name should be noted as examples of Gregorius's "learned" additions. By the Greek tonsure, Gregorius
must be referring to the complete shaving of the head, also known as tonsure
"in the manner of St. Paul." Latin tonsure (or "in the manner of St. Peter")
meant that the head was shaved in the form of a crown.

lacrimis faciem humectabat, et Dominum Ihesum Christum ut se illorum albo quandoque adiungeret, in antro sui pectoris sine inter-
170 stitio suppliciter exposcebat. Sed dum ut praediximus eorum indalmata tueretur, et inflexibilem in tormentis patientiam miraretur, nihilque aliud paene legendo convolveret, nisi quod eius animum ad huiusmodi gloriam inflammaret, quid intrinsecus conciperet, forinsecus reseravit. In eodem autem monasterio talia prosequendo
175 septennium devolvit.

13. Verum antiquissimus draco, illum quidem in Christi dilectione tantum atque taliter se fundasse gravipendens, inconventaneos ei cogitatus et magicorum quos a profano patre didicerat sermonum memoriam callide suggerebat. Ille autem huius modi temptamentis
180 valde affligebatur, et cognita serpentis astutia, omnipotentem Deum quatinus se prosperaret instanter precabatur. Fidissimo quoque abbati omnia sui pectoris latibula retegebat, et ut pro sui ereptione ad Deum preces funderet lacrimans rogitabat. Venerabilis vero abbas sacris cum monitis eum convalidans et aggregatis fratribus
185 Domini pro illo auxilium expostulans, huiuscemodi pugnam prorsus annihilavit.

14. Perpaucis deinde diebus provolutis, Anastasius Dei famulus tali visione meruit consolari. Videbatur quidem ei in cuiusdam montis cacumine seipsum consistere et quendam sibi aureum gemmatum-
190 que cratera porrigentem quatenus accipiens biberet edicere. Quem itaque ut sibi visum est exhausisse tanta alacritate cordis est hylaratus, velut ut si omne desiderium fuisset consecutus. O praedulce et plenissimum mysterii somnium![11] Atqui Dei omnipotentis famu-

---

170 poscebat KE   dum *om.* KE   171 intueretur B uteretur C   173 quid] quod PHTCQ   176 dilectionem KE   177 ei] se Q   181 quatinus] qua P   Fidelissimo PTGQ   182 ereptionem PI exceptione T   183 lacrimas P lacrimis Q   cogitabat KE   184 monitibus KEI   185 auxilium pro illo *transpos.* E *cf.* 411   187 denique KE   188 Videtur KE   quidam E   189 acumine G   sibi] ei B *om.* KE *cf.* 411   190 edicere] ei diceret K et diceret HCI ei liceret Q   191 sibi ut *transpos.* T   est[1] *om.* E   exaudisse KT exaudisset E   191-192 est hylaratus] exhilaratus JE irradiatus K   192 ut *om.* BKE   praedulce] plene dulce KE   193 mysterium omnis (?) E   Atqui] Utqui PTC atque I   Dei *om.* E

11. A brief addition to the Latin version.

lus in excelso montis fastigio se assistere vidit, qui postea contem-
195 plativae vitae tutissimum atque secretissimum cacumen ascendit!
Ubi imperterritus Dei agonitheta instantis vitae curriculum cum
tyrannicis tormentis despiciens, calicem passionis pro Ihesu Christi
nomine devotissime exhausit. Statim itaque consurgens dominica
scilicet die nocturnum psallentium regulariter impleturus, orato-
200 rium cum ceteris fratribus est ingressus; et summovens abbatem
in penitiorem secretarii locum, provolutis genibus lacrimans exposcebat, ut pro se in proximo iam iamque morituro Dominum exoraret. Talibus quoque dictis eum prosequebatur: "Satis mi pater re-
colo quantum in me fatigii miserrimo perpessus fueris, et quantis
205 tribulationibus te quoque fastidierim, et quod te quoque praeduce
de tenebris ad lucem me Christus transtulerit. Sed ut bene incoepta
melius perficias, te nimium deprecor ut pro me Deum poscas." Ad
haec abbas: "Quid est, frater, quod te sic inquietat? vel unde istis
diebus te esse moriturum incunctanter denuntias?" Ille vero reci-
210 tans visionem se fore moriturum sive communi morte sive quomodo libet eum certificabat. Ad martyrium enim se esse emersurum
ne forte increparetur minime praedicebat.

15. Multimodis igitur solaciis et monitibus abbatis roboratus, se-
quentiam psalmodiae cum fratribus implevit. Et post haec sacro-
215 sancti corporis et sanguinis Domini libamina percepit; ac deinde
cum fratribus cibo potuque refectus, pauxillulo sopori suos artus
applicuit. Cum igitur evigilasset, internum sui pectoris ardorem
non sustinens, clanculum de eodem monasterio abscessit. Et nihil
secum devehens excepto indumento, Diospolim abiit. Et exinde in

194 excelsi KE   fastigio se] fastidiose EI   195 secretissimum *om.* H sacratissimum TQ   198 devotissime *om.* ETC   consurgens] exurgens KE
199 regulariter *om.* B   201 penitiorem *om.* E   lacrimis E   202 iam *om.*
JE   iam–morituro *om.* B   203 prosequebatur] exequebatur KE   204 fastigii PHTC   205 fastidierim–quoque *om.* B   quoque] quidem KE *om.* T
207 perficiant E   Deum] Dominum ETQ   208 inquietas T   209 incunc-
tantem TC *corr. ad* incunctanter C   denuntias] prenuntias KE   211 libet]
magis ac magis *add.* KE *cf.* 411   211-212 Ad–praedicabat *om.* KE   212
perdicabat PI praedicabat T   213 monitis BT   214 cum fratribus *om.* B
cum pro fratribus I   hoc E hac TQ   214-215 sacrosancta G   Domini
om. PHTC 216 paxillulo BC paxillum K pauxillum E   suos *om.* JE suo
PCT suos T*corr.*   218 clanculo EG *cf.* 411   218-219 Et–devehens *rep.* E

220 Monte Garizin; et in reliqua sanctorum quae ibi interiacent venerabilium loca oraturus advenit. Hinc quoque divina praeductrice gratia Palestinam Caesaream devenisse contigit; et ibi in ecclesia Sanctae Dei Genetricis semper virginis Mariae duos dies permansit.

16. Interea disponente pie ac sapienter Dei providentia, ad Sanctae
225 Eufemiae orationis causa ecclesiam profectus, in quadam domuncula magos scilicet Persas magice operantes transeundo prospexit.
Divino itaque zelo permotus ad eos quidem divertens, taliter est
aborsus: "Heu miseri, quid erratis et aliis similiter errorem suggeri-
tis?" Illi vero huius modi praeloquentis audacia stupidati, quis vel
230 unde adesset eum interrrogaverunt. Quibus ipse talia increpando
subiunxit: "Ego denique sicut vos erravi aliquando; vestrae quoque
vanitatis maleficia non ignoro." Illi igitur obmutescentes, et eum
quorsum vellet abire dimittentes, ne cui propalaret quae in ipsis
cognoverat tremebundi rogitaverunt.

235 **17.** Cum igitur ab eis paululum discessisset, quidam equites qui se-
debant ad dervas quod erat sellarii praetorium, videntes quidem
eum invicem susurrabant esse exploratorem. Beatus vero Anastasius huiusmodi audiens invicem obloquentes, taliter est affatus:
"Quid garrientes strepitis? Ego quidem minime explorator sed
240 Ihesu Christi servus, et vobis sum melior; et ut vos estis modo, fui
eques aliquando." Insurgentes itaque eum apprehenderunt. Superveniens vero sellarius unde vel quis adesset eum interrogavit; et
omnia quae circa eum aderant curiose rimatus, eum tribus diebus
custodiri praecepit. Sanctus vero Anastasius illorum insidias stu-
245 diose praecavens, tanto temporis intervallo nihil alimoniae ab eisdem accepit.

18. Regresso autem praeside Marzabana—illic enim aberat quando
tentus est sanctus Anastasius—praedictus sellarius Dei famuli cau-

220 Montem E   quae] qui T   223 semperque JKE C   225-226 domun-
culam T domuncula T^corr.   226 transeunte G   228 aborsus] orsus E exorsus C adorsus Q cf. orsus 411   alii HG   230 adesset] esset T esse C
taliter E   233 quorsus E   vellet om. I   234 rogitarent G   237 invi-
cem] iuvenem B   239 explorator] non sum add. T non eras. T^corr.   240
Christi] sum add. T   sum om. E   241-242 Superveniens] Super E   242
adesset] esset E   244-246 Sanctus–accepit om. KE   245 tanti G   247
Barzabana EQ 411 T^corr.

sam illi notificavit. Deinde Marzabanas in suum praetorium eum
250 deduci praecepit. Interea Marzabana aliis sollicitato, quidam vir
Christi amantissimus et sancto Anastasio cognitus ibidem inventus est. In praefata namque Dei Genetricis ecclesia se dudum cogni-
taverant. Iste igitur beatum Anastasium alloquens, et omnia quae
ei insistebant plenissime addiscens, de bono quidem initio eum glo-
255 rificabat, et ut hoc calce tenus perduceret[12] divinis hortaminibus
monitabat, et ut cruciamina vel mortem quae pro Christi nomine
inferentur nequaquam metueret; sed impio Marzabanae fiducialiter responderet. Et hoc quidem creberrimo repetitu salutare tes-
timonium inculcabat, "Qui perseveraverit usque in finem hic sal-
260 vus erit."[13]

19. Interea Anastasius Ihesu Christi famulus impio Marzabanae
repraesentatur. Sed cum eum de more profanissimae gentis flexis
poplitibus minime adorasset, Marzabanas torvo vultu diutissime
eum intuitus dixit: "Unde vel quis es?" Ille ad haec: "Ego, inquit,
265 veraciter christianus sum. Si autem unde sim scire cupis, persarum
genere, de Razech regione, de villa Rasnuni, eques vero et magus

249 Barzabanas HEQ 411 T*corr.*   250 Barzabana EQ 411 T*corr.*   de aliis E
251 Christo T   Christi amantissimus] Christianissimus E   252 ecclesiam
T ecclesia T*corr.*   se] sed E   se dudum] sedulum G   252-253 cognovita-
verant B   254 insistebat E   255 hoc *om.* B   perduret E   hortamini-
bus] oraminibus E hortationibus G   256-257 ut–inferentur] si in crutiamina
vel morte pro Christi nomine inferetur B   257 efferentur E inferrentur TQ
Barzabanae EQ T*corr.*   258 creberrimo–salutare] creberrime repetebat et salutare E   259 usque *om.* Q   261 Barzabanae EQ T*corr.*   repraesentatur]
se (*supra lin. add.*) repraesentavit Q   262 de more *om. sed* more *supra lin.*
add. B   262-263 flexo poplite E   263 Barzabanas EHQ T*corr.*   torvo]
turbo G   266 persarum] Persa sum G   regione *om.* T   villa] videlicet
add. KE

12. The phrase *ut hoc calce tenus perduceret* has no equivalent in the
Greek text. It may have been added by the translator, or may reflect a Greek
model different from the text that has come down to us.
    13. Mt 10.22.

aliquando aderam; sed relictis tenebris veni ad lucem." Ad haec
Marzabanas: "Istum, inquit, errorem desere, et ad pristinum cultum festinus revertere, et tibi quidem cavallos et miliarisia cum
270 magno beneficio donabimus." Ipse vero respondens dixit: "Non
permittat mihi deus meum Christum negare." Marzabanas dixit:
"Placetne ergo tibi habitus quo indueris?" Ille vero respondit: "Iste
quidem habitus mea est gloria." Marzabanas dixit: "Daemonium
habes." Cui beatus Anastasius sic respondit: "Dum essem dudum
275 in errore, habebam daemonium; modo autem persecutorem daemoniorum habeo dominum Ihesum Christum." Item Marzabanas:
"Non metuis imperatorem, ne ubi tuam causam cognoverit faciat
te crucifigi?" Ille vero respondit: "Cur ergo timuerim tuum imperatorem, similiter ut tu es hominem corruptibilem?"

280 **20.** Stomachatus igitur Marzabanas, eum catenatum duci in castrum praecepit, ut sine interstitio lapides devectaret. Et cum hoc
quoque fatigio affligeretur, aliis quoque intolerabilibus angustiis
praemebatur. Quidam enim eiusdem cuius ipse aderat regionis,
propriae confusioni quae contra eum agebantur deputantes, accede-
285 bant quidem ei talia dicentes: "Cur sic nobis fecisti? Nemo quidem
nostrae regionis aliquando factus est christianus; et ecce tantum
nobis intulisti ridiculum." Malesuadis igitur sermonibus, illum an-

---

267 aderam] eram P   ad] veram *add.* H *hic des.* Q   268 Barzabanas EH
T$^{corr.}$X   269-270 cavallos–beneficio] equos et militiam E   269 militaria B
270 respondit E   271 mihi deus meum] Dominus meus me (me *supra lin.*
add. T) TX   Barzabanas EHT$^{corr.}$X   272-273 Placetne–dixit *om.* BC
272 quo] quem E   273 Barzabanas EHT$^{corr.}$X   274 dudum *om.* P   274-
275 dudum–errore] in errorem E   276 dominum *om.* B Ihesum *om.* E
276 Item–cap. 39 (l. 603) *om.* C   Barzabanas EHT$^{corr.}$X   277 metuis]
inquid *add.* E agnoverit BIG   278 vero] autem G   ergo] ego B   timue-
ro T$^{corr.}$X   280 igitur] itaque KE *om.* TX   Barzabanas EHT$^{corr.}$X   280-
281 carcerem E   281 interstitio] intermissione E   282 fastigio PHTX
283 cuius] civis B   284 confusioni] consuetudine K consuetudini E *cf.* contra propriam consuetudinem 411   agebatur TX   285 quidem[1]] quidam
BPI *eras.* T$^{corr.}$ *om.* X   ei] et IX   quidem[2]] quidam TX   286 religionis
JKEI et *om.* TX   286-287 nobis tantum *transpos.* TX   287 Malesuadis]
malesuasis *codd.* (*sed cf. cap. 35, ll. 545-546:* malesuadis blandimentis) malesuadis igitur *om.* KE 411

nitebantur revocare ad seipsos. Ipse vero e contra, eosdem iniurians
repellebat. Illi autem infatuati, cotidie ad eum veniebant. Vesti-
290 menta quoque eius scindentes barbam etiam funditus evellentes,
sine aliquo intervallo eum percutiebant. Et non hoc quidem solum,
verum etiam et saxa quae quattuor illorum deveherent, illi soli sub-
eunda imponebant. Unum insuper convinctum ad tribulationum
congeriem habebat, cum quo unam in collo, alteram vero catenam
295 in pede gestabat. Haec et multo atrociora illis inferentibus, fortissimus Dei adthleta omnia propter Christum gaudenter sufferebat.

21. Iterum Marzabanas iussit eum assisti, et taliter est orsus: "Si
vere ut asseris magi filius fuisti, eandem quoque artem nosti, mihi
aliquid de ea recitato, ut agnoscam utrum vera necne sint quae di-
300 xeris." Ille vero respondit: "Nequaquam permittat Deus aliquid
huiusmodi me ulterius proferre." Dicit ei Marzabanas: "Quid ergo?
In his permanebis? Scribam etenim imperatori de te." Sanctus vero
Anastasius respondit: "Iam scripsisti, et rescripta accepisti; fac igitur quicquid velis." Ad haec Marzabanas: "Nondum scripsi sed scri-
305 bam. Et quaecumque praeceperit, festine perficiam." Ille vero dixit:
"Vade scribe quantacumque volueris mala de me; ego enim fateor
christianum me fieri." Marzabanas igitur eum prostratum ministris
praecepit caedere, ut saltem invitus iussis cogeretur obtemperare.
Sanctus vero Anastasius incipientibus se ligare, sic ait: "Sinite me,
310 non enim vinculis indigeo." Sedens itaque se eis flagellandum

---

288 e *om.* G   iniurias IT iniuriis T$^{corr.}$X   289 infatiati B vafatui E   290
eius *om.* B   barbamque E 411   293 imponerent B   293-294 Unum–
habebat *om.* B   293 coniunctum E   294 cum quo] cumque E   alteram
eras. B   295 gestiebat JKEPTXG *corr. ad* gestabat KB$^{corr.}$H   296 Dei *om.*
PHTX   297 Barzabana E Barzabanas HT$^{corr.}$X   eum] sibi *add.* B *non est
in* g   297-298 et taliter–nosti] et dixit ei "Eandem artem quam nosti B
297 exorsus E   298 vero E   fuisti] et *add.* KE   299 de ea *om.* KE   re-
cita BI recitata G   cognoscam E 411   necne *om.* E   301 dixit PHTXGI
cf. Λέγει   Barzabanas EHT$^{corr.}$X   303 scripsi G   304 Barzabanas EH
T$^{corr.}$X   305 quaecumque] quaeque BK quae E *sed cf.* quaecumque *in cap. 7,
11, 12 etc.*   306 quantacumque] quaecumque G   307 fieri] fore B fieri K
esse E 411   Barzabanas ET$^{corr.}$X   308 praecepit] arcere et *add.* E   ut]
suis *add.* KE 411   iussis *om.* B   310 eis] ad *add.* J   flagellando E

promptificavit, eo situ quo antea ab illis alligari coeperat. Coeperunt igitur eum caedere cum palis; ipse autem dixit: "Exuite me
hunc habitum ut non inhonoretur; et sic me super carnem pro vestro velle caedite. Ista enim fieri ludibunda videntur. Verum et si
315 membratim me discerpseritis, Dominum meum Ihesum Christum
nullatenus negabo." †O perari exemplis[14]† devotissimum martyrem! re vera hostilibus vinculis minime indigebat qui divini ardo-
ris nexibus non carebat. Volebant enim impii invitum extrinsecus
ligando concutere, quem iam Christus ultroneum intrinsecus vin-
320 ciendo coeperat stabilire. Verum qui eum interno ligamine salubriter astringebat, externo eos vinculo ne quid e contra possent
alligare valebat. Sed illis diabolus ut eum vellent vincere rabiem
ministrabat. Ei autem ut minime ab eis ligaretur virtutem patien-
tiae Ihesus Christus inspirabat. O mirae humilitatis exemplum!
325 sanctus quidem se exui habitum rogabat; et se illo indignum quodam modo iudicabat. Sed non sibi vestimenta iam iamque atteren-
da praetulit, sed omnes hunc habitum indutos semet ipsum humi-

---

311 ligari B   312 Exuite] autem *add.* TX   313 hunc habitum *om.* B hoc
habitu T*corr.*X *cf.* τὸ σχῆμα   me *om.* B *cf.* ἐπὶ τῶν σαρκῶν μου   315 discer-
peritis JPI discerpitis TX   316 Operimini B Operari EPTXG   316–351
O perari–redeamus *om.* I   316 exemplum JKE   317 hostibus P hostilis
H 319 concurrere E   322 valebant G   vincirent E   323 virtutum PG
325 sanctum JP sancto T*corr.*X   habitu T*corr.*X   rogavit KE   indigno E
326 iudicavit ETXG iudicabit H   vestimentum E   326-327 adterendo E
327 semet] sed P se TX

14. Here begins a long addition. It echoes Augustine's *Contra Iulianum
opus imperfectum*. Cf., for example, "ista autem contraria, quae medium non
habent, ut puta bonum et malum, iustum et iniustum, innocentia et reatus,
ut uno tempore in unum atque idem convenire non possunt, ita necesse est,
ut altero eorum posito alterum denegetur, id est, ut vel praeceptum vel
consilium vel adiumentum non potest simul uno tempore et iustum et iniustum esse, ita et homo non potest uno eodemque tempore et reus et innocens
et bonus et malus esse" (*Contra Iul. op. imp.* III, 32 [ed. Zelzer, pp. 370-371]).
The opening sentence presents a textual problem. Neither *operari exemplis*
nor *operamini exemplis* make sense here; the use of the accusative *devotissimum martyrem* suggests an exclamatory phrase such as *O mirae humilitatis
exemplum* which follows below in the same chapter.

lians honoravit. O infinitum martyrii desiderium! vestimenta exu-
tus quatinus super carnem caederetur poscebat, quia pro Christi
330 nomine peracto agonismate martyrii coronam maturari volebat.
Sed ne multis auditores fastidiam taceo stabilitatis quam in Christo
habebat fiduciam. Se etenim etiam si nervatim discerperetur, se
numquam abdicaturum Christum proloquebatur. Et hoc non suis
viribus deputabat, sed Dei misericordiae humiliter referebat. Sed tu
335 o cruentissime et ab omni pietate semotissime Marzabana, cur vel
talem et tantam beatissimi martyris patientiam intuitus iram non
mitigasti? vel etiam immensa eius humilitate prospecta, tumorem
tuae mentis minime remisisti? Fortasse tale mihi responsum tu evo-
mas. Quod ideo innocentem virtutibus plenissimum compresseris,
340 quia in eo vitia intrinsecus latitare putaveris; ac proinde quomodo
libet te forte excusabilem decreveris. Conticesce, inquam, miserrime quam quidem ex operum forma patefiunt pectoris antra. Quamvis
igitur rationalis non utaris ratione, rationando tamen probemus
quis nostrum valeat alterum superare. Age igitur; numquid duo
345 contraria unieidemque substantiae simul adesse possunt? velis nolis-
ve negabis. Quin etiam, et virtutibus contraria esse vitia invitus
fateberis. Si igitur beatus Anastasius virtutes habuit, vitiis caruit;
habuit autem virtutes quod ex effectu paruit; vitiis igitur caruit.
Videsne iam miserrime qualiter sis devictus et ab omni veridica ex-
350 cusatione remotus?

329 super *rep.* P   quia] qua TX   330 agonis G   331 fastidiant T   332
nervatum P   333 praeloquebatur PTX   334 humiliter *om.* B   335 et-
semotissime *om.* H   semotissime] saevissime B remotissime TX   335 Barzabana EHTX m *add. supra lin.* T   336 iram] eam E   337 humilitatem
BP   perspecta PTX   tumorem] tu more B *om.* H timorem X   338-339
evomes X   339 ideo] Deo B   innocentem] tuae *add.* K tu *add.* E   com-
plesseris G   340 vitia] etiam JPHTXG   342 quam] quoniam X   ex] et
T$^{corr.}$X   firma PTX   peccatoris TX   343 utaris] imitaris E vitaris TPG
utaris T$^{corr.}$ ratiocinando T$^{corr.}$X   probemus] vitemus G   344 nostrum]
vestrum KE   Age] Ante TX   345 unieidemque] unieidem PH   eius
add. PHTX   347 virtutem E   habuit–caruit *om.* EG   349 devictus] di-
micatus J   ab *om.* TX

22. Sed ut ad propositum redeamus. Marzabanas iterum dicit ei: "Consentito mihi; scribam etenim imperatori de te." Ipse vero respondit: "Vade et scribe imperatori quicquid volueris." Marzabanas dixit: "Non metuis imperatorem?" Beatus Anastasius respondit:
355 "Cur ego timeam imperatorem tuum? Nonne homo est sicut et tu? et sicut tu morieris nonne et ipse morietur? Et sicut tu corrumperis nonne et ipse corrumpetur? Quem igitur potius metuam, illumne corruptibilem, et similem tibi lutum, an caeli et terrae factorem filium Dei Ihesum Christum?" Ille igitur superbus tanta martyris
360 fiducia stupidatus, iussit eum secundo in castrum removeri.

23. Paucis deinde provolutis diebus, iussit eum iterum sibi repraesentari. Primo itaque respectu, sic est eum affatus: "Recepta arte magica, praesentialiter[15] diis sacrifica, ne male moriaris, et hac luce frauderis." Respondens Dei famulus dixit ei: "Quibus diis
365 me iubes sacrificare? Soli an lunae? igni vel aquis?[16] Quid ergo, montibus an collibus? vel aliis quibuslibet similibus? Sed non permittat mihi Deus omnipotens vestras culturas aliquando adorare.

---

351 Barzabanas EHT$^{corr.}$X   igitur] iterum TX   352 Consenti E 411   de te *om.* B *cf.* περὶ σοῦ   352-353 Ipse–imperatori] Sanctus Dei respondit: "Scribe B *cf.* Ἄπελθε, γράψον τῷ βασιλεῖ   353 et *om.* E   Barzabanas EHT$^{corr.}$X   355 ego] ergo E   Nonne–et tu *om.* KE 411   tu *om.* PX ipse *add.* E   metuam *om.* B *cf.* φοβηθῶ   357-358 illumne–similem] illumne an ut tu qui es corruptibilis et similis E   358 factorem *om.* E   360 fiduciam TP fiducia T$^{corr.}$ castro JTX   361-362 praesentari EHTXIG 362 est *om.* TX   363 praesenter JKEPHTXIG   et] ex E   365 an] vel I   similitudinibus G   367 sculturas X

15. The Greek text does not provide evidence to decide between the two variant readings; I have chosen *praesentialiter* following Gregorius's preference for less common words.
16. As the history of the text of the early translation also shows, the addition of the horse to a list of the natural elements worshiped by the Persians was puzzling. Hence, either Gregorius or someone very early in the history of this text corrected what may have been *equis* to *aquis*.

Haec enim omnia cunctisator Deus humano servitio assignanda creavit. Sed quidem homines Deum factorem vestrum ignorantes quadrupedibus et daemonibus errando deservitis. Si enim Dei filium Ihesum Christum cognovissetis, a daemonibus liberati qui vos errare faciunt, ad lucem veniretis." Talia quidem veracissimo Deo, qui os et sapientiam adversariis inexpugnabilem his qui pro suo nomine paterentur promisit, ex ore idiotae et alienigenae ad gloriam et robur suorum fidelium procedere placuit. His igitur divinitus inspiratis sermonibus, adversarios confundebat. Et trina coronatus confessione pro Christi nomine vinculis adornatus, iterum ad castrum reducitur.

24. Abbas itaque eiusdem monasterii quo ipse deguerat, eius quidem confessionis in Christo stabilitatem, et copiosam sine pavore alacritatem, magnam quoque cum perseverantia promptitatem—fama scilicet multivola devehente—comperiens, cum universo suo collegio est nimium laetatus. Et Deum omnipotentem quatenus eius cursum quem in sui nominis confessione coeperat summa tenus perduceret per diis atque nocturnis horis expostulabat. Duos etiam fratres cum adletacis apicibus ad eum roborandum Caesaream direxit.

368 enim *om.* BPHITX quidem G *cf.* Ταῦτα γὰρ πάντα   cunctifactor B cunctis auctor KE cunctorum auctor 411   assignando G   369 Sed] et B vestrum] nostrum B *cf.* τὸν ποιήσαντα ὑμᾶς   370 et daemonibus *om.* KE 411 deservistis B deserviebant H *cf.* δουλεύετε   371 vos] nos B   372 veracissimus Deus T*corr.*X   373 os] nos B hos JT   sapientiam] coram *add.* T*corr.* X   adversis E   374 ad *om.* B et JKE   375 suorum] eorum G   376 inspiratus T*corr.*X   377 nomine] corona KE 411   379-526 Abbas–detulit *om.* I   379 quod JKPT*corr.*X   380 stabilitate B   381 claritatem EPTXIGK *corr. ad* alacritatem K   perseverantiae B perseverantiam KE 382 fama–comperiens *om.* H   fama ... multivola] famam ... multivolam G 383 nimium *om.* X   384 confessionem E ceperit K ceperat TX   384-385 summa tenus] ad finem B quatenus JPHTXG *cf. cap. 31 & 40* summa tenus vidisset/summa tenus provexit   385 diis] diem E dies H horis *om.* G expostulabant BKE *cf.* ἱκέτευεν νυκτὸς καὶ ἡμέρας   386 cum adletacis] cum magnis E athleta sanctas PH *vacuum* + sanctis T tam sanctis X

25. Denique dum Christi martyr catenatus in carcere servaretur, die ac nocte Dominum psalmis, hymnis, et canticis, semper glorifi-
390 cabat. Sed quia uno convincto ut superius diximus, quodam scilicet servo rem ob aliquam comprehenso, nimis impediretur, dum noc-turnis temporibus canonica peracturus psallentia exurgeret ne illum distensione catenarum offenderet; ad collum quidem iacentis sem-per suum inclinabat, et iuxta eius pedem leniter suum figebat. Qua-
395 dam vero nocte dum sanctus Anastasius solicanus Deo psalleret, unus quidem convinctorum, hebraeae scilicet religionis, stemmate praeclarus, moribus quoque probus, eum intentis auribus pervigil auscultabat. Videns quippe illum diurno tempore devectionem lapi-dum miserabiliter perpessum, nocturno quoque conticuo assiduis
400 orationibus deditum quantus vel qualis esset nimis extupescebat.

26. Interea dum delitens in nocturna furvitate pavimento accumbe-ret, subito quosdam splendidissime indutos, et vibrantissimo lumi-ne praefulgidos, ingredientes quidem ergastuli ostium et simul cir-cumdantes beatum Anastasium prospexit. Huiusmodi igitur intuitu
405 stupefactus, apud semetipsum dixit: "Sanctus Deus, isti angeli sunt." Et dum talia convolveret, eosdem crucigeris homoforis circuma-mictos respexit. Et iterum apud se dixit: "Isti episcopi sunt." Intui-tusque martyrem Christi Anastasium, eisdem collucentem similiter aspexit. Cui quidam eximiae gloriae ante sistens iuvenis habens qui-
410 dem turibulum incensum adigebat. Talia vero diutissime prospec-tans, quendam christicolam Scitopolitanae civitatis iudicem, ut et ipsi quae videbat ostenderet, e somno excutere pulsando nitebatur. Quem cum excitare nullomodo valeret, quemamodum exsanguis

---

391 servo rem] fervore BEH fervorem K   nimis] nominis J ne minis E
392 canonica ... psallentia] canonicam ... psalmodiam E   393 catenatus TX
393-394 ad–inclinabat *om.* H   394 leviter J   395 solitus E   396 ebreo
B   religionis *om.* B regionis E   398 devectione JTX   399 continuo E
contiguo XG   400 debitum G   401 delitens] deditus E   furtivitate TX
402-403 indutos–lumine *om.* KE 411   403 ergastulo JPH   405 semetip-
sum] se ipsum BPX   405-407 Sanctus–dixit *om.* E   405 Sancti Dei TX
406 crucigeros T^{corr.}X   406-407 circum amictis PH   407-408 Intuitusque]
Intuitus B Tusque (?) K cumque E   Christi martyrem *transpos.* TX   409
quidem B *cf.* νεανίας τις   gloriae *om.* G   410 adagebat *codd. sed corr. ad*
adigebat B *ad* adaugebat T^{corr.}X

sine flatu manebat, pervigili animo intuens quae videbat. Sed ut
415 illum amplius expergisci cogeret, se quidem soporanti totum super-
posuit. Tandem itaque Scithopolitanus evigilans, nimioque pavore
perculsus, quid hoc esset interrogat. Cui hebraeus: "Videsne hoc?"
inquit, et conspicientibus, nil ulterius paruit. Ac postquam ei hebraeus ante visa narraverat, ambo unanimiter Deum glorificaverunt.

420 **27.** Denique Marzabanas prima et secunda ut supradictum est interrogatione stabilitatem Dei famuli Anastasii expertus, de eo imperatori Chosroae apices destinavit. Perpaucis autem provolutis diebus
imperatoris praeceptum Marzabanas recepit; ac deinde beato Anastasio mittens unum ex suis magnatibus in carcerem sic ait: "En
425 edixit imperator, ut solo quidem verbo te esse christianum abdicis,
et statim te absolvam; et quocumque volueris abire sive monachus
volueris adesse, sive eques ut prius et nobiscum manere, tuae prorsus aderit potestatis." At ille respondit: "Absit a me aliquando
Ihesum Christum negare." Plurimas autem promissiones et innu-
430 meros commonitus per suum magnatem dirigens, nullatenus ei
persuadere valuit.

28. Posthac tamen per eundem remandavit ei dicens: "Scio quidem
te tuos contribules erubescere; et ideo te nolle coram eis negare.
Quia igitur sic iubet imperator, inter me et alios duos equites dic
435 verbum." Cui et ipse respondens, talia remandavit: "Tam coram te
quam coram quibuslibet, absit a me aliquando Christum meum
negare." Tandem itaque Marzabanas per semetipsum dixit ei: "Ecce
iussit imperator, ut catenis devinctus abeas in Persidem." Ad haec

414 pervigili–videbat *om.* H   anima KE   417 interrogans KE   hoc² *om.*
KE   418 paruit] apparuit E 411   420 Barzabanas EHT^{corr.}X   supradictum est] dictum est supra TX   422 Chosdroae B Chosroi TX   423 imperator E   Barzabanas HT^{corr.}X Barzabanae E   recepit] direxit E   425 edi-
xit] dixit KE 411   abdicas *(?)* T abdices EHT^{corr.}X   426-427 abire–volueris
om. E   426-427 sive–adesse *om.* J   428 me] ut *add.* E   aliquando] Dominum *add.* E   429 negem E negari PHT negare T^{corr.}X   430 suos magnates
E   433 tuos *om.* E   434 inter] in B ut inter *sed* ut *eras.* T   et] alios *add.*
B   duos] tuos KE   equites] milites B   435 respondit et B respondit talia
T respondit taliaque T^{corr.}X   437 negari BEPT negare T^{corr.}X *cf. supra cap.*
27 l. 429 et g   Barzabanas ET^{corr.}X   seipsum E   438 devinctus] vinctus
E 411

440 sanctus: "Si me, inquit, dimiseris, ego ipse ultroneus ad imperatorem vadam." Videns itaque Marzabanas beatum Dei martyrem im-
mote assistentem in omne experimentum et neque minis territum
neque blandimentis persuasum, iussit eum cum aliis duobus christicolis publica custodia bullatos carcerari, ut post quinque dies ad
praedictum imperatorem iter simul arriperent.

445 **29.** Interea adveniente exaltationis salutiferae crucis festivitate, beatus quidem Anastasius cum duobus ex suo monasterio fratribus, et
praefatis christicolis duobus, cum quibusdam de eadem civitate viris venerabilibus psalmis, ymnis, et canticis spiritualibus sollemni-
ter pernoctaverunt, ita quidem ut omnes vincti conglorificantes
450 Deum penitus obliviscerentur suarum calamitatum. Commerciarius
autem vir Christo amabilis, ad impium Marzabanam primo mane
perrexit, nimis eum expostulans, ut beatum Anastasium introeundi
ecclesiam gratia sub pacto restituendi vinculis absolveret. Quo imperato omnes quidem fideles qui ibi intererant infinito gaudio sunt
455 repleti, sicut eo quippe ingrediente ecclesiam de suis periculis statim sunt consolati. Quot quot enim concivium christiani aderant,
in magnam desperationem pariter corruerant; magnis quoque et
inestimabilibus tribulationibus animae eorum coangustatae aderant.

30. Tantam vero beati Anastasii in Christo fidem et sufferentiam
460 videntes, refloruerunt; et prae nimia eius consolatione, quasi denuo
in fide revixerunt. < *** >¹⁷ Et quod dictu est mirabile qui eum

---

440 Barzabanas EH   beatum *om.* E   440-441 immote] in monte K   441 assistente P   442 duobus *om.* TX   443 bullata Tᶜᵒʳʳ·X   ut] et Tᶜᵒʳʳ·(*ex ut?*)X   444 arripiunt TX   445 festivitatem E   447-448 viris *om.* E   451 autem *om.* E   Christi BPH   Barzabanam EHTᶜᵒʳʳ·X   452 perrexit] surrexit TX   453 gratiam E   453-454 impetrato E 411 *corr. ad* imperato E imperator KPG *cf.* τούτου γενομένου   454 fideles *om.* G   qui ibi] quibus PH qui + *eras.* T qui X   455 sicut eo] eo B sicut KEPHTXG *cf.* Statim quippe eo ... 411   quippe] qui per E   455-456 statim *om.* B   456 Quot quot] quo tempore E   concivium] concilium KE convicium G   457 corruerunt E convenerant G   458 eorum *om.* BG   excoangustatae BG *corr. ad* coangustatae B   aderant] erant Tᶜᵒʳʳ·X   459 in Christo *om.* TX   461 dictum E   eum] cum EP

---

17. The Latin omits here a Greek phrase (καὶ ἐπελάθοντο—παράκλησιν). The following Latin sentence, furthermore, does not render fully and accurately the

prius in angustiis ad tempus scilicet fide frigescentes afflixerant, osculantes eius vincula illum postea obsecrabant dicentes: "Et si nos
parati sumus pro te mortem subire, quanto magis tu propter com-
465 munem omnium dominatorem Christum cum omni promptitate
talia debes sufferre." Talem quidem et tantum honorem uterque
sexus devote ac simpliciter erga sanctum demonstrabant. Post per-
acta deinde missarum sollemnia, praedictus commerciarius sanctum
Dei martyrem cum duobus praelibatis e suo monasterio fratribus
470 rogitans et coactans secum deduxit domum. Solutaque inedia, beatum Anastasium in Domino gaudentem Marzabanae carcerandum
restituit. Ceterum in ergastulo quicumque tunc aderant eo regre-
diente valde gratulati omnes unanimiter Deum glorificabant.

31. Post quinque autem dies ut erat iam praestitutum, ille cum
475 duobus aliis christicolis quadam de causa accusatis, Caesaream discessit. Et plurimi civium christiani Persae alienigenae, cum infinitis
lacrimis foras eum comitantes, super eius bona devotione Dominum collaudabant. Unus autem e duobus sui monasterii saepe com-
memoratis fratribus obsequelae et solacii causa abbate praeiubente
480 eum est assecutus. Verum ob hoc maxime, ut quaecumque ab initio

---

462 prius *om.* E   fidei BJKPT*corr.*X   refrigescentes PTX frigentes G
463 vinculis KE   illum ... obsecrebant dicentes] illum ... obsecreantes
dicentes JPHT illumque ... obsecrantes dicebant T*corr.*X   467 devota PH
ac] et GP   470 rogitant P recitans H rogans TX   et coactans *om.* E 411
471 Barzabane JEHT*corr.*X   472 restituit] constituit G   472-473 eo re-
grediente] congrediente G   eo *om.* E   474 iam *om.* TX   475 accusatis]
apud *add.* E   478-479 commemoratus G obsequelae] obsequere K obsequii
E 411

---

meaning of the Greek model, but may represent a correction to make sense
of a problematic text. While here the contrast appears to be in the behavior
of the Christians, in the Greek text the paradox being emphasized is that
"those who in their misfortunes had reneged, and, in time, had fallen into
lukewarm faith, now become as if anointers of the martyr." The Latin text
here may also reflect a misunderstanding of the Greek. In particular, the
image of the Christians oiling the martyr as an athlete before combat may
have not been grasped, explaining its disappearance in this Latin version (cf.
unctores in the early translation).

agonismatis martyrem Dei perpessum summa tenus vidisset, ea
Christo favente supradicto abbati et suggregatis fratribus fidelissime
referret. Cuncta autem cum universis civitatibus loca in adventu
martyris Ihesu Christi gaudebant. Et omnes quidem honorabiliter
485 introeuntem excipientes, foras quoque abeuntem honorabilius ex-
ponebant. Haec autem ipse martyr ab Hieropolitana civitate supradicto abbati litteratim significavit, obnixe depostulans, ut pro suo
certamine consummando, Deum omnipotentem assidue rogaret.
Hoc quoque et a Tygride fluvio destinatis apicibus ab eo depoposcit.

490 **32.** Ingrediente vero martyre Christi Persidem, sine aliquo dilatu
missus est in carcerem, in villa videlicet quae dicitur Bethsaloes,
quae a Discarthas, in quo tunc temporis imperator degebat quasi
sex stadiis dirimitur. Frater autem qui cum eo aderat, in eadem villa mansit, in domo scilicet Cargacti filii Iesdin, primi commerciarii
495 Persarum, qui et ipsi christicolae aderant. Et commorante sancto
martyre aliquot dies cum eis qui ibidem aderant captivatis, suggestum est de eo Chosroae imperatori. Mittens igitur imperator unum
ex principibus, iussit eum diligenter rimatimque indagari.

33. Postmodum vero cum quodam chiliarcho cui cura carceris in-
500 sistebat, veniens in carcerem interrogavit eum, quis, vel unde adesset, vel cur eorum spreta religione, factus esset christianus. Beatus
vero Anastasius eos quidem alloqui persice dedignatus, multum mul-
tumque coactus tandem eis respondit: "O miseri errantes, pro Deo
cunctipotente daemones colentes. Hos equidem aliquando dum er-

481 tenus] attenus T hactenus X   482 praedicto P   segregatis E   fidissime B   483 referre KP   489 a Tygride fluvio] aggrigri defluvido G a gi-
gride fluvido BPH   eodem poposcit BJKEG   491 carcere BJPT$^{corr.}$X
quae] qui T   492 quae a Discarthas *om.* E   tunc *om.* B   temporibus JT
temporis T$^{corr.}$ *om.* H   492-493 quasi–dirimitur *om.* E   494 Cargago E
Iesdin] Gesdin BJKEH Gesdim PG *cf.* 'Ιεσδὶν   494-495 primi–Persarum
om. TX   495 ipse christicola aderat T$^{corr.}$X   496 captivitatis PT*(?)* captivi-
tati T$^{corr.}$ captivati X   497 Chosroae B Chosroi TX   igitur] vero E
499 cum–carceris] quidam chiliarco cuius carceri T$^{corr.}$ (*vacuum* quidam chiliarco *vacuum* cuius carceri) X   cui] cuius BJKEHG   carceri BP   499-
500 insistebant P   500-501 adesset] esset E   501 eorum *om.* B   eorum
spreta] expreta G   504 colentes] colitis T$^{corr.}$X   504-505 dum errarem]
cum errantem K errans tum E

505 rarem colebam; nunc autem Deum omnipotentem colo, qui fecit
caelum et terram, mare et omnia quae in eis sunt. Vestras quoque
culturas errorem et perditionem daemonum esse, indubitanter cognosco." Dixit ei princeps: "Miser, nonne quem colitis vos christiani, crucifixere Iudaei? Quomodo igitur errabundus postposita tua
510 religione factus es christianus?" Ad haec sanctus: "Illum quidem,"
inquit, "a Iudaeis sed sponte crucifixum fuisse non mentiris. Verumtamen ipse est qui fecit caelum et terram, mare et omnia quae in
eis sunt. Et dignatus est in terram descendere, et homo fieri et crucifigi, ut humanum genus ab errore Satanae, qui a vobis colitur li-
515 beraret. Vos autem ignem, et cetera quorum memorari nos pudet,
colentes vana spe ludimini, creaturae scilicet creatore neglecto servientes." Dixit ei princeps: "Quid tibi et istis sermonum ambagibus? En tibi imperatoris sublimitas, zonas aureas cum equis et magna dignitate paravit, suorumque magnatum adiungendi numero po-
520 testatem donavit? Solummodo pristinam religionem tuam culturus,
resipiscas." Cui martyr Ihesu Christi respondens: "Ego," inquit,
"Deum meum nequaquam abnegabo; sed semper eum colam, et semper adorabo; dona vero tui imperatoris pro stercore computabo."

34. Digressus abinde princeps, huiuscemodi dicta imperatori detu-
525 lit. Stomachatus igitur imperator, sequenti die eundem principem
ad puniendum beatum Anastasium destinavit. Abiens autem princeps furibundus, impio scilicet imperatori obsecutus, e carcere de-
trahi Christi famulum iussit; atque putans stabilem deflecti posse
columnam, eum orribilibus minis terrere coepit. Sanctus vero ad
530 haec: "Ne labores," inquit, "neque obnitaris o princeps; me etenim
Christo vigorante nequaquam a mea fide extirpare valebis. Quic-

507 culturas] atque *add.* B quoque *add.* TX   errorem] quoque *add.* H
509 Iudaeis] tentum *add.* E   512 terris G   513 hominem TX   514 ut]
et PH   qui–colitur *om.* H   515 autem] igitur TX   nos *om.* B   516
illudimini TX   creaturae–neglecto] creatorem scilicet neglecto creatures K
creatorem scilicet creaturae neglecto E creaturae scilicet neglecto creatore creaturae TX   517 isti P   sermonis E   521 resipiscas *om.* E   respondit
BE   Deum] Dominum JPHG   522 abnegabo nequaquam *transpos.* TX
sed *om.* KE   semper] eum TX   527 impio ... imperatori] impii ... imperatoris iussum T^{corr.}X   528 deflecti] defrecti P   531 Christo *om.* E   vigo-
rantem E   531-532 Quicquid enim *add.* PG

quid igitur volueris facito." Ferocissimus igitur princeps beatum
Anastasium persico more devinctum, vectibus caedi praecepit. "Et
quando quidem," inquit, "donis et honoribus adquiescere noluisti,
535   amodo iam cognoscito ista te esse habiturum; huiuscemodi namque
te singulis diebus plagis consumam." Sanctus Anastasius respondit:
"Neque donis tui imperatoris adquiesco, neque etiam tuas minas
formido; quicquid igitur velis iam iamque perficito."

35. Tunc impiissimus princeps, multifariae iniquitatis atrocissimus
540   perscrutator, solutum Dei martyrem supinari praecepit; atque eius
tibias superposito ligno, atque duobus fortissimis utrimque supersistentibus viris substringi commandavit. Quis autem nesciat huius
tormenti speciem esse intolerabilem? At gloriosissimus Christi martyr huiusmodi dolores patienter sufferens, Deo omnipotenti gratias
545   referebat. Videns igitur princeps se cum suis malesuadis blandimentis et tyrannicis tormentis adesse parvipensum, sicut enim calidum
ferrum aqua frigida induratur atque temperatur, sic etiam tyro
Christi huiusmodi cruciamentis magis magisque corroboratur. Tandem eum in carcerem retrahi donec iterum imperatori de eo sugge-
550   reret, praecepit.

36. Saepedictus autem coenobialis beati Anastasii frater, non diffi-
dens sellario qui scilicet carcerem providebat, nam et ipse Christianus aderat, alternis eum diebus solacii et obsequii gratia visitabat.
Plurimi quoque christianorum ibidem degentium inter quos et filii
555   Iesdin, introibant ad eum, rogantes, quatenus pro eis ad Dominum

---

532 valueris BI   533 persico–devinctum] per commovere devinctum K iam
invictum E   Et *om.* E   535 ista te] his te BPHTXIG iste JK ista E *cf.*
πρὸς ταῦτα ἔχεις   habiturum] in *add.* TX   538 iam *om.* E   perfice B
perficita G   540 persecutor E   541 tibiam KE   fortissimis] ferocissimus
E   utrique JPH   542 commendavit BET commandavit T*corr.*   542-576
Quis–dereliquit *om.* I   543 esse intolerabilem *om.* JE   At] Atque JKEP
TX *cf.* 'Ο δὲ   545 malesuadi B male suadens J malesuasis EH male suadi
(?) T mali suadere T*corr.*X   547 atque] aquae P   548 magisque *om.* B
549 carcere BP   549-550 retrahi–praecepit] retrudi mandavit E 411   suggereret *corr. ex* suggeret B suggerere H   550 praecepit *om.* E   551-552 diffi-
dens] de *add.* T*corr.*X   553 eum] enim E   diebus *om.* G   gratiam E
555 Gesdin KE

interveniret, et ad sui custodiam aliquod benedictionis monimentum donaret. Sane ipso huius modi preces[18] quasi indigno penitus
abnuente, illi ei vinculorum superposita cera formam exprimentes,
pro benedictione benefidi reservabant.

560 **37.** Paucis deinde interlapsis diebus, idem temerarius princeps remittens ad carcerem, "Quid dicis?" inquit, "obsecundabis iussioni
imperatoris, an forte in eisdem permanebis?" At ille commoto in
eius abominationem capite, respondit: "Semel et bis, saepiusque tibi
dixi, quod sit impossibile a me Christum negari. Quicquid igitur
565 velis maturanter facito." Tunc ipse omni tyrannide barbarieque ple-
nissimus eum ut ante vinctum palis caedi atrociter praecepit. Et
relinquens eum in carcere discessit. Aliquot post haec diebus provolutis, regrediens ad carcerem tum lenesuadis ut pridem sermonibus, tum blanditoriis pecuniae et dignitatum promissionibus, tum
570 terribilibus minis, tum amaris tormentis, sanctum Dei martyrem
in christiani nominis abnegationem provocare nitebatur. Sed cum

---

556-557 et–donaret *om.* E   monimentum] tum *add.* E   557 preve + *eras.*
J prebere EKT*corr.*X praebe PH preve G   558 ei *om.* KE eius T*corr.*X   559
beneficii E *om.* H benefici G   servabant H resonabant X   561 iussionem
EH   562 commotus E   563 capite *om.* E   565 velis] vis T*corr.*X   bar-
bariaque E barbarique G   atrociter *om.* E   567 carcerem BJEPHT(?) carcere T*corr.* *cf.* φυλακῇ   discessit] habiit T abiit X   567-568 discessit–carcerem *om.* B   567 haec] hac PHTX hos KE diebus] dies KEH   568 lenesua-
denus E lenesedis G lenesuadibilibus T*corr.*X   ut pridem *om.* B   570 ama-
ris] amatoribus H amatoris G   Dei *om.* E   571 christiani–abnegationem]
Christi nominis abnegatione E Christi nomine H   abnigatione T*corr.*X
provocat G

18. The Latin expands on the Greek, explicitly stating the reasons for
Anastasius's refusal to provide an "eulogia" for the faithful. The use of the
term "benedictionis monimentum" is an elaboration of "benedictio," the general Latin term corresponding to the Greek "εὐλογία" (which is also found
as a Latin word, but usually in the sense of "blessed food" or "blessed bread"
or Eucharist; cf. s.v. "eulogia" in *CLCLT*). "Benedictiones" were fundamentally relics: objects sanctified by contact with a martyr while s/he was alive or
associated with his/her tomb after death (See McCulloh, "The Cult of Relics
in the Letters and Dialogues of Gregory the Great: a Lexicographical Study,"
156-157).

eius immotissimae mentis coherentissimum christianae fidei stabilimentum perspiceret, iussit eum iam tertio ligatum similiter infestissime caedi. Ac deinde resolutum una manu suspendi subligato pon-
575 derosissimo lapide eius pedi praecepit. Ac sic demum digrediens,
pendulum dereliquit. Ipso autem huiusmodi supplicium quasi duas
horas fortiter sufferente, eum inde deponi destinando mandavit. Ac
deinde immobilitatem et constantiam eius imperatori notificavit.

38. Post haec praemotis quindenis ferme diebus, eundem sibi non
580 disparem[19] principem, et alios nonnullos ad interficiendum Dei
martyrem et plurimos alios christianorum captivos transmisit. Qui
obsequentes, beatum Anastasium cum aliis fere septuaginta christicolis, extra villam Bethsaloes in qua erat carcer extractos, iuxta fluvium praeceperunt exponi, ac deinde omnes singillatim, inter quos
585 et supradictos duos christicolas qui et vincti abeuntem Caesaream
beatum Anastasium comitati fuerant, spectante Christi martyre,
restibus suffocari. Et singulo quoque eorum interempto beato Anastasio dicebant: "Quare vis sicut unus horum male perire? et non
potius ut vivas imperatori acquiescere? et acceptis honoribus sicut
590 unus nostrum in palatio esse ut neque huius vitae dulcedine frauderis, neque acerbae mortis fato praeripiaris?" At Christi victoriosissimus martyr, velut iam sui desiderii compos, omnipotenti Deo
gratias referens, ad haec respondit: "Pro Christi equidem amore, a

---

573 perciperet E   574 manus G manum P   575 pedi] sub pedibus E pede
T^{corr.}X   576 *corr. ex* supplicio E In ipso ... supplicio H   duas] duas per
T^{corr.}X   579 quindecim E   581 alios *om.* E   Cui T^{corr.}X   583 quo
PTX   584 singulatim JHIG   585 duos supradictos *transpos.* TX christianos TX   586 spectantes TX   martyrem TX   587 singulos quosque ...
interemptos E   588 unus] unusquisque T^{corr.}X   589 quiescere TX   591
facto JKPHTXI   593 equidem] eiusdem J quidem E

---

19. Cf. ὁ βασιλεὺς αὐτόν τε τὸν ἄρχοντα, and the early translation's *imperator ipsum quoque iudicem*, which is an accurate rendering of the Greek. The
translation in 411a is difficult to explain. It seems likely that a word such as
imperator is missing. Is *sibi non disparem* a marginal gloss that migrated to
the text proper, or perhaps an alternate translation? Or is it the result of a
corruption in the Greek model available to the translator of 411a?

vobis membratim concidi optaveram. Verum si huius modi quem
595 et vos minamini obitus me commanet, gratias Deo meo inexaustas
replico, qui me suorum martyrum participem gloriae dignatus est
facere tam parvo supplicio." His dictis, gloriosissimus Dei martyr
beatus Anastasius transitoria vita huiuscemodi termino limitata,
voti compos, gaudii plenus, immarcescibili bravio coronatus, ad ve-
600 ram aeternamque vitam quae Christus est meruit pervenire. At
postquam eum suffocaverunt, praetiosissimum caput eius absciderunt. Et deinde bullam accipientes quae vinculis superhaeserat, imperatori secum devexerunt.

39. Sellarius itaque qui ut praelibatum est Christianus atque custos
605 carceris aderat, corpus beati martyris ut esset cognoscibile, semotim
collocare voluit. Sed hoc quaestionarii hebraei scilicet existentes minime permiserunt. Cognoscentes filii Iesdin transitum victoriosi
martyris, pueri namque eorum cum ipse ad martyrizandum ducere-
tur praesentes affuerant, percitato tramite illuc statim concurre-
610 runt, superspectisque eius manibus eum recognoscentes,[20] maximum pondus argenti praefatis quaestionariis clanculum obtulerunt.
At ipsi eis postea deferendi corporis licentiam praebuerunt. Sequenti igitur nocte superius rememoratus de coenobio beati martyris
monachus comitantibus pueris filiorum Iesdin, et quibusdam mona-

---

595 et *om.* P   597-676 tam–puro ac *om.* G (*folium succisum est*)   597 hii
(?) T His T*corr.*   598 sublimitate J limitate E   599 gaudio E   602 Et *om.*
P   604-605 atque–aderat] ad quem carceris adherat cura E   605 ut *om.* E
esse T   remotum E semotum X   607 Cognoscentes] autem *add.* KE
Gesdin KE deiesdin H Iesdim T   609 praecitato P   609-610 cucurrerunt
T*corr.*X   611 clanculo BEH *cf.* clanculum *supra l. 218*   612 eius PHT eis
T*corr.*   613 memoratus KE   614 Gesdin KE deiesdin H Iesdim T   614-
615 monachos T monachus T*corr.*

20. This passage misinterprets the Greek, concluding that the children of
Yesdin recognize the body of the saint from his hands, since his head had
been cut off. This interpretation must be the result of reading ὑπερείδοντες
(from ὑπερείδω) as if it were ὑπερίδοντες (from ὑπεροράω). It is clear from
the early translation that this is also the interpretation given by the first
translator (*super despicientes manus eius*). And in fact the pseudo-Philoxenus
(*CGL*, 464) reads "Ὑπερορω perspicio despicio sprevo."

615 chis qui ibidem aderant, ad tollendum sacratissimum corpus secretissime venit. Cumque illuc venisset, invenit quidem canes interfectorum corpora comedentes, corpus beati Anastasii seorsum iacens penitus intactum. Praetiosa enim in conspectu Domini mors sanctorum eius,[21] et custodit Dominus omnia ossa eorum, unum ex

620 eis conteri non permittit.[22] Corpus igitur beati martyris revolutum praetiosis linteis a filiis scilicet Iesdin datis devexerunt, atque in monasterio beati martyris Sergii quod unius fere stadii intercapedine a praedicto castello dirimitur reposuerunt.

40. Victoriosissimus igitur martyr Anastasius, vicesima secunda

625 ianuariarum die, indictione prima, anno septimo decimo imperii Heraclii piissimi, et quinto decimo Constantini filii eius suum agonisma pro Ihesu Christi nomine summa tenus provexit qui cum patre et spiritu sancto vivit et regnat per infinita saecula saeculorum. Amen.

630 **41.** Sane quid haec sequenti die fuerit assecutum nec scriptoris pigritia, nec auditorum desidia fiat obnubilandum. Quibusdam namque carcere inclusorum duobus se alterno colloquio affantibus, unus alteri dixit: "Scisne," inquit, "qualiter advenientes canes iuxta corpus illius monachi circumsederint, nequaquam videlicet contin

635 gere volentes, sed velut obsequiali pervigilio ei invigilantes. Quos

---

615 tollendam sacratissimam glebam E   615-616 sacratissime PI   617 comedentes] et *add.* TX   corpus] vero *add.* E   618 intactus I   Praetiosa enim] Pratio sacrum P   enim] est *add.* B *om.* TXG   619 eorum] et *add.* BK   620 his TX   permisit E   beati] Anastasii *add.* B   621 scilicet *om.* EH   Gesdin KE deiesdin H Iesdim T   623 deposuerunt E Tunc marzabanas iussit eum capitalem subire sententiam *add.* C   624 vicesima] et *add.* TX   625 ianuarioarum I   decimo anno E   625-626 imperii–decimo *om.* H   626 suum *om.* PTX   626-627 agonisma] gratanter suscepit *add.* P 627 summa–provexit *om.* P   cum] Deo *add.* P   629 Amen *Hic des.* JCI Item miraculum eiusdem *add.* KE   630 hac T^{corr.}X et E   634 circumsederunt BHTX *sed cf.* Videsne ... qualiter sis *supra l. 349* circumsederent KE 635 sed–invigilantes *om.* PHTX *sed cf.* g

21. Ps 116.15.
22. Cf. Ps 34.20.

ego quidem minime recedentes, et nullomodo contingentes, duabus horis attentissime conspexi." Cui alter: "Et ego," inquit, "vesperi e carcere domum abiens, quasi stellam pavimento superlucentem vidi. Et dum gressum concitarem ut quid esset hoc scirem, michi iam iamque appropinquaturo stella nusquam comparuit. Corpus vero illius monachi pavimento accubabat."

42. Haec igitur custodes ergastuli sese propria lingua invicem alloquentes, valde ammirabantur. Quidam vero ibidem carceratorum christicolae non ignari videlicet persicae linguae eosdem auscultabant. Ex quibus duo cum aliis plurimis dimissi, post interfectionem Chosroae, in sanctam civitatem venerunt. Quibus et beatissimus martyr Ihesu Christi Anastasius, dum esset cum eis in carcere et de sui agonis consumatione et de eorum liberatione, et etiam praefati regis ruina, omnino praedixerat, dicens: "Minime vos dilectissimi fratres lateat, me quidem crastina die affore finiendum; vos quoque paucis interiectis diebus dimittendos adesse; iniquum vero atque malignissimum regem interficiendum fore. Sed vestrae[23] fraternitati nimium abflagito, ut cum Deo prosperante sanctam civitatem intraveritis, in monasterium quod appellatur beati Anastasii introeatis; et haec omnia meo abbati ac fratrum collegio plenissime referatis." Ipsi igitur haec omnia a sanctissimo Dei martyre praemoniti, rei quoque gestum suis oculis intuiti, Deum quidem glorifi-

636 ego] ergo E   recedens T$^{corr.}$X   637 aptissime E   vesperi e] vespere E   639 gressu P *non legi potest* H   sciret T   iam *om.* E   640 appropinquanti E 411   641 accubat KE   642 sese] cum B   646 Chosdroae B Chosrohae E   647 cum eis *om.* TX   carcerem *codd.* carcere T$^{corr.}$ 648 suis T   consumationem *codd.* consumatione T$^{corr.}$X   et–liberatione *om.* B   et *om.* TX   etiam] de *add.* E   649 ruinam TX   Minime] neminem TX   651 iniquissimum E   652 malignum E   652-653 vestrae fraternitatis societatem E vestrae fraternitatis P vestrae clementiam fraternitatis T$^{corr.}$X   abflagito] rogito E   properante E   655 ac] et BP   ac–collegio] eorumque omnium collegio fratrum E   657 gestu E   intuitu BPT intuitus T$^{corr.}$X intuito E

23. This phrase is added in the Latin text. The unusual use of the dative with *abflagito*—if indeed that is the correct reading; neither *flagito* nor any other compound forms are found in the text—might explain the variants as attempts at corrections.

cantem se glorificantes unanimiter glorificaverunt. Ac beati Anastasii praecepto obsecuti, haec quoque omnia pleno et veridico relatu
660 nobis enarraverunt.

43. Multotiens autem memoratus monachus qui et eius pedisequus
ac demum sepultor fuerat, in praedicto beati Sergii monasterio ali-
quandiu mansit, excogitans atque secum contractans, quam difficul-
ter ac periculose ad suum a quo missus fuerat abbatem rediturus
665 adesset. Interea praelapsis quasi decem diebus, prima videlicet ianuarii mensis die, piissimum imperatorem Heraclium cum suo exercitu illuc venisse contigit. Quos cum ipse monachus aspexisset,
infinito gaudio est repletus, atque eos latine[24] statim est allocutus;
ipsi autem eum quid ibidem faceret interrogaverunt. Eo autem se-
670 riatim singula referente, Deum omnipotentem unanimiter glorificantes, ut pro eius custodia atque defensione eos comitaretur, eum
commonuerunt. Quandiu igitur morati sunt in Perside, honorifice
cum illis ipse quoque permansit; eosque digredientes assecutus, securo gressu Armeniam pertransiit.

675 **44.** Et sic tandem circumvoluto unius anni spatio ad suum monasterium regressus, haec omnia suo abbati puro ac diligentissimo relatu sicut et viderat enarravit. Colobium quoque sancti Anastasii in
quo martyrizatus fuerat ei offerens, hoc praeclarum et omni laude
dignissimum miraculum retulit. Dum esset, inquiens, in monasterio
680 beati martyris Sergii in quo ut praediximus corpus beati Anastasii

---

658 glorificantem se *om.* KEH glorificantem *om.* TX   Ac] Hoc E   658-
660 Ac–enarraverunt *om.* H   658-659 beato Anastasio EPT beati Anastasii
T^{corr.}X   659 praeceptum B praeceptis E   obsecutis KPT obsecuti T^{corr.}X
quoque *om.* E   662 demum sepultor] demonum persecutor E   663 excogi-
tans] et cogitans PHTX   665 prolapsis E   666 mensi P   669 eum *om.*
E   autem] itaque KEHT ita P   670-671 unanimiter glorificantes] una voce
glorificantes K unaglorificantes E unianimiter glorificantes T   672 moratis
P   673 ipsi P   676 regressus] reversus B   abbati suo *transpos.* TX   di-
ligentissime T   677 et *om.* K eviderat H

---

24. The translator and the editor of this version, like the early translator,
did not understand that ῥωμαϊστί meant the language of the "Romans," that
is Greek, contrasted to the language spoken by the companion of Anastasius,
which was Syriac most likely. See above, p. 298.

reposuerat, quendam ibi commorantium fratrum immundo spiritu atrociter fuisse vexatum; seque ab eiusdem monasterii praeposito rogatum sanctissimi Anastasii colobium eundem infirmum indui concessisse. Sicque statim Dei omnipotentis gratia, eum a daemo-
685 niaca infestatione liberatum fuisse, praestante Domino nostro Ihesu Christo, qui cum patre et spiritu sancto distinctis personis una essentia, maiestas eadem, aeternum imperium, et nunc et semper et in saecula saeculorum. Amen.

682-683 seque–rogatum *om.* H   682 praepositum T praeposito T*corr.* 684 consensisse TX concesse G   eum *om.* TX   686 est *add.* B   686-687 una–imperium] una est eadem gloria aeternum imperium E

3

THE ROMAN MIRACLE
BHL 412

In preparing this edition of the Roman Miracle (*BHL* 412), I have considered the evidence provided by all sixteen manuscripts listed in the *Conspectus Siglorum*. They are arranged in the stemma codicum discussed below. I have omitted from consideration Fiesole's early twelfth-century legendary, since its text of the Roman Miracle was almost certainly copied from Y, and six late *codices descripti*.[1] All these manuscripts are described in the "Descriptive List of Manuscripts."

The Roman Miracle was not subjected to the radical revisions worked upon the versions of the Passion of St. Anastasius, perhaps because it was not used for liturgical reading.[2] However, the text of the Miracle has come down to us as a highly unstable text, riddled with countless, if minor, textual variations. There are constant attempts at correcting the Latin, but, except for V, none of these is significant. Some of these changes and corrections may result from contamination, as hagiographic compilers may have consulted more than one source in putting their collections together. Such cross-fertilization may also explain inconsistent manuscript groupings that frustrate the design of a fully satisfactory stemma codicum.

There are no common mistakes to suggest that all the surviving witnesses originated from a common archetype. The omission of

---

1. These are (all from Rome): BAV, S. Pietro D 190 s. XV, which is closely related to T and G; Biblioteca alessandrina 91, a copy of A; Vallicelliana H 9, copied from L; Vallicelliana H 18 (s. XVI-XVII inc.) copied from M; Vallicelliana H 25 copied from P by Antonio Bosio; Vallicelliana H 28 (s. XV-XVI) copied from L.

2. I have not found the text of the Roman Miracle marked for liturgical reading in any manuscript.

the phrase *nomine Theopentus* (l. 10) by PHMTGAFYUSD segregates these witnesses into one separate branch (=[b]).

There is no similarly conclusive evidence showing that OLNV go back to a common subarchetype. OLNV are joined in common error by the omissions of *apostolus* (l. 48) and of the phrase *Et praecepit Nazarenus* (l. 162). The latter, however, is an eye-skip mistake and could be explained as having occurred independently; the significance of the omission of the single word *apostolus* is diminished by the fact that G, a manuscript of the [b] branch, also omits it. Other errors shared by this group furnish similarly inconclusive evidence.[3] I have constructed a bipartite stemma, which, however, must be considered tentative. LNV could arguably be placed as a sub-group breaking off from the top of the [b] branch, further isolating the only non-Italian witness of the Miracle text (O) in a way parallel to the stemma of *BHL* 411a.

The [a] Branch

The oldest witness, O, presents the text closest to the subarchetype, and the one that has suffered the least corruption. This important manuscript, the only non-Italian witness of the Miracle, is discussed more fully in the "Descriptive List" and also in Chapter IV.

LNV are joined by a few common errors.[4] The relations within the sub-group, however, are not clear. On the one hand, some evidence proposes the grouping of NV against L;[5] on the other, there is support for the grouping LN against V.[6] The grouping of LN against VN is given additional weight by the contents of the legendaries in which the Miracle text occurs. L and N share an interest in texts connected with Spoleto: L includes *BHL* 7453 (S. Sabinus of Spoleto), *BHL* 3677 (S. Gregorius of Spoleto); N contains *BHL* 7451 (S. Sabinus of Spoleto) and also *BHL* 3677 (S. Gregorius of Spoleto). The textual and the contextual evidence taken together suggest the grouping of L and N as parallel witnesses of the dif-

---

3. (l. 167) sapientia viva] via sapientiae ONV; (l. 214) omnibus] hominibus OLNV MF.

4. For example, the common omission of *me coniuravi* (ll. 111-112).

5. For example, (l. 257) milites–est in *om.* NV; (l. 123) caderet frangere N caderet et frangeret V.

6. For example, the omission by LN of *turbis* in l. 184.

fusion of the Miracle text to the northeast and southeast of Rome, an area to which they are connected both by their contents and by their script.[7] V, on the other hand, which constitutes part of the passionary of S. Maria in Trastevere, remains a witness to the presence of the text in Rome.

The text of the Roman Miracle in V has undergone substantial editorial revisions.[8] Two important variants in V's text deserve special notice. One is the addition *quod et sancti andreae dicitur* in cap. 1 to identify more fully the monastery *sancti Cassiani* (l. 20) in which Theopentus places his daughter. Although there is no other evidence to support the identification of "S. Cassianus" with "S. Andrea," the recent suggestion that V in fact is part of the legendarium of S. Maria in Trastevere would lend credibility to the information provided in this addition.[9] The other important variant is V's *alapam* while all other manuscripts have *palmam* (l. 151). Clearly, *alapam* is the more precise word and would have to be preferred as the *lectio difficilior* under normal circumstances. As the Greek passage is missing, there is no way to ascertain whether V's editor could have emended his Latin text by direct access to the Greek.[10] It seems prudent to allow the possibility that he had access to the Greek text, or perhaps to another Latin copy no longer surviving, although a clever emendation on the editor's

7. N's script is a Bari-type Beneventan, which comprises the southeastern portion of the Italian peninsula; L's script suggests that it was written in central Italy.

8. See, for example (ll. 33-37) anima ... et dicit] Anima enim orthodoxa et catholica habet intra se fidem quam dominus in evangelio commendans dicens: Si habueritis fidem ut granum synapis dicetis monti transferte in mare et transfertur, et habens purae fidei conscientiam cum fiducia currit ad divinum auxilium et dicit: "Exaudi deus orationem meam" ... ; or (ll. 283-286) nec pro ... Secutus] sed dei virtute qui est mirabilis in sanctis suis. Nec corporis vitam religio complectebatur humana, sed regni celestis gloria dimicabat. Hic enim nec tirannicae subici potuit voluntati nec laqueo collum praebere formidavit. O pastor bonus, o martir fortissimus, magnus est quem nos nimis parva voce laudamus. Iste secutus ... . These two cases show V's editor revising, not always clearly, the confused original.

9. See the commentary in n. 7 to my edition.

10. Perhaps the addition of *turbis* in V (l. 184), which had been omitted by LN, is further evidence that V had access to the Greek, or at least to another Latin manuscript.

part, in keeping with his attempts to clarify and improve the text he was copying, cannot be completely excluded. There is, in addition, some slight evidence, beginning in cap. 9, suggesting contamination between V and YSD.[11]

The [b] Branch

The manuscripts at the top of the [b] branch include its oldest Roman witnesses—P, the legendary from St. Peter's Basilica; and H, from the Ospedale di S. Salvatore—as well as other witnesses connected with the city. All of these manuscripts, except for the late M, also contain the "Roman" version of the *Passio*, *BHL* 411a. A, attributed to the Romano-Umbrian area, and F, from Arezzo, are the result of the movement of the text of the Roman Miracle further afield, and particularly toward the northwest and Tuscany. The Miracle is attached in these two witnesses to the *BHL* 408(s) version of the text, which circulated in central and northern Italy. The closely related lower group of witnesses—YUSD—could be called the Florentine version of the text. Despite its stemmatic separation from the archetype, however, this final group includes the oldest witness of the Miracle text, Y, a manuscript from the Badia of Florence copied perhaps as early as the late tenth century. None of these manuscripts contains the *Passio*.

P, the important legendary from St. Peter's Basilica, is joined to H and M by a few common errors.[12] The segregation of HM from P is suggested by a few shared variants, but it does not appear certain.[13] P transmits the most correct version of the text in this branch of the stemma.

A series of common errors delineates very clearly the group of manuscripts T(X)GAFYUSD [=f].[14] Within this cluster, a discer-

---

11. (l. 238) Dominus *om.* VYSD; (l. 244) sicut antea *om.* VAYSD, etc. (U's text ends with cap. 8).

12. Most important are (l. 165) non–flectere *om.* PM cepit H; and (l. 284) subire] subripere PHM.

13. For example, (l. 31) exponere] quaerere PM; (l. 190) tutare eam] extinguere VHM; (l. 278) Debacchabatur] Exvacuabatur HM.

14. (l. 2) quarti *add.* V TGAFYUSDX; (l. 31) exponere] aut exponere TGAY FUS aut ponere D anteponere X; (l. 170) requiem] veniam TGAFYUSDX.

nible textual group is formed by TXG.[15] The textual relationship among these three codices is paralled by their association with the *BHL* 411a version of the *Passio*. They all originate, as well, from the Roman area, T from the church "SS. Johannis et Pauli de urbe," G perhaps from S. Pancrazio or its possession in Roman Tuscia, S. Michele in Subripa. X, the self-proclaimed copy of the legendary of S. Cecilia (=Q),[16] took the Roman Miracle, however, as well as a large portion of *BHL* 411a from T or a copy of T.

The other well-defined manuscript group in this branch is constituted by AFYUSD,[17] whose stemmatic relationship is confirmed by these manuscripts' ties to the Tusco-Umbrian geographic area already mentioned above. A, the twelfth-century legendary from the Ambrosian Library on which Poncelet's edition of the Miracle was based, has been tied by its hagiological program to F.[18] F is a gigantic, decorated legendary from the fourth quarter of the eleventh century whose origin has been placed in southeast Tuscany or western Umbria and specifically in the region centering on the bishoprics of Chiusi and Orvieto.[19] The close relationship revealed by the sanctoral of these two legendaries is confirmed by the text of the *Miraculum S. Anastasii*, for A and F clearly form a sub-branch of their own as they share many peculiar errors.[20]

15. TXG is defined by such common errors as: (l. 23) impleret] compleret TXG; (l. 40) vir *om.* TXG; (l. 74) est qui possit me] me potest TX potest me G; (l. 195) Pridie–kalendas] Igitur TXG; (l. 239) et alia multa *om.* TXG. TX is further segregated by, for example, (l. 151) palmam] palmas in faciem TX.

16. See pp. 301-303.

17. E.g. (l. 35) pectoris] corporis AFYUSD; (l. 87) cynophagum] signofagum AFYUSD; (l. 108) te dicis *om.* N AFYUSD.

18. Garrison, *Studies in the History of Mediaeval Italian Painting* III, 281 n. 3. A is also dated to the "third or fourth quarter of the [eleventh] century" by Garrison, who, however, does not subject it to as thorough a study as F. The style of decoration also links these two codices.

19. Garrison, *Studies* III, 281-284. Garrison's dating to the "fourth quarter of the eleventh century" (p. 281) is more precise than a broader twelfth-century date, but is based on both script and decoration.

20. Most notably, (l. 67) ipsum sanctum] ipsa in sancta AF; (l. 67) sicut (non) *add.* AF; (l. 72) ad cruciandum *om.* AF; (l. 101) calcaret] collocaret AF; (ll. 186-187) et hominum] omnium sanctorum AF.

Y, U, S, and D originated in the Florentine area. They present a text that is clearly distinct, and restricted geographically; their further segregation into the groups USD and SD is made quite evident by common errors.[21] These relationships are underscored by the diffusion of the *Passio*: A and F contain the *Passio* (*BHL* 408), while YUSD do not. Given the close affinity of the group YUSD and Y's antiquity, the question arises whether Y could be the direct model of USD (i.e. [l]). While possible, this hypothesis appears to be countered by at least a couple of readings.[22]

The stemma expresses the relationships discussed above:

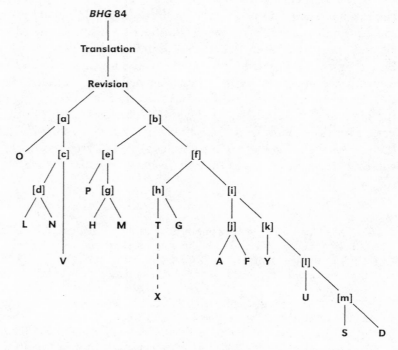

21. For YUSD and USD—very closely related groups—see, for example, (l. 19) quia-Dei *om.* YUSD; (l. 34) intra] infra USD; (l. 101) illa] in illius USD; (ll. 110-119) Nolite-dicebat *om.* YUSD; (l. 139) hostis-generis *om.* YUSD. For SD, (l. 52) ibi *om.* SD; (l. 82) martyris *om.* SD. The omission of ll. 89-91 (Et violenter-coronam meam) is due to an eye-skip mistake.

22. (l. 142) iudicare] vivos et mortuos et *add.* H AFUSD (but the addition can be explained by liturgical echo); (l. 172) hominibus] hominis US hominem D; (l. 172) unigenite] piissime USD.

I proposed in Chapter IV that the Miracle's text as it has come down to us in all its Latin witnesses represents a version already significantly revised by the addition of the last chapter, the probable elimination of the original preface, and most likely also a correction of the text. I argue that this first, early revision was accomplished at the time when the text of the Miracle was added to that of the Roman version of the *Passio S. Anastasii* (*BHL* 411a) to create the *libellus* of a Roman martyr, emphasizing the miraculous cure of the afflicted girl that took place in the complex of St. Anastasius *ad Aquas Salvias*. My examination and collation of all manuscript witnesses in preparation for the critical edition of this text have shown that the text of the Roman Miracle continued to be revised and corrected. Some of the witnesses, and most especially H, an early witness, were inexpertly copied. The large number of eye-skip omissions suggests great carelessness on the part of scribes. Many witnesses incorporate various attempts at improving the text throughout the centuries. V represents the most drastic effort, but all manuscripts to various degrees are riddled with minor textual variants aiming both at improving the text and also shortening it (e.g. by the omission of *et, autem* and similar inconsequential words). These would have to be described not as errors but as willful changes.

The two-sided stemma codicum constructed above therefore cannot be relied upon mechanically to establish the text because many variants are not the result of common error, and do not appear to fit into the stemmatic model. These mistakes—both willful and negligent—occur most frequently in the [b] branch. I have therefore given greater weight to the [a] branch of the stemma as represented by the manuscript from Orléans (=O), which appears the least corrupted. P, the manuscript at the top of the [b] branch, has been the other principal witness for this edition. Since the inclusion of the extensive *apparatus criticus* would be typographically distracting and critically unnecessary, in most cases when my edition follows one of these two primary witnesses, I have included only any deviation of the other. In cases where I consider the text of O and P to be corrupt, my *apparatus criticus* justifies my choice, by referring to other manuscripts as necessary. The Greek source, which has been kept at hand in the establishment of the Latin text, is frequently cited to support my text. I have noted the major differences between the two linguistic versions in the notes. There are some Latin passages that make little sense, and others that are obviously marred by omissions; I have noted these in the body of the text and discussed them in the notes. My chapter divisions follow those of Flusin's Greek text.

Conspectus Siglorum

A   Milan, Biblioteca ambrosiana B 49 Inf.

D   Florence, Biblioteca medicea laurenziana, Aediles 135

F   Florence, Biblioteca nazionale centrale II I 412

G   Biblioteca apostolica vaticana, Chigianus P VIII 15

H   Rome, Archivio di Stato, S. Salvatore 996

L   Rome, Biblioteca vallicelliana Tomus V

M   Biblioteca apostolica vaticana, Archivio di S. Maria Maggiore 1 (A)

N   Naples, Biblioteca nazionale VIII B 6

O   Orléans, Bibliothèque municipale 342 (290)

P   Biblioteca apostolica vaticana, Archivio di S. Pietro A 2

S   Rome, Biblioteca nazionale Vittorio Emanuele II, Sessoriani 5 (alias XXIX, olim 118)

T   Biblioteca apostolica vaticana, Vaticanus latinus 1195

V   Biblioteca apostolica vaticana, Vaticanus latinus 1193

U   Florence, Biblioteca medicea laurenziana, Plutei XX, Codex I

X   Biblioteca apostolica vaticana, Vaticanus latinus 6075

Y   Florence, Biblioteca medicea laurenziana, Conventi soppressi 182

g   *BHG* 89, Flusin ed.

INCIPIT MIRACULUM[1] ANASTASII INCLITI MARTYRIS quod factum est temporibus beatissimi papae Constantini urbis Romae, et temporibus[2] piissimi imperatoris Anastasii Constantinopolitani indictione undecima et duodecima, in monasterio quod appellatur Aqua Salvia.[3] In nomine Domini Dei et Salvatoris Iesu Christi.

1. Imperante domino nostro piissimo perpetuo[4] augusto Anastasio magno imperatore anno primo et post consulatum eiusdem serenitatis anno primo, temporibus sanctissimi et beatissimi et apostolici summi pontificis Constantini papae urbis Romae, **[2]** fuit quidam episcopus nomine Theopentus,[5] natione Syrus, de civitate quae ap-

---

1 Incipiunt miracula P   2 beatissimi *om.* P *cf.* ἀγιωτάτου (Flusin 1.19)   2-4 et–duodecima *om.* P   4-5 Aquas Salvias O *cf.* ll. 48-49   5 In–Christi *om.* P *cf.* Κύριε Εὐλόγησον (Flusin *Tit.*, p. 165)   6 nostro *om.* P   7 post consulatum] consulatu O *cf.* μετὰ τὴν ὑπατείαν   8 et[1] ac P   et[2] *om.* P   9 fuit *om.* O *cf.* Ἦν τις ἐπίσκοπος   10 nomine Theopentus *om.* P

1. It is not certain whether the Greek source used the singular θαῦμα or the plural θαύματα in its title (cf. Flusin's *apparatus criticus* and note 1). I would suggest a different interpretation for ἐν μερικῇ διηγήσει than given by Flusin ("Relation partielle ..."). μερικός can also mean "particular, individual, special" (Liddell and Scott, s.v., II). The writer surely could not mean that this is a partial narrative, an abbreviation or extract from a longer version of the Miracle. Rather, the title refers to the fact that this is a special miracle, because it took place in Rome most likely, rather than because it was one miracle out of many. The Greek subtitle, περὶ τῆς θυγατρὸς ... , might also recall the organization and titles of the ancient miracles (Flusin I, 116-153). See below (n. 20) for another reference to the ancient miracles.

2. Only O retains *indictione undecima et duodecima*, which I believe represents a relic of the original translation, corresponding to the Greek τῆς παρούσης δωδεκάτης ἰνδικτιῶνος.

3. The precise location of the Miracle in the Roman monastery is not found in the Greek manuscripts.

4. *Perpetuo* does not correspond at all to εἰρηνοποιοῦντος, which should have been translated with *pacificus* or the like. A textual corruption?

5. The omission of *nomine Theopentus* in the entire [b] branch is the major distinction between the two textual branches of the Latin text. The name of the bishop is also omitted in the transmission of the Greek text. The preservation of the bishop's name is evidence of the generally greater faithfulness to the original text by some of the witnesses of the [a] branch.

pellatur Constantia.[6] Qui ante istos modicos annos deveniens in hac civitate romana, habens filiam parvulam quam dare visus est in monasterio ad discendas sacras litteras. Quae cum erudita fuisset in psalmis et hymnis et canticis et lectionibus, et facta fuisset puel-
15 la in vultu decora et pulchra nimis, multi eam in matrimonio postulare a praedicto patre eius voluerunt, non tantum pro specie et pulchritudine puellae, sed magis propter divitias patris eius. Erat enim vir venerabilis episcopus locuples valde. Quod considerans vir venerabilis episcopus pater eius, quia bona res esset ancilla Dei
20 praevidens, consecravit eam in monasterio sancti Cassiani[7] inter ancillas Christi. Et coepit ipse episcopus substantiam suam erogare pauperibus et per loca pia.

11 ante isto modico anno O ante modico anno P ante hos modicos annos LV cf. πρὸ τούτων τῶν βραχέων χρόνων   12 hanc civitatem romam O cf. ἐνταῦ-θα ἐν τῇ Ῥωμαίων πόλει   13 Qui O   14 et⁴] cum *add.* P   16-17 pro-puellae] pro specie pulchritudine + *ras.* P

6. Constantia (Constantina) d'Osrohene was a stop on the translation of the relics of Anastasius (Flusin 3.2; I, 101; II, 374 and n. 114). Had Theopentus become familiar with Anastasius's cult in his native city? If so, this episode would provide an example of the direct importation of cults by the oriental population of Rome.

7. This monastery is identified by both Ferrari (*Early Roman monasteries*, pp. 182-89) and Sansterre (*Les moines grecs* I, 81-82) as the "S. Cassiani" near St. Lawrence Outside the Walls, which Pope Leo IV (847-855) joined to St. Stephen and turned over to a community of Greek monks. In 807 it is listed as housing Latin monks, and before then, at the time of the Miracle, one must assume that it housed Latin nuns. There is no evidence that at this time there were any communities in Rome exclusively for Greek women, and therefore only a Latin convent would have been available for Theopentus's daughter. See Sansterre, *Les moines grecs* I, 81-82 and pertinent notes. There is no support in Ferrari's survey for the addition in V that S. Cassianus was called also "S. Andrea," and it seems unlikely that such knowledge about an important monastic center would not have been preserved. There is a little-documented "Monasterium S. Andreae de Biberatica," whose existence is attested in the early ninth century (and it was founded earlier) and which housed nuns in the fourteenth century (Ferrari, *Early Roman Monasteries*, pp. 49-50); one wonders whether this may have been identified with the earlier S. Cassianus in the Vatican codex. For V, and the contention that it is part of the passionary of S. Maria in Trastevere, see above pp. 341-342.

3. Et dum impleret in monasterio puella menses decem et octo,[8]
ille invidus et hostis antiquus, humani generis inimicus, immisit se
25   in puellam, et coepit eam vexare atque stimulare. Quod multi venientes ad praedictum episcopum, patrem puellae, dicebant, quia[9]
"Faciemus phylacteria et eiciemus istud daemonium de hac puella."
Ille autem coepit coartari nimis. Sed quia necessitas imminebat
internis doloribus, ...[10] †ipsa sibi appetit Dominum maiestatis,
30   nec enim egrediens a Dei consilio mereri contempta secreta non
vadit ad ludi magistrum exponere causam negotiorum, qualiter iudicem invicem possit adire eremum†; sed hoc non facit anima christiana. Anima vero christiana quascumque tribulationes vel tempta-
tiones fuerit absoluta,[11] habens intra se fidem, intra conscientiam
35   cordis sui et intra speluncam pectoris sui collocat sibi dignum con-
sistorium; facit sibi chartam conscientiam, stilum gemitum et lacrimas atramentum. Exstitit[12] interno et proximo consilio et dicit:[13]

24 invidus hostis humani generis inimicus P *cf.* g   25 puella P   Quia P
27 eicimus P   istum P   28 coartari] evitare P   imminebat *omm. codd.*
exc. O *cf.* ἐπειδὴ ἦν ἀνάγκη ἐν ταῖς ἔνδοθεν ὀδύναις   29 doloris P   30
mereri] querer (?) P   31 exponere] quaerere P   32 invicem *om.* P   eremum *om.* P   hoc *om.* P   34 intra se *om.* O   fidem *om.* P   36 faciet
P   carta O   stilo O   37 lacrimis O

8. Because the manifestation of the girl's possession begins in September
713 (see l. 58), this detail establishes that she entered the monastery in March 712.
This date must refer to the time she first went there to study and before her
father decided to consecrate her *in monasterio S. Cassiani inter ancillas Christi*.
It would be difficult to understand a trip to the baths after her consecration.

9. The translation of ὅτι with *quia* is a striking indication of the priority
of the Greek.

10. The Latin, which makes no sense, has a lacuna here as the Greek indicates; the Greek text itself then omits the following, confused Latin passage
(*ipsa ... vero christiana*).

11. The Latin text does not parallel the Greek, and the problematic *fuerit
absoluta* does not seem to correspond to παρατετύχησαν. There is perhaps
a lacuna in the middle of this Latin passage.

12. A poor translation of ἐπέστη, but an attempt most likely to translate
its parts (ἐπί = ex; ἔστη = stitit).

13. The similarity in the Latin phrasing (*dicit–consilio et*) suggests that the
lacuna in the following Greek text results from an eye-skip in the Greek.

"Exaudi Deus orationem meam, auribus percipe lacrimas meas, ne sileas a me."[14]

40   **4.** Sic namque et ille vir venerabilis episcopus, cuius filia vexabatur a diabolo, exstitit interno consilio et apud se dixit: "Surgam et eam ad Dominum nostrum Iesum Christum et ad sanctum martyrem eius Anastasium; potens est enim curare meam filiam a daemoni vexatione. Surrexit vir venerabilis episcopus habens plurimam

45   fidem in Christo et in sancto Anastasio martyre, et assumens filiam suam habentem spiritum immundum, et venit in mansionem sanctae Dei genetricis semperque virginis Mariae, ubi sanctus ac beatus Paulus apostolus decollatus est in loco qui appellatur Aqua Salvia, ubi requiescunt venerabiles reliquiae beati martyris Anasta-

50   sii, et quia in ipso monasterio mulier non ingreditur, iuxta monasterium autem est basilica beati Iohannis Baptistae et praecursoris,[15] intravit ipse episcopus et coepit ibi esse in orationem;[16] adsumens secum presbyterum et diaconum, et postulans abbatem ipsius monasterii, ut reliquiae sancti martyris Anastasii adduceren-

55   tur in basilica sancti Iohannis, ut et omnis congregatio pro ipsa puella genua flecterent et postularent Dominum nostrum Iesum Christum et beatum martyrem Anastasium. Et dum haec fierent die kalendas octobris istius duodecimae indictionis,[17] tunc adductae sunt reliquiae venerabilis martyris, id est caput eius; et positae

60   super altare. Coepit itaque postulare ipse praedictus episcopus ab-

---

41 surgamus et eamus O *cf. g*   43 eius *om.* P   daemonio P   44 maximam P   48 apostolus *om.* O   48-49 Aquas Salvias O *cf.* ᾿Ακουασάλβια 49 reliquias P   53 diaconem O   abbati O ab abbati P abbatem *alii codd.* 54 ut reliquiae] et reliquias P   58 duodecimo O   59 positum est P

14. *Exaudi–meam*: Ps 54.2; *auribus–meas*: Ps 39.13 (*iuxta LXX*); *ne–a me*: Ps 28.1 (*iuxta LXX*).

15. Sansterre uses this passage, and indeed the entire text, to support the view that the monastery through this chapel also functioned as a parish (*Les moines grecs* I, 108).

16. The Greek text makes it clear that Theopentus established himself and his entourage—consisting of pious men, priests, and deacons—in this church.

17. 1 October 713.

batem ipsius monasterii ut acciperet portiunculam de sanctis ac venerabilibus reliquiis ut suspenderet in cervice filiae suae. Et datus est ei unus de venerabilibus dentibus sancti martyris, quem et suspenderunt in collo eius.

65   **5.** Quod ipse nequissimus inimicus per quamlibet occasionem fecit ut periret[18] et non paruit. Et quid multa? Dum adductum fuisset ipsum sanctum ac venerabile caput in sancto altare,[19] sicut supra dictum est, coepit daemon conturbare puellam non dans ei requiem die noctuque et coepit ipse daemon per os puellae loqui
70   blasphemiam in martyres Christi et in servos Dei, dicens: "Quid me adduxistis ad Anastasium, cynophagum[20] istum? Meus enim erat, sed dedit corpus suum ad cruciandum pro Nazareno. Non me potest eicere, quia imperator sum et coronam habeo, et phalangas et patricios habeo et non est qui possit me eicere de isto corpore."
75   Et quidam de congregatione dicit ei: "Eiciet te Dominus noster Iesus Christus et sanctus Anastasius." Daemon autem dicebat: "Non me eiciet Nazarenus, quia illius est caelum, meum autem est aer et terra." Et interrogabant[21] eum fratres dicentes: "Dic nobis, nequissime, quomodo ausus es introire in vas consecratum, ubi corpus et
80   sanguis Domini nostri Iesu Christi introivit?" Daemon respondit: "Quidam me coniuravit ut ingrederer in isto corpore, et ideo ingressus sum."[22] Eicientes[23] autem caput beati martyris Anastasii

---

61-62 sancta ac venerabiles reliquias P   62 cervice] collo O *cf.* τραχήλῳ *et* (l. 64) collo (αὐχένι)   63 de] ex P   quod P   66 Et *om.* P   Dum] autem *add.* P   67 sicut] ut P   70 martirem O *cf.* μάρτυρας   80 domini nostri *om.* P

18. *periret* does not correspond accurately to ἐκπέσῃ. The same peculiar translation is found below (l. 228).

19. The Latin text is shortened here. The omission of τεθῆναι might explain the ablative *in sancto altare.*

20. A calque on the Greek word, which may be, in its turn, a deliberate echo of the ancient Greek miracle collection (Flusin 16.18; I, 149).

21. The Latin text does not follow the Greek closely. Note, for example, the use of direct discourse for the Greek indirect.

22. The Latin omits καὶ ταῦτα ἀκηκοότες παρ' αὐτοῦ.

23. *eicientes* is not an accurate rendition of ἐκβαλόντες in this context. See above, pp. 129-130.

in parapside argenteo, imposuerunt super caput puellae. Mittentes
autem in turibulo thimiama, daemon dicebat: "Ne faciatis hoc quia
85 foetet mihi." Et quidam de congregatione adduxit lutum et odora-
tus dixit: "Ecce odorem meum, nam et ego talem desidero." Clamabat iterum et dicebat: "Non me potest eicere cynophagus iste,
quia meus erat. Et ego coniurationem accepi super coronam meam.
Et violenter ingressus sum, violenter non egredior de hoc corpore,
90 quia non possum confringere coniurationem quae data est mihi
super coronam meam."

6. Nos autem interrogavimus eum dicentes: "Quis est ille qui dedit
tibi coniurationem?"[24] Daemon repondit: "Non dico vobis amicum meum." Nos autem coniurantes eum in nomine Domini nostri
95 Iesu Christi et per iudicium aeternum ut recederet de ipso corpore,
aut diceret quomodo ingressus est. Et daemon coepit dicere quia:
"Ille adulescens, qui eam in matrimonio postulabat, ipse ambulavit
in Sicilia ad quendam[25] in loco qui dicitur Marathodis,[26] et ipse
fecit in nomine meo coniurationem et ligavit in folia fici et adduxit
100 eam apud se. Et dum ambularet istud corpus in balneum,[27] iactavit eam ante ipsam in via; et dum ea calcaret ipsam ligaturam illa
hora ingressus sum in eam et[28] in illa die non eam elisi, neque vo-
lutavi; fuit enim dies secunda mensis augusti, indictionis undeci-
mae; et ipso mense non eam vexavi, neque stimulavi, neque voluta-

---

83 argenteum P   Mittens P   86 tale O   96 Et *om.* P   98 Sicilia O Si-
ciliam *cet. codd. cf.* Σικελίᾳ   locum P   100 valneum P   101 ipsa ligatura
P   103 die P   104 et] in *add.* P   stimulavi neque *om.* O

24. The Latin text suggests the emendation of ἐξουσίαν to ἐξωμοσίαν
(Flusin 6.2).
25. φαρμακὸν καταμένοντα is omitted, helping to explain the corruption
of *in loco* to *in locum*.
26. This locality cannot be identified.
27. The unusually awkward phrasing may be the result of a faulty Greek
original.
28. A long lacuna occurs in the corresponding Greek text. Hence, it is
the Latin version that allows the precise dating of the demonic possession,
on 2 August 713, and the resulting first demonic manifestation on 2 September.

105 vi. In secunda autem die mensis septembris ingressus sum in eam
et coepi cum ea ludere atque exagitare et stimulare." Et quidam de
fratribus dicebat ei: "Nequissime, maledicte, immunde, quomodo
cum te dicis esse imperatorem, coronam te dicis habere, quomodo
manifestas[29] ligatum te esse in folia fici?" Daemon respondit:
110 "Nolite mihi iniuriam facere quia imperator sum et regnare adhuc
habeo. Ideo accepi coniurationem.[30] Per coronam meam me coniuravi quia habeo patricios et phalangas et ecce hic in circuitu meo
adstant, et non possum canones[31] meos solvere. Sed si vultis ut
exeam de isto corpore, ambulate ac solvite ipsas ligaturas et ipsas
115 coniurationes; et exeo de hoc corpore." Et praedictus vir venerabilis episcopus una cum congregatione dixerunt: "Non dimittimus
Dominum nostrum Iesum Christum et istum beatum martyrem
Anastasium, et quaerimus ligaturas daemonum et hominum." Daemon autem dicebat: "Et quid speratis? Anastasius non est hic; in
120 orientem enim ambulavit, quia amicum quendam habet ibi qui et
basilicam ei fabricare visus est. Qui et reliquias eius[32] posuit, ubi
deserviet die noctuque; et per mea argumenta feci, ut dum vellet
transire flumen cecidit et fregit crura sua, et invocavit nomen de
Anastasio, et ibi ambulavit ut praestet illi sanitatem. Sed dico vo-
125 bis, quia per totum istum mensem octobrium non veniet. Si autem
venerit, non est mihi dubitatio,[33] quia non me potest eicere de isto corpore."

---

105 septembri O   ea P   106-107 de fratribus *om.* P   108 imperator P
112 hic *om.* P   113 adstans P

29. *Manifestas* does not render accurately πάσχεις.

30. The Latin phrase *Ideo accepi coniurationem. Per coronam meam me
coniuravi* does not correspond to the Greek exactly. This entire passage may
represent a reworking.

31. *canones* perhaps indicates that ὅρκους should be ememded to ὅρους
(Flusin 6.15).

32. *Qui et reliquias eius posuit* corresponds to καὶ τὰ λείψανα αὐτοῦ
κατέχων and is a looser translation with changed word order, not an addition, to the Latin text (Flusin 6.22).

33. *est ... dubitatio*: an inaccurate translation of οὐ μὴ δειλανδρήσω αὐτόν.

7. Et quid plurima? veniebat frequenter die noctuque hilaris, gaudens et ridens per puellam, quemadmodum qui veniet in convi-
130 vium ad amicum suum, et ingrediebatur in puellam et blasphemias
et iniurias faciebat in maiestatem et in martyres et in episcopos et
in presbyteros et in diaconos et in monachos. Et multotiens dicebat gaudens: "Vah, vah, quid hodie operatus sum? Hodie tria homicidia feci, et ecce gratulor in operibus meis." Et altera occasione
135 dicebat: "Feci hodie ut miles dormiret cum ancilla Dei; et ecce gratulor." Post modicos autem dies iterum dixit: "Modo veni de His-
pania³⁴ et feci ibi homicidia multa et effusiones sanguinum. Et ecce multo magis gratulor in operibus meis." Et quidam de fratribus
dixit ei: "Maledicte, nequissime spiritus, hostis humani generis,
140 quid persequeris hominem qui factus est ad imaginem Dei? Praeparatur tibi gehennae tormentus, flamma inextinguibilis. Da honorem Deo et Iesu Christo filio eius, qui venturus est iudicare
saeculum per ignem." Et daemon respondit:³⁵ "Numquam inclinabo caput meum et coronam meam ante Nazarenum. Sed secundum
145 canones meos sic facio quia aliquem non timeo." Dicentibus nobis:
"Ecce apostoli Domini nostri Iesu Christi Petrus et Paulus, ipsi te
eiciunt de isto corpore." Daemon respondit: "O iste senex malus
Petrus, quid est operatus? Ego feceram ut regnaret Philippicus,³⁶
quia amicus meus erat; et iste ambulavit in die Pentecosten et ordi-

---

129-130 in convivium *om.* P   130 blasphemiam O *cf.* ὕβρεις   137 effusione P   139 iniquissimus P   140 quid] quanto P   143-144 inclino P
145 Dicentibus nobis] Nos ei e contra dicentibus P   147 eicient O *cf.* ἐκβάλλουσιν

34. This is most likely a reference to the contemporary Muslim conquest
of Spain, begun in 711. In 712-713, right before the Miracle was composed,
Seville and Saragossa, among other cities, had fallen. See also Flusin II, 377.
   35. The Greek text adds Ἄπιθι εἰς τὸ σκότος, ἀββᾶ missing in the Latin
tradition.
   36. The emperor who ruled from 11 December 711 to 3 June 713, best
known for his attempt to revive monothelism. The Latin text alone preserves
(or adds?) the name Petrus (*O iste senex malus Petrus* ...); cf. the Greek κακόγηρος (Flusin 7.15). The passage has been seen as a reflection of the strong
reaction in Rome against Philippicus (Llewellyn, *Rome in the Dark Ages*, pp.
164-165).

150 navit alium.[37] Haec operatus est in me; sed de isto corpore eicere
me non potest." Et unus de fratribus dedit palmam puellae dicens:
"Non facias iniurias in maiestatem et in martyres." Daemon dixit:
"Caedite, quid mihi pertinet de corpore isto?" Et non cessabat in
blasphemia contra martyres[38] et servos Dei, similia, et alia multa
155 quae per singula enarrare longum est.

8. Cum autem compleret ipsa puella in basilica sancti Iohannis dies
viginti quinque,[39] frequentabat ipse daemon in puellam stimulan-
do illam. In ipsa autem nocte, hora quasi secunda, venit ipse nequissimus spiritus in ipsa puella et coepit per illam exclamare di-
160 cens: "Ecce dico vobis, quia Maria et Paulus et Andreas obtulerunt
de isto sene malo episcopo et de istis monachis lacrimas ante Nazarenum. Et praecepit Nazarenus, et dedit potestatem Anastasio, et
ipse veniet et eiciet me de isto corpore in kalendas novembris." Ille
autem vir venerabilis episcopus una cum abbate et omni congrega-
165 tione non cessabat die noctuque flectere genua, caput humo con-
tundere, manus expandere, oculos ad caelum levare, pectus contun-
dere, clamans et dicens: "O dilectissime Domine, tu sapientia viva,
tu fons vitae,[40] tu es sol iustitiae, tu verissimus lumen, miserere
mei et effunde largitatis antidotum,[41] qui solvis contritos[42] a pec-
170 cato. Da veniam peccatis, qui donas requiem lapsis. Suscita meam
filiam a mortuis,[43] et erue eam ab iniquissimis poenis. Quia sic

154 blasphemiam P   157 puella P *cf. g*   160 a Maria et Paulo et Andrea
P   161 senece P   isto monacho   lacrimans P   162 Et–Nazarenus *om.*
O   163 iste P   165 non–flectere *om.* P   cessabant O *cf.* ἐπαύετο
flectendo *add.* P   167 via sapientiae O *cf.* σοφία ζῶσα   169 contritis P

37. The orthodox Anastasius II, crowned on Pentecost 713 (4 June).

38. V's addition (*martyres dicere*) finds a correspondence in προσφέρων.
As I suggest above (p. 341), it seems possible that V relied to a certain extent
on a copy of the Greek.

39. The Greek text specifies twenty-six days instead. The date would correspond to 25 (26) October 713.

40. Cf. Prv 13.14.

41. A loose rendering of τῆς δαψιλείας σου τοὺς οἰκτιρμούς.

42. Cf. Ps 33.19; 146.3.

43. The Latin omits ποτε τὸν υἱὸν τῆς χήρας καὶ τὸν τετραήμερον Λάζαρον.

descendisti de caelis ut hominibus miserearis. O Domine unigenite, suscita quod fecisti, propter corpus quod in terris induisti. Adimple quod dixit propheta: 'Qui sanat contritos corde et alligat contritio-
175 nes eorum.'[44] O Domine unigenite, nobis per evangelium promisis-ti dicens: 'Quaerite et invenietis, petite et accipietis, pulsate et aperietur vobis.'[45] O Domine unigenite, quaero, peto, pulso tuam misericordiam ut meam cures filiam ut non cum ea interam. Do-mine beate, scio quia tu quatriduanum Lazarum a mortuis suscitas-
180 ti, socrum tui discipuli Petri a febribus liberasti et centurionis puerum iam mortuum sanasti, apparuisti medicus caelestis, filiam principis[46] suscitasti a mortuis et filiam Chananeae a daemonio liberasti; mulierem a profluvio sanguinis sanasti et ut bonus Domi-nus ostendisti turbis tuam deitatem. O Domine, tu aspice meas la-
185 crimas; tribue mihi auxilium ut salvam recipiam meam filiam post diaboli oppressionem. Quia te credimus Dominum angelorum et hominum, qui vivis et regnas in saecula saeculorum. Amen.'[47]

9. Et sicut supra diximus, ante ipsas venerabiles reliquias assidue candela ardens erat die noctuque et quolibet argumento ille nequis-
190 simus, maledictus invidus daemon tutare eam visus est. Erat enim hora diei circiter tertia. Quod videns vir venerabilis episcopus con-tristatus est nimis, et mandavit in monasterio puerum ut adduceret lumen. Et[48] ecce subito accensa est candela a semetipsa cum mag-no splendore. Hoc autem factum est tertio kalendas novembris.[49]

---

172 misereris P   177 peto *om.* P   181 sanasti *om.* O   183 fluvio P   li-berasti OP sanasti *alii codd. cf.* ἰάσω   188 superius P   189 qualibet P

44. Ps 146.3.
45. Cf. Mt 7.7.
46. The Greek text clearly refers here to the story as told in Mk 5.22ff as is made clear by the use of the word ἀρχισυναγώγου (= *archisynagogus* in the Vulgate). The use here of *principis* recalls instead Mt 9.18 and 23-26; it may be a further indication of the Latin translator's lack of familiarity with the Latin biblical text. See above, p. 132.
47. The Latin text abbreviates the formulaic ending.
48. Latin omits τοῦ παιδὸς ἀπιόντος.
49. 29 October 713; the Greek adds a short phrase (καὶ πάντες ... Ἀναστασίου [Flusin 9.8-9]).

195 Pridie autem kalendas postulavit vir venerabilis episcopus abbatem
monasterii[50] ut omnis congregatio in eadem basilica sancti Iohannis vigilias atque matutinas celebraret. Quod et factum est. Mane
autem facto die kalendarum[51] exierunt fratres et reversi sunt in
monasterio, et remanserunt cum episcopo presbyter et diaconus[52]
200 et tres monachi. Et subito veniens ipse nequissimus immundus
spiritus introivit in puellam et coepit stimulare eam. Et tenentes
monachi manus eius, duxerunt eam ante sanctum altare ubi erant
venerabiles reliquiae. Et usque quasi hora una[53] coepit daemon va-
nitates per ipsam puellam loqui. Deinde coepit dicere: "Anastasius
205 adduxit me ad stimulandum et cruciandum, et iam non facio iniurias neque in Anastasio, neque in episcopo, neque in presbyteris,
neque in diaconibus, neque in monachis." Continuo autem mandavit praedictus episcopus et venit omnis congregatio. Et dum omnes[54] flecterent genua et dicerent simul "Kyrie eleison," coepit
210 daemon per puellam clamare et dicere: "Anastasi, quid me adduxisti in spectaculo ante homines ut me stimules et crucies?" Et coepit
se puella flectere dextra laevaque, tamquam qui flagellatur durissime et voce magna clamare: "Vae! Vae mihi! quid patior propter
istud corpus maledictum, quia veni in derisionem coram omnibus?
215 Sub violentia ingressus sum, exeo,[55] non stabo in isto maledicto
corpore." Et nos dicentibus illi: "Exi, maledicte," daemon respondit: "Non possum exire, quia ligatum me habet Anastasius. Heu
me! heu me! quid patior!"

10. Et post paululum suspensa est a terra; daemon qui semper hila-
220 rem faciebat puellam, nunc autem tristem, et qui ridere et gaudere

---

195 abbatis O   197 matutinum P   celebrarent O   198 kalendarum *om.*
P   203 reliquias P   206 Anastasium ... episcopum ... presbyteros ... diacones ... monachos *cf. g*   214 istum O   hominibus O *cf.* ἐναντίον πάντων

50. The name of the abbot, Theodosius, is preserved in the Greek.
51. Yet one more precise date is given in this chapter, 1 November 613.
52. Cf. πρεσβύτεροι καὶ διάκονοι καὶ μοναχοὶ τρεῖς.
53. Cf. ὡσεὶ μιᾶς ὥρας διάστημα.
54. The Greek adds παραγενέσθαι πρὸς αὐτὸν ἐν τῷ σεπτῷ εὐκτηρίῳ.
55. The Greek adds βιαίως ἐξέρχομαι.

eam faciebat, nunc autem flere et lacrimare. Coepit[56] ... et dum
suspenderetur, clamabat daemon: "Heu me, Anastasi." Iterum facta
est puella capite deorsum. Et daemon clamabat: "Quid me suspendis
capite deorsum, Anastasi? Exeo de isto corpore." Et nos dicentibus
225   illi: "Exi et recede, maledicte, de plasmate Dei et sponsa Christi."
Et daemon dixit: "Ligatum me habet Anastasius, quia in vesperum
iterum in me poenas exercere volet, plus propter illum dentem
eius, quem feceram ut periret."[57] Nos autem diximus ei: "Et quid
factus est ipse dens?" Daemon dixit: "Quando venit Anastasius,
230   tunc adduxit eum et levavit et posuit eum in loco suo."[58] Et nos
diximus ei: "Et quando venit sanctus Anastasius?" Daemon dixit:
"Quando accensa est candela a semetipsa, tunc ingressus est Anastasius et revocavit eum in loco suo." Episcopus dixit: "Mentiris, maledicte." Daemon dixit: "Quaerite in arca ubi sunt reliquiae et cog-
235   noscetis." Et dum aperta fuisset arca, inventum est inter ceteras.
Et rememorati sumus, quia fidelis Dominus in verbis suis,[59] quod
locutus est per prophetam: "Dominus custodit omnia ossa eorum:
unum ex eis non contéretur."[60] Et Dominus in evangelio ait:
"Non periet capillus capitis vestri,"[61] et alia multa.

---

222 daemon *omm. codd. exc.* N *cf.* g   228 Et *omm. codd. exc.* L *cf.* g   229
ipsum dentem P   231 Et *omm. codd. exc.* H *cf.* g   234 reliquias P   235
inventa O *cf.* αὐτὸν   ceteros O   239 de capite vestro P

56. A lacuna in the Latin text: πάλιν–κλίνασα (Flusin 10.3-4).

57. V's reading (*perdiretur* for *periret*) is more accurate and closer to the
Greek text, providing further evidence that this witness was edited, perhaps
with the aid of the Greek text.

58. *tunc adduxit eum et levavit*, although awkward, corresponds to the
Greek τότε ἦρεν αὐτὸν ὅθεν ἔκειτο.

59. Cf. Ps 144.13.

60. Ps 34.20.

61. Cf. Lc 21.18. This sentence is not found in the Greek text, but the
wording of the biblical verse which departs from the text of the Vulgate ("Et
capillus de capite vestro non peribit") here indicates that it is a translation,
and not a Latin addition. The variant readings of some of the manuscripts,
including P, attempt to conform to the Vulgate text.

240 **11.** Et[62] dum perficeretur opus Dei, non est locutus per puellam daemon ullum verbum, sed erat in silentio ante altare. Et dum reversi essent monachi ad reficiendum, remansit episcopus et presbyter, et diaconus, et tres monachi. Et dum facta esset hora undecima,[63] coepit iterum daemon sicut antea clamare et dicere: "Quid

245 me crucias, Anastasi? Scio quia sanctus es." Et clamabat cum ululatu magno dicens: "Vae, vae, vae mihi! sancte Anastasi, scio quia sanctus es, non tibi peccavi, stimula per quem in isto corpore ingressus sum." Et iterum sicut antea, coepit puella flectere se dextra laevaque, sicut qui flagellatur durissime in praetorio. Daemon cla-

250 mabat: "Exeo de corpore hoc cum omni vitio meo." Et modice tacebat, et iterum cum ululatu clamabat: "Exeo. Nam iuro per eum quem tu veneraris et adoras, quia non periuro." Et iterum tacebat, et iterum cum ululatu clamabat, dicens: "Per quod portas, quia non periuro, exeo; et numquam in hoc corpore revertar. Heu me, heu

255 me ! quia veni in derisionem inter homines." Et iterum clamabat: "Sancte Anastasi, exeo; et numquam in presbyteros tuos, neque in diaconos tuos, neque in milites tuos, id est in monachos tuos, quia milites tui sunt, iniuriam facio. Et ecce dico atque confiteor vobis quia nihil sum. Ventus sum, spiritus nequam et immundus sum, et

260 nihil sum.[64] Sed ubi verus christianus est, fugio ab ipso, et aliquid illi mali facere non possum." Et flentibus nobis omnibus, daemon dicebat: "Nolite flere, quia, cum videt sanctus Anastasius lacrimas vestras, plus me incendit et exercet in me tormenta. Sed, sicut iuravi, exeo et numquam revertor in hoc corpore." Et quidam de fra-

265 tribus dixit: "Non facias aliquid malum, dum exieris." Daemon respondit: "Sic mihi praecepit sanctus Anastasius ut sine aliqua tri-

---

240-241 per–daemon *om.* P   244 et dicere *omm. codd. exc.* A *cf.* g   Quid] quanto P   246 magno *om.* O   dicens *omm. codd. exc.* N *cf.* g   250 modicum P   252 veneras P   253 Per–portas *om.* O   254 revertor P   257 diacones O   tuos *om.* P   258 iniuriam] numquam *add.* O   261 nos P   263 et exercet] exercens O *cf.* ἐπιτίθει   265 aliquod P   266 sanctus] beatus P

62. The Latin text deviates from the Greek in this sentence.
63. Another precise chronological indication.
64. The Latin omits ἀλλὰ ἀδυνατῶ πρὸς τοὺς ἁγίους τοῦ Θεοῦ (Flusin 11.20).

bulatione relinquam corpus istud." Et haec dicens, tacuit quasi hora una. Inclinans caput suum puella ante altare et venerabiles reliquias tacens, nos autem coepimus dicere: "Maledicte, exi." Daemon
270 respondit: "Sinite me, quia satisfacio⁶⁵ sancto Anastasio qualia tormenta patiar si reversus fuero in isto corpore." Et factum est in
hora tertia noctis flexit puella genua ante vultum⁶⁶ Domini nostri
Iesu Christi quasi hora semis; et erexit se sana mente sanoque corpore, et stetit ante sanctum altare, et suscepit corpus et sanguinem
275 Domini nostri Iesu Christi et salva facta est puella ex illa hora.

[12.⁶⁷ Et ideo debemus mirabilia et laudem beati martyris Anastasii suaviter enarrare, qui post saeculi pompas profectus est ad caeli
coronam. Debacchabatur in eo tyrannicus furor insanus et eius
corde divinus fulgebat aspectus. Vir iniquus Marzabanas carnifex
280 secabat sancti Anastasii membra et in eius corde reficiebat infatiga-
bilis medicina. Marzabanas inimicus eius torquendo⁶⁸ deficiebat;
et beatus Anastasius patiendo vincebat. Non enim viribus certatur
humanis nec pro corporis vita †complectitur regio†⁶⁹ et regnis
caelestibus dimicabat. Hic enim nec subire potuit, nec laqueo colla
285 componere formidavit. O pastor bonus, quem parva cum voce lau-
demus. Secutus est aeterni pastoris vestigia Domini nostri Iesu
Christi. Mercabatur de morte ad vitam accipere gloriae coronam.

---

268 et] ad O; *cf.* καὶ   270 quales P   272 flectit O *cf.* ἔκαμψεν   274 accepit P   275 puellam O   278 coronas O   Devacabatur O   280 sancto
anastasio O   283 vitae O   284 Hic] Sic O   subiri O subripere PM subire *cett. codd.*   285 parva cum voce] par ut contra voce O parva echo (?) P
parve contra voce LAF parva contra H parve voce contra TGYSD

65. Not an accurate translation of the specific ἐγγράφως ποιῶ. Perhaps *satis*
is a corruption of the original translation of ἐγγράφως (*scriptum? scripte?*).
66. V's reading *imaginem* is more precise, and renders the Greek more
accurately.
67. This final chapter is not found in the Greek. See above, pp. 141ff.
68. This construction is frequently found in *BHL* 411a. Cf., for example,
(ll. 318-320), "Volebant enim impii invitum extrinsecus ligando concutere,
quem iam Christus ultroneum intrinsecus vinciendo coeperat stabilire."
69. Although the general sense of this passage is obvious, the exact meaning of *complectitur regio et regnis caelestibus* is puzzling.

O magnum genus admirationis! Occiditur corpus ut nascatur martyrum fructus. O mors pretiosa! per quam fit de confessione victo-
290 ria. Fit innocens reus, dum non attenditur Deus. Occiditur iustus
et in suis crucifigitur Christus. Elegit mortem praesentem propter
salutem vitae aeternae. Stabat beatus Anastasius vexillo crucis armatus et lorica fidei munitus. Pugnabat iustus, non tantum laboris
sudore, sed sanguinis effusione. Vicit corpus inter supplicia et ani-
295 ma invicta emisit cruorem pro Domino salvatore. Fratres carissimi,
contremiscit cor meum et renes mei resolvuntur quotienscumque
recordor ista mirabilia, quae fecit Dominus noster Iesus Christus
per martyrem suum beatum Anastasium. Mirabilis Deus in sanctis
suis faciens prodigia. Ecce quid meruerunt, qui Dominum Iesum
300 Christum non negaverunt. Videte, fratres, quantum meruerunt martyres fide, †tantum invenitur confessione†.[70] Dignetur ergo et nos
Dominus unigenitus per orationes beati martyris sui Anastasii
omnes eripi ab ipsius oppressione inimici ut per ipsum Dominum
nostrum Iesum Christum gratias agamus Deo patri et Spiritui sanc-
305 to nunc et semper et in aeterna saecula saeculorum. Amen.]

288 magnus P   289 de qua P   289-290 victoriam P   292 vexillum P
293 loricam P   294 effusionem P   294-295 animae invictae P   297
quem OP quae *cett. codd.*   301 martyrum OP martyres/martyris *cett. codd.*
fides P   confessio *codd. exc.* H   et *om.* P   303 oppressiones O ut *om.*
O   305 sancto *om.* O   et² *om.* P

70. The Latin text appears to be corrupt.

4

THE *BHL* 408(p) REDACTION

The Three Major Redactions (p, r, s)

The *Passio S. Anastasii* numbered *BHL* 408 survives today in about fifty manuscript witnesses from the ninth to the fifteenth century. It is the version of the *Passio S. Anastasii* that achieved the greatest dissemination. The edition published in the second volume of the *ASS*[1] can be considered neither the original recension, nor a text that was in actual use, for it is a reconstruction based on two manuscripts, each representing a distinct revision of the original recension.[2] It is my purpose in this discussion to identify the earliest recensions of this text, to propose an explanation of their evolution, and to justify my choice of p as the original redaction, deriving directly from the early translation, *BHL* 410b.

The transmission of *BHL* 408 was increasingly marked by the contamination and fluidity that is characteristic of hagiographic texts. In addition, the manuscript tradition of this version incorporates corrections and elisions by scribes and hagiographic compilers, who repeatedly attempted to perfect those passages that the original redactor, Bede, as I argue in Chapter VI, was unable to clarify, and yet was loath to cut out. Some of the texts that result from these corrections and revisions are quite different from those contained in the earliest surviving manuscripts. I have identified three versions that are so far removed from the earliest sources that they must be considered new redactions: the "Abbreviation r_1," the "Roman Revision" ($=r_2$), and the version that survives in Paris, Bibliothèque nationale de France, lat. 9741 ($=p_1$). If we exclude the few, highly localized manuscripts that contain these later

---

1. Ian. II, 426-431; 3rd ed. III, 39-45. I will refer to the third edition.

2. Jean Bolland noted that his two manuscripts represented different redactions (p. 35). See Appendix 1 to Chapter VII.

redactions,[3] the remaining manuscript witnesses of *BHL* 408 can be divided into three major groups according to variant readings. I will use the terms "recension" or "redaction" of the *BHL* 408 version of the *Passio S. Anastasii* to refer to these manuscript groups, even though these terms may suggest greater distinctiveness than actually exists among these three manifestations of the same text. I cite each redaction as transmitted in its oldest complete witness:

p = the text as transmitted in BAV, Palatinus latinus 846, s. IX first half (=Pl);

r = the text as transmitted in BAV, Reginensis latinus 516, s. IX ex. (=Rg);

s = the text as transmitted in Stuttgart, Württembergische Landesbibliothek, HB XIV 13, s. IX ex. (=St).

The fluidity of these redactions and the consideration that the oldest complete exemplar of each redaction antedates the next oldest witness by a considerable span—about two centuries—make this approach not only expedient, but also necessary.[4]

The text of the p-redaction survives in eleven manuscripts, all of which were written along a swathe stretching from Freising to northeastern France and Flanders.[5] The oldest witness is a fragment of a passionary copied in Freising at the very beginning of the ninth century (Trier, Stadtbibliothek 190 [1246]). The oldest *complete* witness is a passionary comprising the entire year, from

3. These versions are discussed in Chapter VII, and two of them, p_1 and r_2, are edited below. The *BHL* singles out another redaction of 408 and numbers it 409, but its main difference from 408 is the absence of the preface.

4. The alternative to this approach would be to reconstruct critically each redaction individually by using all its manuscripts separately. I have rejected this course for several reasons. First, I do in fact present the critical edition of one of the three redactions, p, which I judge to be the original one, by considering all its manuscript witnesses separately. Furthermore, the original redaction r would be almost exactly the text transmitted by Rg (whose readings are included in p's *apparatus criticus*) since there are only three later witnesses of this redaction that have been greatly altered. Finally, s, as I argue below, is an interpolated version, dependent on p and r.

5. See below, p. 386. All the manuscripts are included in "Descriptive List."

January to December, copied in the first half of the ninth century, most likely at Lorsch (BAV, Pal. lat. 846). There is then a long hiatus in the textual transmission. The next oldest manuscript is a legendary from the eleventh century, from Rheims or Troyes (Troyes, Bibliothèque municipale 1171), followed then by a twelfth-century codex now in Vienna (Lat. 377). The remaining witnesses to the p-redaction are seven closely related exemplars of the large Cistercian hagiographic compilation known as the *Liber de natalitiis* from the twelfth to the fourteenth century, originating in northeastern France and Flanders. They are preserved today in the Bibliothèque nationale de France.

The oldest witness of the r-redaction is BAV, Reginensis latinus 516, the only surviving volume of a two-volume legendary written at the end of the ninth century. Its origin is uncertain, but its close affinity to the other early passionaries and legendaries transmitting *BHL* 408 is clear.[6] Chartres 506, from the tenth century and closely related to the Reginensis, also contained the r-redaction. It was destroyed during World War II. The other surviving witnesses of the r-redaction are three legendaries from central and northern Italy, directly connected to each other by their contents and dating to the period from the twelfth to the thirteenth century.[7]

The oldest witness of the s-recension is a two-volume legendary copied toward the end of the ninth century at Reichenau (Stuttgart, Württembergische Landesbibliothek, HB XIV 13). About twelve other legendaries, all from central or north-central Italy copied during the eleventh and twelfth century, also transmit this recension.[8]

---

6. See pp. 377-381, below.

7. Rome, Biblioteca vallicelliana, Tomus V (s. XI); BAV, Vat. lat. 6073 (s. XII); BAV, Arch. S. Maria Maggiore 1 (s. XII-XIII); see "Descriptive List."

8. These are Vercelli, Archivio capitolare LXIX (s. XI); Florence, Biblioteca nazionale, Fondo nazionale II I 412 (s. XI); Biblioteca laurenziana, Amiatinus 2 (s. XI); Bologna, Biblioteca universitaria 2205 (s. XI); Perugia, Biblioteca capitolare 40 (s. XI-XII); Naples, Biblioteca nazionale VIII B 2 (s. XI-XII); Spoleto, Archivio capitolare Tomo I (s. XII ex.). The following transmit a version of the Passion that has been further corrected: Bergamo, Biblioteca Mons. Radini Tedeschi 227 (s. XI); Ivrea, Biblioteca capitolare 112 (s. XI); Rome, Archivio storico del Vicariato, Later. 79 (s. XII[1]); Milan, Biblioteca ambrosiana B 49 Inf. (s. XII); Lucca, Biblioteca capitolare C (s. XII); Perugia, Biblioteca augusta 3270 (s. XII). See "Descriptive List."

The variant readings that identify each redaction and that emerge most consistently in the later witnesses are as follows:[9]

(cap. 1 [=p ll. 6-7, 15])
> mortis atque corruptionis tyrannicae potestati subiectum Pl
> sub mortis atque corruptionis tyrannicae potestatis subiectum Rg St
> in caelestibus Pl
> in caelestia Rg St

(cap. 11 [=p ll. 152, 161])
> perduxit eum ad monasterium Pl
> ad monasterium *om.* Rg St
> docuit eum litteras Pl St
> docuit eum litteras grecas Rg

(cap. 15 [=p ll. 220-221])
> nisi eam vestem qua indutus erat Pl
> nisi ea quam indutus erat Rg
> nisi quae indutus erat St

(cap. 21 [=p l. 313])
> caedebant eum Pl St
> caedebant eum fustibus Rg

(cap. 34 [=p l. 503])
> cum ira foris carcerem Pl
> cum ira et iussit eum trai foris carcerem Rg
> cum ira foris ad carcerem St

(cap. 35 [=p l. 517])
> supra metam duarum partium ligni Pl
> supra duarum partium ligni Rg St

The Relation of the Three Earliest Recensions and the Early Translation

The task of reconstructing the original redaction of *BHL* 408 must begin with a comparison of the three redactions p, r, s. The early translation *BHL* 410b (=t, as edited above) plays a central role in the establishment of the original recension of 408 because it is the source from which 408 derives.[10] According to this paradigm, then, we would normally theorize that, in cases of disagreement among

9. Not every single witness of course will share every reading, since each witness may have been further corrected.

10. The author/editor of *BHL* 408, as one would expect, had a manuscript of t that differed in some details with our only witness of t, the Bobbio codex (=T). Also, it is clear that 408's editor could not or did not consult the Greek original in any significant way. See Chapter V, pp. 166ff.

the ancient witnesses representing the recensions, whichever agrees with t should be considered to have preserved the reading of the archetype, or original recension. Hence, t's evidence generally would have to be given the highest authority in establishing the "correct" (in the parlance of stemmatics) or original redaction of *BHL* 408.

One can immediately see the difficulty of this approach, given t's problematic Latinity. In the case of a lacuna or missing detail, or in cases where there is a difference in factual information, the evidence of t would be easily acceptable. But when a redaction agrees with t in a grammatical or syntactical error, the shortcomings of this procedure become obvious. Are instances of poor Latin usage to be considered authentic because they agree with t? This is the question that the following discussion will be concerned with.

The redaction that agrees most consistently with t where there are disagreements among the ancient witnesses is r, as is illustrated in the following examples:

1. (cap. 7 [=p ll. 97-98])
   Deus Christianorum ... hic veniret t
   quomodo Deus Christianorum in hac cruce, quae huc advenit Pl St
   quomodo Deus Christianorum in hac crucem, qui hic advenit Rg

Rg keeps Christ, to whom the *qui* refers, as the subject of the verb, following t (and the Greek text, g, which t follows very closely).[11] In St and Pl, however, *quae* and hence the cross become the subject of the verb, thus altering the meaning. One might conclude from this that Rg preserves a more primitive, less revised text.

2. (cap. 11 [=p l. 161])
   docuit eum tam litteras grecas t
   docuit eum litteras Pl St
   docuit eum litteras graecas Rg
3. (cap. 21 [=p l. 313])
   ferire in eum fustibus t
   caedebant eum Pl St
   caedebant eum fustibus Rg
4. (cap. 34 [=p ll. 502-503])
   veniens ... cum ira iussit trahere eum foris carcerem t
   veniens ... cum ira foris (ad *add.* St) carcerem Pl St
   veniens ... cum ira et iussit eum trai foris carcerem Rg

---

11. g can often be used to establish the authenticity of t, helping to identify possible scribal or editorial intervention.

In the above three examples, only Rg preserves details supported by t. Rg's text would have to be considered the "correct" text, while St and Pl would be joined in a common error by their omissions.

5. (cap. 2 [=p l. 17])
   de sublimis uirtutem induti t
   de sublimi virtute induti Pl St
   de sublimis virtutem induti Rg

6. (cap. 6 [=p l. 85])
   Sanctae autem ciuitati excidioni factae t
   Sanctae autem civitatis desolatione facta St Pl
   Sanctae autem civitatis desolatione factae Rg

7. (cap. 26 [=p ll. 381-382])
   iuuenis ... incensum mittentem t
   iuvenis ... incensum mittens Pl St
   iuvenis ... incensum mittentem Rg

8. (cap. 27 [=p l. 393])
   discens t
   dicens Rg St
   videns Pl

9. (cap. 31 [=l. 458])
   gaudium et laetitiam his t
   erat eis gaudium et laetitia Pl St
   erat eis gaudium et laetitiam Rg

10. (cap. 32 [=p l. 468])
    qui est a stadiorum sex t
    quod est miliario sexto Pl St
    quod est a miliario sexto Rg

In these last examples (5-10), whose number could easily be increased, Rg appears over and over to be more faithful to t, repeating t's problematic and ungrammatical text,[12] while St and Pl present a text more distant from t but generally more grammatically correct. While it is true that Rg is often carelessly written,[13] its agreements with t's problematic text are too numerous to be attributed to scribal incompetence or carelessness alone.

A possible explanation is that Rg preserves a more primitive text, a first revision of t, which was then itself further corrected, and

---

12. See, for example, numbers 7, 8, 9 above.
13. See BAV, Reg. lat. 516 in "Descriptive List."

that this later, more thoroughly revised redaction has come down
to us in St and Pl, which agreee in all the examples cited above.

There are other cases, however, in which St agrees with the apparently more primitive readings of Rg and t, while Pl presents a
text that is grammatically more consistent and at the same time
further distanced from t, as in the following examples:

1. (cap. 1 [=p ll. 6-7])
   sub mortis atque corruptionis t Rg St
   mortis atque corruptionis Pl
2. (cap. 3 [=p ll. 42-43])
   Nihil enim deterius horum (orum Rg) t Rg St
   Nihil enim deterius Pl
3. (cap. 3 [=p ll. 46-47)
   addebatur ... numerum t
   additur (addetur Rg) ... numerum copiosum Rg St
   additur ... numerus copiosus Pl
4. (cap. 6 [=p ll. 80-81])
   Filius vero erat magi quoddam (quondam St) Bau nomine t Rg St
   Filius vero erat magi cuiusdam Bau nomine Pl
5. (cap. 14 [=p ll. 205-206])
   quasi futurum se mori t
   quasi moriturus esset Rg St
   quod moriturus esset Pl
6. (cap. 19 [=p l. 265])
   ritum quod t Rg St
   ritum qui Pl
7. (cap. 31 [=p ll. 452-453)
   super bonum eius propositum t
   super eius bonum propositum Rg St
   super eius bono proposito Pl
8. (cap. 35 [=p l. 517])
   supra duarum partium ligni t Rg St
   supra metam duarum partium ligni Pl
9. (cap. 37 [=p l. 536])
   abominauit t [Rg has a lacuna] St
   abominabatur Pl
10. (cap. 38 [=p ll. 568-569])
    comminatis t
    minatis St Rg
    minamini Pl

These examples could be taken to indicate that St is a witness to a first correction of the text transmitted in Rg, and that Pl, with which St agrees in the first set of examples cited above, represents a further vertical development of the text. These relations could be described by the following stemma:

If this were in fact the relationship among the three redactions and t, we would expect Rg and St never to depart from t when Pl is faithful to it, for a departure from t would have to be considered a "common error," and faithfulness to t the "correct" or authentic reading. However, there are several instances in which Pl and t agree against Rg and St, as the following examples show:

1. (cap. 1 [=p l. 15])
   fecit et consedere nos in caelestibus t
   et consedere nos in caelestibus iussit Pl (caelestia Rg St)

This is a biblical phrase in which the language of t is very similar to that of the Vulgate (Eph 2.6 "et consedere fecit in caelestibus"). Hence, given the agreement among t, Pl, and the biblical passage, *caelestia* must be considered an error, shared by Rg and St.[14]

2. (cap. 2 [=p l. 22]) illam t   illa Rg St   illum Pl

The reading that would suit the grammar is *illum* (to agree with *errorem*). Hence, Pl's *illum* seems a more plausible correction of t's *illam*, than the transformation of *illam* to *illa* (Rg St) to *illum* (Pl).

3. (cap. 5 [=p l. 74]) obligaturas t   adepturi Rg St   adepturas Pl

Pl's reading must be considered the correct text because it parallels t's *obligaturas*, which is a close translation of g's ἀναδησαμένας (from ἀναδέω=to bind), and modifies *mulieres*.

---

14. Nor does it seems likely that the reading of the original translation was *caelestia*, later changed in t and Pl under the influence of the biblical language, because the Greek text (ἐν τοῖς ἐπουρανίοις) confirms t's ablative and eliminates the only possible support for an original *caelestia* in t.

4. (cap. 6 [=p l. 82]) magicam artem t Pl   magica arte Rg St
5. (cap. 9 [=p l. 134]) mereretur t Pl   dignaretur Rg St
6. (cap. 11 [=p l. 152]) in mansionem t   ad monasterium Pl *om*. Rg St
7. (cap. 31 [=p l. 457]) tamque t   tamquam Pl   quamquam Rg St
8. (cap. 42 [=p l. 605]) in carcere t Pl   in carcerem Rg St

In all these examples, the readings common to Rg and St cannot be considered correct. Rather, in all cases, Pl's readings appear correct because they are shared by t, and also because they make more sense. Rg and St again are joined in common error.

To conclude: according to a paradigm positing agreement with t as the correct reading and departure from t as the error, St is joined sometimes with Pl and sometimes with Rg. Pl and Rg, on the contrary, never agree against the agreement of St and t, indicating that Pl and Rg share no common error. The simplest explanation for this textual relationship is to regard St as the result of contamination of the Pl and Rg tradition,[15] and that Pl and Rg have a parallel relationship to t. Furthermore, such a scheme might also explain why Rg preserves the correct readings at times (and here we define correct as agreeing with t) and Pl preserves them at other times:

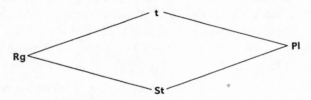

This stemma gives equal weight to the evidence of Rg and Pl. In deciding which of the two manuscript witnesses has more authority, t would be crucial. As a consequence, Rg, which in so many cases is closer to t and repeats t's grammatical and lexical infelicities, would have to be accorded greater weight in reconstructing the original redaction.

15. See West, *Textual Criticism and Editorial Technique*, pp. 12ff. and 35ff., for a discussion of contamination. Another specific example illustrating that Rg > St > Pl is not possible is provided by the reading *quasi* Pl *quae quasi* Rg *quae* St t (cap. 2 [=p l. 22]).

This solution, however, is not congruent with the basic nature of *BHL* 408. The same editor who is to be credited for transforming the early translation into 408, a text that for the most part is intelligible and in places even artful,[16] would have to be held responsible also for retaining the grammatical mistakes shared by Rg (and St in some cases) and t. For example, the editor who changed t's *cultoribus vestris* into the allusive *sculptilia vestra* (l. 334) or who, in l. 635, clearly distinguished the usage of the reflexive pronoun by writing "de eius glorioso fine and de sui itineris labore"[17] would have to have kept t's *primatos* for the accusative plural (as it is in Rg) and not changed it to *primates* (as it is in Pl).[18] Such inconsistent practice is implausible.

A more convincing solution to this dilemma is provided by a horizontal rather than vertical or developmental relationship among the three recensions and t. To simplify our analysis, St\s, which appears to result from contamination between the two traditions, can be excluded from consideration for the moment. We must then explain, in the simplest terms, why the p-redaction presents the more consistently acceptable text, while r has a closer relation to t, manifested by its preservation of the details omitted by p (i.e. *litteras graecas, fustibus, et iussit eum tra[h]i* in examples 2, 3, and 4 above), and by its frequent agreements with t's ungrammatical text.

If we assume that the text of *BHL* 408 transmitted by Pl represents the original version, the recension prepared by the editor who revised t, then r can be seen as the result of the contamination between t and p, for r is indeed a composite of p and t. According to this view, a scribe or editor who had a copy of the early translation came in possession of a copy of p and entered corrections in his copy of the early translation, perhaps over the line, perhaps in the margin. t and 408 follow each other so careful-

16. See Chapter V, pp. 166-177.

17. This phrase is particularly noteworthy because it is added by the editor of 408 and not found in g or t or 410. Hence, it must be remarked that the 408 editor differentiated quite carefully in the use of the third person pronoun. For a problematic attempt at correcting t's grammar, see cap. 14 (=p l. 197) and n. 43.

18. Cap. 33 (=p l. 496).

ly that this can be easily visualized. In some cases, this scribe or editor did not correct fully or precisely. He failed to follow p in changing the ending of some words and let the earlier reading of r stand. In other cases, he might not have marked his corrections clearly enough.[19] When, at a later time, another scribe copied from this exemplar the corrected version of the early translation, some of the text from the original translation—generally words or endings—were retained through confusion or carelessness.[20] The resulting text would have been p contaminated by the early translation, or r, in other words. The origin of the s-redaction might either be found in another copy of the t\p text just described, or in further contamination.[21] Such textual contamination is not

19. There are examples of scribes correcting one manuscript witness against another, and of new hagiographic texts written directly over older versions (see, for example, the legendary of St. John the Lateran ["Descriptive List," p. 528]). An occurrence that is very similar to the procedure I am describing here might be the two versions of Bede's metrical Life of St. Cuthbert. Michael Lapidge has advanced the very convincing theory that a ninth-century manuscript from western Germany in fact contains the earlier, less proficient redaction of Bede's poem, which a later scribe has changed in accordance with the second redaction. The copy of the second redaction against which the corrections were made may also have survived (Lapidge, "Bede's Metrical *Vita S. Cuthberti*," p. 79 n. 13).

20. Another explanation for the relation of r to t, with p postulated as the original redaction, would be to assume that the editor who created *BHL* 408 in fact did it on his copy of t, in much the same way as I describe the origin of r above. In other words, he wrote his revisions in the margin, perhaps also above the line or correcting over some words directly. From this copy, one copy was made which will ultimately turn up in Rg. Its original scribe copied the new text, but in some cases he did not catch the corrections and left instead the words of the t-text. Another copy, with fewer words copied from t, resulted in s. The text contained in Pl, on the other hand, is the end product of a copy that followed the corrected text most closely. The problem with this solution, however, is that there are no common error agreements between Pl and Rg and t against St, as we would expect.

21. There is not enough clear evidence to suggest which possibility is more likely. The fact that Rg and St agree in common errors against Pl in several cases where t does not support the error (and therefore the origin of their common error cannot be ascribed to their joint partial origin from t) does not necessarily mean that s's origin must go back to r and not to t\p. For these cases of common errors shared by St and Rg against t (and p) could simply go back to t\p itself.

unique. There are other examples of hagiographic texts for which a horizontal transmission, and double readings, both marginal and interlinear, have been similarly postulated.[22]

In places, a detailed comparison of t with the three old redactions of the *Passio S. Anastasii* reveals the textual strata that constitute r and s. An example is found at the very beginning:

(cap. 1 [=p ll. 6-7])

  t : sub mortis atque corruptionis tyrannide (tyrannice?) subjectum[23]
  Pl : mortis atque corruptionis tyrannicae potestati subjecto
  Rg : sub mortis atque corruptionis tyrannicae potestatis subjectum
  St : sub mortis atque corruptionis tyrannicae potestatis subjectum

This analysis begins with the assumption that *BHL* 408 is a revision of t. If we follow a developmental or vertical model of transmission, the comparison of the three redactions would lead to the conclusion that the first reviser, who produced r, either changed a perfectly good phrase (if *tyrannide* is the correct reading) into nonsense; or, if the original translation read *tyrannice*, that he attempted to revise a text that he perceived to be defective by adding a genitive noun (*potestatis*) to what he took to be a genitive adjective (*tyrannice*). The resulting phrase is no better or clearer. The next editor, of s, did not attempt in this case to correct the text, but simply copied r. Finally p's editor made sense of the phrase by eliminating *sub* and changing one of the genitive phrases into a dependent dative. This solution presumes a degree of skill and another of ignorance on the part of the r editor that are incompatible.

If the horizontal model of textual transmission is considered, on the other hand, p's reading can be explained either as a clever correction of the original translation (*tyrannice*), or as a reasonable editiorial expansion of the original idea (*tyrannide*). If we accept p as the original 408 recension, then the text in Rg can be seen to contain all the elements present in t and all those present in p,

22. Chiesa, *Le versioni latine*, pp. 67ff., esp. 67-68, for the *Passio Febroniae*; and Maggioni, "La *Vita sanctae Theodorae* (BHL 8070). La revisione imperfetta di una traduzione perfettibile," pp. 205-206. Both are translations from the Greek.

23. The possibility that the original translation may have read "tyrannice subjectum" is discussed above. See t l. 6 and note.

with an additional scribal error (*potestatis*). The source of r, according to this textual history, could have been a copy of t with p
added as interlinear or marginal corrections. Rg would derive from
such a mixed textual tradition. St may represent a witness to another
redaction, from another copy more faithful to the p text than to
r, or a further contaminated development from it.

Another reflection of the layers of corrections represented in
these redactions may be the following:

cap. 11 (=p l. 160)
   t : unum de eius germanis discipulis
   Pl : unum eiusdem congregationis fratrem
   Rg St : unum de eiusdem congregationis (congregatione St) fratrem

Here, it is easy to imagine that the editor who added p over the
earlier text simply did not scratch out *de* from his copy of t as he
added the new phrase from p. The other possibility, that Rg is a
witness to an initial correction of t, does not make sense since this
would mean that the editor of r would have taken a clear phrase
in his original and transformed in into an ungrammatical one.[24]
Evidence in support of this model is also provided by a few instances
in which p—and not t—can be shown to have influenced or preceded
r. One such occurrence is found in cap. 25 (=p ll. 366-370]):

t : ... auscultabatur ei quidam de uinctis, Hebraeus quidem religione
et de nobilioribus, clemens autem moribus, sicut didicimus. Et uidens
beatum martyrem die quidem in lapidum asportatione miserantem,
nocte uero deprecatione Dei sustinente, stupebat ...

Pl : ... auscultabat eum quidam de vinctis qui ibi erat, Hebraeus
quidem religione, et nobilis genere. Mitissimus autem et beatus martyr
per diem quidem in lapidum fatigatione, nocte autem in Dei laudibus
perseverans stupebat ...

24. Nor can the possibility that t does not represent the original trans-
lation (and that Rg does) be accepted in this instance, for the reliability of
Bobbio's text is confirmed both by *BHL* 410 ("unum de eius germanis disci-
pulis") and by the Greek text (ἕνα τῶν ἑαυτοῦ γνησίων μαθητῶν [11.11]).
Another example revealing r's layers is found in cap. 12 (=p l. 176):
   t : desiderium malens
   Pl St : desiderio accensus
   Rg : desiderium accensus

Rg : ... auscultabat eos quidam de vinctis qui ibi erat, Hebraeus quidem religione, et nobili genere, mitissimus autem. Videns autem beatum martyrem per diem quidem in lapidum fatigationem, nocte autem in Dei laudibus <u>perseverans</u>, stupebat ...

St : ... auscultabat eum quidam de vinctis qui ibi erat, Haebreus quidem religione et nobili genere. Mitissimum autem beatum martyrem per diem quidem in lapidum fatigatione, nocte autem in Dei laudibus <u>perseverans</u>, stupebat ...

It is difficult to reconcile the addition of *perseverans*, found in all three recensions of *BHL* 408, with the view that posits Rg as representing a text closer to t, and St and Pl as later revisions. The participle *perseverans* has no support in t, but suits the grammar and meaning of Pl's text, and not Rg's. The best explanation for the textual history of this passage is to posit the anteriority of the p-redaction. We must assume that the text of the original translation available to the editor of p omitted a crucial passage, leading to the misunderstanding found in Pl. Alternatively, we might suppose that p's original text had been corrupted by the time it was available to r (and also to Pl's direct ancestor). The p text was then written over a copy of the early translation. The r text, combining t and p, took *perseverans* from p, and kept *videns beatum martyrem* from t. The text that resulted is confused and ungrammatical. Another consequence of the model here proposed is the possibility that the text of t available to r was different from the text of t available to p. This might explain why Rg preserves details missing from Pl and St.[25]

The relations among these major recensions and their earliest manuscript witnesses could be represented by the following diagram:

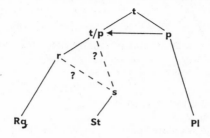

25. I.e. (l. 161) (litteras) graecas; (l. 313) (caedebant eum) fustibus; (l. 503) et iussit eum trai.

The high degree of cross-fertilization among different versions of the same text required by this scheme appears improbable if we maintain a fairly rigid view of textual transmission. Hagiographic texts, as many have remarked and the present study amply illustrates, are, however, extraordinarily fluid. The compiler of every passionary or legendary was not merely a scribe, but also an editor. The texts he chose to include in his collection had to suit many requirements, and he made use of a broad variety of sources.[26] Some texts were taken from already formed collections; some from independent *libelli*; others from non-hagiographic materials. In this process of collecting and compiling, many texts were edited, shortened, improved. The oldest passionaries that transmit the *Passio S. Anastasii* have been localized in the same geographical area, as is discussed further in the next section, and cross-pollination among these texts could have more easily occurred.

The horizontal evolution of the three redactions is presented as an alternative to the relationship that might at first appear to be self-evident, a vertical link that posits Rg as preserving the primitive redaction of *BHL* 408, and Pl its ultimate correction. The horizontal alternative is not definitively established. But it explains textual inconsistencies that the vertical relationship among the three early witnesses would leave unexplained. Most importantly, it allows for the possibility that p, a text that is coherent and self-consistent, is the "authentic" text, and it provides a plausible explanation for the inconsistencies and self-contradictions of r.

In practical terms, the p-recension is not very different from the r-recension. Beyond issues of grammar and style, r is different from p in preserving details in three passages.[27] It could even be argued that these details fell out of p's tradition and should be restored in its edition. The presence of these details in *BHL* 410, which may have been available to the original redactor of p, supports this view.[28] But as there is no evidence for them in p's

26. Philippart, *Légendiers*, pp. 101ff.

27. See above, n. 25.

28. One should compare these omissions, for which no sound editorial reason can be found, to the omission of *latine* in cap. 43 not only in p, but in the entire *BHL* 408 tradition. This omission does not occur in *BHL* 410, and may reflect a deliberate editorial decision by p's editor (p. 174).

tradition, their addition would create a text that as far as we know never existed.

The Early Diffusion of BHL 408

The affiliation among the three ancient redactions of *BHL* 408 (p, r, and s) as represented by their oldest complete witnesses (Pl, Rg, and St) has been constructed in the previous section solely from the textual evidence of the *Passio S. Anastasii*. In this section, I will map the relationship among these manuscripts through their contents within the historical development of formal hagiographic collections. The results of this analysis will support the conclusions derived from the textual comparison of the redactions of the *Passio S. Anastasii*.

The oldest surviving witnesses of *BHL* 408—Tr, Pl, Rg, and St— have been identified as belonging to a cluster of nine ancient passionaries, closely related through their overlapping sanctorals, all put together before the year 1000, and most, if not all, in Bavaria or German Switzerland.[29] We know that the *Passio S. Anastasii* (*BHL* 408) was also included in the two collections of this group that no longer exist, Chartres 506 (144), burned during the last world war, and the reconstructed *Passionarium minus* of St. Gall. We may also infer that the *Passio S. Anastasii* once appeared as well in the three other members of this group that have survived in defective form: in Bollandianus 14, whose initial leaves, on which the *Passio* would have been found, have been lost; and in the missing first volumes of Karlsruhe, Aug. XXXII from the ninth century and of the lost Passionary of Fulda written around 900 in southern Germany. Each of these passionaries represents a distinctive stage in the transformation and development of this cluster of hagiographic collections over more than a century.

Pl and Tr are the most primitive or simplest collections in the entire group of nine. Each passionary is comprised of one single

---

29. Dolbeau, "Le passionaire de Fulda" provides a thorough survey of this hagiographic cluster. Philippart (*Légendiers*, p. 102 n. 186; "Catalogues récents de manuscrits," pp. 200-201) had already pointed out the strong connections between St, Bollandianus 14, Chartres 506 (144), and Rg and promised a further study. See also "Descriptive List."

volume, which encompasses the entire year; both passionaries exclude the Passions of the Apostles.[30] Pl as it now stands (from 1 January to 7 December; the last folia are missing) includes only forty-eight texts. The strong connection between Pl and Tr, exposed through their overlapping sanctoral by Dolbeau, is confirmed by my study of the text of the *Passio S. Anastasii*. Pl contains the *BHL* 408(p) redaction, as does the Tr fragment. The position of the p-redaction as the original recension of *BHL* 408 parallels the older format of the two manuscripts that preserve it.

Bollandianus 14, Chartres 506, and St. Gall's *Passionarium minus* represent intermediate stages in the transformation of this cluster. These passionaries are much larger than Pl and Tr, containing almost double the number of texts, as well as the Passions of the Apostles. Still, like Pl and Tr, each one of them is comprised in one volume. None of these collections unfortunately provides us today with a text of the *Passio S. Anastasii*. But we can be certain that at least one of them, the Chartres passionary destroyed in World War II, contained *BHL* 408 in the r-redaction.[31] I argue above that the r-redaction represents a second, intermediate stage in the development of 408.

Rg and even more strikingly St, together with the lost passionary of Fulda, make up the most developed collections of this group of nine passionaries. These compilations have grown much bigger, containing double the number of texts of the first group, and incorporating also the celebrations of the apostles, as does the second group. Each of these collections occupies two volumes to cover the entire complement of feast days, unlike the earlier collections, each of which is contained in one volume. The *Passio S. Anastasii*, recorded for 22 January, always occurs in the first volume of the

---

30. It is assumed that at an earlier time, when the passionaries did not include the apostles, there were separate apostles' passionaries that complemented the others. Some of these apostles' passionaries have survived. Philippart, *Légendiers*, pp. 31, 90-93.

31. The close relationship between the lost Chartres codex and Rg is indicated most spectacularly by their common lacuna in the text of the *Passio S. Anastasii*, which we know thanks to the care of De Smedt's catalogue ("Descriptive List").

collection.[32] Rg contains thirty-five texts for the period for which Pl contains only twenty-two. Six of the thirty-five texts included in Rg concern the apostles (Iacobus Maior, Philippus, Matthaeus, Bartholmaeus, Iacobus Minor, Petrus & Paulus). St's sanctoral is even larger, comprising forty-four figures for the first half of the year,[33] including six apostles. The version of the *Passio S. Anastasii* preserved in St is, according to my conclusions above, farthest removed from the original redaction.

The relationship of the surviving witnesses of *BHL* 408 to each other within the development of this cluster of hagiographic collections can be further refined by superimposing the lists of their contents. All of the texts in Pl are included in St, but not all of them are contained in Rg (see chart on pp. 508-510).[34] All of the texts contained in Rg are contained in St with the exception of the Passion of Georgius (martyred in Cappadocia; *BHL* 3379), which is not found in Pl either.[35] Hence, one could assume that the collection now represented by Pl and another now represented by Rg were incorporated into St, and that Pl and Rg have a parallel, not vertical relationship, since they share only part of their contents.[36]

---

32. The second semester volumes of Rg and St have not survived, or at least not been identified yet.

33. There are two additional feasts included at the end, but they are outside the order of the sanctoral and must not have been part of the original compilation. The first is Aurelius (celebrated on 14 September and 4 November), the fourth century Armenian bishop who was patron of the monastery at Hirsau. His *Vita et translatio* (*BHL* 819) is included here as is *BHL* 820, the *Vita et translatio auctore Willirammo ab. Ebersbergensi.* The other text is *BHL* 4178, the *Exaltatio S. Crucis.*

34. Missing are: Pontianus (*BHL* 6891); Iohannes Penariensis (*BHL* 4420); Torpes (*BHL* 8307); Conon (*BHL* 1912); Gethulius (*BHL* 3524); Symphorosa (*BHL* 7971). All of the above of course are contained in St.

35. I assume therefore that this text was an addition peculiar to Rg.

36. These conclusions are based only on the general information provided by manuscript catalogues. Only the systematic comparison of the texts themselves can provide more definite results. Still, even the published catalogues on occasion provide more precise information. The text for SS. Basilides et soc., for example, included in Pl and St is *BHL* 1019, while in Rg it is *BHL* 1018 (*ASS* Iun. III, 6-7; 7-8). St appears to have a different version of the life of the apostle Jacob the Greater (*BHL* 4089 part II) than that in Rg (*BHL* 4093). Such details corroborate my general conclusions.

St, in addition to containing all of the texts found in Pl and nearly all the texts included in Rg, includes five texts not found in either Pl or Rg.[37] It is reasonable to deduce that St must have had at least another source besides the two represented by Pl and Rg. The relationship among these three collections, defined solely on the basis of contents, could be described by the following tree:[38]

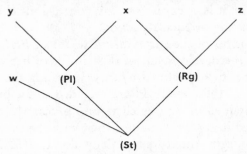

This tree corresponds completely to the *stemma redactionum* established above from the three ancient witnesses of the *Passio S. Anastasii*, Pl, Rg, and St. It confirms that the Passion of Anastasius found in St can be seen as the result of the contamination between p and r. The tree allows the possibility that the original version of the Passion of Anastasius contained in (x) was r, which would have then been reworked into p in Pl and remained r into Rg; or p, which would have been transformed into r through contamination with t. These conclusions are not certain, but the history and nature of these collections lean in support of p's antiquity. Pl represents an earlier and more primitive stage than Rg in the evolution of the cluster of related hagiographic legendaries to which they both belong. The precedence of the p-redaction over

37. Concordius (*BHL* 1906); Vincentius (*BHL* 8628); Thecla (*BHL* 8024); Gregorius papa (*BHL* 3639); Eleutherius & Antia (*BHL* 2451).

38. By using the manuscript *sigla* I do not wish to imply that there is a direct relationship beween these collections as there would be in a stemma codicum (this could only be claimed through an extensive textual study), but rather to indicate the *type* of relationship that is suggested by the contents. The lost Chartres codex appears to have contained all of Rg's texts and to have all of its texts included in St, and it could occupy a similar position as Rg in the scheme above.

r is supported as well by the date of the manuscripts, since Pl and Tr are older, from the first half of the ninth century, while Rg is more recent, from the end of the ninth century. Given no evidence to the contrary, one would have to assume that Pl rather than Rg preserves older versions of their common texts.

About This Edition
The text of the p-redaction survives in at least eleven manuscripts, written between the early ninth century and the fourteenth within a territorial band stretching from Freising to northeastern France and Flanders. These provide the direct evidence on which my edition is based.[39]

Tr, from the beginning of the ninth century, is the oldest witness for the *Passio* (in any redaction, Latin or Greek), but it consists of a single folio, cut from its original binding so that words in the inside margin have been trimmed. It preserves the section of text *respondit ei dicens–dicebat sancto martyri: Quare dispo* (ll. 506-561). Its reconstructed sanctoral overlaps completely that of Pl, the oldest complete witness; its fragmentary text of p agrees completely with Pl. Ty introduces some changes into the standard p text, most notably the consistant substitution of *sanctus* for *beatus*. The *Passio S. Anastasii* contained in Vn was copied from an exemplar that must have been misbound, since the order of text is transposed, with the second and third part of the text (each of these parts being equal in length) copied in reverse order.[40] This sug-

---

39. All witnesses of every recension of *BHL* 408 known to me are discussed in the "Descriptive List," including manuscripts that are today lost or destroyed. I have used the distinguishing variants I single out above to classify the redaction found in almost all the manuscripts of *BHL* 408. In a few cases, this has not been possible because of the high degree of contamination among the redactions (especially for the s-redaction), and in a few others, because the surviving evidence is fragmentary. I do not discuss as fully late manuscripts that do not contribute to the establishment of the critical text.

40. Fols. 73v-76r middle contain the text from the beginning to l. 154 (... *et multum rogans*); fols. 76r middle to 79r middle contain the section from l. 327 to l. 500 (*autem superbus ille–et intimavit imperatori*); fols. 79r middle to 82r middle contain ll. 154-326 (*cum aliis praedicti–Stupefactus*); fols. 82r middle to 84v contain the last section of the text, beginning with l. 501 (*Chosroi. Furore*–end).

gests that a group of pages—perhaps a quire?—in the immediate or an earlier model had been copied, or bound, in the wrong order. There is no indication that the scribe of this Vienna codex noticed, or attempted to correct, the mistake.

A group of seven codices housed today in the Bibliothèque nationale de France, ranging in date from the twelfth to the fourteenth century, contain a nearly identical text of the p-redaction. Five of these codices, 5291, 5319, 5341, 16736, 17003, are copies of the Cistercian legendary named the *Liber de natalitiis*, whose development begins in northeastern France and Flanders in the twelfth century.[41] The other two codices, 5300 and 5318, are closely related to this group.[42] The largest collection is represented in 5318, containing 104 hagiographic texts and covering the months January through March. It includes almost all the texts found in the other six codices, each one of which covers, by and large, the month of January alone. One sub-group is constituted by 5319, 16736, and 17003, which have an almost identical set of sixty-six texts[43] that is quite similar to the first part of the larger group represented by 5318. Closely related to this sub-group is the collection represented in 5341.[44] Finally, all of the Lives copied into 5291 (forty-two texts) and twenty-eight of the thirty Lives of 5300 are also present in 5318. Given the similarity in the text transmitted by

41. Levison, "Conspectus codicum hagiographicorum," pp. 547-550. Dolbeau, "Notes sur la genèse et sur la diffusion du 'Liber de Natalitiis'," pp. 143-195; Rochais, *Un légendier cistercien de la fin du XIIe s.: le 'Liber de Natalitiis' et de quelques grands légendiers des XII et XIIIe s.* Rochais does not differentiate clearly enough between the various versions of the *Passio S. Anastasii* (Part 2, p. 19). The redaction found in the *Magnum legendarium austriacum* is not *BHL* 408 but *BHL* 410; the one found in the Trier Legendary is a revised version of *BHL* 408 (=p₁); and the one found in Brussels, Bibliothèque royale 207-8 is a slightly revised version of *BHL* 408 (see pp. 230-231 and "Descriptive List").

42. In addition, this same form of the *Passio S. Anastasii* was contained in a lost legendary of St. Melaine Abbey in Rennes (Dolbeau, "Notes sur la genèse," p. 154).

43. Poncelet, *Catalogus ... parisiensi* II, 354, 386.

44. Poncelet, *Catalogus ... parisiensi* II, 264.

this group of witnesses, I have included in my *apparatus criticus* only the three twelfth-century witnesses.[45]

The indirect evidence contributes significantly to the establishment of p's text and to the understanding of its history. My reconstruction of p has been constantly informed by a comparison with t, its direct source. t's readings are included in the *apparatus criticus* whenever they can help in justifying the choice of reading among variants. The variant readings of Rg (and of its later corrector Rg²) and St, which fairly represent the redactions I label r and s, are also provided in the critical apparatus. I have also included the readings of *BHL* 410, which may have been used by the editor of p, on relevant occasions. The complete apparatus of the p-recension, which combines both the direct and indirect evidence, can serve to reconstruct s and r, evaluate my reconstruction of the history of 408, and determine the affiliation of manuscripts that may have eluded my search.

The relationship among the direct and indirect witnesses can be summarized by the following stemma:

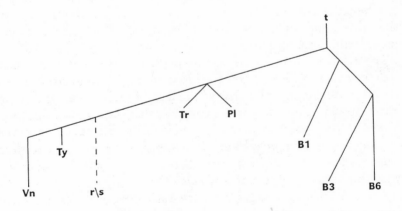

45. The text of the *Passio S. Anastasii* preserved in the Cistercian legendary was also copied in the fifteenth century into Cambrai, Bibliothèque publique 816 (721), fols. 78r-85r. This codex has the mark of the Benedictine Abbey of the Holy Sepulchre of Cambrai, where it was probably compiled. As its text of *BHL* 408 was copied from that preserved in the Cistercian tradition, I have not used this very late witness in my critical apparatus.

The text common to Pl Tr Ty Vn r s = π
The text common to B1 B3 B6 = β

The relationships expressed by the stemma can be justified by the following observations. The left branch, constituted by the oldest witnesses, namely Pl, Tr, Ty, and Vn, and r and s can be separated from β principally by the following common errors:

(l. 12) corruptionis] corruptione Pl Ty Vn   corruptionem Rg   corruptionum St

(l. 91) metus] moechatur π

(l. 124) praefectum] perfectum π

Within the π branch, Vn and Ty depart from the rest in their common errors *intentio* for *contentio* (l. 430), *multo* for *magno* (l. 571). Of these, only *intentio* is significant, while the other could be attributed to chance or independent emendation. Pl and Tr can be grouped together—despite the very fragmentary evidence provided by Tr—because of their common error *immortalis* (*importabilis* cet.) (ll. 517-518). On the whole, however, it must be emphasized that a striking characteristic in the transmission of this redaction is its absence of significant variants—that is variants that cannot be attributed to independent editors—and the abundance, on the other hand, of minor variants, mostly confined to word endings attributable to editors who wanted to improve the text.

The relation of the s and r-redactions (as represented by their oldest witnesses, St and Rg) to this stemma is also difficult to establish with certainty because of the lack of truly meaningful variants. However, one may safely conclude that these redactions originated in the π branch because s and r share with this branch the reading *corruptione, moechatur, perfectum.* Furthermore, the reading *intentio* and *multo*, which they share with Ty and Vn, indicate that their separation point was below Pl.

The β branch is segregated most clearly from the other branch by the following errors that are shared by all the manuscripts belonging to this group:[46]

(l. 59)   corporibus] pecoribus β

(l. 328) castellum] custodiam β

---

46. I.e. not only the ones I cite in my *apparatus criticus.*

(l. 388) comperit] requisivit β

By and large, all the witnesses in this group present a uniform text. The variations among them are quite minor, and there is no clear evidence that any of these manuscripts has been copied from another. I have not attempted to define the relationship among all of them, but only among the three from the twelfth century, lat. 5318 (=B1), lat. 16736 (=B6), and lat. 17003 (=B3) which I cite in my stemma. The grouping of B3 and B6 apart from B1 is indicated, for example, by the following shared variants:

(l. 5)   qui *om.* B3 B6
(l. 20)   praedicantes] pradicaverunt B3 B6
(l. 34)   aetheris] aethere B3 B6
(l. 36)   per (eos) *add.* B3 B6
(l. 319) ipse] ille B3 B6
(l. 462) erant *om.* B3 B6

It is always difficult to assign authority properly in a two-sided stemma. In this case, the antiquity of the left branch of the stemma has to be balanced at times against the more grammatical polish of the right.[47] While in many cases β's readings ought to be considered revisions due to the fluidity of hagiographic texts, the correctness of this branch is sometimes upheld by important, though seemingly minor, clues. One is found in ll. 394-395. Here, while the π branch reads *Et contigit infra dies paucos suscipere imperatoris iussionem*, β reads *Et contigit infra dies paucos suscipere eum imperatoris iussionem*, which agrees completely with t, and should be considered the correct reading. A similar agreement is provided by the reading *relinquens* of both t and β (l. 477) as opposed to *reliquit* of the other branch.[48] As a result of these considerations, I have not followed a rigid position. Rather, I have weighed each case separately, using every piece of direct and indirect evidence.

---

47. But I wish to emphasize that most of the variants are minor. The one significant variant is *moechatur/metus* (l. 91), but even in this case the correct reading of the BN manuscripts could have been arrived at by a scribe intent on improving the text available to him. And in fact, even in Pl a later scribe added the correction over the line.

48. Another small example is the *et* in both β and t of l. 542.

In many cases, however, one must admit, a different conclusion could have been sustained.

My *apparatus criticus* is a negative one for the manuscripts transmitting p and for St and Rg; it includes therefore only those readings of these manuscripts that differ from what I judge to be the authentic text of the p-redaction. The readings of t and g, the Greek source, are supplied in the *apparatus criticus* only when they bear on the choice of reading; otherwise it is omitted.

My division into chapters follows that of Flusin's Greek text; I have indicated in brackets the divisions of the text of *BHL* 408 as published in the *ASS*. I have standardized the orthography, with a note in the *apparatus criticus* only in cases of unusual spelling.

CONSPECTUS SIGLORUM

Tr	Trier, Stadtbibliothek 190 (1246)
Pl	Biblioteca apostolica vaticana, Palatinus latinus 846
Ty	Troyes, Bibliothèque municipale 1171
Vn	Vienna, Österreichische Nationalbibliothek, Latinus 377
B1	Paris, Bibliothèque nationale de France, latinus 5318
B3	Paris, Bibliothèque nationale de France, latinus 17003
B6	Paris, Bibliothèque nationale de France, latinus 16736
Rg	Biblioteca apostolica vaticana, Reginensis latinus 516
St	Stuttgart, Württembergische Landesbibliothek, HB XIV 13
π	Pl Tr Ty Vn Rg St
β	B1 B3 B6
codd.	= π β
t	*BHL* 410b *supra editum*
g	*BHG* 84, Flusin ed.
ASS	Acta edita in *ASS* Ian. II, 426-431 (3rd ed. III, 39-45).
410	*BHL* 410 *infra editum*

INCIPIUNT ACTA ET PASSIO
BEATI ANASTASII MARTYRIS
EX PERSIDA CIVITATE MENSE IAN. DIE XXII

1. Unigenitus filius et verbum Dei per quem omnia facta sunt,
qui coaequalis atque consubstantialis patri et sancto atque vivificatori spiritui misertus est generi humano perituro et mortis atque
corruptionis tyrannicae potestati subiecto, inclinavit autem caelos,
et descendit,[1] secundum quod scriptum est. Per virginem autem
natus, formam servi suscipiens,[2] conversatus est cum hominibus,[3]
omnia dispensans semper ad salutem generis nostri, et quidem
propria morte destruens eum qui habebat mortis imperium.[4] †Tri-
duano[5] autem eius corpori sepultura iacens†, corruptionis emundationem faciens, atque inferni descensione quae multa temporum de-
licta retinebant claustra subvertens,[6] ita gloriosa eius resurrectio
nos consurgere fecit, et consedere nos in caelestibus[7] iussit, sicut
Apostolus ait.

1 Incipit (Incipiunt *corr. supr. lin.* Pl) Pl Rg St   5 qui *om.* B3 B6   atque[2]]
et B1   constantialis Rg   6 et] sub *add.* Rg St   7 potestatis Rg St subjectum π Rg St t   9 accipiens Pl t   11-12 Traduano Rg Triduo ... corpus
in sepultura iacens β   12 sepulturae Rg St t   corruptione Pl Ty Vn corruptionem Rg corruptionum St *cf.* corruptionis t   12-13 emendationem Pl
13 in inferni *codd. exc.* B3   15 caelestia Rg St *cf.* caelestibus t

1. 2 Sm 22.10.
2. Cf. Phil 2.7. Both Pl and t quote the Vulgate text's *accipiens*, followed
also in 410. But *suscipiens* may represent the *lectio difficilior*.
3. Cf. Bar 3.38.
4. Cf. Heb 2.14.
5. The text here as transmitted by the oldest codices is very problematic,
and in fact has been corrected in various ways in later witnesses (cf. *In triduana autem sui corporis sepultura jacens ASS; triduana sui corporis sepultura* 410).
Certainly, despite the close adherence of t to g, the ultimate meaning of the
text must have been easy enough for any editor to deduce, and the problematic text here is the result of corruption probably, rather than misunderstanding or lack of skill.
6. This is a good example of the way in which the editor of p attempted
to revise the relative pronoun translating the Greek article.
7. Cf. Eph 2.6.

2. Ex hoc quippe de[8] sublimi virtute induti, hi qui per semetipsos prospecti et ministri verbi facti sunt,[9] atque eius passionis testes[10] beati apostoli, universum mundum peragrantes, divina mandata praedicantes, convenerunt autem ex Dei pietate per civitates et regiones, nationes et populos; tribubus et linguis praedicaverunt. Et illum quidem quasi paternae traditionis et multis temporibus impietatis errorem quo tenebantur radicitus evellentes, angelicam vero conversationem homines habere docuerunt. Ex hoc repleta iam bono cuncta in mundo[11] ut cognoscerent Dominum creatorem suum, secundum quod scriptum est, sicut aqua multa cooperiet mare.[12] Ex hoc terrestria caelestibus coniuncta sunt, et vita aeterna mundo concessa est. Ex hoc universa hominum natura magnis et ineffabilibus Dei donis laetatur.

3. Sed †quia†[13] humanae vitae a principio insidiator et fraudator atque dolosus et iustorum inimicus diabolus non habens qualiter induceret in tam amplam bonitatem, quae per Christi gratiam in hominibus fiebat, et magnum donum mundo datum videret, cernensque seipsum proiectum ab aetheriis, invenit concinnationem

---

17 de] pede Rg   sublimis virtutem Rg t   semetipsi Rg t   20 praedicaverunt B3 B6   22 illa Rg St illam t   quidem] quae *add.* Rg St t   quasi *om.*
St t   24 hominibus Rg St   24-25 bona Rg St   mundo] sunt *add.* B1 B3
26 quooperiet Rg   33-34 cernens quae Rg   34 aetheris *codd. exc.* aethere
B3 B6 caelestibus t

8. Rg's reading could represent either a repetition of (*quip-)pe* or a relic of t's *que de.*

9. Cf. Lc 1.2.

10. Cf. 1 Pt 5.1.

11. The addition of the phrases *iam bono* and *in mundo* removes the sense of p even further from g.

12. Cf. Is 11.9.

13. The grammar and meaning of the text here are problematic. *Quia* is perhaps an attempt to make sense of t's *qui* (which translates the Greek article). The phrase *et magnum donum mundo datum videret* in l. 33 is p's revision (cf. *magnale donum*), and arguably one could emend †*quia* ...† to *cum ... haberet* to parallel it.

35　eius malignitatis.[14] Nihil autem magnum eos qui pietatis[15] sunt
enutriti laedere posse, sed magis prodesse quod maximum est. Eos
enim qui tunc tenebant sceptra regalia varietate et multis modis
semetipsum disseminans, insurgere quidem fecit universam persecutionem adversus ecclesiam Dei, et hoc[16] quod super seipsum cunc-
40　tum orbem pervertit quasi confundens. Melior[17] autem †ei† restitit ad eius inmissionem. Quamvis parve tamen nihil nocuit Dei
cultores, maxime tamen hactenus ipse confunditur. Nihil[18] enim
deterius qui olim eum praeterminantium sanctorum apostolorum,
victoriosorum martyrum tolerantiam abiectus est dolosus; et
45　rursum proprium pietatis ornatum Christi recepit ecclesia, et quod

---

35 eius *om.* Rg *cf.* eius t　　malignitatis dignam t　　pietati Rg t pietate B6
36 est] Per *add.* B3 B6　　39 seipso Rg t　　40 convertit St subvertit t　　ei]
et Rg　　41 tamen] usque *add.* Rg St　　43 deterius] orum *add.* Rg *add.* horum St sanctorum] -que *add.* π　　44 martyrum] per *add.* B3 B6　　45 pro-
prium] -que *add.* Rg proprium quae t

---

14. The entire 408 tradition as represented in the manuscripts I have examined omits *dignam* ("a plan worthy of his malignity"). But it is found in
the *ASS* edition of 408 suggesting that Bolland emended the text to reflect the
Greek. The omission of this word in all redactions of 408 and 410 (but not
in t) illustrates again that t is derived from a different branch of the original
translation than 408 and 410.

15. The phrase *pietatis sunt enutriti* perhaps represents a double, but incomplete, correction of t's *pietati sunt alumnos*. p's editor may have first corrected *pietati* to *pietatis* to suit *alumnos*, but then changed *alumnos* to *enutriti*
without going back to alter *pietatis*. Several later manuscripts (and also the
ASS text) read *pietate*.

16. In this problematic passage p is very close to t (*et hoc quod super se
ipso*). Later manuscripts show attempts at improvement such as *ex hoc* (cf.
also the *ASS*).

17. p is unclear here, not surprisingly since t (*in meliori autem ei circumstetit ea quas inmissionis sunt*) makes absolutely no sense. Perhaps, the editor
meant the text to read *melior autem restitit ad eius inmissionem*, and *ei* (t's word)
was meant to be erased. The text remains unclear until the end of the chapter.

18. p repeats almost verbatim the confused text of t, as usual an awkward
calque of the Greek, unintelligible in Latin. *Propriumque*, preserved only by
Rg, is, I believe, a remnant of t's *proprium quae*, a rendering of τὸν οἰκεῖον
τῆς (εὐσεβείας), following t's general approach to the translation of the
Greek article (discussed on pp. 56ff.).

Dei est gratia, cotidie floret atque additur singulis temporibus numerus copiosus, protegente gratia Dei.

4. Satietatem[19] autem quae in nobis facta est ex Deo omnium bonorum accipientes homines, magnorum et ineffabilium Christi do-
50   norum < *** > languentes atque omnium aegrotationum varietate seu multis modis delictorum catena constricti, et sanguinum effusione terram satiantes, fornicationibus vero atque adulteriis seu aliis innumeris vitiis, atque malis actionibus iram Dei adversus semetipsos exardescentes, totam, ut dicam, super nos Dei manum discipli-
55   nae traximus. Unde tradidit quidem nos in manibus nequissimorum inimicorum, et regi iniusto et iniquo et maligno paene universam terram,[20] civitates et regiones omnes, quasdam igni traditas, quasdam autem radicitus evulsas, et captivum omne quod electum erat et desiderabile in corporibus quoque et in pecuniis, in perni-
60   ciem autem fecit universum quod derelictum est insatiabili insania.

---

46 tottidie Rg   addetur Rg   46-47 numerum copiosum Rg St numerum
t   48 Salus *codd.*   Dei Rg   omnium *om.* Rg t   49 magnarum *codd.*
50 varietas *codd.* varietate *corr.* B3 variate t   51-52 effusionem Pl Rg   52
terram satiantes] terram satiata Pl Ty B1 B6 terra satiata Vn B3 terram satiatam Rg St terram rubrantes t   56 inimicorum *om.* Rg inimicorum nequissimorum t   58, 59 omnem ... desiderabilem St   59 erat *om.* Rg St
corporibus] pecoribus β

19. This passage is also a very close rendering of t's difficult text. The change of t's *satietatem* (Κόρον = *satietas*) to *salus* in the manuscripts of 408, however, obfuscates the meaning even more, and it seems possible to take *Salus autem*, which is the reading of the manuscripts, as a corruption of *Satietatem*. I posit a word or so missing after *donorum* that would have corresponded to t's *oblivionem perfectam* magnarum et ineffabilium Christi donorum. The phrase *omnium aegrotationum* added in p has no equivalent in t, and can be considered perhaps attached more directly to *languentes*, to which (rather than to *constricti*) it is more clearly suited. Also problematic is the reading *varietas*, which is not a good rendering of t's adverb *variate*; *variatim* is suggested as a possibility. Finally, I have emended *satiata/m* to *satiantes* on the model of t's *rubrantes*. The *ASS* text is highly edited and no surviving manuscript I have examined supports it.
    20. Cf. Dn 3.32.

Derelicti sumus.[21] Non tamen usque in finem despexit benignus atque amator humani generis Deus, sicut manifestant res ipsae, sed suaves habere nos spes dedit, ut usque nunc glorificari[22] inter proprios et fideles eius servos et martyres.

65   **5.** Oportunum autem hic sermonem facturi secundum magni apostoli vocem dicentis, O altitudo divitiarum et sapientiae atque scientiae Dei, quam inscrutabilia iudicia eius et investigabiles viae eius! [23] Etenim Persis[24] quidem tradidit ad correptionem eos qui[25] eius secundum gratiam filii atque heredes < sunt >. Ex Persida autem
70   martyrem sibi elegit usque ad sanguinem, qui in eum est caritatem, fidem, atque confessionem ostensurus, et quod melius est quia non solum viros, sed et mulieres omnes ostensuras agonem et certamen, et usque in finem pro Christi fide per crucis exemplum coronam

---

61 Derelicti] quoderelictum *codd.* quod derelictum t   63 suavem ... spem St *cf.* suaves spes t   ut] et B3   65 hinc β   66 et *om.* β St   atque] et β   67 scrutabilia Rg   viae *om.* Pl   68 Persis *aut* Persibus Pl Persibus *codd.* t   eos qui eius] suos β   69 filios *codd.*   71 ostensuris Rg St t

     21. The phrase *derelicti sumus* is added in the 408 tradition, but it is difficult to see how it improves the text. It was, very possibly, a marginal comment or note that found its way into the text. The *ASS* text adds *Adeo derelicti sumus*, but there is no support for this variant in the manuscripts I have examined.

     22. *Ut ... glorificari* is the same construction used by t, a calque on g (τῷ ... ἐνδοξάζεσθαι) left uncorrected in p. The *ASS* text (*ut glorificati simus*), for which there is no evidence in the manuscripts available to me, represents a further departure from the meaning of g, where it is God who is glorified among his servants and martyrs.

     23. Cf. Rm 11.33.

     24. The usage of this word is inconsistent. Since Pl considers it most of the times a word belonging to the first declension, and that is also the usage of all the manuscripts for the genitive plural, I have regularized its use.

     25. This phrase, *qui–heredes*, repeats t's text verbatim, except for the absence of the verb *extiterunt*, which may have been a later addition in t's tradition, since it has no equivalent in g. I have chosen to emend *filios* to *filii* and to add *sunt* on the assumption that this may be another example of incomplete correction; cf. p₁ (*filii sunt eius ...*). β's text must be considered a further correction of the problematic passage.

adepturas. Horum unus extitit et noster coronator Anastasius,
75 huius vitam quam ab initio usque ad finem scribere iussus sum,
ipsum praeponens testem quem ipse confessus est, Deum et Dominum Ihesum Christum, et sic incipiam enarrationis sermonem,
Domino protegente.

6. Hic quidem erat de Persidis regione Razech vocabulo, de fundo
80 Rasnuni, nomen autem ei Magundat. Filius vero erat magi cuiusdam Bau nomine, qui etiam doctor extiterat magicae artis. Erudivitque eum pater suus a pueritia magicam artem. [*7. ASS*] Factus
est autem iuvenis. Contigit ergo militare eum in tyronatu cum aliis
multis, et esse in regia civitate Persarum sub Chosroe imperatore.
85 Sanctae autem civitatis desolatione facta, et venerabilibus[26] atque
adorandis locis igni concrematis in praedicta ira, quam pro nostris
peccatis perpessi sumus, honoranda vero atque vivifica ligna pretiosae crucis Domini nostri Ihesu Christi captiva deducta sunt in Persidam.[27] O admiranda res! Captiva quidem ducebatur Domini crux
90 ad illorum insipientiam; captivabat autem magis corda infidelium.

---

74 adepturi Rg St obligaturas t   77 et sic *om.* B6   79 Racech St   functo
Pl   80-81 quoddam Rg t quondam St   82 magica arte Rg St *cf.* magicam
artem t   83 militari π   tyro] -cinio *add. supra lin.* Rg²   84 est Rg *cf.*
esse t   Chosdroe *corr.* Rg²   85 factae Rg t   venerabilia atque adoranda
loca concremata sunt in π   88-89 Persida Rg St t   89 admirande St
autem] enim Pl Vn *cf.* autem t

26. t's confused text (*venerandorum atque adorandorum locorum igni combustis in praedicto irae propter peccata nostra sumpta sunt et onoranda ...*) does
not provide clear support for either branch's reading. I have chosen to follow
β because of t's mixture of ablative and genitive absolute, but π's *sunt* may
be a remnant of t's *sumpta sunt.*

27. The usage of this word is inconsistent in the manuscripts: *Persidis* is
found for the genitive, *Persida* is always used for the ablative, but *Persidam*
(once *Persidem*) is found for the accusative in Pl and *Persida* a couple of times
in St. I have followed the general usage of Pl.

7. Metus autem et stupor invadebat[28] infideles, gaudio vero atque
laetitia corda fidelium coruscabant. Fama autem ubique de ea in
omni Persida diffamabatur. [8. *ASS*] Interea audiens praefatus tyro
Magundat, qui et Anastasius, famam atque virtutem pretiosae cru-
95 cis Domini nostri Ihesu Christi, interrogavit de ea, quomodo aut
qualiter esset mysterium venerandae crucis. Et discens a fidelibus
eius virtutem, atque ab aliis dicentibus quomodo Deus Christianorum in hac cruce, quae huc advenit,[29] †in ea†[30] pependit pro salute generis humani; statim sicut terra bona, suscepta pluvia ad
100 producendum fructum praeparata, ita et ille tunc suscipiens per
auditum ineffabilem virtutem[31] Domini nostri Ihesu Christi < atque > mirabile nomen, in intimo cordis sui suscipiebat monita
vitae, cogitans qualiter Deum magnum, qui habitat in caelo, quem
Christiani colunt, ad culturam eius pertingeret.[32] Diligenter autem

91 Moechatur π (metum *corr. supra lin.* Pl) metum t   stuporem π gaudium π   92 coruscabunt St   in *om.* Rg t *add.* Rg²   95 nostri *om.* Rg
96 a] ad Rg   98 crucem Rg   qui hic advenit Rg hic veniret t   98-99
salutem Rg   100 praeparatam Rg   tunc *eras.* Rg   101 ineffabilem] atque
add. Rg St

28. The text here is problematic. There is t's support for the readings *metum ... stuporem*, which, however, would require a different verb than *invadebat*. Both t and 410 have *imponebat* translating ἐνετίθει. *Moechatur* is indication that this passage has undergone corruption in the π branch.

29. Only Rg interprets the subject of *advenit* to refer to Christ as do g,
t, and 410. But one can see how *advenit* can be easily taken to refer to the
cross: for it is the cross that has been brought to Persia, where Anastasius
sees it. And this seems to make sense, and to be the work of a good editor.

30. Clearly, this is an unnecessary addition in 408, and in fact it has been
eliminated in the Roman revision, cf. p. 474 l. 89. Could it have been a marginal note, which made its way into the text?

31. The addition of *virtutem*, which is not in g or t, presents a problem
for this text. I have chosen to add *atque*, on the assumption that the addition
of *atque* in Rg and St a little before might in fact represent a misplacement
of this word, present originally. Cf. also the expansion of t by the addition
monita vitae in ll. 102-103.

32. p presents a reasonable interpretation of t's poor translation of g.
Hence, t's *inveniret hic* is an attempt to render ἥκει ἐνταῦθα, but both p and
410 (*inveniret*) take *invenio* in its common meaning of "to find." But still, the
two objects (*Deum* and *ad culturam eius*) are problematic. They could be ex-

105 perquirebat a quibusdam,[33] quomodo ipsa est crux, in qua Christus filius Dei crucifixus est, quem Christiani adorant; et vehementer admirans, decrevit Dei famulus Anastasius ad religionem christianam pertingere. Et quanto plus per auditum quae veritatis sunt
percipiebat, tanto magis ab eius corde magicae artis seductio absce-
110 debat. Sicut enim effugiunt tenebrae a luce, a sole autem umbra, et
ab igne fumus, ita et fallacia exterminatur a doctrina veritatis.

8 [9 *ASS*]. Habebat[34] autem fratrem carnalem beatus Anastasius
†qui militans et pergens in exercitu cum eo cognomento Sain,
princeps exercitus Persarum, et† venit usque Carchedonia. At vero
115 sanctae recordationis et divinae memoriae Philippico circumvallante[35] eum, ingressus est Persidam. Audiens vero Sain reversus
est post tergum suum. Et sic contigit famulum Dei Anastasium

---

105 quomodo *add. supra ras.* Rg² esset St *cf.* est t 106 Dei *om.* B1
113 qui *om.* Rg *cf.* Habens ... fratrem ... militem t militantem *corr. supra
lin.* Rg² exercitu] exercitum Pl Ty Vn *cf.* exercitu t 114 Carchedona]
Carcedona Rg Charcedona St B1 B6 t 115 et *om.* St 115-116 circumval-
lante] circumvallanti Rg St t 116 Persidam] Persida St 117 Anastasium]
ut *add.* Rg²

---

plained, again, as an unclear correction or notation, in which *ad culturam eius
pertingeret* could be seen as either an addition or alternative to t's text or a
marginal explanation that made its way into the text.

33. In Rg, there is something scraped off between *quibusdam* and *ipsa*,
and *quomodo* is added by the corrector above the line. I suggest that *(et) didicit* might have been scraped off, which is t's and 410's reading.

34. The text here is unclear, and in fact later editors corrected it. The
Roman Revision, for example, reads *Habebat autem fratrem carnalem beatus
Anastasius cum quo militabat et pergebat in exercitu, cui nomen Sayn, et hic
erat princeps exercitus Persarum.* And the Gladbach manusript used in the *ASS*
has *Habebat autem fratrem carnalem B. Anastasius militantem, et pergentem in
exercitu cum eo, cognomento Sain, Principem exercitus Persarum ... .* Although
t is ungrammatical, its meaning is not too difficult to extract, and it was
followed quite closely by 410.

35. As a result of t's mistranslation of ἀντιπερισπάω ("to divert, draw
out"—in a military sense), the Latin text is not an accurate reflection of the
Greek. p's change of the second ablative absolute into a finite clause causes
additional confusion.

cum Persarum exercitu devenire in partibus Orientis. Et exinde recessit ab exercitu, et derelinquens proprium fratrem venit ad Hie-
120 ropolim, et devertit ad quendam Christianum Persam malleatorem, et mansit apud eum. Didicit autem apud eum et ipse artem, et operabatur cum eo.

9 [10 *ASS*]. Cum ergo abundaret in eo amor et gratia atque deside-rium ut inluminaretur, multum rogabat praefatum malleatorem, ut
125 eum instrueret qualiter ad gratiam sancti baptismatis perveniret. At ille intra se cogitans[36] propter metum Persarum ne periclitaretur, metuebat. Tamen cum illo ibat ad ecclesiam sanctorum martyrum, et orabat. Et picturas sanctorum et historias[37] conspiciebat, et re-quirebat ab eo quidnam hoc esset. Et audiebat ab eo sanctorum
130 certamina, sive mirabilia quae fecerunt, sive atrociora tormenta quae a tyrannis perpessi sunt et eorum tolerantiam, et mirabatur pavens. Manens igitur per parvum tempus apud praedictum chris-tianissimum virum, optimum desiderium perceptum est in animo suo ut Hierosolymam adveniret, et illic sancti mereretur baptisma-
135 tis consecrationem adipisci.

10 [11 *ASS*]. Et habens propositum in Dei amore, devenit ad sanc-tam civitatem, et mansit apud quemdam Christi amabilem virum, item malleatorem, et patefaciens omne suum desiderium, quomodo

---

118 devenire] deveniret Rg St *cf.* venire t   119 exercitu] exercito Rg *cf.* exer-citu t   120 Persam] Persum Rg St *cf.* Persam t   123 habundaret Rg 124 inluminaretur] miraretur *corr. ex* imminaretur Rg² praefatum] perfec-tum π (praefatum *corr. ex* perfectum Rg²) *cf.* praedictum t 410   126 cogita-ret Rg cepit cogitaret Rg² cogitavit *cet. mss cf.* suspectus t   132 pavens-igitur *add. in marg.* Rg   per *om.* St Rg t   133 percepit β preceptum Rg perceptus St t   134 meretur] dignaretur Rg St *cf.* mereretur t   135 conse-cratione St   136 Et] hoc *add.* Rg   de(venit?) *erasum est* Rg deinde venit Rg²   137 Christo Rg t   138 item] et ipsum *supra lin. add.* Rg²

---

36. I have emended *cogitavit* both because t also has a participle (*suspectus*) and because the root of the scribal mistake can be easily understood. The *ASS* text also reads *cogitans*.

37. The addition of *historias* to the *picturas sanctorum martyrum* of t is peculiar to 408.

vult Christo coniungi, ut mereretur gratiam sancti baptismatis
140 accipere, et perductus est ab eo Heliae sanctissimo presbytero
Sanctae Resurrectionis, qui eum tamquam a Deo praedestinatum
suscepit filium. Et postea indicavit de eo Modesto sanctissimo
presbytero et vicario apostolicae sedis, et fecit eum baptizari simul
cum aliis[38] qui et ipsi de eadem regione erant qui etiam et ipsi
145 beatum finem pro Christo suscipientes in Edessa civitate martyrio
coronantur.

11 [12 *ASS*]. Detentus vero beatus Anastasius a sanctissimo presbytero Helia in domo sua vel octo dies. Exhortans eum in proposito
bono persistere, interrogabat eum praedictus sanctissimus presbyter
150 Helias dicens quid cogitasset erga se de reliquo. Ipse vero rogavit
eum, dicens ut monachum eum ordinaret. Post depositas vero albas,[39] continuo perduxit eum ad monasterium sanctae recordationis
Anastasii Abbatis quod quarto miliario distat a sancta civitate, et
multum rogans cum aliis praedicti venerabilis monasterii fratribus
155 Iustinum Praepositum, virum valde mirabilem, per omnia quaeque
prudentem et plenum quae Dei sunt praeceptis, tradidit ei Dei famulum Anastasium. Qui etiam suscipiens eum suae congregationi
sociavit. Hoc autem factum est per indictionem octavam domini
Eraclii piissimi atque christianissimi imperatoris anno decimo.
160 Dedit autem ei et magistrum unum eiusdem congregationis fratrem

139 mereretur] dignaretur Rg St digne accipere t   gratiae Rg   140 accipere *om.* Rg *cf.* digne accipere gratiam sancti baptismatis t   141 Sanctae *eras.*
non legi potest Rg   Resurrectionis *eras.* surrettis *(?)* Rg   144 de *om.* Rg
add. Rg²   qui²] et *add.* Rg   145 beatam Ty Vn Rg St t   146 autem B1
147 vel *om.* β   dies] Et *add.* β 148 persisti Rg   152 ad monasterium *om.*
Rg St (*sed* ad *add.* Rg *aut* Rg²) *cf.* in mansionem t ad mansionem 410   153
Anastasio Abbati St   qui Rg   155 Iussinum Rg -ti- *supra lin. add.* Rg²
156 praecepta Rg St   ei et Rg   158-159 per–imperatoris] indictione octava
imperante domino Eraclio piissimo atque christianissimo imperatore Rg St
159 imperatoris] domini *add.* Pl Vn β   160 unum] de *add.* Rg St *cf.* unum de
eius germanis discipulis t congregatione St

38. The 408 tradition changes some of the details: g, t (and 410) all say
that Anastasius was baptized with one companion, not with *aliis*.
39. A learned conjecture in p referring to the custom of wearing white cloth-
ing for a week after baptism. For a fuller discussion, cf. Chapter V, p. 175.

virum prudentem, qui etiam docuit eum litteras[40] simul et placentes Dei doctrinas, simul cum psalterio, et tondens eum tradidit ei sanctum habitum atque ut filium adoptavit.

12 [13 *ASS*]. Fecit autem omne ministerium, et per omnia officia
165 pertransivit in praedicto monasterio beatus Anastasius, placens omnibus per Domini gratiam. Erat enim sedulus valde in ministerio fratrum et in opere manus, et prae omnibus in regulam monachicam intentus et in Missarum solemniis frequentans. Et audiens sine intermissione sanctas ac divinas scripturas, ac vitam sanctorum Pa-
170 trum attentius legebat, et ponebat studium diligenter. Et si aliquid non intellegebat, interrogabat suum magistrum, idoneum virum, prudentem, in omnibus ornatum, et discebat ab eo quae requirebat, et admirans glorificabat Deum. Adsidue autem legebat in cella secretius certamina vel agones sanctorum martyrum, et cotidie lacri-
175 mas effundebat et cogitabat atque aestuabat secretius in corde suo, ac desiderio accensus, ut eum Dominus ad martyrii palmam vocare dignaretur; quatenus eum dignaretur[41] fieri socium servorum suorum qui pro eius nomine passi sunt, ad laudem et gloriam Domini nostri Ihesu Christi. Perseveravit autem in eadem mansione per an-
180 nos septem.[42]

13 [14 *ASS*]. Videns autem antiquus hostis et inimicus humani generis tanta perseverantia in Christi servitio atque amore famulum Dei Anastasium persistere, et volens eum a bono proposito revoca-

---

161 litteras] graecas *add.* Rg t   161-162 placenta Rg placentia *corr.* Rg *aut* Rg² St   162 doctrinam Rg doctrina St   165 pertransibit Rg pertransibat *corr.* Rg²   166 Domini] Dei St   enim] autem Rg *cf.* enim t   167 manu Pl (*sed* -um *add. supra lin.*) manuum St manens Vn *cf.* manus t   169 ac^(1&2)] hac ... hac Rg   vitas Rg St t   174 et *om.* Rg   175 infundebat Pl   176 desiderium Rg desiderium malens t   179 mansionem Rg   per *om.* St   182 tantam perseverantiam Rg St atque] circa *add. in marg.* Rg²   183-184 revocari St

---

40. See above, pp. 365 and 376, on the omission of *graecas*.

41. p here repeats the point made in t *(Ut et eum dignum efficiat quandoque coequari sanctorum certaminis ad laudem)*; it seems possible that one may have been an editor's note that made its way into the text.

42. p and 410 suggest that a phrase corresponding to Διετέλεσεν–μονῇ has dropped out of t's tradition.

185 re, et de praedicto monasterio suadere exire, immisit ei cogitationes iniquas, etiam ut ad memoriam ei revocaret magicam artem, quam a suo patre didicerat. Ipse vero videns iniquissimi diaboli astutiam sese in orationem dedit, et enixius Dominum deprecabatur, ut eum eriperet ab insidiis adversarii. Abbati vero monasterii sui indicavit cordis sui secreta, et lacrimabiliter deprecabatur eum, ut pro se Do-
190 mino effunderet preces, ut eum liberaret de faucibus adversarii. Quod et faciebat iam praefatus abbas. Admonebat quoque eum et confortabat in Domino secundum quae data illi fuerat in Domino gratiam, et faciens orationem pro eo coram omnibus fratribus in ecclesia, effugavit ab eo pugnam diabolicam.

195 **14 [15 *ASS*].** Post dies autem modicos somnium vidit per noctem Dei famulus Anastasius, ita. Videbat seipsum in monte stare excelso, et quendam ad eum[43] venientem et porrigentem sibi poculum aureum plenum vino, et dicentem: "Accipe, et bibe." Quem suscipiens, bibit. Statim autem vigilans et interpretatus est intra se som-
200 nium quod viderat, hoc esse quod cupiebat. Qui protinus surgens ad ecclesiam perrexit ad matutinales ymnos explendos, adlucescente sancto Dominico die. Et expletis vero ymnis matutinalibus, rogavit abbatem monasterii ut ei secretius loqueretur. Et ingressi in sacrario cecidit ad pedes eius, rogans cum lacrimis ut Domino effunderet
205 preces pro eo, ut eum dignum susciperet, sperans quod moriturus esset in ipsis diebus. Dicebat tamen abbati: "Scio, Pater, quantos labores habuisti in me miserum, et quia multum te tribulavi, et quia

---

184 de *om.* Rg   185 etiam ut] ut etiam *corr.* Rg[2]   quod Rg St quorum t 188] insidias Rg *cf.* insidiis t   188-189 indicavit cordis sui *rep.* Rg   190 inimici Pl   191 *corr. ex* faciens Rg[2]   193 gratia *codd.*   194 effugavit] et fugabat *aut* exfugavit Rg   196 ita *eras. et add.* Rg *aut* Rg[2]   196-197 montem ... excelsum St   stare excelso] se excelsum Rg   198 quod St t 199 et *om.* β *cf.* et t   interpretavit Rg St   intra] in St   200 *corr. ex* videbat Rg *aut* Rg[2]   201 at luciscente Pl Vn St allucescente Ty inlucescente *corr. ex* adlucescente Rg delucescente t   202 et *om.* Rg St   vero *om.* β   205 quod] quasi Rg St t   206 tamen] autem Pl   207 tribulavit Rg[2]

---

43. *ad eum ... sibi*: This may be an instance of uneven grammar, or perhaps an attempt by the editor of p to make sense of t's *ad eum venientem et porrigentem ei* with as little change as possible by assuming that *eum* refers to *montem* and *ei* to Anastasius (hence the change to *sibi*).

per te adduxit me Deus de tenebris ad veram lucem. Sed rogo, Pater, ut pro me Dominum exores." Dicit ei abbas: "Quae est enim
210 causa, fili mi? et unde nosti, quia in his diebus egrediaris de hoc saeculo?" Ipse vero narravit ei somnium quod viderat, et confirmans asserebat quia per omnia moriturus esset in ipsis diebus, sive propria morte, sive per martyrium, quomodo cupiebat. Timebat tamen palam dicere de martyrio ut non increparent eum fratres.

215 **15 [16 *ASS*].** Abbas vero blande consolabatur eum multis admonitionibus. Missarum vero sollemnia celebrans cum fratribus, et percipiens divina mysteria, sumpsit cibum cum eis. Soporatusque est modicum, et evigilans, non ferens cordis sui incendium, volens adimplere desiderium suum quod erat placitum Domino, egressus
220 est clam de monasterio, nihil secum tollens nisi eam vestem qua indutus erat, et abiit Diospolim. Exinde profectus est causa orationis in montem Garizin, atque exinde profectus est ad alia venerabilia loca. Deductus est autem per Domini gratiam, et devenit usque Caesaream Palestinam, et mansit in domo beatae et
225 intemeratae Dei genetricis Mariae diebus duobus.

16 [17 *ASS*]. Secundum vero praedestinationem Dei quae a Deo illi fuerat data, perrexit usque ad Beatam Euphemiam ad orationis modum. Cumque pergeret transiens per quendam locum, vidit in domo cuiusdam Persae magicam operantes artem. Et zelo Dei ductus
230 ingressus est ad eos, et dixit eis: "Quid erratis, et errare facitis animas hominum in maleficiis vestris?" Stupentes autem viri illi in sermonibus et in constantia ipsius, interrogaverunt eum dicentes: "Quisnam es tu qui hoc dicis?" Ipse vero ait eis: "Et ego aliquando erravi, sicut et vos, et cognovi aliquando istam nefandam artem at-
235 que de vestris incantantionibus conscius sum." Et arguens eos, obmutuerunt, et rogaverunt eum, ne detraheret aut divulgaret de arte eorum cuiquam, et dimisit eos.

209 *corr. ex* quid Rg *aut* Rg² quid t   210 egrederis St   214 diceret Rg
increparent] in *add.* Rg   215 Abba St   218 non–volens *om.* Rg   220
eam vestem qua] ea quam Rg quae St   221 habiit Rg   causam Rg   221-
222 causa–profectus est *om.* St   224 domum Rg   226 quam St   227 Euphoniam Rg   228 pergeret] et *add.* Rg St   quoddam Rg St   228-229 domum Rg t   229 Persae] *emendavi* Persi *codd.*   232 inconstantiam Rg super ... constantiam t   235 sum] *om.* π

17 [18 *ASS*]. Et praeteriens modicum ab illis et videntes eum quidam de officio sedentes ante ianuam praetorii et transeuntem illum
240 dixerunt propria lingua inter se: "Iste delator est." Audiens autem
beatus Anastasius haec verba inter se ad invicem conferentes, intuens
eos, dixit: "Quid inter vos verba confertis? Ego impostor non sum
sed servus sum Domini mei Ihesu Christi. Nam et melior vestri
sum, quia illius merui esse servus, qui pro peccatoribus de caelo de-
245 scendere dignatus est. Nam et ego aliquando in officio fui, sicut et
vos." At illi surgentes tenuerunt eum. Et exiens primarius eorum,
et inquirens unde esset < et >[44] diligenter investigans, iussit eum
custodiri tribus diebus, in quibus nullatenus usus est de eorum alimentis, memorans dolositatem eorum in maleficiis ipsorum.

250 **18** [19 *ASS*]. Veniente autem Barzabana in Caesaream (non enim
ibidem erat quando tentus est beatus Anastasius) et suggerens de eo
primus officiorum, adduxit eum in praetorium suum. Occupato vero Barzabana circa alia negotia, inventus est ibi quidam Christianus,
qui cognovit beatum Anastasium cum esset in domo beatae Dei
255 genetricis Mariae semper virginis. Et colloquens ei secretius, ac requirens quam ob causam detentus ab eis fuisset, et cognoscens rei
causam, beatificavit eum de bono proposito, et confortavit in Domino divinis sermonibus monens eum ut non metueret tormenta,
et non timeret mori pro nomine Domini nostri Iesu Christi, sed
260 fortiter atque fiducialiter responderet Barzabanae ad ea quae interrogatus esset ab eo, memorans ei et sermonem quem Dominus in
sancto Evangelio dixit: Quia qui perseveraverit usque in finem hic
salvus erit.[45]

---

240 delarator Rg impostor *supra lin. add.* Rg[2]   242 vos] eos Rg v *supra lin.*
add. Rg[2]   243 sum *corr. ex* suum Rg   et] ego *add.* St   244 meruit Rg
249 dolositates β   250 Venientem Rg   251-252 de–officiorum] de officiorum Rg de officio St   255-256 secretius–rei *om.* Rg   255 ac] et St   260
fiducialiter] fideliter St   261 ab] hab Rg   Dominus *om.* Rg

---

44. Cf. *et discutiens eum unde esset* et *omnia diligenter quae erga eum erant
examinans* t; et *diligenter investigans* p₁; et *diligenter eum examinans* 410
45. Mt 10.22.

19 [20 *ASS*]. Introductus est autem Dei famulus Anastasius, et stans
265 coram Barzabana non adoravit eum secundum ritum qui ab eis te-
nebatur. Et intuens in eum Barzabanas, dicit ei: "Unde es? et quis
vocaris?" Ipse vero ait: "Ego Christianus sum. Si autem cupis discere quantum ad genus, Persa de regione Razech, de villa Rasnuni.
Officialis eram et magus; et reliqui tenebras, et veni ad veram lucem.
270 Nomen autem meum prius Magundat, Christianitatis < *** >[46]
vero Anastasius vocor." Dixit ei Barzabanas: "Dimitte hunc errorem et convertere ad primam tuam religionem, et praebemus tibi
pecuniam, et possessiones plurimas." Ipse vero respondens ait:
"Non mihi contingat negare Dominum meum Ihesum Christum."
275 Dixit ei Barzabanas: "Ergo placent tibi vestimenta talia, qualibus
uteris?" Beatus Anastasius dixit: "Hoc indumentum angelicum et
gloriosum est." Dixit ei Barzabanas: "Daemonium habes." Respondit beatus Anastasius, et dixit ei: "Quando in errore eram, habui
daemonium. Nunc autem habeo Dominum Ihesum Christum Sal-
280 vatorem meum, qui destruit daemonia." Dixit ei Barzabanas: "Non
metuis imperatorem? Nam si de te cognoverit quae erga te sunt,
iubebit te crucifigi." Beatus Anastasius dixit: "Quare timeam illum?
Homo est corruptibilis, sicut et tu."

20 [21 *ASS*]. Tunc indignatus Barzabanas iussit eum in vinculis fer-
285 reis duci in castrum, et lapides sine cessatione deportari fecit. Et
multas atque innumeras tribulationes perpessus est famulus Christi
Anastasius.[47] Quidam enim de regione eius, videntes quae in eum
fiebant, erubescebant et increpabant eum, dicentes: "Quid hoc face-

---

265 quod Rg St t   268 Persas Pl Persus Rg St   regione] regno Pl   270
priore Rg priorem St Magundas Rg   273 pecunia St   275 quibus B3 B6 qualia Rg St   277 Respondens B3 B6   278 et *om.* B3 B6   280 destruet *corr. ex*
destruat Rg *aut* Rg²   285 castro Rg St t   deportare β *cf.* asportari t   286
est] *om. codd. exc.* B3 B6   287 videntes] eum *add.* Rg *cf.* videntes eum t

46. This passage, in which Anastasius discusses his names, is added by the
408 tradition. Most likely, a word connected to *Christianitatis* is missing. The
ASS text adds *nomine* (cf. *nomine* p₁).

47. For the similarity of this passage—and particularly *in vinculis* and *perpessus*—to Bede's Chronicle's *et multa diu verbera inter carceres et vincula Marzabana iudice perpessus* (t: *sustineret*), see Chapter VI, p. 190.

re voluisti? Nemo aliquando de regione nostra factus est Christia-
290 nus; et ecce fecisti nobis ridiculum." Atque aliis verbis fallacibus
suadebant ei. Ipse vero expellebat eos a se. In insaniam autem conversi percutiebant eum absque pietate et trahebant ei barbam, et
scindebant vestimenta eius. Non solum autem istud Dei famulo faciebant, sed et lapides magnos quos quatuor homines non poterant
295 volvere ei in collo ponebant. Et vinctus sic faciebat opus: unam[48]
catenam ad collum eius, aliam vero in pedes, et multa atrociora et
saeva tormenta ei contulerunt. At vero fortissimus athleta Dei
Anastasius omnia sustinuit gaudens pro Christi nomine.

21 [22 *ASS*]. Iterum autem iussit Barzabanas eum ante se adsisti, et
300 dixit ei: "Si veraciter, sicut dixisti, magi filius fuisti, et scis magicam
artem, dic mihi a quo didiceris vel aliqua ex eis, ut ego cognoscam." Ipse vero ait: "Ne permittat Deus ultra ut egrediatur quicquam ex ore meo de tali re." Dicit ei Barzabanas: "Quid ergo, permanes in his? Convertere in illam primam religionem, nam pro te
305 suggeram Chosroi Imperatori." Ipse vero ait ad eum: "Scripsisti, et
suscepisti rescripta. Fac quod vis." Et ait Barzabanas: "Non scripsi,
sed scribo, et quicquid mihi praecipiet facio." Sanctus vero Anastasius respondit: "Vade, scribe quanta volueris mala de me. Ego enim
Christianus sum." Barzabanas dixit: "Prosternatur in terra, et tam-
310 diu caedatur quousque perficiat quod ei iubetur." Anastasius Dei
famulus dixit: "Sinite me, non habeo necesse vincula." Et exprimens signum[49] sibi sanctae crucis fecit in fronte, et sedens in terra

---

291 ad insania St Illi autem (in insania) *add.* Rg² 292 pietatem Rg 294
famuliis Rg 296 in collo B3 B6 aliam B3 B6 alia *cet.* in] ad Rg a t
297 intulerunt β Dei] Christi Rg 299 eum *om.* π *cf.* eum t ante se
om. Rg 302 Non St ultra ut] *transpos.* Rg 305 imperatoris Rg 307
praecipiat Rg St praeciperit ... faciam *corr.* Rg² 310 ei iubetur *corr. ex* ei-
betur Rg 311 *corr. ex* famulum Rg habeo] abeo Rg

---

48. t's participle *ferentem* governing *unam catenam ... aliam* has no equivalent in the early 408 tradition. Some later manuscripts show attempts at
improvements, as does the *ASS* text, which adds *imponebant*.

49. In t there is no mention of the sign of the cross but that is how p's editor, attempting to make sense of this passage, understood *designavit semetipsum*.

ligaverunt eum et caedebant eum.[50] Sanctus vero Anastasius dixit
eis: "Expoliate me habitum, quo sum indutus, ut non patiatur iniu-
315 riam, et sic caedite carnes meas. Ista enim quae facitis lusus sunt.
Ego enim si membratim abscidar, numquam negabo Dominum
meum Ihesum Christum."

22. Dicit ei Barzabanas: "Adquiesce mihi, nam scribo pro te imperatori." At ipse respondens dixit: "Vade, scribe imperatori tuo quic-
320 quid volueris." Et ait Barzabanas: "Ergo imperatorem non times?"
Beatus Anastasius dixit: "Quare timeam imperatorem tuum? Aut
non est homo sicut et tu? Aut non moritur sicut et tu? Aut non
videt corruptionem sicut et tu? Quem autem dicis ut timeam, illum, qui corruptionem videt similem tibi luto? Aut Dominum Ihe-
325 sum Christum, qui fecit caelum et terram, mare et omnia quae in
eis sunt, qui numquam vidit corruptionem?" [23 *ASS*]. Stupefactus
autem superbus ille Barzabanas in responsione martyris, item iussit
eum duci in castellum.

23. Et post dies paucos fecit eum sibi praesentari, et dixit ei: "Re-
330 cordare magicae artis, et sacrifica, ut non male moriaris et frauderis
hac luce." Respondens autem Dei famulus dixit ei: "Quibus diis iubes me sacrificare? Soli, et lunae, et igni, et mari, monti et colli,
ceterisque omnibus elementis, et metallis? Ne praestet mihi Dominus ut adorem sculptilia[51] vestra aliquando. Haec enim omnia Chris-
335 tus Dei filius fecit ad servitium nostrum. Vos vero erratis, serviendo daemonibus et quadrupediis. Homines facti,[52] ignoratis Deum

---

313 eum] fustibus *add.* Rg *cf.* ferire in eum fustibus t   314 me *om.* π me t
quod Rg   *corr. ex* indutum Rg[2]   314-315 iniuria Rg   315 Ista] ita St
ludi sunt Vn lusus sum St ludibria sunt t   319 ipse] ille B3 B6   320 imperatores Rg   322 moritur] est moriturus Pl morietur β *cf.* moritur t
324 lutus B1 lutum B3 B6   327 responsionem Rg   328 custodiam β castello Rg castro t   330 frauderis] de *add.* Rg   334 sculptilibus vestris Rg
cultoribus vestris t   336 demonis Rg *cf.* daemonibus t

---

50. For the omission of *fustibus*, see above, pp. 365ff.
51. p's editor revised t's *cultoribus* to echo Ps 96.7 (*iuxta LXX*) *confundantur omnes qui adorant sculptilia.*
52. The *ASS* text adds *ad imaginem Dei*, which is most appropriate, but
none of the manuscripts I have consulted includes that phrase.

qui vos fecit. Si enim cognovissetis Christum qui vos fecit, quandoque converti habuissetis ad veram lucem, et erui a daemonum potestate qui vos errare faciunt, et credere Deo, qui non mentitur his
340   qui credunt in nomine eius, dicens eis: Ego[53] dabo vobis os et sapientiam, cui non potuerunt resistere omnes adversarii vestri.
Voluit autem ex idiota et alienigena habere servum sibi autem ad
gloriam, fortitudinem autem praestans credentibus in se." Haec et
his similia prosequente sancto Anastasio bonis sermonibus, stupen-
345   tibus autem et mirantibus < *** >[54]; Dei martyr Anastasius tribus iam vicibus coronatus, in confessione Christi certator fortissimus, statim ad castellum reducitur vinculis constrictus.

24. Cognoscens autem sanctissimus abbas praefati monasterii, in
quo beatus Anastasius sanctum habitum susceperat, stabilitatem at-
350   que confessionem eius quae in Christo erat, et quia sine metu fortiter decertaret, et eius alacritatem atque perseverantiam, gavisus est
gaudio magno una cum universa congregatione sibi commissa, et
Dominum benedicebat, atque supplicabat die noctuque cum omni
congregatione, ut eius cursum dirigeret, et usque in finem perseve-
355   raret. Direxit autem duos ex fratribus monasterii in Caesaream ad
beatum Anastasium cum letteris consolatoriis, confortans animum
eius in Domino.

25. Cum vero esset in custodia castri[55] martyr Christi Anastasius,
non cessabat psalmis et ymnis diebus ac noctibus glorificare Deum
360   omnipotentem. [25 *ASS*]. Habens vero secum et alium in vinculis

---

342 autem *om.* β   et] ex *add.* Rg²   344 prosequente *rep.* Pl prosequenti Rg
345 autem] omnibus β   348 abba St   351 atque perseverantiam *om.* Rg
corr. ex gavisum Rg *aut* Rg² *cf.* gavisus t   358 castris Rg   359 ac] hac Rg²

53. Cf. Lc 21.15. The p text is modified so that a much fuller biblical
quote can be given than that provided in t.
54. The β group omits *autem* and adds *omnibus*, thus completing the ablative absolute. But this is most likely a late correction, since *omnibus* seems
a poor rendition of t's *contrarios*. Furthermore, the repetition of *Dei martyr
Anastasius* is awkward, as well as grammatically problematic. The *ASS*'s *et mirantibus adversariis* has no support in the early manuscript tradition.
55. Only the 408 tradition preserves g's τοῦ κάστρου (t and 410 omit).

iuvenem constitutum, quendam servorum Barzabanae pro quadam causa tentum, et non volens contristare eum, surgens itaque noctu famulus Christi ut celebraret ymnos matutinales in Dei laudibus, inclinabat vero collum suum ad collum eius, et pedem suum ad
365 pedem eius ut non per catenarum extensionem laborem praestaret Dei famulo.[56] Una igitur nocte, psallente eo, auscultabat eum quidam de vinctis qui ibi erat, Hebraeus quidem religione, et nobilis genere. Mitissimus autem et beatus martyr per diem quidem in lapidum fatigatione, nocte autem in Dei laudibus perseverans, stu-
370 pebat autem ille dicens: "Quidnam vult hoc esse?"

26. Tamdiu ergo intuens in eum, iacens super pavimentum in noctis silentio, stans[57] beatus martyr et psallens matutinales ymnos, vidit subito aliquos in vestibus albis ingredientes per ostium carceris, et circumdantes beatum martyrem, quibus et lux copiosa inful-
375 sit in carcere. Amens vero factus praefatus vir super visione, dixit intra se: "Sanctus Deus, isti angeli sunt." Hoc autem aspiciens, vidit hos ipsos pallia circumdatos, habentes cruces in manibus,[58] et ait

---

361 servum β *cf.* servorum t   362 causam Rg   surgens] surgebat Rg t itaque *om.* β   noctuque β noctum Rg   363 cum famulo π   364 vero *om.* β   365 extensione Pl Vn t   366 nocti Pl St   psallentes cum eo Rg eum] eos Rg   367 erant β *corr.* Rg   quidem] autem quidam *corr.* Rg² 367 nobili Rg St   368 Mitissimus autem et beatus martyr] Videns autem (valde *corr.* Rg²) beatum martyrem Rg Mitissimum autem beatum matyrem St 369 fatigationem Rg   perseverantem *corr.* Rg²   370 autem ille *om.* Rg 371 Tunc diu β *cf.* Tamdiu t   371-372 iacentem ... stabat ... et psallebat β 372 stans] cum staret *add. in marg.* Rg²   375 vero *om.* St   visionem Rg St 377 palliis β St *cf.* pallia t

56. By changing *praestaret ei* to *praestaret Dei famulo* the tradition of 408 confuses the original meaning. It is Anastasius who does not want to disturb his companion as he gets up to pray, and it is he who bends over to create slack in the chain, as β indicates. Cf. p_1 and r_2.

57. One would expect an ablative absolute, as in t, or a similar construction, such as the one attempted by Rg's corrector, here. The *ASS* text uses the ablative absolute, and β emends to finite verbs, which, however, obscure the meaning of the sentence (... *stabat beatus martyr et psallebat ... et vidit subito* ...).

58. The phrase *in manibus* is also in 410, but not in t nor in g, suggesting a connection between 408 and 410 (see Chapter V, pp. 180-184).

in semetipso: "Isti episcopi sunt." Admirans autem de his, intuens in martyrem Christi Anastasium, et qui cum illo erant,[59] immen-
380 sum lumen, et candidis vestibus eum indutum cum eis qui ei appa-ruerant. Et ecce iuvenis quidam in magna gloria stetit ante eum, habens thuribulum aureum et incensum mittens. Aspiciens autem vir qui contemplabatur, pulsabat manu proximum suum dormien-tem, qui erat Christianus, iudex Cytopolim, qualiter ei ostenderet
385 quae videbat, et non poterat, quia graviter dormiebat. Ille autem attendebat quae videbat, corpore quidem manens immobilis, tamen iactans se super proximum cum quo iacebat. Et expergefactus, quandoque comperit ab eo quid hoc esset. Dicit ei Hebraeus: "Consideras aliquid?" Et intuentes iam nihil viderunt. Insinuavit
390 autem ei omnia quae viderat, et glorificaverunt simul Dominum Ihesum Christum.

27 [26 *ASS*]. Quia vero, sicut superius memoravimus, a prima et secunda interrogatione videns Barzabanas constantiam famuli Dei Anastasii, scripsit imperatori Chosroi, quae de eo gesta sunt. Et
395 contigit infra dies paucos suscipere eum imperatoris iussionem. Et transmisit ad eum in carcere per domesticum suum, dicens: "Ecce iussit imperator ut verbo solum dicas, quia non sum Christianus, et statim te dimitto, ut ubi volueris vade, sive monachus vis esse, esto, sive equestris, sicut fueras antea, aut esse nobiscum, ut vis
400 fac." Respondit autem martyr Christi et dixit: "Ne fiat mihi negare

378 semetipsos Rg   autem–intuens *om.* Rg   his] et *add.* β *non est in* t
379 martyre Pl Vn circa martirem β *cf.* martyrem t   380 *corr. ex* candidi
Rg² 382 mittentem Rg t   383 vir *om.* Pl St B6 *cf.* vir t   384 Scytho-polis β Scytopolim Rg Scythopoleos t   387 iactansque Rg   expergens fac-tus Rg   388 comperit] requisivit β *cf.* comperit t   389 Insinuavit] Enarra-vit *add. supra lin.* Rg²   390 autem] *om.* B3 B6   392 commemoravimus Pl
393 videns] dicens Rg St discens *corr.* Rg² discens t   394 iscripsit Rg scripsi
St   Chosdroi *corr.* Rg² Chosdrohi t   395 diebus paucos Rg diebus paucis
St *cf.* dies paucos t   eum *om.* π *cf.* eum t   396 carcerem β Rg St   397
Christianum Rg   398 te dimitto ut] dedit mitto Rg et dimitto te *corr.* Rg²
monachos Rg   399 aut] et B3 B6 Rg t   400 negari Pl Rg St *cf.* negare t

59. Although the meaning is clear, the awkward grammar may reflect t's clumsy text.

me Christum." Dum ergo multas promissiones et suasiones ei direxisset per domesticum suum, et nullatenus adquiesceret, **28.** postmodum vero direxit illi per praefatum domesticum suum, dicens:
"Scio quia erubescis propter concives tuos, et ideo non vis negare
405   coram eis. Sed quia iussio imperatoris urguet, si vis, coram me et
aliis duobus dic sermonem, et dimittam te." Ipse vero martyr per
superscriptum missum direxit ei, dicens: "Absit a me. Neque coram
te, neque ante alios aliquando negabo Dominum meum." Tunc dixit
ei per semetipsum: "Ecce iussit imperator, ut ferro vinctus vadas in
410   Persidam." Beatus vero martyr Christi Anastasius dixit: "Si volueris
me dimittere, ego solus vadam ad imperatorem tuum." Ut autem
audivit beatum martyrem fortiter persistentem, neque minas paventem, neque blandimentis suaderi, bullatum eum iussit duci in carcerem. Et post quinque dies direxit eum cum aliis duobus Christianis
415   quibus et ipsis bullam expressit.

29 [27 *ASS*]. Approximabat autem interea dies festus exaltationis
venerandae crucis Domini nostri Ihesu Christi. Ipse autem beatus
martyr, et duo fratres monasterii eius, et duo christianissimi viri,
et quidam de civitate fideles in psalmis et ymnis et canticis spirituali-
420   bus pernoctantes, ita ut obliviscerentur habere sibi vincula, glorificantes Dominum nostrum Ihesum Christum, qui[60] tantam longanimitatem dat sperantibus in se. Diluculo autem ingressus dispositor quidam rebus publicis, et ipse vir christianissimus, ad Barza-

---

402-403 post modicum Rg *cf.* postmodum t   405 urget β 407 suprascrip-
tum β direxit] dixit Rg mandavit *corr. supra lin.* Rg^2 remandavit t   410
Persida St   412-413 *corr. ex* paventes Rg   413 blandimentis] posse *add.*
Rg^2 suadi *codd.*   bullatum] vinctum *add. in marg.* Rg^2 414 quinques
Rg   415 et *om.* π *cf.* quos etiam bullatos t   exprexit Rg   416 Adproxi-
mante ... die festo St   419 fidelibus π fideles *corr.* Rg   420 obliviscerent
Rg St   sibi] se β vinculas Rg   421 nostrum *om.* Rg   423 vir *om.* Rg

---

60. This phrase (*qui–se*) is the first of four in this section that are added
by p and have no correspondence in t. This and the next two (*tantummodo–
in custodiam; Et permisit Barzabanas*) are attempts at making the strange request and the marzabanas's even stranger agreement more understandable.
But the last addition (*Facta est–infidelibus*) is obscure.

banam, rogavit eum, ut vincula ei tollerentur, et eum in ecclesiam
425 deduceret tantummodo pro die festo, subiungens, quia: "Ego iterum reduco in custodiam." Quod et factum est. Et permisit Barzabanas. Et deductus in ecclesia gaudium magnum factum est universis fidelibus et consolatio, agentibus Deo gratias super certamen
martyris Christi et de eius crebris tribulationibus, quae sustinebat.
430 Facta[61] est autem et contentio inter populum de civitate eadem
de eo per fideles cum infidelibus.

30. Et quidem stupentes de eius tribulationibus, quas tolerabat famulus Dei Anastasius, et convaluerunt et confortati sunt fideles in
Christo de eius longanimitate et perseverantia; et in multis sermo-
435 nibus consolatus est fideles martyr Christi Anastasius. Et hi qui de
fide christiana se desperabant, de eius alacritate convaluerunt, osculantes eius vincula, et quasi victores[62] facti dicebant beato Anastasio: "Si tu propter Dominum nostrum Ihesum Christum mori disposuisti, quanto magis nos tecum mori debemus?" Et consolaban-
440 tur eum in Domino et honorem maximum ei praebebant, viri pariter et mulieres. Et expletis Missarum sollemniis, vim faciens ei dispositor perduxit in propriam domum ut victum aliquem caperet
cum duobus fratribus monasterii eius. Et cum sumpsissent cibum
pariter confortati sunt, et conloquentes de divinis sermonibus uter-
445 que aedificati sunt in Domino. Et postmodum iterum gaudens et
exultans quasi ad convivium perrexerunt in carcerem, et ibi glorificabant Dominum Ihesum Christum, qui tantam gratiam contulit
servis suis.

---

428 agentes St   *corr. ex* certaminis Rg[2]   **430** intentio Ty Vn Rg St   **431**
per *om.* Rg   **432** quas] quod Rg   **433** in *om.* Rg   **434** longanimitatem
... perseverantiam Rg   **435** fideles *om.* B1 fidelis Rg   **436** se *om.* β   **439**
debuimus Rg   **439-440** *corr. ex* solabantur Rg[2]   **442** victum aliquem] vinctum aliquid Rg

61. This passage corresponds to t's unclear *et enim multam uenerunt desidiam hii qui de civitate erant uiri*. 410 omits the passage completely.

62. p departs from the Greek in this passage. In particular, g's ἀλείπται,
rendered as *unctores* in the original translation but already changed to *iunctores* in T, has been completely lost in 408.

31 [28 *ASS*]. Expletis vero quinque diebus egressus est de civitate
450 Caesarea cum praefatis duobus christianissimis viris[63] et uno fratre de monasterio eius. Et multi qui eum noverant viri ac mulieres
cum multarum lacrimarum effusione glorificabant Deum super eius
bono proposito, quod disposuerat mori pro Christo. Et ivit unus,
ut dictum est, de monasterio eius frater cum eo, secundum iussio-
455 nem praepositi ad solatium atque ministerium eius, plurimum autem ut ea quae cognovisset de eo usque in finem per Domini gratiam detulisset tamquam sanctissimo abbati suo, nec non et cunctae
eius congregationi. Multum enim erat eis gaudium et laetitia qui
eum excipiebant per civitates et oppida fideles viri in adventum
460 eius, et glorificabant Dominum omnium creatorem, suscipientes
eum cum honore, et osculabantur vincula eius, et tribuebant[64]
quaeque necessaria erant. Scripsit autem beatus Anastasius litteras
deprecatorias abbati suo ab Hieropoli, ut pro se Dominum exoraret, et effunderet preces ut eum dignum susciperet, et eius cursum
465 consummaret. Et de fluvio Tigride similiter ei direxit.

32. [29 *ASS*]. Ingrediens autem in Persidam civitatem beatus Anastasius, missus est in carcerem in praedio quod vocatur Bethsaloe,
quod est miliario sexto de Discarthas, in quo erat imperator. At
vero frater qui cum eo erat mansit in eodem praedio, in domo
470 Cortacii filii Dejesdim primi dispositoris publicis rebus Persarum,

---

449 quinques Rg   450-451 unus frater π uno frater Rg   452 effusionem
Rg   453 bonum propositum Rg St bonum eius propositum t   457 tam-
quam] tam β quamquam Rg St tamque t   458 laetitiam Rg t   459 accipiebant B1   viri] et *add.* Rg   adventu β   461 tribuebat π   462 quae-
que] quidquid Rg quaecumque St   erant *om.* B3 B6   463 Hieropolim Rg
t   465 Trigride Pl Tigri de Rg   466 Persida civitate St   467 Bethsaloch
β   468 est] a *add.* Rg a stadiorum sex t   Discartas β Discardas St   470
Cartacii St Cortac t   Deiestim Rg

63. p omits t's phrase *super quadam causa accusatis,* which is kept by 410.
But its editor added *uno fratre,* which is not in the Greek or any other Latin
tradition, making his addition even more obvious by adding *ut dictum est* below. This addition suggests an emphasis on the eyewitness testimony on
which the *Acta* are based.

64. This phrase is added by p, as is the subsequent detail *litteras deprecatorias*
(ll. 462-463).

qui erat Christianus. Et morante beato martyre per dies aliquot cum eis qui ibidem devenerant captivorum, suggestum est Chosroi imperatori quae erga eum erant. Et mittens unum ex iudicibus suis, iussit examinari eum.

475 **33.** Qui etiam veniens in carcerem cum tribuno qui erat super carcerem, et interrogavit eum, quis esset et unde advenisset et quamobrem relinquens eorum religionem, factus est Christianus. Martyr autem Christi Anastasius respondit ei per interpretem (non enim locutus est ei persica lingua), et quidem multum coactus, dixit eis:
480 "Erratis vos daemones pro Deo colentes. Et ego enim aliquando, cum essem in errorem, hos colebam. Nunc autem adoro omnipotentem Dominum Ihesum Christum, qui fecit caelum et terram, mare et omnia quae in eis sunt, et scio diligenter quia culturae vestrae perditio et error daemonum sunt." Dicit ei iudex: "Miser,
485 numquid quem colitis vos Christiani, Iudaei eum crucifixerunt? Quomodo ergo errasti relinquens religionem tuam, et factus es Christianus?" Sanctus vero Anastasius ait: "Quoniam quidem crucifixus est a Iudaeis, verum dicis; quia vero sponte, quare non dicis? Ipse est enim qui fecit caelum et terram, mare et omnia quae in eis
490 sunt, et voluit descendere in terris et incarnari ex Spiritu sancto et Maria Virgine, et crucifigi et liberare genus hominum de errore Satanae, qui a vobis colitur. Vos autem colitis ignem et cetera elementa, et quod dici nefas est, servientes creaturae potius, quam creatori." [30 *ASS*] Dixit ei iudex: "Quid tibi et sermonibus istis?
495 Ecce pietas imperatoris paravit tibi dignitatem et zonas aureas, et equos et ut sis inter primates eius. Tantum convertere in primam tuam religionem." Beatus Anastasius dixit: "Ego numquam negabo Dominum meum Ihesum Christum, sed magis eum totis viribus adoro et colo. Dona vero imperatoris tui ut stercora computabo."

---

471 moranti *codd. exc.* B3 B6   beato martyri Pl beati martyri Rg   aliquod St   472 est] autem *add.* π *non est in* t   Chosdroi *corr.* Rg² 476 et¹ *om.* B3 *cf.* et t   venisset St   477 reliquit π *cf.* relinquens t   479 persica lingua] per syriacam linguam Pl Ty Vn β persiriaca Rg *cf.* persica lingua t 480 daemonia St *cf.* daemones t   Et *om.* St   485 Christiani] non *add.* St eum *om.* St   488 dicis²] dicitis St   491 et liberare] ut liberaret Rg t   495 dignitates Rg t   496 aequos Rg   primatos Rg t

500 **34.** Abiit[65] praefatus iudex, et haec omnia intimavit imperatori
Chosroi. Furore vero repletus imperator iussit mitti eum in carcerem, in crastinum volens eum poenis affici. Veniens autem alia die
ex iussu imperatoris praefatus iudex cum ira[66] foris carcerem et
coepit minas ei promittere atque inferre, ut eum terreret, putans
505 eum per poenas adquiescere a tali proposito. Sanctus vero martyr
Anastasius respondit ei dicens: "Ne labores, domine iudex, neque
fatigeris. Me enim Christo confortante, non adquiescam tibi, neque
recedere facies a fide quam cepi. Sed si quid facere velis, fac." Tunc
iussit eum vinctum secundum morem Persarum fustibus caedi abs-
510 que pietate, dicens: "Honoribus et donis imperatoris non adquiescis? Nunc modo cognosces per singulos dies iram eius. Sic enim te
cotidie perficiam, donec consumaris." Respondit autem sanctus
martyr Anastasius, et dixit: "Nec donis imperatoris tui adquiesco,
neque minas tuas timeo. Quicquid ergo vis, fac."

515 **35 [31 *ASS*].** Tunc iussit eum solvi et poni deorsum, et lignum super tibias eius imponi, et iubens duobus viris fortissimis stare supra
metam duarum partium ligni. Omnes vero novimus quod importabilis est huius tormenti species. Sanctus vero martyr Christi Anastasius agens gratias omnipotenti Deo, sustinebat dolores fortiter.
520 Videns autem iudex quia nihil proficeret, sed magis huiusmodi do-

---

500 Haec omnia (omni Pl) abiit praefatus iudex et intimavit *omnes codd.* Haec
autem omnia abiens intimavit t   501 Chosdroi *corr.* Rg^2 503 iussum Rg
foris carcerem] et iussit eum trai foris carcerem Rg foris ad carcerem St iussit
trahere eum foris carceris t   505 adquiescere] eum *add. codd.*   506 ei] *hic
inc.* Tr   508 *corr. ex* quis Rg^2 509 vinctum *om.* β   511 enim *om.* Rg
cf. enim t   517 metam *om.* Rg St supra duarum partium ligni t   517-518
immortalis Pl Tr   520 *corr. ex* qui Rg^2

65. The text as transmitted is not grammatically correct, but its meaning
is clear. I have chosen therefore to emend by changing the word order, on
the assumpiton that the p editor meant to rearrange t's word order when
changing *abiens* to *abiit*. The *ASS* text reads *Abiit praefatus iudex et intimavit*.
66. The copy of the translation available to the editor of p may have
omitted part of this phrase, or it may have dropped out of its tradition. Note
that 410 does not have this small lacuna, suggesting that the latter is perhaps
more likely; cf. p$_1$. See the discussion in Chapter V, pp. 180ff, and p. 375.

loribus, sicut ferrum frigidis aquis limabatur, per divinam gratiam et confortabatur, iussit eum iterum retrudi in carcerem, donec iterum intimaret imperatori de eo.

36. Sellarius vero qui erat super carcerem, dum esset Christianus, et frater monasterii qui comitabatur cum martyre Christi, ingrediebantur ad eum, consolantes et admonentes eum in bonum. Multi vero Christiani qui ibidem erant, in quibus et Deiesdim filii, ingrediebantur ad eum et corruebant ad pedes eius, et osculabantur vincula eius, et rogabant ut dignaretur pro eis orare, et ut daret eis aliquam benedictionem ad custodiam eorum. At vero spernebat eos beatus martyr, ne talia dicerent. Ipsi vero ceram superponebant vinculis eius expressis,[67] in benedictionem hoc percipiebant.

37 [32 ASS]. Iterum ergo post dies paucos ingressus est iudex ad beatum Anastasium in carcerem, et dicit ei: "Quid dicis? Facis iussionem imperatoris aut permanes in his?" Sanctus vero Anastasius movens caput suum, quasi abominabatur eum dicens: "Et semel et secundo et saepius tibi dixi, quia impossibile est negare me Christum Dei filium. Quod ergo vis, fac citius." Tunc temerator ille barbarus iussit eum ligari sicut prius, et diutius caedi fustibus, et derelinquens eum in carcerem recessit. Post dies autem paucos, iterum ingressus est ad eum, suadens ut negaret Christum Dei filium, aliquando blandimentis atque promissionibus pecuniae et dignitatibus, aliquando minis et tormentis. Cum vero vidisset quia famulus Christi nec terrore concutitur, nec blandimento seducitur, sed perseveravit in Christi fide, iussit eum iterum ligari et caedi sicut prius, et iussit eum solvi et suspendi ex una manu, et saxum magnum ligari ad pedem eius, et sic derelinquens eum, abiit. Sustinente

---

521 ferrus Rg t   frigidi aqua Rg frigida aqua St frigidi aquae t   elimabatur Rg elimatur St limabitur t   522 et *om.* Rg   iterum] iudex *add.* π *non est in* t   carcere Pl Rg   525-558 qui comitabatur–universos iusserunt *om.* Rg 534 dixit St   536 abominabatur *non legi potest* Tr abominavit St t   539 sicut *om.* β *cf.* sicut t   542 et *om.* π *cf.* et t   544-545 perseveraret β

---

67. t's text, *exprimentesque eam*, seems clear. The *ASS* text remains very close to it (*et expressam*) but is not supported in any surviving manuscript witnesses.

autem martyre Christi huiusmodi supplicium quasi horarum duarum spatio, et postmodum iussit eum deponi. Et abiit et suggessit
550 imperatori de proposito mentis eius, et de perseverantia quam habebat in Christo.

38 [33 *ASS*]. Et post dies quindecim misit imperator ipsum iudicem
et alios cum eo ad interficiendum beatum martyrem, et plurimos
Christianos cum eo, nec non et captivos. Qui venientes iusserunt
555 eos educi foras praedio[68] Bethsaloe, in quibus beatum Anastasium
cum aliis circiter septuaginta viris iuxta ripam fluminis. Et prius
illos[69] sanctissimos viros coram sancto martyre funes mitti in gutture eorum, et sic suffocari universos iusserunt, inter quos erant et
praedicti duo christianissimi viri qui comitati fuerant a Caesarea
560 cum sanctissimo martyre Christi Anastasio. [34 *ASS*] Et cum inter-
ficeret eos, dicebat sancto martyri: "Quare disposuisti ut tam pessimam mortem ducas, sicut isti? Sed magis adquiesce imperatori et
vive et accipe honorem ab eo, et esto in palatio sicut unus ex nobis, et ne careas hac luce et dulci vita." At vero victoriosissimus
565 Christi martyr Anastasius aspiciens in caelum gratias agebat Deo,
qui consummavit cursum eius, et adimplevit eius desiderium. Et
respondens ait ad eos: "Ego putabam[70] membratim concidi a vobis propter amorem Christi. Quia vero ista est mors quam minamini mihi, gratias ago Domino meo Ihesu Christo, quia per modi-
570 cum dolorem participem me fecistis gloriae sanctorum eius." Et ita
cum magno gaudio atque alacritate suscepit gloriosam passionem,
atque simili morte defunctus est. Postquam autem suffocaverunt
eum, absciderunt eius pretiosum caput, et tollentes bullam perdu-
xerunt ad imperatorem.

558 quos] quibus Rg t   561 disposuisti *hic des.* Tr   564 hac] ac Rg
dulcem vitam Rg dulciam vitam hanc t   567 respondit Pl Ty Vn *β cf.* respondens t   ait *om.* B3 B6   568 ista *rep.* St   568-569 minatis Rg St comminatis t   571 magno] multo Ty Vn B3 B6 Rg St t

68. The use of *foris/foras* follows t (with the accusative in l. 503 and the
ablative here).
69. The repetition of the object (*illos sanctissimos viros* ... *eorum* ...
universos) suggests an incomplete or poorly transmitted revision.
70. t's *optabam* is found only in the *ASS* text; perhaps Bolland's emendation was suggested by p_1's *cupiebam*. See Chapter VII, Appendix 1.

575 **39 [35 *ASS*]**. Christianus igitur cum esset qui super carceres praeerat tribunus, sicut prius iam dictum est, voluit corpus martyris
seorsum ponere. Et[71] cognitum est a quaestionariis. Et cognoscentes filii Deiesdim finem sancti martyris, quia et pueri eorum simul
secuti erant beatum Anastasium quando ducebatur ad mortem ut
580 viderent exitum rei, et dederunt clam quaestionariis infinitam pecuniam, et permiserunt separatim reponi corpus eius sanctum. Et
sequenti nocte accipiens secum frater qui eum secutus fuerat de
monasterio sancti viri pueros de filiis Deiesdim, et quosdam monachos qui ibidem erant, ut tollerent corpus sancti martyris, et inve-
585 nerunt canes edentes corpora interfectorum, corpus vero martyris
separatim iacens intactum. Pretiosa est enim in conspectu Domini
mors sanctorum eius,[72] et custodit Dominus omnia ossa eorum,
unum ex eis non conteretur. Accipiens igitur corpus martyris et
involvens linteaminibus pretiosis, quos dederant filii Deiesdim,
590 deducens sepelivit in monasterium sancti martyris Sergii, miliario
uno distans a praefato castro.

40. Finitum est autem certamen et cursus, et in Christo confessio
victoriossimi martyris Anastasii vicesima et secunda die mensis
Ianuarii, indictione prima, anno septimo decimo imperii piissimi
595 Eraclii, et quinto decimo anno Constantini eius filio.

41 [36 *ASS*]. Alia autem die post transitum sancti martyris Anastasii, duo quidam in custodia confabulabantur ad invicem, dicens
unus ad alterum: "Scis quia venerunt canes et sederunt iuxta corpus

---

580-581 infinita pecunia Rg infinitas pecunias St   581 sanctum *om.* Rg t
582 accipientes *codd. cf.* accipiens t   secum] et *add.* Pl Ty Vn β   fratrem
Ty   583 viri] et *add.* β   filios dei estum Rg   et *om.* Rg *cf.* et t   583-
584 monachos *eras.* Rg   erant] rogavit *supra lin. add.* Rg[2]   587 eorum] et
add. Pl Ty (*sed postea eras.*) Vn *non est in* t   588 igitur] praefatus frater *add.*
β   589 *corr. ex* lenteaminibus(?) Rg[2]   *corr. ex* dederat Rg[2]   Deiestim
Rg   596 Alii Pl   598 alterum] alium Rg

---

71. p departs from t in some of the details, omitting, for example, the
fact that the *quaestionarii* were *Hebraei*.
72. Ps 115.15.

de illo monacho et non contingebant ei, sed custodiebant illud?"[73]
600 Item alius socius dixit ad eum: "Et ego quando supplevi vigiliam
meam, et ambulavi in domum meam, vidi sicut stellam lucidam super pavimentum, et pergens ut viderem quid esset, iam iam stellam
non vidi, sed repperi corpus monachi illius ibidem iacens." Haec
quidem custodes inter se dicebant.

605 **42.** Alii autem Christiani captivi qui erant in carcere inclusi, dum
ergo cognovissent aliquid de locutione Persica ipsi nobis retulerunt
quid inter se custodes confabularentur. [37 *ASS*] Absoluti vero a
vinculis et venientes in sanctam civitatem hoc diffamabant ubique;
sed et aliud adiungentes dicebant, quia: "Dum esset beatus Anasta-
610 sius nobiscum in carcere, sic nobis fasus est dicens: Ut sciatis fratres, quia per Dei gratiam ego quidem crastino die finior, et transeo de hoc saeculo. Post paucos autem dies vos relaxabimini. Iniquus autem et malignus rex interficietur. Sed Domino prosperante
ambulantibus vobis in sanctam civitatem, ite ad mansionem quae
615 dicitur Abbatis Anastasii et dicite abbati meo et fratribus haec."
Viri autem qui audierunt ex ore sancti viri et rerum exitum cognoscentes, Dominum glorificaverunt, qui glorificat glorificantes
eum. Mandatum vero sancti martyris impleverunt, et propriis oculis quae viderunt et cognoverunt,[74] diligenter nobis innotuerunt.

620 **43.** Praedictus autem frater mansionis, qui eum obsecundabat,
sepeliens corpus sancti martyris, et cum omni diligentia reponens
in praefato monasterio Sancti Sergii, mansit ibidem pertractans
qualiter sine periculo remearet ad abbatem, et mansionem suam.

---

599 de–monacho] illius monachi β *cf.* de illo monacho t   illud] illum Rg *cf.* illud t   600-601 vigilia mea Rg   602 esset] et *add.* Rg St t   603 iacentem Rg
t   604 dicentes π *cf.* dicebant t   605 carcerem β Rg St   606 ergo *om.* β
Persiaca Rg St   608 hic *codd.*   609 aliud] alii Rg   610 fasus *eras. non legi
potest* Rg locutus Rg² confessus St   Ut *om.* β *cf.* ut t   612 vos] vox Rg
615 dicitur Pl   618 eum] se β   619 et] que *add.* Rg   623 et] ad *add.* St

73. A phrase from t, *Et mansi–eius,* is omitted here, but is partially preserved in 410.

74. The phrase *et propriis–cognoverunt* is added, emphasising the eyewitness account.

625

630

[38 *ASS*] Et post dies decem, prima die mensis Februarii coniunxit in eisdem partibus christianissimus et piissimus Eraclius imperator cum exercitu. Quos cum vidisset frater gavisus est valde, et ipsi diligentius inquisierunt eum, quid ibidem faceret, et insinuavit eis minutius.[75]1At illi glorificaverunt Deum, et fratri quidem dixerunt: "Surge et veni nobiscum, et salva animam tuam." Et erat cum eis in multo honore cum essent in Persida, et cum eis reversus est per Armeniorum regionem.

635

640

44. Post anniversarium vero reversus ad propriam mansionem, deferens secum et colobium sancti martyris Anastasii, et intimavit diligenter praeposito et fratribus minutius quae circa martyrem acciderant, et de eius glorioso fine, et de sui itineris labore, et glorificaverunt Deum, qui salvat sperantes in se. Factum est autem primum signum per colobium beati martyris Anastasii. Erat quidam iuvenis in monasterio, qui nequiter vexabatur a spiritu immundo. Qui[76] < *** > accipiens praepositus colobium sancti martyris Anastasii induit eum. Qui etiam protinus salvatus est per Domini gratiam et interventu beati Anastasii martyris ad gloriam et laudem omnipotentis Dei et Domini nostri Ihesu Christi, qui glorificatur in sanctis suis, cui est honor gloria et potestas atque maiestas per immortalia secula seculorum. Amen.

645

Explicit passio sancti Anastasii mart.

626 exercitum Rg *cf.* exercitu t   629 eram B3 B6   630 esset Rg   631 Armeniorem St   635 gloriosa fine Pl Vn *corr. ex* gloriosam finem Rg[2] suis itineribus St   637 colabium Rg   639 praepositum Pl Rg propositum St   640 etiam *om.* St   643 suis] eius β t   honor] et *add.* St

75. 408 omits t's ... *et locutus est latine,* included in 410. See Chapter V, pp. 174-175.
76. t and *BHL* 410 suggest a lacuna in 408.

5

THE REVISION *BHL* 410

BHL 410 *and Its Manuscript Circulation*

BHL 410, a direct revision of the early translation (*BHL* 410b), survives today in at least thirteen manuscripts, all of which go back to a common archetype.[1] The diffusion of these witnesses can be traced to the region of southwestern Germany or northwestern Switzerland in the late ninth century.[2] The earliest surviving manuscript (Vienna, lat. 357 = V), which may be as early as the late ninth century, was copied most likely in this area. A copy (= G) from it or its direct descendant was made in the twelfth century at Gregorienmünster in Münster (Alsace). These two manuscripts form one branch of the stemma constructed below.

The witness closest to the apograph on the other side of the stemma is a twelfth-century legendary (= N) from the Abbey of Einsiedeln (Stiftsbibliothek 249), and it provides further evidence of *BHL* 410's early geographical diffusion in the border area between western Germany and Switzerland. All the other manuscripts of this branch were copied in Austria and Bavaria during the twelfth and thirteenth centuries. They divide themselves into two groups. One group includes among its five witnesses the voluminous legendary (Clm 22240 = I) written at the Premonstratensian abbey of Windberg in Bavaria in the second half of the twelfth century.[3] The other group consists entirely of five exemplars of the *Magnum legendarium austriacum*, an even larger hagiographic compendium copied in Benedictine and Cistercian houses in southern Bavaria

---

1. All witnesses share a lacuna in cap. 10 (see p. 432 n. 8).

2. See chapters V, pp. 180ff. and VI, p. 193 for a discussion of this version's possible circulation in Anglo-Saxon England.

3. The Windberg Legendary occupies six volumes (Munich, Bayerische Staatsbibliothek, latt. 22240-22245).

and Austria from the end of the twelfth century and through the thirteenth.[4]

The [b] Branch

The segregation of V and G (Colmar, Bibliothèque de la Ville 356) from all the other witnesses is illustrated by their common errors, and most visibly by their common omissions in capp. 14 ([ll. 125-126] *Ipse–visionem*), 19 ([l. 165] *et aureos*), 22 ([ll. 208-209] *et–metuam*), 32 ([l. 311] *in–Gesdim*). G is so close to V that it must be considered a direct copy. It shares all of V's errors (except a few that can be easily supposed to have been corrected by the scribe), and all of V's omissions. G has been corrected by a slightly later scribe who may have had a copy of a text from the α sub-branch (=SLDZM),[5] and who filled in most of V's omissions in the margins of G. I indicate these corrections in my textual notes.

This branch, and specifically V (since G is irrelevant as a *codex descriptus*) preserves the text closest to the exemplar, except for the omissions. The accuracy of V's readings is constantly confirmed by its agreement with the early translation.

The [c] Branch

N, the legendary from Einsiedeln, preserves a text that has very few scribal errors. It frequently joins V (and G) in readings whose correctness is supported by the text of the early translation. But it is segregated into the other branch [c] of the stemma with all the other manuscripts by a few common errors:

4. The fundamental studies of these legendaries remain Poncelet, "De legendario Windbergensi" and "De *Magno legendario austriaco*." A sixth exemplar of the *Magnum legendarium austriacum* (Vienna, lat. 336, from the thirteenth century) is incomplete, lacking January among other months (Poncelet, "De *Magno legendario austriaco*," p. 36). Its later revision at Klosterneuburg (Philippart, "Legendare," col. 649) does not contain the *Passio S. Anastasii*, as I was able to ascertain from a description of the manuscript (Cod. 710) in a handwritten catalogue available in photocopy at the Hill Monastic Manuscript Library (Collegeville, MN).

5. This is best illustrated in the correction of *ornatus* to *oneratus* of ll. 223-224. G also may have been contaminated from *BHL* 408, but only briefly in the opening chapter, and perhaps in ll. 398-399 (*fideles digesdim*). See my *apparatus criticus*.

419 | 5 *The Revision BHL* 410

(cap. 14, ll. 124-125) Dicit–diebus *add. in marg.* N *om.* α
(cap. 26, l. 255) Enarravit] narravit N αβ *cf.* t
(cap. 39-40, ll. 398-399) Gesdim] gesdin V gestum N αβ

The omission in cap. 14 is actually an eye-skip mistake, which must have been corrected in the branch's exemplar through a marginal note. The scribe of N must have realized his exemplar's error, for he too copied the skipped passage in the margin.[6] Only one (β=HEWIA) of the two sub-branches of this branch of the stemma followed the exemplar's correction. The minor error in cap. 26 is self-explanatory. The reading of capp. 39-40 *fideles Gesdin/fideles gestum* represents different errors stemming from the early translation's *filii de Gesdim*. Most likely, a corrupted reading was present already at their common apograph.

In a few cases where N contains details omitted in the *BHL* 410 transmission, its wording betrays contamination from the *BHL* 408 tradition, as shown by this example from cap. 6, ll. 25-26:[7]

410 : Erat quidam de Persida Razehe vocabulo, nomen autem ei Magundat.

N : Erat quidam de Persidis regione Razech vocabulo, de fundo Rasnuni, nomen autem ei Magundat.

t : Hic regionis quidam erat de Persida Razech uocabulo, de fundo autem Rasnuni, nomen autem ei Magundat.

p : Hic quidem erat de Persidis regione Razech vocabulo, de fundo Rasnuni, nomen autem ei Magundat.

The editor/compiler responsible for the contamination must have had available a copy of *BHL* 408, which clearly presented a better text than the one provided by his copy of *BHL* 410, and he revised his own text accordingly. It is important to note that in this example of correction, or contamination, as well as in all the others, the text of *BHL* 410 remains closer to the early translation,[8] while N betrays its similarity to *BHL* 408.[9] The editor responsible for

6. It is clear that N's marginal correction is not a contamination from *BHL* 408, which presents a very different reading here.

7. The other cases are found in capp. 8, 11, 16, 33, 39-40. I note them in the *apparatus criticus*.

8. As illustrated here by the agreement of t and 410 in *quidam, Persida*.

9. Note in particular the agreement of p and N (against t) in *de Persidis regione, de fundo Rasnuni*.

the contamination did not collate the two texts available to him consistently, however; most notably, he missed the opportunity to fill the lacuna of cap. 10, for example. He seems, rather, to have consulted *BHL* 408 in places where he thought his text was not clear. Why did the editor responsible for the contamination simply not copy *BHL* 408? The most likely answer is, I think, that the corrections were entered on an already existing copy of *BHL* 410, as marginal notes or corrections over erasures, and the next copyist made a fair copy of the corrected text, which has come down to us as N. Despite these examples of contamination, N's witness to the text of 410 is of primary importance, for it confirms or challenges the correctness of V.

Relationships within α (*"Magnum legendarium austriacum"*)
The manuscripts of the *Magnum legendarium austriacum* (S, L, D, Z, M) segregate themselves into one group of witnesses (=α), as is shown by a number of common errors, among which are:[10]

(l. 17)	per Christi gratiam] per Christi sanguinem α
(ll. 124-125)	dicit–diebus om. α
(l. 160)	quis existeris] quid profiteris α
(l. 223)	ornatus] oneratus α

In general, the *Magnum legendarium austriacum* preserves a more polished version of the *Passio S. Anastasii*, one that has been consistently corrected and improved. Its importance for the establishment of *BHL* 410 is therefore not significant. However, the *Passio S. Anastasii* can be used as evidence for clarifying the history of this large and important hagiographic compendium and the relationship among its various witnesses.

In his study of the monumental Great Austrian Legendary, Albert Poncelet grouped its manuscripts according to the contents of their sanctoral. Poncelet found that none of the surviving witnesses of the *Magnum legendarium austriacum* could be the archetype, not even its oldest exemplar from the Cistercian house of Heiligencreuz (=S). He found, however, that S, L (Lilienfeld, Stiftsbibliothek 58), and Z (Zwettl, Stiftsbibliothek 13)—all originating in Cistercian

---

10. In all of these cases, the correct reading is confirmed by t. See my *apparatus criticus* for further examples.

houses—form one group, while the two Benedictine exemplars, D (Admont, Stiftsbibliothek 25) and M (Melk, Stiftsbibliothek 388), form another. According to Poncelet, these last two copies of the *Magnum legendarium austriacum* are segregated from the Cistercian cluster both by their omission of a batch of documents at the end of February and also by their choice of different redactions of several texts.[11] Furthermore, Poncelet maintained that both the Lilienfeld and the Zwettl legendaries were derived from the legendary of their mother-house, Heiligencreuz.

The same conclusions regarding the relationship among the Cistercian exemplars of the *Magnum legendarium austriacum* have more recently been presented also by Charlotte Ziegler in her catalogue of the Zwettl manuscripts.[12] She maintains that the Zwettl exemplar of the *Magnum legendarium austriacum* is dependent on that of Heiligencreuz on paleographic and art historical grounds. She rejects, however, earlier views that the *Magnum legendarium austriacum* originated in southern Germany or Austria, and proposes that the source of the *Magnum legendarium austriacum* lies within the Cistercian tradition.[13] She identifies the great legendary of Cîteaux of the first quarter of the twelfth century as the source of the Heiligencreuz and Zwettl exemplars of the *Magnum legendarium austriacum*.[14] Hence, the stemmatic relationship established among the witnesses of the *Magnum legendarium austriacum* by the collation of the *Passio S. Anastasii* is in fact a test of the conclusions Poncelet and Ziegler arrived at.

11. Poncelet, "De *Magno legendario austriaco*," p. 31.

12. Ziegler, *Zisterzienserstift Zwettl. Katalog der Handschriften des Mittelalters* I, xi, 31-43, 55-59, esp. 38; III, xxiii.

13. For the claims that Salzburg or Admont in Austria, or Prüfening in Bavaria were the birthplace of the *Magnum legendarium austriacum* see Philippart, "Legendare," with earlier bibliography.

14. Ziegler does not comment on Poncelet's conclusions, nor even refer to his study. Van der Straeten, in a thorough review of Ziegler's *Katalog* in light of Poncelet's earlier discussion, asks whether Heiligencreuz should now be considered the "cradle of the *Magnum legendarium austriacum*" ("Le 'Grand Légendier Autrichien' dans les manuscripts de Zwettl"). Poncelet had rejected this possibility ("De *Magno legendario austriaco*," p. 25).

The collation of the *Passio S. Anastasii* confirms that the exemplars of the *Magnum legendarium austriacum* form a segregated group going back to a common apograph [i], as illustrated in the stemma codicum below. Furthermore, the copy of the *Passio S. Anastasii* in the Lilienfeld codex (=L) shows without a doubt that it was copied directly from the Heiligencreuz codex (=S). The Zwettl copy (=Z), however, is not directly dependent on the Heiligencreuz exemplar, as both Poncelet and Ziegler maintained. Rather, the stemma developed below shows that S and Z simply go back to a common exemplar [i] as all the witnesses of the *Magnum legendarium austriacum* do, and that while S might be a direct copy of this common exemplar, Z is twice removed from it. Z shares its direct exemplar, [k], with one of the Benedictine codices (M), while D, the other Benedictine codex, in fact is closer to S than Z is. These relationships can be illustrated by the occurrence of common errors.

The direct dependence of L, the Lilienfeld exemplar, from S, the Heiligencreuz exemplar, is shown by the fact that L contains all of S's mistakes and adds some of its own as well.[15] It should be emphasized that the Zwettl exemplar (Z) does not follow S in these mistakes, indicating that it cannot have been copied from it. DZM rather are grouped together by a number of common errors;[16] each has peculiar mistakes[17] precluding the possibility of direct dependence among them. Finally, a number of errors common to Z and M segregates these two witnesses into a group.[18]

---

15. For example, (l. 69) percepit] concepit SL; (l. 129) canonem] orationem S orationes L; (l. 190) aliqua] aliquid L; (l. 223) coronatus] honoratus SL; (l. 229) consummaret] confirmaret L; (l. 329) de caelis in] de caelo ad L. Other examples could be cited as well.

16. For example, (l. 23) scribere] describere DZM; (l. 40) inferebat] infundebat DZM; (l. 80) de reliquo] de reliquo esse DZM; (ll. 212-213) ducit-iussit eum *om.* DZM

17. Taking only some examples of omissions: (l. 116) sibi *om.* D; (l. 165) et–argenteos *om.* D; (l. 263) et dixit *om.* Z; (ll. 321-322) et scio–sunt *om.* M; (l. 450) me *om.* Z (on the significance of this last reading, see below).

18. For example, (ll. 49-50) desinebat] sinebat ZM; (l. 194) rescripta] scripta ZM; (ll. 363-364) citius *om.* ZM.

The Relationships within β

The Windberg Legendary's text (I) joins with the other manuscripts from Bavaria (Clm 2570=A; Clm 17137=H; and Clm 22020=E), and Codex 72 from Zwettl in lower Austria (W) to form a discernible group (=β) as is illustrated by common errors.[19] Common errors also isolate the groups EWIA,[20] WIA[21] and IA.[22] None of the witnesses in the β branch can be the archetype for this group because each one contains mistakes peculiar to itself.[23]

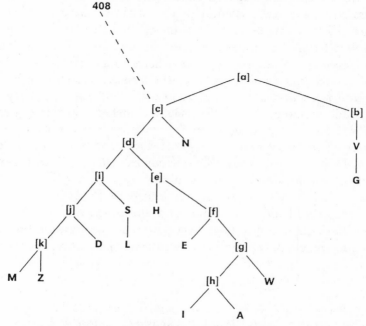

19. E.g. (l. 113) diaboli] inimici HEWIA; (l. 148) verbositatis] verbositatis HEWIA; (l. 443) salva] salvamus HEWIA. A in particular seems more likely to expand the text, change the word order, etc.

20. E.g. (l. 207) tuum *om.* EWIA; (l. 244) circumdantes] circumstantes EWIA; (l. 268) imperatoris] regis EWIA.

21. E.g. (l. 54) et venit *om.* WIA; (l. 198) confiteatur] fateatur se WIA; (l. 307) flumine] fluvio WIA; (l. 316) quam ob rem] quare WIA.

22. E.g. (l. 146) sellarii] callarii IA; (l. 249) splendide] splendore IA.

23. E.g. (l. 19) laedere] reddere N; (l. 29) in tyrone] et introire N; (l. 30) regia *om.* A; (l. 32) sumpta] ablata A; (l. 78) Faciente vero] Faciebat autem A; (l. 161) discere] scire E; (l. 200) ut non] ne E; (l. 255) iam] eum H; (l. 289) fuimus] sumus H; (l. 311) in domo–Gesdim *om.* G; (l. 381) sanctum *om.* I; W is clearly isolated by its textual revision at the beginning of cap. 9 (*At ille sumpto ... sanctorum*).

In his study of the sources for the Windberg Legendary and the *Magnum legendarium austriacum*, Albert Poncelet postulated the existence of a legendary that had supplied about two hundred documents to both collections. These are texts not contained in the other identifiable sources of the Windberg Legendary and the *Magnum legendarium austriacum*.[24] Poncelet pointed out that this source-legendary must have been put together after 1065 because it comprised texts composed at this time, and that it need not necessarily have been assembled in Austria or Bavaria, since it included a very rare text—an epitome of the Life of St. Germanus compiled from Venantius Fortunatus—found also in an eleventh-century codex of St. Bertin in northern France.[25] Since a very similar redaction of the *Passio S. Anastasii* is found in both the *Magnum legendarium austriacum* and the Windberg Legendary, it is possible to speculate that *BHL* 410 was included in this source.[26] *BHL* 410 has a very circumscribed circulation; it has not survived outside of the very narrow range of these closely related collections. In its nature as an abbreviated text, *BHL* 410 displays a characteristic common to these compilations that may in fact have been already peculiar to the source legendary.[27]

On the other hand, the stemma codicum of the *Passio S. Anastasii* indicates that the Windberg Legendary and the *Magnum legendarium austriacum* do not go back to an immediate, direct ancestor.

24. Poncelet, "De *Magno legendario austriaco*," pp. 24-25; "De legendario Windbergensi," pp. 98-99. The principal known sources are Wolfhard's Martyrology (for both *Magnum legendarium austriacum* and Windberg, but different texts culled by each compiler); and the works of Gregory of Tours, Bede's *Ecclesiastical History*, and the so-called "Datiana historia ecclesiae Mediolanensis" (for the *Magnum legendarium austriacum* only).

25. "De legendario Windbergensi," pp. 99-100.

26. Poncelet cautioned against assuming that every text common to both compilations, and not included in the common sources already identified, was drawn from the postulated common legendary; hagiographic *libelli* also may have been used by the compilers. Philippart's study of the *Passio Cypriani* shows that the compiler of the *Magum legendarium austriacum* used a different redaction of this text than the source used by the Windberg Legendary (*Légendiers*, p. 104).

27. See p. 178.

The Windberg Legendary, from the second half of the twelfth century, is at several removes from their common source, which has a much closer relationship to the surviving manuscripts of the *Magnum legendarium austriacum*. If the *Passio S. Anastasii* derived from the collection of two hundred texts, one would have to assume that this legendary was copied several times in a century.[28] This is not impossible, for the various exemplars of the *Magnum legendarium austriacum* were copied with minor changes many times over a similar period. If the *Passio S. Anastasii* was part of this collection—whether defined as the original compilation (perhaps [i] in our stemma) or the two-hundred-text legendary-source (which could be [d] in our stemma)—it would argue against Ziegler's proposal of a Cistercian origin for the *Magnum legendarium austriacum*. The redaction of the *Passio S. Anastasii* found in the Cistercian tradition is *BHL* 408, while the *Magnum legendarium austriacum* and its related collections, including the Windberg Legendary, contain *BHL* 410.[29] Paleographical or other codicological influences cannot be isolated from the contents of these manuscripts; in fact, codicological similarities do not necessarily imply similarity in contents. The dependence of one hagiographical collection on another can be ascertained provisionally by a

28. These copies would be [e], [f], [g] in the stemma. Another possibility is that [e] is actually the original Windberg Legendary, which was then transformed as it was being transmitted. Eis, "Legendarium Windbergense" (*Verfasserlexikon*, col. 607), has questioned whether the Windberg manuscripts in fact represent the original compilation. A thorough study of the other witnesses of the β branch of *BHL* 410 might provide further elucidation.

29. See p. 000 for my discussion of the Cistercian *Liber de natalitiis*. Since Ziegler completely ignores the numerous studies, based on the collections' contents, that have placed the legendaries of Cîteaux within the development of the *Liber de natalitiis*, including recent works by Rochais and Dolbeau, and older ones by Levison and Poncelet, it is not clear whether she would identify her Cistercian source with Poncelet's two-hundred-texts legendary. In his list of sources of the *Magnum legendarium austriacum*, Dolbeau describes Ziegler's Cistercian source as a "French Cistercian legendary," distinct from the model that served also as a source for the Windberg Legendary, but his words express doubt ("... enfin, un légendier de cisterciens français, si l'on accepte la suggestion récente de Madame Ch. Ziegler ..." ["Les prologues de légendiers latins," pp. 354 and n. 30]).

study of the contents of the compilations and, more assuredly, by the production of stemmata of common texts.[30] This work remains unfinished for the *Magnum legendarium austriacum* and the *Liber de natalitiis*.

About This Edition

My edition is based on the thirteen witnesses to the text *BHL* 410, all of which go back to a common archetype.[31] As this version of the *Passio S. Anastasii* like that of *BHL* 408 is a reworking of the original translation *BHL* 410b, both of these other works have been used to establish the text of 410. It is also possible, as I discuss in Chapter V, that 410 may have been available to the editor of the 408, or p redaction.

As is made clear by the above discussion, V and N, despite its contamination from 408, are most important in the establishment of the text. If the two of them agree, I have generally followed their lead. In case of disagreement between them, t's evidence, if relevant, has been the guide, and I have indicated the reading in my critical notes.

The other witnesses play only a minor role in the establishment of the text. α as a group has undergone revision early on in its history, most likely at point [i] in my stemma. Most of these revisions are minor ones, meant to improve the text primarily by lexical change, although grammatical improvements are also occasionally found in the α tradition.[32] The manuscripts of the β branch, on the contrary, go back on the whole to a "purer" apograph, closer to the original text. However, given the availability of N and V, the textual evidence of β is important only for understanding the textual trasmission of this version, and the relationships among these legendaries. The great number of textual variants in this version of the *Passio S. Anastasii* is witness to the constant tinkering

---

30. This is well pointed out by Dolbeau: "Pour qui veut préciser les relations de parenté existant à l'intérieur d'un groupe, la superposition de différents stemmata, scientifiquement établis à partir de textes particuliers, est indispensable" ("Liber de Natalitiis," p. 178). See also p. 424 n. 26 for the evidence of the *Passio Cypriani*.

31. See p. 417 n. 1.

32. For example, l. 234, where α changed *cum surgebat* to *cum surgeret*.

the text was subjected to by scribes and editors as it moved away chronologically and geographically from its point of origin.[33]

I have divided the text according to the chapter divisions in Flusin's Greek version, followed also in my edition of *BHL* 410b and *BHL* 408, i.e. t and p.

CONSPECTUS SIGLORUM

A   Munich, Bayerische Staatsbibliothek, Clm 2570 (Ald. 40)

D   Admont, Stiftsbibliothek 25

E   Munich, Bayerische Staatsbibliothek, Clm 22020 (Wess. 20)

G   Colmar, Bibliothèque de la Ville 356 (121)

H   Munich, Bayerische Staatsbibliothek, Clm 17137 (Scheftl. 137)

I   Munich, Bayerische Staatsbibliothek, Clm 22240 (Windberg Legendary)

L   Lilienfeld, Stiftsbibliothek 58

M   Melk, Stiftsbibliothek 388 (F8)

N   Einsiedeln, Stiftsbibliothek 249 (381)

S   Heiligencreuz, Stiftsbibliothek 11

V   Vienna, Österreichisches Nationalbibliothek, Latinus 357

W   Zwettl, Stiftsbibliothek 72

Z   Zwettl, Stiftsbibliothek 13

t   *BHL* 410b *supra editum*

p   *BHL* 408 (p) *supra editum*

α   = S L D Z M (*Magum legendarium austriacum*)

β   = H E W I A

---

33. It should be noted that the manuscripts group themselves not according to the religious affiliation of the abbey that produced them, or used them at least (Cistercian, Benedictine, Premonstratensian, etc.), but rather according to geography, with the Austrian all on one side, for example, and the Bavarian on the other.

PASSIO SANCTI ANASTASII MARTYRIS

1. Unigenitus filius et verbum Dei per quem omnia facta sunt, qui coaequalis atque consubstantialis patri et vivificatori spiritui sancto est, miseratus generis humani quod sub mortis atque corruptionis
5 tyrannide subiacebat, inclinavit caelos·et descendit secundum quod scriptum est, per nativitatem vero ex virgine formam servi accipiens et cum hominibus conversatus est dispensans omnia ad salutem generis nostri. Et quidem propria morte destruxit eum qui habebat mortis imperium triduana sui corporis sepultura ac gloriosa
10 resurrectione et in caelos ascensione.

2. Et hinc quippe ministri verbi eius atque passionis testes facti sunt beati apostoli qui repleverunt cunctum orbem praedicatione divina. De qua re universa hominum natura magnis et inenarrabilibus Dei donis laetatur.

15 **3.** Sed qui humanae vitae a principio insidiator dolosus est non habuit qualiter malum induceret in tantam bonorum multitudinem quae per Christi gratiam ad fidem est congregata. Videns autem semet ipsum de caelo eiectum ab electorum consortio, quaesivit concinnationem malignitatis, sed nihil eos qui pietatis sunt alumni laedere
20 potuit. Unde eos qui tunc tenebant Romana sceptra insurgere fecit, qui persecutiones universales adversus Dei ecclesiam agitarent.

1 Anastasii Martiris XII die ian V Passio S. Anastasii monachi et martyris GH Incipit Passio S. Anastasii ND Passio S. Anastasii monachi A   2 qui *om.* A   3-7 sancto atque vivificatori spiritui misertus est generi humano perituro et sub mortis atque corruptionis tyrannicae potestatis subiectus inclinavit autem caelos et descendit secundum quod scriptum est per virginem autem natus formam servi suscipiens cum hominibus conversatus est G *cf.* p 4 misertus generi humano α misertus generis humani A miseratus genus hominum t   5 iacebat VZ   7 et *om.* LW   hominibus] omnibus W   8 Et quidem] equidem Z   11 Ex α   eius *om.* αβ   12 repleverunt *transpos. post* divina A   cunctum] totum VG *cf.* cunctum t   13 magnis] magis W 14 Dei *om.* SL   laetabatur DI   15 quia VG *cf.* qui t   dolosus] diabolus L   17 per *om.* W   Christi *transpos. post* gratiam A   gratia G sanguinem α   18 deiectum G   electo W   18-19 inconcinnationem M   19 laedere] reddere N   20 qui] ut VG A quo α   21 persecutionem universalem VG *cf.* uniuersales persecutiones t

5. Quo in tempore inventus est religiosissimus ac beatissimus Anastasius, cuius vitam ab initio usque ad martyrii finem scribere iussus
sum,[1] ipsum propono sermoni qui ab eo confessus est Deum et
25 Dominum nostrum Ihesum Christum, ac sic incipiam enarrare.

6. Erat quidam de Persida Razehe vocabulo, nomen autem[2] ei Magundat. Filius autem erat magi quondam Bau nomine qui etiam et
doctor extiterat magicae disciplinae, erudivitque eum a pueritia magica arte. Facto autem iuvene contigit teneri eum in tyrone cum
30 aliis multis et esse in regia civitate Persarum sub Chosrue rege.
Sanctae autem civitati excidione facta et venerandorum atque adorandorum locorum in praedicta ira propter peccata nostra, sumpta
sunt adoranda ligna vivificatricis et preciosae crucis Christi introducta sunt in Persidam. O admiranda res! Captiva quidem duceba-
35 tur Domini crux; captivabant sibi autem magi[3] quod digni non
erant in salutem habere.

---

22 ac] et α   23 describere DZM   24 sum] *om.* SLZM   Deum et *om.*
DZM   26 Persida–vocabulo] Persidis regione Razech vocabulo de fundo
Rasnuni N p (Raznuni p)   de Perside α   Razaeae vocabulum VG (vocabulo *corr. alt. manus*) EWIA   27 autem] vero N   qui etiam *om.* αβ etiam
om. G   29 Factus autem iuvenis VG   teneri eum *transpos.* N α   in
tyrone] et introire N tyronem α   30 et esse] ut esset N et erat A   regia
om. A   Chosrue] Chosdrohe *corr. ex* Chusrue G Chosdra H Chosdre A
rege] Persarum *add.* A   31 civitatis α   excidio facto α excidioni facta t
32 sumpta] ablata A   33 Christi] et *add.* α   34 Persida VH   34-35 Domini ducebatur *transpos.* α   35 captivant α (35-37 captivabant–crux *om.* D)
β   autem *om.* W Sed magi captivant sibi quod A

1. Although the Greek text has a simple participle, t and p both have *iussus sum*, indicating that this was the reading of the original source of the Latin tradition, preserved also in the 410 revision.

2. This *autem*, translating the Greek δε, is not preserved in 410b's unique
manuscript witness, but its presence in 408 indicates that it was in the original Latin translation. Cf. my edition of t.

3. The editor of the original *BHL* 410 must have revised the puzzling
text: t's *magis ibidem* must have been transformed into *magi sibi* at some
stage because of Anastasius's earlier description as a *magus*.

7. Superstans enim ut dictum est civitati Persidae honoranda crux salvatoris quae gratia atque virtute eius radians ac splendens[4] ubique metum et stuporem infidelibus imponebat, gaudium vero atque
40 laeticiam cordibus fidelium conferebat. Fama autem in tota regione personante de vero Deo, interrogabat praedictus tyro Magundat qui et Anastasius quid hoc esset. Et audiens quomodo Deus Christianorum illuc veniret, statim sicut terra bona suscepta pluvia efficitur ad fructificationem idonea, ita et ipse suscepit per auditum
45 nomen Dei. Deinde cogitans in semetipso qualiter Deum verum qui habitat in caelo quem Christiani colunt inveniret, didicit a quibusdam quomodo ipsa est crux in qua Christus filius Dei fuerat cruxifixus quem Christiani adorant. Admirans autem et obstupescens super hoc praedestinatus Dei famulus Anastasius, non desine-
50 bat de Christianitate inquirere, et quanto plus per auditum quae veritatis sunt percipiebat, tanto magis ab eius corde magicae seductiones abscedebant.

8. Habebat autem fratrem carnalem beatus Anastasius militem qui ducebatur cum eo et venit usque ad Calcedoniam. At vero Philip-

37 honoranda] ignorata SLZM ignoranda β   38 quae *om.* α A et E virtus α   ac] atque DZM   39-40 vero–fidelium] vero fidelium laeticiam cordibus W   40 conferebat] inferebat SL β infundebat DZM   41 Deo vero *transpos.* L   42 qui *om.* Z   Et audiens] Audiens autem A   43 venisset A   44 fructificationem] edificationem N fructificandum DZM *cf.* fructificationem t   ita *om.* SL   suscepit] cepit fructificare A   45 nomen] verbum *add.* I verbi *add.* A   46 qui–caelo *om.* A   caelis α HEI   48 Admirans] audiens α   48-49 obstupefactus I   49 praedestinatus] praedictus α *om.* A   49-50 sinebat ZM   50 quantum VG   51 percipiebant M magicae] magis M   51-52 seductionis M seductionesque W   54 ducebatur] in exercitu *add.* N   et venit usque *om.* VG et venit *om.* WIA   ad *om.* β   54-55 Philippico–reversus] Philippo circumvallante eum ingressus est Persidam. Audiens vero Sain frater eius reversus N Philippico introeunte Persidam abiens inde reversus α Philippico introiens in Persidam audiens autem (autem *om.* + clam *supra lineam add.* A) inde (*om.* VG) reversus A β VG (*cf.* Philippico circumvallanti eum et introgresso eo in Persida audiens Sain reversus est t)

4. t's original unclear text (*Superstans enim ut dictum est ciuitati Persidae honoranda atque uiuifica crux saluatoris et quae gratiae atque uirtutis eius rádia explendens ...*) was more thoroughly revised in the α branch, as is usual.

55 pico introeunte in Persidam, audiens inde reversus est post tergum
eius,[5] et sic contigit famulum Dei Anastasium cum Persarum exercitu venire in partibus orientis. Et inde recedens ab exercitu, dereliquit fratrem suum et venit in Ierapolim, et devertit ad quemdam
Christianum Persam argentaricae artis magistrum, et mansit apud
60 eum. Didicit quidem et ipse artem et operabatur cum eo.

9. Rogabat autem praedictum virum ut indicaret ei qualiter mereretur gratiam sancti baptismatis adipisci. At ille suspectus propter
metum Persarum ne periclitaretur ob hoc occultabatur.[6] Verum
tamen cum eo ibat ad ecclesias et orabat, et videns picturas sancto-
65 rum martyrum siscitabatur ab eo quidnam haec essent. Audiens
vero ab eo sanctorum mirabilia et atrociora tormenta quae eis fuerant a tyrannis inlata, et eorum tollerantiam mirabatur et pavebat.[7] Manens igitur parvo tempore apud praedictum Christo amabilem virum, optimum desiderium percepit in animo venire Ieroso-
70 limam ut illic gratiam baptismatis perciperet.

56 et sic] sicque W   famulum Dei *om.* A   57-58 reliquit M   58 in *om.*
Z   59 argentariae NH   60 Didicit] vero *add.* W   quidem *om.* A   62-
66 At ille–Audiens vero] sumpto eo venit ad ecclesiam et orabat cum eo.
Cumque Anastasius sanctus prospexisset picturas sanctorum martyrum mox
sciscitabatur ab eo quid nam haec essent. At ille intimavit ei omnia per ordinem. Audiens vero sanctus W   63 metus G   ob hoc occultabatur] ad hoc
occultabatur N occultabat α occultabatur HE oboccultabatur WIA   65 ab
eo *om.* A   hoc VGZ   66 vero] autem A   tormenta] fore *add.* A   67
et eorum] simul et eorum audiens A   tollerantia W   67-68 *emendavi* et
faciebat VGHEIA pavens sciebat et tabescebat N et stupebat α magis W *cf.*
et mirabatur pavens p et pavebat t   68 igitur] autem *add.* W   praedictum
om. A   69 percepit] concepit SL

5. The omission of Saim, the name of the commander of the army in
which both Magundat and his brother were enrolled, obfuscates the rest of
the chapter. N has been corrected with the use of *BHL* 408.

6. This passage shows how the α group represents a more revised version
of the original *BHL* 410 text, which is kept, although in a garbled version,
by β.

7. *Pavens* in N may be a relic of the original text, or the result of contamination from *BHL* 408.

10. Devenit autem in sanctam civitatem et mansit apud quemdam cultorem Christi argentarium, et manifestavit ei omne desiderium suum qualiter ad Christum cupiebat accedere. Oblatus est autem ab eo Helyae sanctissimo presbytero qui tunc vicarius apostolicae sedis erat[8] fecit eum baptizari cum socio eiusdem regionis qui etiam et ipse beatum finem pro Christo suscipiens in Edissa civitate martyrio coronatus est.

11. Faciens vero in domo eius octo dies pro illuminatione sua, interrogabat beatum Anastasium sanctissimus presbyter Helias quid nam vellet de reliquo. At vero ipse rogabat eum dicens: "Fac me monachum." Abbas[9] continuo adsumens eum perduxit eum ad mansionem[10] abbatis Anastasii quae a quarto miliario sanctae civitati adiacet. Igitur praedicti monasterii praepositus Iustinus vir in omnibus illustris et plenus quae a Deo sunt bonis suscepit Anastasium et connumeravit eum sanctae congregationi in indictione VIII imperante Heraclio anno decimo. Dedit autem ei et magistrum[11]

---

71 autem] ergo A   72 et manifestavit] aperiens A   73 Oblatusque W
74 sanctissimo presbytero] sanctissimo viro presbytero N presbytero sancto A   75 erat] qui *add.* α H qui ... mox *add.* W et *add.* A   78 Faciente vero α β (Faciebat autem A)   illuminatione] vero *add.* A   80 reliquo] esse *add.* DZM   81 Abbas] Helias Z At ille NW   assumens eum continuo W eum[2] *om.* VGH   81-82 mansionem] nomen loci *add.* N   82 Anastasii *om.* W   a quarto miliario] quarto miliario α ad quatuor milia EWI ad iiii miliaria A   85 connumeravit] connumerabat IA   eum *om.* EIA   86 Heraclio] imperatore *add.* Z   86-88 magistrum de eadem congregatione, fratrem virum prudentem. Qui etiam docuit germanum eum literis graecis atque N magistrum unum eiusdem congregationis fratrem virum prudentem qui etiam docuit eum litteras [graecas] p

8. The phrase naming Modestus as the one *qui tunc vicarius apostolicae sedis erat* has fallen out of the 410 tradition, probably through conflation of t's *sanctissimus presbyter ... sanctissimo presbytero*. The addition of *qui* by α, *et* by A, and *qui ... mox* by W represent attempts to make the Latin clearer.

9. Does *BHL* 410's *abbas* suggest that the original Latin translation read *albas*? The *BHL* 410 tradition, particularly the variants of Z, N and W, indicates that the text was corrupt.

10. The phrase *nomen loci* must have been a marginal note that made its way into the text of N.

11. Another of N's corrections from *BHL* 408.

unum de eius germanis discipulis. Abbas vero intellectu plenus docuit[12] eum graecis litteris atque psalterio. Et tondens eum in sancto monachorum habitu induens ut filium educabat.

90   12. Fecit autem administrationes diversas beatus Anastasius tam de
coquina quam etiam de horto, placens eis per Domini gratiam.
Erat enim sedulus valde in ministerio fratrum et in opere manum
et in regula prae omnibus. Audiens quidem sine intermissione divinas scripturas et vitam sanctorum patrum ponebat mentem suam
95   diligenter, et si quid forte non intellegebat interrogabat idoneum
virum qui praeerat fratribus et discens quae requirebat mirabatur
glorificans Deum. Legens autem intra semetipsum in cella certamina martyrum lacrimabatur multum, et orabat ut eum dignum effi-
ceret Deus quandoque sancto certamini ad laudem gloriae Christi.
100   Hoc autem novimus cum miraretur ac stuperet perseverantiam
sanctorum et paene nihil aliud legeret nisi haec quae inflammabant
desiderium eius. Perseveravit autem beatus Anastasius in mansione
illa annis vii.

13. Videns vero malignus spiritus tantam in Christo caritatem, co-
105   nabatur evertere et in desperationem abducere famulum Dei Anastasium. Inmisit ei cogitationes malignas et memoriam magicorum
verborum quibus a patre suo edoctus fuerat. At ipse cognoscens
dolosi astuciam orabat quidem Deum eripi se ab insidiis diaboli.

---

87 germani *codd. cf.* germanis t   87-88 Abbas–eum] a quo edoctus est W
88 psalterium HA   Et] Insuper W   in] ac α   88-89 in sancto–induens]
induit sanctum monachorum habitum et eum A   89 induens] induit W educa-
vit α   91 Domini] Dei WIA   92 valde *om.* α   94 vitas αβ   96 discens–
requirebat] dicens quod quaerebat N   98 Legens–semetipsum] intra semetipsum
autem legebat A   98 orabat] Deum *add.* A   99 Deus] Dominus W *om.* A
Christi] suae α   101 et] quia SL *om.* A   legebat A   inflammarent α   104
vero] ergo EWIA   Christo] eo A   104-105 conabatur] eum *add.* W   105
Dei famulum *transpos.* EWI   106 Inmisit ei] Nam immisit W Immisit enim ei
A   107 doctus ZW   108 dolosi] inimici *add.* α   quidem] frequenter A
eripere α

12. Again, a lacuna or shortening in the *BHL* 410 tradition changes the details of the story. It is not the abbot, but a confrere appointed by the *praepositus*
Justinus who instructs Anastasius.

Abbati vero denudans omnia cum multis lacrimis ut dignaretur
110 orare pro eo ad Deum rogabat quatenus liberaret eum ab insidiis
adversarii. Admonens quoque eum et confortans secundum quae
data est ei a Deo intelligentiam praepositus monasterii, et faciens
orationem pro eo coram ecclesia effugavit ab eo insidias diaboli.

14. Post dies autem paucos videbat se Dei famulus per visionem
115 stare in monte excelso et quendam ad se venientem ac porrigentem
sibi poculum vini aureum et gemmis ornatum et dicentem sibi:
"Accipe et bibe." Quem suscipiens bibit. Statim igitur suspectus
factus est se impetrasse quod cupiebat. Et surgens venit ad ecclesiam nocturna psalmodia inlucescente sancto domenico die; et
120 adortans abbatem monasterii ingredi in ministerialem locum, cecidit ad pedes eius rogans cum lacrimis ut oraret pro eo et dicit ei:
"Scio pater quantos labores in me miserabili habuisti et quia per te
adduxit me Deus de tenebris ad lucem; sed nunc peto ora pro me
ad Dominum quia sum moriturus in his diebus." Dicit ei abbas:
125 "Et unde scis quia moriturus es in his diebus?" Ipse vero narravit
ei visionem confirmans per omnia quod moriturus esset in proximo sive comuni morte, seu aliter. Metuebat enim palam dicere ut
non increparet eum.

109 vero] ergo A   109-110 ut–rogabat] rogabat eum ut pro eo dignaretur
Deum orare A   111 adversarii] diaboli α   111-112 Admonens–faciens]
Abbas vero monasterii faciens W Praepositus autem monasterii admonebat
et confortabat eum secundum quae data est ei intelligentiam et faciens A
112 ei–praepositus] ei sapientia a Deo abbas α   113 coram ecclesia *om.* W
diaboli] inimici β   114 autem] vero A   114-115 paucos–quendam] paucos
famulus Dei Anastasius per visionem videbat se stare in monte excelso et vidit quendam A   115 se *om.* W   116 sibi *om.* D   et dicentem] et *om.* N
dicentemque E   117 Quem] qui β   Statim] Statimque Z Autem H   igi-
tur] autem D *om.* M   117-118 suspectus–est] suspensus factus est WI expergefactus intellexit A   118 se *om.* WI   118-119 ad–psalmodia] ad ecclesiam
(et *add. supra lin.*) nocturnam psalmodiam G ad nocturnam psalmodiam W
119 sancto *om.* WIA   120 adortans] adorans N   locum] et mox *add.* A
121 rogans] eum *add.* A   dicens WIA   122 et *om.* A   123 adduxit]
duxit α HEIA eduxit W   124 ad *om.* SL   124-125 Dicit–diebus *om.* α
Dicit ei abbas: "Et unde moriturus es in his diebus?" *add. in marg.* N *cf.* et
unde scis quia futurus es mori in his diebus? t   125 scis quia *om.* β   125-
126 Ipse–visionem *om.* V *add. in marg. alt. man.* G   127 seu] siue
EWIA   127-128 ut non] ne Z   128 increpasset E

15. Abbas vero eius multis admonitionibus consolatus est eum.
130 Sanctus vero Anastasius complens canonem cum fratribus missa
facta percepit de divinis mysteriis et prandens cum fratribus sopo-
ratus est modicum. Statimque surgens et non deferens cordis incendium exiit clam de monasterio, nihil omnino accipiens nisi ea
quibus vestiebatur, et abiit. Qui deductus gratia Dei per veneranda
135 loca pervenit Caesaream Palestinae, et mansit in domo semper lau-
dabilis Dei genitricis Mariae per dies duos.

16. Procedens autem ad sanctam ecclesiam beatae Eufemiae orationis causa, vidit in quadam domo Persarum magice operantes, et
zelo deifico ductus, ingressus ad eos dixit: "Quid erratis et errare
140 facitis in maleficiis vestris?" Stupentes autem hi viri super eius constantia interrogabant eum quis esset, vel unde, et quare hoc diceret
ad eos. Ipse vero ait eis: "Ego quidem sicut et vos fui aliquando, et
scio incantationes vestras." Et incipiente eo arguere illos, obmutuerunt illi, et rogabant eum ne divulgaret eos, et dimiserunt eum.

145 **17.** Post haec autem viderunt eum quidam de cavallariis sedentes
ante derbas quod est praetorium sellarii, et dicunt intra se propria
lingua: "Iste delator est." Audiens vero beatus Anastasius haec eos
dicentes ait: "Quid verbosatis? Ego delator non sum, sed servus
sum Ihesu Christi et melior vestri. Nam et ego aliquando sicut et

129 vero] autem A   eius *om.* Z   130 canonem] orationem S orationes L
131 percepit de divinis] perceptis divinis α   fratribus] confratribus L   132
deferens] differens VG α ferens H   133 de *om.* E   135 pervenit] venit Z
137 autem] inde *add.* W   138 vidit] itidem L   quadam–operantes] domo
cuiusdam Persi magicam operantes artem N domo cuiusdam Persae magicam
operantes artem p   et *om.* E   139 dicit WI   139-140 et errare facitis]
et errare alios facitis α et quare errare facitis alios W et quare errare facitis I
et quare facitis errare A   140 hi viri] viri illi A   140-141 constantiam NW
141 vel] et αβ   hoc *om.* VG   142 ait] dixit WI respondit A   fui] filii
I   143 arguere] coarguere S arguens L   illos] eos LA et *add.* E   144
eum] illum E   145 cavallariis] caballariis G cavillariis α calvariis EWIA
146 derbas] rerbas Z thermas EWIA   sellarii] callarii IA   intra se] inter
M   147 vero *om.* A   148 Quid verbosatis] Quid inter vos musitatis α
Quid verbositatis β   149 Nam et ego] Ego enim A   et[3] *om.* DZM

150 vos cavallarius fui." At illi surgentes, tenuerunt eum. Et exiens
sellarius discutiebat eum unde esset, et diligenter eum examinans,
custodivit per tres dies. In quibus diebus non adquievit suscipere
quicquam ab eis alimenti.

18. Marzabanas vero non erat in Caesarea quando tentus est famu-
155 lus Dei Anastasius. Veniente ergo eo, suggessit illi praedictus sellarius quae egit erga sanctum Anastasium, et adduxit eum ad praetorium eius.

19. Beatus vero Anastasius cum stetisset coram Marzabana non
adoravit eum secundum ritum qui habetur ab eis. Intuens autem
160 eum Marzabana dicit ei: "Unde es et quis existeris? Ipse vero respondit: "Christianus sum. Si autem velis discere unde sim Perso
quidem genere de regione Razehe de villa Rasnuni. Cavallarius
vero eram et magus, sed reliqui tenebras et veni ad lucem." Dicit
ei Marzabanas: "Dimitte errorem hunc et convertere ad primam
165 tuam religionem, et praebemus tibi iumenta et argenteos et aureos,
et continentiam magnam." Ipse vero respondens ait: "Non det mihi
Deus negare Christum meum." Dicit ei Marzabanas: "Ergo placet
tibi vestiri scemate quo indutus es?" Ipse vero ait: "Iste habitus gloria mea est." Dicit ei Marzabanas: "Daemonem habes." Respondens
170 beatus Anastasius: "Quando fui in errore habui daemonem; nunc
vero habeo Christum qui persequitur daemones." Dicit ei Marzabanas: "Non metuis imperatorem? ne quando didicerit quae erga te

150 cavallarius] caballarius G cavillarius α EWIA   Et exiens] Cumque com-
prehensus esset, statim exiens W   152 custodivit] eum *add.* E   diebus *om.*
A   154 vero *om.* A   154-155 famulus Dei *om.* A   155 ergo] autem E
illi] ei ZWIA   156 adduxit] duxit VG   ad] in H   158 vero *om.* A
Marzabana] eo A   159 habebatur VG   ab eis] apud eos *et transpos. ante*
habetur A   160 eum *om.* VGWI   dixit E   quis existeris] quid profiteris
α   vero] autem L   161 discere] discutere Z scire E   sum VL   Persa
Z   162 Razeae VG Racehe D Razeche EWIA   Rasunni W   cavillarius
α calvarius EW   164 errorem hunc] errores S   165 et–argenteos *om.* D
et³ *om.* M   et aureos *om.* V *add. supra lin.* G   166 respondens *om.* A
168 ero *om.* A   Iste *om.* D enim *add.* SLZM EWIA vero *add.* H   169
Daemonium EW   170 Anastasius] dixit *add.* N α (*supra lin. alt. man.*) G
inquit *add.* E ait *add.* A   daemonium W   171 vero] autem EA *om.* I
172 ne *om.* W

sunt iubeat te crucifigi?" Ipse vero dixit: "Quare habeo timere imperatorem? Homo est corruptibilis sicut et tu."

175   **20.** Tunc indignatus Marzabanas iussit eum ferro alligari, et duci in castrum, et asportari lapides sine cessatione. Cum vero asportaret lapides multos atque insufferentes tribulationes sustineret famulus Dei, quidam enim de regione eius videntes quae in eo fiebant accesserunt ad eum dicentes: "Quid hoc fecisti? Nemo enim de re-
180   gione nostra factus est Christianus, et ecce fecisti nobis ridiculum." Ipse vero iniuriabat eos et repellebat. At illi versi in insaniam, et per singulos dies accedentes evellebant barbam eius, et percutientes eum scindebant vestimenta eius. Sed et saxum magnum quod quatuor ex eis baiolabant imponebant ei habenti unam catenam in
185   collo et aliam in pedibus, adiungentes ei etiam multa et acriora tormenta. Fortissimus autem athleta ferebat haec omnia gaudens propter Christum.

21. Tunc iussit iterum Marzabanas adduci eum et dicit ei: "Si veraciter ut dixisti magi filius fuisti, et scis artem magicam, dic mihi
190   aliqua ex eis ut cognoscam." Ipse vero respondens ait: "Non det mihi Deus ut egrediatur quicquam huiusmodi ex ore meo." Dicit ei Marzabanas: "Ergo permanes in his? Convertere in primam tuam religionem. Nam si nolueris scribam imperatori de te." Beatus Anastasius dixit: "Scripsisti et recepisti rescripta; fac quod vis." Cui
195   Marzabanas ait: "Non scripsi sed scribam et quidquid iusserit mihi faciam." Cui beatus Anastasius respondit: "Vade et scribe quanta volueris mala de me. Ego enim Christianus sum." Dicit Marzabanas: "Ponatur et caedatur usque dum confiteatur facere quae ei

---

173 crucifigi] cruci affigi H   dixit] ait EWI respondit A   176 asportare
αβ *ex* asportari *corr. alt. man.* G   vero] ergo WIA   176-177 portaret A
177 insufferentes] intolerabiles α   sustinuisset α sustinuit EWIA   178
enim *om.* α HIA autem E tunc quidam W   179 enim *om.* W   181 Ipse
vero] At ille E Ipse autem A   184 habenti *om.* W   185 et aliam] aliamque
E   pedibus] pellibus D   188 dixit αβ   189 scies SLEI sciens A   190
aliquid L   191 ex] de WIA   192 in²] ad EWIA   193 Beatus] Sanctus A
194 accepisti E   scripta ZM   Cui *om.* A   195 ait] dixit HEIA   mihi
om. M   196 Cui *om.* EA *sed vide infra*   respondit] dixit ei A   et *om.*
EWIA   197 enim *om.* WIA   198 confiteatur] fateatur se WIA

iubentur." Cumque cepissent eum fustibus caedere dixit sanctus
Anastasius: "Expoliate me ut non iniurientur vestimenta mea, et sic
caedite carnes meas. Haec enim quae facitis ludibria sunt. Me autem si membratim abscidatis non negabo Christum meum."

22. Iterum dicit ei Marzabanas: "Adquiesce mihi. Nam scribo imperatori de te." Beatus Anastasius respondit: "Vade scribe imperatori tuo quicquid volueris." Et Marzabanas ad eum: Quid igitur?
Non times imperatorem?" Beatus Anastasius respondit: "Quare
habeo timere imperatorum tuum? Numquid non est homo sicut et
tu? Et sicut morieris non morietur? Et sicut corrumperis non corrumpitur? Quem ergo magis metuam, illum qui corrumpitur sicut
et tu similem tibi lutum, aut Christum qui fecit caelum et terram
mare et omnia quae in eis sunt?" Stupefactus autem superbus ille
super fidutia martyris, iussit eum duci in castrum.

23. Et post dies paucos iussit eum assisti coram se et dicit ei: "Accipe magicam tuam et sacrifica ut non moriaris." Respondit Dei
famulus et dicit ei: "Quibus diis iubes me sacrificare? Soli et lunae
et igni et montibus et collibus? Haec omnia Christus fecit ad hominum servitium. Vos vero errando servitis daemonibus ignorantes
Deum qui fecit vos. Si enim novissetis Christum, habuissetis converti ad lucem et erui a daemonibus qui errare vos faciunt. Et
qui non mentitur Deus verus qui promisit pro nomine suo passuris
dare os et sapientiam quibus non poterunt resistere adversarii eorum."

199 iubentur] praecipiuntur WIA   eum] omnes Z   dicit α   200 Anas-
tasius] eis *add.* A   ut non] ne E   iniurient W   201 facitis] fecistis M
202 meum *om.* Z   203 Iterum *om.* A   scribam L   204 Beatus–respon-
dit] sanctus dicit ei A   Vade] et *add.* β   205 quidcumque Z   igitur] ergo WI inquid *add.* H   206 Anastasius *om.* A   respondit] at eum Z   207
habeo] debeo W   tuum *om.* EWIA   homo *om.* E   208-209 Et¹-metuam
om. V *add. ad calcem alt. man.* G   non¹ *om.* E   non² *om.* Z   209
corrumpetur α IA   210 et¹ *om.* α   212 fidutia] fidem α   212-213 duci-
iussit eum *om.* DZM   214 magica tuam G   et sacrifica *om.* W   214-
215 Respondit–dicit] Sanctus A. respondit dicens A   215 Dei] ei ME   216
et collibus *om.* N   217 vero] autem A   219 erui *om.* WIA   faciunt] recedere *add.* W   Et *om.* A   220 qui] quia N αβ *cf.* Haec qui t   qui²]
quae H   221 dare *om.* WIA   poterint SL possunt Z

Loquente beato Anastasio stupebant contrarii Dei. Martyr vero trinis coronatus confessionibus ducebatur ad castrum vinculis ornatus pro Christo.

225 **24.** Cognoscens autem sanctissimus abbas monasterii de quo erat martyr Christi stabilitatem et copiosam alacritatem perseverantiae eius in Christo, gavisus est gaudio magno cum universa congregatione sua, et supplicabat Deo die noctuque cum universis fratribus ut consummaret cursum eius. Et dirigens duos fratres in Caesaream 230 ad beatum Anastasium litteris athleticis confortavit alacritatem eius.

25. Cum vero esset in custodia martyr Christi Anastasius non cessabat psalmis et hymnis glorificare Deum. Habens secum convinctum iuvenem quendam pro quadam causa, et nolens contristari cum surgebat ut celebraret consuetum canonem Dei, superinclina-235 bat se vincto iacenti tenens pedem suum iuxta pedem eius, ut non per catenarum extensionem faceret ei laborem. Una igitur noctium psallente beato Anastasio quidam de vinctis Hebraeus professione clemens nobilior moribusque honestis videns beatum Anastasium martyrem die quidem in lapidum asportatione laborantem nocte 240 vero deprecationem Dei facientem stupebat admirans quid nam esset hoc.

26. Et diu intuens in eum iacens super pavimentum subito vidit aliquos veste dealbatos per hostium carceris in matutinis horis cum

---

222 Loquente] Haec loquente W Loquente haec A   beato] sancto W Dei] eius β   223 coronatus] honoratus SL   223-224 ornatus] oneratus α *alt. man. corr. ex* ornatus G   226 perseverantiae *om.* A   228 Deo *om. et* Deum *add. post* noctuque A   fratribus] suis *add.* SL   229 consummaret] confirmaret L   230 athleticis] allectitiis N ac decretis α encleticis H ad cleticis E athleticis (*correc.*) W ad clericis I adcleticis A   confortabat WIA 231 vero *om.* L autem A   232 Habuit A   232-233 convinctum] coniunctum D   233 contristari] contristare eum α   234 surgeret α   ut] et Z quidem *add. ante* ut E   consuetum] quidem *add.* NA   235 se *om.* W suum iuxta pedem *om.* N   236 per *om.* WIA   extensione EWIA   237 de vinctis Hebraeus] de vinctis Hebraeis SLZM devinctus Hebraeus E   238 moribusque–videns] moribus quam vestibus videns α   Anastasium *om.* A 239 quidem] quadam IA   240 vero] autem A   Deo α   241 esset hoc] hoc esset SZHA beatus esset L   242 subito *om.* W

esset in silentio noctis ingredientes ac circumdantes beatum Anasta-
245 sium martyrem et lux copiosa refulsit. Amens vero factus super
contemplatione hac, dixit intra se: "Isti angeli sunt." Hoc autem
existimans, vidit eos palliis circumdatos, habentes cruces in manibus et dicit in semetipso: "Isti episcopi sunt." Intuens autem martyrem Christi Anastasium, vidit eum splendide indutum sicut et
250 caeteros et iuvenem quendam in multa gloria stantem ante eum et
habentem turibulum et incensum mittentem. Aspiciens autem haec
omnia cepit manu pulsare proximum suum ut ostenderet ei quae
videbat, et non poterat quia manebat amens. Territus vero factus,
interrogabat ab eo quid hoc esset. Dicit ei Hebraeus: "Cernis hoc."
255 Et intuentes iam nihil viderunt. Enarravit ergo ei ille omnia quae
viderat et glorificaverunt unanimiter Deum.

27. Et quia ut superius dictum est in prima et secunda interrogatione didicit Marzabanas immobilitatem servi Dei Anastasii scripsit
imperatori de eo. Contigit autem intra paucos dies suscipere Mar-
260 zabanan imperatoris iussionem, et transmittens ad eum, mandavit
ei: "En iussit imperator ut verbum dicas 'non sum Christianus' et
statim te demitto; et ubi volueris vade." Respondit autem martyr
Christi et dixit: "Nec fiat mihi ut negem Christum Dominum
meum." Multas vero promissiones faciebat ei, sed non valuit per-
265 suadere illi.

28. Post hoc autem mandavit ei dicens: "Scio quia confunderis
propter congentiles tuos, et ideo non vis coram eis negare. Sed quia
iussio imperatoris est ut coram me et aliis duobus sellariis dicas

---

244 circumstantes EWIA   245-246 super–hac] super contemplationem hanc
α ex contemplatione hac EWIA   246 autem] ita *add.* E   247-248 manibus]
suis *add.* E   248 dixit EWIA   in semetipso] ad semetipsum E   249
splendide] splendore IA   indutus L   250 multa] magna α   eum *om.* D
et^2 *om.* E   251 mittentem] immittentem β   253 viderat EWIA et] sed A
vero] et ille *add.* A   254 ab eo] eum A   255 intuens VGZ iam] eum H
Enarravit] Narravit N αβ *cf.* Enarravit t   ei–quae] ille ei quae WIA   256
glorificabant DZM   257 superius] iam *add.* SL   258 Anastasii] et *add.* WI
262 ubi] ubicumque E   autem] ei W   263 et dixit] *om.* Z et ait E et dixit
ei WA   Ne EWIA   263-264 Dominum meum] Deum Z Deum meum E
264 valuit] potuit W   265 illi] ei α WIA   266 haec N   autem *om.* ZA
268 imperatoris] regis EWIA   ut *om.* ZA vel M

verbum et dimittam te." Et ipse remandavit ei dicens: "Absit a me
270 ut coram te vel aliis aliquando negem Dominum meum." Tunc dicit ei per semetipsum: "Ecce iussit imperator ut ferro vinctus vadas
in Persidam." Ad haec martyr Christi respondit: "Si dimiseris me,
ego solus vadam ad imperatorem." Ut autem vidit beatum Anastasium ad omne experimentum fortiter stantem, neque minis terri-
275 tum neque blandimentis suasum, iussit eum duci in custodia publica, ut post quinque dies iter faceret cum duobus Christi amabilibus
viris quos etiam vinctos cum eo transmisit.

29. Adproximans autem dies festus exaltationis crucis Domini, fecerunt sanctam sollempnitatem in carcere beatus Anastasius et duo
280 fratres monasterii eius ac praefati duo Christo amabiles viri et quidam de civitate reverentissimi psalmis et hymnis totam noctem
ducentes in tantum ut obliviscerentur universorum vinculorum
glorificantes communem Deum. Diluculo autem ingrediens commerciarius vir Christo amabilis ad Marzabanam postulavit tolli a
285 beato Anastasio vincula ut eum duceret in ecclesiam. Quo facto,
magnum gaudium erat universis fidelibus Christi et consolatio multa.

30. Cernentes tantam beati martyris fidem in Christo, et refloruerunt et revixerunt fidei ita ut obliti essent suarum tribulationum,
et osculantes vincula martyris dicebant: "Si nos parati fuimus mori
290 pro te, tu magis propter communem Dominum Christum debes cum
magna alacritate hoc sustinere." Commerciarius vero rogans sanctum Anastasium et vim faciens ei perduxit ad propriam domum

269 et¹ *om*. E   Et ipse] Ipse autem A   remandavit] mandavit VG *cf*. remandavit t   270 vel] et W   271 vadas] eas E   272 Christi *om*. Z   274
neque] nec Z   275-276 custodiam publicam αβ   278 Adproximans–festus]
Adproximante autem die festo N α Adpropinquans autem dies festus E Adproximans autem erat dies festus A   exaltationis] sanctae *add*. ZEWIA Domini *om*. ZH   279 beatus] sanctus IA   280 Christi VSLZWI   281 noc-
tem] pervigilem *add. supra lin*. A   282 ut *om*. M   universorum] cunctorum E   285 vinculum N *om*. VGHα   288 fidei] fideli WI in fide A
289 et *om*. E   dixerunt α IA   fuimus] sumus H   mori *om*. N
290 Dominum] Deum β (nostrum *add*. E)   291 Commerciarius] Camerarius
W   291-292 vero–sanctum] autem rogabat beatum E   292 perduxit] eum
add. E   propriam *om*. D

suam cum duobus fratribus monasterii eius, et convescens cum eis
restituit eum in carcerem gaudentem et exultantem in Domino.

295 **31.** Expleto autem termino quinque dierum, exiit de civitate Caesarea cum duobus Christo amabilibus viris de quadam causa accusatis, cum multis lacrimis civium Christianorum et aliorum gentilium pariter glorificantium Deum super eius bonum propositum.
Ivit autem cum illo unus de duobus fratribus monasterii eius, se-
300 cundum iussionem praepositi ad solatium atque ministerium eius,
ut ea quae sequerentur in eo ab initio usque in finem referret tam
sanctissimo abbati quam etiam cunctae congregationi. Multum enim
gaudium et laeticia per civitates et fideles fiebat super adventum
martyris. Scripsit autem ipse martyr ad[13] Hierapolim praeposito
305 monasterii sui rogans orare pro se, ut incommutabilem eum Dominus super huiusmodi honorem et gloriam custodiret. Scripsit ei et
a Tygride flumine similiter, rogans obsecrare Dominum finiri eius
cursum in gloria nominis sui.

32. Ingrediens autem in Persidam Christi martyr Anastasius missus
310 est in carcerem. At vero frater eius qui cum eo erat mansit in eodem praedio in domo Cortach filii de Gesdim primi commerciarii
Persarum qui erat Christianus. Et faciente sancto martyre dies aliquos cum eis qui ibidem capti erant suggestum est imperatori Chosroi. Qui mittens unum de iudicibus iussit examinari eum.

---

293 suam *om.* E   294 gaudentem et *om.* ZE   296 viris] et aliis pro
add. W   quadam *om.* HEIA α   298 Deum] Dominum L   eius] huius E   bono proposito VG *cf.* bonum propositum t   299 Ibat β
300 iussionem] praeceptum α   atque] ad WIA   301 in] ad WIA
302 cunctae *om.* β   302-303 Multum–laeticia] Multa enim laetitia gaudiumque SLDM Laetitia enim multa gaudiumque Z Magnum autem gaudium multaque laeticia A   303 et laeticia] laeticiaque HEWI   304 au-
tem] etiam A   306 ei] autem E   307 flumine] fluvio WIA   rogans]
eum *add.* W   310 erat] venerat E   311 praedio] loco SLZM   in-
Gesdim *om.* VG   Cortach filii] Cartacii N cortaphili α   312 Et faci-
ente] Faciente autem A   313 eis] his E   capti erant] capti sunt EWI
capti fuerant A captivi erant Z   313-314 Chosdroe HA

13. All the manuscript witnesses read *ad*, a mistake most likely occa-
sioned by the ending of *Hierapolim*.

315 **33.** Quique adveniens in carcerem interrogavit eum quis esset et unde, et quam ob rem relinquens eorum religionem factus esset Christianus. Respondit martyr Christi per interpretem—non enim dignatus est eis loqui persica lingua—et ait: "Erratis vos daemones pro Deo colentes. Et ego aliquando cum in errore essem hos cole-
320 bam; nunc autem colo omnipotentem Deum qui fecit caelum et terram, et omnia quae in eis sunt. Et scio diligenter quia culturae vestrae perditio et error daemonum sunt." Dicit ei iudex: "Miser homo! Numquid quem colitis vos Christiani non eum crucifixe-runt Iudaei? Quomodo ergo errasti relinquens religionem tuam, et
325 factus es Christianus?" Beatus Anastasius respondit: "Quoniam cru-cifixus est a Iudaeis salvator mundi verum dicis, quia sponte voluit pati pro humani generis salvatione.[14] Ipse autem est verus Deus qui fecit caelum et terram, mare et omnia quae in eis sunt, et des-cendit de caelis in terram, et homo factus est et crucifixus ut libera-
330 ret genus hominum de errore Satanae qui colitur a vobis. Vos vero colentes ignem et caetera quae dicere erubesco vanam habentes spem, colentes creaturam et non creatorem." Dicit ei iudex: "Quid mihi et sermonibus istis? Ecce divinitas imperatoris paravit tibi dignitates magnas, ut sis inter primates eius; tantum convertere in
335 pristinam religionem tuam." Respondit beatus Anastasius et dixit: "Ego Deum meum non negabo, sed magis adoro et colo. Dona ve-ro imperatoris tui ut stercora computabo."

315 Quique adveniens] Quinque adveniens E Qui veniens A   315-316 quis–unde] quis aut unde esset Z   316 quam ob rem] quare WIA   religionem eorum *transpos.* WIA   317 Respondens SW Respondens vero L   318 et *om.* SL   Errantes E   319 Deo] Domino L   colentes] colitis E   320 omnipotentem Deum *om.* M *transpos.* SL   321 terram] mare *add.* α   321-322 Et scio–sunt *om.* M   321 diligenter] vere SLDZ   322 vestrae] tuae SLDZ   324 erras VG   tuam] nostram WIA   et *om.* Gβ   325 Beatus] Sanctus vero N   Quoniam] quidem *add.* N   326 salvator mundi *om.* N   quia] vero *add.* N   327 pro–salvatione] quare non dicis? N *cf.* quare non dicis? p   salvatione] salute αβ   329 caelis in] caelo ad L   330 hominum] humanum αβ   331 colentes] colitis W   caetera] alia β   332 colentes] colitis α   creaturas ZMD   333 istis *des.* A   334 eius] suos Z   335 tuam *om.* VG   et dixit] ei *add.* G dicens HEWI   336-337 vero] etiam HEWI   337 computabo] deputabo WI

14. This passage clearly shows N's correction based on *BHL* 408; it is diffi-cult to determine whether the original was *salute* as in αβ or *salvatione* as in VG.

34. Haec autem omnia intimavit imperatori praedictus iudex. Qui statim furore repletus misit eum in carcerem. Veniens ergo iudex
340 cum ira iussit trahi eum de carcere, et coepit minis terribilibus concutere eum. Sanctus vero martyr respondit ei dicens: "Ne labores iudex neque fatigeris. Me enim Christo confortante non facies recedere a fide Christi; quicquid ergo volueris fac." Tunc iussit eum ligatum secundum morem Persarum fustibus caedi et dicit ei: "Quia
345 honoribus et donis imperatoris non es adsentiens, cognosce quia amodo te per singulos dies his plagis consumam." Respondit sanctus martyr et dixit ei: "Nec donis imperatoris tui acquiesco, nec minas tuas timeo. Quidquid vis facito."

35. Tunc iussit eum solutum poni supinum et lignum super tibias
350 eius imponi, et duos viros fortes stare super utraque capita ligni. Sanctus autem martyr Christi gratias agebat Deo sustinens dolores fortissimos. Videns vero iudex quia nihil ei proficit, iussit eum mitti in carcerem donec iterum intimaret imperatori de ipso.

36. Sellario vero existente Christiano qui erat super carcerem, in-
355 grediabatur frater monasterii ad eum consolans eum et adhortans in bonum. < Multi > Christianorum qui ibidem erant inclinantes atque osculantes vincula eius, rogabant ut dignaretur orare pro eis et dare eis benedictionem in Christo.

37. Post dies autem paucos, iterum ingrediens idem iudex in carce-
360 rem, dicit beato Anastasio: "Quid dicis? facis iussionem imperatoris

---

339 statim] in *add.* E   mis̄it–carcerem] remisit eundem iudicem dicens: "Si non sacrificaverit diversis eum poenis interfice." α   341 Ne] Non SLZ
342 neque fatigeris *om.* E   enim *om.* HEWI   non facies] ne facias E
344 et dicit ei] dicens ei E dicens illi WI   345 adsentiens] consentiens Z
346 te *postpos. ante* consumam αE   346-347 sanctus martyr] sanctus martyr Christi α martyr Christi EWI   347 dixit ei] ei *om.* α ait (ei *om.*) EWI adquiescam WI   348 facito] Fac ergo quod vis α Quicquid vis fac H quicquid volueris fac E Quidquid vultis facite WI   349 et lignum] lignumque EWI   350 imponi] poni H   351-352 fortissimos dolores *transpos.* WI
352 ei proficit] in eum profecit α proficit WI nihil plus exigit t nihil proficeret p   353 ipso] eo E   355 ad eum *om.* G   356 in] ad WI   Christianorum] Christiani HEWI *cf.* Multi uero Christianorum t   357 atque] et WI
358 in] pro HEWI   359 idem] isdem VG   360 dixit E   imperatoris *om.* W

aut permanes ut coepisti?" Sanctus vero martyr movens caput suum, abominavit eum dicens: "Semel, secundo, et saepius iam dixi tibi quoniam impossibile est negare me Christum. Quicquid vis fac citius." Tunc temerarius ille et barbarus iussit ligari eum quemad-
365 modum et primum et caedi eum diutius fustibus et derelinquens eum in carcerem recessit. Revertens autem post dies aliquos, rursum ingrediens ad eum his ipsis sermonibus utens ad negationem provocabat sanctum martyrem, aliquando quidem blandimentis et promissionibus pecuniarum et dignitatum, aliquando autem minis
370 et terribilibus amarisque tormentis. Cum vero vidisset eius immutabilem mentem atque soliditatem fidei in Christo, iussit ligari eum sicut et semel et bis, ac caedi fustibus, et post haec solutum iussit eum suspendi ex una manu et saxum magnum alligari in pede eius, et sic derelinquens eum abiit. Sustinuit autem fortiter martyr
375 Christi Anastasius hoc supplicium quasi horarum duarum spacium. Tunc mittens iussit deponi eum et vadens suggessit imperatori fiduciam eius.

38. Post dies autem quindecim misit imperator ipsum iudicem et socios cum eo, qui interficerent sanctum martyrem et multos Chris-
380 tianorum captivos. Qui veniens iussit eos adduci foras in praedium in quo existebat carcer, ipsumque sanctum martyrem et septuaginta viros secus amnem, et sic coram sancto martyre funibus suffocari.[15] Inter quos erant praedicti duo Christo amabiles viri qui cum eo venerant a Caesarea, et per unumquemque qui interficiebantur,

---

361 aut] an E   ut] ubi VG   movit EWI   362 abominavit] abhominatus est α abhominavitque I   iam *om.* ZM   363 me *om.* H   363-364 citius *om.* ZM   364 eum *om.* SL   365 et³] sic *add.* W   366 aliquos dies *transpos.* WI   366-367 rursumque WI   369 pecuniarum] multarum *add.* EWI   370 terribilibus] terroribus α   370-371 immutabilem] immobilem N   371 soliditatem fidei] confortatum W   372 eum *om.* D   et¹ *om.* SLDZ HEWI   373 alligari] ligari W   375 Anastasius] et *add.* M   380 eos *om.* WI   381 existebat] stetit EWI   sanctum *om.* I   et] multos Christianorum *add.* Z   382 funibus] fustibus N   382-383 suffocari] iussum est *add.* VGN iussi sunt α iussus est EI iussit eum W   383 Christo *om.* DZM HEWI   384 a Caesarea] Caesaream EWI   unumquemque] eorum *add.* α

---

15. The reading of the best manuscripts (*iussum est*) may be a corruption or correction of t's *iusserunt,* following *veniens (venientes iusserunt* t).

385 dicebant sancto Anastasio: "Vis sicut horum unus male perire? Adquiesce imperatori, et vive, et accipe ab eo honores, et esto in palacio eius sicut unus ex nostris, et ne derelinquas dulcem vitam hanc." At vero Christi martyr Anastasius aspiciens in caelum gratias egit Deo quoniam implebatur desiderium eius, et respondens

390 ait ad eos: "Ego optabam membratim concidi a vobis pro caritate Christi. Si vere iste est exitus meus quem comminatis mihi, gratias ago Deo meo quia per modicum dolorem participem me fecistis gloriae martyrum eius." Et ita cum magno gaudio atque alacritate defunctus est simili morte. Postquam autem suffucaverunt eum,

395 absciderunt preciosum caput eius, et detulerunt illud imperatori.

39-40. Igitur sellarius qui erat super carcerem existens ut dictum est Christianus voluit corpus martyris seorsum poni et non sinebant eum quaestionarii cum essent Hebraei. Cognoscentes vero fideles Gesdim finem sancti martyris et pueri eorum dederunt clam quaes-

400 tionariis argenteos multos, et permiserunt eos separatim poni corpus eius. Sequenti vero nocte accipiens frater de mansione martyris secum pueros de Gesdim et quosdam monachos qui ibidem erant venit auferre corpus sancti martyris, et invenit canes corpora edentes interfectorum, corpus vero martyris de parte proxime iactatum

405 integrum atque intactum, quoniam Dominus custodit omnia ossa sanctorum suorum et unum ex his non contereretur,[16] quoniam preciosa est in conspectu Domini mors sanctorum eius.[17] Accipiens

---

385 Vis] Si non vis α Quare vis t   horum unus] unus eorum HE   387 eius *om*. SLZ   ne] nec WI   390 ait] dixit SL   391 vero WI   comminatis] comminastis G comminamini (*ex*. comminavi *corr*. M) α   392 quia ... fecistis] qui ... fecit α HEWI   393 eius] suorum α   magno] multo α   395 illud *om*. H   397 ponere α   398-401 Cognoscentes–eius *om*. E   399 Gesdim] gesdin V digesdim G gestum N αβ   et *om*. H   400 ponere αβ   402-403 secum–auferre *om*. E   402 de Gesdim] degesdin V digesdim G   403 sancti martyris corpus *transpos*. EWI   403-404 edentes] comedentes α   404 proxima α proximae HWI   406 sanctorum *om*. α sanctorum eorum WI   ex his *om*. W   quoniam] quia N   407 est *om*. β   et *om*. E

16. Cf. Ps 34.20.
17. Ps 116.15.

igitur corpus sancti martyris, et involvens illud linteis preciosis reposuit in monasterio Christi martyris Sergi a miliario ferme uno
410 praedicti castelli, vigesima et secunda die mensis ianuarii prima indictione, anno septimo decimo imperii Heraclii et quinto decimo anno Constantini imperatoris.

41. Accidit autem post mortem sancti martyris ut duo quidam qui erant in custodia loquerentur inter se, et unus diceret ad alterum:
415 "Venerunt canes, et sederunt iuxta corpus monachi illius, et non tetigerunt eum, sed custodientes erant illud per horas fere duas, et neque recedebant neque contingebant corpus eius." At vero socius eius respondit ei: "Et ego vespere vadens in domum meam, vidi sicut stellam lucentem super pavimentum. Abiens vero ut viderem
420 quid hoc esset, mox ut propinquus factus sum stella nusquam comparuit, corpus vero monachi vidi iacere super pavimentum.

42. Quidam vero captivorum qui erant in carcere viri Christiani scientes persicam linguam auscultabant eos. Ex quibus duo dimissi cum aliis multis venerunt in sanctam civitatem post interfectionem
425 Chosroe regis, quibus praedixerat sanctus martyr Anastasius dum esset cum eis in custodia, dicens eis: "Scitote fratres quia Dei gratia die crastina finior. Post paucos autem dies vos relaxabimini, iniquus vero atque malignissimus rex interficietur. Sed Domino prosperante advenientes in sanctam civitatem ite ad mansionem quae
430 dicitur abbatis Anastasii, et dicite abbati meo simul et fratribus

---

408-409 involvens–reposuit] involvens in linteaminibus preciosis quae dederunt filii Deiesdim deducens sepelivit N *cf.* involvens linteaminibus pretiosis quos dederant filii Deiesdim deducens sepelivit p   408 illud] eum HI in W   409 reposuit] -que *add.* E eum *add.* WI   Christi] sancti NWI a *om.* α   410 praedicti castelli] a praedicto castello SLDZ apud dicto castello M   vigesimo et secundo die SLDM XXII Z   413 mortem] obitum E sancti *om.* SL   416 eum] illud V illius G *cf.* eum t   illud] istud WI   417 neque ... neque] nec ... nec L   eius] illius E   418 vadens] adveniens EWI 419 stellam] caeli *add.* WI   419-421 Abiens–pavimentum *om.* D   vero] ergo E   420 stellae H   421 vero] autem α   422 captivi α   Christiani *om.* D   423 duo *om.* VG   425 Chosrue α (Chosdrue Z)   martyr *om.* WI   426 fratres] mei *add.* W   427 crastino α   428 interficietur] occideretur Z   429 advenientes *emendavi* adveniente VGN adveniente me α HE advenientibus vobis WI *cf.* advenientes t   429-430 quae dicitur *om.* Z   430 simul *om.* α

haec omnia quae vidistis." Illi autem viri audientes ista ab Anastasio et propris oculis exitum rerum cernentes, glorificaverunt Deum, et mandatum sancti martyris implentes, proprio ore haec omnia nobis narraverunt.

435 **43-44.** Et enim memoratus frater sepeliens corpus martyris, et reponens decenter in praefato monasterio sancti Sergi mansit ibidem, tractans qualiter absque periculo remearet ad transmissorem suum. Et post dies decem, prima die mensis februarii adproximavit piissimus atque Christo amabilis imperator Heraclius cum exercitu.
440 Quod cernens frater gavisus est gaudio magno, et locutus est latine. At illi interrogaverunt eum: "Quid facis hic?" Et insinuavit eis omnia per ordinem. Illi vero glorificantes Deum dixerunt ei: "Surge, veni nobiscum, et salva animam tuam." Et erat cum eis in magno honore, et cum eis exiens per Armeniorum regionem, (44) adpro-
445 pinquans ad monasterium per annum unum. Intimavit vero praeposito universa quae acta sunt erga sanctum Anastasium cum omni diligentia, ostendens ei etiam colobium martyris in quo finivit martyrium suum, enarrans ei et hoc: "Erat quidam frater iuvenis in monasterio, in quo depositum est corpus sancti martyris, qui vexa-
450 batur atrociter a spiritu immundo. Rogavit vero me praepositus monasterii illius, et accipiens colobium martyris, induit eum qui paciebatur, et confestim sanus factus est gratia Dei in gloria eius, qui glorificatur in sanctis suis." Finivit vero certamen in Christi confessione sanctus martyr Anastasius sicut iam supra praemisimus
455 vigesima et secunda die mensis Januarii, indictione prima, anno septimo decimo imperii Heraclii, et quinto decimo Constantini. Regnante domino nostro Ihesu Christo cui est honor et gloria in saecula saeculorum. Amen.

431 haec *om.* E   431-432 ab Anastasio] a sancto viro α   432 rei α   435 corpus] sancti *add.* EWI   436 decenter] eum cum omni diligentia N mansit] -que *add.* EW   439 Christo *om.* SL   440 Quod] Quem E   est[1] *om.* W   et *om.* W   est[2]] eis *add.* E   441 eis] illis E   442 vero] ergo E   glorificaverunt H   dixerunt ei] dicentes Z dixeruntque ei H   443 salvamus HEWI   444-445 adpropinquans] pervenit α   445 monasterium] suum *add.* E   per annum unum] post annum α   448 iuvenis] vivens α HEI   449 est *om.* W   450 atrociter] acriter WI   vero] ergo E   me *om.* Z   451 colobium] sancti *add.* W   452 sanus factus] sanatus E   Dei] Domini HW   453 certamen] vitam G   454 praemisimus] memoravimus G   456 decimo] anno *add.* E

6

THE REVISION p₁

About This Edition

This edition is in essence a transcription of the exclusive witness that preserves this version of the *Passio S. Anastasii*, Bibiothèque nationale de France, lat. 9741 (fully described below in the "Descriptive List"). I have kept the spelling of the manuscript, with the exception of diphthongs, and emended the text in only a few cases, noting it always in the *apparatus criticus*. The chapter divisions follow those in Flusin's edition of the Greek text.

CONSPECTUS SIGLORUM

cod.	Paris, Bibliothèque nationale de France, lat. 9741
p	*BHL* 408(p), *supra editum*
π B3 B6	*vide p. 386 supra*

PASSIO SANCTI ANASTASII MARTYRIS

ex codice manuscripto 9741 Bibliothecae Nationalis Parisiensis

1. Unigenitus Filius et Verbum Dei per quem facta sunt omnia, qui coaequalis et consubstantialis Patri et sancto Spiritui paraclito, misertus est generi humano quod sub mortis atque corruptionis diaboli tyrannica potestate erat subiectum. De virgine autem carnem humanam et servi formam suscipiens[1] inter homines conversatus,[2] omnia quae sunt hominis absque peccato sustinuit, videlicet famem, sitim, sompnium, et omnia ad salutem humani generis quaeque fecit miracula pia dispensatione operatus est. Equidem propria morte destruens eum qui habebat mortis imperium,[3] triduoque eius corpus in sepulchro iacens, resurgens tertia die iam ultra non moriturus, inferni autem claustra sua descensione subvertens, animas quae multo tempore ob delictum primae praevaricationis ibi detinebantur liberans secum ad caelos evexit. Ita ergo sicut apostolus ait gloriosa eius resurrectio nos consurgere et consedere in caelestibus fecit.[4]

2. Ex hoc quippe de sublimibus Spiritu sancto inflammati, hi qui per seipsos non valuerunt et ministri verbi facti sunt[5] atque eius passionis testes,[6] videlicet sancti apostoli totum mundum peragraverunt, divina mandata praedicantes, et illa quidem quae paternae traditionis ex multis temporibus impietatis errore tenebantur radicitus evellentes, et angelicam conversationem homines habere docentes. Ex hoc est repletus iam bonis omnibus mundus ut cognoscerent cuncti creatorem suum Dominum, secundum quod scriptum est, In novissimis diebus erit preparatus mons domus domini in vertice montium, et elevabitur super colles et fluent ad eum omnes gentes[7] et cetera. Ex hoc igitur terrestria caelestibus coniuncta sunt et vita aeterna hominibus concessa est. Ex hoc universa quaeque natura hominum magnis et ineffabilibus Dei donis laetatur.

---

1. Cf. Phil 2.7.
2. Cf. Bar 3.38.
3. Cf. Heb 2.14.
4. Cf. Eph 2.6.
5. Cf. Lc 1.2.
6. Cf. 1 Pt 5.1.
7. Is 2.2. This text is not cited in other versions.

3. Sed quia humanae vitae a principio insidiator et fraudator atque dolosus et omnium inimicus iustorum diabolus nesciens qualiter se induceret in tam amplam bonitatem, quae per Christi gratiam in hominibus fiebat, et cum invideret tam magno dono huic mundo dato, cernens etiam se alienatum ab aethereo honore quem de terra homines adquirebant, invenit concinnationem eius malignitas. Nihil enim magnum egit contra eos qui Dei pietate sunt defensi nec eos potuit laedere sed quod maximum est magis prodesse. In eos qui tunc tenebant sceptra regalia varie et multimodis se disseminans, et maliciam suam artibus malignis aperiens, insurgere quidem fecit cunctam persecutionem contra Dei ecclesiam, et omnem christianam fidem quam extinguere et confundere volens. Ad hanc autem inmissionem eius persequutionis melior pars ei restitit quamvis parva. Tamen nil Dei cultoribus nocuit sed tamen usque hactenus maxime ipse confunditur. Nihil enim deterius eorum qui ipsum olim diabolum propter persequutionem comminantium in se receperunt. Tamen per sanctorum apostolorum et per victoriosorum martyrum tolerantiam ipse serpens antiquus devincitur et rursum proprium pietatis et fidei ornatum recepit Christi ecclesia. Quod vero gratia Dei cotidie floret atque additur diebus singulis numerus copiosior christianorum divina misericordia est.

4. Salus enim quae in nobis est facta non ex nostris meritis sed ex Dei bonitate venit. Acceperunt etenim homines magna satis et ineffabilia Christi dona, scilicet omnium aegrotantium languores sanare ac multimodis delictorum catheniis astrictos resolvere. Nos vero qui istis temporibus videmus de sanguinum effusione terram satiatam, hoc ob fornicationibus et adulteriis seu innumeris criminibus et immundiciis quae homines perpetrare non timuerunt, iram Dei adversum se exardescentes persenserunt, et ut vere dicam totam super nos Dei manum disciplinae traximus. Unde tradidit nos in manus iniquissimorum inimicorum et super cunctos reges regi iniusto et iniquo et maligno[8] qui civitates et regiones omnes dissipavit, quasdam quidem igne exussit, quasdam autem radicitus evulsit, et captivavit omne quod dilectum et desiderabile erat in omni

---

47 Tamen] Qui tamen *cod.*   63 quasdam] quas dein *cod.*

8. *Unde–maligno*: cf. Dn 3.32.

65   suppellectili. In pernitiem autem tradidit omne quod derelictum est, et insanabili paene plaga percussi sumus. Nec tamen usque in finem benignus et humani generis amator Deus nos despexit sicut res ipsae manifestant sed suaves hostes[9] ipsos nobis fecit, et usque nunc glorificari inter praecipuos et fideles suos servos plurimos et
70   martyres ex nostris concessit.

5. Et quia secundum apostoli vocem dicentis, inscrutabilia sunt iudicia Dei et investigabiles viae eius,[10] oportunum sermonem ut nobis visum est perfecimus. Eos etenim Persis tradidit ad correptionem qui secundum gratiam filii sunt eius atque heredes regni
75   ipsius. Ex Persida autem martyrem sibi elegit qui quantum in eo fuit per caritatem et fidem et confessionem ostendit se fidelem usque ad sanguinis effusionem et mortem. Et quod melius est non solum viros sed et mulieres Christus elegit, omnes ostensuras agonem et certamen, et pro ipsius domini fide usque in finem decer-
80   tantes coronas promeruerunt aeternas. Horum unus exstitit et noster martyr Anastasius. Huius vitam quam ab initio usque in finem scribere iussus sum ipsum praeponens testem quem ipse confessus est, Deum et Dominum Ihesum Christum, et sic enarrationis incipiam, sermonem Domino protegente.

85   **6.** Hic quidem fuit de Perside regione Razech vocabulo, de fundo Rasnuni, nomen autem ei Magundat. Filius vero erat magi cuiusdam Bau nomine, qui etiam doctor extiterat magicae artis. Erudivitque eum pater suus a pueritia arte magica. Factus autem iuvenis, contigit militare eum in tyrocinio cum multis aliis, et esse in regia
90   civitate Persarum sub Chosroe Imperatore. Sanctae autem civitatis desolatione facta, et venerabilia atque adoranda loca igne sunt concremata in praedicta ira, et una cum praeciosa cruce domini nostri Ihesu Christi captiva asportata sunt cetera sancta[11] in Persida. O

---

73 etenim] *ex* enim *corr. cod.*

9. This reworking of p's phrase (*suaves habere nos spes dedit*) suggests that the text available to the revisor was defective.
10. Cf. Rom 11.33.
11. The additional information that other things besides the Holy Cross were brought to Persia is not in *BHL* 408. This phrase recalls information contained also in Bede's *Chronica* ("inter ornamenta locorum vel sanctorum

admiranda res! Captiva quidem crux Domini ducebatur ad illorum
95   insipientiam; infidelium autem magis corda captivabat.

7. Maeror[12] autem et stupor invadebat corda infidelium, gaudio
vero et laetitia corda fidelium coruscabant. Fama autem ubique de
ea in tota coruscabat Persida. Interea audiens praefatus tyro Magundat, qui et Anastasius, famam et virtutem sanctae crucis Christi
100   domini, interrogavit de ea, quomodo aut qualiter esset mysterium
venerandae crucis. Et discens a fidelibus eius virtutem, atque ab
aliis dicentibus quomodo Deus Christianorum in hac cruce pependit pro salute generis humani, statim sicut terra bona, suscepta
pluvia ad producendum fructum praeparata, ita et ille tunc susci-
105   piens per auditum ineffabilem virtutem Christi Domini mirabiliter
in intimo corde suscipiebat monita vitae, cogitans qualiter ad culturam christianam et fidem Christi pertingere possit. Diligenter
autem addiscens si ipsa vere esset crux in qua filius Dei pependit
vehementer decrevit ad religionem christianam accedere. Et quanto
110   plus quae veritatis sunt audiebat, tanto magis ab eius corde magicae
artis seductio abscedebat. Sicut enim effugiunt tenebrae a luce, a
sole autem umbrae, et ab igne fumus, ita et fallacia exterminatur
a veritatis doctrina.

8. Habebat autem fratrem carnalem beatus Anastasius militantem,
115   et pergens in exercitum cum eo, cognomento Sain, princeps exercitus Persarum, et venit usque Carchedona. At vero sanctae recordationis divinaeque memoriae Philippico circumvallenti eum, ingressus est Persidam. Audiens vero Sain reversus est post tergum
suum. Et sic contigit famulus Dei Anastasius cum Persarum exerci-
120   tu deveniret in partibus Orientis. Et exinde recessit ab exercitu, et
derelinquens proprium fratrem venit ad Hieropolim, et divertit ad
quendam Christianum Persum malleatorem, et mansit apud eum.
Didicit autem apud eum et ipse artem, et operabatur cum eo.

98 choruscabat *cod.*

---

vel communium, quae abstulere, etiam vexillum dominicae crucis abducunt.").
It is highly possible that the revisor knew the Chronicle, or that this would
be a natural inference from the story.
    12. Cf. moechatur π in the *BHL* 408 tradition.

9. Cum ergo habundaret in eo amor et gratia, atque desiderium ut
125 inluminaretur, multum rogabat praefatum malleatorem, ut eum
instrueret qualiter ad gratiam sancti baptismatis perveniret. At ille
dum intra se cogitaret propter metum Persarum ne periclitaretur,
tamen cum illo ibat ad ecclesiam sanctorum martyrum, et orabat.
Et picturas sanctorum et historias conspiciebat, et requirebat ab eo
130 quidnam hoc esset. Et audiebat sanctorum certamina, sive mirabilia
quae fecerunt, sive tormenta crudelia quae a tyrannis perpessi sunt
et eorum tolerantiam, et mirabatur pavens. Manens igitur parvo
tempore apud praedictum christianissimum virum, optimum
desiderium percepit in animo ut Hierosolym adiret, et illic
135 mereretur baptismatis sancti consecrationem adipisci.

10. Et habens propositum in Dei amore, devenit ad sanctam civitatem, et mansit apud quemdam Christo amabilem item malleatorem, et aperiens omne suum desiderium petebat ut ei daret gratiam
sancti baptismatis quatinus christianis posset associari. Perductus
140 autem est ab eo Heliae sanctissimo presbytero Sanctae Resurectionis, qui eum tamquam a Deo praedestinatum suscepit filium. Et
postea indicavit de eo Modesto sanctissimo presbytero et vicario
apostolicae sedis, et fecit eum baptizari simul cum aliis, qui et ipsi
de eadem regione erant. Sed et ipsi etiam beatum finem pro Chris-
145 to suscipientes in Edissa civitate martyrio coronati sunt.

11. Detentus vero beatus Anastasius a sanctissimo presbytero Helia
in domo sua octo diebus, exhortabatur eum in bono proposito persistere. Interrogabat autem eum sanctissimus presbyter Helias dicens quid cogitasset erga se de reliquo. Ipse vero rogavit eum,
150 dicens ut monachum eum ordinaret. Post depositas autem albas,
continuo perduxit eum ad sanctae recordationis Anastasium abbatem qui quarto miliario distat a sancta civitate, et multum rogans
venerabilibus fratribus monasterii et Iustinum praepositum, virum
valde mirabilem per omnia atque prudentem et plenum quae Dei
155 sunt praeceptis, tradidit ei Dei famulum Anastasium. Qui etiam
eum suscipiens suae congregationi sociavit. Hoc autem factum est
per indictionem octavam imperatoris piissimi Eraclii atque christia-

---

125 praefatum] perfectum *cod.*, cf. *BHL*408(π)   155 praeceptos *cod.*

nissimi anno decimo. Dedit autem ei et magistrum unum de eadem congregatione fratrem, virum prudentem, qui etiam docuit eum
160 litteras simul et doctrinam Deo placitam cum psalterio, et tondens eum tradidit ei sanctum habitum atque in filium adoptavit.

12. Fecit autem eum adimplere omne ministerium, et per omnia officia pertransivit monasterii sanctus Anastasius, placens Deo et omnibus fratribus. Erat autem sedulus valde in servitio fratrum et
165 in opere manuum, et prae omnibus in regulam monachicam intentus et in Missarum solemniis frequentissimus. Et auditor indefessus sanctarum scripturarum, ac vitas sanctorum Patrum diligentius auscultabat et legebat. Et si quid non intellegebat a magistro suo prudentissimo viro in omnibus addiscebat, et admirans glorificabat
170 Deum. Secretius autem in cella legebat assidue certamina vel agones martyrum sanctorum et lacrimas effundens cogitans aestuabat in corde suo et deprecabatur desiderio accensus, ut eum Dominus ad palmam martyrii vocare dignaretur; quatenus existeret socius servorum suorum qui pro eius nomine passi sunt, ad laudem et gloriam
175 Domini nostri Ihesu Christi. Perseveravit autem in eadem mansione annos septem.

13. Videns autem antiquus hostis et inimicus humani generis tantam eius perseverantiam in Dei servitio, volens eum a bono proposito revocare, et a praedicto monasterio expellere, immisit ei cogita-
180 tiones iniquas, ut etiam ei ad memoriam revocaret magicam artem, quam a suo patre didicerat. Ipse vero perspitiens iniquissimi diabuli astutiam erga se moveri, sese in orationem dedit, et obnixius Dominum deprecabatur, ut eum eriperet ab insidiis adversarii. Abbati vero monasterii indicavit cordis sui secreta, et lacrimabiliter eum
185 deprecabatur, ut pro eo effunderet preces Domino, quatinus a diabolicis ipsis eriperetur temptationibus. Quod etiam praefatus abbas fecit devote. Atque confortabat et monebat dominum secundum datam sibi a Christo sapientiam. Fratres autem unanimiter pro eo facientes orationem effugata est ab eo pugna diabolica.

187 dominum] in Domino p

190 **14.** Post paucos vero dies sompnium vidit per noctem idem Dei famulus Anastasius. Videbat enim se in montem excelsum stare, et quendam ad se venientem et aureum sibi poculum porrigentem vino plenum, et dicentem: "Accipe, et bibe." Quem suscipiens, bibit. Statim autem evigilans intellexit poculum quod viderat, hoc 195 esse quod cupiebat. Qui statim surgens ad matutinales ymnos explendos adlucescente sancto die Dominico ad ecclesiam perrexit et ipsis ymnis matutinalibus expletis, rogavit abbatem monasterii ut ei secretius loqueretur. Et ingressi in sacrario cecidit ad pedes eius, rogans cum lacrimis ut Domino pro eo orationes funderet sperans 200 quod in ipsis diebus moriturus esset. Dicebat autem abbati: "Pater, scio quantos labores suscipisti pro me miserum, et quia multum te tribulavi, et quia per te adduxit me Deus de tenebris ad veram lucem. Ne cesses ergo orare pro me." Dicit ei abbas: "Quomodo nosti, quod in proximis diebus debeas migrari?" Enarravit ergo ei 205 sompnium, et asserebat confirmans quod sine dubio moriturus esset in ipsis diebus, sive per propriam mortem, sive per martyrium, quomodo cupiebat. Timebat tamen palam dicere de martyrio ut non increparent eum fratres.

15. Abbas vero multis admonitionibus blande eum consolabatur. 210 Missarum igitur sollemnia celebrans cum fratribus, et percipiens divina mysteria, sumpsit cibum cum eis. Soporatusque est modicum, post evigilans, et cordis sui incendium non ferens, volens quod erat Domino placitum desiderium adimplere, clam de monasterio egressus nihil secum tollens nisi quibus indutus erat vestibus, 215 abiit Diospolim. Et exinde profectus est causa orationis in montem Garizin, atque exinde perrexit ad alia loca venerabilia. Deductus est autem per Domini gratiam et devenit usque ad Caesaream Palestinam, et mansit in domo beatae et intemeratae Dei genetricis virginis Mariae duobus diebus.

220 **16.** Secundum vero praedestinationem Dei quae ab eo illi fuerat data, perrexit ad sanctam Euphemiam ob orationis gratiam. Cumque pergeret, transivit per quendam locum, et vidit in domum Persi cuiusdam magicam artem operari. Et ingressus zelo Dei ductus dixit: "O homines, quid erratis, et errare facitis alios in maleficiis 225 vestris?" Stupentes autem viri illi in sermonibus et in constantia ipsius, interrogaverunt eum dicentes: "Quisnam es tu qui hoc dicis?"

Ipse vero dixit eis: "Ego aliquando in hac arte mala erravi, et cognovi aliquando eam nefandam esse et sum de vestris incantationibus conscius." Arguente vero eo illos, obmutuerunt, et rogaverunt
230   eum, ne detraheret aut divulgaret eos alicui.

17. Dimissis vero illis et secedens modicum ab eis, videntes eum quidam ex officio qui erant ante ianuam praetorii sedentes. Et eo transeunte dixerunt propria lingua invicem: "Hic delator est." Audiens autem beatus Anastasius haec verba illos inter se dicentes
235   intuens eos, ait: "Quare haec verba asseritis? Ego namque impostor non sum sed servus Domini mei Ihesu Christi. Nam et melior vestri sum, quia illius merui esse servus, qui pro peccatoribus in terram de caelo descendere est dignatus. Et ego enim sicut et vos in hoc officio fui." At illi surgentes tenuerunt eum. Et exiens eorum
240   primarius, et inquirens unde esset et diligenter investigans, iussit eum custodiri tribus diebus, in quibus nullatenus usus est de eorum alimentis, memorans eorum dolositatem in maleficiis.

18. Veniens autem Barzabana in Caesarea (non enim ibidem erat quando sanctus Anastasius est tentus), et suggerens de eo primus
245   officii fecit eum in praetorium suum adduci. Occupato vero Barzabana circa alia offitia, inventus est ibi quidam Christianus, qui recognovit sanctum Anastasium, cum esset in monasterio sanctae Dei genetricis semperque virginis Mariae. Requirens autem ille ab eo causam detentionis et cognoscens rei causam, beatificavit eum de
250   bono proposito, et confortavit in Domino, sanctis exemplis eum monens ut non metueret tormenta et mortem sed pro nomine et fide Christi fiducialiter ageret contra Barzabanam, rememorans ei sermonem quem Dominus in sancto Evangelio dixit: "qui perseveraverit usque in finem hic salvus erit."[13]

255   **19.** Adductus autem sanctus Domini coram Barzabana non adoravit eum secundum ritum eorum. Barzabana autem intuens in eum ait: "Unde es? et quis vocaris?" Ipse vero dixit: "Ego Christianus sum. Quantum ad genus, Persus de regione Razech, de villa Rasnuni. Officialis autem eram et magus; reliqui tenebras, et veni ad ve-
260   ram lucem. Nomen autem meum primum Magundat, Christiani-

13. Mt 10.22.

tatis vero nomine nunc Anastasius vocor." Dixit ei Barzabanas: "Dimitte hunc errorem et converte ad primam tuam religionem, et dabimus possessiones tibi et pecunias multas." Ipse autem respondens ait ei: "Non mihi contingat relinquere et negare Ihesum

265 Christum Deum vivum et verum." Barzabanas dixit: "Ergo placent tibi talia vestimenta quibus indutus est?" Respondit sanctus Anastasius: "Hoc indumentum gloriosum et angelicum est." Dixit ei Barzabanas: "Daemonium habes." Sanctus Anastasius respondit: "Quando in errore eram, daemonium habebam. Nunc autem habeo

270 salvatorem Dominum Ihesum Christum, qui omnem potestatem destruit daemoniorum." Dixit ei Barzabanas: "Non metuis imperatorem? Nam si de te cognoverit et quae erga te sunt, iubebit te crucifigi." Beatus Anastasius ait: "Non eum timeo quia homo corruptibilis est ut et tu."

275 **20.** Tunc indignatus Barzabanas iussit eum in vinculis ferreis mitti et in castrum duci, et lapides sine cessatione eum deportari fecit. Et ipso tempore multas et innumeras tribulationes est perpessus sanctus Dei famulus. Quidam ergo de regione eius, videntes ea quae in eum fiebant, erubescebant et increpabant eum, dicentes:

280 "Quid hoc facere voluisti? Nemo aliquando de regione nostra factus est Christianus; et ecce de omnibus nobis ridiculum." Et his ac aliis verbis cupiebant eum seducere. Ipse vero repellebat eos a se. At illi in iram versi percutiebant eum pugno impie et trahebant ei barbam, et vestimenta eius scindebant. Non solum autem hoc Dei

285 famulo faciebant, sed et lapides magnos quos quatuor homines nequibant volvere in collo eius imponebant et faciebant ferre et unam ei catenam in collum, aliam vero in pedibus miserunt. Saeva quoque et atrociora mala ingesserunt. At vero sanctus Anastasius cuncta pro Christi nomine gaudens sustinebat.

290 **21.** Iterum Barzabanas iussit eum ante se adduci, et dixit ei: "Si vere ut dixisti magi filius fuisti, et ipsam artem si scis, vel a quo didiceris aliquam partem dic mihi ut cognoscam si verum asseris." Respondit ei sanctus Dei: "Non permittat Deus ut de tali re amplius os meum polluatur." Dicit ei Barzabanas: "Quid ergo, perma-

266 quibus] qualibus p, *sed cf.* quibus B3 B6.

295 nes in his insanis adhuc? Rogo convertere iam ad primam religionem, et pro te bona suggeram Chosdroe Imperatori." Respondit ei
sanctus Domini: "Iam scripsisti, et rescripta suscepisti. Fac quod
vis." Barzabanas ait: "Non scripsi, sed scribam, et quicquid mihi
praeciperit agam." Sanctus Anastasius respondit: "Quantacumque
300 volueris de me mala scribe. Christianus enim sum et Christum
confiteor." Barzabanas dixit suis: "Prosternatur in terram, et
tamdiu caedatur quousque perficiat quod ei iubetur." Anastasius ait
cum ligare eum vellent: "Sinite, non est opus me ligare." Sedens
autem in terra signum sibi sanctae crucis in fronte fecit. Illi vero
305 ligantes eum coeperunt caedere. Dei autem famulus dixit eis: "Habitum quo sum indutus me expoliate ne patiatur iniuriam, et sic
carnes meas caedite. Ista enim quae facitis michi nocere non poterunt. Ego enim si membratim abscidar, numquam negabo Dominum Ihesum Christum."

310 **22.** Dicit ei Barzabanas: "Adquiesce mihi, nam scribo de te imperatori." Anastasius respondit: "Quicquid volueris, scribe." Barzabanas
ait: "Ergo imperatorem non times?" Sanctus Dei respondit: "Imperator homo est sicut et tu et moriturus est ut et tu et corrumpetur
velut tu. Ideo eum non timeo. Timeo autem illum qui corruptio-
315 nem nullam passus est scilicet Deum Dei patris filium Ihesum
Christum qui fecit caelum et terram, mare et omnia quae in eis
sunt." Stupefactus autem superbus ille Barzabanas in constantissima
responsione martyris, iterum iussit eum duci in castellum.

23. Et post dies paucos fecit eum sibi praesentari, et dixit ei: "Re-
320 cordare magicae artis, et sacrifica, ut non male moriaris et frauderis
de hac luce." Respondens autem sanctus Dei dixit ei: "Quibus diis
iubes me sacrificare? Soli, et lunae, et mari, montibus et collibus,
ceterisque omnibus elementis, et metallis? Ne ergo concedat Deus
et Dominus omnium Christus ne talia umquam adorem quia ipsa
325 omnia Christus fecit ad servitium nostrum. Vos ergo erratis, serviendo daemonibus et quadrupedibus et sensati homines facti, ignoratis Deum qui vos fecit. Si enim cognosceretis eum statim de tenebris converteretis vos ad veram lucem, et festinaretis credere ipsi
qui illuminat omnem hominem venientem in hunc mundum qui-
330 que clamat hominibus dicens: 'Ambulate dum lucem habetis ne

tenebrae mortis vos comprehendant.'[14] Et iterum: 'Dum lucem habetis credite in lucem ut filii lucis sitis.'[15] Ista ergo lux me alienigenam sua misericordia illuminavit et dignata est servum sibi habere." Haec et his similia prosequente sancto Anastasio, stupebant omnes et mirabantur. Dei autem martyr Anastasius tribus iam vicibus auditus et cruciatus in confessione Christi perdurans iterum vinculis constrictus ad castellum reducitur.

24. Cognoscens autem sanctissimus abbas praefati monasterii in quo sanctissimus Anastasius habitaverat perseverantiam eius in fide et martyrio cum omni fratrum congregatione gaudio magno gavisus est, communiterque omnes benedicebant Dominum. Per diem quoque et noctem pro eo orabant ut eius cursum Dominus dignaretur ad laudem et gloriam sui nominis bene consummare. Direxit autem ei duos fratres de monasterio cum letteris consolatoriis, confortans animum eius in Domino et monens ut sine metu decertaret quoniam, ut ait apostolus, non sunt condignae passiones huius temporis ad superventuram gloriam quae revelabitur in nobis.[16]

25. In custodia ergo castri positus martyr Christi non cessabat in ymnis et psalmis laudare nomen Domini. Habens vero secum et alium iuvenem[17] in vinculis constitutum Barzabanae servum pro quadam causa tentum, cum surgeret Dei famulus ad horas et ad matutinales ymnos dicendos ipse iuvenis nolens eum contristari vel fatigari inclinabat collum suum ad collum eius, et pedem suum ad pedem eius ne gravaretur sanctus Dei propter extensionem catenarum quibus uterque erant vinculati. Una igitur nocte sancto Dei psallente, quidam hebraeus mitissimus et religiosus ac nobili genere quem tunc ibi vinxerant auscultabat eum. Videns autem beatum martyrem per diem quidem in lapidum deportatione, nocte autem in Dei perseverantem laudibus, stupens mirabatur valde.

---

14. Cf. Jn 12.35; p₁ differs from other traditions in its biblical citations here.
15. Jn 12.36.
16. Rom 8.18; a p₁ addition.
17. Some of the details in this story are different from the one transmitted in the p-tradition as it has come down to us. In the original version of the story, it is Anastasius who slackens the chain so as not to trouble his fellow prisoner, but correctly, and contrary to the p-tradition, it is the Jew who witnesses the apparition.

360   **26.** Hic ergo in noctis silentio super pavimentum cum iaceret et stantem sanctum Anastasium atque psallentem, ut diximus, auscultaret, vidit subito quosdam in albis vestibus ingredientes per ostium carceris, ad quorum ingressum lux copiosa in carcere refulsit ipsis qui etiam beatum martyrem circumdederunt. Super hanc ergo
365   visionem immo ille amens effectus aiebat intra se: "Isti sancti angeli sunt." Hoc autem aspiciens vidit hos ipsos palliis circumdatos, habentes cruces in manibus, in semetipso quoque dicebat: "Isti episcopi sunt." Ipsos ergo diu intuens et beatum Anastasium, cum illis candidis vestibus indutum et immensum lumen erga illos, ecce iu-
370   venis quidam in magna gloria venit et stetit ante eum, habens aureum thuribulum incenso vaporantem et sancto viro offerentem.[18] Vir ergo ille qui haec contemplabatur, pulsabat manu quemdam proximum sibi dormientem, ut et ipse videret quae videbat. Sed evigilare non poterat, quoniam graviter dormiebat. Quandoque
375   vero expergefactus quaerebat ab hebraeo quid hoc fuisset. Ille vero dixit ei: "Consideras aliquid?" Qui respicientes iam nihil viderunt. Dixit ergo ei omnia quae viderat, et glorificaverunt simul Dominum Ihesum Christum.

       27. Quia vero, sicut superius memoravimus, in prima et secunda
380   interrogatione Barzabanas videns constantiam famuli Dei, scripsit Imperatori Chosdroe quae de eo acta sunt. Et contigit intra dies paucos ut reciperet imperatoris iussionem. Transmisit autem ad famulum Dei domesticum suum in carcerem mandans et dicens: "Ecce iussit imperator ut verbo solummodo dicas, non sum Chris-
385   tianus, et dimitteris, et si volueris monachus permanere sive equestris, ut ante eras, aut nobiscum stare, conceditur tibi." Respondens vero Christi famulus dixit: "Absit ut negem Deum et Dominum meum Christum." Dum ergo neque promissionibus neque suasionibus ullis Barzabanae adquiesceret, **(28)** adhuc iterum per domesticum
390   suum mandavit ei dicens: "Scio quia erubescis propter concives tuos, et ideo non vis negare coram eis. Sed quia iussio imperatoris urget, si vis, coram me et aliis duobus dic negationem, et dimitte-

---

360 Hic] his *cod.*   364 ipsis] ipso *(?) cod.*

18. *et sancto viro offerentem*: a detail added in this version.

ris." Sanctus autem martyr per missum ipsum remandavit ei, dicens: "Neque coram te, neque coram aliquo, nec secrete nec aperte
395 aliquando negabo Deum meum Ihesum Christum." Tunc Barzabanas per seipsum dixit ei: "Ecce iussit imperator, ut ferro vinctus
vadas in Persidam." Respondit sanctus Anastasius: "Si dimittas per
me solum pergam ad imperatorem. Neque enim timeo eum." Ut
ergo vidit sanctum Anastasium viriliter persistentem, neque
400 minas pavere neque blandimenta accipere, bullatum eum iterum
iussit duci in carcerem. Post quinque autem dies cum aliis
Christianis duobus similiter bullatis eum direxit.

29. Interea vero approximante festo exaltationis dominicae crucis
ita sanctus martyr et duo fratres monasterii eius, et alii duo chris-
405 tianissimi viri, et quidam de civitate qui fideles erant pernoctantes
in psalmis et ymnis et canticis spiritalibus ut obliviscerentur sibi
habere vincula, glorificantes Christum Dominum, qui tantam longanimitatem dat sperantibus in se. Diluculo autem ingressus dispositor quidam in rebus publicis, et ipse vir christianissimus, ad Bar-
410 zabanam, rogavit eum, ut vincula ei permitteret tolli pro die festo,
tantummodo permittens quod ipse eum iterum reduceret in custodiam. Quod et permisit. Deductus est ergo in ecclesia sanctus
Anastasius et gaudium et consolatio magna facta est fidelibus agentium Deo gratias qui semper adiuvat se invocantes et in sua miseri-
415 cordia sperantes. In civitate autem eadem extitit contentio inter
populum fidelem et infidelem de eo quia stupebant omnes de tanto
eius certamine et passionum irrogatione.

30. Fideles vero confortabantur multum videntes eius longanimitatem et perseverantiam. Martyr vero Domini Anastasius plurimis
420 et dulcissimis sermonibus consolabatur fideles qui autem de fide
christiana desperabant, de eius alacritate convaluerunt, osculantes
eius vincula, et quasi victores facti dicebant sancto Anastasio: "Si
tu propter Dominum Ihesum Christum mori disposuisti, quanto
magis nos tecum mori debemus?" Et consolabantur eum atque ma-
425 ximum honorem praebebant ei, tam viri quam mulieres. Expletis
Missarum sollemniis, multum eum obsecrans dispositor perduxit
in propriam domum ut cibum ipse et fratres duo de eius monaste-

---

399 viriliter] fortiter p   403 adproximante St   413-414 agentium *sic cod.*

rio secum caperent. Cum ergo pariter sumpsissent cibum confortati
sunt, et conloquentes de divinis sermonibus aedificati sunt simul
430   in Domino. Post modicum dum vero gaudentes et exultantes et
quasi ad epulas redierunt ad vincula et ad carcerem.

31. Expletis igitur quinque diebus egressus est de Caesarea civitate
cum praefatis duobus viris Christianissimis et cum uno fratre de
monasterio suo. Viri autem et mulieres qui eum noverant cum
435   multarum lacrimarum perfusione longuscule persecuti sunt eum et
glorificabant Deum pro passione quam sustinebat. Ad solatium vero missus erat ille praefatus monachus ab abbate suo ut ei serviret
et ea quae de eo videret postmodum sibi et fratrum congregationi
referret. Laetitia ergo et gaudium multum erat eis qui eum per ci-
440   vitates[19] excipiebant et oppida et creatorem omnium collaudabant, suscipientes eum cum honore, et osculantes vincula eius.
Postque tribuebant ei quaeque erant necessaria. Sanctus vero Anastasius direxit suo abbati ab Hieropoli litteras deprecatorias, ut pro
eo preces effunderet Domino quatinus cursum dignum et benepla-
445   citum Christo mereretur consummare. Similiter et a fluvio Tigri
alias litteras pro hac ipsa re direxit.

32. Igitur beatus Anastasius ingressus Persidam civitatem, in loco
qui vocatur Bethsaloc, quod est a miliario sexto de Discarthas in
quo erat imperator, missus est in carcerem. At vero frater qui cum
450   eo aderat mansit in eodem praedio, in domo filii Cortacii Dejesdim
dispositoris primi in publicis rebus Persarum, qui erat christianus.
Et morante beato martyre per dies aliquot cum eis qui ibidem ad-
ducti fuerant captivis, suggestum est Chosdroe Imperatori de eo.
Et mittens unum ex iudicibus suis, praecepit examinari eum.

455   **33.** Qui iudex veniens cum tribuno qui erat super carcerem, interrogavit eum, quis esset et unde advenisset et ob quam rem suam
religionem reliquisset, et quare Christianus factus esset. Martyr autem Christi Anastasius nolens ei loqui persica lingua per interpretem respondit ei dicens: "Vos multum erratis daemonia pro Deo
460   colentes. Et ego aliquando, cum essem in errore, hos colebam.

---

19. BN 9741 here reads *percunctantes*, which has no equivalent in p. I
would suggest that *percunctantes* is actually a corruption of *per civitates*, thus
duplicating p's text if not its word order.

Nunc adoro Deum omnipotentem, qui fecit caelum et terram, mare et omnia quae in eis sunt, et vere scio quia cultura vestra perditio est et seductio daemonum." Dicit ei iudex: "Miser, Deum quem
vos colitis Christiani, Iudaei crucifixerunt. Quoniam ergo errasti
465   relinquens religionem tuam, et factus es Christianus?" Sanctus vero
Anastasius ait: "Quod cruciatus vero est a Iudaeis, verum dicis;
quia vero sponte, quare non dicis? Ipse est enim qui fecit caelum
et terram, mare et omnia quae in eis sunt, et voluit descendere ad
terras et incarnari ex Spiritu sancto et Maria virgine, et inter homi-
470   nes conversari et pro eorum salute crucifigi ut liberaret genus hominum de errore Satanae, cuius adhuc cultores vos estis, qui etiam
colitis ignem et cetera elementa, et quod dici nefas est, servitis potius creaturae, quam creatori." Dicit ei iudex: "Quid tibi et sermonibus istis? Ecce pietas imperatoris paravit tibi dignitates et zonas
475   aureas, et equos et vult ut sis inter primates eius tantum ut conver-
taris in primam tuam religionem." Respondit sanctus Anastasius:
"Ego numquam negabo Dominum meum Ihesum Christum, sed
totis viribus ipsum colere et servire non omittam. Dona vero imperatoris tui ut stercora computo."

480   34. Iudex ergo omnia ista imperatori renuntiavit. Furore vero repletus imperator iussit eum in carcerem mitti, volens in crastinum
poenis eum affici. Veniens autem ex iussu imperatoris praefatus
iudex cum furore magno coepit sancto Dei minas et poenas promittere, ut eum terreret, putans eum taliter a sancto proposito re-
485   vocare. Martyr vero Christi ait ei: "Ne labores, bone iudex, neque
fatigeris. Christo enim me adiuvante, non recedam a fide quam ei
promisi in baptismate. Sed quicquid volueris age de meo corpore;
nam animae meae nil vales facere." Tunc absque misericordia caedi
iussit vinctum secundum morem Persarum, dicens: "Quare dona
490   et honores ab imperatore tibi promissos respicis, quare iterum iussa
eius contempnis, modo cognoscere habes insipientiam tuam et sen-
tire iram eius. Sic enim tibi cotidie fiet, donec male consummeris."
Sanctus Anastasius ait ei: "Nec dona nec iussa imperatoris volo,
neque minas eius timeo. Quicquid autem vis, fac de me."

463 iudex] dux *cod.*

35. Tunc iussit eum solvi et extendi supinum, et lignum super tibias eius imponi, et duos fortissimos viros stare hinc et inde super capita ligni. Omnes vero novimus quod importabilis est huius tormenti species. Martyr vero Christi Anastasius Deo omnipotenti gratias agens, sustinebat dolorem illum fortiter ita ut omnes mirarentur valde. Videns vero iudex quia nihil proficeret, sed magis Anastasius confortaretur et Deum laudaret, fecit eum iterum retrudi in carcerem et sic abiens renuntiavit cuncta imperatori.

36. Sellarius vero qui erat super carcerem, cum esset Christianus, et frater monasterii qui comitabatur cum martyre Christi, consolabantur eum in carcere ipso, et multi Christiani qui ibi erant, in quibus et filii Deiesdim, veniebant et procidentes ad pedes eius, osculabantur vincula eius, et petebant ut pro eis dignaretur orare et benedictionem aliquam impartire ut esset eis ad salutem contra insidias inimici. At vero sanctus Dei ne talia sibi dicerent rogabat. Illi vero ceram superponebant vinculis eius et expressam in benedictionem eam percipiebant.

37. Iterum post paucos dies ingressus iudex ad sanctum Anastasium in carcerem, dixit ei: "Quid dicis? Num iussionem imperatoris non facies aut in tua duritia persistis?" Sanctus autem Anastasius movens caput respondit ei dicens: "Saepius dixi tibi, quoniam impossibile est michi negare Deum meum filium Dei vivi. De me vero quicquid volueris, age." Tunc iudex ille iniquissimus fecit eum ligari sicut prius, et diutius caedi fustibus, postque minas ei inferens multas reliquit eum in carcere et abiit. Diebus autem paucis exactis, regressus cepit suadere eum iterum ut negaret Deum multimodis blandimentis et suasionibus et promissionum dignitatibus. Cum vero videret quod Christi famulus nec terrore concuteretur, nec blandimento seduceretur, nec curaret de suis monitis sed semper maneret firmus et immobilis, iterum ut prius iussit eum ligari et diutissime asperius caedi. Post flagellationem autem fecit eum per unam manum suspendi et ad pedem eius saxum magnum ligari, sicque relinquens eum, abiit. Sustinente autem beato martyre huiusmodi supplicium quasi duarum horarum, postmodum iussit et fecit eum deponi. Et de perseverantia eius suggestum est imperatori.

510 expressa *cod.*

530 **38.** Qui imperator post dies quindecim misit iudicem et cum eo alios ad interficiendum sanctum Anastasium et alios Christianos plurimos nec non et captivos. Qui venientes fecerunt eos foras eduici in praedio Bethsaloc, et beatum Anastasium cum aliis circiter septuaginta viris iuxta ripam fluminis eduxerunt. Et omnes illos 535 sanctissimos viros coram sancto viro funes per guttur fecerunt traicere, et sic suffocari universos et occidere iusserunt, inter quos erant praedicti duo viri christianissimi qui a Syria eum fuerant comitati. Cum autem interficerentur, iudex dicebat sancto martyri: "Recogita de tua salute et noli tam pessimam mortem ut isti susti- 540 nere. Sed magis iussis imperatoris adquiesce et vives semper cum magno honore, et eris in palatio eius nobiscum." At vero victoriosissimus Christi martyr Anastasius, respiciens in caelum gratias agebat Deo, qui adimplere dignatus est eius semper desideratum desiderium et quod iam appropinquasset certaminis eius cursus et 545 aiebat iudici: "Ego a vobis membratim cupiebam discerpi pro nomine Domini mei Ihesu Christi. Quia vero minima est mihi haec mors quam minatis, gratias ago Deo meo, quia per modicum dolorem participem me fecistis gloriae sanctorum eius." Ita ergo cum multo gaudio et alacritate animi suscepit similem mortem et per 550 gloriosam confessionem et passionem pervenit ad beatorum martyrum adiuvante Christo societatem. Suffocato vero eo, praeciderunt a corpore caput preciosum, et tollentes atque bullantes pertulerunt imperatori.

39. Christianus vero cum esset tribunus qui super carceres praeerat, 555 ut iam praefati sumus, seorsum ponere voluit sancti martyris corpus. Et cognitum est a quaestionariis. Cognoscentes autem filii Ciesdim finem sancti martyris, quia et eorum filii secuti fuerant sanctum martyrem quando ducebatur ad mortem ut exitum rei viderent, et dederunt clam quaestionariis pecuniam infinitam, et 560 permiserunt corpus sancti martyris et recipere et separatim reponere. Tribunus ergo ille sequenti nocte accipiens secum fratrem qui martyrem Christi secutus fuerat puerosque de filiis Ciesdim, et quosdam monachos qui ibidem erant, perrexit ad corpus sancti martyris tollendum. Invenerunt autem canes edentes corpora inter-

535-536 traicere *sic cod.*

565 fectorum, beati vero Anastasii corpus separatim iacentem intactum.
Benedicentes vero omnes Dominum et cantantes versum hunc:
"Pretiosa in conspectu Domini mors sanctorum eius, quia verum
custodit Dominus omnia ossa eorum, unum ex eis non conteretur."[20] Levantes involuerunt eum linteaminibus pretiosis, et sepe-
570 lierunt in monasterio sancti Sergii martyris, miliario uno distante
a castro praefato.

40. Finivit autem certamen gloriosum et cursum beatus martyr
invictus Anastasius vicesima et secunda die mensis Ianuarii,
indictione prima, anno vicesimo septimo imperii Eraclii piissimi,
575 et quinto decimo anno Constantini eius filii.

41. Alia igitur die post interfectionem martyris, duo custodes cor-
porum interfectorum coeperunt invicem confabulari et dicere unus
alteri: "Vidi canes venire et sedere iuxta corpus illius monachi in-
terfecti sed non tetigerunt sed magis illud custodierunt." Alter res-
580 pondit: "Ego quando vigiliam meam complevi et vellem redire in
domum meam, vidi stellam lucidam illuc ubi corpus iacebat et pergens ut viderem quid hoc esset, iam stella ab oculis meis evanuit,
sed et corpus illius monachi intactum ut dicis reperi."

42. Haec audientes captivi quidam qui ab ipsis custodibus custodie-
585 bantur retulerunt nobis ista. Et postea absoluti a vinculis venientes-
que in sanctam civitatem diffamaverunt martyrium sancti viri ubique; atque adiungebant prophetiam eius dicentes: "Dum esset beatus vir in carcere nobiscum, quadam die sic affatus est nobis dicens:
'Sciatis quia ego revelante mihi Domino die crastina finiar, et de
590 hoc saeculo transeo. Post paucos vero dies vos relaxabimini. Iniquus autem et malignus rex post non modicum interficietur. Sed
prosperante Christo cum perrexeritis in sanctam civitatem, ite ad
mansionem quae dicitur Abbatis Anastasii et nuntiate ipsi et fratribus quaeque cognovistis de me.'" Illi ergo oboedientes iussis eius
595 et omnia quae cognoverunt et propriis oculis viderunt diligenter
nobis innotuerunt.

565 iacentem *sic cod.*

20. Ps 115.15. Cf. Ps 34.20.

43. Praedictus autem frater Minutius[21] nomine sepeliens corpus sancti martyris cum omni diligentia in praefata ecclesia Sancti Sergii, manensque ibi pertractabat apud se qualiter sine periculo ad monasterium unde transmissus fuerat in obsequium sancti martyris remeare valeret. Post hac ergo re erat obnixe orans Dominum et merita sancti Anastasii deprecans. Ordinante autem Deo post dies decem venit in eisdem partibus christianissimus Imperator Eraclius cum exercitu. Quod cum comperisset frater ille gavisus est valde. De exercitu autem honorati viri videntes eum requisierunt ab eo quid ibidem faceret. Ille vero narravit eis omnia et de sancto Anastasio et de seipso quod actum esset. At illi glorificaverunt Deum, et dixerunt ei: "Redi nobiscum, et in tuo monasterio salva animam tuam." Adherens ergo eis in multo honore habebatur apud eos per totam Persidam, atque cum eis per Armeniorum regionem post anni circulum reversus est ad propria.

44. Detulit autem et secum sancti Anastasii colobium, et ex ordine totum praeposito monasterii et fratribus narravit quod sancto martyri acciderit, videlicet et gloriosum eius finem et sui itineris laborem, et omnes simul glorificaverunt Deum, qui salvat sperantes in se. Per colobium autem sancti martyris hoc primum a Domino ostensum est signum. Iuvenis quidam erat in eodem monasterio, qui nequiter vexabatur a spiritu immundo. Accipiens autem praepositus colobium sancti Anastasii fecit eum indui. Et protinus effugit ab eo daemonium et salvatus est de reliquo misericordia Christi et meritis sancti martyris qui per bonam confessionem suscepit sanctorum testium in caelis societatem praestante salvatore nostro qui cum patre et Spiritu sancto vivit et regnat Deus per omnia saecula seaculorum. Amen.

Explicit passio sancti Anastasii mart.

21. This is the most egregious misreading in this version. The name *Minutius* must have been taken from the following phrases in p: *et insinuavit eis minutius* and *et intimavit diligenter praeposito et fratribus minutius.*

7

THE ROMAN REVISION (r_2)

About This Edition

The version of the *Passio S. Anastasii* that I call "The Roman Revision"[1] derives from the r-redaction of *BHL* 408, discussed in my introduction to the text of *BHL* 408, p-redaction, above.[2] The Roman Revision of the *Passio S. Anastasii* survives only in three manuscript witnesses that originated in the Roman area and are closely related to each other.[3] The sanctoral of Vat. lat. 1196 (Vc) and 5696 (Vt) is nearly identical in the parts of the year that overlap;[4] the titles of the texts are quite similar in several instances.[5] If the contents of Vat. lat. 1193 (Va) are compared to the corresponding parts of 5696 and 1196, all three share a similar hagiographical program.[6]

---

1. See Chapter VII, p. 234.

2. The clearest indication of this derivation is the reading *qui docuit eum litteras graecas* (l. 161). For a fuller discussion of the relation of r to p, cf. pp. 365ff.

3. Vat. lat. 1193 (s. XI-XII) together with Vat. lat. 1194, 1191, and 10999 makes up the legendary of S. Maria in Trastevere; it also contains the Roman Miracle, *BHL* 412. Vat. lat. 1196 (s. XI-XII) and Vat. lat. 5696 (s. XII) were also compiled for Roman churches.

4. It is in fact identical from the *Passio S. Margaritae* to the *Vita Mariae Aegyptiacae*. The only slight discrepancy occurs for early January: Vat. lat. 1196 does not contain the *Miraculum S. Basilii* (*BHL* 1022; instead it has the *Vita S. Basilii episcopi*, *BHL* 1024), nor the *Passio SS. Iuliani et Basilissae et Celsi et aliorum* (*BHL* 4532). Vat. lat. 5696, on the other hand, omits the *Vita S. Basilii episcopi* (*BHL* 1024), the *Vita S. Macharii confessoris* (*BHL* 5104), the *Passio Concordii*, and the *Vita S. Pauli eremitae* (*BHL* 6596).

5. For example, *Vita B. Paulae, matris Eustochiae edita a B. Hieronymo presb.* (Poncelet, *Catalolgus ... vaticanae*, pp. 60, 138).

6. This was also noted in Garrison, *Studies* IV, 284. Va omits the Life of Antony (*BHL* 609), the Passion of S. Valentinus (*BHL* 8463), the Life of Constantia (*Cf. BHL* 1927), the Life of S. Gregory I (an abbreviation of *BHL*

A collation of the text of the Passion of Anastasius transmitted in these three manuscripts confirms the relationship suggested by the sanctoral of these codices. Vt and Vc separate themselves from Va most clearly by their common omission in cap. 31.[7] Neither one could have been copied from the other or its direct tradition.[8] In addition, Vt and Vc omit the preface, but Va includes it. The manuscripts' affiliation can be expressed by the following stemma:

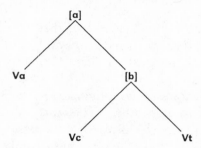

My edition is based on the stemma above, as well as on the indirect evidence of p and the r-redaction as represented by its oldest manuscript witness, Reginensis latinus 516 (Rg) of the Vatican Library. In cases where the two branches differ from each other, I have followed the reading supported by the source text if it is relevant. Those cases where p and Rg agree in supporting the reading of one branch over the other are not cited in my *apparatus criticus*.[9] But whenever variant readings are supported by the Reginensis and not by p, I have indicated this explicitly in the apparatus to illustrate the dependence of this revision on the r-redaction. Similarly, in cases where the choice of a variant reading is un-

---

3641), and the Life of St. Benedict (*BHL* 1102). But it has many more texts than those represented in the two other codices, four texts concerning Aquila and Prisca, for example, while the other two have only two. It also commemorates saints excluded by the other two such as Ignatius (Rufinus, *Historia ecclesiastica* III, 36) and Pygmenius (*BHL* 6849).

7. (l. 440) *et—erant.*

8. Vt contains an omission (*cursum–ademplivit* [ll. 544-545]) not shared by Vc, which, in turn, has several peculiar readings of its own, e.g. *exercitum* (l. 100), *servitium* (l. 325), *errans* (l. 464).

9. The apparatus of my critical edition of p includes the Reginensis's variants.

certain, I have added the reading of p (and if different, also Rg) in the apparatus. As usual, I have standardized the spelling, except for proper nouns, or unusual words. The division into chapters follows that of the Greek text.

Conspectus Siglorum

Va   Biblioteca apostolica vaticana, Vaticanus latinus 1193

Vc   Biblioteca apostolica vaticana, Vaticanus latinus 1196

Vt   Biblioteca apostolica vaticana, Vaticanus latinus 5696

Rg   Biblioteca apostolica vaticana, Reginensis latinus 516

p   *BHL* 408(p) *supra editum*

Passio sancti Anastasii martyris

1. Unigenitus filius et verbum Dei per quem omnia facta sunt,
coaequalis atque consubstantialis Patri et sancto atque vivifico Spiritui, misertus generi humano perdito et sub mortis atque corrup-
5 tionis condicione subiecto, descendit secundum quod scriptum est,
per virginem natus formam servi suscipiens,[1] conversatus cum hominibus[2] omnia dispensans ad salutem nostram. Nam sua tempo-
rali morte destruxit nostram mortem aeternam. Triduo autem in
sepulcro iacens, sine corruptione nostrae corruptionis emunda-
10 tionem fecit, atque in infernum descendens iustorum inde reduxit
animas quas detinebat claustra subvertens. Denique gloriosa sua
resurrectione secum nos consurgere fecit, et consedere nos in caelestibus iussit,[3] sicut apostolus dicit.

2. Et post eius gloriosam ascensionem sublimi Spiritus sancti virtu-
15 te induti, hii qui per semetipsos prospectores et ministri verbi in-
carnati facti sunt[4] atque eius passionis testes[5] beati apostoli universum mundum peragraverunt divina mandata efficientes. Praedicaverunt autem ex Dei pietate per civitates et regiones, nationi-
busque et populis tribubus et linguis illam ydolatriae quasi pater-
20 nam traditionem ex multis temporibus et impietatis errorem quo
detinebantur radicitus evellentes, angelicam conversationem homines habere docuerunt. Ex hoc facto iam bonis cunctis repletus est
mundus in cognoscendo Dominum creatorem suum secundum
quod scriptum est in epistula Petri dicentis: In cognitione domini
25 nostri Ihesu Christi omnia ministrabuntur vobis.[6] Ex hoc caelestia
terrestribus iuncta sunt et vita aeterna in mundo concessa est. Ex
hoc hominum natura magnis et ineffabilibus Dei donis letatur.

20 herrorem Va

1. Phil 2.7.
2. Cf. Bar 3.38.
3. Cf. Eph 2.6.
4. Cf. Lc 1.2.
5. Cf. 1 Pt 5.1.
6. Cf. 2 Pt 1.8-11.

3. Sed videns hoc humanae vitae insidiator diabolus, et invidens bonitati quae per Christi gratiam fiebat hominibus, et cernens seip-
30   sum proiectum ab aethereis sedibus, invenit malignitatis consilium quo arbitratus est ea quae pietatis sunt posse delere. Sed magis prodesse inventum est. Eos enim qui tunc tenebant sceptra regalia varie et omnibus modis venena sua disseminans insurgere fecit per diversas persecutiones adversus ecclesiam. Et tamen hoc faciendo
35   nichil profecit. Provexit enim Dei martyres, non devicit. Nam unde existimavit adversarius diminuere christianorum ecclesiam, inde auctus est numerus sanctorum. Maximeque ipse confunditur dum Dei ecclesiam confundere nititur et per sanctorum apostolorum ac victoriosorum martyrum tolerantiam dolosus abiectus est, et divi-
40   nae institutionis ornatum Christi recepit ecclesia cum per gratiam eius cotidie cresceret singulisque temporibus numerus copiosior fidelium fieret usque adeo ut ipsi etiam orbis terrarum principes et imperatores romani qui eam antea persequebantur postea proni ac curvi venerarentur et donis magnis et innumerabilibus eam dita-
45   rent. Quod factum regis qui Abrahae uxorem abstulit[7] significavit, quam amare quidem potuit, violare non potuit, potiusque intactam et ducentos syclos argenti ei donans viro reddidit.

4. Nec autem nostris iniquitatibus exigentibus Dei super nos iram contraximus. Unde tradidit nos in manus inimicorum impiorum
50   et regis iniusti qui civitates nostras et regiones quasdam tradidit igni quasdam autem radicitus evulsit et captivos multos duxit. Non tamen nos usque in finem despexit benignus atque amator humani generis Deus sed suam nos habere spem dedit, etiam nunc glorificare proprios fideles et suos servos non destitit ac multos martyres
55   efficere non cessavit.

5. Unde exclamare in laudem eius placet secundum magni apostoli vocem dicentis: O altitudo divitiarum sapientiae et scientiae Dei, quam inscrutabilia sunt iudicia eius et investigabiles viae eius.[8] Etenim persis quidem tradidit ad correptionem eos qui eius secundum
60   gratiam filii erant atque heredes. Ex Persida autem martyrem sibi elegit gloriosum atque egregium qui caritatem, fidem, atque confes-

7. Gn 20.1ff., with different dietails. Cf. Augustine, *Contra Faustum* XXII, 38.
8. Cf. Rm 11.33.

sionem eius firmiter atque magnanimiter usque in finem retinens coronam adeptus est incorruptibilem. Sancti igitur Anastasii huius vitam quam verissime usque ad finem scribere devovi ut iussus
65 sum, ipsum primum invoco testem et eum quem confessus est Deum ac Dominum Ihesum Christum, et sic narrationis seriem Deo iuvante suscipiam.

6. Hic quidem erat de Persidis regione Razech vocabulo, de villa Rasnuni, nomen eius autem Magundat. Filius vero erat magi cuius-
70 dam Bau nomine, qui etiam doctor extiterat magicae artis. Erudivit itaque eum pater suus a pueritia magica arte. Factus autem iuvenis, contigit militare eum cum aliis multis, et esse in regia civitate sub Chosroe rege persarum. Sanctae autem civitatis desolatione facta per Chosroe impiissimum, venerabilia et sacra loca concremata
75 sunt in praedicta ira quam pro nostris peccatis perpessi sumus. Honoranda vero atque vivifica ligna pretiosae crucis Domini nostri Ihesu Christi captiva translata sunt in Persidam. O admiranda Dei omnipotentia! Captiva quidem ferebatur Domini crux ad illorum insipientiam; captivabat autem ipsa magis corda infidelium a diabo-
80 lo ea separando, et Dei Ihesu Christi fidei adiungendo, qui in ea pro omnium salute pependit.

7. Quapropter tristitia et stupor invadebat infideles, gaudium vero atque laetitia in cordibus fidelium choruscabant. Fama autem ubique de ea in omni Persida discurrebat. Igitur audiens praefatus tyro
85 Magundat, qui et Anastasius famam atque virtutem pretiosae crucis Domini nostri Ihesu Christi, interrogavit de ea quomodo aut qualiter esset mysterium venerandae crucis, et discens a fidelibus eius virtutem atque ab aliis dicentibus quoniam Deus christianorum in hac cruce quae huc delata est pependit pro salute generis humani
90 statim sicut terra bona suscepta pluvia ad producendum fructum praeparata, cor eius per auditum suscipiens mirabilem atque ineffabilem virtutem Domini nostri Ihesu Christi et susceptam vehemen-

---

68-69 Beatus quidem Anastasius de Persidis (Persidi Vt) regione, Razech vocabulo extitit oriundus de villa Vc Vt   68 razach Va   69 autem *om.* Va
70 doctor] gentium *add.* Vt   71 itaque *om.* Va   72 civitati Vc   75 in praedicta *om.* Vc Vt   83 in cordibus–choruscabant] cordium coruscabant fidelium Va   85 Anastasius] dicitur *add.* Vt   89 quae] qui Vc

ter diligens decrevit iam Dei famulus ad religionem christianam
pertingere. Et quanto plus per auditum quae veritatis sunt percipie-
95 bat, tanto magis ab eius corde magicae artis seductio abscedebat.
Sicut enim fugunt tenebrae a luce, a sole autem umbra et ab igne
fumus, ita et fallatia exterminantur a doctrina veritatis.

8. Habebat autem fratrem carnalem beatus Anastasius cum quo militabat et pergebat in exercitu, cui nomen Sayn, et hic erat princeps
100 exercitus Persarum. Itaque venit cum eo usque ad Calcedonem. At
vero dignae recordationis Philippico circumvallanti eum, immo
praeteregredienti et ingresso Persidam, Sayn reversus est post tergum suum, et sic contigit famulum Dei Anastasium cum Persarum
exercitu redire in partes Orientis. Sed exinde recessit ab exercitu et
105 derelinquens proprium fratrem venit Iheropolim et devertit apud
quendam christianum persam malleatorem et mansit apud eum.
Didicit autem apud eum et ipse artem et operabatur cum eo.

9. Cum ergo abundaret in eo amor et gratia atque desiderium ut
illuminaretur, multum rogabat praefatum malleatorem ut eum ins-
110 trueret qualiter ad gratiam baptismatis perveniret. At ille votum
eius nequaquam implevit propter metum Persarum quem ne periclitaretur habebat. Tamen cum illo ibat devotus Deo Anastasius ad
ecclesiam sanctorum martyrum, et orabat et picturas eorum conspi-
ciens addiscebat quidnam hoc esset, et audiens ab eo sanctorum
115 certamina sive mirabilia quae fecerunt sive atrociora tormenta quae
a tyrannis perpessi sunt et eorum tolerantiam mirabatur pavens.
Manens igitur parvum tempus apud praedictum virum christianum,
optimum desiderium divinitus percepit in animo suo ut Iherusoli-
mam adveniret ut illic sancti baptismatis consequeretur gratiam.

120 10. Et hoc habens propositum in mente, devenit ad sanctam civitatem et mansit apud quendam Christo amabilem virum malleatorem, ei patefaciens omne suum desiderium quoniam vult Christo
coniungi et pervenire ad gratiam sancti baptismatis. Perductus est
ergo ab eo Helyae sanctissimo presbytero Sanctae Resurectionis qui

---

96 autem *om.* Va   et *om.* Va   99 nomen] erat *add.* Va   Sain Vc
100 exercitum Vc   104 exercitum Vc   107 cooperabatur Va   111 nec
Vc Vt   122 eique Va   123 sancti baptismatis *om.* Vt   124 ab eo *om.* Vt

125 eum tamque a Deo sibi praedestinatum suscepit filium, et postea
indicavit de eo Modesto sanctissimo presbytero et vicario apostolicae sedis, et fecit eum baptizari simul cum aliis qui et ipsi de
eadem regione erant qui etiam beatum finem pro Christo suscipientes in Edessa civitate martyrio coronati sunt.

130 **11.** Detentus vero est beatus Anastasius a sanctissimo Helia in domo sua per octo dies qui exhortabatur eum in proposito bono persistere et interrogabat eum quid cogitasset se de reliquo facturum. Ipse
vero rogabat eum dicens ut monachus ordinaretur. Post depositas
vero albas continuo perduxit eum Sanctae Recordationis Helias
135 presbyter ad quoddam monasterium quod quarto miliario distat a
sancta civitate, et multum rogans cum aliis praedicti monasterii venerabilibus fratribus Iustinum propositum, virum valde mirabilem
et prudentem plenumque Dei gratiae ad observanda sacra praecepta, tradidit ei Dei famulum Anastasium. Qui libenter suscipiens eum
140 suae congregationi sociavit deditque ei et magistrum unum de eadem
congregatione fratrem virum prudentem qui etiam docuit eum litteras graecas simul et placentem Deo doctrinam cum psalterio, et
tondens tradidit ei sanctum habitum atque ut filium adoptavit.

12. Ferebat autem magnam obedientiam per omnia officia imperata
145 in praedicto monasterio beatus Anastasius, placens omnibus per
Domini gratiam. Erat enim sedulus valde in ministerio fratrum et
in operibus manus, et prae omnibus in regula monachica observanda in missarum sollempniis frequens aderat. Audiebat sane attentius sanctas ac divinas scripturas ac vitas sanctorum patrum et
150 interrogabat suum magistrum virum prudentem et bonis moribus
ornatum, et discebat ab eo quae requirebat et admirans glorificabat Deum. Assidue autem legebat in cellula secretius certamina vel
agones sanctorum martyrum et legendo lacrimas effundebat. Et
cogitabat atque aestuabat secretius in corde suo hoc desiderio ac-
155 census ut eum Deus ad martyrii palmam vocare dignaretur, quatenus in libro vitae ascriberetur socius servorum suorum qui pro

---

128 etiam] et ipsi *add.* Vt   131 eum *om.* Vc Vt   persistere] consistere Va
136 praedictis monasterium Vt   140 sotiavit Vt   142 graecas *cf.* Rg   146
valde *om.* Vc Vt   151 quae requirebat] qui querebat Vt

eius nomine passi sunt. Perseveravit autem in eodem monasterio per annos septem.

13. Videns ergo hostis et inimicus humani generis tantam perseve-
160   rantiam in Christi servitio atque in Christi amore famulum Dei
Anastasium persistere, et volens eum a bono proposito revocare et
a praedicto monasterio eum exire, immisit in illum cogitationes
iniquas etiam ut ad operandam remearet magicam artem quam a
suo patre didicerat. Ipse vero videns impiissimi diaboli astutiam
165   sese in orationem dedit et enixius Dominum deprecabatur ut eum
eriperet ab insidiis adversarii. Abbati vero monasterii sui indicavit
cordis sui secreta et lacrimabiliter deprecabatur eum ut pro se
Dominum exoraret quatenus eum liberaret de faucibus adversarii.
Quod et faciebat ille pius pater. Ammonebat quoque eum et con-
170   fortabat in Domino secundum quae data illi fuerat in Domino gratia. Praeterea faciens orationem pro eo cum omnibus fratribus in
ecclesia, effugavit ab eo pugnam diabolicam.

14. Post paucos autem dies somnium vidit per noctem Dei famulus
Anastasius ita. Videbat se ipsum in monte stare excelso et quendam
175   ad eum venientem et porrigentem sibi calicem aureum plenum vino et dicentem: "Accipe et bibe." Quem suscipiens bibit. Statim
autem evigilans interpretatus est intra se somnium quod viderat
hoc esse quod cupiebat. Qui protinus surgens ad ecclesiam perrexit
matutinales hymnos explendos. Adlucescente sancto dominico die
180   expletis iam hymnis matutinalibus rogavit abbatem monasterii ut
ei secretius loqueretur. Et ingressus in secretarium cecidit ad pedes
eius rogans cum lacrimis ut ad Dominum funderet preces pro eo
ut eum dignaretur suscipere quia sperabat se moriturum in ipsis
diebus. Dicebat autem abbati: "Scio pater quantos labores habuisti
185   in me misero, et quia multum te tribulavi et quia per te adduxit
me Deus de tenebris ad veram lucem. Sed rogo ut pro me Dominum exores." Dicit ei abbas: "Quae est causa fili mi quam dicis? et
unde nosti quia in his diebus egredieris de hoc saeculo?" Ipse itaque
narravit ei somnium quod viderat et confirmans asserebat per om-

---

158 per *om.* Va Vc   159 hostis et *om.* Va   159-160 tantam perseverantiam
cf. Rg   163 ad *om.* Va   164 impii Va iniquissimi *cf.* p Rg   174 ita *om.*
Va   178 esset Vc   181 in *om.* Va   186 rogo] oro Vc Vt

190 nia quia moriturus esset in ipsis diebus sive communi morte sive per martyrium quomodo cupiebat. Tamen timebat palam dicere de martyrio ut non increparent eum fratres.

15. Abbas vero consolabatur eum blande et multis ammonitionibus confortabat in Domino. Igitur beatus Anastasius missarum sollem-
195 niis celebratis cum fratribus, et percipiens divina mysteria sumpsit cibum cum eis. Soporatusque est modicum et evigilans non ferens cordis sui incendium volens adimplere desiderium suum quod erat placitum Domino egressus est clam de monasterio nichil secum fe-rens nisi ea quae indutus erat et abiit Diospolim. Exinde abiit causa
200 orationis in montem Garizim ad quendam venerabilem locum qui illic erat. Inde profectus est ad alia venerabilia loca. Deductus est autem per Domini gratiam et devenit Caesaream Palestinam secun-dum praedestinationem Dei quia ibi praeparatum est illi princi-pium martyrii. Et mansit apud ecclesiam beatae et intemeratae Dei
205 genitricis Mariae duobus diebus.

16. Postea perrexit ad beatam Euphemiam causa orationis. Cumque transiret per quendam locum vidit in domo cuiusdam persae homi-nes magicam operantes artem, et zelo Dei ductus ingressus ad eos dixit eis: "Quid erratis et errare facitis animas hominum in malifi-
210 ciis vestris?" Stupentibus autem viris illis in sermonibus et in con-stantia ipsius interrogaverunt eum dicentes: "Quisnam es tu qui hoc dicis?" Ipse vero ait eis: "Et ego aliquando erravi sicut vos nunc erratis et operatus sum istam nefandam artem atque vestra-rum incantationum sum conscius." Et eo arguente illi trepidi ob-
215 mutuerunt. Tamen multum ante rogatus ne divulgaret de arte eorum cuiquam dimisit eos.

17. Et dum separaretur modicum ab illis, videntes eum quidam de officio principis terrae ante ianuam praetorii ipsius sedentes dixe-runt propria lingua inter se: "Iste explorator est." Audiens autem
220 beatus Anastasius haec verba inter se ad invicem conferentes in-

---

190-191 sive–cupiebat] sive quomodo cupiebat martirio Va   199 et *om.* Vc
Vt   204 et–Dei *om.* Va   207 transisset Va. *cf.* pergeret p Rg   208 ad eos
om. Va   210 viris *om.* Vt   213 et *om.* Vc   213-214 nostrarum Vt
214-215 commutaverunt Vc   218 sedentem Vc

tuens eos dixit: "Quid inter vos talia verba confertis? Ego explorator non sum, sed servus sum Domini mei Ihesu Christi. Itaque ob hoc vobis melior sum quia illius merui esse servus qui pro peccatoribus de caelo descendere dignatus est. Fui tamen et ego in militari
225 officio sicut et vos nunc estis." At illi audito quod christianus esset insurgentes tenuerunt eum. Exeunte primate officii et inquirente quis esset, cum cognovisset Christi esse cultorem, iussit eum custodire tribus diebus in quibus nullatenus est de alimentis eorum refectus. Sanctus vero Anastasius magis de illorum impietate quam
230 de sua dolebat indigentia.

18. Revertente autem Barzabana domino illorum in Caesaream, non enim ibi erat quando tentus est beatus Anastasius, ergo suggerens de eo primus officiorum adduxit illum in praetorium. Occupato vero Barzabana circa alia negotia, inventus est ibi quidam
235 christianus qui cognovit beatum Anastasium cum esset in ecclesia beatae Dei genitricis Mariae semper virginis, et colloquens ei secretius ac requirens quam ob causam detentus ab eis fuisset. Et cognoscens causam, beatificavit eum de bono proposito et confortavit in Domino divinis sermonibus monens eum ut non metueret tor-
240 menta, et non timeret mori pro nomine Domini nostri Ihesu Christi, sed fortiter atque fiducialiter responderet Barzabanae ad ea quae interrogatus esset ab eo, memorans ei et sermonem quem Dominus in sancto evangelio dixit, quia qui perseveraverit usque in finem, hic salvus erit.⁹

245 **19.** Introductus est autem Dei famulus Anastasius et stans coram Barzabana non adoravit eum secundum nefandum ritum gentis persarum qui detinebatur ab illis. Intuens itaque eum Barzabanas superbissimus cum iracundia dixit: "Unde es tu? Et quis vocaris?" In primis vero ipse ait: "Ego christianus sum." Deinde dixit: "Si cupis
250 discere unde sim, quantum ad genus persa de regione Razech de villa Rasnuni, officialis eram et magus et reliqui tenebras et veni ad

---

231 Revertenti Va   247 detinebantur Va   247-248 superbissimus cum iracundia *om.* Va   249 Ego *om.* Va

9. Mt 10.22.

veram lucem. Nomen autem meum prius Magundat, Christianitatis vero Anastasius." Dixit ei Barzabanas: "Dimitte hunc errorem et convertere ad primam tuam religionem et praebemus tibi pecunias
255 et possessiones plurimas." Ipse vero respondens ait: "Non mihi contingat negare Dominum meum Ihesum Christum." Dicit igitur ei Barzabanas: "Ergo placent tibi vestimenta talia qualibus uteris?" Beatus Anastasius dixit: "Hoc indumentum angelicum et gloriosum est." Dicit ei Barzabanas: "Daemonium habes." Respondit ei beatus
260 Anastasius et dixit: "Quando in errore eram, habui daemonium; nunc autem habeo Dominum Deum Ihesum Christum salvatorem meum qui destruit daemonia." Dicit ei Barzabanas: "Non metuis regem Persarum Chosroem? Qui si de te cognoverit ista iubebit te crucifigi?" Beatus Anastasius dixit: "Quare timeam illum? Homo
265 enim est corruptibilis sicut et tu."

20. Tunc indignatus Barzabanas iussit eum in vinculis ferreis duci in castrum, et lapides sine cessatione deportari ad opus castri. Ita multas atque innumeras tribulationes patiebatur martyr Christi Anastasius, non solum ab extraneis sed etiam a notis. Quidam
270 enim de regione eius, videntes quae in eum fiebant, erubescebant et increpabant eum, dicentes: "Quid hoc fecisti? Nemo enim aliquando de regione nostra factus est christianus; et ecce fecisti nobis ridiculum." Et in his atque aliis verbis fallacibus suadebant ei et decipere nitebantur. Ipse vero expellebat eos a se. In insaniam au-
275 tem illi conversi percutiebant eum absque pietate et trahebant barbam eius, et scindebant vestimenta eius. Ministri autem Barzabanae non solum ad portandos lapides eum cogebant, sed tam magnos quos quatuor homines non poterant volvere in collo ei ponebant. Et tamen vinctus sic faciebat opus, unam catenam in collo habens,
280 aliam in pedibus. Illi quidem multa acriora et saeva tormenta ei intulerunt. At vero fortissimus athleta Christi Anastasius omnia sustinuit gaudens pro Christi nomine.

252 veram *om.* Va   christianitate Va   256 igitur ei] ergo Vc Vt   258 Beatus *om.* Va   259 ei *om.* Va   259-260 Respondit-et] Anastasius Va 263 iubet Va   264 Beatus *om.* Va   267 deportare Va   274 In *om.* Vc Vt 276 eius² *om.* Va   281 intulerant Va   Fortissimus vero Va

21. Iterum autem iussit eum Barzabanas ante se adsisti, et dixit ei: "Si veraciter sicut dixisti magi filius fuisti, et scis magicam artem, dic mihi a quo didiceris vel quid ex ea nosti ut ego cognoscam." Ipse vero ait: "Non permittat Deus ut ultra egrediatur quicquam ex ore meo de tali re." Dicit ei Barzabanas: "Quid inquam, permanes in his? Convertere in illam primam religionem, nam pro te suggeram Chosroi regi." Ipse vero ait ad eum: "Scripsisti, et suscepisti rescripta. Fac quod vis. Ego christianus sum." Barzabanas ait: "Non scripsi, sed scribam, et quicquid mihi praeceperit faciam." Sanctus vero Anastasius respondit: "Vade scribe quanta volueris mala de me. Ego certe christianus sum." Barzabanas dixit: "Prosternatur in terra, et tamdiu caedatur quousque perficiat quod ei iubetur." Cumque vellent eum ligare dixit: "Sinite me, non habeo necesse vincula." Et exprimens sibi signum sanctae crucis fecit in fronte, et sedit in terra. Illi vero ligaverunt eum et caedebant fustibus. Sanctus vero Anastasius dixit eis: "Expoliate me habitu, quo sum indutus ut non patiatur iniuriam, et sic caedite super carnes meas. Ista enim quae facitis lusus sunt. Ego enim si membratim abscidar, numquam negabo Dominum Ihesum Christum."

22. Dicit ei Barzabanas: "Adquiesce mihi, nam scribam de te accusationem regi." At ipse dixit: "Vade scribe regi tuo quicquid volueris." Et ait Barzabanas: "Ergo regem meum non times?" Beatus Anastasius dixit: "Quare timeam regem tuum? Annon est homo sicut et tu? et non morietur aut non videbit corruptionem sicut et tu? illum qui corruptionem videbit simile tibi lutum et respuam Dominum Ihesum Christum qui fecit caelum et terram, mare et omnia quae in eis sunt qui numquam vidit corruptionem?" Stupefactus autem Barzabanas super tam constanti responsione martyris, item iussit eum duci in castellum.

283 adsisti] adduci Vc Vt   286 ait] dixit Va   quicquam *om.* Va   289 ait ad eum] dixit Va   290 ait] dixit Va   292 vero *om.* Va   294 quod ei *om.* Vt   295 me *om.* Vc Vt   habeo *om.* Vt   sibi *om.* Vc Vt   296-297 fecit–et *om.* Va   297 Attamen illi Vc Vt   297-298 fustibus *cf.* Rg   298 vero *om.* Va   eis *om.* Va   298-300 me–Ista] me ut mei vestimenti habitus nullam patiatur iniuriam, sed carnes caedite quia ista Va   303-304 voles Va   304 Et *om.* Va   Beatus *om.* Va   306 moritur Va

23. Et post dies paucos fecit sibi praesentari eum, et dixit ei: "Recordare magicae artis, et sacrifica, ut non male moriaris et frauderis hac luce." Respondit autem famulus Dei et ait: "Quibus diis iubes
315 me sacrificare? Soli aut lunae aut mari? monti aut colli, ceterisve helementis seu metallis? Non permittat mihi Dominus ut adorem sculptilia vestra. Namque in principio haec omnia Christus filius Dei fecit ad servitium nostrum. Vos ergo erratis, serviendo daemonis et quadrupedibus homines facti, et ignoratis Deum qui vos
320 fecit. Si enim cognovissetis Christum qui vos fecit quandoque converti habuissetis ad veram lucem et erui a daemonum potestate qui vos errare faciunt, et credere Deo qui non mentitur his qui credunt in nomine eius dicens eis: Ego enim dabo vobis os et sapientiam cui non poterunt resistere et contradicere omnes adversarii ves-
325 tri.[10] Hic voluit me ex ydiota et alienigena habere servum sibi ad suam gloriam, fortitudinem omnibus praestans credentibus in se." Haec et his similia prosequente sancto Anastasio bonis sermonibus, stupebant et mirabantur audientes. Dei autem martyr Anastasius tribus iam vicibus coronatus in confessione Christi certator fortis-
330 simus statim ad castellum reducitur vinculis constrictus.

24. Cognoscens autem sanctissimus abbas praefati monasterii in quo beatus Anastasius sanctum habitum susceperat stabilitatem eius atque confessionem quae in Christo erat, et quia sine metu fortiter decertaret, eius quoque alacritatem atque perseverantiam, gavisus
335 est gaudio magno una cum universa congregatione sibi commissa, et Dominum benedicebant atque supplicabant die noctuque ut eius cursum dirigeret et usque in finem perseveraret. Direxit etiam duos ex fratribus monasterii in Caesaream ad beatum Anastasium cum litteris consolatoriis confortans animum eius in Domino.

340 **25.** Cum ergo esset in custodia castri martyr Christi non cessabat psalmis et hymnis diebus ac noctibus glorificare Deum omnipotentem. Habens secum et alium in vinculis constitutum iuvenem

---

323 eius] suo Vc Vt   325 servitium Vc   340 castris Vc *cf.* Rg   Christi *om.* Va   341 diebus ac noctibus *om.* Va   ac *om.* Vt   341-342 omnipotentem *om.* Va

10. Lc 21.15.

quendam ex servis Barzabanae pro causa tentum, et nolens contristare eum cum surgebat famulus Christi ut celebraret hymnos matu-
345 tinales in Dei laudibus, inclinabat collum suum ad collum eius et
pedem suum ad pedem eius ut non per cathenarum extensionem
laborem praestaret ei. Una igitur nocte psallente eo abscultabat
eum de vinctis qui ibi erant hebraeus quidam nobili genere, mitissimus tamen, et videns beatum martyrem per diem quidem in lapi-
350 dum fatigationem, nocte autem in Dei laudibus perseverantem stupebat dicens: "Quid nam vult hoc esse?"

26. Ergo intuens eum iacens super pavimentum in noctis silentio
stantem et psallentem matutinales hymnos, vidit subito aliquos in
vestibus albis ingredientes per ostium carceris et circumdantes bea-
355 tum martyrem cum quibus et lux copiosa fulsit in carcere. Amens
itaque factus praefatus vir super visione dixit intra se: "Sanctus
Deus, isti angeli sunt." Iterum admirans videbatur ei cernere hos
ipsos palliis circumdatos habentes cruces in manibus, et ait in semetipso: "Isti episcopi sunt." Sed et servum Dei candidis vestibus
360 indutum cum eis qui ei apparuerunt et iuvenem in gloria magna
stantem ante eum et incensum mittentem. Vir autem qui contemplabatur pulsabat manu proximum suum dormientem qui erat
christianus ut vigilaret quatenus ei ostenderet quae videbat, et non
poterat quia graviter dormiebat. Quapropter iactavit se super eum
365 qui expergere factus tandem quaesivit ab eo quid hoc esset. Dicit
ei hebraeus: "Considera et vide." Et intuentes iam nihil viderunt.
Insinuavit tamen ei omnia quae viderat et glorificaverunt simul
Dominum Ihesum Christum.

27. Quia vero sicut supra memoravimus a prima et secunda inter-
370 rogatione videns Barzabanas constantiam Dei famuli Anastasii
scripsit Chosroi de eo. Itaque contigit intra dies paucos suscipere

---

343 quendam *om.* Va   345 suum] eius Va   eius] suum Va   347 praestaret ei] sibi praestaret Va   349 et] hic Va   beatum] Dei Va   quidem *om.*
Va   in *om.* Va   350 in *om.* Va   352 Intuens igitur Va   iacens–in *om.*
Va   357 isti *om.* Vc Vt   357-358 admirans–habentes] mirabatur cernere
quid hos ipsos videbat palliis circumdatos habentes Vc Vt   362 manu] manum Vt proximum *om.* Vt   370 videns] autem *add.* Vt

regis iussionem ut transmitteret martyrem in Persidam. Sed ille posse prius avertere sensus eius putans deque fide Christi deicere in qua fundatus erat, misit ad eum in carcerem per domesticum
375 eius dicens: "Ecce iussit rex ut verbo solo dicas quia non sum christianus, et statim te dimitto et quo volueris vade, sive esse monachus vis, esto, sive eques sicut fueras antea, et esse nobiscum. Ut vis fac." Respondens autem martyr Christi dixit: "Non fiat mihi negare Christum."

380 **28.** Cumque multas promissiones et suasiones ei direxisset per domesticum suum, et ille nullatenus acquiesceret, postmodum vero direxit illi dicens: "Scio quia erubescis propter concives tuos et ideo non vis negare coram eis. Sed quia iussio regis urguet, si vis coram me et aliis duobus dic sermonem et dimittam te." Martyr vero per
385 suprascriptum missum direxit ei dicens: "Absit a me. Neque coram te neque ante alios aliquando negabo Dominum meum." Tunc dixit ei per semet ipsum: "Ecce iussit rex ut ferro vinctus vadas in Persidam." Beatus vero Christi Anastasius martyr dixit: "Si volueris me dimittere solus ego vadam ad regem tuum." Ut autem audivit
390 beatum martyrem fortiter persistentem neque minas paventem neque blandimentis suadi bullatum eum iussit duci in carcerem. Et post quinque dies direxit eum cum aliis duobus christianis quibus et ipsius bullam expressit.

29. Approximante interea die festo exaltationis venerandae crucis
395 Domini nostri Ihesu Christi ipse beatus martyr et duo fratres monasterii eius et duo christianissimi viri et quidam de civitate fideles in psalmis et hymnys et canticis spiritualibus pernoctanctes erant ita ut obliviscerentur habere sibi vincula, glorificantes Dominum nostrum Ihesum Christum qui tantam longanimitatem dat sperantibus
400 bus in se. Diluculo autem ingressus dispensator quidam rerum publicarum et ipse vir christianissimus ad Barzabanam, rogabat illum ut vincula eius tollerentur, cupiens eum in ecclesiam deducere tantummodo pro die festo, subiungens quia: "Ego eum iterum reduco

373 posse *om.* Vt   376 te dimitto et] dimissus Va   esse] te Vt   378 Respondens–dixit] Respondit martyr Va   386 negare Va   388 Beatus–martyr] Sanctus Anastasius Va   394 Appropinquante Vc Vt   395 Domini–Ihesu *om.* Va   402 eius] eorum Vc   403 adiungens Va

in custodiam." Quod et factum est. Et permisit Barzabanas et de-
405 ductus est in ecclesiam. Gaudium igitur factum est universis fidelibus et consolatio agentibus Deo gratias super certamina martyris
Christi et de eius crebris tribulationibus quas sustinebat. Facta est
autem et contentio inter populum de civitate eadem pro eo. Con-
tendebant quippe fideles cum infidelibus.

410 **30.** Et quidam stupentes de tribulationibus quas tolerabat martyr
Christi Anastasius convaluerunt, et confortati sunt scilicet fideles
in Christo de eius longanimitate et perseverantia et in multis sermonibus consolatus est eos fidelis martyr Christi Anastasius. Et hii
qui de fide christiana desperabant pro eius alacritate convaluerunt,
415 osculantes eius vincula et quasi victores facti dicebant beato Anastasio: "Si tu propter Dominum nostrum Ihesum mori disposuisti,
quanto magis nos tecum mori debemus?" Et consolabantur in Domino et honorem ei praebebant viri pariter et mulieres. Expletis
vero missarum sollemniis vim faciens ei dispensator perduxit in
420 propriam domum ut victum caperet cum duobus fratribus monasterii. Et cum sumpsissent cibum pariter confortati sunt et collo-
quentes de divinis sermonibus inter se aedificati sunt in Domino.
Et postea iterum gaudentes et exultantes quasi ad convivium perrexerunt ad carcerem, et ibi glorificabant Dominum nostrum Ihesum
425 Christum qui tantam gratiam contulit servis suis.

31. Expletis vero quinque diebus egressus est de civitate Caesarea
cum praefatis duobus christianissimis viris et unus quidem frater
de monasterio eius et multi qui eum noverant viri ac mulieres cum
multa eum lacrimarum effusione prosequentes glorificabant Domi-
430 num semper super eius bono proposito quod disposuerat mori pro
Christo et reversi sunt. Alter vero frater habens comites illos duos
viros christianos ivit cum eo secundum iussionem praepositi sui ad
solatium atque ministerium eius, potissimum autem ut ea quae cognovisset de eo usque in finem per Domini gratiam detulisset tam
435 sanctissimo abbati suo quam et cunctae congregationi. Eunte igitur

---

406 certaminibus Vc Vt *cf.* certamen p Rg^corr. 408 civitatis–pro *om.* Vc Vt
412 in² *om.* Va 413 fidelis *om.* Va *cf.* fidelis Rg 414 convaliderunt Vc Vt
416 propter–Ihesum] domino Va 419 eis Vc Vt 422 de *om.* Vt 432
christianissimos Va

fortissimo et glorioso martyre cum devotissimo et alacri corde multum erat eis etiam gaudium et laetitia qui eum excipiebant per civitates et oppida fidelibus viris et in adventum eius magnificabant
Dominum omnium creatorem, suscipientes eum cum honore et os-
440   culabantur vincula eius et tribuebant ei quae necessaria erant.
Scripsit autem beatus Anastasius litteras deprecatorias abbati suo ab
Ierapoli ut pro se Dominum exoraret et effunderet preces ut eum
digne susciperet et suum cursum consumaret. Item de fluvio Tygride ei similiter litteras direxit.

445   **32.** Ingrediens autem in Persidam beatus Anastasius missus est in
carcerem in praedio quod vocatur Bethsaloe quod est longe miliario sexto de Discarthas in quo erat rex. At vero frater qui cum eo
ierat mansit in eodem praedio in domo Cortacii filii cuiusdam hominis nomine Gesdim primi dispensatoris publicarum rerum Persa-
450   rum, qui etiam erat christianus. Et morante beato martyre per dies
aliquot cum quibusdam qui illuc devenerant captivis, suggestum est
Chosroi regi de eo. Qui mittens unum ex iudicibus suis iussit examinari eum.

33. Ille vero veniens in carcerem cum tribuno qui erat super carce-
455   rem interrogavit eum quis esset et unde advenisset et quam ob rem reliquisset regionem et ubi factus est christianus. Martyr autem Christi
respondit ei per interpretem, non enim locutus est ei ille persica
lingua, et quidem multa coactus dixit ei: "Erratis vos daemones pro
Deo colentes. Et ego enim aliquando cum essem in errore hos cole-
460   bam. Nunc autem adoro omnipotentem Dominum Ihesum Christum qui fecit caelum et terram, mare et omnia quae in eis sunt. Et
scio diligenter quia culturae vestrae perditio et error daemonum
sunt." Dicit ei iudex: "Miser, numquid quem colitis vos christiani
non Iudaei crucifixerunt? Quomodo ergo errasti, reliquisti ritum
465   tuum et factus es christianus?" Sanctus vero Anastasius ait: "Quo-

436 cum *om.* Va   437 etiam *om.* Va   439 omnium *om.* Va   440 et–
erant *om.* Vc Vt   443 et] quo Va *om.* Vt   consumare Vt   445 in *om.*
Va   beatus] sanctus Va   446 carcere Vc Vt   454 vero *om.* Vc Vt
455 et² *om.* Va   456 autem] igitur *add.* Vc Vt   457-458 persica] per
syriacam Va *cf.* per siriaca lingua Rg   458 Herratis Va   459 Et *om.* Va
Vc   errorem Vt   464 errans Vc   465 et *om.* Vt   vero *om.* Va

niam crucifixus est a Iudaeis, verum dicis; quia vero sponte quare
non dicis? Ipse est enim qui fecit caelum et terram, mare et omnia
quae in eis sunt et voluit descendere in terras et incarnari de Spiritu sancto ex Maria virgine et crucifigi et liberare genus humanum
470   de errore Sathanae qui a vobis colitur. Vos autem colitis ignem et
cetera helementa et quod dici quoque nefas est servitis creaturae
potius quam creatori." Dixit iudex: "Quid tibi et sermonibus istis?
Ecce pietas regis parabit tibi dignitatem et zonas aureas et equos ut
sis inter primates eius. Tantum convertere in primam tuam religio-
475   nem." Beatus Anastasius dixit: "Ego numquam negabo Dominum
meum Ihesum Christum sed magis eum totis viribus adoro et colo.
Dona vero regis ut stercora computo."

34. Haec omnia audiens praefatus iudex intimavit Chosroi. Furore
ergo repletus rex iussit mitti eum in carcerem in crastinum volens
480   eum poenis interficere. Veniens autem alia die ex iussu regis praefatus iudex cum ira iussit eum trahi foras de carcere et coepit ei
minas prodere atque inferre ut eum terreret, putans eum per poenas discedere a tali proposito. Sanctus vero Anastasius martyr respondit ei dicens: "Ne labores domine iudex neque fatigeris. Me
485   enim Christo confortante neque acquiesco tibi neque recedere facies a fide quam cepi, sed siquid velis facere fac." Tunc iussit eum
vinctum secundum morem Persarum fustibus caedi absque pietate
dicens: "Honoribus et donis regis non adquiescis? Ammodo cognosces per dies iram eius. Sic enim cotidie in te faciam donec con-
490   sumaris." Respondit autem sanctus martyr Anastasius et dixit:
"Nec donis regis tui acquiesco nec minas tuas timeo. Quicquid
ergo vis fac."

35. Tunc iussit eum solvi et poni deorsum et lignum super tibias
eius imponi et duos viros fortissimos stare super utrasque extremas

---

466 vero *om.* Vc Vt   quare] vero Vt   467-468 caelum–sunt] omnia Va
468 in] ad Va   472 Dixit] autem *add.* Vc Vt   475 Beatus] Sanctus Va
478 omnia *om.* Va   480-483 Veniens–proposito] Alia autem die iussit eum
rex trahi de carcere comminans ei ut plurimum terreret putans illum per poenas a tali proposito separare Va   483 Anastasius *om.* Va   484 ei dicens
om. Va   486 velis] vis Va   489 per] in Va   Sicut Vc Vt   490
respondit–dixit] Anastasius dixit Va   491 tui *om.* Va

495   ligni partes. Omnes autem novimus quod importabilis est huius
tormenti species. Sanctus tamen martyr Christi Anastasius agens
gratias omnipotenti Deo sustinebat dolores fortiter. Videns autem
iudex quia nichil proficeret sed magis huiusmodi doloribus sicut
ferrum frigida aqua induratur ita per divinam gratiam eius animus
500   confortabatur, iussit iterum retrudi in carcere donec ista regi intimaret Chosroi.

36. Sellarius vero simul et tribunus qui erat super carcerem dum
esset christianus necnon et frater monasterii qui comes eius erat in
Christo ingrediebantur ad eum consolantes et admonentes eum in
505   bonum. Multi vero christiani qui ibidem erant cum quibus et de
iam dictis Iesdim filiis ingrediebantur ad eum et corruebant ad pedes eius et osculabantur vincula eius et rogabant ut dignaretur pro
eis orare et ut daret eis aliquam benedictionem ad custodiam eorum. At vero prohibebat eos beatus martyr ne talia dicerent. Ipsi
510   vero ceram superponebant vinculis impressam et pro benedictione
hanc accipiebant.

37. Iterum ergo post dies paucos ingressus est iudex ad beatum
Anastasium et temptans dixit ei: "Quid dicis? Facis iussionem regis
an permanes in his?" Sanctus vero Anastasius movens caput suum
515   quasi abhominatus est eum dicens: "Et semel et secundo et saepius
dixi quoniam impossibile est me negare Christum Dei filium.
Quod ergo vis, fac citius." Tunc temerator ille barbarus iussit eum
ligari sicut prius et diutius caedi fustibus et derelinquens eum in
carcere recessit. Transactis vero diebus paucis iterum ingressus est
520   ad eum seducens ut negaret Christum filium Dei aliquando blandimentis atque promissionibus pecuniae, simul et dignitatibus; aliquando poenarum minis et tormentis. Cum ergo vidisset quia famulus
Dei nec terrore concutitur nec blandimento seducitur sed perseve-
rat in Christi fide iussit eum iterum ligari et caedi sicut prius. Post
525   haec iussit eum solvi et suspendi ex una manu et saxum magnum

---

496 Christi Anastasius *om.* Va   497 omnipotenti *om.* Va   499 animus]
animum *codd.*   500 confortabatur] confortari et confirmari Vc confortatus
et confirmari Vt   Iussus est Va   506 corruentes Va   507 et¹ *om.* Va
eius² *om.* Va   509 vero *om.* Va 512 beatum] martyrem Va   514 vero *om.*
Va   518-519 in carcere *om.* Va   521 aliquando] blandimentis *add.* Vt

ligari ad pedes eius et sic derelinquens eum abiit. Sustinente autem martyre Christi huiusmodi supplitium quasi horarum duarum spatio postea reversus fecit eum deponi et abiens suggessit regi de proposito mentis eius et de perseverantia quam habebat in Christo.

530   **38.** Et post dies quindecim misit rex eundem iudicem et alios cum eo ad interficiendum beatum Anastasium martyrem et plurimos christianos cum eo nec non et captivos. Qui venientes iusserunt eos educi foras praedium Bethsaloe, scilicet beatum Anastasium et alios circiter septuaginta viros iuxta ripam fluminis. Et prius qui-
535   dem illis sanctissimis viris coram sancto martyre funibus illaqueari guttura et suffocari universos iusserunt, inter quos erant praedicti duo viri christianissimi qui comitati fuerunt a Caesarea cum sanctissimo martyre Christi Anastasio. Cum interficerentur hii dicebant sancto martyre nimio pavore perterriti et non confidentes for-
540   titudinem mentis eius: "Quare disposuisti istam vitam pessimam ut mortem ducas sicut isti? Immo magis acquiesce regi et vive et accipe honorem ab eo et esto in palatio sicut unus ex nobis et ne careas hac luce et dulci vita." At vero victoriosissimus Anastasius aspiciens in caelum et gratias agens Deo qui consumavit cursum eius
545   et adimplevit eius desiderium, respondens ait ad eos: "Ego putabam membratim concidi ab istis propter amorem Christi. Quia vero ista est mors quam minantur michi, gratias ago Deo meo Ihesu Christo quia per modicos dolores participem me faciet gloriae sanctorum eius." Et ita cum multo gaudio atque alacritate suscepit gloriosissi-
550   mam passionem atque simili morte fune suffocatus defunctus est. Cui ergo in hac turpi morte eum similem dixerimus nisi redemptori nostro de quo dixerunt impii iudaei: "morte turpissima condem-

---

526 sic derelinquens] relinquens Va   530 Et *om.* Va   535 illis *om.* Vt 535-536 illis–erant] omnes illos viros sanctissimos gutture laqueato funibus coram sancto martyre suffocari iusserunt. Et quoniam intererant praedicti Va 536 inter–erant] et quam intererant Vc   537-538 cum–Anastasio] sanctissimum martyrem Anastasium Va   539 et *om.* Vc   542 et¹ *om.* Vt   et²] ut Vt   544 in *om.* Va   544-545 cursum–ademplivit *om.* Vt   544 eius] suum Va   545 respondens–eos] dixit eis Va   551 diximus Va

nemus eum"?[11] Postquam autem suffocaverunt eum, absciderunt eius pretiosum caput et tollentes bullam detulerunt ad regem.

555 **39.** Christianus igitur cum esset qui super carcerem praeerat tribunus sicut prius iam dictum est voluit corpus sancti martyris seorsum ponere sed non potuit quia res innotuit quaestionariis. Cognoscentes vero filii Iesdim finem sancti martyris quia et pueri eorum simul secuti fuerant beatum Anastasium quando ducebatur
560 ad mortem ut viderent exitum rei, dederunt clam quaestionariis magnam pecuniam et iusserunt separatim reponi corpus sanctum. At sequenti nocte accipiens secum frater qui eum secutus fuerat de monasterio sanctos viros pueros filiorum Iesdim et quosdam monachos qui ibidem erant ut tollerent corpus sancti martyris invene-
565 runt canes edentes corpora aliorum interfectorum, corpus vero martyris separatim iacens intactum. Pretiosa enim est in conspectu Domini mors sanctorum eius[12] et custodit Dominus animas sanctorum atque ossa eorum, unum ex eis non contereter.[13] Accipiens igitur corpus martyris et involvens linteaminibus pretiosis quae de-
570 derant filii Iesdim deferens sepelivit in monasterium sancti martyris Sergii miliario uno distans a praefato castro.

40. Finitum est autem certamen et cursus et in Christo confessio victoriosissimi martyris Anastasii vicesima et secunda die mensis Ianuarii tempore piissimi Heraclii et quinto decimo anno Constan-
575 tini eius filii.

41. Alia autem die post transitum sancti martyris Anastasii duo quidam in custodia positi confabulabantur ad invicem dicens unus alteri: "Scis quia venerunt canes et sederunt iuxta corpus illius monachi et non contingebant sed custodiebant illud?" Alter vero ait:

---

566 iacens intactum] iacebat in loco Va   conspectum Vc Vt   567 animas] animam Vc Vt   568 eorum] vel *add.* Va   569 corpus] sancti *add.* Vc Vt 570 filiis Vc Vt   sepelivit] *om.* Vt   monasterio Va   574 tempore] imperante Vc Vt   576 autem *om.* Va   579 non *om.* Vt

11. Sap 2.20.
12. Ps 115.15.
13. Cf. Ps 34.21-23.

580 "Et ego quando supplevi vigiliam meam et ambulabam in domum meam vidi stellam lucidam super pavimentum et pergens ut viderem quid esset stellam non vidi sed repperi corpus monachi illius ibidem iacens."

42. Haec quae a custodibus dicebantur intelligentes quidam chris-
585 tiani captivi qui erant in carcere inclusi dum novissent aliquid de locutione persica ipsi nobis retulerunt. Absoluti enim a vinculis et venientes in sanctam civitatem haec diffamabant ubique. Sed et alii de inclusis adiungentes dicebant quia: "Dum esset beatus Anastasius nobiscum in carcere sic nobis fassus est dicens: 'Ut sciatis fratres
590 quia pro Dei gratiam ego quidem crastino die finior et transeo de hoc saeculo. Post paucos dies vos relaxabimini. Iniquus autem et malignus rex interficietur et Domino prosperante ambulabitis in sanctam civitatem. Ite ad mansionem quae dicitur abbatis Anastasii.'" Viri itaque illi qui audierunt haec ex ore viri sancti, rerum
595 exitus cognoscentes Dominum glorificaverunt qui beatificat speran-
tes in se. Mandatum quoque sancti martyris impleverunt et quae propriis viderunt oculis et cognoverunt diligenter nobis innotuerunt.

43. Praedictus autem frater monasterii qui ei obsecumdabat sepeliens corpus sancti martyris et cum omni diligentia reponens in prae-
600 fato monasterio sancti Sergii mansit ibidem pertractans qualiter sine periculo remearet ad abbatem et monasterium suum. Et post dies decem prima die mensis Februarii pervenit in easdem partes christianissimus et piissimus Heraclius imperator cum exercitu. Quos cum vidisset frater gavisus est valde et ipsi diligentius inqui-
605 sierunt eum quid ibi faceret. Ille autem notificavit eis omnia. At illi glorificaverunt Deum et fratri quidem dixerunt: "Surge et veni nobis-
cum et salva animam tuam." Qui erat apud eos in multo honore cum esset in Persida et cum eis reversus est per Armeniorum regionem.

44. Post anniversarium vero reversus ad proprium monasterium
610 deferens secum et colobium sancti martyris Anastasii intimavit diligenter praeposito et fratribus minutius quae circa martyrem accide-

---

581-582 ut viderem] videre Vc Vt   583 monachi *om.* Vt   584 ibidem *om.*
Vc Vt   587 et *om.* Va   590 crastinum Vt   604 cum] dum Va   606
quidem *om.* Va   et *om.* Va   608 esset in *om.* Vt   611 quae] qui Vt

rant et de eius glorioso fine atque de sui itineris labore pariterque glorificaverunt Deum qui salvat sperantes in se. Factum est autem primum signum per colobium beati martyris Anastasii. Erat qui-
615 dam iuvenis in monasterio qui nequiter vexabatur a spiritu immun-do quem accipiens praepositus colobio sancti martyris Anastasii induit. Qui protinus salvatus est per Domini gratiam et interven-tum beati martyris Anastasii ad laudem et gloriam omnipotentis Dei et domini nostri Ihesu Christi qui glorificatur in sanctis suis.
620 Cui est honor et gloria in saecula saeculorum. Amen.

612 pariterque] et pariter Va   613 in] de Va   618 beati–Anastasii *om.* Va
618-619 ad–suis *om.* Va

8

THE REVISION
BHL 411d

About This Edition

My edition is based on the two manuscript witnesses to this version, discussed in Chapter VII and in the "Descriptive List." The text preserved in B is more corrupt than in A.[1] Could B have been copied from A? As there is no positive evidence in favor of this view and slight evidence against it,[2] it seems more reasonable to conclude that A and B have a parallel rather than a direct relationship.[3] I have divided the text into chapters, indicating as well the corresponding divisions in the Greek text. As usual, I have standardized the spelling, except for proper nouns, and for consistent mispellings (e.g. *praetiosus*).

CONSPECTUS SIGLORUM

A   Monte Cassino, Archivio della Badia 141, fols. 329-335

B   Benevento, Biblioteca capitolare 7, fols. 77ra-81vb

---

1. B's mistakes—e.g. the confusion of "s" for an "r" in *Persarum* (l. 43), and of "r" for an "f" in *effatis* rather than *erratis* (l. 100)—suggests a Beneventan exemplar.

2. I.e. the fact that B does not repeat the reading *Bethsaltes* (l. 161) nor *mundamini* (for *minamini* [l. 169]).

3. This view is also supported by the study of the transmission of two other texts contained in these two codices: the Latin translation of the *Martyrium antiochenum* and Ignatius's letters to the Romans descend from the same exemplar (Mallet and Thibaut, *Les manuscripts en écriture bénéventaine de la Bibliothèque capitulaire de Bénévent*, p. 278).

PASSIO SANCTI ANASTASII MARTYRIS

1. [Flusin 6-7] Beatus Anastasius natione persa, arte magus, nomine primo Magunda, et magi filius, tempore Chosroes Persarum regis et Heraclii christianissimi imperatoris extitisse dinoscitur. Eo
5 igitur tempore, cum lignum salutiferae crucis a nequissimo Chosroe asportatum fuisset in Persidem, fama rei tantae Anastasio per ordinem cognita, Deo faciente qui eum salvum facere disponebat, paulatim de corde eius innatus error abolescere, et rectae fidei veritas in eius coepit pectore pullulare.

10 **2. [Flusin 8-11].** Erat autem illi germanus commilito nomine Saym, quem simul cum militia deserens, mutato habitu abiens Ierapolim, apud quendam christicolam argentarium hospitatus est, a quo perplura christianae fidei dogmata didicit. Inde post dies aliquot Ierusolimam profectus, et ibi salutari unda baptismo rege-
15 neratus, Magunda mutatus in Anastasium est. Atque post octo dies illuminationis suae ferventi nimium desiderio, monasticae etiam professionis habitum est indeptus.

3. [Flusin 12-13]. Factus igitur monachus, tantae protinus oboedientiae, humilitatis seu continentiae, ceterarumque virtutum est fas-
20 tigium assecutus, ut cum esset iunior omnium, omnes in virtutum studiis anteiret. Super haec litterarum scrutator nimium avidus, quotiens victoriales martyrum triumphos apud se relegebat, oborsis affatim lacrimis humectabat, et ex intimis visceribus crebra trahens suspiria, martyrum regem ut se in martyrum sortem per tormento-
25 rum tolerantiam quandoque dignaretur assumere indesinenter orabat. Temptabatur autem saepissime a satana, magicarum artium memoria et nefariis illecebrosisque cogitationibus angebatur. Set tam prece ad Deum assidua quam confessione ad abbatem purissima ad nichilum universa diaboli figmenta ducebat.

30 **4. [Flusin 14-15]** In talibus igitur transacto septennio, quadam nocte dormiente illo videbatur ei in cuiusdam se montis cacumine stare, et virum quendam aureum sibi calicem propinare. Quo ut videbatur ebibito, tanta protinus cordis est alacritate affectus, ac si

---

6 Anastasius *codd.*   7 cognitam B   8-9 veritatis B   14 salutaris *codd.*
17 adeptus B   22 quoties B   28 concessione B

omne fuisset desiderium assecutus. Mox revelata visione abbati, et
35 multis ab eo monitis ac solaciis roboratus, internum tandem pectoris ardorem non sufferens, clam de eodem monasterio exiit profec-
tusque Diospolim est.

5. [Flusin 16-19] Post haec autem cum orationis gratia diversa ea-
rumdem partium oratoria circumiret, tentus a quibusdam satelliti-
40 bus Barzabanae praesidi impiissimo praesentatus est. Quem cum
ritu profanae gentis minime adorasset, torvo illum praeses vultu
contuitus, quis vel unde esset exquirere coepit. Cui beatus Anastasius miti voce respondit: "Ego," inquiens, "persa sum genere, eques
aliquando, arte magus, sed miserante Deo, errore cum omni vani-
45 tate relicto, et christianam fidem et religionis ut vides assumpsi
professionem." Praeses dixit: "Immo istum errorem paenitendo depone, et ad pristinam artem militiamque revertere, et ditabimus te
thesauris et equis atque mancipiis multis." Respondit sanctus: "Absit me aliquando vel Christum Deum et Dominum meum negare,
50 vel vestrae vanissimae participare stultitiae." Et praeses: "Placetne,
inquit, tibi habitus iste turpissimus?" Respondit sanctus: "Habitus
iste mea est gloria." Praeses dixit: "Insaniam pateris." Et sanctus:
"Dum in vestro," inquit, "versarer errore, vere patiebar insaniam;
postquam vero nefarium errorem divina miseratione refutavi, iam
55 insaniam aliquam pati non merui." Praeses dixit: "Non times regem, ne si forte ista cognoverit, iubeat te interfici?" "Et cur ego,"
ait sanctus, "tuum timeam regem, tui videlicet similem hominem?"

6. [Flusin 20-23] Indignatus ad haec Barzabanas iussit eum vinctum catenis in castrum duci et indesinenter vecturis lapidum aliis-
60 que suppliciis fatigari, quae ille omnia velut athleta fortissimus
sustinebat. Iterum autem praeses sibi eum sisti praecipiens, coepit
cum eo agere, ut si quid artis magicae nosceret ostenderet. Quo
prorsus negante et eius monita recusante, iussit eum praeses impius
cum palis diutissime caedi, fecitque illum in castrum rursum redu-
65 ci. Post paucos vero dies iterum iussit eum ante se duci et dixit ei:

36-37 prophetusque B   42 contuitus] est *add. codd. sed eras.* A   43 persa sum]
persarum B   56 iube B   57 timeam *om.* B   59 necturis A nocturis B

"Depone iam, infelix, pertinaciam tuam, et recepta simul militia et arte, offer sacrificia diis nostris, ne male moriaris et hac luce frauderis." Respondens autem Dei famulus dixit: "Quibus, oro, diis me iubes sacrificare? Soli vel lunae, igni vel aquis vel similibus ceteris?
70 Sed non permittat michi aliquando Deus omnipotens vestris meas portentis inclinare cervices. Quin magis, iuxta quod imprecatur propheta: Similes illis fiant qui faciunt ea, et omnes qui confidunt in eis." (*Ps 113.16 [iuxta LXX]*) His et huiuscemodi sermonibus Dei famulus adversarios confundebat. Et trina coronatus confessione,
75 pro Christi nomine vinctus iterum ad castrum reducitur.

7. [Flusin 27-28] Tandem Barzabanas, Dei martyris expertus constantiam, Chrosroe de eo litteras destinavit. Quem cum ad se transmitti Chosroes imperasset, mandavit ei praeses dicens: "Ecce rex iussit ut si verbo tantummodo christianum te abneges, protinus te
80 dimittam, et sive eques ut prius, sive monachus esse volueris, facultatem tibi tribuam liberam." Cui sanctus: "Absit, inquit, a me, ut Deum et dominum meum Ihesum Christum aliquando abnegem." Et preses: "Scio equidem quoniam propter gentis tuae socios id palam facere erubescis; et iccirco privatim coram me tantum et aliis
85 duobus nega Christum Deum esse, et liber abscede." Constantissime autem hoc Dei famulo recusante, iterum ei temptator nequissime mandat: "Iam quid facias videris; nam Chosroes vinctum te ad se in Persidem transmitti mandavit." Ad haec sanctus: "Profecto videbo quid faciam; nam si me dimiseris, ego ipse ad regem spontaneus
90 pergam." Cernens igitur Barzabanas Dei martyris insuperabilem prorsus constantiam, iussit eum cum aliis duobus christicolis publica custodia mancipari. Dehinc post quinque dies ad praefatum regem transmisit.

8. [Flusin 31-33] Profectus itaque beatus Anastasius a Caesarea in
95 Persidem, factaque de illo regi subgestione, trudi protinus in custodiam iussus est. Et post aliquot dies mittens ad eum idem rex unum de principibus, fecit causam illius diligenter exquiri. Interrogatus igitur ab eo quis vel unde esset, vel cur deorum contempta religione christianus fieri voluisset, per interpretem ita respondit:

67 affer B   69 ceteris] terris B   87 Iam] Nam B   92 prephatum B

100 "Heu miseri, quid erratis, ac pro Deo rerum omnium creatore por-
tenta quaedam turpia et vana numina colitis? Eram plane aliquando
vestri in hac stultitia similis, sed agnita vera luce quae Deus est,
ipsum semper colo et veneror, qui fecit caelum et terram et mare,
et omnia quae sunt in eis." Ad haec princeps: "Nescis, inquit, quae
105 loqueris, miser. Nonne etenim illum, quem vos christiani Deum
asseritis Iudaei crucifixerunt?" Respondit sanctus: "Crucifixum quidem a Iudaeis Christum dominum nostrum nec vos mentimini, nec
nos utique < dissentimur >. Verumtamen ipse est creator omnium
visibilium et invisibilium, qui de sinu benedicti et coaeterni patris
110 a summis caelorum est dignatus descendere, carnemque humilitatis
nostrae ex intemeratae virginis utero sumere, ad postremum vero
pro redemptione generis humani crucem mortemque suscipere, ut
mundum universum ab errore satanae, qui a vobis colitur, liberaret." Dicit ei princeps: "Quid multis sermonum ambagibus niteris?
115 Ecce tibi rex noster et dignitates maximas et dona multiplicia re-
promittit, siquidem paratus fueris et christianorum errores abicere,
et ad deorum cultum redire." Respondit sanctus: "Ego certissime
neque Christum Deum meum aliquando negabo, neque ad daemonum cultum aliquando repedabo, neque dona vestra et dignitates
120 quantumvis sint magna recipio, sed ac si lutum quod pedibus calca-
tur despicio. Facite quod facere vultis; ex me enim nichil aliud aliquando audietis."

9. [Flusin 34] Tunc abiens princeps retulit haec omnia regi. Rex
vero his cognitis, iussit eum ab eodem principe sequenti die puniri.
125 Princeps ergo eiectum martyrem Christi de carcere, minis terrere
terribilibus coepit. Sed nec terroribus frangere, nec rationibus eum
praevalens superare, iratus vectibus eum caedi more persico iussit.
"Quandoquidem," inquit, "donis et honoribus adquiescere noluisti,
iam cognoscito te singulis diebus quamdiu supervixeris huiusce-
130 modo tormento esse multandum." Sanctus Dei respondit: "Iam tibi
dixi: fac quod facturus es; ex me enim nichil quam dixi superius
es auditurus."

---

100 effatis B   106 asseritis B   108 differtemur (?) A confitemur B
111 ad *om*. B   112 suscipere] dignatus est *add*. B   130 tormenta B   Dei
om. B   131 fac quod *om*. B

10. [Flusin 35, 37] Tunc impius princeps iterum iussit eum supinari atque eius tibias super posito ligno a duobus viris utrimque constringi. Martyr autem fortissimus tantos dolores patientissime sufferens, Deo omnipotenti gratias indesinentes referebat. Videns igitur princeps se cum tormentis suis simul ac blanditiis superatum, tandem eum in carcerem retrudi praecepit, et iterum de eo regi suggessit. Item vero post dies paucos remittens idem princeps ad carcerem, utrum suis monitis consentiret an in priori pertinacia permaneret exquirit. Athleta autem Dei commoto capite, "Semel," inquit, "et bis ac saepius vobis iam dixi nequaquam me aliquando facturum quod dicitis; quid est quod iterum et iterum eadem replicatis? Pro certo non sum facturus quod dicitis, facite quae facturi estis." Rursum nequissimus princeps vinctum ut antea palis eum caedi atrociter imperavit, et retrudens in carcerem recessit. Post aliquantos iterum dies regressus ad carcerem, tum benesuadis ut pridem sermonibus, tum pecuniae dignitatumque pollicitationibus, tum terribilibus minis, tum amaris tormentis, sanctum Dei martyrem in christiani nominis abnegationem provocare instantius nitebatur. Sed cum nullo unquam modo Christi martyris flectere constantiam posset, similiter ut superius fecit eum infestissime caedi, ac deinde resolutum una manu suspendi, subligato eius pedi saxo ingenti et ita pendulum derelinqui. Quod cum per duas horas magnanimiter sustinuisset, fecit eum deponi et regi iterum omnia intimari.

13. [Flusin 38] Quindecim post ista diebus exactis, idem rex principem praefatum ad Dei famuli peremptionem direxit, et ut ceteros quoque christicolas simul convinctos una cum illo necaret, ira dictante mandavit. Veniens ergo princeps ad carcerem, beatum Anastasium et septuaginta fere alios christicolas extra villam Bethsalaes educi praecepit, ac iuxta fluvium exponi. Dehinc omnes singulatim spectante Christi martyre restibus suffocari, dicendo illi per singulos: "Quare vis tam pessima morte perire, et non potius in honore multo et gloria una nobiscum in regis palatio vivere?" Beatus au-

---

144 quae] *corr. ex* quod B   147 bene blandis B   150 Christi B   158 perimitionem B   159 similiter B   160 veniente *codd.*   161 villas B   Bethsaltes A

tem Anastasius veluti iam desiderii sui compos effectus, confortabatur et gratulabatur in Domino dicens: "Pro Christi equidem amore
membratim a vobis concidi optaveram; verum si me is quem vos
minamini obitus manet, gratias Deo meo maximas refero, qui me
170 suorum participem martyrum dignabitur facere tam parvo supplicio." Et his dictis sanctissimus martyr mox a nequissimis satanae
ministris crudeli laqueo suffocatus, temporalem mortem perpetua
vita mutavit, et sic immarcescibili laurea coronatus, de manibus im-
piissimorum hominum in manus translatus est angelorum, cantans
175 et psallens: "Anima nostra sicut passer erepta est de laqueo
venantium. Laqueus contritus est, et nos liberati sumus; adiutorium
nostrum in nomine Domini, qui fecit caelum et terram." (*Ps 123.7-
8 [iuxta LXX]*) Sed nequam homines nequaquam adhuc tanto sce-
lere satiati, postquam suffocaverunt eum, praetiosum caput ipsius
180 a corpore absciderunt et ad crudelissimum regem sicut iussi fuerant
detulerunt.

14. [Flusin 39] Carcerarius itaque cum esset clanculo christianus,
corpus beati martyris ut a ceteris posset discerni semotim ponere
voluit, sed hoc prohibentibus quaestionariis, facere non est permis-
185 sus. Cognito igitur transitu sancti martyris, quidam christicolae,
qui et in carcere posito multotiens ministraverunt, protinus cucurrerunt, et ex manibus ipsius diligenter perspectis eum recognoscentes, maximo argenti pondere a quaestionariis redemerunt. Dehinc
praetiosis involutum linteaminibus, extulerunt atque in monasterio
190 beati Sergi martyris quod uno fere stadio a praedicta villa dirimitur
posuerunt.

15. [Flusin 40] Passus est autem sanctus et praetiosus martyr
Christi Domini Anastasius secunda et vicesima die kalendarum
ianuariarum, anno septimo decimo imperii Heraclii piissimi impe-
195 ratoris. Regnante Domino nostro Ihesu Christo cum Deo patre et
Spiritu sancto ante omnia et per omnia saecula saeculorum. Amen.

169 mundamini A   172-173 perpetua–mutavit] perpetuam vitavit B   189
involutum *om.* B

9

ABBREVIATED VERSIONS

Abbreviation A

I have preserved the spelling of the manuscripts for this late text (e.g. *profocatus* [l. 122]); I have not spelled out the diphthongs, nor corrected proper nouns.

CONSPECTUS CODICUM ET REDACTIONUM

E London, British Library, Egerton 2902, fragment at the beginning of the codex

V Rome, Biblioteca vallicelliana, Tomus VII, fols. 87v–89

411a *BHL* 411a *ut supra editum*

EODEM DIE BEATI ANASTASII. Lectio iiii. Beatus igitur Anastasius de quadam Persidis regione que Rachel nuncupatur extitit oriundus. Ex villa videlicet Rasnuni, proprium quoque nomen eius Magundag fuit; filius vero cuiusdam magi nomine Bau qui et eum a crepundiis
5 magicam disciplina < m > docuisse dinoscitur. Cum itaque Phoca romanis imperante perse sub Chosroe rege Ierosolimam invasissent, et inter ornamenta sacra quae abstulerunt etiam lignum vivifice crucis in Persidem abduxissent, Magundag audito quod de cruce Domini acciderat rimari de christianismo penitus non cessabat, et
10 quo magis auditu preceptabat eo magis de eius corde magicum proludium discedebat. Tandem relicta Perside venit Ieropolim. Et inde Ierosolimam pervenit, ibique ad Heliam Sancte Resurrectionis presbiterum baptizaturum, et mutatione Anastasius nuncupatur qui in latino resurrectionem sonat. Octava vero die post albas depositas
15 in monasterio sancti Anastasii quod quattuor stadiis distat a Ierusolimam monachus factus per septem annos ibidem est conversatus.

4 filius] eius *add.* V 9 christianissimo V 12-13 presbiterum baptizaturum *emendavi ex* presbitero baptizaturus V

In quo spatio universa que iniungebantur fideliter adimplebat et in lege domini meditando fratres ceteros piis operibus anteibat.

Lectio v. Per paucis denique provolutis diebus cum legendo
20 martyrum agonismata martyrium totis visceribus affectaret, Anastasius Dei famulus tali visione meruit consolari. Videbat siquidem se in cuiusdam montis vertice consistere et quendam sibi aureum gemmatumque cratera porrigentem et dicere quatinus accipiens biberet. Quem itaque ut sibi visum est exaurisset ita cor eius exhi-
25 laratum est velut si omne desiderium fuisset consecutus. Quod cum secreto suo exposuisset abbati dicens se in proximo moriturum et ab eo proficiscendi licentiam impetrasset, sacri corporis et sanguinis domini libamine premunitus clanculum de eodem monasterio abscessit. Et nichil secum devehens excepto indumento Diospolim
30 abiit. Et exinde in monte Garizim et in reliqua sanctorum qui ibi interiacent venerabilium loca oraturus advenit. Hinc quoque divina productrice gratia Palestinam Cesaream <ut> devenisset contigit et ibi in ecclesia sancte Dei genitricis semper virginis Marie duos dies permansit. Cum igitur iter ageret beatus Anastasius, videntes
35 eum quidam milites ad invicem susurrabant. Quibus ait: "Quid garrientes strepitis? Ego quidem explorator non sum, sed Ihesu Christi sum servus et ut estis vos modo miles fui." Insurgentes itaque tenuerunt eum et Marzabane Persidi tradiderunt.

Lectio vi. Interea Anastasius Ihesu Christi famulus impio Marzaba-
40 ne representatur. Sed cum eum de more prophanissime gentis flexis poplitibus minime adorasset, Marzabanas torvo vultu diutissime eum intuitus dixit: "Unde vel quis es?" Ille ad hec: "Ego," inquit, "veraciter christianus sum. Si autem unde sim scire cupis, persa sum genere. Eques vero et magus aliquando, sed relictis tenebris
45 veni ad lucem." Ad hec Marzabanas: "Istum," inquit, "errorem desere, et ad pristinum cultum festinus revertere, et magnis muneribus donaberis." Beatus Anastasius respondit: "Non permittat mihi Dominus meus Christum negare." Stomachatus igitur Marzabanas eum catenis duci in castrum precepit ut sine interstitione lapides
50 vectaret. Aliis quoque intolerabilibus angustiis premebatur.

20 martyrium V   39 viiii V

Quidam enim eiusdem cuius et ipse regionis erat accedentes ei talia dicebant: "Nemo nostre regionis aliquando factus est christianus. Ecce tantum nobis intulisti ridiculum." Ipse vero contra iniuriis repellebat. Illi autem infatuati cotidie vestimenta eius scindentes et
55 barbam funditus evellentes sine aliquo intervallo eum percutiebant. Insuper saxa que quattuor illorum devehebant illi autem soli impendebant. Unum solum convictum ad tribulationum congeriem habebat cum quo unam < in > collo alteram vero in pede catena < m > gestabat. Hec et multa atrociora illis inferentibus for-
60 tissimus athleta animo propter Christum gaudenter sufferebat.

Lectio vii. Iussit igitur Marzabanas beatum Anastasium sibi presentari et dixit ei: "Set ut asseris magicam artem nosti michi aliquid ea recitato ut agnoscam si vera sunt que asseris." Beatus Anastasius respondit: "Nequaquam permittat Deus aliquid me ulterius profer-
65 re." Dixit ei Marzabanas: "Quid ergo? in hiis permanebis? Scribam etenim imperatori de te." Sanctus Anastasius respondit: "Iam scripsisti et rescripta accepisti; fac quod vis. Ego enim me fateor christianus." Marzabanas iussit eum palis cedi. Sed cum ministri vellent eum ligare dixit: "Sinite me, non enim vinculis indigeo. Verumta-
70 men exuite me hoc habitum ut non inhonoretur et sic me nudum cedite." Sedens itaque se eis flagellandum prebuit quasi esset ligatus. Ministri autem cum palis eum sicut sibi iussum fuerat cedunt. Iterum interrogat eum Marzabanas iterum si suis dictis preberet assensum et inveniens eum invincibilem iussit eum secundo
75 in castrum removeri. Denique tertio presentatus interrogatur, auditur et in carcere inclusus divina visitatione consolatur. Perpaucis autem provolutis diebus imperatoris preceptum Marzabanas recepit et mittens beato Anastasio ubi erat in carcere, ait illi: "Hoc mandavit imperator ut solo verbo neges te christianum et dimitteris." At
80 ille respondit: "Absit ut ego aliquando negem Ihesum Christum." Videns itaque Marzabanas illum immotum ad omnem experimentum post quinque dies cum duobus aliis christicolis eum ad imperatorem direxit.

Lectio viii. Ingressus igitur beatus Anastasius Persidem, statim mit-
85 titur in carcerem. Mittens igitur imperator unum ex principibus

61 iussit *add. in marg.* V   73-74 *hic inc.* E   83 dixerit V

iussit eum diligenter indagari. Sed cum idem princeps nec promissis nec·terroribus illum posset aliquatenus commovere que dixerat et audierat retulit imperatori. Stomachatus igitur imperator sequenti die eundem principem ad puniendum beatum Anastasium destina-
90   vit. Ferocissimus igitur princeps beatissimum Anastasium persico more devictum vectibus cedi precepit. Deinde solutum supinari iussit atque eius tybias subposito ligno duobus fortissimis utrique supersistentibus viris substringi commendavit. Quod genus tormenti ipse gratias agens patienter ferebat. Videns igitur princeps se cum
95   suis blandimentis et penis pariter parvipensum iussit eum in carcerem retrahi donec iterum de eo imperatori suggereret. Paucis deinde interlapsis diebus idem temerarius princeps remittens in carcerem, "Quid dicis," inquid, "obsecundabis iussioni imperatoris?" At ille commoto in eius abhominatione capite respondit: "Semel et bis sepius-
100 que tibi dixi quod sit impossibile a me Christum negari. Quicquid igitur velis maturanter facito." Tunc iussit eum ut prius palis fortiter cederetur. Sed cum eius immotissime mentis coherentissimum christiane fidei stabilimentum prospiceret precepit eum tertio cesum una manu suspendi, ligato ad pedem eius ponderosissimo saxo
105 ac sic demum digrediens pendulum dereliquit. Ipsum denique huius modi supplicio quasi duas horas fortiter sufferentem deponi mandavit ac deinde constantiam eius imperatori notificavit.

Lectio viiii. Post hec prolapsis quindenis ferme diebus imperator eundem principem et alios nonnullos ad interficiendum Dei marty-
110 rem et plurimos alios christianorum captivos transmisit. Qui mandatis obsequentes beatissimum Anastasium cum aliis septuaginta christicolis extra villam Bethsaloes in qua erat carcer extractos iuxta fluvium preceperunt exponi ac deinde omnes singillatim spectante Christi martyre restibus suffocari. Et singulo eorum interempto
115 beato Anastasio dicebant: "Quare vis sicut unus horum male perire et non potius ut vivas imperatori acquiescere?" Quibus beatus Anastasius respondit: "Pro Christi equidem amore a vobis membratim concidi optaveram. Verum si huiusmodi quem et vos mina-

87 queque E   88-93 igitur–commendavit *non legi potest in* E   96 trahi V *cf.* carcerem retrahi donec iterum imperatori 411a   102 cederetur] cedere *corr. ex* cedi *(?)* E   105 sic] si V   110-112 transmisit–extractos *non legi potest in* E

mini obitus commanet, gratias Deo meo inexaustas replico qui me
120 suorum martyrum participem gloriae dignatus est facere tam parvo
supplicio." His dictis gloriosissimus Dei martyr beatus Anastasius
profocatus in flumine immarcescibili bravio coronatus ad veram
eternamque vitam que Christus est meruit pervenire. At postquam
eum suffocaverunt, pretiosissimum caput absciderunt. Quidam mo-
125 nachus de cenobio eius iubente abbate eum usque ad mortem secutus ipsius passionem diligenter descripsit. Reliquie corporis eius
una cum capite primo ad monasterium suum deinde Romam delate
venerantur in monasterio ad Aquas Salvias.

Abbreviation B

This text is based exclusively on its single witness, Rome, Biblioteca nazionale Vittorio Emanuele II, Cod. Sessorianus 4, fols. 25v-
28r, dated to the fourteenth century. I have not standardized or
corrected the spelling (e.g. *in scalore* [l. 104]) and have kept the
awkward grammar (cf. *Deus autem temporibus nostris precibus exigentibus* [ll. 21-22]), but have used capital letters and standardized
the punctuation.

IN NATALE SANCTI ANASTASII. Incipit prologus beati Gregorii papae < *** > beati Anastasii monachi. Lectio i.

Anastasio gratia Dei venerabili abbati Gregorius clericorum infi-
mus perpetuam in Christo salutem. Vestrae benignitatis excellentia
5 nos †pulum† rogavit ut beati Anastasii martirium regulari digestu
componerem. Quod onus bina excusatione repellere volueram. Sed
tandem confisus de divino suffragio et prephati sanctissimi martiris et vestri interventu aggrediar quod rogastis. Ceterum tam vos
quam quoslibet hoc opusculum inspecturos suppliciter exposco ut
10 gloriosissimum Dei martirem Anastasium devote invocent quatinus
id sibi dicatum devote accipiat. Ad eum per quem hoc promeruit
et a quo coronatus est pro nobis intercedat Dominum nostrum
Ihesum Christum cui cum patre et spiritu sancto semper inest gloria in saecula saeculorum. Amen.

124 caput] capud V eius *add.* E   127 capite] patre V

2 *eras.; non legi potest*   11 dictatum *cod.*

15 Lectio ii. Incipit < *** > beati Anastasii martiris.
Beatus itaque Anastasius de quadam regione Persidis quae Razech
nuncupatur extitit oriundus, de villa videlicet Rasnuni; proprium
nomen eius Magundagh primum fuit, filius cuiusdam magi nomine
Bau qui eum < a > crepundiis magicam doctrinam docuisse dignos-
20 citur. Regnante igitur Chosroe in imperiali persarum civitate, hunc
effectum iam iuvenem tironicae professionis contigit affuisse. Deus
autem temporibus nostris precibus exigentibus Ierusalem civitas
sancta capta et destructa est, ac preciosissimum vivifice crucis lignum in Persidem est devectum. Cumque de presentia christiani et
25 miraculis crucis dominice letarentur et concursus fieret populorum,
prephatus Magundagh videns et audiens que fiebant, tamquam granium seminis in terra non sterili germinanda suscipiebat videlicet
quicquid ad Christi †pot† ac pertinere.

Lectio iii. Audiens itaque christianus de Christo tanto plus in divi-
30 num amorem accendebatur et a magico preludio discedebat. Tandem
in eo spiritu divino irruente, ipse Magundagh postpositis sociis et
militari offitio ingressus civitatem Ierapolim apud quendam persem
argentificem christicolam mansit, circuiens cum illo ecclesias et oratoria et se quantum(?) poterat muniens doctrinam fidei christianae,
35 accipiebat gladium salutis quod est verbum Dei. Sed cum prephatus
argentarius timore infidelium ipsum renuerat baptizare, discedens
inde venit Iherosolimam, ibique venerabili Helye presentatus est.
Qui tamquam donum optimum hunc suscipiens sancto Modesto
episcopo ierosolimitano rem serie tenus enarravit; qui episcopus
40 instructum in fide Magundagh baptizavit et competenti sibi nomine Anastasius appellatus est.

Lectio iiii. Octavo igitur die post baptismum prephatus sanctus
Helyas perduxit eum ad sancti Anastasii monasterium a Ierusalem
civitate quattuor ferme stadiorum iter habens. Huius quoque mo-
45 nasterii abbatem Iustinum videlicet Dei gratia et sanctitate refertum
ut eum fraterno aggregare < t > collegio affectuose rogavit. Qui libenter acquiescens sanctum Anastasium sue congregationi attitulavit. Unum quoque de suis discipulis divina scientia imbutum eidem

15 *vacuum reliquit cod.*   28 potest?

instruendo assignavit, qui eum tam grecas litteras quam psalterium
50 perfecte docuit. Sicque beatus Anastasius attonsis capillis, monasti-
co indutus habitu, tam doctrine magistri quam obedientiae prelati,
nec non et fratrum servitio insudabat.

Lectio v. Beatus Anastasius suam resurrectionem pretendit in nomine, quia de infirmitate magica surrexit ad eminentiam vite mo-
55 nastice. Anastasius namque grece latine resurrectionem sonat. Vel
dicitur Anastasius quasi sursum stans. Ipsa enim humilitas que suos
sequaces exaltat in tantum hunc evexit ad altitudinem virtutum
quod divina iuvante gratia diversis offitiis coquine videlicet et orti,
aliorum quoque vilium ministeriorum actu caritatis offitio fungeba-
60 tur. Tante quippe efficacie et servitii erat ut obsequio fratrum et
laboribus manuum agilis insisteret et ceteros fratres in divino offitio et institutis regularibus anteiret. Sacras vero scripturas legentibus sic aures et animum applicabat ut eas corde sedulo intelligeret
et ea que difficiliora erant a magistro suo vel ceteris fratribus intel-
65 ligentibus interrogabat.

Lectio vi. Quando beatus Anastasius victoriosas martyrum passiones sicut fuerat assuetus in propria cella legebat, affluenti ubertate
lacrimarum faciem humectebat suppliciter rogans Dominum Ihesum
Christum ut imitando eos per penas martirii corporales ipsum eum
70 posset cruce sequi. Nichilque aliud libentius legebat quam quod ac-
cendere eum poterat ad amorem martirii. In eodem autem monasterio talia prosequendo septennium fecit. Illo autem in tempore
Anastasius Dei famulus tali visione meruit consolari. Videbatur
beato viro quod in quodam montis cacumine consistens videret
75 quendam aureum gemmatumque < calicem > porrigere ut acciperet
et biberet dic < ere >. Quem calicem accipiens bibit tanta alacritate
cordis est ylaratus ac si omne desiderium fuisse < t > assecutus. O
predulce et plenissimum misterii sompnium. Qui enim in excelso
montis fastigio se stare vidit, postea contemplative vite tutissimum
80 atque sacratissimum cacumen ascendit.

Lectio vii. Consurgens itaque post prefatam visionem dominica die
nocturnum offitium expleturus vir sanctus oratorium cum ceteris
fratribus est ingressus et advocans abbatem flexis genibus in loco

55 resurrectonem *cod.*

secreto cum lacrimis exposcebat ut pro se in proximo iam morituro
85 Dominum exoraret. Ad quem abbas, "Unde frater sic te in proximo moriturus?" Ille vero recitans prefatam visionem comuni morte
seu quomodo libet se consumaturum predicebat. Iturum ei ad martirium celabat se timens ne impediretur. Consolatione ergo ab abbate recepta residuum psalmodie implebat. Et post hec sacrosancti
90 corporis et sanguinis domini tanquam future vie viaticum percipiens ardorem martirii non substinens, de monasterio recessit. Et
nichil nisi habitum secum portans Diospolim civitatem ingrediens,
visitavit loca sancta et sanctorum ibi quiescentium et in monte Garizim corpora. Et post multa sanctorum locorum visitationes Pales-
95 tinam Caesaream ingressus est sanctaque loca visitans, ingrediens
ecclesiam sanctae Eufemie videns postea magos magice operantes
zelo fidei constanter reprehendit. Unde dicti malefici indignati sibi
insidias tetenderunt et eum exploratorem dixerunt.

Lectio viii. Beatus Anastasius intelligens se exploratorem a quibus-
100 dam nominari respondit, "Quid garrientes? Ego minime explorator
sum sed christianus et servus Domini nostri Ihesu Christi." Quod
audientes pagani, irruentes in eum apprehenderunt, et vinctum tradiderunt sellario qui eum precepit in carcere custodiri. Fuit ergo
sanctus Anastasius in scalore carceris per tres dies non manducans
105 neque bibens. Regresso autem preside Barzabana (non enim ibi erat
quando detemptus est sanctus Anastasius), dictus sellarius nuntiavit
sibi quod sanctus esset in carcere. Qui Marzabanas in suum preto-
rium eum deduci precepit. Presentatur ergo famulus Dei prefato
presidi sed cum nollet eum flexis genibus adorare Marzabanas tor-
110 vo vultu eum intuitus dixit: "Unde vel quis es?" Cui sanctus: "Ego
veraciter christianus sum. Si autem unde sim scire cupis, genere
sum persa, equus et magus aliquando sed relictis tenebris veni ad
lucem." Cui preses: "Istum errorem desere et ad pristinum cultum
festinus revertere et tibi caballos et militaria magno benefitio dona-
115 bimus." Cui respondit sanctus Anastasius: "Non permittat me dominus meus Ihesus negare fidem christianam."

Appendix

THE SANCTORAL OF Pl, Rg AND St

The following chart compares the contents of the three oldest, complete manuscript witnesses of *BHL* 408: BAV, Palatinus latinus 846 (= Pl), BAV, Reginensis latinus 516 (= Rg), and Stuttgart, Württembergische Landesbibliothek HB XIV 13 (= St). Its purpose is to illustrate the development of these three passionaries and to support the anteriority of the p-recension (for further discussion, see pp. 377-381). Only Pl covers the entire year; the others were part of two-volume passionaries whose second volumes have not survived. The order of saints are given as they appear in the manuscripts. Saints' names have been standardized to reflect the spelling in the *Bibliotheca Hagiographica Latina*. I have added *BHL* numbers, dates, and cross-references. For further discussion of the manuscripts see pp. 362-364 and Descriptive List.

DATE	Pl	Rg	St
Ian 1	Martina 5588 Pontianus 6891	Martina 5588	Martina 5588 Concordius 1906
Ian 13		[see Ian 22]	Iulianus & Basilissa 4532
Ian 14	Felix 2885	Felix 2885	Felix 2885 Pontianus 6891
Ian 16	Marcellus 5235	Marcellus 5234 Sebastianus 7543	Marcellus 5235 Sebastianus 7543
Ian 19		Marius & soc. 5543	Marius & soc. 5543
Ian 21		Agnes 156	Agnes 156
Ian 22	Anastasius 408	Anastastius 408 Vincentius 8631 Iulianus & Basilissa 4532	Anastasius 408 Vincentius 8628, 8631 Blasius 1370
Feb 5		Agatha 133	Agatha 133
Feb 7		Iuliana 4523	Iuliana 4523

DATE	Pl	Rg	St
Feb 3	Blasius 1371a	Blasius 1370	[*see* Ian 22]
Feb 14		Valentinus 8460	Valentinus 8460 Thecla 8024
Mar 9	XL 7538	XL 7538	XL 7538 Gregorius papa 3639
Apr 23		Georgius & soc. 3379	Iohannes Penar. 4420
Mar 19	Iohannes Penar. 4420		Eleutherius & Anthia 2451
Apr 25		Marcus ev. 5276	Marcus ev. 5276
Apr 28	Torpes 8307	Vitalis, Gerva-sius, Protasus 3514	Vitalis, Gervasius, Protasus 3514 Torpes 8307
Mai 1		Iacobus ap. 4093 Philippus ap. 6814	Iacobus ap. 4093 Philippus ap. 6814
Mai 3	Alexander papa 266	Alexander papa 266	Alexander papa 266
Mai 6		Mattheus ap. 5690	Mattheus ap. 5690
Mai 10	Gordianus 3612	Gordianus 3612	Gordianus 13612
Mai 12	Nereus & Achilleus 6058-6066	Pancratius 6421 Nereus & Achil-leus 6058-6066, 1515	Pancratius 6421 Nereus & Achilleus 6058, 6060-61, 6063/64, 6066 Caesarius 1515
Mai 14		Bonifatius 1413	
Mai 19	Pudentiana 6991	Pudentiana 6991	Pudentiana 6991
Mai 20	Conon m. Iconii 1912	Marcellinus & Petrus 5231	Conon m. Iconii 1912
Iun 2	Bonifatius 1413	Erasmus 2578 [*see* Mai 14]	Marcellinus & Petrus 5231 Erasmus 2578 Bonifatius 1413
Iun 8	Primus & Felicianus 6922	Primus & Felicia-nus 6922	Primus & Felicianus 6922

DATE	Pl	Rg	St
Iun 9	Getulius 3524		Getulius 3524
Iun 12	Basilides & soc. 1019	Basilides & soc. 1019	Basilides & soc. 1019
Iun 13		Bartholomaeus ap. 1002	Bartholomaeus ap. 1002
Iun 15	Vitus & soc. 8712	Vitus & soc. 8712	Vitus & soc. 8712
Iun 22		Iacobus ap. 4057	Iacobus ap. 4057
Iun 26	Iohannes & Paulus 3236, 3238	Iohannes & Paulus 3236, 3238	Gallicanus, Iohannes & Paulus 3236, 3238
Iun 27	Symphorosa 7971		
Iun 29		Petrus & Paulus app. 6657	Symphorosa 7971 Petrus & Paulus app. 6657

Iul 2	Processus & Martianus 6947
Iul 10	Rufina & Secunda 7359; Felicitas 2853
Iul 21	Praxedis 6920
Iul 24	Victorinus 7659
Iul 29	Simplicius & soc. 7790; Felix papa 2857; Seraphia 7586
Aug 7	Donatus ep. (m. Aretii) 2289
Apr 30	Donatus ep. Epiro 2304
Aug 11	Susanna 7937
Aug 12	Euplus 2729
Aug 14	Eusebius 2740
Aug 18	Agapetus 125
Sep 9	Iacynthus 4053
Sep 14	Cyprianus & Iustina 2047, 2050
Sep 16	Lucia & Geminianus
Oct 14	Calixtus 1523
Nov 8	Simpronianus & soc. 1837
Nov 9	Theodorus 8077
Nov 11	Mennas 5921
Nov 23	Clemens [miracula] 1855; Aliud miraculum 1857
Dec 4	Barbara m. 913
Dec 6	Nicolas 6119
Dec 7	Savinus 7451?

Descriptive List of Manuscripts

This Descriptive List is arranged according to city, library, and shelf number, followed by the date and place of origin of the manuscript, if known. I report the dating given to the manuscripts according to the bibliography as cited; this precluded the imposition of a uniform system. The meaning of the abbreviations, however, is clear: ex. = exeunte; inc. = incipiente; the superscript numbers refer to the quarter century. The list also indicates which of the various texts on Anastasius each manuscript contains, and the siglum, in square brackets, if the manuscript was used in any of the editions.

ADMONT
Stiftsbibliothek 25
s. XIII; Admont
fols. 94-96v = *BHL* 410   [D]
BIBLIOGRAPHY: Poncelet, "De *Magno legendario austriaco*," pp. 31-32.
Part of Admont's exemplar of the MLA, this volume contains saints' Lives for January-March.

BENEVENTO
Biblioteca capitolare 7[1]
s. XII[1]; Benevento
fols. 77-81v = *BHL* 411d   [B]
BIBLIOGRAPHY: Mallet and Thibaut, *Manuscrits en écriture bénéventaine* I, 162-168; Poncelet, "Catalogus codicum ... cathedralis beneventanae," pp. 355-357; Lowe and Brown, *Beneventan Script* II, 18.
This volume was part of the hagiographic collection of the Cathedral of Benevento arranged *per circulum anni*.[2] It covers the period from 17 January to 16 February; its texts were regularly marked for reading by the original

---

1. This is the number assigned it in the Mallet and Thibaut catalogue; its older number, based on the shelving in the library building destroyed in 1944, is III 7; in Poncelet, it is numbered V.

2. An entire group of nine codices that can be connected to the cathedral is studied in Mallet and Thibaut, *Manuscrits*, pp. 35-53. The series—incomplete for the period from May 25 to July 28—of which Codex 7 is part consists today of five surviving volumes. See esp. p. 42.

scribe. This book has been called a "lectionaire hagiographique."³ More precisely, however, this collection is an example of the fusion of the homiliary and legendary, for it contains not only hagiographic texts but also sermons and Gospel readings. This type of combination book is much rarer than its sources, but there are other surviving examples from south-central Italy.⁴

BERGAMO
Biblioteca Mons. Radini Tedeschi 227 (olim 4)
s. XI; Milan province?
fols. 38v-46 = *BHL* 408(s)
BIBLIOGRAPHY: Franchi de Cavalieri, "Il Codice 4 di S. Alessandro in Colonna."
A large legendary whose sanctoral suggests that it originated in the province of Milan. The *Passio S. Anastasii* has been extensively corrected.

BERN
Burgerbibliothek 24
s. XI (post-1054); Toul (St. Epure?)
fols. 86-92v = *BHL* 411a   [B]
BIBLIOGRAPHY: Hagen, *Catalogus Codicum Bernensium*, pp. 14-18.
Although dated in the Hagen catalogue "s.XIin." this manuscript must have been copied at the earliest in the second half of the twelfth century since it contains several pieces by Widricus of Toul, abbot of St. Epure,⁵ and the Life and Miracles of Leo IX (1049-1054), former bishop of Toul, by his contemporary Humbert (or Wimbertus), archdeacon of Toul (*BHL* 4818). This codex contains sixty-three hagiographic pieces arranged *per circulum anni* from 8 December through June, and must therefore be only half of a two-volume legendary. It was certainly produced in the region of Toul (Alsace), perhaps in the Abbey of St. Epure itself, given its highly localized sanctoral.

---

3. Mallet and Thibaut, *Manuscrits*, p. 162. Following Dolbeau, "Notes sur l'organization interne des légendiers latins," I prefer to reserve the term "hagiographic lectionary" for collections of extracts to be read at the Office, not for collections of complete, though abbreviated, texts.

4. For a discussion of this type of book, see Dolbeau, "Notes sur l'organisation," p. 14, and idem, "Les manuscrits hagiographiques de Gubbio," pp. 359-360 for an example from Gubbio.

5. Including three texts on S. Gerardus, bishop of Toul (†994), and a letter to Bruno, bishop of Toul and later Pope Leo IX.

BOLOGNA
Biblioteca universitaria 2205 (olim 729 et aula III, B, 9)
s. XI; Bologna region?
fols. 42v-46v = *BHL* 408(s)
BIBLIOGRAPHY: Poncelet, "Catalogus codicum ... universitatis bononiensis,"
pp. 354-357.
This book is a collection of forty-one hagiographical fragments bound together. No significant indications about its origin can be garnered from its
fragmentary sanctoral. The *Passio S. Anastasii* is one of several texts to come
from the same legendary. Given its inclusion in this collection, and the diffusion of this redaction, it seems most likely that its source legendary was also
written in this region.

BRUSSELS
Bibliothèque des bollandistes 14
s. IX-X; Bavaria or German Switzerland
fols. ? = *olim BHL* 408
BIBLIOGRAPHY: Moretus, "Catalogus ... Bibliothecae bollandianae," pp. 432-
439; Coens, "La Passion de S. Sauve," pp. 138-139; Dolbeau, "Le passionaire
de Fulda," pp. 526-529.
This is a manuscript whose initial pages, now missing, almost certainly contained the *Passio S. Anastasii*. It is part of a group of hagiographic collections
put together before the year 1000, and clearly related by their contents as
well as origin. See further, "The Early Diffusion of *BHL* 408," pp. 377-381.

Bibliothèque royale de Belgique 207-8
s. XII (Poncelet); XIII (Levison; Colgrave); Trier region
fols. 75v-79v = *BHL* 409
BIBLIOGRAPHY: Poncelet, *Catalogus ... regiae bruxellensis*, I, 135-157; van den
Gheyn, *Catalogue des manuscrits de la Bibliothèque royale de Belgique* V, 60-65
(no. 3132); Colgrave, *Two Lives*, pp. 18-19; Levison, "Conspectus codicum
hagiographicorum," pp. 537, 563.
This book constitutes the first volume of a three-volume legendary (the
others are 98-100, 206), related most closely to the Arnstein compendium
(London, British Library, Harley 2800).[6] Like Harley, 207-8 also covers
January to 8 June. It contains 125 items, only a few of which are missing

6. Colgrave considers the Harley and Brussels collections "two copies of a
great legendary" (*Two Lives*, p. 18). Levison calls it a copy of a legendary of
which Harley is also a copy, but whose origin is unknown ("Conspectus," pp.
537, 543).

from the Harley volume, and it omits only a few of the texts contained in Harley.

CAMBRAI
Bibliothèque publique 816 (721)
s. XV; Cambrai
fols. 78-85 = *BHL* 408(p)
BIBLIOGRAPHY: *Catalogue général des manuscrits des bibliothèques publiques de France* XVII, 301-305; Levison, "Conspectus," p. 570; Colgrave, *Two Lives*, pp. 33-34.
This legendary has the mark of the Benedictine Abbey of the Holy Sepulchre of Cambrai, where it was probably compiled during the fifteenth century.

CAPE TOWN
The South African Public Library, Grey Collection, Ms 48 b 4
s. XII inc.; S. Cecilia (Rome)
fols. 46-47v = *BHL* 411a   [Q]
fols. ? = *olim BHL* 412
BIBLIOGRAPHY: *Medieval and Renaissance Manuscripts in the Grey Collection*, p. 16; Casson, "The Manuscripts of the Grey Collection," p. 150; Dolbeau, "Le légendier de Sainte-Cécile," p. 302.
This is one half (9 January-24 August)[7] of the two-volume legendary of S. Cecilia in Rome. Only the first part of the *Passio S. Anastasii* (up to the middle of cap. 19) is preserved here, for a number of following pages are missing. They must have contained the rest of the *Passio* and the *Miraculum*, as well as the first part of the *Vita* of S. Paula Romana. A copy of this legendary was made in 1601 and is preserved today as BAV, Vat. lat. 6075 (=X; see below). Already by that time, however, these pages were missing. There are a few corrections to the text all made in a hand other than the scribe's, as well as a few glosses in the margin by yet a later hand; both sets of changes were followed by the copyist of Vat. lat. 6075.[8]

---

7. The other volume is also found today in the Grey Collection, MS 48 b 5. The Grey Collection catalogue (p. 16, as above) indicates that the volume covering the second part of the year is the first half of the legendary, but without explanation. I have not examined the codex itself, but have only photographs of the pages containing the Passion of Anastasius.

8. The glosses seem to be explicatory. Hence, e.g. on fol. 46v the note *.i. vestigia* refers to *orbitam*; on fol. 47r the note *intervallo* refers to *inter capedine*.

CHARTRES
Bibliothèque municipale 506 (144)
s. X; Dreux?
fols. 49v-56v = *olim BHL* 408(r)
BIBLIOGRAPHY: Philippart, *Légendiers,* pp. 15, 102 n. 186; de Smedt, "Catalogus codicum ... civitatis carnotensis," pp. 125-36; Dolbeau, "Le passionaire de Fulda," pp. 527-529.
This manuscript was burned in 1944; only a few pages had been photographed, but we have a list of the contents from de Smedt's catalogue. It is part of the group of legendaries copied before 1000 in Bavaria or German Switzerland, all of which included *BHL* 408. There seems little doubt that this was a witness to the r-recension since de Smedt notes an omission in the text of the *Passio S. Anastasii* found also in BAV, Reginensis latinus 516.[9]

COLMAR
Bibliothèque de la Ville 356 (121)
s. XII; Gregorienmünster (Münster, in Alsace)
fols. 76v-81v = *BHL* 410   [G]
BIBLIOGRAPHY: Philippart, *Légendiers,* p. 15.
The text of the *Passio Anastasii* was most likely copied from Vienna 357.

EINSIEDELN
Stiftbibliothek 249 (381)
s. XII; Einsiedeln
fols. 404-424 = *BHL* 410   [N]
BIBLIOGRAPHY: Meier, *Catalogus ... Einsidlensis ...* I, 212-215
A legendary encompassing texts arranged from 31 December (S. Silvester) to 5 February (S. Agatha). The vast majority of the saints included here are early and universal martyrs. Its most particular text is the *Passio S. Meginradi Heremitae* (pp. 377-387), suggesting that this book—which must be but one volume of a collection—was composed for Einsiedeln itself.[10] Despite

---

9. De Smedt (p. 126) notes: "Om. inde a nu. 31 med. (*qui comitabatur...*) ad num. 33 extr. (*suffocari universos jusserunt*)." Furthermore, the sanctoral for the overlapping period in the Carnotensis and Reginensis is nearly identical, with the latter omitting only Iulianus, and Basilissa and Caesarius found in the former.

10. Meinrad was a monk and priest at Reichanau who in 829 moved to Einsiedeln to be a hermit. In 861 two visitors looking for treasures battered him to death. The body of Meinrad was enshrined at Reichenau. In the tenth century, Einsiedeln was refounded as a Benedictine monastery, and such it has remained (Cottineau, *Répertoire* I, cols. 1034-39). There are two other noteworthy characteristics in the sanctoral, namely, the great attention paid

Meier's remarks ("Codex est valde similis Bruxellensi 207-208," p. 212), there are no striking similarities in the contents of these books, except that they both contain many standard passions. But if the rarer texts are considered, then it is significant that Brussells 207-208 does not contain the Passion of Meinrad, for example, nor does Einsiedeln 249 contain the Life of Cuthbert. The *Passio S. Anastasii* as contained in this codex has been significantly contaminated by *BHL* 408.

FIESOLE
Archivio capitolare XXII 1
s. XII[1]; Fiesole
pp. 235-241 = *BHL* 412
BIBLIOGRAPHY: Verrando, "I due leggendari di Fiesole."
This is a complete legendary *per circulum anni* from 30 November (Andreas Apostolus) to 27 November. Its version of the Roman Miracle was copied most likely from Florence, Biblioteca medicea laurenziana, Conventi Soppressi 182.

FLORENCE
Biblioteca medicea laurenziana, Conventi soppressi 182
s. X ex.; Florence
fols. 160-165 = *BHL* 412   [Y]
BIBLIOGRAPHY: Verrando, "I due leggendari di Fiesole," p. 459,
Described as "one of the oldest Florentine hagiographic codices" by Verrando, this manuscript includes fourteen texts, mostly ancient passions, with the notable exception of Zeno of Verona. Its origin in Florence's Benedictine Badia (Monastero di S. Maria) seems assured. It is closely related in its contents to Fiesole's legendary.

Biblioteca medicea laurenziana Aediles 135
s. XI; southeast Tuscany
fols. 486-490 = *BHL* 412   [D]
BIBLIOGRAPHY: Bandinius, *Bibliotheca leopoldina* ... I, 299-310; Garrison, *Studies* I, 38 and n. 3; IV, 175.
This legendary is part of what Garrison calls a "group of carelessly written Passionaries and Lectionaries of the later 11th century" from southeast Tuscany, perhaps from S. Michele a Martiri, since it contains the rare life of S. Flavianus.

to St. Hilary of Poitiers (several texts are included, pp. 183-222) and the Life of Sulpitius, the seventh-century bishop of Bourges (pp. 262-272).

Biblioteca medicea laurenziana Monte Amiata 2
s. XI; Monte Amiata
fols. 130v-136v = *BHL* 408(s)
BIBLIOGRAPHY: Bandinius, *Bibliotheca leopoldina* ... I, 618-637; Garrison, *Studies in the History of Mediaeval Italian Painting* I, 38 and n. 3.

Biblioteca medicea laurenziana Plutei XX, Codex I
s. XI-XII; Florence
pp. 83v-84v = *BHL* 412   [U]
BIBLIOGRAPHY: Bandinius, *Catalogus ... Bibliothecae mediceae laurentianae* I, 583-596; Garrison, *Studies* I, 27 and III, 292.
A legendary originating from Florence, covering 30 November to the end of January. This witness does not include the last chapter of the Roman Miracle.

Biblioteca medicea laurenziana Strozzi I
s. XIII
fols. 135v-138v = *BHL* 408, r₁ revision
BIBLIOGRAPHY: Bandinius, *Bibliotheca leopoldina* ... II, 269.

Biblioteca nazionale centrale, Fondo nazionale II I 412
s. XI-XII; Arezzo?
fols. 35-39v = *BHL* 408(s)
fols. 39v-41v = *BHL* 412   [F]
BIBLIOGRAPHY: Berg, *Studies in Tuscan Twelfth-Century Illumination*, passim; Garrison, *Studies* III, 281-284.
A giant passionary originating in southern Tuscany, perhaps Arezzo.

HEILIGENCREUZ
Stiftsbibliothek 11
s. XII⁴; Heiligencreuz
fols. 69v-71 = *BHL* 410   [S]
BIBLIOGRAPHY: Poncelet, "De *Magno legendario austriaco*," pp. 27-28.
This codex, containing saints' lives for January-March, is part of the exemplar of the MLA copied at the Cistercian abbey of Heiligencreuz after 1181.

IVREA
Biblioteca capitolare 112 (catal. 55)
s. XI
fols. XLIXv-L = *BHL* 408(s)
BIBLIOGRAPHY: Poncelet, "Catalogus ... Bibliothecae eporidiensis," p. 342.
A passionary covering January to June. Only the very end of the *Passio S. Anastasii* has been preserved (*gratias ago Domino*—end) since fols. XLVII-XLIX were erased in the twelfth century. Furthermore, even the little that

is left is difficult to read.[11] There is little text to compare thus, but there are numerous readings common to the manuscripts of the 408(s) redaction.[12]

LILIENFELD
Stiftsbibliothek 58
s. XIII; Lilienfeld
fols. 78-81 = *BHL* 410   [L]
BIBLIOGRAPHY: Poncelet, "De *Magno legendario austriaco*," pp. 28-29.
Part of the Lilienfeld copy of the MLA, this volume contains saints' lives for January-15 February.

LONDON
British Library, Egerton 2902
s. XIII; Rome (S. Croce in Gerusalemme)
fragment added at beginning of codex = Abbreviated Version A   [E]
BIBLIOGRAPHY: *Catalogue of the Additions ... (1911-1915)*, pp. 416-419.
The fragment of one leaf containing the *Passio S. Anastasii*, "apparently written in Italy, 13th cent., in double columns of 36 lines ..." was added to this "Sacramentary apparently executed for a monastery connected with Jerusalem," dated to the early thirteenth century from Italy with additions by hands of the thirteenth and fourteenth centuries. I think we can conclude that the Roman monastery with connections to Jerusalem is most likely S. Croce di Gerusalemme *in aedibus sessorianis*.[13]

This added leaf has been cropped both at the top and at the outside margin. Three of its four columns contain the last section of the Passion of Anastasius, marked into readings by the original scribe, followed in the last column by the beginning of the *Passio S. Emerentianae* (*ex BHL* 156).

British Library Harley 2800
s. XII-XIII; Arnstein (Trier)
fols. 63-65v = *BHL* 409
BIBLIOGRAPHY: *A Catalogue of the Harleian MSS ...* II, 712-13; Levison, "Conspectus," pp. 537, 603; Colgrave, *Two Lives*, pp. 18-19; Petitmengin, "Les Vies latines de sainte Pélagie. Inventaire ...," p. 296.

---

11. I have used only a microfilm copy, not the original.

12. For example: (cap. 39) *infinitas pecunias*; (cap. 42) *carcerem*; (cap. 42) *Persiaca*; (cap. 42) *confessus*.

13. Since much of the Sessoriana Library ended up at the Phillips collection at Chelthenham, I suspect that to be the route by which this codex arrived in England.

This is the first volume of a three-volume legendary, completed by Harley 2801 and 2802, from the Premonstratensian monastery of Arnstein in Limbourg, in the diocese of Trier.[14] Harley 2800 encompasses 128 items, from January to 8 June, and was written ca. 1200. It is closely related to Brussels, Bibliotèque royale 207-8 above.

LUCCA
Biblioteca capitolare C
s. XII; Lucca
fols. 72v-76 = *BHL* 408(s)
BIBLIOGRAPHY: Garrison, *Studies* I, 115-125.
Characterized by Garrison as "among the finest manuscripts produced in Italy in the 12th century" (p. 115), this passionary was produced at Lucca, as both its hagiological program,[15] which corresponds almost exactly to that of Rome, Archivio storico del Vicariato, Lateranenses A 79/81, below, and the style of its illustrations reveal.

MELK
Stiftsbibliothek 388(F8)
s. XIII ex.; Melk
fols. 156-159v = *BHL* 410   [M]
BIBLIOGRAPHY: Poncelet, "De *Magno legendario austriaco*," pp. 32-33.
Part of Melk's copy of the MLA, it contains saints' lives for January-14 February.

MILAN
Biblioteca ambrosiana B 49 Inf. (olim R, 978)
s. XII; Umbro-Roman region
fols. 72v-73v = *BHL* 408(s)
fols. 73v-75v = *BHL* 412   [A]
BIBLIOGRAPHY: Poncelet, "Catalogus codicum ... Bibliothecae ambrosianae," pp. 224-231; Garrison, *Studies* III, 51, 281 n. 3.
The *Passio S. Anastasii* is only partially preserved in this codex, which cuts out the entire central portion of the work (i.e. *Manens igitur parvum tempus* [cap. 9]—*derelinquens eum in carcerem recessit* [cap. 37]), without any indica-

---

14. Numerous books from Arnstein are found today in the British Library.

15. For example, S. Senesius on 4 May; S. Teodorus, Bishop of Lucca, on 19 May.

tion, however, that any portion of the text has been eliminated.[16] The Bollandists' edition of the Roman Miracle was based on this witness.

MONTE CASSINO
Archivio della Badia 123
s. XI²; Monte Cassino?
fols. 255-261 = *BHL* 411
BIBLIOGRAPHY: Newton, *The Scriptorium and the Library at Monte Cassino*, plate 105; Lowe and Brown, *Beneventan Script* II, 69 with further bibliography; Inguanez, *Codicum casinensium manuscriptorum catalogus* I, 203-205.
This is a composite book. The fourth section containing the *Vita S. Anastasii* and written in Beneventan script consists of five hagiographical texts.

Archivio della Badia 141
s. XII inc.; Benevento
fols. 329-335 = *BHL* 411d   [A]
BIBLIOGRAPHY: Newton, *Scriptorium and Library*, p. 407; Lowe and Brown, *Beneventan Script* II, 71; Inguanez, *Catalogus* I, 225.
This is a legendary covering the period from 30 November (S. Andreas Apostolus) to 3 February (S. Blasius), but as this last text is incomplete, we do not know how far the calendar reached. It was written in the Benevento territory, as a note at the bottom of p. 1 says: "Liber sancti nycolai turre pagane," which is in Benevento.

Archivio della Badia 144
s. XI²; Monte Cassino
fols. 500-526 = *BHL* 411
BIBLIOGRAPHY: Newton, *Scriptorium and Library*, plate 20 and p. 334, and passim; Lowe and Brown, *Beneventan Script* II, 71 with further bibliography; Inguanez, *Catalogus* I, 230.
A legendary in Beneventan script from the Desiderian period, including Passions and Lives from S. Nicholas to S. Blasius (3 February), with pages missing at the end.

Archivio della Badia 145
s. XI²; Monte Cassino
fols. 295-309 = *BHL* 411
BIBLIOGRAPHY: Newton, *Scriptorium and Library*, plate 113 and p. 361, and passim; Lowe and Brown, *Beneventan Script* II, 72 with further bibliography; Inguanez, *Catalogus* I, 230-232

---

16. Nor are there any obvious reasons why this central portion should have been excluded, except that perhaps the model was defective.

A legendary in Beneventan, covering the period from 30 November through June.

Archivio della Badia 146
s. XI ex.; Monte Cassino
fols. 412-431 = *BHL* 411
BIBLIOGRAPHY: Newton, *Scriptorium and Library*, plate 114 and p. 361, and passim; Lowe and Brown, *Beneventan Script* II, p. 72; Inguanez, *Catalogus* I 232-234.
A legendary, written in Beneventan script, from 30 November through June, from the Oderisian period, perhaps used at S. Maria de Albaneta.[17]

MUNICH
Bayerische Staatsbibliothek Clm 2570 (Ald. 40)
s. XII-XIII; Aldersbach (Diocese of Passau)
fols. 100v-105 = *BHL* 410   [A]
BIBLIOGRAPHY: *Catalogus ... monacensis* I [III], 2, p. 9.
This book came to Munich from Aldersbach, founded as a house of Augustinian Canons Regular in 1123 but turned Cistercian in 1146. Clm 2570 is a miscellany, containing, among other pieces, nine saints' lives of which the incomplete *Vita S. Anastasii* is the last, thus suggesting that the codex has been mutilated at some time. The text on Anastasius departs significantly from the archetype; its word order is frequently changed and a hand other than the original scribe's has corrected it.

Bayerische Staatsbibliothek Clm 17137 (Scheftl. 137)
s. XII; Schäftlarn
fols. 82-86 = *BHL* 410   [H]
BIBLIOGRAPHY: *Catalogus ... monacensis* II [IV], 3, p. 82.
A miscellany including several saints' lives,[18] from Schäftlarn, in the diocese of Freising, on the River Isar, in upper Bavaria. Originally a Benedictine priory founded in 762, Schäftlarn became Premonstratensian in 1140.[19]

---

17. The dependent church of Monte Cassino, as is indicated by a later note written on the title page: "Codex Seculi X desinentis vel XI incipientis forsan S. Marie de Albaneta."
18. There are thirty-one texts, the first twenty-three of which commemorate by and large saints venerated in January; the rest do not appear to be organized according to any principle.
19. Cottineau, *Répertoire topo-bibliographique des abbayes et prieurés* II, 2974-2975.

Bayerische Staatsbibliothek Clm 22020 (Wess. 20)
s. XII; Wessobrunn
fols. 129-34 = *BHL* 410   [E]
BIBLIOGRAPHY: Philippart, *Légendiers*, p. 18; *Catalogus ... monacensis* II [IV], 4, p. 19.
This volume contains a passionary of the twelve apostles followed by a group of other saints' Lives gathered according to no discernible principle. It came to Munich from the Benedictine monastery of SS. Peter and Paul in Wessobrunn, in the diocese of Augsburg in Upper Bavaria.

Bayerische Staatsbibliothek Clm 22240
1141-1191; Windberg
fols. 115v-121 = *BHL* 410   [I]
BIBLIOGRAPHY: Poncelet, "De legendario Windbergensi," pp. 97-122.
This is a volume of the Windberg Legendary. The dating of this collection is based on a note indicating that Abbot Gebhardus, who held office from 1141 to 1191, ordered its composition.

NAPLES
Biblioteca nazionale Vittorio Emanuele III, VIII B 2
s. XI (Poncelet)-XII (Philippart); border region between Umbria, Tuscany, and the Marches
fols. 83-88 = *BHL* 408(s)
BIBLIOGRAPHY: Poncelet, "Catalogus ... neapolitanarum," pp. 150-154; Philippart, *Légendiers*, pp. 13, 102 n. 186.
A passionary covering the entire year beginning on 30 November, written in Caroline minuscule. It was once in the possession of Aemilius Iacobus Cavalerius, bishop of Troia.

Biblioteca nazionale Vittorio Emanuele III, VIII B 3
s. XII; XI (Dolbeau); Troia region (Apulia)
fol. 104v-144v (olim cclxxxxviii-cccviii) = *BHL* 411a   [E]
BIBLIOGRAPHY: Poncelet, "Catalogus ... bibliothecarum neapolitanarum," pp. 154-157; Lowe and Brown, *Beneventan Script* I, 77, II, 103; Cavallo, "Struttura e articolazione della minuscula beneventana libraria tra i secoli X-XII," p. 365; Dolbeau, "Le rôle des interprètes," p. 157.
This is the second volume of a legendary (the first part is VIII B 4), written in Beneventan script and produced in a scriptorium in the Troia region for the use of the local clergy.

Biblioteca nazionale Vittorio Emanuele III, VIII B 6
s. XI; Troia region (Apulia)
fols. 214-217v = *BHL* 412   [N]

BIBLIOGRAPHY: Poncelet, "Catalogus ... bibliothecarum neapolitanarum," pp. 162-165; Lowe and Brown, *Beneventan Script* I, 151; II, 103; Cavallo, "Struttura e articolazione," p. 354.

This is a legendary covering the months of December and January, although not in strict chronological order, and with several additional texts at the end that do not follow the calendar.[20] The title of the text is given as "Passio S. Anastasii sacerdotis"(!). The codex is written in Beneventan script of the Bari-type "in its most accomplished form" (Cavallo). It once belonged to Aemilius Iacobus Cavalerius, bishop of Troia. Although it has not been identified as a codex written in Troia, its relation to the Troia area may be quite close because its sanctoral includes the *Passio* of S. Eleutherius (*BHL* 2450) whose relics were kept in the city.

Biblioteca nazionale Vittorio Emanuele III, VIII B 9
s. XV
fols. 131-131v = *BHL* 411a [Extracts]
BIBLIOGRAPHY: Poncelet, "Catalogus ... bibliothecarum neapolitanarum," pp. 168-173.

The first section of this book contains the last part of the *Legenda Aurea*; the rest is taken up with a mixture of hagiographic texts, both ancient and recent. There does not appear to be any order in this collection.[21]

ORLÉANS
Bibliothèque municipale 342 (290)
s. X-XI; Fleury (pp. 69-232)
pp. 210-221 = *BHL* 412   [O]
BIBLIOGRAPHY: van der Straeten, *Les manuscrits hagiographiques d'Orléans, Tours et Angers*, p.73; 342; Mostert, *The Library of Fleury*, p. 180.

This codex is composed of three separate parts, bound together before the eighteenth century. The Roman Miracle is found in the third, main part of the codex (pp. 69-232), containing a varied assortment of hagiographic pieces.

---

20. It is not clear to me whether the Roman Miracle follows the calendar or not; it is placed right after the *Passio S. Sabinae* (29 January) and before the Passion of St. Antonina (4 May!) where the order truly breaks down.

21. There are several texts concerning St. Thomas Aquinas including the privilege and bull of canonization, the Life and Miracles of St Louis (*BHL* 5043 and 5044), but also the Lives of numerous ancient popes. The codex is written by several hands.

This main part was copied at Fleury, not England, as it has been stated.[22] This is shown by the script and the presence of musical notations in both the older Fleury style and in the new calligraphic style introduced at the abbey at the end of the tenth or early in the eleventh century.[23] Also, the presence of a *Sermo in exaltationis S. Crucis* on pp. 183-200 provides further evidence of the manuscript's origin, for the abbey's martyrology indicates that on 24 February the reception of the relics of the Holy Sponge and a piece of the True Cross was commemorated at Fleury.

PARIS
Bibliothèque nationale de France, latinus 5291
s. XIII; Foucarmont
fols. 141v-144v = *BHL* 408(p)

Bibliothèque nationale de France, latinus 5300
s. XIII; unknown origin
fols. 50-54 = *BHL* 408(p)

Bibliothèque nationale de France, latinus 5318
s. XII; ecclesiastical province of Tours
fols. 125-129 = *BHL* 408(p)   [B1]

Bibliothèque nationale de France, latinus 5319
s. XIV; Fontevrault
fols. 97v-202v = *BHL* 408(p)

Bibliothèque nationale de France, latinus 5341
s. XIII; Mortemer-en-Lyons
fols. s.n. = *BHL* 408(p)

Bibliothèque nationale de France, latinus 16736
s. XII; Chaâlis
fols. 135v-139v = *BHL* 408(p)   [B6]

---

22. Mostert, p. 180, citing Lowe, *Codices Latini Antiquiores* VI, no. 820, p. 35. But Lowe here is discussing the second part of the codex (i.e. pp. 1-68), a palimpsest whose lower script is characterized as Anglo-Saxon minuscule of the eighth century and which was "used in the eleventh century for re-writing, apparently in England to judge by the script."

23. For the script, see Samaran and Marichal, *Catalogue des manuscrits en écriture latine* ... VII, 571. For the script of Fleury in general, see Barker-Benfield, "A ninth century manuscript from Fleury," pp. 155-156. I thank Dr. Barker-Benfield, who confirmed by letter that the script on the pages containing the Roman Miracle is not English.

Bibliothèque nationale de France, latinus 17003
s. XII; Le Val?
fols. s.n. = *BHL* 408(p) [B3]
BIBLIOGRAPHY: Poncelet, *Catalogus codicum ... parisiensi* I, 536-541; II, 21-23, 174-182, 191-196, 263-267; III, 354-357, 386-389; Levison, "Conspectus," pp. 547-550; Dolbeau, "Notes sur la genèse," pp. 148-149, 154-155, 159-160, 161, 163; Rochais, *Un légendier cistercien* ... I, 67-68, 70, 74, 80-81, 87.

These seven legendaries, ranging in date from the twelfth to the fourteenth century, contain a nearly identical text of the *Passio S. Anastasii*. Five of these codices, 5291, 5319, 5341, 16736, 17003, are copies of the Cistercian legendary referred to as *Liber de natalitiis*, which was developing in northeastern France and Flanders in the twelfth century. The other two, 5300 and 5318, are closely related to the Cistercian legendary.[24]

Bibliothèque nationale de France, latinus 9741
ca. 1235; St. Maximin in Trier.
pp. 302-314 = *BHL* 408, p_1 revision [single witness]
BIBLIOGRAPHY: Poncelet, *Catalogus codicum ... parisiensi* III, 584-88; Colgrave, *Two Lives*, p. 19; Levison, "Conspectus," pp. 536; 685ff; Poncelet, "Le Légendier de Pierre Calo," p. 11; Rochais, *Un légendier cistercien* ... I, 4-5.

This is the first volume of a nine-volume hagiographic collection, "the most comprehensive of all the legendaries written on German soil" (Colgrave). 9741 includes the saints of the month of January.[25] The legendary was clearly composed for the Benedictine monastery of St. Maximin in Trier, for it

24. BN 5318 is Benedictine and is one of the sources of the *Liber de natalitiis*; 5300 appears to be a collection prepared to complement an already existing legendary and is related to the *Liber de natalitiis* (Dolbeau, "Notes sur la genèse," p. 173). The close connection among all these manuscripts is highlighted most strikingly by their similar contents. In addition, this same form of the *Passio S. Anastasii* was contained in a lost legendary of St. Melanie Abbey in Rennes, also Benedictine (Dolbeau, p. 154).

25. Besides this first volume for January, the fifth (August) is also preserved in Paris; the second volume (February, March, and April), the third (May), the fourth (June and July), and the seventh (October) are in the Trier public library; the sixth volume (September) and the eighth (November) are in the Priesterseminar also at Trier. The ninth volume is apparently lost. This January volume contains a few non-January saints, namely the first two (S. Fulgentius and S. Eufrosyna), SS. Macharius and Eugenius (pp. 448-450), and the Donatist saints Dativus and Saturninus (pp. 386-396). Bolland used this codex for his edition of several texts and refers to it as "pervetusto Codice MS. monasterii S. Maximini Treviris" (*Passio S. Dativi, Secundini et al., ASS* Feb. II, 514); see further pp. 248-249. See Poncelet's catalogue for references to Bolland's editions.

contains several texts concerned with saints venerated particularly in this city and at the abbey, including, for example, a text entitled "De sancto Maro, ab Euchario XI Trevirensi archiepiscopo, qui jacet post altare quod est ad australem partem chori sancti Paulini archipraesulis Trevirensis et martyris."[26]

The contents of 9741 have a large overlap with the corresponding volumes of the Cistercian Legendary, the manuscripts representing the β branch of the transmission of *BHL* 408(p). For example, of the fifty-five Lives[27] contained in this codex, thirty-two are also contained in 5318 (which holds Lives for January-March and includes most of the January saints represented in the other BN manuscripts, legendaries for the month of January). But the most characteristic saints of Trier present in 9741 are not included in 5318. Hence, the translation of S. Agricius in Trier, the *Vita S. Popponis*, and that of S. Maximinus, and the last text on S. Marus are all missing.[28] One may perhaps conclude that the similarities in contents between these two collections go back to their circulation in the same geographical area, and that the Trier compilation was particularized to serve the needs of S. Maximinus. This inference is supported by the textual comparison of the texts relating to St. Anastasius, although this evidence is rather limited by the revised nature of the redaction preserved in 9741. None of the characteristic "errors" of the β text is found in 9741, but rather here one encounters a greater similarity with the other members of this group (= π).[29] The Passion of St. Anastasius suggests a parallel relationship between the Trier and Cistercian collections in this case.

PERUGIA
Biblioteca augusta comunale 3270 N. 3
s. XII; Umbria/Tuscany
BIBLIOGRAPHY: Verrando, "Frammenti e testi agiografici ... ," pp. 274-275.

---

26. A note on p. 452 of the first volume further reads, "Liber Sancti Maximini Treverensis archiepiscopi. Si quis eum abstulerit vel invaderat, anathema sit in aeternum. Amen. Hunc librum comparavit bonae memoriae prior Fridericus." This suggests that the prior Fridericus had bought the volume, or, more likely, commissioned it, given the particular association of the sanctoral with Trier. Other saints in this January volume connected with Trier and St. Maximin's Abbey are S. Agricius, S. Poppo, and S. Maximinus.

27. The *Vita S. Irminae virginis* (pp. 139-140) was added in the fifteenth century (Poncelet, *Catalogus ... parisiensi* III, 584).

28. Also missing in the February section of the BN 5318 group is the Passion of the Donatist saints Dativus, Saturnius et al.

29. (l. 59) corporibus : pecoribus β: suppelectili 9741; (l. 124) perfectum π 9741 : praefatum β; (l. 328) in castellum π 9741 : in custodiam β.

This fragment of two folia from a legendary contains only the very beginning of *BHL* 408, following the end of the *Passio S. Vincentii.* It is not possible to determine which of the three redactions was contained here, but given the origin of the codex it was most likely *BHL* 408(s).

Biblioteca capitolare, Codex 40
s. XI/XII; Perugia
fols. 58-70 = *BHL* 408(s)
BIBLIOGRAPHY: Philippart, *Légendiers,* p. 13; Caleca, *Miniature in Umbria,* pp. 153-159; de Gaiffier, "Saints et légendiers de l'Ombrie," pp. 235-256.
This very large legendary, written in Perugia, is incomplete both at the beginning and at the end.

RENNES
Benedictine Abbey of St. Melaine
BIBLIOGRAPHY: Dolbeau, "Fragments métriques consacrés à S. Melaine de Rennes," pp. 117-118.
A legendary belonging to this abbey disappeared during the fire of 1665 that partially destroyed the buildings. Its contents were identical to those of the first 160 folia of Paris, BN lat. 5318. Hence, it is most probable that this lost witness belonged to the β sub-group of *BHL* 408(p).

RIMINI
Biblioteca del Seminario diocesano
Codex s.n.; fragmentary legendary of Rimini Cathedral
s. XII inc.; Rimini
fol. 102 = *BHL* 408, r_1 revision
BIBLIOGRAPHY: Gattucci, "Codici agiografici riminesi ... ," pp. 711-773.
This fragmentary legendary compiled for the use of the cathedral of Rimini is constituted by sixty-four loose sheets discovered after World War II in the old cathedral archives. It covered the entire year, beginning on 30 November. Only the very end of the *Passio S. Anastasii* is preserved (*pedem eius et sic derelinquens eum abiit. Sustinente—foris predio Bethsaloe, in quibus beatum Anastasium cum aliis circiter LXX viris interfecerunt, propter nomen D.N.I.C. Qui vivit et regnat.*)

ROME
Archivio di stato, Ospedale di S. Salvatore 996
s. XI[1]; Rome
fols. 130-138v = *BHL* 411a   [H]
fols. 138v-142v = *BHL* 412   [H]
BIBLIOGRAPHY: Supino Martini, *Roma e l'area grafica romanesca,* pp. 301-302; Barré, *Les homéliaires carolingiens de l'École d'Auxerre,* pp. 117-118.

A legendary-homeliary covering the period from Advent to Easter, written in a hybrid Romanesca. The texts on Anastasius are very carelessly copied; even basic abbreviations are confused, with the accusative and the genitive, for example, often mixed up. The prologue to Gregorius's text is omitted. The Ospedale di S. Salvatore (at the Lateran) was founded at the beginning of the thirteenth century by Cardinal Giovanni Colonna. There are two related hagiographic codices in this same collection, 994 and 995. This book was in use well into the fourteenth century as numerous marginalia indicate (including notes about liturgical readings).

Archivio storico del Vicariato, Lateranense 79 (alias B)
s.XII[1]; Lucca
fols. 99v-104v = *BHL* 408(s)
BIBLIOGRAPHY: Poncelet, *Catalogus ... romanarum*, pp. 55-62; Supino Martini, *Roma*, p. 49 n. 20; Franklin, "Roman Hagiography," pp. 875-876; Garrison, *Studies* I, 177-191; Ermini, "I passionari lateranensi," pp. 99-108; Grandsen, "Abbo of Fleury's 'Passio Sancti Edmundi,'" p. 73 and n. 320.
This volume and codex 81 constitute a legendary that belonged to the canons of S. Frediano of Lucca, to whom the Basilica of St. John the Lateran had been entrusted. The hagiological program is almost identical to that of the legendary of the Cathedral of Lucca, above. The version of the *Passio S. Anastasii* has been emended and corrected by a hand perhaps only slightly later than the original one by scraping off the inital script and writing over it with a much darker ink.[30]

Archivio storico del Vicariato, Lateranense 67
s. XIII; Rome
fols. 39-40 = *BHL* 411a [Extracts]
BIBLIOGRAPHY: Poncelet, *Catalogus ... romanarum*, pp. 49-52; Supino Martini, *Roma*, p. 49 n. 20.
A lectionary containing a large number texts extracted from the *Liber pontificalis*, Ado's Martyrology and also the *Legenda Aurea*.

Biblioteca alessandrina (universitaria) 91
fols. 367-375 = *BHL* 411a Extracts for the Office
fols. 377-384v = *BHL* 411a

---

30. The corrector is blunt about his motives in a note to the preface: "Hic prologus Penitus nullius utilitatis est." It is difficult at times to be certain of the underlying text, but it is clearly part of the s-recension and appears related to Naples VIII B 2 and Bologna 2205 discussed above—e.g. l. 12 *triduo* (like Naples VIII B 2), l. 17 *de subliminibus* (like Bologna 2205).

fols. 385-388v = *BHL* 412
BIBLIOGRAPHY: Poncelet, *Catalogus ... romanarum*, pp. 135-143.
This paper manuscript contains texts on the saints of January and February collected by Costantino Gaetano (1560-1650). The texts on Anastasius were copied from S. Pietro A 3 and A 2.

Biblioteca casanatense 718 (alias B.I.3)
s. XI/XII; Tuscany
fols. 114-115 = *BHL* 408, r₁ revision
BIBLIOGRAPHY: Poncelet, *Catalogus ... romanarum*, pp. 231-236; Garrison, *Studies* I, 172-173, 177 n. 2
This is the first tome, covering the period 30 November-16 June, of a two-volume legendary. Casanatense 719 is the second volume. Tuscany, and specifically the area around Lucca and Pistoia, has been proposed as its place of origin.[31] The *Passio Anastasii* is missing the first part; it begins with cap. 12 (*transivit in praedicto monasterio ...*). Since the preceding text, the *Passio S. Vincentii*, ends incomplete at the bottom of fol. 113v, one may conclude that at least one leaf is missing between the leaves now numbered 113 and 114.

Biblioteca casanatense 726 (alias B.I.11)
s. XI-XII; Pisa
fols. 138-144v = *BHL* 411
BIBLIOGRAPHY: Poncelet, *Catalogus ... romanarum*, pp. 243-246; Garrison, *Studies* IV, 295-296.
A legendary written in common minuscule covering roughly the first three months of the year, beginning with 31 December, the *Vita* of S. Silvester, and ending with the *Passio SS. Faustini et Iovitae*, which stops incomplete as pages are missing at the end.[32] This collection most certainly originated in Pisa, prepared perhaps for the monastery of SS. Gorgonio, Vito, and Milzia-

---

31. The contents of the sanctoral, which includes S. Iventius of Pavia (*BHL* 4619), S. Vitalis (*BHL* 8700) and S. Severus of Ravenna (*BHL* 7683), S. Geminianus of Modena (*BHL* 3300), S. Apollenaris (*BHL* 623, in the second volume), suggest that it was produced in the area bordering the Po river. Garrison says that the hagiological program of Casanatense 718 indicates that it was made in Pistoia, but the one of 719 suggests Lucca. He concludes that it is best to call it "Tuscan."

32. The only text that appears out of order is the *Passio S. Isidori in Chio*, inserted around 9 January, but I wonder if this commemorates the translation to Venice which took place in 1125.

de or that dedicated to S. Maria and S. Gorgonio on the island of Gorgona, off the Pisan coast.[33]

Biblioteca nazionale centrale Vittorio Emanuele II, Sessoriani 4 (alias XXVIII, olim 119)
s. XIV; Tre Fontane (Rome)
fols. 25v-28 = Abbreviated Version B
BIBLIOGRAPHY: Poncelet, *Catalogus ... romanarum*, pp. 97-98.
This book is described by Poncelet as a *lectionarius* that belonged once to the monastery of SS. Vincenzo e Anastasio ad Aquas Salvias in which are found several hagiographic works, including the *Passio S. Anastasii*.[34] The texts were divided into readings by the original scribe. The Passion is arranged into readings i-viii, and is followed immediately by the Sermon of St. Augustine "in natale S. Vincentii martiris,"[35] also divided into readings.

Biblioteca nazionale centrale Vittorio Emanuele II, Sessoriani 5 (alias XXIX, olim 118)
s. XI (Poncelet); s. XII med. (Garrison); Florence area
fols. 68v-70v = *BHL* 412   [S]
BIBLIOGRAPHY: Poncelet, *Catalogus ... romanarum*, pp. 98-103; Garrison, *Studies* I, 167-168.
A legendary covering the entire year. According to Poncelet, it originated in the Benedictine abbey of San Salvatore in Settimo, in the neighborhood of Florence.[36] Garrison also points out that its Florentine origin is proved by its sanctoral, especially the inclusion of St. Zenobio, bishop of Florence, for 25 May, and St. Alexander, bishop of Fiesole, on 6 June.[37]

---

33. The origin is proposed by Garrison, who points out particularly as signs of Pisan origin (besides the decoration of the initials) the celebration of S. Miltiades papa on 10 January (while elsewhere it occurs on 10 December), and the inclusion on 13 February of S. Euphrasia, little known in Italy but to whom a church was dedicated at Pisa. In support of the monastic origin of the collection I would add the presence of a large number of monastic and heremitical figures: out of thirty-one texts, about eleven concern monks or nuns, including Donatus of Fiesole's Life of St. Bridget of Ireland.

34. This is not simply a "legendary" but a "lectionary," including, for example, also indications for Gospel readings.

35. Sermo 276 (PL 38, 1255-1257).

36. Because of its similarity to other codices from San Salvatore.

37. Bertelli, "Caput," p. 21, n. 2, reports that an inventory of the codices of Santa Croce in Gerusalemme "riuniti da Ilarione Rancati (Bibl. Vaticana, Chig. R II 64)" declares this codex to come from Tre Fontane. Its origin in the Florentine area seems assured, however.

Biblioteca vallicelliana G 98
s. XII in.
fol. 25v = *BHL* 411 [Extracts]
BIBLIOGRAPHY: Poncelet, *Catalogus ... romanarum*, pp. 398-399; Lowe and Brown, *Beneventan Script* II, 130.
This is a miscellany of fragments put together by Antonio Gallonio (1556-1605) and now bound together. Fol. 25, derived *a quodam antiphonario-legendario*, is written in Beneventan script and thus accords with the circulation of *BHL* 411; on its verso it contains the fragment from the *Passio S. Anastasii*. The page's outer margin has been trimmed so that part of the second column is missing. It consists of extracts from 411 as is made clear by the phrase *Post haec transactis qui[ndenis ferme] diebus* ... There is no prologue; but perhaps these extracts were taken from throughout the work, not only from the central chapters, for the first reading is from the very beginning of the text.[38] The second reading, beginning with the opening words of the execution scene ends incomplete.[39]

Biblioteca vallicelliana H 9 (Gallonii L)
s. XVI-XVII
fols. 266-276 = *BHL* 412
BIBLIOGRAPHY: Poncelet, *Catalogus ... romanarum*, pp. 424-429.
This codex is a collection of hagiographic texts. The Roman Miracle was copied from Vallicelliana Tomus V.

Biblioteca vallicelliana H 16 (Gallonii S)
fols. 27-32v = *BHL* 408, r_1 revision
fols. 253-258v = *BHL* 408(r)
BIBLIOGRAPHY: Poncelet, *Catalogus ... romanarum*, pp. 436-438.
Transcribed by Antonio Gallonio (1556-1605) from Codex A of the Archivio di S. Maria Maggiore (now in BAV), and Vat. lat. 5696.

Biblioteca vallicelliana H 18 (Gallonii V)
fols. 225-226v = *BHL* 412
BIBLIOGRAPHY: Poncelet, *Catalogus ... romanarum*, pp. 440-442.
Transcribed by Antonio Gallonio (1556-1605) from Codex A of the Archivio di S. Maria Maggiore (now in BAV, as below, p. 535).

---

38. *Beatus Anastasius de quadam regione* (cap. 1 [Flusin 6]) and continues up to ... *eius pectore annihilabat* (cap. 2 [8]).

39. cap. 33 [38] *Post haec transactis qui[ndenis ferme] diebus* and ends with ... *Deo gratias referens* (cap. 33 [38]).

Biblioteca vallicelliana H 25
fols. 24-32v = *BHL* 411a
fols. 32v-34v = *BHL* 412
BIBLIOGRAPHY: Poncelet, *Catalogus ... romanarum*, pp. 443-447.
A collection of hagiographic texts copied by Antonio Bosio (1575-1629) from various Roman legendaries. The texts on St. Anastasius were copied from S. Pietro A 2 (now in BAV).

Biblioteca vallicelliana H 28
fols. 99-103v = *BHL* 412
BIBLIOGRAPHY: Poncelet, *Catalogus ... romanarum*, pp. 447-448.
A collection of hagiographic texts copied in the sixteenth and seventeenth centuries; the Roman Miracle was copied from Vallicelliana Tomus V.

Biblioteca vallicelliana Tomus V
s. XI^2; Rome
fols. 130v-138 = *BHL* 408(r)
fols. 138-141v = *BHL* 412 [L]
BIBLIOGRAPHY: Vichi and Mottironi, *Catalogo dei manoscritti della Biblioteca vallicelliana* I, 64-73; Poncelet, *Catalogus ... romanarum*, pp. 306-310; Garrison, *Studies* IV, p. 280; Supino Martini, *Roma*, pp. 121-122.
This legendary covers the period December-April. The writing in Romanesca and a reference to the church of S. Lorenzo in Damaso may indicate that the codex was written in Rome and perhaps at the church itself. But one also must note the strong Benedictine character of the sanctoral (including Bertharius's homily on Scholastica on fols. 175v-182 and the Life and Miracles of Benedict on fols. 204-212), and the striking presence of saints from Spoleto. In the thirteenth century, the book came to belong to the monastery of S. Sebastiano "ad Catacumbas" as a note on fol. 224v reveals.

Biblioteca vallicelliana Tomus VI
s. XIII-XIV; Benevento area?
fols. 204-210 = *BHL* 411
BIBLIOGRAPHY: Poncelet, *Catalogus ... romanarum*, pp. 311-315.
A legendary from the beginning of December (S. Barbara, 4 December) to the incomplete life of St. Barbatus (16 February), the seventh-century bishop of Benevento.[40]

Biblioteca vallicelliana Tomus VII
s. XIII/XIV; Rome?
fols. 87v-89 = Abbreviated version A [V]

---

40. There is also a fragment of the Life of St. Benedict in the very last folio.

BIBLIOGRAPHY: Poncelet, *Catalogus ... romanarum*, pp. 315-329.
Poncelet described this book as a lectionary intended for use at the Divine Office in which are gathered saints' Lives, homilies and similar works. It includes a full complement of 263 texts arranged *per circulum anni* from 29 November (S. Saturninus).[41] The *Passio S. Anastasii* is divided by the original scribe into readings iiii-viiii, supplementing the three readings provided by the *Passio S. Vincentii* also for 22 January, as its rubric confirms.[42]

There are several indications from the contents that this collection was put together for a Roman church. There is first of all the presence of an unusually large number of popes venerated as saints. There are also other Roman hagiographic texts, such as the interpolated Life of St. John the Evangelist (*ex BHL* 4321) relating to the Roman church of S. Giovanni *ante portam latinam*.[43] There are finally several topographical references to Rome.[44]

Biblioteca vallicelliana Tomus X
s. XII-XIII; Rome
fols. 35v-40 = *BHL* 411a   [I]
BIBLIOGRAPHY: Vichi and Mottironi, *Catalogo ... della Biblioteca vallicelliana* I, 162ff. with further bibliography; Poncelet, *Catalogus ... romanarum*, pp. 337-344.
A legendary covering the entire year, from January to December; several texts are shortened or summarized. The sanctoral, which includes the standard Roman martyrs and popes as well as rarer texts connected with the city's churches,[45] suggests that this book originated in the city. The *Passio S. Anastasii* has been shortened by several excisions in the body of the text.

SPOLETO
Archivio capitolare, Legendarium S. Felicis de Narco (Tomo I)
s. XII ex.; Spoleto
fols. 119-122 = *BHL* 408(s)

---

41. It also contains both the *Proprium sanctorum* (fols. 315-318) and the *Commune sanctorum* (fols. 318-350v).

42. *Eodem die Beati Anastasii lectio iiii.*

43. Poncelet, *Catalogus ... romanarum*, p. 319 (no. 98).

44. Such as, for example, "... cuius corpus [S. Paulini] nunc videtur esse coniunctum corpori beati Bartholomaei apostoli Roma in insula Lycaonia in ecclesia Sancti Alberti, quae nunc vocatur ecclesia Sancti Bartholomaei ..." (p. 321 [no. 126]); or the note referring to S. Marina: "Apud Ardeam est locus ubi beata Marina quiescit, et ipsa triginta duobus milibus distat ab urbe" (p. 322 [no. 143]).

45. In particular, the Life of S. Constantia (Constantina) in a form found only in this and another manuscript from Rome (*BHL* 1927b; see *BHL. Supplementum*, p. 222).

BIBLIOGRAPHY: de Gaiffier, "Les légendiers de Spolète," pp. 313-348, esp. 313, 322.

A legendary in two volumes that was written for the monastery of S. Felice de Narco in the region of Spoleto.[46]

ST. GALL
Passionarium minus
s. X; St. Gall
BIBLIOGRAPHY: Munding, *Das Verzeichnis der St. Galler Heiligenleben ...*, pp. 68-69; Dolbeau, "Le Passionaire de Fulda," pp. 528-529.

This lost passionary was part of the group produced before the year 1000 in Bavaria and German Switzerland. It contained *BHL* 408.

STUTTGART
Württembergische Landesbibliothek HB XIV 13
s. IX ex.; Reichenau
fols. 87-98v = *BHL* 408(s)   [St]
BIBLIOGRAPHY: Buhl and Kurras, *Die Handschriften des ehemaligen Hofbibliothek Stuttgart*, pp. 104-105; Dolbeau, "Le Passionaire de Fulda," pp. 527-529; Quentin, *Les martyrologes historiques du moyen âge*, pp. 643-649; Philippart, *Légendiers*, p. 102 n. 186 with further bibliographic references.

This is the first volume of a two-volume passionary; it covers the first semester of the year. See further Chapter V.

SUBIACO
Biblioteca del monastero di S. Scolastica II 2
s.XII²; Subiaco
fols. 159-164v = *BHL* 411a   [K]
BIBLIOGRAPHY: Supino Martino, *Roma*, p. 183; Mazzatinti, *Inventari dei manoscritti delle biblioteche d'Italia* I, 161; Federichi, *I monasteri di Subiaco* II, 4 no. 24.

A "legendarium sanctorum" copied in common Caroline that already presents Gothic characteristics according to Supino Martino's analysis.

Biblioteca del monastero di S. Scolastica IV 4
s. XIII; Subiaco
fols. 64v-66 = *BHL* 411a, capp. 1-8 (no Prologue)
BIBLIOGRAPHY: Mazzatinti, *Inventari* I, 162; Federichi, *I monasteri* II, 5 no. 34.

---

46. The monastery's history is quite obscure. From the sixteenth century at the latest, its manuscripts have been in the Spoleto cathedral. The *Passio Anastasii*, ends, incomplete, at the bottom of the first column of fol. 122 (cap. 43).

An Office lectionary written in early Gothic script. The first eight chapters of the *Passio* of Anastasius are marked into four readings, numbered IX-XII. The text was copied from Subiaco II 2.

Biblioteca del monastero di S. Scolastica X 10
1065-1120; Subiaco
fols. 47v-54 = *BHL* 411a   [J]
BIBLIOGRAPHY: Supino Martino, *Roma*, pp. 36 and n. 27, 170-171, 181 and n. 106; Mazzatinti, *Inventari* I, 163; Federichi, *I monasteri* II, xxvii, 4, no. 12.
A legendary written in Romanesca during the abbacy of John V. The text of the *Passio* omits the last section (cap. 36—end), most likely because in its exemplar these chapters were segregated as a "Miraculum" as is the case in the closely related witnesses K and E.

TRIER
Stadtbibliothek 190 (1246)
s. IX in.; Freising
fragment = *BHL* 408(p)   [Tr]
BIBLIOGRAPHY: Coens, "Appendice au Catalogue des manuscripts de Trèves," pp. 213-215; Bischoff, *Die südostdeutschen Schreibschulen* ... , p. 98 n. 36; Dolbeau, "Le passionaire de Fulda," pp. 527-529.
This is the oldest surviving witness for the *Passio S. Anastasii*, in any version. It consists of one folio, cut from its original binding. This passionary's sanctoral, as can be reconstructed, can be superimposed onto that of Pal. lat. 846. See further Chapter V.

TROYES
Bibliothèque municipale 1171
s. XI; Rheims? Troyes?
fols. 72-87 = *BHL* 408(p)   [Ty]
BIBLIOGRAPHY: Philippart, *Légendiers*, pp. 15, 80.
A Rheims legendary adapted for the use of Troyes. See Chapter V for further discussion.

TURIN
Biblioteca nazionale universitaria F III 16 (Ottino, no. 24)
s. IX-X; Bobbio
fols. 14-23 = *BHL* 410b   [T]
See Chapter II for full discussion.

VATICAN CITY
Biblioteca apostolica vaticana, Archivio di S. Maria Maggiore 1 (A; EE I 1)
s. XII-XIII; Rome?

fols. 139v-145v = *BHL* 408(r)
fols. 145v-148 = *BHL* 412 [M]
BIBLIOGRAPHY: Poncelet, *Catalogus ... romanarum.* pp. 81-85; Garrison, *Studies* III, 107 n. 1; Supino Martini, *Roma*, pp. 323-324.
A legendary covering the year from 30 November to 30 September. Its origin in the Roman or Umbro-Roman region is suggested by the great number of Roman saints, including Petronilla (*BHL* 6061, 6062), and Aquila and Prisca (*BHL* 654n).

Biblioteca apostolica vaticana, Archivio di S. Pietro A 2 (alias A)
s. XI ex.; Rome (S. Peter's Basilica)
fols. 136-143v = *BHL* 411a [P]
fols. 143v-146v = *BHL* 412 [P]
BIBLIOGRAPHY: Poncelet, *Catalogus ... romanarum*, pp. 1-6; Supino Martini, *Roma*, pp. 68-71; Franklin, "Roman Hagiography," pp. 866-868.
This is the first volume of the legendary used in the Basilica of St. Peter, written in Romanesca. Two other volumes survive, S. Pietro A 4 and A 5; at least one is missing.

Biblioteca apostolica vaticana, Archivio di S. Pietro A 3 (alias B)
s. XII ex.; Rome (St. Peter's Basilica)
fols. 110-111 = *BHL* 411a [Extracts]
BIBLIOGRAPHY: Poncelet, *Catalogus ... romanarum*, p. 6-10; Franklin, "Roman Hagiography," p. 862.
This is a lectionary for use at the Office comprising 133 texts (from 1 October, most likely,[47] to the end of September), some complete, but most either abbreviated or in extracts. Its principal source was the great legendary of the basilica, preserved in S. Pietro A 2, A 4, and A 5.

Biblioteca apostolica vaticana, Archivio di S. Pietro A 7 (alias F)
s. XIII-XIV; Rome (St. Peter's Basilica)
fols. 65-65v = *BHL* 411a [Extracts]
BIBLIOGRAPHY: Poncelet, *Catalogus ... romanarum*, pp. 24-28.
This book contains readings for matins (*ad matutinum*) both for the temporal and the sanctoral intermingled with each other.

Biblioteca apostolica vaticana, Archivio di S. Pietro A 8 (alias G)
s. XV; Rome (St. Peter's Basilica)
fols. 54v-55 = *BHL* 411a [extracts]
BIBLIOGRAPHY: Poncelet, *Catalogus ... romanarum*, pp. 28-38.

---

47. The first fourteen folia are lost. The saints' feasts begin with 7/9 October.

Biblioteca apostolica vaticana, Archivio di. S. Pietro A 9 (alias H)
1339[48]; Rome (St. Peter's Basilica)
fol. 29 = *BHL* 411a [extracts]
BIBLIOGRAPHY: Poncelet, *Catalogus ... romanarum,* pp. 29-38.
Codd. A 8 and A 9 contain the saints' legends read, as is indicated on A 8,
in sacrosancta basilica principis apostolorum de Urbe in matutinali officio. [49]

Biblioteca apostolica vaticana, Archivio di. S. Pietro D 190
s. XV; Rome
fols. 138-142 = *BHL* 412
BIBLIOGRAPHY: Poncelet, *Catalogus ... romanarum,* p. 44.
A parchment codex containing a variety of hagiographic texts. The Roman
Miracle is closely related to the copy found in Vat. lat. 1195 and Chigianus
P VIII 15.

Biblioteca apostolica vaticana, Chigianus P VIII 15
s. XIII; Northern Latium or Roman Tuscia
fols. 119v-127[50] = *BHL* 411a   [G]
fols. 127-130v = *BHL* 412   [G]
BIBLIOGRAPHY: Poncelet, *Catalogus ... romanarum,* pp. 271-276; Dolbeau,
"Notes sur deux collections," pp. 407-417, 407, n. 3 for bibliography.
The contents of this manuscript argue in favor of its proposed origin in
northern Latium or Roman Tuscia, perhaps at the Monastery of S. Michele
de Subripa, or a Roman establishment that had possessions in this area, such
as S. Pancrazio, which received Subripa in 1246. It consists of various hagiographic pieces for saints' days, homilies and sermons for the temporal, all arranged chronologically and covering the period from Advent through April.

Biblioteca apostolica vaticana, Palatinus latinus 846
s.IX[1]; Lorsch?
fols. 74-79 = *BHL* 408(p)   [Pl]
BIBLIOGRAPHY: Poncelet, *Catalogus ... vaticanae,* pp. 272-276; Bischoff, *Die
Abtei Lorsch im Spiegel ihrer Handschriften,* pp. 41-44; Dolbeau, "Le Passionaire de Fulda," pp. 527-529.[51]

---

48. As is indicated on fols. 264v-265.
49. Fols. 1 and 111.
50. There is a lacuna between fols. 126 and 127.
51. Garrison (*Studies* IV, 158 n. 5, 394 nn. 2 and 3, 400 n. 7) considers it a
Tusco-Umbrian-Sabine passionary of the second half of the eleventh century, and
connects it to Naples, VIII B 2 and Florence, Amiatinus 2. But, while Garrison's
conclusions are based mostly on the sanctoral (a fairly general one as expected for
this early date, as I discuss in "The Early Diffusion of *BHL* 408," pp. 377-381),

This passionary comprises the entire year, from 1 January (S. Martina) to 23 December (S. Victoria). This manuscript is part of a group of codices written in the St. Vaast script style, but most likely at Lorsch.[52] See Chapter V for further discussion.

Biblioteca apostolica vaticana, Reginensis latinus 516
s. IX ex.; uncertain origin[53]
fols. 32-40v = *BHL* 408(r)   [Rg]
BIBLIOGRAPHY: Poncelet, *Catalogus ...vaticanae*, pp. 344-346; Dolbeau, "Le Passionaire de Fulda," pp. 527-529; Cross, "Saints' lives in Old English," p. 46 and n. 9.
This is the first volume of a two-volume passionary, whose second volume has not survived. See Chapter V for further discussion.

Biblioteca apostolica vaticana, Vaticanus latinus 1193
s. XI-XII; Rome
fols. 73v-82 = *BHL* 408, r_2 revision   [Va]
fols. 82-86 = *BHL* 412   [V]
BIBLIOGRAPHY: Poncelet, *Catalogus ... vaticanae*, pp. 50-53; Laurent, *Codices 1135-1266*, pp. 98-101; Dolbeau, "Notes sur deux collections," pp. 398-407; Garrison, *Studies* IV, 277; Supino Martini, *Roma*, p. 315.
Together with Vat. lat. 1194, 1191, and 10999 this codex makes up the legendary of S. Maria in Trastevere.

Biblioteca apostolica vaticana, Vaticanus latinus 1195
s. XI ex.; Rome (SS. Giovanni e Paolo)
fols. 98-106 = *BHL* 411a   [T]

Bischoff's are based on paleographical evidence. Dufourcq ("Le Passionaire occidental au VIIe siècle") studied this manuscript together with other early passionaries in his effort to prove that Vienna 357 contained a Roman passionary from the time of Gregory I, a thesis that has been rejected. See, most recently, Dolbeau, "Le Passionaire de Fulda," p. 528 n. 80.

52. The connection between the scriptoria of Lorsch and St. Vaast (Arras) is explained by the identification of Abbot Adalung of Lorsch with the Adalung who was also abbot of St. Vaast in 808. Palatinus lat. 846 is one of three manuscripts from Lorsch written completely in the St. Vaast style script, not a mixed St. Vaast-Lorsch script, as are some others. Hence, its origin in the Lorsch scriptorium is not as certain (Bischoff, *Die Abtei Lorsch*, as above). (It should be noted that the part under discussion here is the main body of the codex; fols. 1-61, on the other hand, were written by several Lorsch hands [s. IX-X]).

53. This is Dolbeau's evaluation ("Le Passionaire de Fulda," p. 528), but Cross ("Saints' lives," p. 46 and n. 9) tentatively locates it in Brittany on information provided by B. Bischoff.

fols. 98-106 = *BHL* 411a [T]
fols. 106-109v = *BHL* 412 [T]
BIBLIOGRAPHY: Laurent, *Codices 1135-1266*, pp. 104-112; Poncelet, *Catalogus ... vaticanae*, pp.55-59; Supino Martini, *Roma*, pp. 123-124 and n. 49.
Most likely, this codex belonged to the church of SS. Giovanni e Paolo al Celio because its dedication and the patronal feast day are particularly marked (fols. 253v, 259). It is a legendary covering the months January through June. It is highly probable that this codex was used by the scribe of Vat. lat. 6075 (=X).

The text of the *Passio S. Anastasii* has been corrected occasionally by scraping off the old text and writing over it or by small additions over the line by a different hand than the original scribe's.[54]

Biblioteca apostolica vaticana, Vaticanus latinus 1196
s. XI-XII; Rome?
fols. 65-70 = *BHL* 408, r$_2$ revision [Vc]
BIBLIOGRAPHY: Poncelet, *Catalogus ... vaticanae*, pp. 59-63; Laurent, *Codices 1135-1266*, pp. 112-119.
A legendary covering the first six months of the year, from the *Vita S. Basili* (1 January) to the *Passio* of the apostles Peter and Paul.[55] It omits the preface of the *Passio S. Anastasii*.

Biblioteca apostolica vaticana, Vaticanus latinus 1197
s. XI ex. (Lowe and Brown); s. XII inc. (Supino Martini); Abruzzi
fols. 126-133 = *BHL* 411
BIBLIOGRAPHY: Lowe and Brown, *Beneventan Script* I, 76; II, 143 with further bibliography; Laurent, *Codices 1135-1266*, pp. 119-123; Poncelet, *Catalogus ...vaticanae*, pp. 63-66; Supino Martini, *Roma*, pp. 158-59.
A legendary covering the months from December through March, but with some texts apparently out of order. Written in Beneventan script, it was most likely composed at or for the church of Valva and Sulmona in the

---

54. The corrector tried to conform his hand to that of the original scribe when writing over the scraped words, but the additions over the line betray a different hand, albeit not a much later one.

55. This legendary includes those saints' Lives that generally indicate Roman origin, namely Johannes Calovita, Macharius Romanus, Abbacyrus and John. The very last piece, an extract from the miracles of Thomas à Becket, was added from another manuscript (Poncelet, *Catalogus ...vaticanae*, p. 59; Laurent, *Codices 1135-1266*, p. 118). The cult of the English martyr reached central Italy very early. Already in the twelfth century, a fresco of his martyrdom had been painted in the church of SS. Giovanni e Paolo in Spoleto, and the Spoleto legendary discussed above includes him.

Abruzzi because of its hagiological program, which includes, for example, S. Polinus.

Biblioteca apostolica vaticana, Vaticanus latinus 5696
s. XII inc. (Poncelet); s. XII³ (Garrison); Rome
fols. 245v-252 = *BHL* 408, r₂ revision   [Vt]
BIBLIOGRAPHY: Poncelet, *Catalogus ... vaticanae*, pp. 135-139; Garrison, *Studies* IV, 283-288.
A legendary constituted by two fragments of legendaries, the first one (up to fol. 95) covering the month of November; the second, the period from 30 November to 28 April. The script and decoration are closely related and contemporary. Both parts were made for Roman use, and the hagiological program leads Garrison to consider the two parts as constituting a whole.[56] The *Passio S. Anastasii* lacks the preface.

Biblioteca apostolica vaticana, Vaticanus latinus 6073
s. XII; Ravenna?
fols. 63r-68r (quondam 94-99) = *BHL* 408(r)
BIBLIOGRAPHY: Poncelet, *Catalogus ...vaticanae*, pp. 159-164; Philippart, *Légendiers*, p.14; Garrison, *Studies* I, 100.
A large legendary covering most likely the entire year. It may originate from Ravenna, as is suggested by the presence of texts relating to Ravenna's particular saints, such as Ursicinus (*BHL* 8410; fols. 30v-34v), Barbatianus (*BHL* 972; fols. 72v-76v), Severus (*BHL* 7683; fols. 106v-112r) as well as Vitalis (*BHL* 8700; fols. 152v-153) and Apollenaris (*BHL* 623; fols. 204-208). The first twenty-nine folia are missing; it begins in the middle of the Life of St. Lucy and continues to 27 September (SS. Cosma and Damian). There is also a missing folio between modern page numbers 64v and 65r (earlier numbering xcv verso and xcvi recto), in the middle of the *Passio S. Anastasii*. This creates a lacuna in the text from cap. 13 to cap. 20 (*cogitationes iniquas etiam—videntes quae in eum fiebant*). I calculate from the amount of missing text that only one folio is lost, torn off before binding and numbering.

Biblioteca apostolica vaticana, Vaticanus latinus 6075
1601; Rome
fols. 48-53 = *BHL* 411a   [X]
BIBLIOGRAPHY: Poncelet, *Catalogus ... vaticanae*, pp. 170-176.
This book and Vat. lat. 6076 are copies made in 1601 of the legendary of S. Cecilia in Trastevere, now found in Cape Town (=Q above). Since Q was

---

56. Poncelet adds that a note indicates that this codex came to the BAV ultimately from S. Maria ad Martyres (i.e. S. Maria Rotonda, or the Pantheon), but Garrison states that "its place of production remains occult."

already missing the folia containing the latter part of the *Passio S. Anastasii* and the Roman Miracle, Vat. lat. 1195 or its copy supplied the missing text.

Biblioteca apostolica vaticana, Vaticanus latinus 6933
s. XII²; Pisa?
fols. 23-29v = *BHL* 411
BIBLIOGRAPHY: Poncelet, *Catalogus ... vaticanae*, pp. 186-204; Garrison, *Studies* IV, 357.
This is a legendary in common minuscule beginning with the acephalous *Passio* of Pope Marcellus on 16 January and continuing until 19 June, but including other Lives and Passions out of order. It was likely put together in the area of Pisa, for it includes S. Miltiades papa on 10 January (rather than 10 December), S. Euphrasia, and S. Rossorius, whose relics were in Pisa and to whom were dedicated a church and monastery in the city.

Biblioteca apostolica vaticana, Vaticanus latinus 13012
s. XI-XII; Assisi
fols. 54-56 = *BHL* 411a   [C]
BIBLIOGRAPHY: Mercati, "Codici del Convento di S. Francesco in Assisi nella Biblioteca vaticana," p. 117; Mercati, "Altri codici del sacro Convento di Assisi nella Vaticana," p. 496.
A passionary from the Convento di S. Francesco in Assisi. The *Passio S. Anastasii* was not copied in its entirety; the preface is omitted; the entire middle section of the text is skipped (from the middle of cap. 14 to the end of cap. 34), and a sentence is added to connect the two parts together. This was clearly done in an awkward effort to abbreviate the text.

VERCELLI
Archivio capitolare LXIX (Arab. 129)
s. XI; Vercelli?
fols. 62v-72v = *BHL* 408 (s)
BIBLIOGRAPHY: Mazzatinti, *Inventari* XXXI, 94.
A legendary arranged per *circulum anni*, but excluding the period from July to November.

VIENNA
Österreichisches Nationalbibliothek, Latinus 357
s. IX ex.; southwestern Germany/northwestern Switzerland
fols. 29-36v (235-242v) = *BHL* 410   [V]
BIBLIOGRAPHY: *Tabulae codicum ... in Bibliotheca Palatina Vindobonensi ... ,* p. 53; Dufourcq, *Études sur les Gesta martyrum romains*, pp. 8, 88; Levison, "Conspectus," p. 697; Philippart, *Légendiers*, p. 103 n. 186; Pilsworth, "Dating the *Gesta martyrum*," pp. 320-323, with bibliography.

This composite codex is the oldest witness to this version of the *Passio Anastasii*. It contains an important collection of texts relating to early Roman martyrs, believed by Dufourcq to be a copy of a passionary known to Gregory the Great. While this identification has been convincingly challenged, the manuscript still awaits a thorough codicological and textual investigation.[57] Its origin in southwestern Germany or northwestern Switzerland is supported by the transmission of *BHL* 410. The surviving witnesses closest to the apograph are V and N, copied at Einsiedeln in the twelfth century. A copy of V was made at Gregorienmünster (Alsace) in the twelfth century (Colmar 356 = G).

Österreichisches Nationalbibliothek, Latinus 377
s. XII (after 1160)
fols. 74-84v = *BHL* 408(p)   [Vn]
BIBLIOGRAPHY: *Tabulae codicum* ... , p. 58.
This hagiographic collection (seventy-four texts) can be dated by its inclusion of a version of the *Acta S. Demetrii* composed around the year 1160.[58]

ZWETTL
Stiftsbibliothek 13
s. XIII[1]; Zwettl
fols. 68-70 = *BHL* 410   [Z]
BIBLIOGRAPHY: Poncelet, "De *Magno legendario austriaco*," p. 30; Ziegler, *Zisterzienserstift Zwettl. Catalog* I, 31-37.
Part of the Zwettl exemplar of the MLA, it contains saints' Lives for January-March. Ziegler misidentifies the *Passio S. Anastasii* as *BHL* 408.

Stiftsbibliothek 72
s. XII[4]; Zwettl
fols. 2-6v = *BHL* 410   [W]
BIBLIOGRAPHY: Ziegler, *Zisterzienserstift Zwettl. Catalog* I, 136-137.
A collection of saints' Lives arranged in no apparent order. The *Passio S. Anastasii* has been corrected by the original scribe. Ziegler misidentifies the *Passio S. Anastasii* as *BHL* 408.

57. Pilsworth's discussion provides no precise codicological description, and no detailed list of contents, on which any study of the manuscript must be firmly based.
58. (A Bollandist), "De versione latina Actorum S. Demetrii saeculo XII confecta," p. 66 and n. 2. It could not have been copied in the eleventh century as the Vienna catalogue says. The *Passio S. Anastasii* was copied from an exemplar that must have been misbound since the order of text is transposed. See further my edition of the text.

Bibliography

Acta Conciliorum Oecumenicorum iussu atque mandato Societatis scientiarum argentoranensis. Vol. I.1, part 3. Edited by Edward Schwartz. Berlin/ Leipzig, 1922-30.

[Ado of Vienne.] *S. Adonis viennensis Chronicon in aetates sex divisum.* PL 123, 23-138.

——. Dubois, Jacques, and Renaud, Geneviève. *Le Martyrologe d'Adon. Ses deux familles. Ses trois recensions.* Paris, 1984.

Alexakis, Alexander. *Codex Parisinus Graecus 1115 and Its Archetype.* Dumbarton Oaks Studies 34. Washington, DC, 1996.

[Anastasius Bibliothecarius]. *Anastasii bibliothecarii epistolae sive praefationes.* Edited by E. Perels and G. Laehr. *MGH. Epistolae* VII (Karolini aevi V), 95-442. Berlin, 1928.

Arnaldi, Girolamo. "Anastasio Bibliotecario." In *Dizionario biografico degli italiani* III, 25-37. Rome, 1961.

[Augustine]. *S. Aureli Augustini Contra Iulianum opus imperfectum.* Edited by Michaela Zelzer. Corpus Scriptorum Ecclesiasticorum Latinorum 85. Vienna, 1974.

—— *S. Aurelii Augustini De Trinitate Libri XV.* Edited by W. J. Mountain. CCSL 50-50A. Turnholt, 1968.

Auzépy, Marie-France. "L'évolution de l'attitude face au miracle à Byzance (VII-IXe siècle)". In *Miracles, prodiges et merveilles au Moyen Age.* XXVe Congrès de la S.H.M.E.S. (Orléans, juin 1994), pp. 31-46. Publications de la Sorbonne. Paris, 1995.

Ayres, Larry M. "The Italian Giant Bibles: Aspects of their Touronian Ancestry and Early History." In *The Early Medieval Bible. Its Production, Decoration and Use,* pp. 125-154. Edited by Richard Gameson. Cambridge, 1994.

Bandinius, A.M. *Catalogus codicum latinorum Bibliothecae mediceae laurentianae.* 5 vols. Florence, 1744-1778.

——. *Bibliotheca leopoldina laurentiana seu Catalogus manuscriptorum qui iussu Petri Leopoldi ... in Laurentianam translati sunt ...* 3 vols. Florence, 1791-1793.

Barker-Benfield, R.C. "A ninth century manuscript from Fleury: Cato de senectute cum Macrobio." In *Medieval Learning and Literature: Essays Pre-*

sented to R.W. Hunt, pp. 145-165. Edited by J.J.G. Alexander and M.T. Gibson. Oxford, 1976.

[Barbiero, A.]. S. Paolo e le Tre Fontane. XXII secoli di storia messi in luce da un monaco cisterciense (trappista). Rome, 1938.

Baronio, Cesare. Annales Ecclesiastici. 12 vols. Lucca, 1742.

——. Martyrologium Romanum. Roma (ex typ. D. Bassae), 1586.

Barré, Henri. Les homéliaires carolingiens de l'École d'Auxerre. Studi e testi 225. Vatican City, 1962.

Beda Venerabilis. Bede's Ecclesiastical History of the English People. Edited by Bertram Colgrave and R.A.B. Mynors. Oxford, 1969.

——. Chronica maiora. Edited by Theodore Mommsen. In Chronica Minora. Vol. III. MGH. Auctores antiquissimi XIII, 231-327. Berlin, 1898 (reedited by Charles W. Jones in CCSL 123B, 461-545. Turnhout, 1977).

——. The Ecclesiastical History of the English People; the Greater Chronicle; Bede's Letter to Egbert. Edited with an introduction by Judith McClure and Roger Collins. Oxford, 1994.

——. Epistola prima ad Albinum Abbatem. PL 94, 655-657.

——. Expositio in Actus apostolorum et Retractatio. Edited by M.L.W. Laistner. Cambridge (Mass.), 1939.

——. In Lucae euangelium expositio. Edited by David Hurst. CCSL 120, 1-425. Turnhout, 1960.

——. In Marci euangelium expositio. Edited by David Hurst. CCSL 120, 427-648. Turnhout, 1960.

——. In primam partem Samuhelis libri IIII. Edited by David Hurst. CCSL 119, 1-272.

——. Vita Sancti Cuthberti Auctore Beda. In Two Lives of Saint Cuthbert. A Life by an Anonymous Monk of Lindisfarne and Bede's Prose Life. Edited and translated by Bertram Colgrave, pp. 141-307. Cambridge, 1940.

Beeson, Charles. "Paris Lat. 7530: a Study in Insular Symptoms." In Raccolta di scritti in onore di Felice Ramorina, pp. 199-211. Pubblicazioni del l'Università cattolica del Sacro Cuore. Milan, 1927.

Belardi, Giovanni, et al. Abbazia delle Tre Fontane: il complesso, la storia, il restauro. Rome, 1995.

Berg, Knut. Studies in Tuscan Twelfth Century Illumination. Oslo-Bergen-Tromsö, 1967.

Bernt, G. "Die Quellen zu Walahfrids Mammas-Leben." In Festschrift B. Bischoff zu seinem 65. Geburtstag, pp. 142-152. Edited by Johanne Autenrieth and Franz Brunhölz. Stuttgart, 1971.

Berschin, Walter. "Bonifatius Consiliarius. Ein römischer Übersetzer in der byzantinischen Epoche des Papsttums." In Lateinische Kultur im VIII. Jahrhundert. Traube-Gedenkschrift, pp. 25-40. Edited by Albert Lehner and Walter Berschin. Erzabttei St. Ottilien, 1989.

——. *Greek Letters and the Latin Middle Ages. From Jerome to Nicholas of Cusa.* Translated by Jerold C. Frakes. Washington, D.C., 1988.

——. *"Opus Deliberatum ac perfectum:* Why Did the Venerable Bede Write a Second Prose Life of St. Cuthbert?" In *St. Cuthbert, His Cult and His Community to AD 1200,* pp. 95-102. Edited by Gerald Bonner, David Rollason, and Clare Stancliffe. London, 1989.

Bertelli, Carlo. "'Caput Sancti Anastasii'." *Paragone: Mensile di arti figurative e letteratura* XXI, 247 (1970), 12-25.

——. "L'enciclopedia delle Tre Fontane." *Paragone: Mensile di arti figurative e letteratura* XX, 235 (1969), 24-49.

Bertolini, Ottorino. *Roma di fronte a Bisanzio e ai longobardi.* Storia di Roma 9. Bologna, 1941.

——. *Roma e i Longobardi.* Rome, 1972.

Biblia Sacra iuxta vulgatam versionem. Edited by Robert Weber OSB. 2 vols. Stuttgart, 1969; 1975.

Bibliotheca casinensis seu Codicum manuscriptorum qui in tabulario casinensi asservantur series. Vols. I-V.1. Monte Cassino, 1873-1894.

Bibliotheca Sanctorum. 12 vols. Rome, 1961-1970.

Birch, Debra J. *Pilgrimage to Rome in the Middle Ages. Continuity and Change.* Studies in the History of Medieval Religion 13. Woodbridge, 1998.

Bischoff, Bernhard. *Die Abtei Lorsch im Spiegel ihrer Handschriften.* Lorsch, 1989.

——. *Latin Palaeography. Antiquity and the Middle Ages.* Translated by D.Ó Cróinín and David Ganz. Cambridge, 1990.

——. *Die südostdeutschen Schreibschulen und Bibliotheken in der Karolingerzeit.* Vol. 1: *Die bayerischen Diozesen.* Leipzig, 1940; 2nd ed. Wiesbaden, 1960.

——, and Lapidge, Michael. *Biblical Commentaries from the Canterbury School of Theodore and Hadrian.* Cambridge Studies in Anglo-Saxon England 10. Cambridge, 1994.

Blaise, Albert. *Lexicon Latinitatis Medii Aevi.* Corpus Christianorum. Continuatio Mediaevalis. Turnhout, 1975.

Bloch, Herbert. *Montecassino in the Middle Ages.* 3 vols. Cambridge, Mass., 1986.

Bock, Franz. *Das Heiligthum zu Aachen.* Cologne and Neuss, 1867.

Boehm, Barbara Drake. "Body-Part Reliquaries: The State of Research." *Gesta* 36,1 (1997), 8-19.

[A Bollandist]. "De versione latina Actorum S. Demetrii saeculo XII confecta." *Analecta Bollandiana* 16 (1897), 66-69.

Braun, Joseph. *Die Reliquiare des Christlichen Kultes und ihre Entwicklung.* Freiburg im Breisgau, 1940.

Broccoli, Ugo. *L'abbazia delle Tre Fontane. Fasi paleocristiane e altomedievali del complesso 'ad Aquas Salvias' in Roma.* Trani, 1980.

Brock, Sebastian. "Aspects of Translation Technique in Antiquity." *Greek, Roman and Byzantine Studies* 20 (1979), 69-87.

Brown, Michelle. "Paris, Bibliothèque Nationale, lat. 10861 and the Scriptorium of Christ Church, Canterbury." *Anglo Saxon England* 15 (1986), 119-157.

Brown, T.J. "An historical introduction to the use of Classical Latin Authors in the British Isles from the Fifth to the Eleventh Century." In *La Cultura antica nell'occidente latino dal VII al XI secolo. 18-24 aprile 1974.* Settimane di Studio del Centro italiano di studi sull'alto medioevo 22. II, 237-293. Spoleto, 1975.

Brunhölzl, Franz. *Histoire de la litterature latine du Moyen Age.* 2 vols. Louvain, 1990-1996.

Buhl, Maria Sophia, and Kurras, Lotte. *Die Handschriften des ehemaligen Hofbibliothek Stuttgart.* 4,2: *Codices physici, medici, mathematici etc. (HB XI 1-56), Poetae (HB XII 1-23), Poetae Germanici (HB XIII 1-11), Vitae Sanctorum (HB XIV 1-28).* Wiesbaden, 1969.

Bynum, Caroline Walker. *The Resurrection of the Body.* New York, 1995.

Caleca, Antonino. *Miniature in Umbria* I: *La Biblioteca capitolare di Perugia.* Florence, 1969.

Cameron, Alan. *The Greek Anthology from Meleager to Planudes.* Oxford, 1993.

Campbell, James. "Bede." In *Latin Historians,* pp. 176-184. Edited by T.A. Dorey. London, 1966.

Casson, L.F. "The Manuscripts of the Grey Collection in Cape Town." *The Book Collector* 10 (1961), 147-155.

Catalogue général des manuscripts des bibliothèques publiques de France. Départments. Vol. XVII. *Cambrai.* By Auguste Molinier. Paris, 1891.

Catalogue of the Additions to the Manuscripts in the British Museum (1911-1915). London, 1925.

Catalogue of the Harleian MSS in the British Museum. 4 vols. London, 1808-1812.

Catalogus codicum latinorum Bibliothecae regiae monacensis. 2nd ed. Vol. I [III] 1, 2. Munich, 1892-1894; edited by C. Halm, G. Laubmann, et al. Vol. II [IV], 3, 4. Munich, 1878, 1881.

Cavallo, Guglielmo. "Struttura e articolazione della minuscula beneventana libraria tra i secoli X-XII." *Studi Medievali* 11 (1970), 343-368.

Chiesa, Paolo. "*Ad verbum* o *ad sensum?* Modelli e coscienza metodologica della traduzione tra tarda antichità e alto medioevo." *Medioevo e rinascimento* I (1987), 1-51.

——. "Il dossier agiografico latino dei santi Gurias, Samonas e Abibos." *Aevum* 65,2 (1991), 221-258.

——. "Le traduzioni dal greco: l'evoluzione della scuola napoletana nel X secolo." *Mittellateinisches Jahrbuch* 24/25 (1989/90), 67-86.

——. *Le versioni latine della 'Passio Sanctae Febroniae.' Storia, metodo, modelli di due traduzioni agiografiche altomedievali.* Biblioteca di *Medioevo Latino*. Spoleto, 1990.

——. "Traduzioni e traduttori a Roma nell'alto medioevo." In *Roma fra oriente e occidente. 19-24 aprile 2001.* Settimane di studio del Centro italiano di studi sull'alto medioevo 49, pp. 455-492. Spoleto, 2002.

Cipolla, Carlo. *Codici bobbiesi della Biblioteca nazionale universitaria di Torino con illustrazioni.* Milan, 1907.

——. *Codice diplomatico del monastero di S. Colombano di Bobbio fino all'anno MCCVIII.* Rome, 1918.

Coens, Maurice. "Appendice au Catalogue des manuscripts de Trèves." *Analecta Bollandiana* 60 (1942), 213-215.

——. "La Passion de S. Sauve, martyr à Valenciennes." *Analecta Bollandiana* 87 (1969), 133-187.

Colgrave, Bertram. *Two Lives of Saint Cuthbert. A Life by an Anonymous Monk of Lindisfarne and Bede's Prose Life.* Cambridge, 1940.

Collura, Paolo. *La precarolina e la carolina a Bobbio.* Fontes ambrosiani 22. Milan, 1943 (repr. Florence, 1965).

Commena, Anna. *Alexiad.* Edited by August Reifferscheid. 2 vols. Leipzig, 1884.

Copeland, Rita. *Rhetoric, Hermeneutics, and Translation in the Middle Ages: Academic Traditions and Vernacular texts.* Cambridge Studies in Medieval Literature 11. Cambridge, 1991.

Cottineau, L. H. *Répertoire topo-bibliographique des abbayes et prieurés.* 2 vols. Macon, 1939.

Cross, J.E. "On the library of the Old English martyrologist." In *Learning and Literature in Anglo-Saxon England. Studies presented to Peter Clemoes on the occasion of his sixty-fifth birthday*, pp. 227-249. Edited by Michael Lapidge, and Hartmut Gneuss. Cambridge, 1985.

——. "Saints' lives in Old English: Latin manuscripts and vernacular accounts: the *Old English Martyrology.*" *Peritia* 1 (1982), 38-62.

——. "Two Saints in the *Old English Martyrology.*" *Neuphilologische Mitteilungen* 2/78 (1977), 101-107.

——. "The Use of a *Passio S. Sebastiani* in the Old English Martyrology." *Mediaevalia* 14 (1988), 39-50.

Curtius, E.R. *European Literature and the Latin Middle Ages.* Translated by W.R. Trask. Princeton, 1973.

Davis, Raymond. *The Lives of the Eighth-Century Popes.* Liverpool, 1992.

De Rubeis, Flavia. "Le iscrizioni dei re longobardi." In *Poesia dell'alto medioevo europeo: manoscritti, lingua e musica dei ritmi latini. Atti delle euroconferenze per il Corpus dei ritmi latini (IV-IX sec.)*, Arezzo 6-7 novembre 1998 e Ravello 9-12 settembre 1999, pp. 223-237. Florence, 2000.

Dekkers, Eligius. "Les traductions grecques des écrits patristiques latins." *Sacris erudiri* 5 (1953), 193-233.

Delehaye, Hyppolite. *Commentarius Perpetuus in Martyrologium Hieronymianum ad recensionem Henrici Quentin O.S.B. ASS* Nov. II, pars posterior. Brussels, 1931.

——. *Étude sur le Légendier Romain.* Subsidia Hagiographica 23. Brussels, 1936.

——. "Hagiographie Napolitaine." *Analecta Bollandiana* 57 (1939), 5-64; 59 (1941), 1-33.

——. "Les martyrs d'Égypte." *Analecta Bollandiana* 40 (1922), 5-154.

Devos, Paul. "L'oeuvre de Guarimpotus, hagiographe napolitain." *Analecta Bollandiana* 76 (1958), 151-187.

Dictionnaire d'archéologie chrétienne et de liturgie. Edited by F. Cabrol and H. Leclercq. 15 vols. Paris, 1903-1953.

Dictionnaire d'histoire et de géographie ecclésiastiques. Edited by Alfred Baudrillart, et al. Paris, 1912- .

Dionisotti, A.C. "Greek Grammars and Dictionaries in Carolingian Europe." In *The Sacred Nectar of the Greeks: the Study of Greek in the West in the Early Middle Ages*, pp. 1-56. Edited by Michael Herren in collaboration with Shirley Ann Brown. King's College London Medieval Studies 2. London, 1988.

——. "On Bede, Grammars, and Greek." *Revue Bénédictine* 92 (1982), 111-140.

Dolbeau, François. "Fragments métriques consacrés à S. Melaine de Rennes." *Analecta Bollandiana* 93 (1975), 115-125.

——. "Le légendier de Sainte-Cécile retrouvé au Cap." *Analecta Bollandiana* 102 (1984), 302.

——. "Les manuscrits hagiographiques de Gubbio." *Analecta Bollandiana* 95 (1977), 358-388.

——. "Notes sur la genèse et sur la diffusion du 'Liber de Natalitiis.'" *Revue d'histoire des textes* 6 (1976), 143-195.

——. "Notes sur l'organinisation interne des légendiers latins." In *Hagiographie, cultures et sociétés IVe-XIIe siècles*, pp. 11-31. Actes du Colloque organisé à Nanterre et à Paris (2-6 mai 1979). Paris, 1981.

——. "Notes sur deux collections hagiographiques conserves à la Bibliothèque vaticane." *Mélanges de l'École française de Rome.* Moyen Age-Temps Modernes 87 (1975), 397-424.

——. "Le passionaire de Fulda." *Francia. Forschungen sur Westeuropäischen Geschichte* 9 (1981), 515-530.

——. "Les prologues de légendiers latins." In *Les prologues médiévaux.* Actes du Colloque international organisé par l'Academia Belgica et l'École française de Rome avec le concours de la F.I.D.E.M. (Rome, 26-28 mars 1998), pp. 345-393, edited by Jacqueline Hamesse. Turnhout, 2000.

——. "Le rôle des interprètes dans les traductions hagiographiques d'Italie du sud." In *Traduction et traducteurs au Moyen Age*, pp. 145-162. Colloque international du CNRS. IRHT, 26-28 mai 1986. Paris, 1989.

——. "La vie latine de saint Euthyme: une traduction inédite de Jean Diacre napolitain." *Mélanges de l'Ecole française de Rome* (Moyen âge—Temps modernes) 94 (1982), 315-335.

——. "Une Vie inédite de Grégoire de Nazianze (BHL 3668 d), attribuable à Jean de Gaète." *Analecta Bollandiana* 107 (1989), 65-127.

Dubois, Jacques. *Le martyrologe d'Usuard. Texte et commentaire.* Subsidia hagiographica 40. Brussels, 1965.

——. *Les martyrologes du Moyen Âge latin.* Typologie des Sources du Moyen Âge Occidental 26. Turnhout, 1978.

——, and Renaud, Geneviève. *Édition pratique des martyrologes de Bède, de l'Anonyme lyonnais et de Florus.* Institut de recherche et d'histoire des textes. Bibliographies—Colloques—Traveaux préparatoires. Paris, 1976.

——, and Renaud, Geneviève. *Le Martyrologe d'Adon. Ses deux familles. Ses trois recensions.* Paris, 1984.

Du Cange, Charles Du Fresne, sieur. *Glossarium mediae at infimae latinitaits* ... . Edited by G.A.L. Henschel. Graz, 1954.

Duchesne, Louis, ed. *Le Liber pontificalis.* Vols. I-II. Paris, 1886-1892. Vol. III (edited by C. Vogel). Paris, 1955-1957.

——, and Rossi, G.B. de. *Martyrologium hieronymianum. ASS* Nov. II, pars anterior. Brussels, 1894.

Duemmler, E. *Tituli saeculi VIII.* In *Poetae Latini aevi Carolini* I. *MGH. Poetae* I. Berlin, 1881.

Dufourcq, Albert. *Études sur les Gesta martyrum romains.* 4 vols. Paris, 1900-1907.

——. "Le Passionnaire occidental au VIIe siècle." *Mélanges d'archéologie et d'histoire* 26 (1906), 27-65.

[Eddius.] *Vita Wilfridi I episcopi eboracensis auctore Stephano.* Edited by W. Levison. *MGH. Scriptores rerum merovingiarum* VI, 163-263. Hanover and Leipzig, 1913.

Eis, Gerhard. "Legendarium Windbergense." *Die deutsche Literatur des Mittelalters. Verfasserlexicon* 5, cols. 606-609. Berlin, 1955.

Ermini, Filippo. "I passionari lateranensi." In *Medio evo latino.* Istituto di filologia romanza della R. Università di Roma. Studi e testi. Modena, 1938.

——. *Storia della letteratura latina medievale dalle origini alla fine del secolo VII.* Spoleto, 1960.

Esposito, Mario. "The Ancient Bobbio Catalogue." *The Journal of Theological Studies* 32 (1931), 337-344.

[Evagrius]. *Vita Beatri Antonii Abbatis auctore sancto Athanasio ... interprete Evagrio.* PL 73, 125-168.

Evans, Helen C. and Wixom, William D. *The Glory of Byzantium. Art and Culture of the Middle Byzantine Era. A.D. 843-1261.* New York, 1997.

Federichi, Vincenzo. *I monasteri di Subiaco.* Vol. II: *La biblioteca e l'archivio.* Rome, 1904.

Ferrari, Guy. *Early Roman monasteries. Notes for the history of the monasteries and convents at Rome from the V through the X century.* Studi di antichità cristiana 23. Vatican City, 1957.

Ferrari, Mirella. "Manoscritti e cultura." in *Atti del 10o Congresso internazionale di studi sull'alto medioevo. Milano 26-30 settembre 1983.* Spoleto, 1986.

——. "Spigolature bobbiesi. I. In margine ai *Codices latini antiquiores.*" *Italia medievale e umanistica* 16 (1973), 1-14.

Flusin, Bernard. *Saint Anastase le Perse et l'histoire de la Palestine au début du VIIe siècle.* I *Les Textes*; II *Commentaire. Les moines de Jérusalem et l'invasion perse.* Paris, 1992.

Follieri, Enrica. "I rapporti fra Bisanzio e l'Occidente nel campo dell'agiografia." In *Proceedings of the XIII International Congress of Byzantine Studies*, pp. 355-362. Oxford, 1967.

Franchi de Cavalieri, P. "Il Codice 4 di S. Alessandro in Colonna." *Note agiografiche.* Fasc. VI, 49-56. Studi e testi 33. Vatican City, 1920.

Franklin, Carmela Vircillo. "Bilingual Philology in Bede's Exegesis." In *Medieval Cultures in Contact*, pp. 3-17. Edited by Richard F. Gyug. New York, 2003.

——. "The Epigraphic Syllogae of BAV, Palatinus Latinus 833." In *Roma, Magistra Mundi. Itineraria culturae medievalis. Mélanges offerts au Père L.E. Boyle à l'occasion de son 75e anniversaire*, pp. 975-990. Edited by Jacqueline Hamesse. Louvain-la-Neuve, 1998.

——. "Hagiographic Translations in the Early Middle Ages (7th-10th centuries)." In *Les traducteurs au travail. Leurs manuscripts et leurs méthodes.* Actes du Colloque international organisé par le "Ettore Majorana Centre for Scientific Culture." (Erice, 30 septembre-6 octobre 1999), pp. 1-18. Edited by Jacqueline Hamesse. Turnhout, 1999.

——. "Roman Hagiography and Roman Legendaries." In *Roma nell'alto medioevo, 27 aprile-1 maggio 2000.* Settimane di studio del Centro italiano di studi sull'alto medioevo 48, pp. 857-895. Spoleto, 2001.

——. "The restored *Life and Miracles of St. Dominic of Sora* by Alberic of Monte Cassino." *Mediaeval Studies* 55 (1993), 285-345.

——. "Theodore and the *Passio S. Anastasii.*" In *Archbishop Theodore. Commemorative Studies on His Life and Influence*, pp. 175-203. Edited by

Michael Lapidge. Cambridge Studies in Anglo-Saxon England 11. Cambridge, 1995.

——, and Meyvaert, Paul J. "Has Bede's Version of the *Passio S. Anastasii* Come Down to Us in *BHL* 408?" *Analecta Bollandiana* 100 (1982), 373-400.

Gaiffier, Baudouin de. "La lecture des actes des martyrs dans la prière liturgique en Occident. À propos du Passionaire hispanique." *Analecta Bollandiana* 72 (1954), 134-166.

——. "La lecture des passions des martyrs à Rome avant le IX s." *Analecta Bollandiana* 87 (1969), 63-78.

——. "Les légendiers de Spolète." *Analecta Bollandiana* 74 (1956), 313-348.

——. "Saints et légendiers de l'Ombrie." In *Ricerche sull'Umbria tardo antica e pre-romanica. Atti del II Convegno di Studi Umbri. Gubbio, 24-28 maggio 1964*, pp. 235-256. Perugia, 1965.

Ganz, David. "Roman Manuscripts in Francia and Anglo-Saxon England." In *Roma fra oriente e occidente. 19-24 aprile 2001*. Settimane di studio del Centro italiano di studi sull'alto medioevo 49, pp. 607-647. Spoleto, 2002.

Garrison, E.B. "Notes on Certain Italian Mediaeval Manuscripts." *Bibliophilia* 68 (1966), 1-29.

——. *Studies in the History of Mediaeval Italian Painting*. 4 vols. Florence, 1953-1962.

Gattucci, Adriano. "Codici agiografici riminesi. Il Passionario frammentario della cattedrale." *Studi Medievali* 11 (1970), 711-773.

Geertman, H. *More veterum: il 'Liber Pontificalis' e gli edifici ecclesiastici di Roma nella tarda antichità e nell'alto medioevo*. Archaeologica Traiectina 10. Groninger, 1975.

Gheyn, J. van den. *Catalogue des manuscrits de la Bibliothèque royale de Belgique* V: *Histoire. Hagiographie*. Brussels, 1905.

Giles, J.A. *Venerabilis Bedae Opera quae supersunt omnia*. Vol. IV. London, 1843.

Giorgi, I. "Il Regesto del monastero di S. Anastasio ad Aquas Salvias." *Archivio delle Reale società romana di storia patria* 1 (1878), 47-77.

Giovanelli, Germano. *Gli inni sacri di S. Bartolomeo Juniore*. Grottaferrata, 1955.

Godfrey of Viterbo. *Pantheon*. Edited by G. Waitz. *MGH. Scriptores* XXII, 107-307. Hanover, 1872 (repr. Stuttgart, 1976).

Goffart, Walter. *The Narrators of Barbarian History (A.D. 550-800): Jordanes, Gregory the Great, Bede, and Paul the Deacon*. Princeton, 1988.

Gorman, Michael. "Wigbod and the *Lectiones* on the Hexateuch Attributed to Bede in Paris Lat. 2342." *Revue bénédictine* 106 (1996), 343-345.

Grabar, André. "Le reliquaire byzantin de la cathédral d'Aix-la-chapelle." In *L'Art de la fin de l'antiquité et du moyen âge* I, 427-433. Paris, 1968.

Grandsen, Antonia. "Abbo of Fleury's 'Passio Sancti Edmundi.'" *Revue bénédictine* 105 (1995), 20-78.

Grégoire, Réginald. *Manuale di agiologia. Introduzione alla letteratura agiografica.* Bibliotheca Montisfani 12. Fabriano, 1987.

[Gregory I]. *Gregorii I Papae Registrum Epistolarum.* Edited by P. Ewald and L. M. Hartman. 2 vols. *MGH. Epistolae* II. Berlin, 1899 (repr. 1978).

——. *S. Gregori I Magni Moralia in Iob.* Edited by Marcus Adriaen. CCSL 143-145. Turnholt, 1979.

——. *XL Homiliarum in Evangelia libri duo.* PL 76, 1075-1314.

[Gregory of Tours]. *Gregorii Episcopi Turonensis Liber in gloria martyrum.* Edited by B. Krusch. *MGH. Scriptores rerum merovingiarum* I,2, 35-111. Hanover, 1885 (repr. 1959).

Grimme, Ernst G. *Der Aachener Domschatz.* Düsseldorf, 1972.

——. *Der Dom zu Aachen: Architektur und Ausstattung.* Aachen, 1994.

Guillou, André. *Recueil des inscriptions grecques médiévales d'Italie.* Collection de l'École française de Rome 222. Rome, 1996.

Hagen, Hermann. *Catalogus Codicum Bernensium (Bibliotheca Bongarsiana).* Bern, 1875; repr. Hildesheim, N. Y., 1974.

Hahn, Cynthia. "The Voices of the Saints: Speaking Reliquaries." *Gesta* 36/1 (1997), 20-31.

Harper, John. *The Forms and Orders of Western Liturgy from the Tenth to the Eighteenth Century. A Historical Introduction and Guide for Students and Musicians.* Oxford, 1991.

Henry of Auxerre. *Vita S. Germani.* PL 124, 1131-1207.

Herrmann-Mascard, Nicole. *Les reliques des saints. Formation coutumière d'un droit.* Société d'histoire du droit. Collection d'histoire institutionelle et sociale 6. Paris, 1975.

Herzfeld, George. *An Old English Martyrology.* London, 1900.

Hohler, Christopher. "Theodore and the Liturgy." In *Archbishop Theodore. Commemorative Studies on His Life and Influence,* pp. 222-235. Edited by Michael Lapidge. Cambridge Studies in Anglo-Saxon England 11. Cambridge, 1995.

Inguanez, Mauro. *Codicum casinensium manuscriptorum catalogus.* 3 vols. Monte Cassino, 1915-1940.

[Isidore.] *Isidori Hispalensis Chronica.* Cura et studio Jose Carlos Martin. CCSL 112. Turnhout, 2003.

Jackson, Peter and Lapidge, Michael. "The Contents of the Cotton-Corpus Legendary." In *Holy Men and Holy Women. Old English Prose Saints'*

Lives and Their Contexts, pp. 131-146. Edited by Paul E. Szarmach. Albany, NY, 1996.

James, M.R. *The Abbey of St. Edmund at Bury*. Cambridge Archaeological Society 28. Cambridge, 1895.

Janson, Tore. *Latin Prose Prefaces. Studies in Literary Conventions*. Studia Latina Stockholmiensia 13. Stockholm, 1964.

——. *Prose Rhythm in Medieval Latin from the Ninth to the Thirteenth Century*. Studia Latina Stockholmiensia 20. Stockholm, 1975.

Jeauneau, Edouard. "Jean Scot Erigène et le grec." *Bulletin du Cange. Archivum latinitatis medii aevi* 41 (1979), 5-50.

Jerome. *Hebraicae quaestiones in libro Geneseos*. Edited by P. de Lagarde. CCSL 72, 59-161. Turnhout, 1959.

——. *Liber de optimo genere interpretandi (Epistula 57)*. Edited by G.J.M. Bartelink. Leiden, 1980.

——, ed. *Eusebii Pamphili Chronicorum liber secundus S. Hieronymo interprete et ampliatore*. PL 27, 223-507.

Johannes Diaconus. *Descriptio Ecclesiae lateranensis*. PL 194, 1543-1560.

[Johannes Scotus.] *Iohannis Scotti Eriugenae Carmina*. Edited by Michael W. Herren. Scriptores latini Hiberniae 12. Dublin, 1993.

Jones, Charles W. *The Saint Nicholas Liturgy and Its Literary Relationships (Ninth to Twelfth Centuries)*. Berkeley, 1963.

Jones, Putnam Fennell. *A Concordance to the Historia Ecclesiastica of Bede*. Cambridge, Mass., 1929.

Jounel, Pierre. *Le culte des saints dans les basiliques du Latran et du Vatican au douzième siècle*. Collection de l'École française de Rome 26. Rome, 1977.

Kamesar, Adam. *Jerome, Greek Scholarship, and the Hebrew Bible. A study of the Quaestiones hebraicae in Genesim*. Oxford, 1993.

Kaczynski, Bernice M. "A Ninth-Century Latin Translation of Mark the Hermit's *Peri Nomou Pneumatikou* (Dresden, Sächsische Landesbibliothek, Mscr. A 145b)." *Byzantinische Zeitschrift* 89 (1996), 379-388 and plates XIII-XIV.

——. "Review Article: The Seventh-Century School of Canterbury: England and the Continent in Perspective." *The Journal of Medieval Latin* 8 (1998), 212.

Kehr, F. *Italia Pontificia*. Berlin, 1906.

Kelly, Louis. *The True Interpreter: A History of Translation Theory and Practice in the West*. Oxford, 1979.

Kessel, Johann Hubert. *Geschichtliche Mitteilungen über die Heiligthümer der Stiftkirche zu Aachen nebst Abbildung und Beschreibung der sie bergende Behälter und Einfassungen. Festschrift zur Heiligthunsfahrt von 1874*. Cologne and Neuss, 1874.

Kirby, D.P. *Bede's Historia Ecclesiastica Gentis Anglorum: Its Contemporary Setting*. Jarrow Lecture 1992 (1993).

Kitrowo, Sofiia Petrovna [Mme B. de Khitrowo], trans. *Itinéraires russes in Orient*. Société de l'Orient latin. Publications. Série géographique 5. Geneva, 1889.

Kotzor, Günter. *Das altenglische Martyrologium*. 2 vols. Munich, 1981.

Kramer, J. *Glossaria bilinguia in papyris et membranis reperta*. Bonn, 1983.

Krautheimer, Richard. *Rome. Profile of a City, 312-1308*. Princeton, 1980.

Laistner, M.L.W., and King, H.H. *A Hand-List of Bede Manuscripts*. Ithaca, New York, 1943.

Lampert of Hersfeld. *Annales*. In *Lamperti Monachi Hersfeldensis Opera*. Edited by O. Holder-Egger. *MGH. Scriptores rerum germanicarum in usum scholarum*, pp. 1-304. Hanover and Leipzig, 1894.

Lapidge, Michael. "Aelfric's *Sanctorale*." In *Holy Men and Holy Women. Old English Prose Saints' Lives and Their Contexts*, pp. 115-130. Edited by Paul E. Szarmach. Albany, NY, 1996.

——. "Bede's Metrical *Vita S. Cuthberti*." In *St. Cuthbert, His Cult and His Community to AD 1200*, pp. 77-93. Edited by Gerald Bonner, David Rollason, and Clare Stancliffe. London, 1989.

——. "Editing Hagiography." In *La critica del testo mediolatino. Atti del Convegno: Firenze 6-8 dicembre 1990*, pp. 239-258. Edited by Claudio Leonardi. Biblioteca di *Medioevo Latino* 5. Spoleto, 1994.

——. "The Lost 'Passio Metrica S. Dionysii' by Hilduin of Saint-Denis." *Mittellateinisches Jahrbuch* 22 (1987), 56-79.

——. "The Saintly Life in Anglo-Saxon England." In *The Cambridge Companion to Old English Literature*, pp. 243-263. Edited by Malcolm Godden and Michael Lapidge. Cambridge, 1991.

——. "Some Remnants of Bede's Lost *Liber Epigrammatum*." *English Historical Review* 90 (1975), 798-820.

Laurent, M.-H. *Codices Vaticani Latini: Codices 1135-1266*. Città del Vaticano, 1958.

Le Bourdellès, H. *L'Aratus Latinus. Étude sur la culture et la langue latine dans le Nord de la France au viiie siècle*. Université de Lille III. Travaux et recherches. Lille, 1985.

Leonardi, Claudio. "L'agiografia romana nel secolo IX." In *Hagiographie, cultures et societés IVe-XIIe siècles*. Actes du Colloque organisé à Nanterre et à Paris (2-6 mai 1979), pp. 471-490. Paris, 1981.

Levison, Wilhelm. "Conspectus codicum hagiographicorum." In *MGH. Scriptores rerum merovingiarum* VII, 529-706. Berlin, 1920.

——. *England and the Continent in the Eighth Century*. Oxford, 1946.

Liddell, H.G., and Scott, Robert. *A Greek-English Lexicon*. Oxford, 1989.

Llewellyn, Peter. *Rome in the Dark Ages*. New York and London, 1970.

Lot, Ferdinand. *Hariulf. Chronique de l'Abbaye de Saint-Riquier.* Paris, 1894.

Lowe, E.A. *The Beneventan Script.* 2nd edition revised and edited by Virginia Brown. Rome, 1980.

——. *Codices Latini Antiquiores.* Part VI: *France: Abbeville-Valenciennes.* Oxford, 1953 (repr. 1982).

——. *Paleographical Papers.* Vol. II. Oxford, 1972.

Lucchesi, Giovanni. "Il sermonario di s. Pier Damiani come monumento storico, agiografico e liturgico." *Studi gregoriani per la storia della "Libertas ecclesiae"* 10 (1975), 7-68.

Mabillon, Jean. *Museum Italicum seu Collectio* ... Paris, 1687 (repr. Rome, 1971).

Maggioni, G.P. "La *Vita sanctae Theodorae* (BHL 8070). La revisione imperfetta di una traduzione perfettibile." *Hagiographica* 6 (2000), 201-268.

Mai, Angelo. *Spicilegium Romanum.* 10 vols. Rome, 1839-1844.

Mallet, Jean and Thibaut, André. *Les manuscrits en écriture bénéventaine de la Bibliothèque capitulaire de Bénévent.* Paris, 1984.

Maltby, Robert. *A Lexicon of Ancient Latin Etymologies.* ARCA. Classical and Medieval Texts, Papers and Monographs 25. Leeds, 1990.

Mansi, J.D. *Sacrorum conciliorum nova et amplissima collectio.* Florence and Venice, 1767-1773.

Marsden, Richard. *The Text of the Old Testament in Anglo-Saxon England.* Cambridge Studies in Anglo-Saxon England 15. Cambridge, 1995.

Martin von Tropau. *Chronicon pontificum et imperatorum.* Edited by Ludwig Weiland. *MGH. Scriptores* XXII, 377-482. Hanover, 1872.

Mayr-Harting, Henry. *The Coming of Christianity to Anglo-Saxon England.* London, 1972.

Mazzatinti, Giuseppe. "Subiaco. Biblioteca dell'Abbazia." In *Inventari dei manoscritti delle biblioteche d'Italia* I, 161-230. Forli, 1890 (repr. Florence, 1955).

McCormick, Michael. *Origins of the European Economy. Communications and Commerce AD 300-900.* Cambridge, 2001.

McCulloh, J.M. "The Cult of Relics in the Letters and Dialogues of Gregory the Great: a Lexicographical Study." *Traditio* 32 (1976), 145-184.

Medieval and Renaissance Manuscripts in the Grey Collection. A Preliminary Catalogue. South Africa Library, Grey Bibliographies 12. Cape Town, 1984.

Meier, Gabriel, O.S.B. *Catalogus codicum manu scriptorum qui in Bibliotheca Monasterii Einsidlensis O.S.B. servantur.* Einsiedeln, 1899.

Mercati, Giovanni. "Altri codici del sacro Convento di Assisi nella Vaticana." In *Opere minori* IV, 486-505. Studi e testi 79. Vatican City, 1937.

——. "Codici del Convento di S. Francesco in Assisi nella Biblioteca vaticana." In *Miscellanea Francesco Ehrle. Scritti di storia e paleografia.* V, 81-127. Studi e testi 41. Vatican City, 1924.

Metzer, Nancy. "Willibrord's Scriptorium at Echternach and its Relationship to Ireland and Lindisfarne." In *St. Cuthbert, His Cult and His Community to AD 1200*, pp. 203-212. Edited by Gerald Bonner, David Rollason, and Clare Stancliffe. London, 1989.

Meyvaert, Paul [J.]. "Bede and the Church Paintings at Wearmouth-Jarrow." *Anglo-Saxon England* 8 (1979), 63-77.

——. "Bede's *Capitula lectionum* for the Old and New Testaments." *Revue Bénédictine* 105 (1995), 348-380.

——. "Bede's Text of the *Libellus Responsionum* of Gregory the Great to Augustine of Canterbury." In *England Before the Conquest. Studies in Primary Sources presented to Dorothy Whitelock*, pp. 15-33. Edited by Peter Clemoes and Kathleen Hughes. Cambridge, 1971. Reprinted in Meyvaert, Paul J. *Benedict, Gregory, Bede and Others.* Variorum Reprints. London, 1977.

——. "Bede the Scholar." In *Famulus Christi. Essays in Commemoration of the Thirteenth Centenary of the Birth of the Venerable Bede*, pp. 40-69. S.P.C.K. London, 1976. Reprinted in *Benedict, Gregory, Bede and Others*. London, 1977.

Moore, W.J. *The Saxon Pilgrims to Rome and the Schola Saxonum.* Freiburg, 1937.

Moretus, Henri. "Catalogus codicum hagiographicorum latinorum Bibliothecae bollandianae." *Analecta Bollandiana* 24 (1905), 425-472.

Mostert, Marco. *The Library of Fleury: A provisional list of manuscripts.* Hilversum, 1989.

Munding, Emmanuel. *Das Verzeichnis der St. Galler Heiligenleben und ihrer Handschriften in Codex Sangall. N.566.* Beuron, 1918.

Narducci, E. *Catalogus codicum manuscriptorum praeter orientales qui in Bibliotheca alexandrina Romae adservantur.* Rome, 1877.

Newton, Francis. *The Scriptorium and the Library at Monte Cassino, 1058-1105.* Cambridge Studies in Palaeography and Codicology 7. Cambridge, 1999.

[Nicholas I.] *Nicolai I Papae Epistolae.* Edited by Ernst Perels. *MGH. Epistolae* VI (Karolini Aevi IV), 257-690. Berlin, 1925 (repr. Munich, 1978).

Ó Carragáin, Éamonn. *The City of Rome and the World of Bede.* Jarrow Lecture 1994 (1995).

Ó Cróinín, Dáibhí. "Is the Augsburg Gospel Codex a Northumbrian Manuscript?" In *St. Cuthbert, His Cult and His Community to AD 1200*, pp. 189-201. Edited by Gerald Bonner, David Rollason, and Clare Stancliffe. London, 1989.

Ordericus Vitalis. *Historia Ecclesiastica.* PL 188, 15-984.

Ortenberg, Veronica. *The English Church and the Continent in the Tenth and Eleventh Centuries: cultural, spiritual, and artistic exchanges.* Oxford, 1992.

Ottino, Giuseppe. *I Codici bobbiesi nella Biblioteca nazionale di Torino.* Turin, 1890.

The Oxford Dictionary of Byzantium. Edited by Alexander P. Kazhdan, et al. Oxford, 1991.

Panella, Clementina, and Saguí, Lucia. "Consumo e produzione a Roma tra tardoantico e altomedioevo: le merci, i contesti." In *Roma nell'alto medioevo, 27 aprile-1 maggio 2000.* Settimane di studio del Centro italiano di studi sull'alto medioevo 48, pp. 757-820. Spoleto, 2001.

Panvinio, Onofrio. *Le sette chiese romane.* Italian translation by Marco Antonio Lanfranchi. Rome, 1570.

Parkes, Malcolm B. "The Manuscript of the Leiden Riddles." *Anglo-Saxon England* 1 (1972), 207-217.

——. *The Scriptorium of Wearmouth-Jarrow.* Jarrow Lecture 1982 (1983).

Paulus Diaconus. *Historia Langobardorum.* Edited by G. Waitz. *MGH. Scriptores rerum Langobardorum.* Hanover, 1878.

Pertusi, Agostino. "L'encomio di S. Anastasio martire persiano." *Analecta Bollandiana* 76 (1958), 5-63.

[Peter Damian]. *Sancti Petri Damiani sermones.* Edited by Giovanni Lucchesi. Corpus Christianorum. Continuatio mediaevalis 57. Turnhout, 1983.

Petitmengin, Pierre. "La diffusion de la 'Pénitence de Pélagie.' Resultats d'une recherche collective." In *Hagiographie, cultures et societés IVe-XIIe siècles.* Actes du Colloque organisé à Nanterre et à Paris (2-6 mai 1979), pp. 34-47. Paris, 1981.

——, et al. *Pélagie la Pénitente. Métamorphoses d'une légende.* 2 vols. Paris, 1981.

——, et al., "Les Vies latines de sainte Pélagie. Inventaire des textes publiés et inédits." *Recherches Augustiniennes* 12 (1977), 279-305.

Philippart, Guy. "Legendare." *Die deutsche Literatur des Mittelalters. Verfasserlexicon* 5, cols. 644-657. Berlin and New York, 1985.

——. *Les légendiers latins et autres manuscrits hagiographiques.* Typologie des sources du Moyen Âge occidental 24-25. Turnhout, 1977. *Mise à jour,* 1985.

Piazza, Carlo Bartolomeo. *Hieroxenia overo, Sagra pellegrinazione alle sette chiese di Roma. Con le due d'antichissima divozione, che fanno le Nove chiese.* Rome, 1694.

[Pietro dello Schiavo, Antonio di]. *Il Diario Romano di Antonio di Pietro dello Schiavo dal 19 ottobre 1404 al 25 settembre 1417.* Edited by Francesco Isoldi. *Rerum Italicarum Scriptores. Raccolta degli storici italiani dal cinquecento al millecinquecento* XXIV, part 5. Città di Castello, 1917.

Pilsworth, Clare. "Dating the *Gesta martyrum*: a manuscript-based approach." *Early Medieval Europe* 9 (2000), 309-324.

Poncelet, Albert. *Catalogus codicum hagiographicorum Bibliothecae regiae bruxellensis.* Pars I: *Codices latini membranei.* 2 vols. Brussels, 1886-1889.

———. "Catalogus codicum hagiographicorum Bibliothecae universitatis bononiensis." *Analecta Bollandiana* 42 (1924), 320-370.

———. *Catalogus codicum hagiographicorum latinorum antiquioroum saeculo XVI qui asservantur in Bibliotheca nationali parisiensi.* 4 vols. Brussels, 1889-1893.

———. "Catalogus codicum hagiographicorum latinorum Bibliothecae ambrosianae." *Analecta Bollandiana* 11 (1892), 205-368.

———. "Catalogus codicum hagiographicorum latinorum Bibliothecae capituli ecclesiae cathedralis beneventanae." *Analecta Bollandiana* 51 (1933), 337-377.

———. "Catalogus codicum hagiographicorum latinorum Bibliothecae eporidiensis." *Analecta Bollandiana* 41 (1923), 326-356.

———. "Catalogus codicum hagiographicorum latinorum Bibliothecae nationalis taurinensis." *Analecta Bollandiana* 28 (1909), 417-475.

———. *Catalogus codicum hagiographicorum latinorum Bibliothecae vaticanae.* Subsidia Hagiographica 11. Brussels, 1910 (repr. 1983).

———. "Catalogus codicum hagiographicorum latinorum bibliothecarum neapolitanarum." *Analecta Bollandiana* 30 (1911), 137-251.

———. *Catalogus codicum hagiographicorum latinorum bibliothecarum romanarum praeter quam vaticanae.* Subsidia Hagiographica 9. Brussels, 1909 (repr. 1981).

———. "De legendario Windbergensi." *Analecta Bollandiana* 17 (1898), 97-122.

———. "Le Légendier de Pierre Calo." *Analecta Bollandiana* 29 (1910), 5-116.

———. "De *Magno legendario austriaco*." *Analecta Bollandiana* 17 (1898), 24-96.

———. "La vie et les oeuvres de Thierry de Fleury." *Analecta Bollandiana* 27 (1908), 5-27.

Priscian. *Institutiones grammaticae.* In *Grammatici Latini*, ed. H. Keil. Vol. II. Leipzig, 1855 (repr. 1981).

Quentin, Henri. *Les martyrologes historiques du moyen âge. Étude sur la formation du Martyrologe Romain.* Rome, 1908.

Rabbow, Paul. "Zur Geschichte des urkundlichen Sinns." *Historische Zeitschrift* 126 (1922), 58-79.

Riedinger, Rudolf, ed. *Concilium Lateranense a. 649 celebratum. Acta conciliorum oecumenicorum.* 2nd ser. Vol. 1. Berlin, 1984.

Rochais, Henri. *Un légendier cistercien de la fin du XIIe s.: le 'Liber de Natalitiis' et de quelques grands légendiers des XII et XIIIe s.* Documentation Cistercienne 15, 1-2. Rochefort, 1975.

Rönsch, Hermann. *Itala und Vulgata. Das Sprachidiom der Urchristlichen Itala und der Katholischen Vulgata.* Marburg, 1875.

Rossi, G.B. de. *Inscriptiones christianae urbis Romae septimo saeculo antiquiores.* 2 vols. Rome, 1861-1888.

Rice, Eric North. "Music and Ritual in the Collegiate Church of Saint Mary in Aachen 1300-1600." Ph.D. diss., Columbia University, 2002.

Rouse, Richard. "Boston Buriensis and the Author of the *Catalogus Scriptorum Ecclesiae.*" *Speculum* 41 (1966), 471-499.

Samaran, Charles, and Marichal, Robert. *Catalogue des manuscrits en écriture latine portant des indications de date, de lieu ou de copiste.* 7 vols. Paris, 1959-1984.

Sansterre, Jean-Marie. "Le monachisme Byzantin à Rome." In *Bisanzio, Roma e l'Italia nell'alto Medioevo, 3-9 aprile 1986.* II, 701-746. Settimane di studio del Centro italiano di studi sull'alto medioevo 34. Spoleto, 1988.

——. *Les moines grecs et orientaux à Rome aux époques byzantine et carolingienne.* 2 vols. Brussels, 1980.

Saunders, W.B.R. "The Aachen Reliquary of Eustathius Maleinus (969-970)." *Dumbarton Oaks Papers* 36 (1982), 211-219.

Schramm, Percy Ernst, and Mütherich, Florentine. *Denkmale der deutschen Könige und Kaiser.* 2nd ed. Munich, 1982.

Siegmund, Albert. *Die Überlieferung der griechischen christlichen Literatur in der lateinischen Kirche bis zum zwölften Jahrhundert.* Bayerische Benediktiner Akademie. Munich, 1949.

Siffrin, Peter. "Das Walderdorffer Fragment saec. viii und die Berliner Blätter einer Sakramentars aus Regensburg." *Ephemerides Liturgicae* 47 (1933), 201-224.

Simon, Gertrud. "Untersuchungen zur Topik der Widmungsbriefe mittelalterliche Geschichtsschreiber bis zum Ende des 12.Jahrhunderts." *Archiv für Diplomatik* 5/6 (1959/60), 73-153.

[Smedt, Charles de]. "Catalogus codicum hagiographicorum bibliothecae civitatis carnotensis," *Analecta Bollandiana* 8 (1889), 125-136.

Stancliffe, Clare "Cuthbert and the Polarity Between Pastor and Solitary." In *St. Cuthbert, His Cult and His Community to AD 1200*, pp. 21-44. Edited by Gerald Bonner, David Rollason, and Clare Stancliffe. London, 1989.

Stevenson, Jane. *The 'Laterculus Malalianus' and the School of Archbishop Theodore.* Cambridge Studies in Anglo-Saxon England 14. Cambridge, 1995.

Straeten, Joseph van der. "Le 'Grand Légendier Autrichien' dans les manuscrits de Zwettl." *Analecta Bollandiana* 113 (1995), 321-342.

——. *Les manuscrits hagiographiques d'Orléans, Tours et Angers avec plusiers textes inédits.* Bruxelles, 1982.

Strunk, Gerhard. *Kunst und Glaube in der lateinischen Heiligenlegende.* Medium Aevum 12. Munich, 1970.

Supino Martini, Paola. *Roma e l'area grafica romanesca (s. X-XII).* Biblioteca di *Scrittura e civiltà* 1. Alessandria, 1988.

Tabulae codicum manu scriptorum praeter graecos et orientales in Bibliotheca Palatina Vindobonensi asservatorum. Edited by Academia Caesarea Vindobonensis. 10 vols. Vienna, 1864-1899.

Usener, H. ed. *Acta m. Anastasii Persae.* Bonn, 1894.

Valentini, R., and Zucchetti, G. *Codice topografico della città di Roma.* 2 vols. Fonti per la storia d'Italia 88. Rome, 1942.

Verrando, Giovanni Nino. "I due leggendari di Fiesole." *Aevum* 74 (2000), 443-491.

———. "Frammenti e testi agiografici isolati in manoscritti italiani." *Hagiographica* 6 (1999), 257-310.

Vezin, J. "Leofnoth: un scribe anglais à Saint-Benoît-sur-Loire." *Codices Manuscripti* 3 (1977), 109-120.

Vichi, Anna Maria Giorgetti and Mottironi, Giorgio. *Catalogo dei manoscritti della Biblioteca vallicelliana.* Vol. I. Rome, 1961.

Wampach, Kamill. *Geschichte der Grundherrschaft Echternach im Frühmittelalter.* Vol. I, 2. Luxembourg, 1930.

Weber, Robert. *Le Psautier romain et les autres anciens psautiers latins.* Collectanea Biblica Latina 10. Rome, 1953.

Wentzel, Hans. "Das byzantinische Erbe der ottonischen Kaiser: Hypothesen über den Brautschatz der Theophano." *Aachener Kunstblätter* 43 (1972), pp. 11-96.

West, Martin L. *Textual Criticism and Editorial Technique.* Stuttgart, 1973.

Wilson, H.A. ed. *The Calendar of St Willibrord from MS Paris. Lat. 10837. A Facsimile with Transcription, Introduction and Notes.* Henry Bradshaw Society 55. London, 1918.

Wormald, F. *English Calendars before A.D. 1100.* London, 1934.

Ziegler, Charlotte. *Zisterzienserstift Zwettl. Katalog der Handschriften des Mittelalters.* Vol. I. Vienna-Munich, 1992.

Zucchetti, G. ed. *Il «Chronicon» di Benedetto monaco di S. Andrea del Soratte e il «Libellus de imperatoria potestate in urbe Roma».* Fonti per la storia d'Italia 55. Rome, 1922.

Index

INDEX OF MANUSCRIPTS